Lecture Notes in Information Systems and Organisation

Volume 75

Lecture Notes in Information Systems and Organization—LNISO—is a series of scientific books that explore the current scenario of information systems, in particular IS and organization. The focus on the relationship between IT, IS and organization is the common thread of this collection, which aspires to provide scholars across the world with a point of reference and comparison in the study and research of information systems and organization. LNISO is the publication forum for the community of scholars investigating behavioral and design aspects of IS and organization. The series offers an integrated publication platform for high-quality conferences, symposia and workshops in this field. Materials are published upon a strictly controlled double blind peer review evaluation made by selected reviewers.

LNISO is abstracted/indexed in Scopus

Daniel Beverungen · Christiane Lehrer ·
Matthias Trier
Editors

Solutions and Technologies for Responsible Digitalization

Proceedings of the 18th International Conference on Wirtschaftsinformatik, Paderborn, Germany, 2023, Vol. 2

Springer

Editors
Daniel Beverungen
Department of Information Systems
Paderborn University
Paderborn, Nordrhein-Westfalen, Germany

Christiane Lehrer
Department of Digitalization
Copenhagen Business School
Frederiksberg, Denmark

Matthias Trier
Department of Information Systems
Paderborn University
Paderborn, Nordrhein-Westfalen, Germany

ISSN 2195-4968 ISSN 2195-4976 (electronic)
Lecture Notes in Information Systems and Organisation
ISBN 978-3-031-80121-1 ISBN 978-3-031-80122-8 (eBook)
https://doi.org/10.1007/978-3-031-80122-8

This Springer imprint is published by the registered company Springer Nature Switzerland AG
The registered company address is: Gewerbestrasse 11, 6330 Cham, Switzerland

Organization

Conference Chairs

Prof. Dr. Daniel Beverungen, Paderborn University, Germany
Prof. Dr. Dennis Kundisch, Paderborn University, Germany
Prof. Dr. Milad Mirbabaie, Paderborn University, Germany
Prof. Dr. Oliver Müller, Paderborn University, Germany
Prof. Dr. Guido Schryen, Paderborn University, Germany
Prof. Dr. Simon Thanh-Nam Trang, Paderborn University, Germany
Prof. Dr. Matthias Trier, Paderborn University, Germany

Program Committee Chairs

Prof. Dr. Daniel Beverungen, Paderborn University, Germany
Prof. Dr. Christiane Lehrer, Copenhagen Business School, Denmark
Prof. Dr. Matthias Trier, Paderborn University, Germany

Doctoral Consortium Chairs

Prof. Dr. Martin Matzner, Friedrich-Alexander-Universität Erlangen-Nuremberg, Germany
Prof. Dr. Guido Schryen, Paderborn University, Germany
Dr. Miriam Stumpe, Paderborn University, Germany
Dr. Sandra Zilker, Friedrich-Alexander-Universität Erlangen-Nuremberg, Germany

Local Arrangement Chair

Prof. Dr. Dennis Kundisch, Paderborn University, Germany

Sustainability Chair

Prof. Dr. Simon Thanh-Nam Trang, Paderborn University, Germany

Website and Social Media Chair

Prof. Dr. Milad Mirbabaie, Paderborn University, Germany

Preface

This volume comprises papers accepted for publication and presented at the 18th Internationale Tagung Wirtschaftsinformatik (Wi23)—the International Conference of the German-speaking Information Systems Community—held from 18 to 21 September 2023 in Paderborn, Germany. Leaving behind two years of virtual conferences due to the COVID-19 pandemic, the Wi23 took an important role in re-uniting our community, enabling the attendees to meet "old" colleagues—many of them friends—and new people in an on-premise conference setting. In this sense, the Heinz-Nixdorf MuseumsForum, home to the world's largest computer museum, provided an ideal setting for this conference, in which the history and future of the digital society converged.

The conference theme—Digital Responsibility: Social, Ethical, Ecological Implications of Information Systems—acknowledged the crucial role of normative principles in navigating the rapidly accelerating pace of technological change. While digital technologies offer immense opportunities, they also pose significant risks. As markets and innovations outpace regulations, concerns about privacy, fairness, and societal impact continue to grow. Digital responsibility addresses how individuals, organizations, and governments can ensure ethical, inclusive, and sustainable digital development. In information systems, digital responsibility emphasizes moving beyond mere legal compliance, urging stakeholders to consider the broader social, environmental, and ethical consequences of digital transformation. Issues such as avoiding algorithmic bias, assuring data privacy, and providing equitable access to digital services are central to this approach.

The Wi23 program featured 20 scientific tracks. Apart from a track dedicated to the conceptualization and implications of digital responsibility itself, many tracks explored the opportunities and challenges digital transformation presents while many also highlighted the importance of responsible practices. The breadth of topics covered research areas such as business models, digital markets, human–computer interaction, service science, enterprise modeling, and business process management. Specific tracks also examined digitalization prospects in industry, retail, smart cities, education, health, and logistics, alongside focused discussions on the philosophy of science, innovative prototypes, and student contributions.

Focusing on these tracks, we received a reassuring number of 214 full paper submissions and 65 research-in-progress papers. Reflecting the WI conference's role as the premier academic conference of the German-speaking Information Systems/ Wirtschaftsinformatik community, all manuscripts were subjected to an in-depth peer-review process. Each manuscript was assigned to at least two reviewers and one associate editor, assessing the manuscripts scientific rigor and relevance in 953 reviews. The review process resulted in acceptance decisions on 86 full papers and 16 research-in-progress papers, reflecting an overall acceptance rate of 33% across all papers submitted.

This selection of high-quality papers is more than can be included in a single volume. Therefore, we decided to split the conference proceedings into three volumes:

1. The first volume, *Conceptualizing Digital Responsibility for the Information Age*, comprises papers that focus on establishing and clarifying the conceptual ramifications of digital responsibility and its principles in connecting with information systems. A particular focus is also the role of humans and organizations in a digital transformation that is responsible.
2. The second volume, *Solutions and Technologies for Responsible Digitalization*, comprises papers focusing on digital technologies' actual design. It includes foundational topics of our discipline, like information modeling, business process management, and digital infrastructures, but also topics that have emerged more recently, such as data science, prescriptive analytics, and distributed trust. This volume also comprises papers from the conference's industry track, presenting innovative prototypes that can provide immediate business value.
3. The third volume, *Transforming the Digitally Sustainable Enterprise*, comprises papers that focus on the domain tracks of the conference, bringing concrete perspectives and transformation journeys in different industries to the foreground. This volume includes papers on IT strategy, service innovation, and new business models. A particular focus is set on current opportunities and challenges related to digital technologies in health, education, industry and retail, smart cities, and mobility.

Besides the conference tracks, the scientific program of Wi23 included many other formats for presentation and discussion. These included a keynote presentation, a panel discussion, a Chief Information Officers' (CIO) panel, a doctoral consortium, and various ancillary workshops and community meetings. A particular focus of these events was, once again, establishing digital responsibility as a normative guideline for the further digital transformation of society. To initiate and focus discussions, we performed a Delphi study with most of the track chairs before the conference to pinpoint how digital responsibility can be positioned in the broader information systems community. We posit that these results left a strong mark on the community by introducing the concept of digital responsibility and discussing its ramifications.

Organizing the first post-pandemic conference of our community, we also took the liberty to introduce and prototype some administrative innovations that we envisioned would make the conference more interactive, inspiring, and fun. First, regarding paper presentations, we invited the authors to present their research in three different presentation formats, comprising thought-provoking paper sessions, pitch paper sessions, and classic paper sessions. We take the positive feedback as evidence that the new formats spiced up the presentations, while attracting a greater audience and promoting more inspiring discussions. Second, regarding diversity, the Wi23 was the first WI conference to establish diversity in all track chair teams in terms of gender and age. As a program committee, we approached eleven women and nine men to serve as heads for our 20 tracks and asked them to assemble their track chair teams in line with two guidelines: Each track should include men and women, as well as involve at least one young scientist as track chairs. Third, perhaps most notably, we moved the conference from winter to September to avoid the pandemic's repercussions to interfere with the conference once again.

We want to thank all authors, track chairs, associate editors, reviewers, and committee members for devoting their valuable time to organizing and hosting the Wi23. Particular thanks are also due to the entire organizing team from Paderborn University, who worked with all their hearts and souls to welcome our community to Paderborn for a conference that is inspiring, fun, and an asset for developing strong professional and personal relationships.

Finally, we sincerely thank the sponsors who generously supported our conference. Their commitment made it possible to provide a conference experience that we found unique. Special thanks apply to our gold sponsors DATEV eG and the Software Innovation Campus Paderborn (SICP), our silver sponsors 20Forward, Arvato, Finanz Informatik, Heinz Nixdorf Stiftung Westfalen, UNITY, Weidmüller, and our bronze sponsors myConsult, Springer, and SpringerGabler. KONTOR N and Störtebecker Braumanufaktur helped us to make the conference reception a truly memorable event.

As the program committee of the Wi23 conference, we wish you an insightful read of the proceedings. May the research published at this conference stimulate fresh thinking, inspire you to develop new ideas, and build an appreciation for the normative principles that digital transformation can offer as guidance for the further progress of digital transformation. We are convinced that in a world that is transforming at incredible speed, it is on us to envision and build the type of society we desire.

Paderborn, Germany — Daniel Beverungen
Frederiksberg, Denmark — Christiane Lehrer
Paderborn, Germany — Matthias Trier
September 2024

Contents

About the Editors

Daniel Beverungen is Professor of Information Systems and Enterprise Systems at Paderborn University, Germany. His research interests include service research, business process management, and the design of innovative information systems.

Christiane Lehrer is Associate Professor at the Department of Digitalization at Copenhagen Business School, Denmark. Her research interests include data-driven innovation, user behavior, and sustainable information systems.

Matthias Trier is Professor of Information Systems and Social Computing at the University of Paderborn, Germany, and Visiting Professor at Copenhagen Business School, Denmark. His research interests include digital social user behavior such as the appropriation of social media and collaboration platforms in companies' digital participation, the influence of electronic discourse, cooperation in virtual reality, and event-driven dynamic network analysis.

Distributed Trust, Security and Privacy

Requirements for a Federated Learning System to Strengthen IT Security in Human Resource Management

Lisa Kolb, Steffi Rudel, and Ulrike Lechner

Abstract Federated Learning is a decentralized approach to Machine Learning that preserves privacy by sharing models rather than data. This paper examines the requirements for a Federated Learning system as part of an IT service to strengthen IT security in Human Resource Management, especially in the recruitment process, while meeting the business needs of different stakeholders. Our research design is guided by design science research. This paper presents one iteration with a mixed-method approach consisting of a survey with $n = 110$ data sets, a workshop, and ten expert interviews. The result shows up two requirements catalogs for service design and user experience.

Keywords Federated learning · Human resource management · IT security · Requirements

1 Introduction

The risk of companies falling victim to cyber-attacks has steadily increased in recent years. Vulnerabilities in systems, social engineering, and non-robust systems allow attackers to penetrate companies in an increasingly targeted manner. In addition, a growing number of modern ransomware variants and phishing attacks extract data and crash systems (Bundesamt für Sicherheit in der Informationstechnik 2022). The recruitment process in Human Resource Management (HRM) handles sensitive data and, at the same time, opens up many attack possibilities, as companies must

L. Kolb (✉) · S. Rudel · U. Lechner
University of the Bundeswehr Munich, Neubiberg, Germany
e-mail: lisa.kolb@unibw.de

S. Rudel
e-mail: steffi.rudel@unibw.de

U. Lechner
e-mail: ulrike.lechner@unibw.de

D. Beverungen et al. (eds.), *Solutions and Technologies for Responsible Digitalization*, Lecture Notes in Information Systems and Organisation 75,
https://doi.org/10.1007/978-3-031-80122-8_1

permanently enable open interfaces to external applicants, thus increasing the risk of malware infiltration. Social engineering, ransomware hidden in multimedia application documents, or drive-by attacks in background checks are malware attacks that complicate recruiters' work and compromise security. Experimental analyses have demonstrated that Federated Learning (FL) as a subcategory of Machine Learning (ML) can benefit IT security while complying with data protection regulations like the General Data Protection Regulation (GDPR) (Council of European Union 2018) when collecting data to augment the learning system (Li et al. 2020; Alazab et al. 2021). This research focuses on integrating an FL system to enhance IT security in HRM and addresses, in particular, the diverse requirements associated with this integration. The analysis highlights the dynamic nature of these requirements, which vary based on the different stakeholders involved in the HRM processes. As part of our comprehensive design science study to create models and an architecture for an IT security service, we first captured the business processes in HRM in our previous research (Verlande et al. 2023). This allowed us to gain an understanding of the level of IT security knowledge of HRM staff. In parallel, we explored the necessary design of FL services. In this study, we take the next step in our design research towards FL service and capture the requirements for an FL system in HRM, as is more common in service science (Alter 2001), due to the limited information base in the literature. Horkoff (2019) shows that non-functional requirements must be reconsidered in ML, and Habibullah & Horkoff (2021) even connect the requirements with industrial challenges. Vogelsang & Borg (2019) gathers requirements from the perspective of data scientists and notes that changing development processes are accompanied by changing requirements. Thus, in our case study, we also see the need to capture the requirements of an FL system. Using a mix of methods, including a survey, a workshop, and expert interviews, the specific users' and applicability requirements of an FL system are explored. This paper provides two catalogs of requirements (artifacts)—service design and user experience—to identify the needs for an FL system that can strengthen IT security in HRM. Therefore, we want to answer the following questions:

- RQ1: Which stakeholder requirements must an FL system for increasing IT security in HRM fulfill from a service design perspective?
- RQ2: Which stakeholder requirements must an FL system meet for increasing IT security in HRM from the user's perspective?

This paper is organized as follows. After this introduction, we present the theoretical background. This is followed by the research design, the studies' evaluation results, and the requirements catalogs. The article concludes with a discussion and an outlook.

2 Theoretical Background

2.1 IT Security in HRM

The importance of raising IT security within HRM has increased due to the introduction of data protection regulations (e.g., DSGVO, BDSG (German)) (Hoofnagle et al. 2019) and increased IT security regulations (e.g., ITSIG, BSI guidelines)(Bundesamt für die Sicherheit in der Informationstechnik (BSI) 2019, Zweites Gesetz zur Erhöhung der Sicherheit informationstechnischer Systeme 2021). And although IT security in HRM should be an essential topic, one can hardly find any scientific literature. Zafar (2012) focuses on the security of Human Resource Information Systems (HRIS). The paper describes some potential threats that can affect such a system and questions how such a system can be made more (IT-)secure. However, as there is very little research on this topic so far, the authors pose possible research questions and recommend that further research be done on potential threats to the system. Zafar et al. (2011) look specifically at "Human Resources Security Risk Management (HRSRM)" and examine differences in the perception of IT security risks between management and employees. The study concludes that effective cooperation between HRM, IT, and management is necessary and "that additional security training and awareness are needed for HR professionals in order to have successful HRSRM" (p. 505). According to Verhoeven, the central security problem in recruitment is the so-called overtrust effect, which makes recruiters more vulnerable to attacks (Verhoeven 2020). Attackers exploit the predicament of recruiters, who are forced to work with external documents from unknown senders daily and take advantage of their lack of technical expertise. Recruiters may receive application e-mails with modified attachments that seem well-worded and harmless at first glance but open the way into the company for the hacker.

However, HRM must maintain open interfaces while taking additional security and data protection precautions, e.g., contacting applicants in the recruitment process. The security of communication channels is critical to prevent cyber-attacks while maintaining good system performance. Our previous research has shown that HRM's (dominant) communication channels with applicants can be classified into two categories: via e-mail or a so-called Applicant Tracking System (ATS). The dominance of email-based systems or Applicant Tracking Systems depends on company size, industry, application volume, and security requirements (Verlande et al. 2023). In HRM, storing applications received via email on internal file systems can encourage the spread of malware, especially in small companies without secure workspaces. An ATS that operates independently of core systems can help reduce the attack surface. However, both approaches allow, for example, the possibility of a social engineering attack. Despite the great importance of digitization and a corresponding organizational culture, companies do not sufficiently qualify their staff through professional development, technical training, or personal skills. Thus, digitizing HRM processes and workflows is still challenging in digital transformation (Schellinger et al. 2021).

2.2 Federated Learning

Federated learning (FL) is a decentralized machine learning (ML) approach. Figure 1 illustrates how an FL system works. The central server first sends an initial model to each participating entity. Then each entity trains its local model using the initial model and entity-specific data sets. The training data is kept within the entity, and only the trained local model is sent back to the central server. The collected local models are then combined on the central server into a global model, which, once confirmed, is sent to all participating entities for use (McMahan et al. 2017). FL shares models rather than data. This ensures learning is compliant with privacy regulations. Models and not potentially sensitive data are being shared. Moreover, FL enables the aggregation of numerous small decentralized models into one central model through a central communication architecture. This central hub and initial models are typically provided by a service provider (Liu et al. 2022). FL is most frequently associated with the application fields of healthcare (Xu et al. 2021), urban computing and smart cities (Zheng et al. 2022), as well as edge computing and Internet of Things (Ferrag et al. 2021; Lim et al. 2020). But the use of FL to increase IT security is also already being investigated and has shown positive results in other studies because it reduces risks like data breaches and unauthorized access, and the decentralized approach increases the model accessibility (Alazab et al. 2021; Ghimire & Rawat 2022). In addition, FL can work with other technical approaches such as blockchain or differential privacy (Zhang et al. 2020). However, most of these papers focus on algorithms and simulated implementation and pay less attention to embedding the system in an IT landscape, clearly representing business processes, and integrating it into a service system.

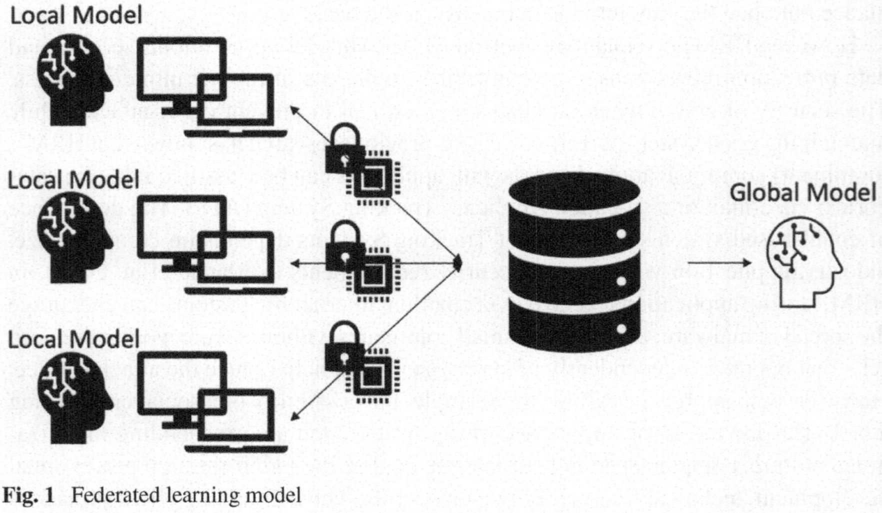

Fig. 1 Federated learning model

3 Research Design

The design science process of Peffers et al. (2007) guides our work. This article focuses on a deep dive into the requirements for an FL system to enhance IT security in HRM. The requirements then guide the design and implementation of the system and the evaluation for usefulness. This research aims to increase the knowledge of service design of FL systems in organizations and the design of IT security systems for HRM.

Requirements engineering offers many methods to the analyst (Pohl 2010). A mixed-methods approach best describes the research design according to Kuckartz (2014) with conceptual models, requirements, and design principles resulting from the design science (Maedche et al. 2019). Our analysis builds on a previous interview study with a conceptual model showing a first approach of design elements (Table 1) for an FL system (Verlande et al. 2023).

To answer RQ1, we choose the first step, a survey. This survey provides an initial overview of the requirements for FL from a system perspective. The survey was subsequently deepened in terms of content in a creative workshop. To design and structure the survey, we determined the focus groups, created questions, conducted pre-tests, collected the data, and carried out a statistical analysis following Lehmann et al. (1998), Müller-Böling & Klandt (1996). A survey with 38 closed questions was created, and 16 filter questions were divided according to the participants' technical knowledge. The survey was conducted in July–August 2022, resulting in $n = 110$ complete data sets and $n = 31$ incomplete data sets, which were included in the analysis. The findings from the survey were then refined in a creative workshop. Six stakeholders: recruiters, IT security experts, technical staff, and data protection officers, participated in a 3-h workshop in September 2022. During the workshop, the service requirements and regulations of the participants were recorded and discussed using a dashboard and post-it notes. Data analysis took place according to Grounded Theory (Glaser & Strauss 2017). The post-it notes were coded as open code, and design elements from previous steps were used as axial codes and were refined in this data analysis. Results from the survey and the creative workshop were analyzed in a cohort analysis; the first session covered the basic unstructured requirements, while the second round focused on adaptation and refinement. The result of this work is the "catalog of Service Design" requirements. To answer RQ2, we conducted an expert interview study to capture user requirements (user experience). To capture the users'

Table 1 Design elements for an FL system (previous research)

Core elements	Support elements	Control elements
Service design	IT security	Compliance
Performance	Awareness	Incentives
	Monitoring	Role concept
	Maintanance	

requirements for software to increase IT security in HRM, expert interviews guided by Lamnek & Krell (2016) were conducted with ten companies in May and June 2022. The interviewed companies were from the energy, semiconductor, food, defense, and mobility sectors, and the interviews lasted an average of 42 min. Interviews were transcribed, coded, and analyzed according to the method of Kuckartz & Rädicker (2022). and resulted in the "User Experience requirements catalog".

4 Results

The results chapter is structured into two sections, the service design and the user experience, presenting and discussing the catalogs. In the case of the survey and the workshop (Sect. 4.1), we used the design elements from the previous paper to cluster the results.

4.1 Service Design

This section shows the survey results and combines them with the workshop results.

Awareness (SD_1): The topic of FL needs to be addressed more strongly within society. Only 13% stated that they had already heard of or were familiar with the term, but the remaining 87% of respondents were unfamiliar with FL. Respondents were also asked about barriers to using FL technology (see Fig. 2). More than half said the most significant barriers were concerns and the lack of knowledge and acceptance (cf. Moody et al. (2018)). Creating more transparency and openness in ML systems is a relevant topic. This can be achieved by integrating Explainable Artificial Intelligence (AI) into the FL system to make system decisions explainable, comprehensible, and transparent. This step strengthens trust, quicker learnability, and, by extension, the system's troubleshooting and maintainability, as also noted by Doshi-Velez & Kim (2017). Raising awareness can help clarify the issues, create understanding, and eliminate ignorance so that digitalization and the integration of new services, in our case with an FL system, are not impaired, as also mentioned by the International Organization for Standardization (2012). Compliance/Contracts (SD_2 and SD_4): Most respondents (42%) desire additional rules, requirements, and restrictions on an FL system with metadata exchange. This statement can also be related to the respondents' concerns about the metadata exchange with third parties.

Thus 19% indicate that they have no confidence in such a system, 42% worry about using a standardized solution, and 12% have concerns regarding the missing readiness for cooperation by third and the not homogeneous data structure. Similarly, respondents see compliance (19%) and legal regulations (15%) as requirements for FL systems to protect IT security, alongside the application of access rights (27%), data security (15%), and lesser aspects such as sustainability and adaptivity. So, all participants must be contractually subject to identical requirements, specifications,

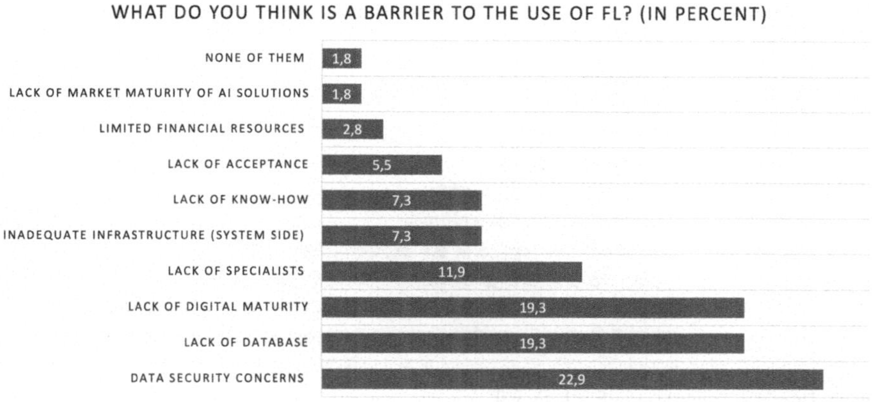

Fig. 2 Barriers to the use of FL

and restrictions when exchanging metadata to avoid conflicts and inconsistencies. Here, examining the possible use of Blockchain to meet the requirements is essential. We discuss in an article that is combining FL and Blockchain eventually increases digital sovereignty (Klare et al. 2023).

Incentives (SD_5): Respondents rate motivation to participate in information sharing as a critical factor; here, incentive schemes can help to increase motivation and fairness through additional features or financial compensation. In addition, 27% of the respondents call for an incentive system as an additional measure when implementing an FL system for sharing metadata between companies' HRM. The use of Blockchain is also suitable for the integration of incentives to increase fairness and motivation.

Role concept (SD_6): Respondents are convinced that access rights are essential, whereby the distribution of rights should be based on the concept of roles. The clarification of responsibilities has a high priority in the role concept, so respondents were also asked in this field for their assessment regarding an FL system to protect IT security in HRM. Overall, 78% stated that technical departments should take care of, while only 22% see the responsibility for such processes and systems in HRM. This assumption is reinforced by the fact that the technical professional group can certainly imagine accepting a higher (45%) to medium (41%) burden for operating with an FL system.

Service design (SD_7, SD_8): Various expectations regarding handling an ML system were queried within the survey. In general, the respondents attach great importance to easy installation and maintenance, as well as their low effort, but simultaneously to the high reliability of the results (see Fig. 3). The results on the expectations of an FL system for IT security protection underline the desire for a fast and effective system. The most important factors mentioned here are memorability (26%), intuitive usability (20%), and flexibility (18%), while transparency, quick learnability, task appropriateness, clarity, and adaptability are significantly lower. In line with these results is the respondents' desire for a fully automated system (81%) in contrast to

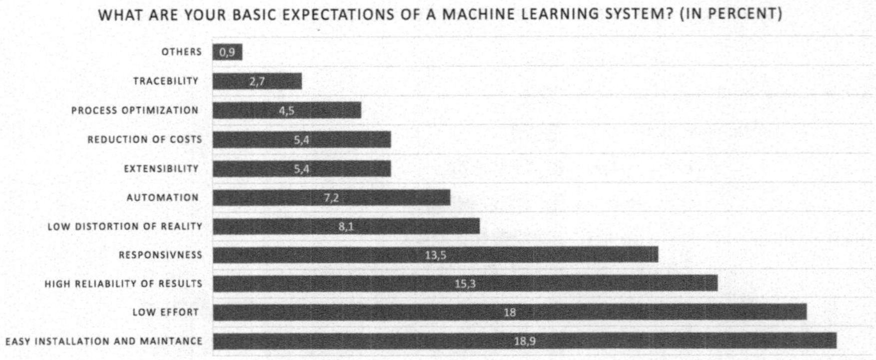

Fig. 3 Basic expectations of an ML system

a partially manual system (19%). Thus, the opposition to approaches like AI Ethics, Human-in-the-loop, and Explainable AI, which seek to increasingly incorporate the human component into the process and decisions of an AI system to control the machine (cf. Jobin et al. (2019), Baum et al. (2022)).

Performance (SD_10 and SD_11): According to the respondents, the systems should be fast, flexible, automated, interoperable, and portable with other services like in other works according to the performance of an ML system (cf. Vogelsang & Borg (2019)). To strengthen the system's performance, the respondents were also asked about ways to minimize the technical effort; again, full automation of the system (35%) and a fast and intuitive presentation (27%) of the system seem to be the most beneficial aspects. In contrast, the documentation of the results and the comprehensibility of the code were rated as less supportive (15%).

Monitoring (SD_12): Above all, monitoring through Key-Performance-Indicators is supported by the majority, followed by general monitoring of training data and control of AI systems and implementing security guidelines and general system transparency (Fig. 4). Thus, monitoring and control of performance must still be considered a fundamental design element.

IT security (SD_3, SD_13 and SD_14): According to the survey, the IT professionals' concerns about ML systems relate primarily to insufficient data protection and worries about industrial espionage, and 42% want additional restrictions to control these areas. Security concerns regarding using an FL system are mainly related to the general exchange of metadata, with exactly half seeing it as rather feasible and the other half seeing it as critical. Since data is primarily needed to create an FL system for IT security, the technical staff was asked what data they could provide. The result shows that policy concepts are usable (57%). But when it comes to monitoring data, only 19% would like to provide security reports, and only a total of 8% would provide documented IT security incidents and IT security audits to train an FL system. The workshop results are highlighted in Fig. 5 and link the axial codes.

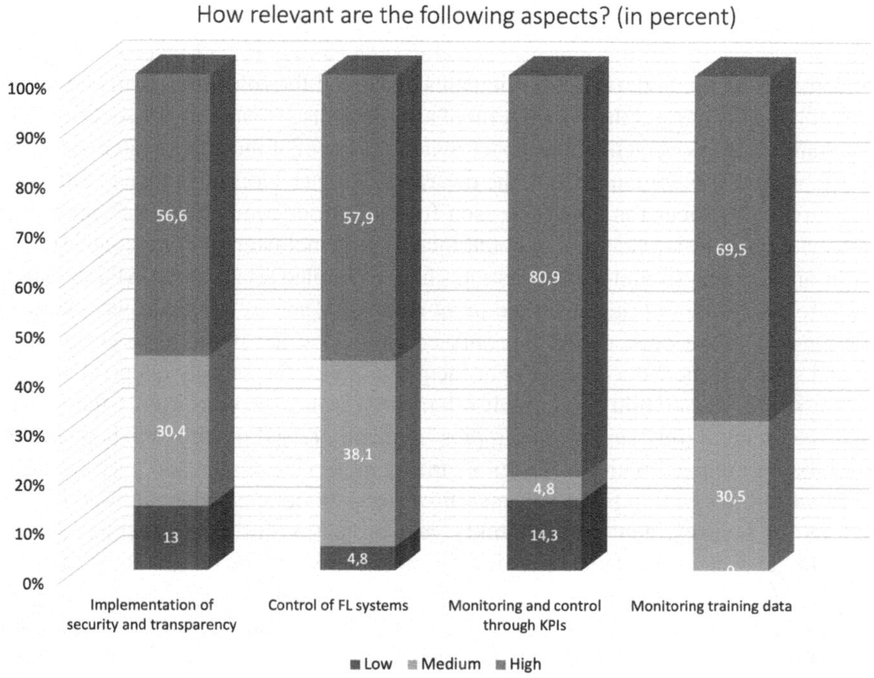

Fig. 4 Relevant aspects for an FL system

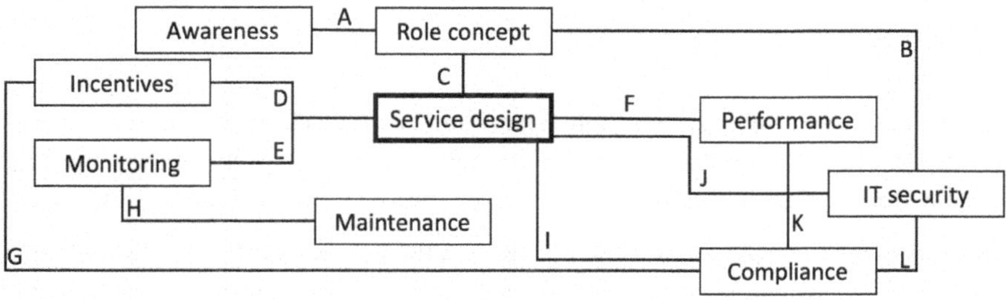

Fig. 5 Results of the selective codes

The open codes are composed of the dashboard post-its created by the workshop participants, where each note was recorded as an independent code. This leads to a total result of 40 open codes (requirements). These codes were linked to the design elements (Table 1), ending with the following nine axial codes: Awareness, Incentive, Compliance/-Contracts, Role concept, Service design, Performance, IT security, Maintenance, and Monitoring.

(A) The increase in awareness in combination with the role concept was mainly demanded by the non-technical staff, who had difficulties imagining integrating an

FL system. From this, the participants recorded the requirements for training, eliminating skepticism and ignorance, increasing understanding, and incorporating the Explainable AI method. (B, C) Participants discussed the role concept in combination with the design and the distribution of access rights provided by IT security. (D) The connection between the open codes and the element of incentive systems cannot be established at first glance. Still, the desire to generate additional added value and the participants' question about a reason for the introduction shows that incentive systems within the service design could increase the inclusion of companies. (E, H) The monitoring and maintenance elements have a coupled relationship. Maintenance reacts to the vulnerabilities identified in monitoring, whereby the terms were named individually in the open codes and only combined by the participants during the second round of the workshop. (F) For the participants, the aspects of speed, delay-free processes, availability, low fault tolerance, resource-saving use of the goods used, and general time-saving were topics frequently raised in the workshop, which are to be harmonized with the design elements of service design and performance. (J) However, integrating protective measures, security policies, manual intervention options for security, general availability, and protection through assigning access rights to the users were also named as relevant and covered the design element of IT security. (G, I, K, L) Compliance with existing regulations was of particular importance not only for the data protection officer but also for the HR specialists and the IT security officer as it influences the possibilities of system implementation and design.

4.2 User Experience

The results were collected through expert interviews. The following categories (Table 2) were in the first step (a priori) formed from the questions in the guideline. These codes were then used on the transcribed interviews to analyze the interviews.

Suggestion for improvement The evaluation of the interviews showed that only half of the respondents could name the IT security software they currently use ("existing systems"). However, all respondents stated they were "satisfied" or "very satisfied" with the current system. This leads to the conclusion that a new (FL-based) system would have to offer clear advantages for the companies to consider a change. Very few suggestions for improvement or disadvantages of the system used so far were mentioned. Among other things, it was mentioned that employees could not always be sure which data were checked by the IT security software, as these were not specially marked. This aspect was included in the requirements catalog (UI_1).

Scope of action for users Regarding the scope of action for the users, almost all respondents agree that they would like to have as little interaction with the software as possible—they do not want to be disturbed in their daily work. Rather, the software should take care of as much as possible, and you should not worry about it. More specifically, we asked how much control or freedom of choice users would want

Table 2 Coding codes for the qualitative analysis

Code		Explanation
Main category	Sub category	
Suggestion for improvement		What potential for improvement is seen in existing systems? What else was mentioned?
Scope of action for users		How much does the user want to be able to/need to interact with the IT security software?
Functions	24h hotline, Personel contact person, Self-guidance, Question-answer System, Reminder services. Placement of warnings. Link check. Forum, Contact form, Chatbot, Training with gamification	How are the following functions valued?
Weighting functions		Which of the functions is rated with which importance?

regarding the data filtered by the security software. Here, too, the picture from the previous question was confirmed—70% of the respondents said they wanted to have as little contact as possible with the security software so as not to be impaired in their daily work. Three respondents concreted their statement: the topic seemed too complex to them, and they would rather have the specialists in the IT department take care of it. These two aspects were included in the requirements catalog (UI_2 and UI_3).

Functions and their weighting Finally, the participants were asked about the additional functions. The weighting was done according to the naming of the participants. The classification was as follows: over seven mentions = high, 4–6 mentions = medium, and 0–3 mentions = low. The "placement of warnings" (UI_8) was named most frequently (eight times). The options "24 h hotline" and "personal contact person" were each mentioned six times. Since these two options are quite similar, they were included as UI_4 in the requirements catalog. Five mentions were given to the "reminder services" and the "automated link check", which were adopted as UI_7 and UI_9. Four respondents saw the "Training with gamification" approach as desirable (UI_13). The fewest nominations received the functions "Self-guidance" (three mentions, UI_5), "Question–answer system" (two mentions, UI_6), "Forum" (zero mentions, UI_10), "Contact form" (two mentions, UI_11) and "Chatbot" (one time mentioned, UI_12).

4.3 Catalogs of Requirements

The following tables depict the requirements catalog for "Service Design" (Table 3) and the requirements catalog for "User Experience" (Table 4). Both include requirements with descriptions, prioritization, and expression measures showing whether it is part of the technical or organizational field.

The requirement catalogs show that users are primarily concerned with service design, user experience, and performance. The ease of use of a new service and the performance and fulfillment of the service description is fundamental. Other design elements are seen as elementary but should support or control convenience and enhance the user's experience so that they have to contribute as little as possible to the service. Dashboards, contacts, reminders, and alerts should also support the user in this. Users find some understanding of the service useful, but this does not necessarily mean a deeper understanding of all the structures and how to deal with the system's decisions and consequences (including ethical consequences), so the system should still function as a black box in its basic. In summary, the general desire of stakeholders is for a system that is integrated into an overall service. Installation, control, and maintenance, as well as information, should b provided, and the relevant systems should operate as required, or contact points should be available in case of conflict.

5 Discussion, Conclusion and Further Steps

As a result of RQ1—Which stakeholder requirements must an FL system for increasing IT security in HRM fulfill from a service design perspective?—we combine the results of the survey and the workshop in the catalog of requirements "Service Design" Table 3. To answer RQ2—Which stakeholder requirements must an FL system meet for increasing IT security in HRM from the user's perspective?—and to demonstrate the requirements for service usability, we conducted expert interviews and designed the "User Experience" catalog, which is shown in Table 4. With our results, we aim to contribute to the knowledge of requirements and service design for an FL system in HRM—to our knowledge, no such research has been done. However, there are many other application areas for FL as privacy-preserving AI, as mentioned in the theoretical background 2.2. The analysis has shown that the integration of an FL system to improve IT security in HRM has different requirements, such as in the areas of service design and performance. The requirements change, especially with the stakeholders, so the challenge is to create a system that meets all aspects. By aligning with established standards and frameworks (e.g., ITIL (AXELOS 2019), BSI guidelines (Bundesamt für die Sicherheit in der Informationstechnik (BSI) 2019)), some of the requirements can potentially be fulfilled through existing measures and practices, especially in IT security, awareness, and compliance. However, certain requirements, including service design, role concept, and

Table 3 Requirements catalog—"service design"

ID	Requirement	Description	Priority	Note	Expression measure
SD_1	Awareness	Eliminate skepticism and ignorance. Provide the participants with information so that they can participate in shaping the project	Medium		Human
SD_2	Contracts	Establish contracts for the participants but also for the service provider in cooperation. Relevant are the design of cooperation and communication, conditions for entry into the system, provision and access rights to be granted, etc.	Medium	Fulfillment by connecting FL and blockchain	Organizational
SD_3	IT security	Ensuring data sovereignty and securing the communication strands. Learning environment should meet current security standards. Data security (data sovereignty) is the focus here	High		Technical
SD_4	Compliance	Compliance with IT security standards (B5I/IS027001), data protection regulations (DSGVO) and, specifically for HRM, the AGG, BVs and TVs	High	Fulfillment by connecting FL and blockchain	Organisational

(continued)

Table 3 (continued)

ID	Requirement	Description	Priority	Note	Expression measure
5D_5	Incentives	Present the incentives (added value of the system) and generate "reward systems" for cooperation. Increase added value and enhance fairness	Low	Fulfillment by connecting FL and blockchain	Technical/ organizational
SD_6	Role concept	Clear statement of the roles required in the company. Description of the activities and the required expertise. Define training concepts for the roles and clearly limit access rights	Medium	Project owner HRM while system owner IT department	Human/ organizational
SD_7	Service design	Handling, operability should be simple, memorable and intuitive. The users do not want to be disturbed in their main processes (invisibility of the system). Complete automation is also desirable, while at the same time ensuring high reliability of the results	High	Because of AI ethics and guidelines, full automation does not seem feasible	Technical
SD_8	Service design	Create a common database among all participants or generate a possibility for learning with heterogeneous data sets	High	Testing within the prototype development	Technical

(continued)

Table 3 (continued)

ID	Requirement	Description	Priority	Note	Expression measure
SD_9	Maintenance	Simple and intuitive, no long processes, no high additional costs for procurement of materials or skilled personnel	Low	Connection to role concept	Technical/ organizational
SD_10	Performance	System should allow interfaces to other IT security software, as well as the file and mail server and the software used in HRM (SAP; ATS)	High	Testing within the prototype development	Technical
SD_11	Performance	Low time expenditure (waiting time/ delay-free communication) for the calculations. Low resource consumption (sustainability)	High	Testing within the prototype development	Technical
SD_12	Monitoring	Monitoring of the systems through KPIs and monitoring of the training data u sed by specialised staff should be in place. Transparency of the system for the supervisor. Quarantine area for rejected applications and Sandbox for testing	Medium	Manual control	Technical/ organizational

(continued)

Table 3 (continued)

ID	Requirement	Description	Priority	Note	Expression measure
SD_13	IT security	It should be possible to check data, especially PDFs and Office files. Due to the already existing security systems, a check of mails is not desired	Medium	Testing within the prototype development	Technical
SD_14	IT security	Elimination of the source of the damage, information about the attack, reduction of successful attacks	Medium	Testing within the prototype development	Technical

monitoring, require further investigation to specify their relevance and applicability to integrating an FL system for enhancing IT security in HRM. For example, examining the User Experience catalog may reveal specific user interaction requirements that have implications for modifying the service design. Specific requirements that are not crucial to the system's main function can be specified during prototype development. Instead of integrating a standalone FL service, we recommend, therefore, examining the possibility of integrating it into existing services, such as IT security service or ATS. This integration has the potential to provide additional value to clients by allowing them to use an already familiar service alongside FL capabilities, so the effort on the part of the customers is also kept as low as possible. In addition, existing services can draw on a larger knowledge base and, thus, a larger amount of data for the initial learning process required to deploy an FL system. As requirements analyses can never be complete, these catalogs show the first general requirements for an IT security FL system in HRM. Considering the domains of Service Design and User Experience, it is important to acknowledge that the sample size in the current study is relatively small—if other experts had been asked, the requirements and weights could have differed. Therefore, repeating the survey with more experts in further research and later in the design process of the system would be desirable to compare the results. Finally, this research contributes to the understanding of services with AI. It provides insights into how business information systems with AI and privacy-preserving AI can be designed and offers perspectives that XAI and privacy only answer in a limited way.

Table 4 Requirements catalog—"user experience"

ID	Requirement	Description	Priority	Note	Expression measure
UI_1	Review visibility	Users in HRM want to be able to recognize what is audited/secure and what is not	Medium	Improvement suggestion	Technical
UI_2	Interaction with security software	Users in HRM want to have to interact as little as possible with the security software or decide for themselves how much to interact. The software should do as much of the work as possible	High	Scope of action for users	Technical
UI_3	No influence on operational work	Users in HRM want to be disturbed as little as possible in their work by security software	High	Scope of action for users	Technical
UI_4	Function: (Emergency) contact person	HRM users wanta 24-hour emergency hotline ora personal contact person	High	Function	Organizational
UI_5	Function: self-guidance	Users in HRM want guidance on how to help themselves	Low	Function	Organizational
UI_6	Function: question-answer system	Users in HRM want a system in which the most frequently asked questions a re answered	Low	Function	Technical
UI_7	Function: reminder services	HRM users would like to be automatically reminded, for example, of password changes or system updates	Medium	Function	Technical
UI_8	Function: placement of warnings	HRM users would like to see a suitable location for warnings of potential phishing e-mails	High	Function	Technical
UI_9	Function: link check	HRM users would like links in e-mails to be automatically checked and marked accordingly	Medium	Function	Technical
UI_10	Function: forum	Users in HRM want a forum to improve IT security software	Low	Function	Organizational

(continued)

Table 4 (continued)

ID	Requirement	Description	Priority	Note	Expression measure
Ul_ll	Function: contact form	Users in HRM would like to be able to write to IT via contact form in case of problems or questions	Low	Function	Organizational
Ul_12	Function: chatbot	Users in HRM would like to chat with a bot when they have questions or problems	Low	Function	Technical
Ul_13	Function: training with gamifikation	HRM users want interesting and motivating training concepts	Medium	Function	Human

Acknowledgements We want to thank Bayern Innovativ for funding the "Federated Learning Enhancing IT Security (FLEIS)" project (DIK 0241_2104_0080), as well as our partners, fellow researchers, and all study participants, as well as the anonymous reviews.

References

Alazab, M., RM, S. P., Parimala, M., Maddikunta, P. K. R., Gadekallu, T. R. & Pham, Q.-V. (2021), 'Federated learning for cybersecurity: concepts, challenges, and future diretions', IEEE Transactions on Industrial Informatics 18(5), 3501–3509.

Alter, S. (2001), 'Which Life Cycle–Work System, Information System, or Software?', Communications of the Association for Information Systems 7(1), 17.

AXELOS (2019), ITIL Foundation - ITIL 4 Edition (DE), Technical report, AXELOS.

Baum, K., Mantel, S., Schmidt, E. & Speith, T. (2022), 'From responsibility to reason- giving explainable artificial intelligence', Philosophy & Technology 35(1), 12.

Bundesamt für die Sicherheit in der Informationstechnik (BSI) (2019), IT-Grundschutz-Kompendium—Edition 2019, Bundesamt für Sicherheit in der Informationstechnik.

Bundesamt für Sicherheit in der Informationstechnik (2022), Die Lage der IT-Sicherheit in Deutschland 2022, Technical report, Bundesamt für Sicherheit in der Information- stechnik (BSI), Bonn.

Council of European Union (2018), 2018 reform of EU data protection rules, Technical report, European Commission.

Doshi-Velez, F. & Kim, B. (2017), 'Towards a rigorous science of interpretable machine learning', arXiv: Machine Learning.

Ferrag, M. A., Friha, O., Maglaras, L., Janicke, H. & Shu, L. (2021), 'Federated deep learning for cyber security in the internet of things: Concepts, applications, and experimental analysis', IEEE Access 9, 138509–138542.

Ghimire, B. & Rawat, D. B. (2022), 'Recent Advances on Federated Learning for Cybersecurity and Cybersecurity for Federated Learning for Internet of Things', IEEE Internet of Things Journal 9(11), 8229–8249.

Glaser, B. G. & Strauss, A. L. (2017), The discovery of grounded theory: Strategies for qualitative research, Routledge.

Habibullah, K. M. & Horkoff, J. (2021), Non-functional requirements for machine learning: understanding current use and challenges in industry, in '2021 IEEE 29th International Requirements Engineering Conference (RE)', IEEE, pp. 13–23.

Hoofnagle, C. J., Van Der Sloot, B. & Borgesius, F. Z. (2019), 'The European Union general data protection regulation: what it is and what it means', Information & Communications Technology Law 28(1), 65–98.

Horkoff, J. (2019), Non-Functional Requirements for Machine Learning: Challenges and New Directions, in 'IEEE 27th International Requirements Engineering Conference (RE)', IEEE, pp. 386–391.

International Organization for Standardization (2012), ISO/IEC 27032:2012(EN) – Information technology — Security techniques — Guidelines for cybersecurity, Technical report, International Organization for Standardization.

Jobin, A., Ienca, M. & Vayena, E. (2019), 'The global landscape of AI ethics guidelines', Nature Machine Intelligence 1(9), 389–399.

Klare, M., Verlande, L., Greiner, M. & Lechner, U. (2023), How Blockchain and Artificial Intelligence influence Digital Sovereignty, in M. Papadaki, P. Rupino da Cunha, M. Themistocleous & K. Christodoulou, eds, 'Information Systems', Springer Nature Switzerland, pp. 3–16.

Kuckartz, U. (2014), Mixed methods: Methodologie, Forschungsdesigns und Analysever- fahren, Springer-Verlag.

Kuckartz, U. & Rädicker, S. (2022), Qualitative Inhaltsanalyse: Methoden, Praxis, Computerunterstützung, Beltz Juventa.

Lamnek, S. & Krell, C. (2016), Qualitative Sozialforschung, Beltz.

Lehmann, D. R., Gupta, S., Steckel, J. H. & Gupta, S. (1998), Marketing research, Addison-Wesley Reading, MA.

Li, B., Wu, Y., Song, J., Lu, R., Li, T. & Zhao, L. (2020), 'DeepFed: Federated deep learning for intrusion detection in industrial cyber-physical systems', IEEE Transactions on Industrial Informatics 17(8), 5615–5624.

Lim, W. Y. B., Luong, N. C., Hoang, D. T., Jiao, Y., Liang, Y.-C., Yang, Q., Niyato, D. & Miao, C. (2020), 'Federated learning in mobile edge networks: A comprehensive survey', IEEE Communications Surveys & Tutorials 22(3), 2031–2063.

Liu, J., Huang, J., Zhou, Y., Li, X., Ji, S., Xiong, H. & Dou, D. (2022), 'From distributed machine learning to federated learning: A survey', Knowledge and Information Systems 64(4), 885–917.

Maedche, A., Gregor, S., Morana, S. & Feine, J. (2019), Conceptualization of the problem space in design science research, in 'Extending the Boundaries of Design Science Theory and Practice: 14th International Conference on Design Science Research in Information Systems and Technology, DESRIST 2019, Worcester, MA, USA, June 4–6, 2019, Proceedings 14', Springer, pp. 18–31.

McMahan, B., Moore, E., Ramage, D., Hampson, S. & y Arcas, B. A. (2017), Communication-efficient learning of deep networks from decentralized data, in 'Artificial intelligence and statistics', PMLR, pp. 1273–1282.

Moody, G. D., Siponen, M. & Pahnila, S. (2018), 'Toward a unified model of information security policy compliance', MIS quarterly 42(1), 285–311.

Müller-Böling, D. & Klandt, H. (1996), Methoden empirischer Wirtschafts- und Sozialforschung: Eine Einführung mit wissenschaftlichem Schwerpunkt, Förderkreis Gründungs-Forschung Köln-Dortmund.

Peffers, K., Tuunanen, T., Rothenberger, M. A. & Chatterjee, S. (2007), 'A design science research methodology for information systems research', Journal of management information systems 24(3), 45–77.

Pohl, K. (2010), Requirements engineering: fundamentals, principles, and techniques, Springer.

Schellinger, J., Tokarski, K. O. & Kissling-Näf, I. (2021), Digital Business: Analysen und Handlungsfelder in der Praxis, Springer Nature.

Verhoeven, T. (2020), Die Risiken der Digitalisierung, in T. Verhoeven, ed., 'Digital- isierung im Recruiting: Wie sich Recruiting durch künstliche Intelligenz, Algorithmen und Bots verändert', Springer Fachmedien Wiesbaden, pp. 225–244.

Verlande, L., Lechner, U. & Rudel, S. (2023), Design of a Federated Learning System for IT Security: Towards Secure Human Resource Management, in 'Proceedings of the 11th Latin-American Symposium on Dependable Computing (LADC 2022)', Association for Computing Machinery, pp. 131–136.

Vogelsang, A. & Borg, M. (2019), Requirements engineering for machine learning: Perspectives from data scientists, in '2019 IEEE 27th International Requirements Engineering Conference Workshops (REW)', IEEE, pp. 245–251.

Xu, J., Glicksberg, B. S., Su, C., Walker, P., Bian, J. & Wang, F. (2021), 'Federated learning for healthcare informatics', Journal of Healthcare Informatics Research 5, 1–19.

Zafar, H. (2012), Exploring Organizational Human Resource Information System Security, in 'AMCIS 2012 Proceedings', Association for Information Systems, p. N/A.

Zafar, H., Clark, J. G. & Ko, M. S. (2011), 'An Exploration of Human Resource Management Information Systems Security', Journal of Emerging Knowledge on Emerging Markets 3(1), 489–510.

Zhang, W., Lu, Q., Yu, Q., Li, Z., Liu, Y., Lo, S. K., Chen, S., Xu, X. & Zhu, L. (2020), 'Blockchain-based federated learning for device failure detection in industrial IoT', IEEE Internet of Things Journal 8(7), 5926–5937.

Zheng, Z., Zhou, Y., Sun, Y., Wang, Z., Liu, B. & Li, K. (2022), 'Applications offederated learning in smart cities: recent advances, taxonomy, and open challenges', Connection Science 34(1), 1–28.

Zweites Gesetz zur Erhöhung der Sicherheit informationstechnischer Systeme (2021), https://www.bsi.bund.de/DE/Das-BSI/Auftrag/Gesetze-und-Verordnungen/IT-SiG/2-0/it_sig-2-0_node.html. Accessed: 06.03.2023.

Implementing Smart Contracts: The Case of NFT-Rental with "Pay-Per-Like"

Alfred Sopi, Johannes Schneider, and Jan vom Brocke

Abstract Non-fungible tokens(NFTs) are on the rise. They can represent artworks exhibited for marketing purposes on webpages of companies or online stores—analogously to physical artworks. Lending of NFTs is an attractive form of passive income for owners but comes with risks (e.g., items are not returned) and costs for escrow agents. Similarly, renters have difficulties in anticipating the impact of artworks, e.g., how spectators of NFTs perceive them. To address these challenges, we introduce an NFT rental solution based on a pay-per-like pricing model using blockchain technology, i.e., smart contracts based on the Ethereum chain. We find that blockchain solutions enjoy many advantages also reported for other applications, but interestingly, we also observe dark sides of (large) blockchain fees. Blockchain solutions appear unfair to niche artists and potentially hamper cultural diversity. Furthermore, a trust-cost tradeoff arises to handle fraud caused by manipulation from parties outside the blockchain. All code for the solution is publicly available at: https://github.com/asopi/rental-project

Keywords Smart contracts · NFT · Rental · Pay-per-like · Value-based pricing

1 Introduction

Since the invention of Bitcoin, blockchain technology has rapidly advanced. Adoption of blockchain technology, especially smart contracts, has also been linked with positive performance, e.g., in an inter-organizational setting (Werner et al., 2021).

A. Sopi (✉) · J. Schneider · J. Brocke
University of Liechtenstein, Vaduz, Liechtenstein
e-mail: alfred.sopi@uni.li

J. Schneider
e-mail: johannes.schneider@uni.li

J. Brocke
e-mail: jan.vombrocke@uni.li

D. Beverungen et al. (eds.), *Solutions and Technologies for Responsible Digitalization*, Lecture Notes in Information Systems and Organisation 75,
https://doi.org/10.1007/978-3-031-80122-8_2

Thus, the time seems more than ripe for widespread adoption. Multiple applications have emerged, and there is a growing body of works that discuss their implementation such as in the energy sector (Kirli et al., 2022), insurance domain (Chondrogiannis et al., 2022), equity market (vom Brocke et al., 2018), and event ticketing (Regner et al. 2019).

However, the full potential of blockchain technology has not yet been explored, in particular, in emerging areas such as digital artworks whose ownership and authenticity can be ensured using non-fungible tokens (NFTs). NFT usage has been growing in the last years (Christodoulou et al., 2022). NFTs might soon be omnipresent.

A non-fungible token is a unique digital identifier that can neither be copied, substituted, nor subdivided (Voshgmir, 2018). It is stored in a blockchain and serves to certify authenticity and ownership. NFTs can be traded or rented. They typically contain references to digital files of various formats, e.g., texts, audio, and images that potentially resemble digital work.

In this work, we focus on an under-explored area, i.e., rental of NFTs with value-based pricing. More specifically, the rental price of artwork is based on the perception of visitors of exhibitions expressed using "likes" as prevalent throughout the digital world, especially, in social media (Ding et al., 2017). NFT renting should enable NFT owners to rent digital assets for temporary use. Especially for art, rental of NFTs is very attractive. For NFT owners, it is lucrative to generate passive income instead of keeping their valuable NFTs locked in their accounts. Renters benefit from the possibility of acquiring the NFT for a limited time, so they do not have to pay high costs compared to purchasing the NFT.

As of now, few organizations are pioneering the NFT rental market, and most solutions have not yet been launched (Beyer, 2023). However, since NFTs are becoming increasingly important and can be very expensive, the need for renting these virtual goods is likely to increase in the upcoming years. Particularly in light of the growing world of virtual assets and the high prices attached to popular NFTs, the need for alternative financing and income-generating methods has increased (J.P.Morgan, 2022).

A rental solution should leverage opportunities of blockchain technology to eliminate typical issues in renting. The most pressing issue for the renter is the return of the item, once the agreed rental period has passed, and being ensured that payments take place. The lender also faces risks. Artwork can trigger a diverse set of reactions, i.e., it can be inspirational, but also trigger disgust or cause no reaction at all. Therefore, it seems advantageous for a renter to pay for positive reactions, e.g., by counting visitors liking the artwork as measured by clicks on a like button. Existing rental solutions are based on a pay-per-use model. They are not able to address fundamental risks of renters or the idea of making payments depending on the reception of an artwork by its audience.

To address these issues, we explore novel solutions using state-of-the-art blockchain technology. Our pay-per-like proposal is analogous to the pay-per-click model, which is one of the modern means of online advertising, wherein an advertiser profits based on the number of clicks made by users on a particular website or an app. There are also a number of challenges in implementing such solutions. For example, click-fraud poses a risk. Each click incurs a cost to the advertiser. Rivals might aim at depleting a competitor's budget through fraudulent clicks or websites hosting 3rd party advertisement have an incentive to generate clicks to increase revenues (Zhang and Guan, 2008). Furthermore, a lender might have to pay a collateral, which poses a risk but also implies that assets are bound for the duration of the rental and cannot be used otherwise.

To develop and evaluate our NFT rental solution, we follow a rigorous design science research (DSR) approach based on Peffers et al. (2007). We leverage existing knowledge through a literature review as well as practitioners' perspectives through an illustrative scenario as common in IS Research (Vom Brocke et al., 2020). By instantiating our framework in a Proof of Concept (PoC) paired with extensive testing, we demonstrate our approach's feasibility and correctness and evaluate its fitness to solve rental-related problems (Hevner et al., 2004). Especially, we address the requirement that the rental price should be value-based, i.e., determined based on feedback from renters.

The key contributions of the paper are: Conceptualizing, implementing and evaluating a value-based rental solution. We also discuss our (and other) solutions in a general setting with three actors, i.e., lenders, renters and consumers. Especially, we unveil a cost-trust trade-off between the actors and negative aspects of high blockchain fees incurred for decentralized Web3 applications, which might manifest as a disadvantage for less established artists.

The paper is organized as follows: We provide background on technology and pricing models, followed by describing the design science process serving as the methodology for our study. The results covering problem analysis, design objectives and implementation, evaluation are stated prior to the discussion and conclusions.

2 Background

Smart Contracts are a computerized transaction protocol that executes the terms of a contract (Szabo, 1994). Smart contracts based on a blockchain are transparent, irreversible, and traceable and do not need intermediaries and human decision-making (Antonopoulos and Wood, 2019, pp. 127–131). However, once deployed on the blockchain, smart contracts cannot be changed, emphasizing the importance of careful development. **Ethereum** provides a blockchain that is well-suited for decentralized applications (Dapps) and smart contracts using Ether (ETH) as currency (Buterin, 2014). The Ethereum virtual machine (EVM) executes code in a global blockchain network. It interprets, stores, and executes smart contracts deployed on the blockchain. Transactions can either be contract creation to deploy the smart contract on the blockchain or message calls to interact with the smart contract (Hirai, 2017).

An account on the Ethereum blockchain is an entity with an ETH balance that can execute transactions. **Accounts** can be user-owned or deployed as smart contracts. Both have the ability to receive, hold, and send ETH and interact with deployed smart contracts (Ethereum Community, 2022b). Anyone can generate an unlimited number of accounts, which correspond to a private and public key pair. The blockchain acts as an enormous ledger with transactions being transferred from one account to another.

Tokens are abstractions representing the ownership of physical or virtual property. They are cryptographically secured on the blockchain. Ownership is associated with certain privileges, such as the right to use or send that property. The tracking of ownership changes is stored on the blockchain and can be viewed and verified transparently by everyone (Solorio et al. 2019, p.23). Tokens are implemented using smart contracts, which typically follow a specific standard called **Ethereum Request for Comments (ERC)**. The ERC-721 introduces the first standard for non-fungible tokens (NFTs) (Ethereum Community, 2022a). The term non-fungible means that the object is unique, not replaceable, and not divisible. An ERC-721 token is used to uniquely identify any content, such as an image, song, or a video. This type of token is used by platforms that offer collectibles, access keys, lottery tickets, etc. Moreover, these unique tokens can be transferred from one account to another. The sender of a transaction must pay a gas fee in ETH depending on computational demands of the transaction (i.e., smart contract) and network utilization (Dr. Wood, 2022,p.8).

A **decentralized application** (Dapp) runs on a peer-to-peer network. Smart contracts are used to implement the backend of such applications, which are then deployed on a blockchain and executed through a frontend or user interface (Zheng et al., 2021,pp.253–280). **Web3** or the decentralized web refers to a distributed internet that aims to eliminate trusted third parties (Antonopoulos and Wood, 2019,p.267). Web2 requires internet users to trust various private companies such as social media platform operators to act in the public's interest. Web3 intends to solve this issue by providing ownership capabilities. The Web3 ecosystem consists of Dapps that adhere to the fundamental principle that users own their data and therefore exert full control over it, unlike applications (and data) managed by centralized organizations.

There are a few **NFT rental** solutions, e.g., IQSpace (2022), Bored Jobs (2022), and reNFT (2022). But none implements an innovative value-based payment solution such as pay-per-click. Typically, the smart contract returns the rented NFT plus the rental fee to the lender after the expiration of the rental period. For collateralized renting, a renter has to deposit a collateral plus the rental fees defined by the lender. The renter then receives the NFT into their account, and the collateral remains in the smart contract, which acts as an escrow account until the renter returns the rented NFT. For collateral-free renting, wrapped NFTs enable the rental of NFTs without a collateral. A wrapped NFT is transferred to the renter's account. Service providers on whose platforms the NFT is to be used can then use the smart contract to verify that the wrapped NFTs originated from a rental deal. For collateral-free, non-wrapped rental the NFT is transferred from the lender's account to the smart contract, the account address from the renter is used to verify and retrieve its rented NFTs.

Pricing Models: The Pay-Per-Use Model (PPU) model also known as the pay-as-you-go usage-based pricing (UBP) model, involves sellers offering identical or comparable goods at different prices, depending on the volume of the goods being purchased (Weinhardt et al., 2009). The PPU model associates service units (e.g., units per time) with fix-priced values so that option prices vary with the volume of service units used (Bauer and Wildman, 2012). The customer pays only for the use of the product or service.

The Pay-Per-Click Model (PPC) model is one of the modern means of online advertising, wherein an advertiser profits based on the number of clicks made by users on a particular website or an app. The advertiser pays for each click collected by the ads, rather than allowing the advertiser to pay a fixed price for a spot on a website. Search engines such as Google or Yahoo exemplify sites with a pay-per-click model (Khraim and Alkrableih, 2015, pp.180–181). One of the most significant limitations of the PPC is the risk of click fraud. The literature recognizes click fraud as the intended and ill-conceived use of PPC when advertising to cause financial damage to another party.

Ives (2005) argued that some individuals use click bots or hit bots to generate invalid clicks on an ad to increase the click count. Click fraud may also include unsatisfied users or employees who willingly click on ads to increase the number of clicks, thereby damaging the company's budget. Attackers can also deliberately cause undesired traffic through scams to damage competitors (Rosso and Jansen, 2010).

3 Methodology

We employ the DSR process by Peffers et al. (2007). Design science aims to conduct research through the development and evaluation of artifacts designed to meet, identify, and leverage business needs (Hevner et al., 2004, pp. 79–80). Design knowledge generated in DSR, can take the form of design entities, e.g. constructs and methods, or the form of design theories. It can be derived inductively, in that the design focuses on situated solutions to situated problems and is, then, further generalized in order to increase the projectability of the design knowledge (Vom Brocke et al., 2020). Specifically, DSR develops prototypes that are demonstrated through iterative analysis, design, and implementation, whether the planned solution can be effectively and efficiently implemented (see Fig. 1). Since DSR supports the generation of knowledge on the design of innovative solutions to real-world problems, DSR has been found particularly suitable in blockchain contexts (Regner et al. 2019, p.5). Knowledge is collected through various methods in several steps. This enables a systematic observation, evaluation, and refinement of the obtained information.

In the first step, we analyze the problem domain based on a literature review, which includes identification of key concepts and terms, and current implementations of smart contract-based solutions, especially rental based-solutions for NFTs to identify shortcomings and their causes. The findings serve as a basis to derive requirements for a tool to address these challenges. The second step comprises the artifact design, which focuses on the development of the Dapp. In the first evaluation step, the two lead authors of this research interacted with the web-based tool prototype,

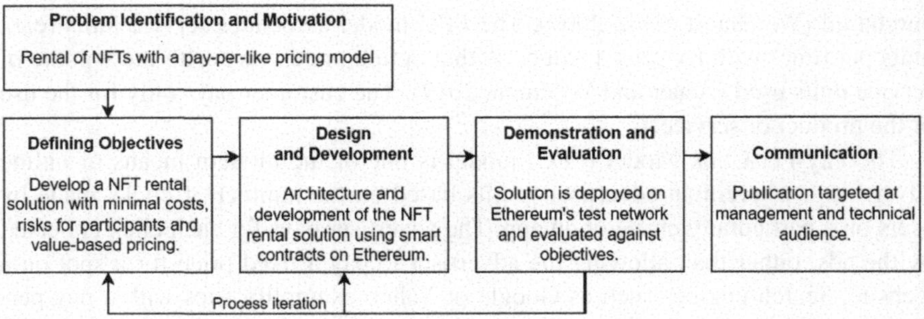

Fig. 1 Design science research methodology for the NFT rental solution

which led to another development cycle to improve shortcomings. For communication, we target management- and technically-oriented audiences. The former can use schematic UML diagrams and reasoning about benefits and challenges, while for the latter we made source code available at: https://github.com/asopi/rental-project

4 Results

We report results for the steps of the DSR process (Fig. 1) in subchapters.

4.1 *Problem Identification, Motivation, and Objectives*

The problem identification and motivation described in the introduction and background were translated into the following design objectives (DOs):

DO (1) Minimal risk for lender and renter, e.g., through non-returned NFTs.

DO (2) Minimal cost for lender and renter, e.g., through opportunity costs due to (large) collaterals, high transactions fees for renter/lender contracts.

DO (3) Value-based rental fees, e.g., based on positive perception, e.g., likes.

DO (4) Easy access, e.g., ideally web-based and mobile friendly.

4.2 *Design and Development*

Design Decisions: We made the following key design decisions. Blockchain technology was chosen since smart contracts allow to address the first three DOs. An assessment tool by Wüst and Gervais (2018), yielded the use of a public permissionless blockchain. Ethereum enjoys a large developer community and ecosystem (easier to find resources), security (It is time-proven and it has undergone multiple security audits), large support of token standards and the supply of popular NFTs is greatest.[1] There are alternatives such as Avalanche or Binance that offer higher throughput and lower transaction fees but come with disadvantages. Generally, they do not meet multiple of the above reasons. For example, Avalanche is less-established (smaller developer community) and newer with fewer security audits and less popular with fewer NFT supply. As the programming language for the backend, we used Solidity (Tikhomirov, 2018). We extended the commonly employed ERC-721 standard by OpenZeppelin (2022). To ensure easy access (DO4), we opted for a mobile-friendly web-based solution as frontend with TypeScript, which builds on top of JavaScript and allows to write type-safe and more readable code. To glue front- and backend, we used the well-established library "web3.js". The Angular Material library was used for UI components due to its ease of use and widespread adoption. We supported two types of wallet software to perform transactions on the blockchain, i.e., we chose MetaMask, which comes as a browser extension and WalletConnect, which is integrated into a mobile app. We opted for a collateral-free variant with a non-wrapped approach. This is because the collateral-free variants entail fewer risks for NFT owners and eliminate the barrier of high collateral costs for renters. Non-wrapped NFTs are considered more authentic, since they are associated directly with the original artwork (and not a copy like for wrapped NFTs). As value-based rental fees, we opted for pay-per-like, where the NFT owner defines the costs for a like. We deemed this more desirable than pay-per-view, since we explicitly aimed to capture positive reactions. To prevent click fraud, we decided to allow an increment only through an authorized party, which could be a service provider that aims to integrate the solution into their project. Commonly, this is the renter itself. The service provider must ensure that "likes" are genuine, e.g., non-fraudulent and non-duplicate. Thus, our solution does not aim to prevent click-fraud directly, but allows to defer it to another neutral entity that can employ any of the existing techniques for click-fraud. Both renters and lenders have an incentive to incorrectly detect non-genuine clicks (to pay less or charge more), while a separate entity per se has no such interest. To ensure the solvency of the renter to eliminate the risk that the renter is not paid due to excessive received likes, the renter must specify a limit with the maximum number of affordable likes and deposit the highest possible price in advance. The solution should then keep the amount until the rent deal is expired, and then the remaining money should be returned to the renter.

Development: Next, we describe the creation of the artifactual solution as a Dapp including use cases that mostly directly translate to function calls (Figs. 2 and 3).

Figure 2 depicts use cases with four human actors: A lender is a person aiming to rent NFTs. The lender opens a rental offer, i.e., an order, by specifying the maximum

[1] https://opensea.io/rankings?sortBy=total_volume (We checked for sales, e.g., in the last 30 days or all on 1st of June 2023).

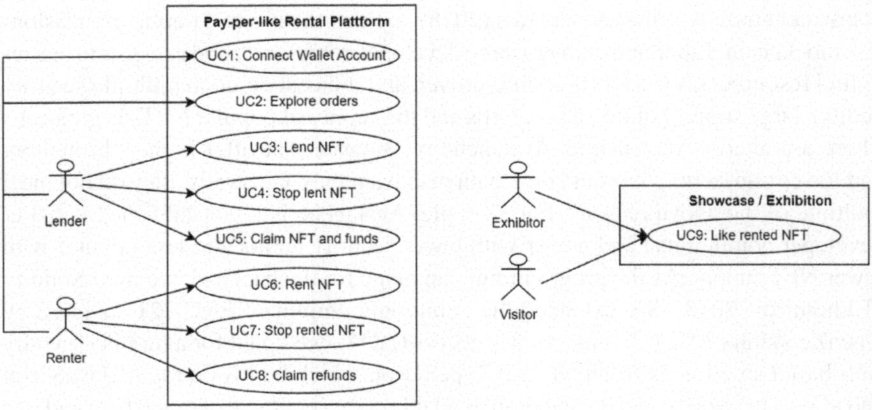

Fig. 2 Use cases

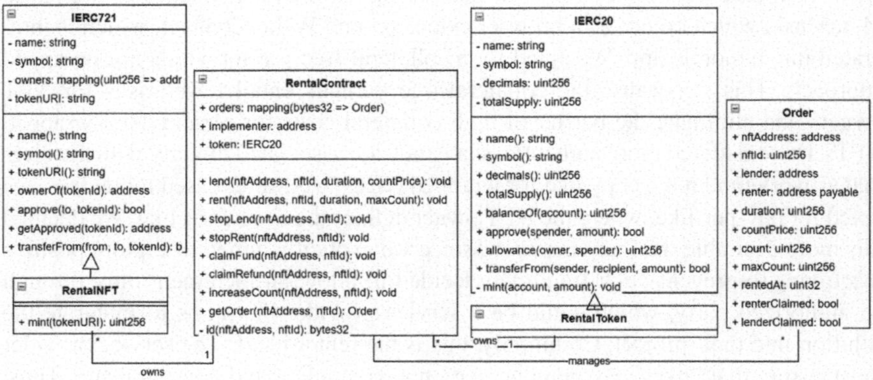

Fig. 3 Class diagram

rent duration and the price per like. Once the lender has created an order, the NFT is transferred to the rental contract. If noone has rented the NFT, the lender can cease the order and reclaim the NFT. After an order is completed, the implementer reclaims the paid rental costs and the NFT. A renter is a person aiming to rent an NFT. The renter accepts a rental order by specifying a maximum rent duration and the maximum number of likes they are willing to pay for. To accept the order, they pay the maximum possible rent price, i.e., the maximum number of likes times the price per like. The order is either stopped by them or when the rent duration expires. After an order is completed, the final rent price is calculated, and the renter reclaims the remaining amount, which is calculated based on the difference between the already paid maximum rent price and the actual rent price.

The exhibitor is a service provider using the rental contract to enable rented NFTs within projects, e.g., to display on a webpage. The exhibitor verifies that an NFT is stored in the rental contract and the associated renter. The exhibitor also offers the functionality to "like" an item, which might trigger additional verification of users that are subject to the exhibitor. The "like" on a rented NFT is captured by incrementing the counter associated with the NFT on the rental contract. Only the exhibitor is authorized to increment this counter.

Use Case Descriptions: **Connect Wallet (UC 1)**: Lenders and renters want to use their accounts stored in their wallet, i.e., (exposed by) MetaMask or WalletConnect. The rental plattform provides a button to connect and disconnect their accounts. The connected account address is displayed in shortened form and associated with a unique profile image derived from the account address, also known as identicon.

Explore Orders (UC 2): Lenders and renters want to have an overview of all lend and rent orders created by them. They can see information about the current RNT balance, the number of open lend orders, and the number of rented and lent NFTs.

Lend NFT (UC 3): Lenders aim to lend their owned NFTs. The rental plattform allows to select an NFT asking for the maximum rent duration in days and the price per like in RNT. By clicking the lend button, the wallet appears and requests to accept or reject the NFT transfer from the lender's wallet to the rental (smart) contract. The rental contract stores the NFT until the order is completed and the lender reclaims it.

Stop Lent NFT(UC 4): The lender wants to stop an opened order which is not yet rented. User can click a "stop lend" which returns the NFT back to the lender's account.

Claim NFT and Funds(UC 5): The lender wants to reclaim the transferred NFT and the funds gained from the order. The lender has to accept or reject the gas fees required for the transaction. **Rent NFT(UC 6)**: The renter aims to rent a listed NFT. The renter selects an NFT and types the rent duration in days up to the maximum duration specified by the lender. The renter indicates the maximum like count they are willing to pay. The renter has to accept the RNT transfer from the lender's wallet to the rental contract.

Stop Rented NFT(UC 7): The renter wants to cancel an already rented order. By clicking the "stop rent" button, the order is canceled, the renter can reclaim the refunds, and the lender can reclaim their NFT plus the funds gained from the rental deal.

Claim Refunds(UC 8): The renter wants to claim the refunds. Upon clicking the "claim refunds" button, the user is asked to accept or reject the gas fees for the transaction.

Like Rented NFT(UC 9): Visitors of an exhibition (or showcase) want to experience and like rented NFTs. The showcase provides access to rented NFTs and to like them, e.g., via a heart icon and a count. The exhibitor must validate clicks and allow the increment of the like counter.

4.3 Demonstration and Evaluation

For demonstration, the smart contracts implementing the use cases were deployed on a test network, called Goerli. We conducted system and unit tests. The end-to-end evaluation of the solution was executed via system tests. For each use case, the solution was operated manually and reviewed on Etherscan to assess whether the associated transactions had been successfully executed on the blockchain and yielded the correct balances for renter and lender and whether the system was easily usable. Figures 4 and 5 illustrate our solution.

Figure 6 shows unit tests for the renter. Overall, all 32 unit tests ran successfully. The tests are divided based on the perspectives of the deployer (which "installs" the solution), lender, renter and the exhibitor or implementer, i.e., which implements the actual exhibition and verifies like clicks. The unit tests achieved 100% coverage in all categories, namely statements, branches, functions, and lines, i.e., we also tested cases such as insufficient funds by a renter.

In order to understand the deployment and execution costs of the smart contracts, an analysis of the gas fees was performed on October 30, 2022 based on an ETH price of 1,597.70 USD and an average gas price of 7 gwei $\left(= 7 \cdot 10^{-9}\text{ETH}\right)$. The Hardhat library retrieves the current Ethereum price and the estimated gas price from the mainnet by fetching the data from the crypto asset price tracking website "CoinMarketCap". Hardhat then analyzes how much gas in gwei the function requires to be executed on the Ethereum blockchain and calculates costs. Execution costs for functions listed in Fig. 3 varied between 0.45 and 2.06 USD. The deployment cost for our smart contract was $28.08, which a service provider must initially pay when integrating the rental solution.

We conclude the evaluation with respect to our design objectives:

DO1(Minimal risk for lender and renter): Using smart contracts, it is automatically enforced that all NFTs are returned and a lender is paid. The renter in turn can prove authenticity of NFTs due to transparency of the blockchain. We defer the detection

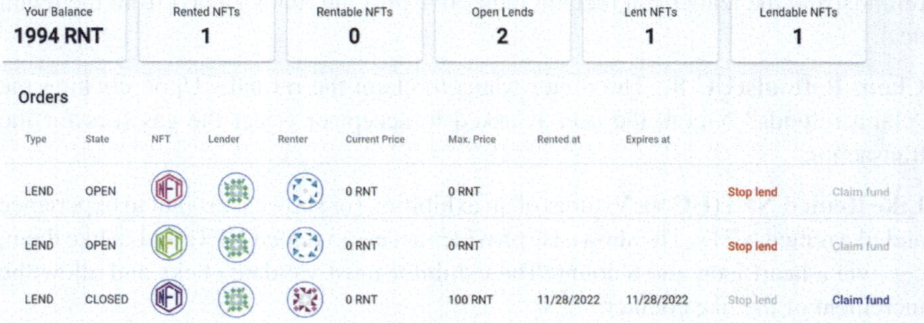

Fig. 4 Dashboard showing lend NFTs: Lending offers for NFTs that are not yet rented can be stopped, while funds can be claimed for completed rentals

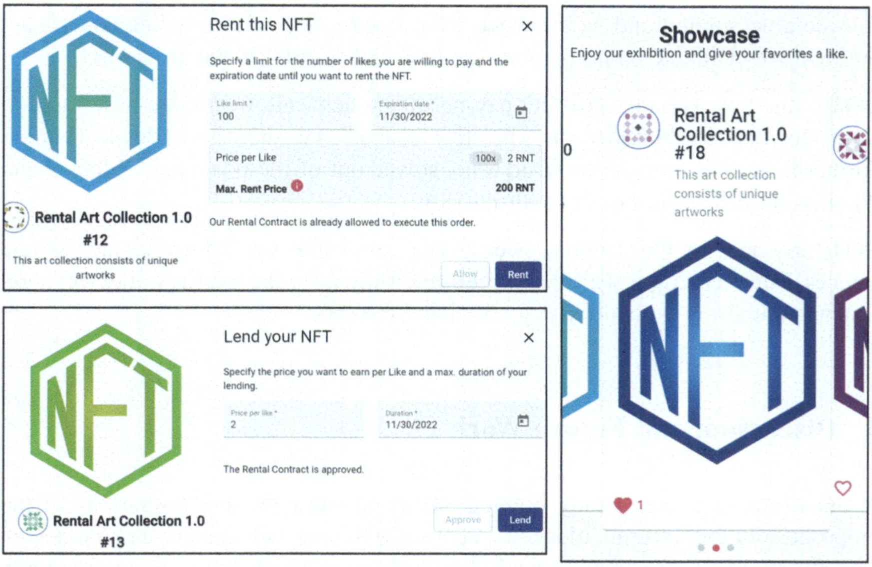

Fig. 5 Screenshots of rental (top left), lending (bottom left) and showcase with a heart button as "like" option

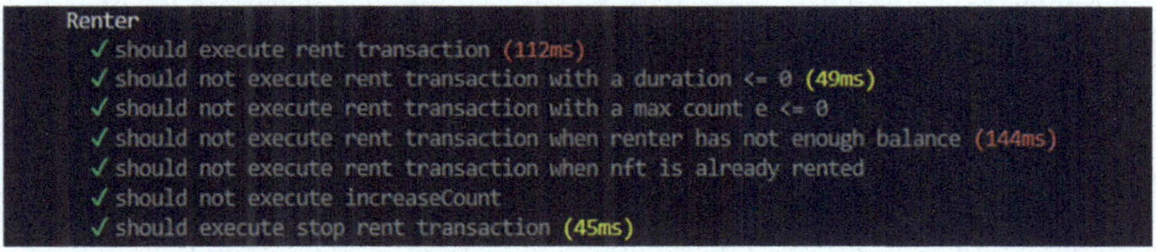

Fig. 6 Subset of unit tests. Overall, all 32 tests covering 100% of code ran successfully

and handling of click fraud to the exhibitor. An exhibitor can control whom to pay. This is fine as long as the exhibitor is an external service provider who favors neither the renter nor the lender. Otherwise, there is a risk of click fraud, either by not recording clicks (in case the renter is favored) or by not properly detecting fraud by others (to favor the lender).

DO2(Minimal cost for lender and renter): Our solution avoids the use of (large) collaterals, which minimizes interest and opportunity costs due to inaccessible assets. Furthermore, our solution is fully digital and, therefore, should be highly cost-efficient. Still, fees are significant. Total costs due to gas fees for deployment are about $28. Executing a lend or rental order on the smart contact costs between $2 and $3. While this is a considerable amount, it is still little compared taking into account that no intermediary is needed and no collateral. However, "a like", i.e., increasing the counter (executing function increaseCount in Fig. 3 cost about $0.45. This is a considerable amount and well beyond what is typically paid in online-advertising settings. We elaborate on mitigations (and their trade-offs) in the discussion.

DO3(Value-based rental fees): Our pay-per-like scheme allows a value-based assessment. However, it is biased towards positive feedback, i.e., there is no "dislike" button. Furthermore, preventing click fraud is not solved out-of-the-box using a blockchain. We present further options in the discussion.

DO4(Easy access): Our solution is easy to access using a web-browser and mobile devices. But interactions with Dapps require additional tools, such as wallet software, which is not always supported, e.g., in older browsers.

5 Discussion and Future Work

In our evaluation, we already pointed out some strengths and limitations of the proposed solution. Overall, blockchain comes with many advantages and our design objectives could mostly be addressed. One challenge of blockchain is that **technology** is still **rapidly evolving**. For example, the (new) ERC-4907 (rentable tokens) offers to grant a time-limited role with restricted rights to a token. As of the writing of this paper, it is not used, since there is no official and reviewed implementation of the interfaces. While it comes with benefits, it remains uncertain whether this standard (potentially well-suited for renting solutions) will find adaptations in the NFT community, making technology decisions difficult.

Another issue not resolved fully with blockchain is dealing with click-fraud. Our solution relies on the exhibitor to ensure that click fraud is detected and handled. That is, it enables the **use of third parties to address fraud**. This is beneficial since the renter and lender in principle do not trust each other, since both have opposite incentives when it comes to counting likes. However, both the renter and lender do not obtain any indicators that might be used to assess if fraud occurred, i.e., they must still trust the third party. In principle, any click on the "like" button (irrespective of whether it is deemed fraudulent or not) could be stored on the blockchain with all kinds of meta-data, such as if the click was deemed fraudulent or not. This might allow verifying the correctness of like classifications as fraudulent or not. However, this would increase gas fees dramatically, even, using just a simple counter that records any "like" clicks could be problematic, since a bot could trigger costs in the form of gas fees with every click. Thus, fraud remains an issue. We observe **a trust-cost tradeoff**. We define the trust costs as the additional costs that occur to capture information that allows to verify actions of another party. In our case, costs are gas fees that arise to capture information on fraud decisions by the exhibitor. The third party could use the same techniques for fraud detection that are currently employed already in the context of online ad click fraud, e.g., (Zhang and Guan, 2008). Such detection techniques can rely on behavioral information or require user authentication. On many online platforms, such as Youtube and StackOverflow, only users with a verified account can like or add comments.

The pay-per-like pricing might not always be preferred, i.e., one might prefer views or other metrics. Our **implementation is generic**; the counters implemented on the smart contract could also be used to count different actions like views, points, or anything else. However, care must be taken with respect to costs. For example, recording views is likely much more expensive than likes, since views are usually at least an order of magnitude larger than likes, i.e., for a large number of views gas fees would also be an order of magnitude larger for counting likes. Gas fees are already problematic when counting likes, i.e., they are about 0.5 USD. **Gas fees can be prohibitive** in many settings. One way to address this issue is to **increment the like counter from time to time**, e.g., only after every 10 verified like clicks. However, even using such ideas, our solution occurs significant gas fees, although all smart contracts are rather simple. Another option to reduce fees is to use a chain with cheaper transaction costs such as Avalanche or Binance instead of Ethereum. However, they tend to have drawbacks compared to Ethereum such as higher costs for implementation (due to lower online resources, fewer standards), less popularity (fewer NFTs), lower security (fewer validators). Furthermore, even if costs are about a factor 20 or so lower than on Ethereum as is roughly the case for Binance[2], they are still a concern - especially if value-based pricing models such as pay-per-view are used. As such, using a blockchain-based approach is not preferable for "cheap" artwork, i.e., taking risks might be more economical than paying fees. Even worse gas fees can exceed potential income. This is problematic, since niche or upcoming artists renting their work do not benefit from the technology in the same way as well-established artists with expensive works, since gas fees take relatively a much larger share of their earnings. That is, for expensive rentals blockchain constitutes a major facilitator, since risks are mitigated and access is simplified. While for artwork that cannot be lend for high prices, blockchains like Ethereum are not an option as gas fees exceed rental income. Thus, **blockchain solutions appear unfair and foster injustices**, i.e., making the rich richer and the poor poorer and contributing to a reduction of cultural diversity. Similar criticism is well-established for other technologies. For example, artificial intelligence is known for its dark sides—especially biases (Meske et al., 2022) and ability to deceive (Schneider, Vlachos and Meske, 2022). For blockchain, to this end only the unfairness of mining mechanisms and rules for proof-of-work based blockchains such as Bitcoin have been mentioned (Ferdous et al., 2021). Generally, it can be said that small transactions are not profitable so that certain pricing models (like pay-per-view) or market participants who cannot charge high rental fees (like niche artists) are excluded. This is in contrast to ordinary centralized web platforms, i.e., Web2, where computations or transactions occur little cost. We call this the **dark sides of large blockchain fees**. Centralized solutions do not occur any coordination costs in contrast to decentralized approaches. Thus, Dapps are inherently inferior from a computational perspective as witnessed by many papers in the field of distributed computing analyzing the costs of decentralized

[2] https://academy.binance.com/en/articles/binance-smart-chain-vs-ethereum-what-S-the-difference We use Binance's on report as a lower bound for Binance fees. They state average transactions costs of 2.46$ for Binance and 68.72$ for Etheruem. Prices fluctuate strongly.

algorithms, e.g., (Harris et al., 2018), especially, consensus algorithms (Chaudhry and Yousaf, 2018).

As future work to improve the current solution one can include chains with lower costs and fraud detection, e.g., by authentication via a blockchain (Patel et al., 2019).

6 Conclusions

We have presented a value-based rental solution for NFTs. Our study showed that blockchain technology has many inherent properties that make it a preferable technology for such a problem, e.g., smart contracts that ensure payments or the return of items without the need for collatorals. However, for handling fraud trust still relies on a third party and we observe a trust-cost tradeoff, i.e., larger costs for more trust. From a societal level, blockchain technology with high fees can appear unfair as it benefits wealthy artists more than non-wealthy ones.

References

Antonopoulos, A.M. and Wood, G. (2019) *Mastering Ethereum: Building smart contracts and DApps*. First edition. O'Reilly.

Bauer, J.M. and Wildman, S.S. (2012) 'The economics of usage-based pricing in local broadband markets'. Available at: https://techliberation.com/wp-content/uploads/2012/12/wildmanreport_web.pdf.

Beyer, H., Seidel, P., Stahlmann, S., & Schoder, D. (2023). Revealing Hidden Self-financed Wash Trading in Non-Fungible-Token Markets.

BoredJobs (2022) 'Hire the perfect NFT for your brand'. Available at: https://www.boredjobs.com/about.

vom Brocke, J. *et al.* (2018) 'Own–The Case of a Blockchain Business Model Disrupting the Equity Market', *Controlling30*, (5), pp. 19–25.

Buterin, V. (2014) 'Ethereum: A Next-Generation Smart Contract and Decentralized Application Platform.' Available at: https://ethereum.org/669c9e2e2027310b6b3cdce6e1c52962/Ethereum_Whitepaper_-_Buterin_2014.pdf.

Chaudhry, N. and Yousaf, M.M. (2018) 'Consensus algorithms in blockchain: Comparative analysis, challenges and opportunities', in *2018 12th International Conference on Open Source Systems and Technologies (ICOSST)*. IEEE, pp. 54–63.

Chondrogiannis, E., Andronikou, V., Karanastasis, E., Litke, A., & Varvarigou, T. (2022). Using blockchain and semantic web technologies for the implementation of smart contracts between individuals and health insurance organizations. Blockchain: Research and Applications, 3(2), 100049

Ding, C. *et al.* (2017) 'The power of the "like" button: The impact of social media on box office', *Decision Support Systems*, 94, pp. 77–84.

Dr. Wood, G. (2022) 'Ethereum Yellow Paper: a formal specification of Ethereum, a programmable blockchain'. Available at: https://ethereum.github.io/yellowpaper/paper.pdf.

Ethereum Community (2022a) 'ERC-721 Non-Fungible Token Standard'. Available at: https://ethereum.org/en/developers/docs/standards/tokens/erc-721/.

Ethereum Community (2022b) 'Ethereum Accounts'. Available at: https://ethereum.org/en/developers/docs/accounts/.

Ferdous, M.S., Chowdhury, M.J.M. and Hoque, M.A. (2021) 'A survey of consensus algorithms in public blockchain systems for crypto-currencies', *Journal of Network and Computer Applications*, 182, p. 103035.

Harris, D.G., Schneider, J. and Su, H.-H. (2018) 'Distributed (Δ+ 1)-Coloring in Sublogarithmic Rounds', *Journal of the ACM (JACM)*, 65(4), pp. 1–21.

Hevner *et al.* (2004) 'Design Science in Information Systems Research', *MIS Quarterly*, 28(1), p. 75. Available at: https://doi.org/10.2307/25148625.

Hirai, Y. (2017) 'Defining the Ethereum Virtual Machine for Interactive Theorem Provers', in M. Brenner et al. (eds) *Financial Cryptography and Data Security*, pp. 520–535. Available at: https://doi.org/10.1007/978-3-319-70278-0_33.

IQSpace (2022) 'What is the IQ Space?' Available at: https://docs.iq.space/nft/general/iq-space.

Ives, N. (2005) 'Web Marketers Fearful of Fraud in Pay-Per-Click'. The New Yourk Times. Available at: https://www.nytimes.com/2005/03/03/business/media/web-marketers-fearful-of-fraud-in-payperclick.html.

JPMorgan (2022) Opportunities in the Metaverse, White Paper. URL: https://www.jpmorgan.com/content/dam/jpm/treasury-services/documents/opportunities-in-the-metaverse.pdf

Khraim, H.S. and Alkrableih, A.A. (2015) 'The Effect of Using Pay Per Click Advertisement on Online Advertisement Effectiveness and Attracting Customers in E-marketing Companies in Jordan', *International Journal of Marketing Studies*, 7(1). Available at: https://doi.org/10.5539/ijms.v7n1p180.

Kirli, D. *et al.* (2022) 'Smart contracts in energy systems: A systematic review of fundamental approaches and implementations', *Renewable and Sustainable Energy Reviews*, 158, p. 112013.

Meske, C. *et al.* (2022) 'Explainable artificial intelligence: objectives, stakeholders, and future research opportunities', *Information Systems Management*, 39(1), pp. 53–63.

OpenZeppelin (2022) 'OpenZeppelin Docs: A library for secure smart contract development.' Available at: https://docs.openzeppelin.com/contracts/4.x/.

Patel, S. *et al.* (2019) 'DAuth: A decentralized web authentication system using Ethereum based blockchain', in *2019 International Conference on Vision Towards Emerging Trends in Communication and Networking (ViTECoN)*. IEEE, pp. 1–5.

Peffers, K. *et al.* (2007) 'A design science research methodology for information systems research', *Journal of management information systems*, 24(3), pp. 45–77.

Regner, F., Urbach, N. and Schweizer, A. (2019) 'NFTs in practice–non-fungible tokens as core component of a blockchain-based event ticketing application', in *International Conference on Information Systems (ICIS)*.

reNFT (2022) 'Rental Infrastructure for the Metaverse'. Available at: https://medium.com/renftlabs/renft-announces-new-funding-round-to-accelerate-growth-of-gamefi-in-web3-830702329085.

Rosso, M.A. and Jansen, B.J. (2010) 'Brand Names as Keywords in Sponsored Search Advertising', in *Communications of the Association for Information Systems*.

Schneider, J., Vlachos, M. and Meske, C. (2022) 'Deceptive AI explanations: Creation and detection', in *International Conference on Agents and Artificial Intelligence (ICAART)*.

Solorio, K., Kanna, R. and Hoover, D.H. (2019) *Hands-on smart contract development with Solidity and Ethereum: From fundamentals to deployment*. First edition. O'Reilly Media Inc.

Szabo, N. (1994) 'Smart Contracts'. Available at: https://www.fon.hum.uva.nl/rob/Courses/InformationInSpeech/CDROM/Literature/LOTwinterschool2006/szabo.best.vwh.net/smart.contracts.html.

Tikhomirov, S. (2018) 'Ethereum: state of knowledge and research perspectives', in *International Symposium of Foundations and Practice of Security*, pp. 206–221.

Vom Brocke, J. *et al.* (2020) 'Accumulation and evolution of design knowledge in design science research: a journey through time and space', *Journal of the Association for Information Systems*, 21(3), p. 9.

Voshgmir, S. (2018) 'Fungible Tokens vs. Non-Fungible Tokens.' Available at: https://blockchainhub.net/blog/blog/nfts-fungible-tokens-vs-non-fungible-tokens/.
Weinhardt, C. *et al.* (2009) 'Business Models in the Service World', *IT Professional*, 11(2), pp. 28–33. Available at: https://doi.org/10.1109/MITP.2009.21.
Werner, F. *et al.* (2021) 'Blockchain adoption from an interorganizational systems perspective–a mixed-methods approach', *Information Systems Management*, 38(2), pp. 135–150.
Wüst, K. and Gervais, A. (2018) 'Do you need a blockchain?', in *Crypto valley conference on blockchain technology (CVCBT)*, pp. 45–54.
Zhang, L. and Guan, Y. (2008) 'Detecting click fraud in pay-per-click streams of online advertising networks', in *International Conference on Distributed Computing Systems*, pp. 77–84.
Zheng, G. *et al.* (2021) *Ethereum Smart Contract Development in Solidity*. 1st edition. Available at: https://doi.org/10.1007/978-981-15-6218-1.

Revealing Hidden Self-financed Wash Trading in Non-Fungible-Token Markets

Henri Beyer, Patrick Seidel, Sven Stahlmann, and Detlef Schoder

Abstract Pricing and sales volumes for non-fungible tokens (NFTs) have seen a meteoric rise and fall in recent years. Partially because of a loss of faith in the true values of NFT assets. Wash trading has emerged to artificially inflate asset prices and trading volumes of NFTs. This not only endangers the integrity of NFT markets but also raises doubts about the authenticity of NFT values. Previous research has identified wash trading actors with techniques such as cyclical trading. Many of the presented techniques, however, can be associated with flaws concerning obviousness or feasibility with constrained capital resources. We propose a method to identify a more intricate and concealed form of wash trading called self-financed trading. Our approach identifies suspicious activities by tracking cash and asset flows between blockchain addresses. This enables us to reveal networks of wash trading designed to reap marketplace rewards or insinuate demand to drive up prices.

Keywords Non-fungible-tokens (NFTs) · Wash trading · Price inflation · Cryptocurrency

H. Beyer · P. Seidel · S. Stahlmann · D. Schoder (✉)
University of Cologne, Cologne Institute for Information Systems, Cologne, Germany
e-mail: schoder@wim.uni-koeln.de

H. Beyer
e-mail: beyer@wim.uni-koeln.de

P. Seidel
e-mail: seidel@wim.uni-koeln.de

S. Stahlmann
e-mail: stahlmann@wim.uni-koeln.de

D. Beverungen et al. (eds.), *Solutions and Technologies for Responsible Digitalization*, Lecture Notes in Information Systems and Organisation 75,
https://doi.org/10.1007/978-3-031-80122-8_3

1 Introduction

With the rise of blockchain technology entire new classes of digital assets have emerged. One of these asset types that has gained a lot of traction recently is Non-Fungible-Tokens (NFTs). NFTs are typically employed to represent a digital certificate of ownership for unique assets (Ethereum Foundation, 2022). These assets can take various forms such as digital art, event tickets (Regner et al., 2019) and collectibles (Tahmasbi & Fuchsberger, 2022) as well as physical assets like real estate.

Decentralized blockchain networks offer benefits such as increased transactional security and privacy (Rejeb et al., 2021). However, the lack of regulation and a high degree of anonymity fosters fraudulent activities such as market manipulation or scams (Eigelshoven et al., 2021).

One popular market manipulation technique is wash trading. Wash trading describes the practice of one or more parties creating artificial transactions in a marketplace for their own gain (Tom C. W. Lin, 2017). As both sides of these trades are colluding the traders are not exposed to any financial risk. Wash trading has the goal to drive prices of assets up or down, deceive unknowing parties to buy assets at artificial prices (Pouncy, 1995), or reap kickbacks from exchanges or brokers (SEC, 2006).

Wash trading in traditional financial markets has been an established research topic in many market environments such as trading at stock exchanges (Cumming et al., 2011, p. 2) and agricultural markets (Culver, 1985, p. 1). The focus has mostly been on the effects on market integrity and market designs. Due to its threat to the stability of said markets, many regulatory bodies such as the Commodity Futures Trading Commission prohibit wash trading activities (CFTC Glossary, 2023).

NFT wash trading is done by trading NFT assets between blockchain addresses (often referred to as wallets) within the realm of control of a single or colluding group of wash traders. Wash trading is employed to artificially increase an asset's price or trading volumes to insinuate inherent value or demand. Since prices of NFTs are determined by unregulated offer and demand of anonymous actors fair values of assets are inherently hard to quantify (Jordanoska, 2021, 716).

Few studies already attempt to identify wash trading activities in NFT markets by tracking the transaction history of NFT assets. These studies apply the concept of cyclical trading to identify malicious trading activities using graph-based methods (Das et al., 2022; Tahmasbi & Fuchsberger, 2022; Wachter et al., 2022). Cyclical trading denotes the concept of trading assets in a circular fashion generating risk-free trading activity at previously set prices. However, we argue that this detection technique is associated with significant flaws. Small cycles are easily visible in the transaction histories on NFT markets and are therefore easily recognizable for end-users, while large cycles of unassociated addresses require increasing capital expenditure. The arbitrary generation of Ethereum addresses also makes circumventing cyclic trading trivial for colluding wash traders.

Therefore, we propose a more comprehensive approach by additionally incorporating the transaction history of blockchain tokens to detect cyclical wash trading activity. Our approach can identify self-financed wash trading which denotes the practice of funding a previously unassociated blockchain address to buy NFTs from oneself. This leads to concealed wash trading activity. Since wash traders need to move capital to execute their artificial trades, we screen the transaction data for value cycles. These value cycles are comprised both of NFT asset transactions and blockchain capital flows for example of ETH. Incorporating the transaction history has certain advantages. First, the arbitrary generation of wallets does not circumvent detection if the trade is self-financed. Second self-financed trades are not easily visible to end users and therefore more likely to be used by malicious actors.

In this study, we analyze transactional data within an NFT collection on the popular Marketplace LooksRare. Using our proposed approach, we are able to find multiple accounts of self-financed wash trading. In this paper, we report the found malicious trading behavior regarding the associated trading volume and asset price developments. Our finding highlights the importance of monitoring suspicious trading activity in unregulated markets such as NFT marketplaces.

2 Theoretical Background

Research regarding wash trading in NFT marketplaces is scarce since it is still in its early stage of adoption (Tahmasbi & Fuchsberger, 2022). Instead, research has focused on a broad range of security issues, such as copycat art (Das et al., 2022) theft of personal information, and shill bidding (Mukhopadhyay and Ghosh, 2021).

Wash trading in traditional markets has been known to be subject to regulatory penalties. Thus, techniques for detecting wash trading are more developed in stock and commodity markets. Research has been focused on market environments such as trading at stock exchanges (Cumming et al., 2011) or agricultural markets (Culver, 1985, p. 1) and examined the effects on market integrity and market designs.

Motivations for wash trading in the NFT realm generally fall into three categories. Firstly, a wash trader might aim to artificially alter prices or trading volumes of assets within his possession. Some marketplaces offer rewards for trading volume generation which opens the possibility of wash trading to reap marketplace rewards (Mukhopadhyay and Ghosh, 2021). Cong et al. (2022) have studied wash trading in the taxation domain concerning cryptocurrencies and NFTs identifying a strategy of tax-loss harvesting during end-of-year periods (Cong et al., 2022).

Initial approaches studied wash trading solely in cryptocurrency trading, e.g. analyzing whether exchanges aim to inflate their trading volume to increase their relevance among other competitors (Cong et al., 2019). The approaches to detect instances of wash trading or flag suspicious behavior can be categorized into anomaly- and graph-based techniques. Cong et al. (2019) follow the anomaly-based approach utilizing first-digit-distributions following Benford's law and transaction roundness (clustering at round sizes) to quantify suspicious transactions totaling an average of 70% at unregulated cryptocurrency exchanges (Cong et al., 2019). Victor and Weintraud (2021) identify cyclical wash trading activity by searching for strongly connected components in transaction graphs to quantify a lower-bound estimate of wash trading frequency in cryptocurrency exchanges (Victor and Weintraud, 2021).

In the context of NFTs Tariq and Sifat (2022) utilize the anomaly-based approach to identify widespread suspicious and non-human-like behavior. Due to the unique non-fungible nature of NFTs mainly graph-based techniques have been considered to detect wash trading in NFT markets. Wachter et al. (2022) have detected closed-cycle trading as well as rapid trading sequences by building transaction graphs. Tahmasbi & Fuchsberger (2022) further expand cycle detection by proposing a more efficient algorithm based on bipartite graphs. All of the above literature only considers the flow of NFT assets which due to the arbitrary generation of Ethereum addresses makes the avoiding of cycles trivial to achieve.

3 Method

To detect self-financed wash trading activity, we will introduce the concept of self-financed trading events and search for such events in the collected data. A self-financed trading event can be described as a directed multigraph, called quiver, consisting of two vertices and two edges in one direction and a third edge in the opposite direction, as can be seen in Fig. 1. More specifically, let $Q = \{V, E\}$ be a quiver, where $V = \{u, v\}$ is a set of two vertices representing Ethereum addresses and $E = \{(u, v), (u, v), (v, u)\}$ is a set of three edges representing token transactions between these addresses. For any edge $e = (u, v) \in E$, u is the source vertex and v describes the destination vertex. The weight $w(e)$ represents the transferred tokens, which can consist of NFTs (ERC-721 tokens) as well as the Ethereum currency wrapped in ERC-20 tokens as WETH. A legitimate NFT sale would be represented by a pair of two edges $\{e_1 = (u, v), e_2 = (v, u)\}$ and the corresponding weights $w(e_1)$ being an NFT asset and $w(e_2)$ being Ethereum currency flow. If a third edge $e_3 = (u, v)$ exists, with $w(e_3)$ being Ethereum currency flow, we define this quiver as a self-financed trading event, since the buying address v receives funds from the selling address u. This allows us to look past the cyclic asset trading and detect cyclic value flows which could be used to conceal wash-trading by hiding it from NFT Marketplace users.

Using the previously defined concept we build a directed multigraph by getting NFT flows and buyer and seller Ethereum addresses from the NFT Marketplace LooksRare as well as payment flow directly from the Ethereum blockchain, utilizing the block explorer Etherscan and the blockchain infrastructure provider Alchemy. The publicly available transaction histories of the selected collection were systematically scraped using LooksRare's API and the seller's Ethereum address, the buyer's Ethereum address, the amount that the buyer paid, and the platform's name of the NFT asset were saved. We used this information to model each sale event in the

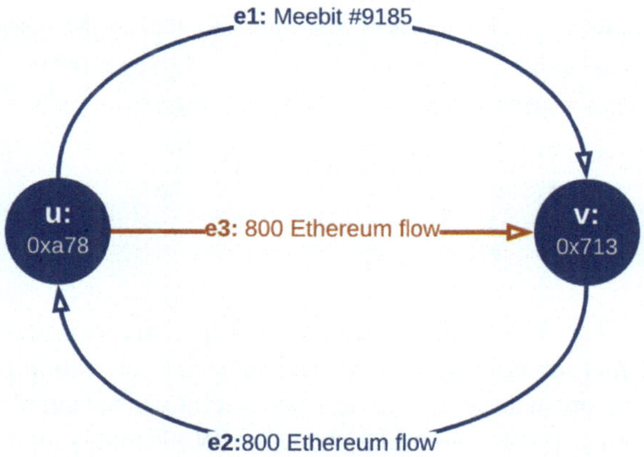

Fig. 1 Graph representation of a self-financed trading event

history of the collection as a quiver of the previously described format with u being the seller's address and v being the buyer's address.

Further, we combined this data with the payment flow data from the Ethereum blockchain. Specifically, for every sale on the NFT marketplace, the buyer's entire Ethereum transaction history was scraped using the public API of Etherscan and enriched it with metadata obtained from Alchemy. It was checked whether any flow of Ethereum currency fitted the description of an edge $e = (u, v)$ with $w(e)$ consisting of the Ethereum funds, meaning the seller's address had funded the buyer's address. These self-financed trading events were recorded and used four our preliminary results.

We focused on a NFT collections with a high amount of trading volume in a short period of time. This was conducted to increase the likelihood of wash trading finds under the hypothesis that wash trading activity leads to spikes in transaction volumes and asset prices. For our preliminary analysis, we chose one collection from this data.

4 Preliminary Results

Following the approach outlined above we were able to successfully identify self-financed wash trading activity. Examples of identified self-financed trades are displayed in Table 1. The first such finding concerns the NFT art piece "Meebit #9185" of the "Meebits" collection. It was sold in January of 2022 at a sale price of 800 ETH. The transaction history displayed on the LooksRare marketplace indicates a regular NFT transaction between the seller's contact address and the buyer's contact address.

Our self-financed wash trading detection approach screened the buyer and seller for previous Ethereum currency flows. This revealed a previous transaction indicating the original seller address funded the subsequent buying side with 800 ETH in a separate transaction mere minutes before the NFT sale.

Table 1 Example instances of self-financed trades in the Meebits collection

Asset name	Previous ETH flow	Sale price (ETH)	Fund date	Sale date
Meebit #9185	800	800	2022-01-28	2022-01-28
Meebit #15377	600	600	2022-01-14	2022-01-14
Meebit #7814	600	600	2022-02-03	2022-02-03
Meebit #15115	392	392	2022-01-17	2022-01-17

This is a severe indication of suspicious wash trading activity as the buyer and seller are connected by a prior financial connection pertaining to almost the exact amount of the asset sale. The close vicinity of the initial funding further deepens suspicions of malicious trading behavior. While highly unlikely, it is theoretically possible that this financial connection is merely a coincidence. This, however, is refuted by the high frequency of suspicious transactions within this collection indicating systematic wash trading activities.

Our analysis revealed 5580 self-financed trading events involving 527 individual Ethereum addresses. The total trading volume of sales that we flagged as suspicious in this collection was 6,068,162,419.74 USD. The funding volume in this single collection shows the potential scale of fraudulent NFT transactions and supports our hypothesis that these activities are potentially fraudulent and aimed at artificially inflating the trading volume and value of the NFT collection.

Our preliminary results provide significant evidence of fraudulent activity in the NFT market, and the potential scale of these transactions highlights the need for action to prevent and monitor this behavior.

However, there are certain restrictions to these results, primarily regarding the financial linkage between the colluding entities. At present, we only monitor for direct capital transfers between the implicated addresses. This detection method could be bypassed by incorporating extra addresses to mask the origin of the funding. With improvements in detection techniques and computational resources, we could also spot these more complex networks. Besides, wash traders might opt to finance their Ethereum addresses off the blockchain, using fiat currency to acquire cryptocurrency via a coin exchange. In such instances, we would be unable to identify financial collusion between the buyer and seller. Nonetheless, this procedure would be incredibly laborious for wash traders, especially those dealing with a significant number of Ethereum addresses.

5 Conclusion and Outlook

In this paper, we propose an approach to identify self-financed wash trading activity and analyze trades of a single collection. Our results indicate that up to 6,068,162,419.74 USD of trading volume in that collection could stem from fraudulent activity. We plan to further extend our study by incorporating a more diverse set of NFT collections. We believe that an expansion of the underlying dataset across a diverse range of NFTs would yield more instances of wash trading activity. Furthermore, applying our approach to a representative sample of NFT transactions we can make a more robust estimate for the overall frequency of self-financed wash trading activity in NFT markets.

A core goal of wash trading is the deception of unassuming buyers to purchase NFTs at artificial prices (Pouncy, 1995). Therefore, the identification of buyers that unknowingly purchased a wash-traded asset is a core future research focus. Precise identification of flagged transactions enables the quantification of the financial damage induced by artificial price inflation. Wash trading activity is associated with cost by the accumulation of transaction fees (gas fees) for each artificial transaction. It is possible to then assess the profitability of wash traders by calculating both their gain resulting from an inflated sale and the "cost of attack" (Wachter et al., 2022) incurred by transaction fees.

Finally, keeping a record of suspicious wash trader accounts in a database would allow us to conduct a more focused search. Rather than randomly sifting through vast amounts of transaction data for signs of wash trading, we could concentrate our efforts on accounts linked to identified wash traders. This approach would likely uncover a greater number of wash trading transactions and reveal extensive networks of colluding wash traders. Additionally, this directed approach would also make the search for value cycles across multiple accounts computationally manageable at a larger scale.

References

CFTC Glossary. (2023, February 28). https://www.cftc.gov/LearnAndProtect/EducationCenter/CFTCGlossary/glossary_wxyz.html

Cong, L., Landsman, W. R., Maydew, E. L., & Rabetti, D. (2022). Tax-Loss Harvesting with Cryptocurrencies. *SSRN Electronic Journal.* Advance online publication. https://doi.org/10.2139/ssrn.4033617

Cong, L., Li, X., Tang, K., & Yang, Y. (2019). Crypto Wash Trading. *SSRN Electronic Journal.* Advance online publication. https://doi.org/10.2139/ssrn.3530220

Culver, J. (1985). Market Integrity Issues and the Agricultural Markets

Cumming, D. J., Zhan, F., & Aitken, M. J. (2011). Exchange Trading Rules, Surveillance, and Insider Trading. *SSRN Electronic Journal.* Advance online publication. https://doi.org/10.2139/ssrn.1990453

Das, D., Bose, P., Ruaro, N., Kruegel, C., & Vigna, G. (2022). Understanding Security Issues in the NFT Ecosystem. In H. Yin, A. Stavrou, C. Cremers, & E. Shi (Eds.), *Proceedings of the 2022 ACM SIGSAC Conference on Computer and Communications Security* (pp. 667–681). ACM. https://doi.org/10.1145/3548606.3559342

Eigelshoven, F., Ullrich, A., & Parry, D. (2021). Cryptocurrency Market Manipulation: A Systematic Literature Review. *ICIS 2021—International Conference on Information Systems*

Ethereum Foundation. (2022, May 14). *Non-fungible tokens (NFT) | ethereum.org*. https://ethereum.org/en/nft/

Jordanoska (2021). The Exciting World of NFTs. A Consideration of Regulatory and Financial Crime Risks. *BUTTERWORTHS JOURNAL of INTERNATIONAL BANKING and FINANCIAL LAW*

Mukhopadhyay, M., & Ghosh, K. (2021). Market Microstructure of Non Fungible Tokens. Advance online publication. https://doi.org/10.5281/zenodo.5654779

Pouncy, C. (1995). *The Scienter Requirement and Wash Trading in Commodity Futures: The Knowledge Lost in Knowing*. Cardozo Law Review, Vol. 16, No. 5, 1995. https://ssrn.com/abstract=1629256

Regner, F., Schweizer, A., & Urbach, N. (2019). NFTs in Practice – Non-Fungible Tokens as Core Component of a Blockchain-based Event Ticketing Application. *Fortieth International Conference on Information Systems, Munich 2019*. https://aisel.aisnet.org/icis2019/blockchain_fintech/blockchain_fintech/1

Rejeb, A., Rejeb, K., & G. Keogh, J. (2021). Cryptocurrencies in Modern Finance: A Literature Review. *ETIKONOMI*, *20*(1), 93–118. https://doi.org/10.15408/etk.v20i1.16911

SEC, U. S. (2006). Commission Opinion: Irfan Mohammed Amanat: SECURITIES EXCHANGE ACT OF 1934 Rel. No. 54708. https://www.sec.govlitigation/opinions/2006/34-54708.pdf

Tahmasbi, N., & Fuchsberger, A. (2022). Non-fungible Tokens - Exploring Suspicious Washtrader Communities in NFT Networks. *ICIS*.

Tariq, S. A., & Sifat, I. (2022). Suspicious Trading in Nonfungible Tokens (Nfts): Evidence from Wash Trading. *SSRN Electronic Journal*. Advance online publication. https://doi.org/10.2139/ssrn.4097642

Tom C. W. Lin (2017). The New Market Manipulation. *Emory Law Journal*

Victor, F., & Weintraud, A. M. (2021). Detecting and Quantifying Wash Trading on Decentralized Cryptocurrency Exchanges. In J. Leskovec, M. Grobelnik, M. Najork, J. Tang, & L. Zia (Eds.), *Proceedings of the Web Conference 2021* (pp. 23–32). ACM. https://doi.org/10.1145/3442381.3449824

Wachter, V. v., Jensen, J. R., Regner, F., & Ross, O. (2022, February 7). *NFT Wash Trading: Quantifying suspicious behaviour in NFT markets*. http://arxiv.org/pdf/2202.03866v1

Data Science and Business Analytics

The Data Collaboration Canvas: A Visual Framework for Systematically Identifying and Evaluating Organizational Data Collaboration Opportunities

Tim Geppert, Alice Dal Fuoco, Ninja Leikert-Boehm, Stefan Deml, David Sturzenegger, and Nico Ebert

Abstract For organizations, the use of Big Data and data analytics provides the opportunity to gain competitive advantages and foster innovation. In most of these data-analytics initiatives, it is clear that data from external stakeholders could enrich the internal data assets and lead to enhanced outcomes. Currently, no framework is available that systematically guides practitioners in identifying and evaluating suitable inter-organizational data collaborations. This paper closes the gap by following an action design research approach to develop the Data Collaboration Canvas (DCC). The DCC was rigorously evaluated by practitioners from Swiss organizations in six different industries, instantiated in four workshops, and used to guide innovative data collaboration projects. This artifact gives practitioners a guideline for identifying data collaboration opportunities and an insight into the main factors that must be addressed before further pursuing a collaborative partnership.

T. Geppert (✉) · N. Leikert-Boehm · N. Ebert
Institute for Business Information Technology, ZHAW Zurich University of Applied Sciences, Winterthur, Switzerland
e-mail: gepp@zhaw.ch

N. Leikert-Boehm
e-mail: leik@zhaw.ch

N. Ebert
e-mail: ebet@zhaw.ch

A. D. Fuoco
PostFinance, Zurich, Switzerland
e-mail: alice.dalfuoco@postfinance.ch

S. Deml · D. Sturzenegger
dq Technologies AG, Zurich, Switzerland
e-mail: stefan.deml@decentriq.ch

D. Sturzenegger
e-mail: david.sturzenegger@decentriq.ch

D. Beverungen et al. (eds.), *Solutions and Technologies for Responsible Digitalization*, Lecture Notes in Information Systems and Organisation 75,
https://doi.org/10.1007/978-3-031-80122-8_4

Keywords Data sharing · Data collaboration · DSR · Canvas

1 Introduction

Organizations are now aware that their data assets can potentially provide an additional value stream, enabling them to remain competitive in their environment (LaValle et al., 2011). Even data collected in the past might provide value for new products and innovations (Constantiou and Kallinikos, 2015). Additional value could be realized by combining data from different sources into data-based products, which satisfy market requirements better than each part alone (Günther et al., 2017). To identify valuable data assets, it is crucial to expand human expertise within the organization and have easy access to the available data (Seddon et al., 2017). This is why organizations have started to extend their strategy toolbox and use data analytics to understand and better utilize their data assets (Woerner and Wixom, 2015). These data analytics initiatives also provide information about the weaknesses within existing data assets; such weaknesses can stem from low-quality data, internal data silos, or a missing data governance structure (Mikalef and Krogstie, 2018). Data analytics can help increase data accessibility by cleaning, normalizing, and centralizing the data (Dinter et al. 2015).

It can also be observed that large corporations have introduced new data governance structures, for example, the role of Chief Data Officer and data governance boards to safeguard valuable assets and oversee the competitive features of these assets (Otto, 2011; Ladley, 2012). Organizations have also realized that they have data blind spots within their assets. Such missing data features cannot be easily acquired, and other strategies are needed to gain access to these missing data so as to keep up with larger tech companies (Gulati and Singh, 1998). An example of a data blind spot might be a small retail company that has data about the shopping behavior of its customers but has no knowledge about the additional items that would complement a customer's shopping basket. In comparison, large tech companies like Google, Amazon, Facebook, Apple, and Microsoft have data assets providing intelligence about customers in a variety of areas (Miguel and Casado, 2016). It is clear that this competitive disadvantage can be an obstacle for small organizations, which is why some operations have started to form collaborative data initiatives (Pouwels and Koster, 2017). Similar to data initiatives within a single organization, it is important to clarify important aspects of inter-organizational data collaboration.

Several visual tools have been described in the recent literature to systematically guide the development of data initiatives within a single organization (Thoring et al. 2019). However, to our knowledge, a systematic framework to facilitate inter-organizational data collaboration is currently missing. Therefore, this paper will address the following research question:

"Can a visual tool facilitate the identification and systematic evaluation of data-based, organizational collaboration?"

To answer this question, this paper will first provide an overview of related visual tools and data-based organizational collaboration (Sect. 2). The research method is explained afterward, followed by a presentation of the "data collaboration canvas" (DCC). Finally, we examine the iterative evolution and instantiation of this novel artifact in an organizational environment and discuss its impact and limitations.

2 Foundation and Related Work

Different theoretical perspectives have been described to explain the formation of inter-organizational relationships (Barringer and Harrison, 2000). These relationships are typically initiated to create additional value for the participating organizations (Liu and Zou, 2019). Mitchell and Singh (1996) described as one possible reason for forming inter-organizational relationships, that the access to critical resources can be essential since it helps gain market power by filling a resource gap. Related to data-based organizational collaborations, this resource gap can be the deficiency of a data asset that can be remedied by fostering inter-organizational relationships to share data (Richter and Slowinski, 2019). Such a relationship could also involve several different partners to create an entire data ecosystem (Oliveira et al., 2018).

Not only resource dependence but also the theoretical perspective of organizational learning could explain the formation of inter-organizational relationships. Powell et al. (1996) wrote that organizations could have a competitive advantage if they interacted to share knowledge. To form a data-based collaboration, it is necessary to share knowledge about data assets and be open-minded concerning the data and processes of the other organizations. This external view on data assets could also promote innovation within the relationship supported, for example, by creativity workshops (Polewsky and Will, 1996). In these workshops, experts from different organizations can learn about best practice procedures from the other partners, but also about relevant data strengths and weaknesses inherent to the participating organizations (cf. Nissen et al. 2014). A shared understanding of each other's strengths and weaknesses can result in unexpected opportunities for new data-driven products (Broek et al. 2015). The current literature on inter-organizational data collaboration highlights that the potential of data ecosystems or collaborations is still not realized (Broek et al. 2015). The main challenges that are identified are in the area of data governance (Abraham et al. 2019). Organizations still struggle to ensure data ownership and control in inter-organizational relationships. These properties have to be clarified as early as possible to enable a commercially successful collaboration. As a prerequisite it is recommended that organizations clarify for themselves what data is available, who is responsible for the data, how this data is produced, used and under which conditions this data can be shared (Lis and Otto, 2020). Data catalogs can help to describe these aspects of internal data (Labadie et al., 2020). But it is still unclear how a commercially viable model for cross-organizational data sharing can be set up (Broek et al. 2015).

To guide a knowledge-sharing process, visual tools such as the business model canvas by Osterwalder et al. (2010) have shown their effectiveness in helping to systemize the development of new ideas and help focus on key areas during ideation (Avdiji et al., 2018). There are already artifacts that have been useful for organizations to understand internal data initiatives (Sammon and Nagle, 2017), facilitate ideation with data (Kronsbein and Mueller, 2019), and support the identification of data service systems (Hunke et al. 2020). Sammon et al. (2017) observed that data-based value creation within internal data initiatives needs a shared understanding and a common participant language. These properties are also necessary for developing new data-based ideas between two organizations as a shared understanding and language cannot be taken for granted.

During our initial exchange with practitioners from various Swiss-based organizations—and an evaluation of the current literature (cf. Thoring et al., 2019)—it became clear that there is currently no visual tool to facilitate communication between two organizations in core areas related to the systematic evaluation of data collaboration. Recent work by Krasikov et al. (2022) support this view and propose a reference process for data sourcing and managing external data. This paper will address these two shortcomings by developing and testing a visual canvas to guide the early stages of a data-sharing partnership.

3 Methodology

Our approach to developing the DCC follows the action design research (ADR) method (Sein et al., 2011). The technique is best suitable in situations where the research process of building, using, and evaluating the artifact is shaped within the organizational context (Sein et al., 2011) and follows four stages; the first three can be iteratively cycled.

First, the problem was formulated as a research question based on initial exchange with practitioners and the current literature on data-based collaborations. Here, we followed the recommendations of Avdiji et al. (2018) to create tools for poorly structured problems. The issue was framed using an ontology. The ontology was used to create a visual representation in the form of a canvas. In the second stage of the ADR, the artifact was evaluated and shaped based on expert feedback and current literature on visual collaboration tools. The second stage included two additional iterations, and each evolutionary phase was followed by a reflection and learning phase. The output of expert workshops and individual practitioner interviews was used to optimize the understandability and usefulness of the framework. The complete iterative process took eight months, from March–October 2021 (Table 1). During this timeframe, five workshops ranging from 2–5 h evaluated the DCC. The workshops started with a short introduction of the DCC. The participants used the DCC in a second phase to identify and evaluate data opportunities. In the last phase of the workshop all participants gave feedback to the understandability and usefulness of the DCC.

The researchers took pictures during the workshops and collected the written feedback. In addition, nine individual expert interviews, ranging from 1–2 h each, were conducted online using the respective version of the DCC. Two senior researchers conducted the semi-structured interviews, but because of confidentiality concerns of the experts, the interviews were not recorded. The interviews addressed first the understandability of the canvas. In a second phase the interviews addressed possible missing points within the current instance of the canvas. Following the interviews, these two researchers noted the critical insights from the discussion and possible adaptions to the artifact. The specialists from different industry sectors in Switzerland, including banking, mobility, retail, and insurance, all had roles (e.g., Chief Data Officer) associated with innovation or data processes within their organizations. We deliberately invited specialists from different industry sectors to get a consensus view on the artifact.

The current version (I3) of the DCC was evaluated in two online workshops (20 and 16 participants, respectively) and an in-person workshop with ten participants (Table 1, W5). Workshop participants always successfully identified novel data

Table 1 Schedule of the DCC iterations with partners (I.: Iteration)

	Date	Partner	ID	Industry	Time (h)
I.1	23.03.21	Workshop (26 Participants—4 groups)	W1	Multiple	2
I.2	16.04.21	Interview w/ Business analyst	P1	Insurance	1
	26.04.21	Interview w/ Data scientist	P2	Insurance	1
	30.04.21	Interview w/ Chief data officer	P3	Retail	1
I.3	19.05.21	Interview w/ Innovation manager	P4	Banking	2
	26.05.21	Interview w/ Data scientist	P2	Insurance	1
	26.05.21	Workshop (4 participants—1 group)	W2	Multiple	1
	07.06.21	Interview w/ Chief data officer	P3	Retail	1
	16.06.21	Interview w/ Head of data	P5	Mobility	1
	17.06.21	Interview w/ Innovation manager	P6	Insurance	1
	28.06.21	Interview w/ IT Architect	P7	Postal service	1
	29.06.21	Workshop (20 participants—3 groups)	W3	Multiple	2
	07.09.21	Workshop (16 participants—2 groups)	W4	Multiple	2
	20.10.21	Workshop (10 participants—3 groups)	W5	Multiple	5

collaboration opportunities using the DCC and provided rigorous feedback on the usability and usefulness of the current artifact. The DCC was used by practitioners, as described in Sect. 5.3, to successfully identify a data collaboration between two organizations and derive a feasible IS/IT alignment (according to Stolze et al. (2011)) to implement the opportunity now used in production.

4 The Data Collaboration Canvas

The following paragraphs describe the DCC in greater detail. The framework is organized into two parts; each part has different components identified as relevant based on the current literature and expert practitioners interviewed during the iterative ADR evolution stages. It is worth mentioning that in Fig. 1, we show a possible collaboration between two organizations. Still, it is also possible that the collaboration partners are organizational units within one organization. It is also easy to extend the canvas to include more than two collaborators, which was also done during workshops when data collaboration that would profit from more than two organizations was identified.

4.1 Idea Generation Within the Data Collaboration Canvas

The idea generation part of the DCC (Fig. 1) is tailored to help identify valuable opportunities for collaborations between organizations ("data collaboration opportunities"). Specifically, this part of the canvas addresses the theory of resource dependence (cf. Mitchell and Singh, 1996), as it aims to fill the potential resource gaps of the organizations. It is an optional first idea generation tool that can identify unique complementary data assets, whose combination could result in a data collaboration opportunity. This part of the DCC also fosters open innovation, as described by Enkel et al. (2009), because both organizations are invited to discuss data weaknesses and strengths openly.

Data strengths: Within this component, each participant in the possible data collaboration must note the available datasets unique to the respective organization. For example, a retailer has information about the shopping baskets of its customers as well as addresses and personal interests. This part of the canvas follows the data-driven approach, where data are of the highest importance, and organizations should first identify their valuable assets (Dinter and Krämer, 2018; Hannila et al., 2019).

Data weaknesses: This part of the canvas highlights areas where an organization has weak spots within its data assets. For example, a retailer does not know where its customers buy other items, so it may be interested in having a complete view of the shopping basket of its customers and extending its portfolio. As for data strength, it is also essential to identify and close gaps within the data assets to improve organizational performance (Kaufmann, 2019).

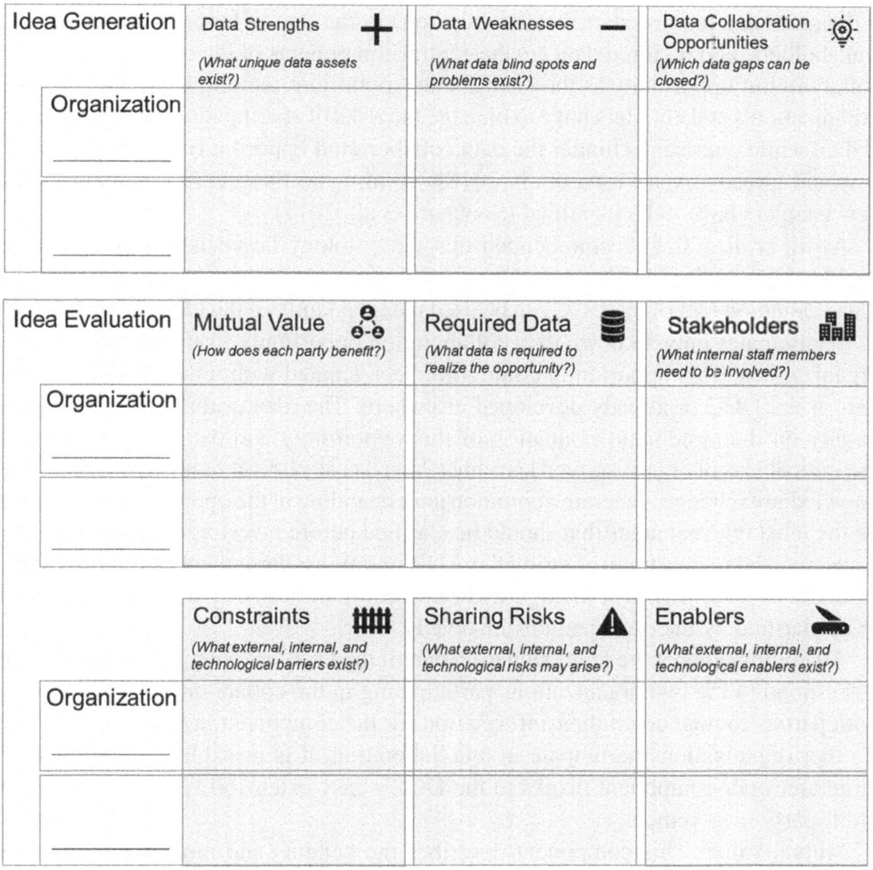

Fig. 1 The DCC is used to identify (idea generation) and to structure (idea evaluation) collaboration opportunities

Data opportunities: As shown in Fig. 1, a simple cross-over of the strength and weakness box can be used to identify areas where the strength of one participant matches a weakness of the other. These areas are called "data collaboration opportunities" and can be termed as such within this component.

4.2 Idea Evaluation Within the Data Collaboration Canvas

To form a relevant collaboration between the participating organizations, a collaboration opportunity that provides mutual value for the participating stakeholders is needed (Osterwalder and Pigneur, 2010). This value can be seen as a competitive advantage for the individual members (Provan and Kenis, 2008). As this collaboration is data-based, it requires data that the stakeholders can share. Hence the mutual value, stakeholders, and required data are the central components of the ontology. The data collaboration opportunity is the central entry point into the ontology (Fig. 2). The organization's stakeholders have to manage the risks of sharing internal data (Meyer, 2018), while constraints hinder the data collaboration opportunity since, otherwise, it would already exist (Tona et al., 2018). To mitigate these constraints and risks, new enablers have to be identified (Sonehara et al., 2011).

Avdiji et al. (2018) recommended that the ontology be visually represented to enable collaborative ideation, and this visual representation is presented in Fig. 1. The idea evaluation part of the DCC can be used independently of the idea generation part as it anticipates only a known data collaboration opportunity from the participating organizations. This opportunity could have been created within the idea generation part of the DCC or already developed elsewhere. The idea evaluation part focuses largely on the systematic evaluation of this opportunity and can be seen with the theoretical lens of organizational learning (Powell et al., 1996). This helps to facilitate knowledge exchange, generate a common understanding of the opportunity, and focus on the most relevant areas that should be clarified before investing in developing the respective data opportunity. During the ADR iterations, these theory ingrained areas emerged as most pertinent to align IS/IT according to Stolze et al. (2011) and need to be clarified by the organizations involved.

All components of the idea evaluation part of the DCC are split into two areas that correspond to the two organizations participating in the collaboration. This enables both parties to note down their information for the component at hand. In addition, if other organizations participate in a collaboration, it is possible to have three or more areas per component thanks to the DCC's easy extensibility to accommodate multi-party involvement.

Mutual value: This component describes the benefits and motivations for data collaboration. Data collaboration requires that all organizations benefit from it, for example, through monetary compensation or data exchanges. Benefits could also be related to offering customers new or better services or improving an organization's reputation. This part of the canvas was significant for all practitioners interviewed during the evolution phase and was also highlighted by Osterwalder et al. (2014)

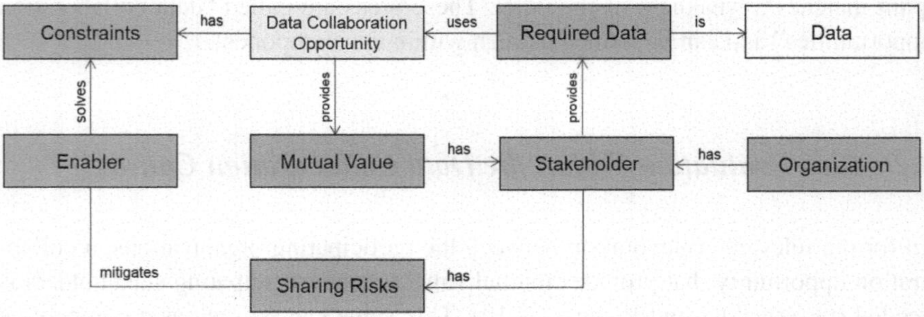

Fig. 2 Ontology for the idea evaluation part of the DCC

Required data: This component holds detailed information concerning the data used. Based on the opportunity generation stage, an initial idea of the data required is typically already available (e.g., customer location data) and is specified in more detail here. For example, ought the data to be granular (e.g., customer records) or at a more aggregate level (e.g., statistics)? The answer will influence subsequent concerns such as risks and constraints. If personal data are needed, this might require additional customer consent. As Kayser et al. (2019) remarked, there can be a variety of data assets, but it is vital to specify precisely the data required in the shared context.

Stakeholder: This component holds all information related to the stakeholder(s) necessary to proceed. These can be internal departments such as marketing or operations and support functions such as IT, legal, or risk management. Stakeholders could also be external vendors. This component also helps to assess the alignment needed between business and IT, as noted by Sabherwal et al. (2019).

Constraints: This component describes what currently prevents data owners from sharing these data. Constraints are typically technological (e.g., no software interface existing), internal (e.g., no processes exist), or external such as data privacy and security (e.g., competition, legal regulations). As Tona et al. (2018) mentioned, ethical reasons could be a constraint for collaboration, underlining the importance of discussing this area at an early stage.

Sharing risks: This component describes the risks for parties in realizing the data sharing opportunity. Fang et al. (2017) and Meyer (2018) both described examples of risks, including data breaches or other breaches of confidentiality, adverse effects on reputation, illegal cooperation (e.g., breaches of antitrust law), and poor-quality data.

Enabler: This component records potential enablers for this data collaboration opportunity. Enablers are typically technical (e.g., secure data transfer, data anonymization), organizational (e.g., non-disclosure agreements, certificates, insurances), or based on the environment (e.g., third parties, legal regulations), as shown by Geppert et al. (2022) and Liu et al. (2019).

5 Evolution

The main discoveries revealed during the evolution of the DCC are shown in Table 2. The workshop participants identified data collaboration opportunities and gave rigorous feedback to the usability and usefulness of the current artifact. Details of this feedback is given in the following paragraphs.

5.1 Iterations 1 and 2

Version 1 of the DCC was created based on the current data collaboration literature and shaped in an initial workshop with industry participants. Based on experiences

Table 2 Conclusions from the evolution leading to the current DCC

	Iteration 1	Iteration 2	Iteration 3
Conclusion	Iteration 1 was useful to start the idea-generation process. It showed clearly that IT/IS alignment is needed for a common understanding of the idea	The interviews highlighted the need for a common language for practitioners. It became increasingly clear that an additional idea generation section is needed. The discussion also showed that the areas are already helpful in mapping out a collaboration but could be simplified	The experts could easily understand the components of the canvas and structure collaboration opportunities using the canvas. Within the workshop setting, the participants could generate and validate opportunities, offering compelling evidence for the usefulness and usability of the DCC

and feedback from this first workshop, a second iteration of the DCC was generated, and this version was discussed with industry experts to evaluate its comprehensibility. It was clear to the experts involved that business value is a critical component and that risks concerning compliance, privacy, and legal issues must be resolved as early as possible.

During the interviews, it became apparent that the organizations were searching for innovative opportunities and needed an additional phase to create potential opportunities. One interviewee commented: "There are always two phases; first you have to identify a partner and then you can evaluate" [P3]. The need for open innovation was also mentioned during the same interview: "We know our assets and can identify partners based on our weaknesses, but this is always driven based on an inside view. Real innovation would first need an open exchange of relevant assets." [P3]. It was also stated that one should start with the value of the opportunity: "There has to be a mutual benefit. Something should come out of the collaboration, and this needs to be discussed first" [P2]. It was apparent during all the interviews that the wording also needs clarification and should be adapted to industry practice. Regarding an early naming of the data collaboration opportunity, one expert articulated, "we would not call the input for evaluation a use-case; it is a possible opportunity" [P4].

5.2 Iteration 3

Feedback from Version 2 was used to further shape the ontology (Fig. 2) and the canvas (Table 2). The updated canvas became the idea evaluation part of the DCC (Fig. 1), and an additional idea generation part was added to the DCC (Fig. 1). This section addresses the need to identify relevant collaboration partners not addressed in the initial design. This latest version was then rigorously evaluated in interviews with specialists as well as in several workshops. The main findings were that experts could easily understand the different areas of the canvas and also grasped the two-step process (Table 2). Indeed, they all saw additional value in the DCC and could imagine a setup for using the canvas within their organizations. Some participants were already using the DCC to structure workshops and present collaborative projects to management for go/no-go decisions.

The idea generation part of the DCC was seen to be extremely useful in itself: "It is interesting to note which unique data we possess and where we miss information" [W5], and useful to facilitate an early-stage discussion of a collaboration: "This seems to be very useful in an early phase of discussions" [W4, P6]. The second part of the canvas was seen to be helpful in structuring a possible collaboration opportunity: "I have the feeling our current work is very unstructured; this would help us structure our process" [P6].

The workshop evaluation gave additional insight into the usability of the DCC. In a short time, participants could always find initial possible opportunities and evaluate them on the DCC. They stated that the tool was very compelling and gave an interesting insight into the assets of different industries in a short time. It was found to support and guide the discussion and help cover the key areas first: "Very comprehensible, and the canvas covers all important aspects" [W5], "Very good as a basis for further discussions; easy to identify the initial opportunity based on the field structure" [W5].

It was also stated that the initial workshop results could easily be verified with internal stakeholders to clarify all the open issues identified and then move ahead following clarification: "Both companies get a checklist for internal clarification, which reduces the number exchanges that we would need if we didn't structure the opportunity" [W2]. This was seen to be valuable as it reduces the cost of an initial proof of concept. The participants were also pleasantly surprised that they could identify and clarify complex cases in such a short time when using the canvas.

5.3 Using the DCC

The following procedure can be followed when instantiating the canvas in a workshop setting. This procedure was tested in workshops in an online setting (Table 1, W1-4), where all participants had access to a shared whiteboard application, and in a physical setting, where all participants had access to real whiteboards (Table 1, W5). The workshops were structured—in line with the canvas structure—in two phases. In the first phase, participants from several different companies, previously unknown to each other, were invited to complete the first part individually.

Following this individual think-phase, the participants were placed in pairs to see if relevant opportunities could be derived by comparing the individually identified strength and weaknesses. We called this part of the workshop "data-driven speed dating" because participants came together for a short amount of time to compare their strengths and weaknesses, identify possible opportunities for future collaboration, and then moved on to the next brief encounter.

Based on the opportunities identified, the second part of the workshop could now begin. In this phase, the DCC facilitates the systematic evaluation of individual collaboration opportunities and enables an assessment from the perspective of two or more participating organizations. Representatives of the different companies involved in the data opportunity completed the second part of the DCC together. Here, they discovered whether the collaborative opportunity was feasible and ought to be discussed further within the organization or discarded altogether (e.g., because no mutual benefit existed). Additional internal and external experts (e.g., legal, risk, and IT departments) can also support this process. Participants were preassigned to a group of 3–6 persons within the workshops, and each group decided which was the best opportunity identified by the phase one pairings. In phase two, only the opportunity selected was evaluated by the entire group.

Two industry partners (a bank and a postal service provider) applied the procedure mentioned above. In this example, a data collaboration opportunity was identified based on the first part of the DCC and then evaluated using the second part of the canvas. In the idea generation part of the DCC, the bank had a data weakness in that up-to-date customer addresses were not always available and that because of this, mailings were not always delivered, thereby increasing the cost of client interaction. The postal service prover had a unique data strength because it offered services to update incorrect customer addresses. As the industry partners were from banking and postal services, several legal constraints were identified in the second part of the canvas; however, these could be mitigated by using novel privacy-enhancing technologies as an enabler. Since all areas were clarified at an early stage (such as finding the stakeholders needed to reduce the risks), the project could be successfully started. The results were incorporated into a white paper for industry experts in the field of data innovation. This white paper—which contains additional information about the use of the DCC and the use-case as a working example—will also be released to the wider practitioner community.

6 Discussion

This paper presents the DCC—a visual framework to facilitate data collaboration between organizations or organizational units within the same operation. As this framework provides a new solution for a practical problem, the ADR approach was followed during its creation (Sein et al., 2011). The project was motivated by the fact that practitioners had no tool to structure and initiate a data-based organizational collaboration. The benefits of the DCC are twofold: First, it can help identify possible collaboration partners and, second, it determines the most beneficial of those opportunities and can lead to maximization of the data value (van den Broek & van Veenstra, 2015). In addition, this approach helps to identify—early in the process—those projects that have no chance of success.

The DCC also helps balance the focus of discussion between collaborative partners to the most relevant areas for data sharing (Reich and Benbasat, 2000; Sabherwal et al., 2019). Using the DCC, organizations can develop a shared understanding of data-based opportunities, helping them form a mental picture of the final project. This also helps to spot potential flaws, which can be clarified together or individually. The design of the DCC incorporates the language of industry experts and aids practitioners in finding a shared language. The structure of the DCC guides the user through a conversation process that assists in speedily overcoming misconceptions and identifying relevant information regarding the opportunity.

The research described in this paper follows the ADR paradigm and, as such, has certain limitations that need to be acknowledged. The artifact is derived from the scientific literature, and the current version has emerged from several workshops. While this is the standard approach to ADR, it would be beneficial to validate the derived components of the DCC further. Moreover, only a limited number of workshops with participants from larger organizations were conducted. Additional workshops would be necessary to assess further the applicability of the framework for small and medium enterprises. A further potential weakness stems from the personal involvement of the researchers in the workshops. Although this is a common feature of action research, such participation could have biased the results of the workshops. To some extent, the expert interviews may have redressed this possible imbalance. Nevertheless, the first application of the DCC in a project within an organization shows it can be applied without the researchers' direct involvement.

The artifact generated by this project provides an important contribution to the IS practice domain as it can be used visually to identify and systematically evaluate innovative data based organizational collaborations. It also helps to align the collaborative work between stakeholders from different companies and backgrounds and facilitates industry workshops in the early phases of evaluating possible data-exchange partnerships. This paper does not focus on forming open data initiatives, which have also been studied, for example, by Conrado et al. (2017). It is evident, however, that the use of open data could further enrich an inter-organizational collaboration.

From an academic perspective, our study is an example of ADR since it solves a significant practical problem, uses rigorous evaluation, and offers valuable commercial benefits. As a research contribution, the artifact amalgamates the most critical components needed to create a successful data collaboration partnership.

Acknowledgements The authors would like to thank all workshop and interview participants for their valuable feedback regarding the DCC's design, usability, and usefulness. The authors of this research paper were supported by the <blinded>.

References

Abraham, R., Schneider, J., & vom Brocke, J. (2019). Data governance: A conceptual framework, structured review, and research agenda. International Journal of Information Management, 49, pp. 424–438.

Avdiji, H., Elikan, D., Missonier, S., & Pigneur, Y. (2018). Designing Tools for Collectively Solving Ill-Structured Problems. Proceedings of the 51st Hawaii International Conference on System Sciences, pp. 400–409.

Barringer, B. and Harrison, J. (2000) 'Walking a tightrope: creating value through interorganizational relationships', Journal of Management, 26(3), pp. 367–403.

van den Broek, T. and van Veenstra, A. fleur (2015) 'Modes of Governance in Inter-Organizational Data Collaborations', in ECIS 2015 Proceedings. ECIS 2015, p. 13.

Conrado, D.J. et al. (2017) 'Open innovation: Towards sharing of data, models and workflows', European Journal of Pharmaceutical Sciences, 109, pp. 65–71.

Constantiou, I.D. and Kallinikos, J. (2015) 'New Games, New Rules: Big Data and the Changing Context of Strategy', Journal of Information Technology, 30(1), pp. 44–57.

Dinter, B. and Krämer, J. (2018) 'Data-driven innovations in electronic markets', Electronic Markets, 28(4), pp. 403–405.

Dinter, B., Schieder, C. and Gluchowski, P. (2015) 'A Stakeholder Lens on Metadata Management in Business Intelligence and Big Data—Results of an Empirical Investigation', in Proceedings of the Twenty-first Americas Conference on Information Systems. Twenty-first Americas Conference on Information Systems, p. 13.

Enkel, E., Gassmann, O. and Chesbrough, H. (2009) 'Open R&D and open innovation: exploring the phenomenon', R&D Management, 39(4), pp. 311–316.

Fang, W. , Wen, X. Z., Zheng, Y., & Zhou, M. (2017) 'A Survey of Big Data Security and Privacy Preserving', IETE Technical Review, 34(5), pp. 544–560.

Geppert, T., Anderegg, J., Frei, L., Moeller, S., Deml, S., Sturzenegger, D., & Ebert, N. (2022). Overcoming Cloud Concerns with Trusted Execution Environments? Exploring the Organizational Perception of a Novel Security Technology in Regulated Swiss Companies. Proceedings of the 55nd Hawaii International Conference on System Sciences, pp. 6822–6829

Gulati, R. and Singh, H. (1998) 'The Architecture of Cooperation: Managing Coordination Costs and Appropriation Concerns in Strategic Alliances', Administrative Science Quarterly, 43(4), p. 781.

Günther, W.A. et al. (2017) 'Debating big data: A literature review on realizing value from big data', The Journal of Strategic Information Systems, 26(3), pp. 191–209.

Hannila, H. et al. (2019) 'Data-driven Begins with DATA; Potential of Data Assets', Journal of Computer Information Systems, 62(1), pp. 29-38.

Hunke, F., Seebacher, S. and Thomsen, H. (2020) 'Please Tell Me What to Do—Towards a Guided Orchestration of Key Activities in Data-Rich Service Systems', in S. Hofmann, O. Müller, and M. Rossi (eds) Designing for Digital Transformation. Co-Creating Services with Citizens and Industry. Cham: Springer International Publishing (Lecture Notes in Computer Science), pp. 426–437.

Kaufmann, M. (2019) 'Big Data Management Canvas: A Reference Model for Value Creation from Data', Big Data and Cognitive Computing, 3(1), p. 19.

Kayser, L., Mueller, R.M. and Kronsbein, T. (2019) 'Data Collection Map: A Canvas for Shared Data Awareness in Data-Driven Innovation Projects', in Prodeedings of the 2019 Pre-ICIS SIGDSA Symposium 18.

Krasikov, P., Eurich, M., & Legner, C. (2022). Unleashing the Potential of External Data: A DSR-based applroach to Data Sourcing, ECIS 2022 Research Papers. 64.

Kronsbein, T. and Mueller, R.M. (2019) 'Data Thinking: A Canvas for Data-Driven Ideation Workshops', in Proceedings of the 52nd Hawaii International Conference on System Sciences. Hawaii International Conference on System Sciences, p. 10.

Labadie, C. et al. (2020) 'FAIR Enough? Enhancing the Usage of Enterprise Data with Data Catalogs', in 2020 IEEE 22nd Conference on Business Informatics (CBI). 2020 IEEE 22nd Conference on Business Informatics (CBI), pp. 201–210.

Ladley, J. (2012) Data Governance: How to Design, Deploy and Sustain an Effective Data Governance Program. 1st edn. Morgan Kaufmann (The Morgan Kaufmann Series on Business Intelligence).

LaValle, S. et al. (2011) 'Big Data, Analytics and the Path from Insights to Value', MIT Sloan Management Review, 52(2), pp. 21–31.
Lis, D. and Otto, B. (2020) Data Governance in Data Ecosystems—Insights from Organizations, AMCIS 2020 Proceedings. 12.
Liu, Q. and Zou, X. (2019) 'Research on trust mechanism of cooperation innovation with big data processing based on blockchain', EURASIP Journal on Wireless Communications and Networking, 2019(1), p. 26.
Meyer, M.N. (2018) 'Practical Tips for Ethical Data Sharing', Advances in Methods and Practices in Psychological Science, 1(1), pp. 131–144.
Miguel, J.C. and Casado, M.Á. (2016) 'GAFAnomy (Google, Amazon, Facebook and Apple): The Big Four and the b-Ecosystem', in M. Gómez-Uranga, J.M. Zabala-Iturriagagoitia, and J. Barrutia (eds) Dynamics of Big Internet Industry Groups and Future Trends: A View from Epigenetic Economics. Cham: Springer International Publishing, pp. 127–148.
Mikalef, P. and Krogstie, J. (2018) 'Big Data Governance and Dynamic Capabilities: The Moderating effect of Environmental Uncertainty', PACIS 2018 Proceedings. 206.
Mitchell, W. and Singh, K. (1996) 'Survival of Businesses Using Collaborative Relationships to Commercialize Complex Goods', Strategic Management Journal, 17(3), pp. 169–195.
Nissen, H.A., Evald, M.R. and Clarke, A.H. (2014) 'Knowledge sharing in heterogeneous teams through collaboration and cooperation: Exemplified through Public–Private-Innovation partnerships', Industrial Marketing Management, 43(3), pp. 473–482.
Oliveira, M.I.S. et al. (2018) 'Towards a meta-model for data ecosystems', in Proceedings of the 19th Annual International Conference on Digital Government Research: Governance in the Data Age. New York, NY, USA: Association for Computing Machinery (dg.o '18), pp. 1–10.
Osterwalder, A. et al. (2014) Value Proposition Design: How to Create Products and Services Customers Want. John Wiley & Sons.
Osterwalder, A. and Pigneur, Y. (2010) Business Model Generation: A Handbook for Visionaries, Game Changers, and Challengers. John Wiley & Sons.
Otto, B. (2011) 'Organizing Data Governance: Findings from the Telecommunications Industry and Consequences for Large Service Providers', Communications of the Association for Information Systems, 29(1).
Polewsky, S. and Will, H. (1996) 'Creativity workshops: Tools for innovation in organizations?', European Journal of Work and Organizational Psychology, 5(1), pp. 43–51.
Pouwels, I. and Koster, F. (2017) 'Inter-organizational cooperation and organizational innovativeness. A comparative study', International Journal of Innovation Science, 9(2), pp. 184–204.
Powell, W.W., Koput, K.W. and Smith-Doerr, L. (1996) 'Interorganizational Collaboration and the Locus of Innovation: Networks of Learning in Biotechnology', Administrative Science Quarterly, 41(1), p. 116.
Provan, K.G. and Kenis, P. (2008) 'Modes of Network Governance: Structure, Management, and Effectiveness', Journal of Public Administration Research and Theory, 18(2), pp. 229–252.
Reich, B.H. and Benbasat, I. (2000) 'Factors That Influence the Social Dimension of Alignment between Business and Information Technology Objectives', MIS Quarterly, 24(1), p. 81.
Richter, H. and Slowinski, P.R. (2019) 'The Data Sharing Economy: On the Emergence of New Intermediaries', IIC - International Review of Intellectual Property and Competition Law, 50(1), pp. 4–29.
Sabherwal, R. et al. (2019) 'How does strategic alignment affect firm performance? the roles of information technology investment and environmental uncertainty', MIS Quarterly, 43(2), pp. 453–474.
Sammon, D. and Nagle, T. (2017) 'The Data Value Map: A framework for developing shared understanding on data initiatives', Proceedings of the 25th European Conference on Information Systems (ECIS), pp. 1439–1452.
Seddon, P.B. et al. (2017) 'How does business analytics contribute to business value?', Information Systems Journal, 27(3), pp. 237–269.
Sein et al. (2011) 'Action Design Research', MIS Quarterly, 35(1), p. 37.

Sonehara, N., Echizen, I. and Wohlgemuth, S. (2011) 'Isolation in Cloud Computing and Privacy-Enhancing Technologies: Suitability of Privacy-Enhancing Technologies for Separating Data Usage in Business Processes', Business & Information Systems Engineering, 3(3), pp. 155–162.

Stolze, C., Zarvic, N. and Thomas, O. (2011) 'Working in an inter-organisational context: The relevance of IT Governance and Business-IT Alignment.', International Journal of Computer Science and Information Security, 9(8).

Thoring, K., Mueller, R.M. and Badke-Schaub, P. (2019) 'Exploring the Design Space of Innovation Canvases', Conference Proceedings of the Academy for Design Innovation Management, 2(1).

Tona, O. et al. (2018) 'Towards Ethical Big Data Artifacts: A Conceptual Design', Proceedings of the 51nd Hawaii International Conference on System Sciences, pp. 4523–4532

Woerner, S.L. and Wixom, B.H. (2015) 'Big Data: Extending the Business Strategy Toolbox', Journal of Information Technology, 30(1), pp. 60–62.

Impact of Data Collection on ML Models: Analyzing Differences of Biases Between Low-Versus High-Skilled Annotators

Johannes Schneider, Daniel Eisenhardt, Christian Utama, and Christian Meske

Abstract Labeled data is crucial for the success of machine learning-based artificial intelligence. However, companies often face a choice between collecting few annotations from high- or low-skilled annotators, possibly exhibiting different biases. This study investigates differences in biases between datasets labeled by said annotator groups and their impact on machine learning models. Therefore, we created high- and low-skilled annotated datasets measured the contained biases through entropy and trained different machine learning models to examine bias inheritance effects. Our findings on text sentiment annotations show both groups exhibit a considerable amount of bias in their annotations, although there is a significant difference regarding the error types commonly encountered. Models trained on biased annotations produce significantly different predictions, indicating bias propagation and tend to make more extreme errors than humans. As partial mitigation, we propose and show the efficiency of a hybrid approach where data is labeled by low-skilled and high-skilled workers.

Keywords Annotators · Machine learning models · Bias · Labeling

---

J. Schneider
Institute of Information Systems, University of Liechtenstein, Vaduz, Liechtenstein
e-mail: johannes.schneider@uni.li

D. Eisenhardt · C. Meske (✉)
Faculties of Mechanical Engineering and Computer Science, Ruhr-University Bochum, Bochum, Germany
e-mail: christian.meske@rub.de

D. Eisenhardt
e-mail: daniel.eisenhardt@rub.de

C. Utama
Department of Information Systems, Freie Universität Berlin, Berlin, Germany
e-mail: christian.utama@fu-berlin.de

D. Beverungen et al. (eds.), *Solutions and Technologies for Responsible Digitalization*, Lecture Notes in Information Systems and Organisation 75,
https://doi.org/10.1007/978-3-031-80122-8_5

1 Introduction

The phrase "data is the new oil" was coined already in 2006 by Clive Humby. It has ever since been confirmed by the area of big data and AI, which learns decision making capability from data (Rodrigues and Pereira, 2018; Schneider et al., 2022). Especially, labeled data has proven useful in the context of supervised learning enabling a variety of applications (Hötter et al., 2022; Saravanan and Sujatha, 2018). Data labeling is the process of assigning labels to raw data. It is essential for supervised machine learning as it provides the necessary information on the ground truth of a data instance for training algorithms to recognize patterns and make accurate predictions.

While unlabeled data is often abundant, data labeling can be costly, since humans typically do it. Humans bare potential biases, alone poor quality data can have a negative impact on the annotator's performance (Cabrera et al., 2014).

Furthermore, human characteristics such as biased decision-making can adversely affect data quality (Barbosa and Chen, 2019; Ding et al., 2022; Hube et al., 2018; Kafkalias et al., 2022). Since personal characteristics and experiences can influence how annotators label data, the skill level of annotators can also influence labeling behavior. For example, highly qualified annotators may have a stronger opinion and thus tend to label data in a more extreme way. In contrast, less qualified annotators may tend to label data more cautiously and thus show a tendency towards the middle. In turn, machine learning models trained on such data can exhibit poor performance, e.g. increasing noise in the data can result in decreasing model accuracies (Caiafa et al., 2020; Barbosa & Chen, 2019; Geva et al., 2019; Zhang et al., 2014; Zhu & Wu, 2004). While there is rich literature on crowdsourcing and biases of annotators, the impact of biases originating from low-skilled and high-skilled annotators on model performance has received only limited attention (e.g., Snow et al., 2008; Wassem, 2016). So far, results have been inconclusive showing that non-expert annotations can outperform expert annotations (Waseem, 2016), can yield acceptable data quality (Irshad et al., 2014; O'Neil et al., 2017; Warby et al., 2014; Zhang et al., 2020), show only little differences to expert annotations (See et al., 2013) or get outperformed by experts (Snow et al., 2008). This calls for additional investigation to understand how biases impact overall performance. There is also a lack of works that analyze how data biases are reflected in model predictions in multi-class settings, where different types of errors might have different consequences. As an example, a website classifier misclassifying an adult site as a children's entertainment site is much more harmful than misclassifying it as a gambling site. Similarly, failing a student that should have passed has different implications than letting a student pass that should have failed (Schneider et al., 2022). With the steadily increasing influence of AI on more and more critical areas, the relevance of the training data, which determines the origin of the tendencies and the performance of such systems, increases. With the previously mentioned increasing need for labeled data, the effects of potential biases of annotators must be investigated in order to avoid the development of potentially harmful systems as early as possible. In this work, we are particularly interested in understanding:

RQ1: How do biases of high-skilled annotators differ during labeling from biases of low-skilled annotators in text sentiment classification tasks?

RQ2: To what extent do biases in annotated training data lead to biases in predictions of ml models and how can these biases be mitigated?

That is, we aim to understand if machine learning models amplify biases in data, dampen them or shift one bias to another. All the evidence so far points to the existence of bias in annotations provided by different groups and its negative effect on model performance but to our best knowledge, very few of the existing studies have looked into its subsequent propagation into model predictions, i.e., whether biases in annotations are reflected in predictions. Therefore, we set out to find evidence in support of this statement by comparing crowdsourced annotations provided by low- and high-skilled annotators. As another (minor) difference to most of the existing studies we segregate annotators based on their apparent skill level on the task at hand, whereas prior compared experts and non-experts or people from different demographic groups. Finally, we also discuss the mitigation of biases. This question is of high practical relevance, since companies can impact data biases through their choice of annotators, i.e., crowd workers. They can employ high or low skilled workers in typical crowdsourcing settings, e.g., by demanding a certain level of education of crowd workers. To answer our question, we employ an empirical approach. This seems well-suited in the context of machine learning, since machine learning models are notoriously difficult to understand (Meske et al., 2022) making a deductive approach challenging. That is, despite significant efforts in the research community to explain machine learning models, many challenges remain (Meske et al., 2022).

We explore the presence of biases in crowdsourced annotations and investigate whether these biases are the same for low- and high-skilled annotators. We also provide empirical evidence to understand to what extent biases and errors in annotations are transferred to ML models. Finally, we show that biases can be reduced by using a mix of high- and low-skilled workers. Thus, our work has tangible implications for practitioners facing the choice of what skill level of workers they should demand. However, in this paper, we provide findings of our work in progress for one common task in machine learning, i.e., annotation of textual data with sentiments, using a state-of-the-art model in NLP, e.g., a transformer-based deep learning model.

The paper is structured as follows. We start with the background and related work on the topics of crowdsourcing in machine learning research, comparing annotations from different sources and training models with biased data. This is followed by a description of the methods we used to derive our analysis, a summary of our results and finally the conclusions drawn and an outlook for future research.

2 Background and Related Work

2.1 Crowdsourcing in Machine Learning Research

In the context of machine learning, crowdsourcing has a multitude of application areas, namely data generation, model evaluation and debugging, hybrid intelligence systems, and behavioral experiments (Vaughan, 2018). For data generation purposes, crowdsourcing is seen as a quick and efficient way to annotate large amounts of data, which could in turn be used to train supervised machine learning models. Although crowdsourcing alleviates the problem of data quantity, there are questions regarding the quality of the data. Annotations or labels collected might be noisy due to spammers providing arbitrary labels to maximize their financial gains (Eickhoff et al., 2012), annotators' malicious behavior (Wang et al., 2013), and cognitive biases (Eickhoff, 2018). In this paper, we adopt the definition of biases as annotators' cognitive biases, i.e., systematic deviation patterns in thinking from the rational causing systematic errors (Haselton et al., 2015). In addition to potential malicious data biases, Liu et al. (2021) found that demographic groups of annotators show similarities in biases within their group and differences across different groups. Meaning different unconscious factors of annotators can influence their labeling behaviour and therefore be the origin of biases that transfer into the data. In recent years, various ways to get around this issue have been studied, including label aggregation techniques (Jagabathula et al., 2014; Zhang et al., 2016), designing tasks and incentive schemes to induce high quality answers (He et al., 2013; Radanovic et al., 2016), and training models with noisy labels (Cordeiro and Carneiro, 2020; Han et al., 2018; Lee et al., 2022; Nomura et al., 2021; Rodrigues and Pereira, 2018). Most works on label aggregation techniques have been based on the general expectation-maximization (EM) framework proposed by Dawid & Skene (1979), although simple majority voting has also been shown to perform robustly in some cases (Saab et al., 2019; Van Atteveldt et al., 2021).

2.2 Comparing Crowdsourced (Non-Expert) and Expert Annotations

Evaluating the quality of crowdsourced annotations is seen as standard practice before using them in downstream applications. To do so, it is common to measure the inter-annotator agreement using some statistical measure such as Krippendorff's alpha (Hayes and Krippendorff, 2007). Snow et al. (2008) evaluated the quality of non-expert annotations and compared them to expert annotations for five natural language tasks. They found that across all tasks, between 4 and 10 non-expert annotations are required to match an expert annotator's performance and for a particular task, a supervised machine learning model trained with non-expert annotations can outperform one trained with expert annotations, indicating the presence of a strong bias in individual labelers. Waseem (2016) compared expert and non-expert annotations collected for a hate speech labeling task and showed that non-expert annotators are more likely to label items as hate speech compared to experts. Comparing the performances of downstream classification models trained on these annotations, it was found that models trained on expert annotations showed superior performance. Long et al. (2021) showed that non-expert annotations from crowdsourcing services could have negative effects on a supervised machine learning model's performance. The study of Shakeri Hossein Abad et al. (2022) supports these findings by showing a fall of at least 8% across all performance measures when using non-expert annotations. Barbera et al. (2020) looked at the task of content truthfulness assessment and explored how the adopted response scale and annotators' own bias affect their responses. Their results showed that annotators tend to be biased towards their beliefs, i.e., items aligned to their political beliefs were marked as truthful more often. These studies hint at the difference in annotation behavior between experts and non-experts. They also suggest that machine learning models trained on either expert or non-expert annotations might vary performance-wise.

2.3 *Training with Biased Data*

Binns et al. (2017) conducted empirical experiments in the context of content and showed that the classifiers trained on men-annotated labels are less sensitive to women-annotated labels and vice-versa. Similarly, Al Kuwatly et al. (2020) investigated annotator bias by training hateful content classifiers on annotations provided by groups segregated by demographic features such as gender, age, education and first language. The results show that except for gender, all other demographic features considered had a significant effect on the predictions, e.g., classifiers trained on annotations provided by native English speakers demonstrate significantly better performance in classifying personal attack comments compared to those trained on non-native speakers-provided annotations. Geva et al. (2019) explored annotator bias in three natural language tasks by training models either with or without annotator identifiers as features and found that model performance is superior in the former case, indicating that models could use the additional information to better replicate annotators' behavior. Moreover, models trained from a pool of annotations provided by certain annotators were also found to perform poorly when tested on data provided by another subset of annotators.

Existing studies have therefore shown the effects of demographic characteristics and domain knowledge by annotators on the accuracy of the resulting models. However, our primary area of interest lies in investigating the transmission of bias, stemming from the labeling procedure of the training data to the corresponding machine learning models.

3 Methodology

Ultimately, we aim to empirically analyze how biases in data impact model predictions using multiple datasets and multiple machine learning models. In this paper, we use one dataset and one machine learning model to gather findings by tackling the problem of sentiment analysis in the realm of natural language processing (NLP) using a state-of-the-art deep learning model.

For our analysis, we utilized a dataset of crowdsourced annotations for weather tweet sentiment analysis collected through Crowdflower. The tweets, which have been presented to the annotators have a ground truth label collected from domain experts outside the crowdsourcing setup, meaning a total of 102 experts were involved in the ground truth labeling process. The raw dataset contains 1000 tweets, and each tweet was annotated by 20 annotators to be classified into one of the following classes based on their sentiment: (1) Negative, (2) Neutral, (3) Positive, (4) I can't tell and (5) Tweet not related to weather condition. Previous research has shown that having many sentiment classes is a challenging task for machine learning models (Bouazizi and Ohtsuki, 2019), which is why we decided to remove the last two classes from the dataset in order to achieve a respectable performance from our subsequent classifier. After removing the last two classes, our final dataset contains 763 tweets and 13,484 annotations. The class distributions for the tweets and annotations are provided in Table 1. It can be seen that both the tweets and annotations are fairly evenly distributed between the three classes.

We classified the 102 annotators into low- and high-skilled annotators based on their annotation performance as measured by the average weighted F1 score, which indicates the skill, and the number of tweets they annotated, i.e., for high-skilled workers we also demanded a minimum amount of experience. Figures 1 and 2 illustrate the distributions of the annotators based on these two variables. For our purposes, we intended to have at least 30 annotators in both groups in order to enable reliable statistical tests for our subsequent analyses and ultimately set a minimum value of 0.8 for the average weighted F1 score and 60 for the number of annotated tweets for an annotator to be classified as highly skilled. This led to 31 high-skilled annotators and 71 low-skilled annotators.

To measure overall biases in the annotations, we utilized the concept of normalized entropy in information theory (Shannon, 1948), the formula for which is given below.

$$H = -\sum_{i=1}^{n} P(x_i) \log_n P(x_i),$$

Table 1 Distribution of tweets and annotations

Class	No. of tweets	No. of annotations
Negative	271	4668
Neutral	261	4486
Positive	231	4330

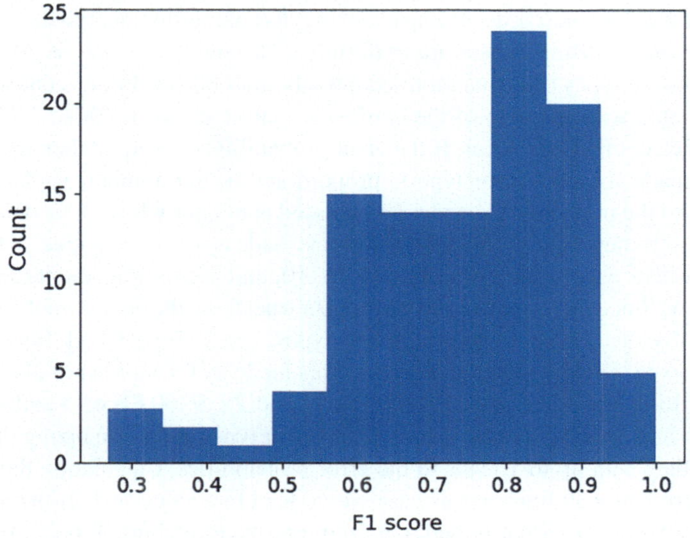

Fig. 1 Annotators' F1 score distribution

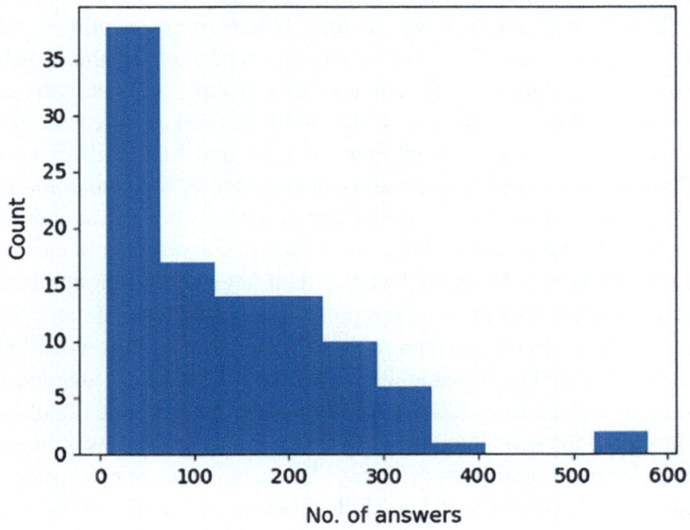

Fig. 2 Annotators' number of answers distribution

where H is the normalized entropy with values in [0,1], i denotes the outcome class and ranges from 1–6, n is the number of possible outcome classes and P(x_i) is the probability of observing the outcome of class i. Meaning P(x_i) equals the relative frequency with which the annotator at hand contributed to the different types of existing errors. A value of one indicates no bias and a value of 0 large bias. If the annotators were not biased, according to our previous definition, we would expect that their errors in confusing classes are uniformly distributed, i.e., there is no tendency to make certain types of errors more commonly than others. In our context, this is best illustrated with the help of the confusion matrix shown in Table 2. There are 6 types of errors that can occur. If the error probabilities are equal then the number of errors made for each error type is proportional to the number of observations belonging to the true class. Consider an unbiased annotator who errs in 10% of their annotations. If they were to annotate 300 tweets made up of 160 negative, 100 neutral and 40 positive tweets, they would make 16, 10, and 4 errors for the three classes, respectively. Since there are two error types per true class, the errors would also have to be equally distributed between the two types, i.e., 8 Type 1 and Type 2 errors each, and so on. Dividing the numbers of errors made by the number of observations belonging to its true class, e.g., 8/160 (Type 1 and 2), 5/100 (Type 3 and 4) and 2/40 (Type 5 and 6), we get equal values for all error types and normalizing the values such that they sum up to 1 leads to the error probabilities. Calculating the entropy from the error probabilities in this case would lead to a value of 1. If the annotator in question were somewhat biased, e.g., more prone to making Type 1 errors than Type 2, the number of Type 1 errors might be higher than that of Type 2—12 versus 4. In this case, the entropy would be equal to 0.976. Hence, the lower the entropy of an annotator is, the more biased their annotations are.

For each high-skilled annotator, we calculated their error probabilities and entropy on the tweets they annotated. As our results are dependent on the dirstibution of ground truth labels among the different annotator groups, we evenly dispensed the true classes across them. To provide a fair comparison, i.e., to ensure the overall number of correct labels is very similar for low- and high-skilled workers, we created ensembles of non-skilled annotators and aggregated their annotations through majority voting. The number of non-skilled annotators ensembles was chosen to equal the number of high-skilled annotators. The number of annotators in each ensemble is set to be the fewest possible as such so that their aggregated annotation achieves a comparable F1 score to that of the corresponding high-skilled annotator (difference < 0.03). The error probabilities and entropies of the ensembles of low-skilled annotators were then calculated in the same way. To find out whether the annotations of the two groups exhibit bias, we conducted a one sample t-test with the population mean set to the entropy of the raw annotations (0.9885). This procedure was chosen to find out whether there is no significant difference between the mean entropy of the high-skilled annotators' (ensembles of low-skilled annotators') annotations and the raw

Table 2 Example confusion matrix for the dataset

True class	Predicted class		
	Negative	Neutral	Positive
Negative	–	Type 1	Type 2
Neutral	Type 3	–	Type 4
Positive	Type 5	Type 6	–

annotations' entropy. Finally, we ran Kolmogorov-Smirnov tests on the following variables to further investigate two scenarios:

- Entropy of the high-skilled annotators' versus ensembles of low-skilled annotators' annotations should indicate if1: there is no bias-wise difference between the high-skilled annotators and the ensembles of low-skilled annotators.
- Error probabilities of the high-skilled annotators versus ensembles of low-skilled annotators should show if2: high-skilled annotators and ensembles of low-skilled annotators are prone to the same types of errors, i.e., there is no significant difference in probabilities across all error types.

To investigate the propagation of annotation bias into model predictions, we fine-tuned smallBERT (Devlin et al., 2019) for 20 epochs with the learning rate set to 1e-4 to classify the tweets using three different sets of annotations as training data: (1) aggregated annotations from all high-skilled annotators, (2) aggregated annotations from all low-skilled annotators and (3) half of the tweets annotated by high-skilled annotators and the other half by low-skilled annotators. For each of the 30 annotators sets (of each skill level), we trained a separate model. We used fivefold cross-validation and recorded the cross-validated accuracies and error probabilities on the predictions. Lastly, we ran pair-wise Kolmogorov–Smirnov tests to compare the error probabilities across all error types for the three annotation sets, with the goal to investigate if: there is no significant difference between the three models' predictions in terms of error probabilities.

4 Results and Discussion

The t-test results for the detection of biases are presented in Table 3. For both low- and high-skilled annotators, biases are detected at a 1% significance level, meaning that both groups tend to make certain types of errors more often as opposed to having equal probabilities for all types of errors. Comparing the two groups, no statistically significant difference is found, suggesting that low- and high-skilled annotators exhibit about the same level of bias. It is intuitive to think that ensembles of low-skilled annotators show less bias due to the aggregation of annotations, i.e., different biases "cancel". However, biases within the group of low-skilled workers exist. Low-skilled workers picked the "Neutral" and "Positive" labels slightly more often than their high-skilled counterparts, while the opposite applies to the "Negative" label. The overall distribution of replies of low and high-skilled workers is given in Table 4.

Figure 3 shows the distributions of error probabilities for annotations provided by high-skilled and low-skilled annotators. The results show that in general, high-skilled annotators demonstrate large variances across all error types, i.e., a certain annotator A might be highly susceptible to Type 1 error and not to other error types. For another annotator B high susceptibility to Type 3 error might be observed. In contrast, ensembles of low-skilled annotators seem to be relatively consistent with

Table 3 One sample t-test results for bias detection

Group	Mean entropy ± std	t-statistic	*p*-value
High-skilled annotators	0.714 ± 0.179	−8.42	2.13e–9
Ensembles of low-skilled annotators	0.719 ± 0.157	−9.36	2.07e–10

Table 4 Distributions of annotations from low- and high-skilled workers

Class	No. of annotations	
	High-skilled annotators	Low-skilled annotators
Negative	1896 (36.8%)	2590 (31.1%)
Neutral	1707 (33.1%)	2961 (35.5%)
Positive	1550 (30.1%)	2780 (33.4%)

regard to the errors they make, in that Type 1 and 6 errors are the most common by far and only small variances are observed. The latter is a consequence of aggregating outcomes of multiple workers.

While it might be tempting to attribute the irregularities of errors as a regression to the mean, i.e., towards "Neutral", it is not the case because having "Neutral" as the aggregated annotation for a certain tweet is only possible if the majority of the annotators actually answered"Neutral" and not when "Positive" and"Negative" annotations are observed in equal measure. Instead, it might be attributed to the tendency of low-skilled annotators to choose the "safe" answer in order to minimize large errors in an estimate. That is, in our case the error is maximal if "Positive" and "Negative" are confused. Choosing "Neutral" avoids such large errors. This tendency

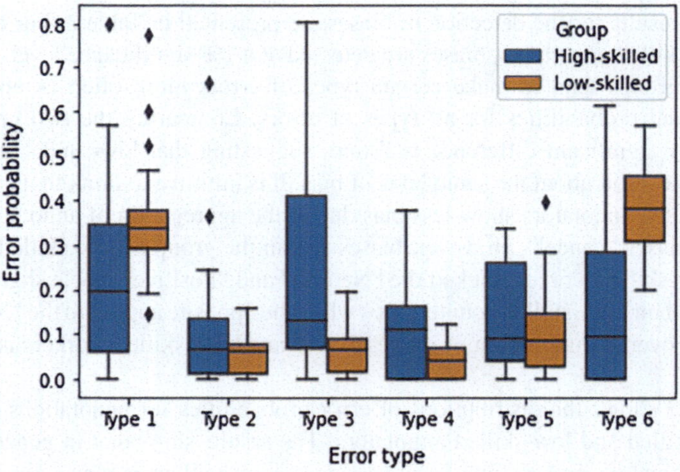

Fig. 3 Distributions of error probabilities for low—and high-skilled annotators

Table 5 KS-test results for the annotators' error probabilities

Error type	Statistic	*p*-value
Type 1	0.484	0.001*
Type 2	0.258	0.256
Type 3	0.452	0.003*
Type 4	0.452	0.003*
Type 5	0.194	0.615
Type 6	0.677	4.62e–7*

is also apparent from the distributions of annotations from the two groups shown in Table 4, where low-skilled workers have a slight preference for neutral labels.

The Kolmogorov-Smirnov test results for comparing the error probabilities between low and high-skilled workers are shown in Table 5. The probabilities of Type 1, 3, 4 and 6 errors between high-skilled and low-skilled annotators are significantly different (at 1% significance level). As is evident in Fig. 3, high-skilled annotators tend to make Type 3 and 4 errors more often than low-skilled counterparts, while the opposite is true for Type 1 and 6 errors. Based on this evidence, it could be argued that high-skilled annotators are more confident in their judgment than low-skilled ones, leading the former to choose the "Negative" and "Positive" labels more often than the latter, although erroneously in some cases. This is in line with the findings of Hube et al. (2019), which state that annotators with strong opinions tend to provide non-neutral options more often, leading to biased annotations. These behavioral tendencies might have their origin in the way experts and novices approach topics and problem solving tasks, as Haerem and Rau (2007) stated that experts predominantly rely on deep structures of the problem and novices on the surface structure. We can also rule out the possibility of this finding being an artifact of the data, as Table 4 shows that in general, high-skilled annotators annotate tweets as "Positive" less often compared to low-skilled annotators.

Results of the empirical experiment on classifiers are summarized in Figs. 4, 5 and Table 6. First of all, it can be seen that the trends of the error probabilities (Fig. 4) are consistent with the ones shown in Fig. 3—classifiers trained on high-skilled annotators' annotations produce Type 3 and 4 errors in their predictions more often than those trained on annotators provided by low-skilled annotators, while the latter group of classifiers is more susceptible to Type 1 and 6 errors. Although the Kolmogorov-Smirnov test results show that only the differences in Type 1 and Type 3 errors are detected at 1% significance level, the overall trend remains consistent when comparing the means of the error probabilities. This is while both classifiers exhibit almost the same level of accuracy: 0.71 ± 0.01 (low-skilled) vs. 0.72 ± 0.01 (high-skilled). Based on these results, it can be concluded that biases in annotations are reflected in model predictions to a considerable extent, indicating that caution should be exercised when gathering crowdsourced annotations for training models. It is also interesting to see that the model makes extreme errors, i.e., Types 2 and 5 confusing "Positive" and "Negative" much more often than humans. We

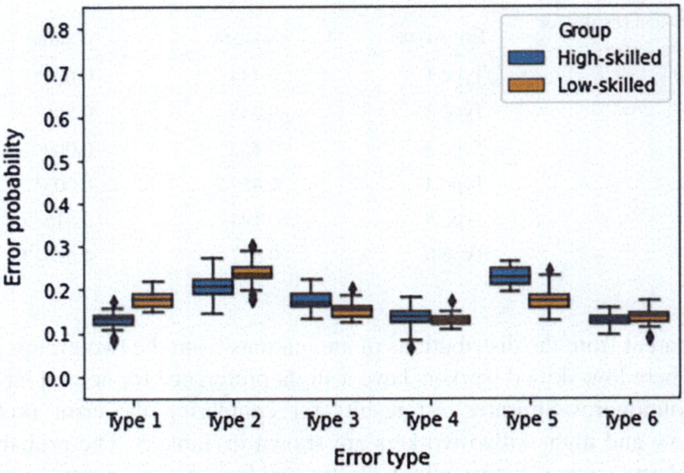

Fig. 4 Distributions of error probabilities for classifiers trained on the low—and high-skilled annotation sets

attribute this to the fact that the classifier is trained on few data and on a specific usecase in contrast to humans, i.e., humans have a more-fine granular understanding of sentiment (and language) originating from similar tasks and other domains (a broughter knowledgebase) reducing the likelihood of large errors. From Fig. 5, it can be seen that the mixed annotation strategy has an averaging effect on the error probabilities—across all error types, the error probabilities of these classifiers are in between the values exhibited by the classifiers trained on the other two annotation sets. In applications where avoiding any extreme error probability is desirable, the results indicate that implementing a mixed annotation strategy might help machine learning models to produce more balanced, hence less biased, predictions.

5 Conclusion and Future Work

We have shown that both low- and high-skilled annotators exhibit certain biases in their annotations. Although there is no evidence of significant difference regarding the extent of bias between the two groups, it was found that they are susceptible to different types of errors. Assuming the same number of errors, high-skilled annotators tend to avoid the "Neutral" label and provide polarized annotations instead, whereas the opposite is true for low-skilled annotators. By training classifiers on biased annotations, we found evidence that biases in the annotations also manifest in model predictions, calling for caution when training models on crowdsourced annotations and different costs are attached to the various types of error. In particular, classifiers tended to show more extreme errors than found in human data, i.e., confusing sentiments of opposite sentiment. As partial mitigation, practitioners might

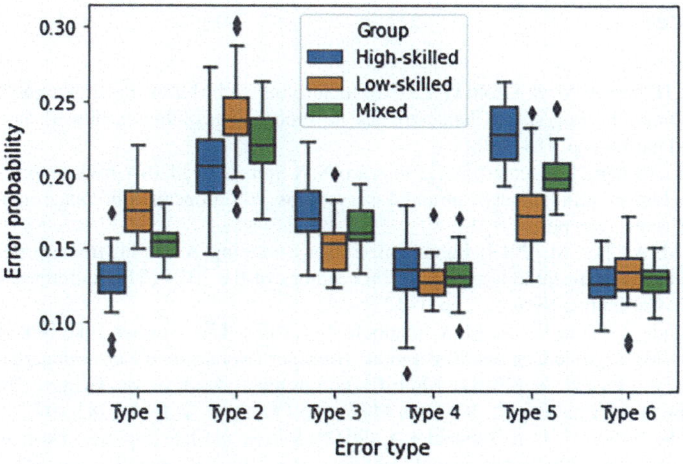

Fig. 5 Distributions of error probabilities for classifiers trained on the low-, high-skilled and mixed sets of annotations

Table 6 KS-test results for the model predictions' error probabilities

Error type	Predicted class		Low versus mixed		High versus mixed	
	Statistic	*p*-value	Statistic	*p*-value	Statistic	*p*-value
Type 1	0.9	5.78e–13*	0.533	2.93e–4*	0.633	5.79e–6*
Type 2	0.567	8.74e–5*	0.433	0.007*	0.3	0.135
Type 3	0.567	8.74e–5*	0.367	0.035	0.333	0.071
Type 4	0.367	0.035	0.233	0.393	0.333	0.071
Type 5	0.867	8.25e–12*	0.667	1.28e–6*	0.567	8.74e–5*
Type 6	0.233	0.393	0.267	0.239	0.167	0.808

employ a mix of low- and high-skilled workers to minimize biases in models as an ex-post optimization approach.

Our results provide a first glance at the presented issue, as they are based on a single dataset and classifier limiting the generalizability of our findings. We plan to conduct similar experiments using further datasets from different tasks and classifiers. In addition, we want to examine different annotator groups e.g. selecting them prior to their annotation task based on their experience and expertise in a task specific field. Furthermore, we want to look into mitigation strategies and measure their effects to further validate our mentioned mixed annotation strategy with possibly other datasets. We hope to contribute to the information systems research community by providing a concise but thorough overview of the propagation of biases into ML model predictions.

References

Al Kuwatly, H., Wich, M. & Groh, G. (2020), Identifying and Measuring Annotator Bias Based on Annotators' Demographic Characteristics, *in* 'Proceedings of the fourth workshop on online abuse and harms', pp. 184–190.

Barbera, D. L., Roitero, K., Demartini, G., Mizzaro, S. & Spina, D. (2020), Crowdsourcing Truthfulness: The Impact of Judgment Scale and Assessor Bias, *in* 'European Conference on Information Retrieval', Springer, pp. 207–214.

Barbosa, N. M., & Chen, M. (2019). Rehumanized crowdsourcing: A labeling framework addressing bias and ethics in machine learning. *in* 'Proceedings of the 2019 CHI Conference on Human Factors in Computing Systems', pp. 1–12.

Binns, R., Veale, M., Van Kleek, M. & Shadbolt, N. (2017), 'Like Trainer, Like Bot? Inheritance of Bias in Algorithmic Content Moderation', *Springer International Publishing*, pp. 405–415.

Bouazizi, M. & Ohtsuki, T. (2019). 'Multi-Class Sentiment Analysis on Twitter: Classification Performance and Challenges', *Big Data Mining and Analytics* **2**(3), pp. 181-194.

Cabrera, G. F., Miller, C. J., & Schneider, J. (2014). Systematic labeling bias: De-biasing where everyone is wrong. 22nd International Conference on Pattern Recognition, pp. 4417–4422.

Caiafa, C. F., Solé-Casals, J., Marti-Puig, P., Zhe, S., & Tanaka, T. (2020). Decomposition methods for machine learning with small, incomplete or noisy datasets. Applied Sciences, **10**(23), pp. 8481-8501.

Cordeiro, F. R., & Carneiro, G. (2020). A survey on deep learning with noisy labels: How to train your model when you cannot trust on the annotations?. *in* '2020 33rd SIBGRAPI conference on graphics, patterns and images, pp. 9–16.

Dawid, A. P. & Skene, A. M. (1979), 'Maximum Likelihood Estimation of Observer Error-Rates Using the Em Algorithm', *Journal of the Royal Statistical Society: Series C (Applied Statistics)*, **28**(1), pp. 20-28.

Devlin, J., Chang, M.-W., Lee, K. & Toutanova, K. (2019), Bert: Pre-Training of Deep Bidirectional Transformers for Language Understanding, *in* 'Proceedings of NAACL-HLT', pp. 4171–4186.

Ding, Y., You, J., Machulla, T. K., Jacobs, J., Sen, P., & Höllerer, T. (2022). Impact of Annotator Demographics on Sentiment Dataset Labeling. *in* 'Proceedings of the ACM on Human-Computer Interaction', pp. 1–22.

Eickhoff, C. (2018), Cognitive Biases in Crowdsourcing, *in* 'Proceedings of the eleventh ACM international conference on web search and data mining', pp. 162–170.

Eickhoff, C., Harris, C. G., de Vries, A. P. & Srinivasan, P. (2012), Quality through Flow and Immersion: Gamifying Crowdsourced Relevance Assessments, *in* 'Proceedings of the 35th international ACM SIGIR conference on Research and development in information retrieval', pp. 871–880.

Geva, M., Goldberg, Y. & Berant, J. (2019), Are We Modeling the Task or the Annotator? An Investigation of Annotator Bias in Natural Language Understanding Datasets, *in* 'Proceedings of the 2019 Conference on Empirical Methods in Natural Language Processing and the 9th International Joint Conference on Natural Language Processing', pp. 1161–1166.

Haerem, T., & Rau, D. (2007). The influence of degree of expertise and objective task complexity on perceived task complexity and performance. Journal of Applied Psychology, **92**(5), pp. 1320-1331.

Han, B., Yao, Q., Yu, X., Niu, G., Xu, M., Hu, W., Tsang, I., & Sugiyama, M. (2018). Co-teaching: Robust training of deep neural networks with extremely noisy labels. Advances in neural information processing systems, pp. 8527–8537.

Haselton, M. G., Nettle, D. & Murray, D. R. (2015), 'The Evolution of Cognitive Bias', *The handbook of evolutionary psychology*, pp. 1–20.

Hayes, A. F. & Krippendorff, K. (2007), 'Answering the Call for a Standard Reliability Measure for Coding Data', *Communication methods and measures* **1**(1), pp. 77-89.

He, J., van Ossenbruggen, J., & de Vries, A. P. (2013). Do you need experts in the crowd? A case study in image annotation for marine biology. *in* 'Proceedings of the 10th Conference on Open Research Areas in Information Retrieval';, pp. 57–60.

Hötter, J., Wenck, H., Feuerpfeil, M., & Witzke, S. (2022). Kern: A Labeling Environment for Large-Scale, High-Quality Training Data, *in* 'Proceedings of the Natural Language Processing and Information Systems: 27th International Conference on Applications of Natural Language to Information Systems', pp. 502–507

Hube, C., Fetahu, B. & Gadiraju, U. (2018), Limitbias! Measuring Worker Biases in the Crowdsourced Collection of Subjective Judgments, *in* 'Proceedings of the 1st Workshop on Subjectivity, Ambiguity and Disagreement in Crowdsourcing'.

Hube, C., Fetahu, B. & Gadiraju, U. (2019), Understanding and Mitigating Worker Biases in the Crowdsourced Collection of Subjective Judgments, *in* 'Proceedings of the 2019 CHI Conference on Human Factors in Computing Systems', pp. 1–12.

Irshad, H., Montaser-Kouhsari, L., Waltz, G., Bucur, O., Nowak, J. A., Dong, F., ... & Beck, A. H. (2014). Crowdsourcing image annotation for nucleus detection and segmentation in computational pathology: evaluating experts, automated methods, and the crowd. *in* 'Pacific symposium on biocomputing Co-chairs', pp. 294–305.

Jagabathula, S., Subramanian, L., & Venkataraman, A. (2014). Reputation-based worker filtering in crowdsourcing. Advances in Neural Information Processing Systems, pp. 2492–2500

Kafkalias, A., Herodotou, S., Theodosiou, Z., & Lanitis, A. (2022). Bias in Face Image Classification Machine Learning Models: The Impact of Annotator's Gender and Race, *in* 'Proceedings of the Artificial Intelligence Applications and Innovations: 18th IFIP WG 12.5 International Conference', pp. 89–100.

Lee, D. M., Kim, Y., & Seo, C. G. (2022). Context-based Virtual Adversarial Training for Text Classification with Noisy Labels.

Liu, H., J. Thekinen, S. Mollaoglu, Da Tang, J. Yang, Y. Cheng, H. Liu & J. Tang (2021), 'Toward Annotator Group Bias in Crowdsourcing'.

Long, H. L., A. O'Neil & S. Kübler (2021), On the Interaction between Annotation Quality and Classifier Performance in Abusive Language Detection, *in* 'Proceedings of Recent Advances in Natural Language Processing', pp. 868–875.

Meske, C., Bunde, E., Schneider, J. & Gersch, M. (2022), 'Explainable Artificial Intelligence: Objectives, Stakeholders, and Future Research Opportunities', *Information Systems Management* **39**(1), pp. 53-63.

Nomura, Y., & Kurita, T. (2021). Robust Training of Deep Neural Networks with Noisy Labels by Graph Label Propagation. *in* 'Frontiers of Computer Vision: 27th International Workshop', pp. 281–293.

O'Neil, A. Q., Murchison, J. T., van Beek, E. J., & Goatman, K. A. (2017). Crowdsourcing labels for pathological patterns in CT lung scans: can non-experts contribute expert-quality ground truth?. *in* 'Intravascular Imaging and Computer Assisted Stenting, and Large-Scale Annotation of Biomedical Data and Expert Label Synthesis: 6th Joint International Workshops, CVII-STENT 2017 and Second International Workshop', pp. 96–105.

Radanovic, G., Faltings, B. & Jurca, R. (2016), 'Incentives for Effort in Crowdsourcing Using the Peer Truth Serum', *ACM Transactions on Intelligent Systems and Technology (TIST)* **7**(4), pp. 1-28.

Rodrigues, F. & Pereira, F. (2018), Deep Learning from Crowds, *in* 'Proceedings of the AAAI Conference on Artificial Intelligence'.

Saab, F., Elhajj, I. H., Kayssi, A. & Chehab, A. (2019), 'Modelling Cognitive Bias in Crowdsourcing Systems', *Cognitive Systems Research* **58**, pp. 1-18.

Saravanan, R. & Sujatha, P. (2018), A State of Art Techniques on Machine Learning Algorithms: A Perspective of Supervised Learning Approaches in Data Classification, *in* '2018 Second International Conference on Intelligent Computing and Control Systems (ICICCS): IEEE', pp. 945–949.

Schneider, J., Richner, R. & Riser, M. (2022), 'Towards Trustworthy AutoGrading of Short, Multilingual, Multi-type Answers', *Int Journal of Artificial Intelligence in Education.*

See, L., Comber, A., Salk, C., Fritz, S., Van Der Velde, M., Perger, C., Schill, C., McCallum, I., Kraxner, F. & Obersteiner, M. (2013). Comparing the quality of crowdsourced data contributed by expert and non-experts, **8**(7).

Shakeri Hossein Abad, Z., G. P. Butler, W. Thompson & J. Lee (2022), 'Crowdsourcing for Machine Learning in Public Health Surveillance: Lessons Learned From Amazon Mechanical Turk', *Journal of medical Internet research* **24**(1).

Shannon, C. E. (1948), 'A Mathematical Theory of Communication', *The Bell system technical journal* **27**(3), pp. 379-423.

Snow, R., O'connor, B., Jurafsky, D. & Ng, A. Y. (2008), Cheap and Fast–but Is It Good? Evaluating Non-Expert Annotations for Natural Language Tasks, *in* 'Proceedings of the 2008 conference on empirical methods in natural language processing', pp. 254–263.

Van Atteveldt, W., van der Velden, M. A. & Boukes, M. (2021), 'The Validity of Sentiment Analysis: Comparing Manual Annotation, Crowd-Coding, Dictionary Approaches, and Machine Learning Algorithms', *Communication Methods and Measures* **15**(2), pp. 121-140.

Vaughan, J. W. (2018), 'Making Better Use of the Crowd: How Crowdsourcing Can Advance Machine Learning Research', *Journal of Machine Learning Research* **18**.

Wang, T., Wang, G., Li, X., Zheng, H. & Zhao, B. Y. (2013), Characterizing and Detecting Malicious Crowdsourcing, *in* 'Proceedings of the ACM SIGCOMM 2013 conference on SIGCOMM', pp. 537–538.

Warby, S. C., Wendt, S. L., Welinder, P., Munk, E. G., Carrillo, O., Sorensen, H. B., Jennum, P., Peppard, P., E., Perona, P. & Mignot, E. (2014). Sleep-spindle detection: crowdsourcing and evaluating performance of experts, non-experts and automated methods. Nature methods, **11**(4), pp. 385-392.

Waseem, Z. (2016), Are You a Racist or Am I Seeing Things? Annotator Influence on Hate Speech Detection on Twitter, *in* 'Proceedings of the first workshop on NLP and computational social science', pp. 138–142.

Zhang, J., Wu, X., & Sheng, V. S. (2014). Imbalanced multiple noisy labeling. IEEE Transactions on Knowledge and Data Engineering, **27**(2), pp. 489-503.

Zhang, J., Wu, X. & Sheng, V. S. (2016), 'Learning from Crowdsourced Labeled Data: A Survey', *Artificial Intelligence Review* **46**(4), pp. 543-576.

Zhang, T., Yu, L., Hu, N., Lv, S., & Gu, S. (2020). Robust medical image segmentation from non-expert annotations with tri-network. *in* 'Medical Image Computing and Computer Assisted Intervention–MICCAI 2020: 23rd International Conference', pp. 249–258.

Zhu, X., & Wu, X. (2004). Class noise vs. attribute noise: A quantitative study. The Artificial Intelligence Review, **22**(3), pp. 177–210.

DataOps as a Prerequisite for the Next Level of Self-service Analytics—Balancing User Agency and Central Control

Henning Baars

Abstract The area of Business Intelligence and Analytics (BIA) has repeatedly oscillated between more central, efficiency-oriented, professionalized approaches and decentral, agility-oriented, user-driven ones. This paper investigates whether and how to alleviate that tradeoff by combining an agility-oriented self-service analytics approach with the professionalization-driven DataOps concept: DataOps aims at transferring ideas from DevOps to the realm of analytics, namely a mutual integration of Development and Operations and a high degree of professionalization and automation. A case study with a series of interviews and a workshop led to insights into the viability of such a combination. These inspire a theoretical concept for capturing the economics behind the approaches that is considering the (opportunity) costs of the components "user agency" and "central control". The concept has been evaluated with representatives from the case study. Based on the results, I argue that the discussed combination can push BIA solutions towards fine-tuned federated environments.

Keywords DataOps · Self-service analytics · DevOps · Analytical capabilities

1 Introduction

The 2010s have radically transformed corporate data landscapes and therefore approaches to Business Intelligence and Analytics (BIA) (Marjanovic and Dinter 2018): The decade was marked by the entrance of Big Data technologies (Chen and Zhang 2014), the emergence of the data lake as a new type of analytical data repository (Fang 2015), the rise of cloud-based BIA platforms (Thomson and van der Walt 2010), as well as significant progress in the field of machine and deep learning (Janiesch et al. 2021). These developments have shifted the attention away from

H. Baars (✉)
Chair of Information Systems I, Universität Stuttgart, Stuttgart, Germany
e-mail: henning.baars@bwi.uni-stuttgart.de

D. Beverungen et al. (eds.), *Solutions and Technologies for Responsible Digitalization*, Lecture Notes in Information Systems and Organisation 75,
https://doi.org/10.1007/978-3-031-80122-8_6

centrally managed, curated data warehouse-based Business Intelligence (BI) infrastructures towards distributed, more flexible, and often cloud-enabled data management approaches (Baars et al. 2014). The new concepts and technologies come with the promise of a "democratization" of data analytics with empowered end-users (Lefebvre et al. 2021) and a federated "mesh" of data resources (Dehghani 2022). A cornerstone here is *self-service analytics*, the idea to equip end users with user-friendly tools to autonomously gather, transform, and analyze data (Michalczyk et al. 2020). In its most far-reaching forms, this allows users to join heterogeneous data sources and even build advanced analytical models (Alpar and Schulz 2016), thereby maximizing *user agency*. However, this is seemingly at odds with older recommendations for centralized and tightly governed BIA solutions to achieve professionalization and efficiency. These approaches stress *central control.*

Since the second half of the 2010s, centrality regained traction, e. g. with the introduction of structured data lakes (LaPlante and Sharma 2016), data lakehouses (Oreščanin and Hlupić 2021), the increased role of a data catalog for central metadata management (Labadie et al. 2020), as well as a general resurgence of governance aspects (Fadler and Legner 2021). It needs to be emphasized that similar swings between central and decentral approaches have taken place since the 1990s under various names.

This paper investigates the possibility of complementing self-service analytics with the novel concept of "DataOps" to alleviate the tradeoff between central control and user agency and move beyond a fruitless back-and-forth. *DataOps* translates the ideas of "DevOps" to the analytics world (Ereth 2018). DevOps is an established approach to IT systems development that marries system development ("Dev") to system operations ("Ops") in an agile and software-supported fashion. It is primarily driven by a rationale of professionalization and is heavily geared towards software support and an automation of the development processes (Ebert et al. 2016).

For our study the discussed issues are condensed to the following research questions:

RQ1: how can DataOps complement a self-service analytics approach?

RQ2: What impact does a combination of DataOps and self-service analytics have on the tradeoff between user agency and central control and how can this relationship be captured economically?

The findings contribute to research by furthering the body of knowledge on BIA by addressing new options for the organization of BIA (RQ1). Additionally, the derived economics-driven rationale of RQ2 can act as a new conceptual tool for capturing and evaluating combinations like the one discussed.

As DataOps is a rather recent approach and its combination with self-service analytics is particularly novel, this study pursues an qualitative and explorative approach that aims at hypothesis generation rather than hypothesis testing (Miles et al. 2014). More concretely, the research is based on an interpretative (single) research case study (Yin 2018; Benbasat et al. 1987; Walsham 1995) at a mid-sized automotive OEM. The approach was explorative and qualitative, as I strived for hypothesis generation rather than hypothesis testing.

The course of the paper is as follows: After a short overview on foundational concepts, Sect. 2 presents a literature review for the identification of related work. Section 3 gives an overview on the applied methodology and the core findings regarding RQ1. The results inspire the presented concept that abstracts the cost rationales behind self-service and DataOps (RQ2) and that was evaluated together with key case participants (Sect. 4). The paper concludes with a discussion and an outlook (Sect. 5).

2 Conceptual Foundation and State of the Research

The term *(data) analytics* is used rather broadly and refers to all kinds of activities relating to the collection, transformation, and analysis of data, as well as its use in reports and analysis models (Davenport and Harris 2007). *Analytics* is now often combined with *Business Intelligence* to *Business Intelligence and Analytics* (BIA) to stress that the subject in discussion goes beyond basic reporting-driven solutions and to highlight that it subsumes all components of an integrated approach to management and decision support (Lim et al. 2014; Sharda et al. 2015, pp. 18–21; Marjanovic and Dinter 2018). Economically, BIA solutions are understood to provide organizations with a certain type of dynamic capabilities, namely "analytics capabilities" (Seddon et al. 2012). An *analytics capability* indirectly contributes to business value by enabling data-related activities for the provision of insights with a defined information quality for a certain type of business task that is itself embedded in a technological and organizational environment (Ereth and Baars 2020).

An established approach for an efficient and consistent provision of analytical capabilities is to combine centralized data stores (esp. data warehouses) with defined governance structures for the roles and responsibilities, processes, BIA portfolios, as well as for rules and regulations. Such solutions stress *central control*. Their main downside is a potential lack of *BIA agility*, i.e., the ability to react to unforeseen requirements swiftly and efficiently (Baars and Zimmer 2013). And while an arsenal of remedies has been proposed to tackle this issue (Krawatzeck and Dinter 2015), a core ingredient for BIA agility was and is the inclusion of end users into the design and the implementation of BIA applications as it is done in self-service analytics. Current self-service approaches allow users to design data extraction, transformation, and analysis routines (Alpar and Schulz 2016) – and potentially even to develop advanced machine learning models ("self-service ML") (Jacquin et al. 2020; Ooms and Spruit 2020). On the solution side, this means to grant the user *agency* over large parts of the analytics process.

"DataOps" appears to bridge fully uncoordinated individual solutions (with maximal user agency) and inflexible "classic" central DW concepts (with maximal central control). In essence, *DataOps* transfers the ideas from the software development approach of DevOps to the realm of data analytics (Ereth 2018): DevOps aims at integrating **D**evelopment and **O**perations. It emphasizes the complete software lifecycle, a customer-oriented perspective, a transparent cooperation of the responsible units, and a culture of cooperation (Sánchez-Gordón and Colomo-Palacios 2018). This is also supported by defined "pipelines" for created artifacts and includes highly professionalized and tool-supported processes for software testing, for the integration of software artifacts into the system landscape (*continuous integration*), for their deployment (*continuous deployment*), as well as for the version management for its infrastructures (*infrastructure as code*) (Ebert et al. 2016).

The term DataOps still lacks some clarity (Munappy et al. 2020; Ereth 2018) and this is exacerbated in self-service environments, where the end-user is the developer of the report or the model (resp. of parts of it). But while DevOps cannot be applied in a one-to-one fashion to the realm of analytics, a tight cooperation between the units that are providing infrastructure, models, and reports (or templates therefore) and the users consuming them (or building up on them) is of central importance here as well.

To identify related work, a structured literature review (Brocke et al 2009; Webster and Watson 2002) was conducted with a search for peer-reviewed papers on the AIS library (112 hits, 3 relevant), IEEE-Explore (1 hit, 0 relevant), the ACM digital library (24 hits, 4 relevant), and the Web of Science (1 hit, redundant) for the search terms (all search fields including keywords, full texts, and abstract):

- "Self-Service" AND ("analytics" OR "Business Intelligence" OR "Machine Learning" OR "Artificial Intelligence") AND ("DataOps" OR "MLOps" OR "DevOps"),
- "DataOps" AND "Agility",
- "DataOps" AND "democratization" AND ("Analytics" OR < "Machine Learning" OR "Artificial Intelligence"), and
- ("DataOps" OR "MLOps") AND "user-empowerment".

I filtered out research in progress papers, solely technical papers, papers that mentioned the search terms without really addressing them, papers that were not connected to the user side as well as papers that were not linked to the operations and support side (e. g. that were merely discussing the local development of a model).

The low number of relevant hits despite the rather wide net of search strings indicates that the subject has not yet been adequately addressed and thus forms a research gap. A closer look into the papers further bolsters that conclusion. While the papers all acknowledge the interplay of self-service analytics and DataOps or related concepts, they do not delve further into this. Nevertheless, the identified literature nevertheless provided additional relevant insights:

Relation to the Subject of the Internet of Things The paper "DataOps for Cyber-Physical Systems Governance" by Garriga et al. (2020) focusses on the development of a single ML solution for the prediction of passenger flows at an airport in a highly distributed environment and under the utilization of selected DataOps concepts (esp. by building end-to-end data pipelines). The authors demonstrate how DataOps techniques facilitate the exploitation of complex Internet-of-Things data sources.

Maturity Levels of DataOps Approaches In their paper "From Ad-Hoc Data Analytics to DataOps" (2020), Munappy et al. develop an evolutionary model based on a case study at Ericsson: They distinguish between the steps "ad-hoc data analysis", "semi-automated data analysis", "agile data science", "continuous testing and monitoring" and "data ops" (as the goal).

DataOps as a Driver of Agility In "Scaling Enterprise Recommender Systems for Decentralization" van der Goes (2021) discuss an MLOps/DataOps based platform for building and operating recommender systems in the federated organizational environment of Heineken. They observed a higher agility of the distributed data science teams.

DataOps as a Conduit for the Digital Transformation Informed by a literature review, the authors Xu et al. (2021) link DataOps to aspects of digital transformation. Their paper argues that the components of DataOps bring stakeholders together in a dynamic and creative fashion and thus strengthen organizational performance.

Relevance of Socioeconomical Factors Mucha et al. (2022) stress the importance socioeconomical dimension of DataOps/MLOps and derive a multi-cyclical development model that highlights non-technical components.

Relevance of Central Support for Self-Service Analytics (as a Linking Pin to DataOps) Both Namyslo and Baars (2022) and Iyer (2021) discuss environments for self-service analytics and the prerequisites for successfully running them. While Namyslo and Baars discuss how end-users can be empowered by self-service ML to conduct complex forecast of warranty costs in the automotive industry, Iyer et al. present a solution for self-service analytics with complex geospatial data. Both illustrate the need to underpin self-service approaches with supporting tools and structures – on the technology (templates, feature and model catalogs etc.) and the organizational side (defined processes, support, quality assurance etc.).

3 Case Study: Methodology and Findings

The following section presents the case study and its immediate results which primarily feed into RQ1. They also lay the groundwork for answers to RQ2, which will be addressed by the concept design in the subsequent Chap. 4.

3.1 Methodology

The company in discussion presented the opportunity to collect relevant and rich insights into the subject matter: A mid-sized German automotive OEM that has already successfully adopted a self-service analytics approach which is now used widely across all business units. After perusing the relevant documentation and reviewing relevant artifacts (esp. the transformation pipelines, analysis models and reports created by the end-users), a series of qualitative, semi-structured interviews with participants from seven different business units was conducted. Methodologically, the interviews followed the recommendations of Meyers and Newman (2007).

The derivation of the interview questionnaires, as well as the coding, were based on a conceptual framework (Ravitch and Riggan 2012) that comprises of the following components: the business context of the self-service analytics (including the background and IT/analytics competences of the users), the concrete analytical tasks tackled with self-service analytics, the state of automation and the DataOps potential in data preparation, data integration, testing, and data management (as potential parts of data pipelines), the cooperation with the central BIA unit, as well as outcomes and trends.

The seven interviews took on average 60 min and were conducted in January–April 2022 (each with two interviewers). The BIA unit identified and contacted the potential interviewees (either business or engineering experts, all self-service adopters) and made sure that all relevant business units of the company were covered. All interviews were recorded and transcribed. The analysis of the transcripts followed the recommendations of Miles et al. (2014) and Mayring (2014) and was based on a stepwise category formation process (Mayring 2014, pp. 79–88). The workshop with the IT department was conducted with the CIO of the company and members of the BIA unit responsible for data analysts, systems operations, and system development, as well as the BIA unit's leader (5 participants in total). In the workshop, I presented, discussed, and enriched the findings in an open discussion (responses were documented in field notes). The focus of the workshop were the processual and technical roles of the IT in the self-service approach, as well as their take regarding on an introduction of DataOps.

The automotive OEM had already implemented a sophisticated BIA architecture backed by a strong analytics team and an established self-service approach. According to the model of Munappy et al. (2020), I see them in between the development steps "semi-automated data analysis" and "agile data science" with a set of state-of the art tools and professionalized processes and already some pipelines in place.

The seven interviews were done in the business units and addressed the core use cases shown in Table 1.

BU1 For sales control, data from heterogenous systems from the areas of finance, retail, and marketing are provided in a specialized sales-oriented data mart by the central BIA unit. This data is already transformed and prepared (assisted by the business unit); data cleansing and integration are therefore subject to a high degree of central control. Report generation, however, rests completely in the hand of the users.

BU2 The subject of BU2 is managerial control, also. Here, indicators and reports are generated based on data from mostly file-based source systems. Unlike in BU1, the main challenges for the users lie in data extraction and transformation.

Table 1 List of interviews

Business unit (BU)	Main use case for self-service analytics
BU1: Managerial control 1	Data preparation and analysis for sales controlling
BU2: Managerial control 2	Data preparation and managerial-control tasks as well as accounting-related analyses
BU3: After sales	Clustering and analysis of complaints
BU4: Research and development (R&D) for powertrain components	Statistical analysis of data from vehicles for the continuous improvement of vehicle design
BU5: Production	Constant monitoring of the quality of assembly processes and descriptive analysis of faults
BU6: Logistic	Inventory management analysis
BU7: Marketing and sales	Preparation and analysis of data on inventory and retail stock levels for different markets

BU3 The data for the user of BU3 (aftersales) primarily come from a single system. Since the analyzed complaints are entered as free text, analysis is not straightforward and data quality is a problem. The interviewed user applies cluster analyses techniques to group complaints. This scenario goes far beyond simple descriptive statistics and requires the domain knowledge of the user and therefore high degrees of user agency.

BU4 Like in BU3, the relevant data in this environment is also extracted from a single system. The data structures in this case are both complex and heterogeneous (vehicles measurement data). Also, data volumes are high, and each analysis is individual and relies on the specialized know-how of the user as a domain expert. This reduces both the potential to automate data analysis and the possible contribution of the central BIA unit beyond a technical support after the data provision.

BU5 In production, a variety of (often embedded) IT source systems from different suppliers are accessed, which leads to considerable challenges during data extraction and integration. Currently, each analysis is done by the users who prepare the source data in a mostly (semi)-manual fashion. The setting bears similarities to the ones presented by Garriga et al. (2020), that have already shown potential for DataOps.

BU6 All necessary data for inventory management come from a single and centrally managed SAP™ system with a guaranteed high degree of data quality. The main challenge in this use case is to access the necessary data form the system in time.

BU7 Marketing and sales have access to a data warehouse provided by the IT department. Similar to BU1, business users develop their own dashboards. The user often adds additional data sources, esp. file-based and crafts her own ETL-tasks.

3.2 Findings

It is noteworthy that the interview partners were all regular employees of the business units and by no means professional data analysts or data scientists – even those who conducted more complex data transformations (BU2, BU4, BU5, BU7) or advanced analytics (BU3, BU4). It was also striking that the users were not using any form of standardized process or relying on a fixed toolset. They employed heterogeneous software products such as MS Excel™, Tableau™, Tableau Prep™, KNIME™, specific tools for analyzing engineering data, as well as VBA or Python programming. Some of the users were working with isolated data from file systems or different transactional systems, while others were building their solutions on top of a centralized data warehouse, data mart, or a big data cluster in the cloud.

Despite an established centralized data warehouse, a Big Data cluster, and a standardized reporting platform, the required BIA capabilities cannot be fully covered by the BIA unit. The high degree of user autonomy is correlated to the variety of use cases that spans both the data and the analysis side. The self-service approach allows the company to react to the heterogeneity of the required analytical capabilities and gives the users as much autonomy as they demand, while keeping central control for infrastructure provision. The users translate the granted degrees of freedom into BIA agility.

Finding 1 *The need for heterogeneous BIA capabilities can be countered by a high degree of user autonomy and supported by a self-service analytics approach.*

The benefits of the self-service approach do not come without caveats: two thirds of the interviewees cited data availability and data provision as their biggest concerns. This is reflected in statements from the interviewees like *"Data can only be downloaded manually in the form of Excel files"* (BU6). *"Data are not always consistent across time and between different analyses, so every time I have to look for the right data"* (BU5). *"Data from different sources must first be integrated"* (BU7).

For the questioned users, a lack of automation in data provision seems to be the greatest pain point and one that binds significant time and costs. The need to pour self-service resources into data preparation was also stated as a reason for the strong focus on descriptive analysis – despite the explicit wish to try more advanced ML techniques. Corroborating this is the fact that the use cases, where more advanced models were already being in use, were also the ones with a single source system, namely BU3 and BU6. The following typical statement illustrates those points: *"I wish, I could concentrate on my business analytics tasks and would not have to spend so much time on data provision and data preparation"*. Such issues came alongside requests for a more centrally managed data integration and storage pipeline and for increased support.

The issue of data preparation was also discussed during the workshop with the IT department: The BIA unit stated to have already begun to address it, e. g. by building special data marts with integrated data for specific business units (as in BU1), standardizing REST APIs, etc. These technical solutions were developed in close cooperation with the business units and incorporated ideas and routines that the users came up with in their self-service routines (esp. in BU2 and BU3). Incorporating DataOps would mean doubling down on this approach by automating data pipelines that are specified and maintained by a joint team of business users and IT. The aim would be an enhanced central control with a minimal reduction of perceived user agency.

Finding 2 *A professionalized data provision (e.g., based on a DataOps approach) can facilitate a more efficient BIA application and potentially free resources for new BIA capabilities. This implies more central control but not necessary a reduction of user agency – as long as the processes remain adequately cooperative and agile.*

The BIA team also pointed out that the issues of data provision run deeper than just fixing the IT side of BIA. A problem was seen in the variety of suppliers of the data sources—some of which are often not even subsumed under the umbrella of IT, e. g. smart machines. As the IT is usually not involved in the selection and implementation for such components, aspects of data interfaces, data formats, and data quality are often neglected during the specification by the business units. The problems surface often at the time that data needs to be analyzed. A stricter data governance that promotes a "analytics by design" thinking could alleviate those issues. This would entail reduced user agency and stronger central control but facilitate self-service.

Finding 3 *A strict, analytics-oriented data governance that encompasses the complete data landscape of the organization can lay the groundwork for a self-service approach, particularly when it comes to potential source systems – which are ideally understood as stubs of future analytics pipelines. This entails curtailing the user agency of the units responsible for acquiring or developing those systems.*

Also problematic were data sources with manually or semi-manually collected data (BU1, BU2, BU3 and BU7), e. g. error reports in after sales (as in BU3). Additionally, an increased number of data sources also correlates with issues of consistency and completeness (BU4, BU5). Some data sources also lack timeliness (BU1, BU2, BU7).

This is a major difference to a centralized approach with a strong governing unit at its core. In self-service analytics with individual solutions built upon individual data transformations, there is an inherent risk of insufficient oversight, of redundant developments of data transformation pipelines, and of a lack of power to enforce changes at the side of the source systems. This would be an anchor for a DataOps approach in which the developing user is working with the BIA unit that operates the infrastructure. The BIA unit could also be made responsible for the continuous integration of the user-developed solutions into the wider analytics environment of the organization.

Finding 4 *Efficiency gains can be unlocked if a unit with central control is overseeing, guiding, and leveraging the development of the users' data pipelines.*

The consensus in the interviews was that the documentation of data sources, data models and formats, data lineage, and analyses was inadequate. In the cases with one or two stable source systems, this does not pose a problem. In the other cases, however, it is seen as one, esp. because of the time needed to find the right data for a given analysis. Most users consider a central metadata management as necessary for self-service analytics. In the workshop, the BIA unit acknowledged this problem and stated that this was one of the reasons for the ongoing development of a company-wide data catalog. There is some skepticism regarding the sustainability of a typical data catalog, however, as most of the important metadata are documented manually. This is thought to lead to a fast loss of topicality of the metadata. Ideally, these aspects are integral parts of the design of data pipelines with high degrees of automation.

Finding 5 *Metadata management is a precondition for a comprehensive usage of self-service-analytics in an organization – and should be part of a dataops approach.*

Since automated testing plays a significant role in both the DevOps and the DataOps literature, it was also addressed it in the study – with rather meagre results: None of the BUs that were encountered in the study has implemented automated testing in their use cases. There were two reasons given for that: Firstly, most of the self-service analytics tasks are by definition ad-hoc and individual, which makes it difficult to systematically define test cases or implement automated testing routines. Secondly, many of the applied data sources are not suited, esp. the ones with manually entered data. The approach to quality assurance chosen by the users were expert assessments, which were stated to identify errors quickly and thoroughly.

Finding 6 *Due to the unique nature of the analyses, self-service analytics is rarely compatible with automated testing routines. However, to capture the spirit behind testing, workflows with expert assessments are a valid alternative.*

One point that came up in the workshop was that issues of compliance and data security require an oversight of the central BIA unit and form a natural limitation of user agency.

Finding 7 *Data governance should be integrated into the DataOps process based on an oversight by a central unit/*

In the workshop, it was intensively discussed among the group of participants in how far the company would benefit from a combination of a DataOps approach with self-service analytics. The CIO in particular questioned if the stated problem and the presented solutions were novel at all. The final consensus of the group, however, was that the unprecedented breadth and the depth of the self-service approach was indeed new. On the one hand, this is fueled both by the competencies of the users and the user-friendliness of the self-service tools. On the other hand, it is driven by the massively increased awareness of both management and users for the business potential of BIA and for relevant use cases – even in units that have had relatively few contacts to the BIA domain before such as logistics, manufacturing, or development. The potential of the combination of self-service analytics with DataOps was seen in the option to further unlock the business potential of an enhanced user agency. Moreover, a stronger and professionalized cooperation between the IT/BIA unit and the end users for both infrastructure operation and the provision of central components (data marts, data catalog) was deemed critical – as was its role for overarching questions of governance.

4 Concept Design and Evaluation

A core theoretical insight I gleaned from the case study was how the nature of centrality of BIA is changed with the introduction of self-service analytics and DataOps. This particularly encompasses the aspects of *central control* and *user agency* as opposing poles. Economically, a reduced user-agency incurs opportunity costs resulting from insufficient alignment of BIA applications with the users' requirements and possibly a lack of acceptance. For example, it became clear that the highly domain-driven, complex solutions of BU3, BU4, or BU5 would incur prohibitive costs without the active involvement of the users. Decreased central control, however, comes at the costs of reduced efficiency and missed overarching benefits. In the case, this can be seen across the use cases in inefficiencies with data provision and transformation, and in the lack of metadata that led to tedious and repeated information seeking activities.

Figure 1 captures these ideas for the examples found in BU1, BU4, and BU5 (that represent different classes of cases with respect to the subject at hand): In each case, the costs of a purely central solution with minimal user agency and a maximum of central control can be lowered by the inclusion of users with self-service approaches. However, a complete handover of the responsibility would also raise costs significantly as this would correspond with the typical inefficiencies of de-central analytics solutions (data stovepipes, duplication of data provision tasks work, tool variety etc.). This leads to the conclusion that the minimal costs are somewhere along the spectrum.

The BU1 case (reports for sales controlling) is a base case as it aligns well with established BI cases that have been around for decades. Here, the (somewhat limited) contribution of the self-service approach primarily comes from a slightly more agile and individual report design and some indicator calculations. A full-fledged self-service, that also includes data provision, would lead to tremendous redundancies.

Providing the analytics capability "monitoring of assembly processes" (BU5) however, heavily depends on the domain knowledge of the users. A full centralization would lead to significant coordination requirements. This moves the point of minimal costs to the right of the axes. In that case, inefficiencies became visible that would normally demand a partly recentralization of those tasks, esp. regarding the provision and preparation of machine data. Similar, the complex statistics in R&D (BU4), requires the expert hand of the users. Note that the lines in all illustrations are so far only meant to be qualitative illustrations rather than measured costs and are in reality comprised of a variety of discrete cost components for different technical and organizational measures.

Figure 2 visualizes the potential effects of (successfully) implementing ideas from DataOps on those cost curves. For BU5, an active involvement of the central BIA unit with control over the central data provision pipeline (including the specification of data interfaces and standards for non-IT-components), as well as a stronger and professionalized automation of the data transformation, could lower the costs of the current self-service approach. The minimal cost point would move to the left towards

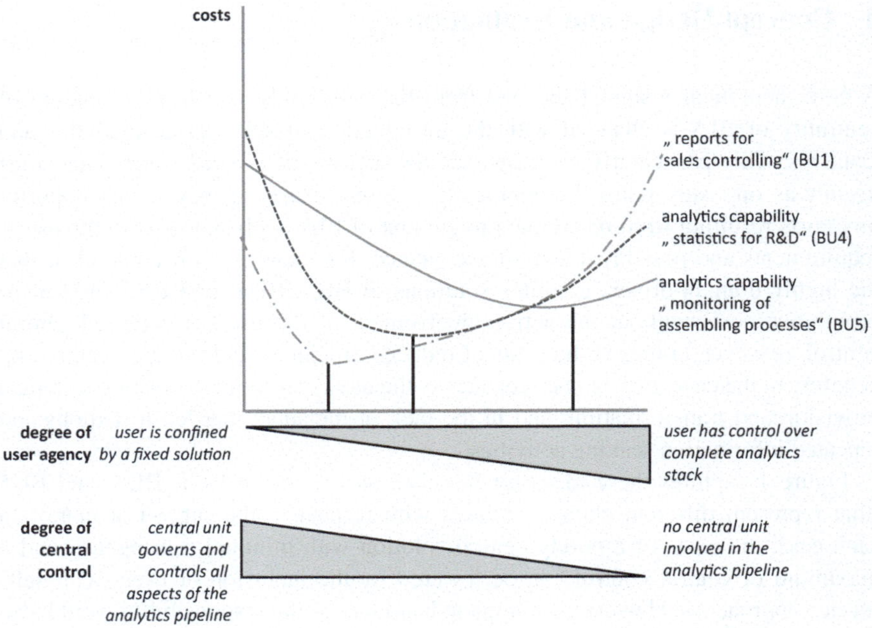

Fig. 1 DataOps and centralization of analytics

the central unit. In contrast to that, for BU4 (R&D) the point would move to the *right* as a stronger support makes room for advanced analytics.

These ideas were evaluated in two interviews in March 2023 with the head of the BIA unit and a representative of the R&D team, because the cost curve of that unit was the most atypical. We discussed the understandability and plausibility of

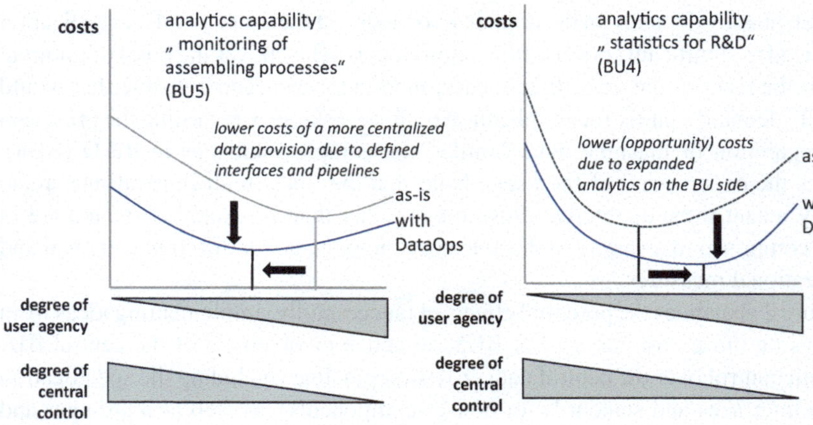

Fig. 2 Potential of introducing DataOps to BU5 and BU4

the approach and selected cost curves, comprehensiveness, practical usefulness, and the need for further research.

The interviewees saw all those criteria as fulfilled, apart from smaller corrections on the cost curves of BU5 (which became flatter). Both considered it relevant to include the competencies of the users as a relevant factor. The BIA head also stressed the factor time (esp. one-time reports vs. development of an operationalized model). As for practicability, the head of analytics plans to apply the concept for BIA portfolio management, in individual investment decisions, and for policy design. This is why the company currently sets up on a follow-up study for further operationalizing the approach.

5 Discussion and Outlook

The results of the presented study highlight the increased awareness for BIA of users across a variety of domains, their acceptance of BIA solutions and their willingness to engage in a self-service approach. This is undeniably fostered by technical advances and can be expected to be unspecific for the given company. Here, however, the approach was additionally enabled by a supporting BIA unit with close ties to the user departments and an eye for innovations – the need for the support was stressed across all interviews. This is a first step towards DataOps, that will be implemented in the future.

The case also demonstrates the viability of a self-service analytics approach that is rolled out across heterogeneous business units, and it highlights how a DataOps-based professionalization of data pipelines (including those designed by the users) and a tightly controlled data and meta data management can unlock further business potential, esp. by freeing resources. While some DataOps concepts are by definition rather hard to employ in a self-service environment (esp. automatized testing), adapting the ideas behind DataOps can indeed propel self-service towards higher degrees of efficiency – either by enabling more central control where needed or by enabling more self-service. Prerequisites are a motivated and capable user base as much as an active and professional IT provision and support. All these insights contribute to RQ1.

This paper proposes to capture the impact of the topic in discussion with a cost-based rationale that is built up on of the components "central control" and "user agency" and the (opportunity) costs introduced by them. The concept underwent a preliminary evaluation with representatives from the case study. All this feeds into answers to RQ2.

The main contributions to research lie in the insights on self-service analytics and its DataOps-based professionalization, as well as in the cost-based concept for its evaluation. The evaluation indicates that the concept is also relevant to practice as they provide a conceptual toolset for discussing the benefits, prerequisites, and impacts of different degrees of central control, user agency and professionalization measures like DataOps.

A core limitation is that the results are based in one case only. Although this is already addressed by disseminating the results, further studies are advisable. Also, the derived concept needs further fleshing out, esp. regarding the measurement of the dimensions and the cost calculation. Given the oscillations in BIA for or against centrality, I regard the approach as a first suggestion on how to settle the debate for good one day.

References

Alpar, P. & Schulz, M. (2016). 'Self-Service Business Intelligence', *Business & Information Systems Engineering* **58**(2), pp. 151-155.

Baars, H. & Zimmer, M. (2013), A Classification for Business Intelligence Agility Indicators, *in* 'Proceedings 21st European Conference on Information Systems', ECIS, Utrecht, Netherlands.

Baars, H., Felden, C., Gluchowski, P., Hilbert, A., Kemper, H. G. & Olbrich, S. (2014), Shaping the next incarnation of business intelligence, *Business & Information Systems Engineering*, **6**(1), pp.11-16.

Benbasat, I., Goldstein, D. K., & Mead, M. (1987), The Case Research Strategy in Studies of Information Systems, *MIS Quarterly*, **11**(3), pp. 369–386.

Chen, C. & Zhang, C. (2014), Data-intensive applications, challenges, techniques and technologies – A survey on Big Data, Information Sciences **275**, 314-347.

Davenport, T.H. & Harries, H.G. (2007), *Competing on Analytics: The New Science of Winning*. Harvard Business Press.

Dehghani, Z. (2022), *Data Mesh: Delivering Data-Driven Value at Scale*. O'Reilly.

Ebert, C., Gallardo, G., Hernantes, J. & Serrano, N. (2016), DevOps, *IEEE Software*, **33**(3), pp. 94-100.

Ereth, J. (2018), DataOps-Towards a Definition, *in* 'Proceedings of the Lernen, Wissen, Daten, Analysen' LWDA, CEUR Workshop Proceedings, **2191**, Paper 13, pp. 104-112.

Ereth, J. & Baars, H. (2020), A Capability Approach for Designing Business Intelligence and Analytics Architectures, *in* 'Proceedings 53rd Hawaii International Conference on System Sciences', HICSS, Maui, USA.

Fadler, M. & Legner, C. (2021), Toward big data and analytics governance: redefining structural governance mechanisms, *in* 'Proceedings 534th Hawaii International Conference on System Sciences', HICSS, Kauai, USA

Fang, H (2015), Managing data lakes in big data era – what's a data lake and why has it became popular in data management eco-system? *in* 'Proceedings of the IEEE International Conference on Cyber Technology in Automation, Control, and Intelligent Systems', Shenyang, China.

Garriga, M., Aarns, K., Tsigkanos, C., Tamburri, D.A., van den Heuvel, W.J. (2020), DataOps for Cyber-Physical Systems Governance: The Airport Passenger Flow Case, *ACM Transactions on Internet Technology*, **21** (2), 1-25.

Iyer, C. V. K. (2021), Trinity: A No-Code AI platform for complex spatial datasets". *In*' Proceedings of the 4th ACM SIGSPATIAL International Workshop on AI for Geographic Knowledge Discovery (GEOAI '21), Beijing, China.

Jacquin, S., Pawlewitz, J. & Doyle, A. (2020), Democratizing Data with Self-Service Analytics, *in* 'Proceedings Offshore Technology Conference', Houston, USA.

Janiesch, C., Zschech, P. & Heinrich, K. (2021), Machine learning and deep learning, *Electronic Markets* **31**, pp. 685–695

Krawatzeck, R., & Dinter, B. (2015), Agile business intelligence: Collection and classification of agile business intelligence actions by means of a catalog and a selection guide, *Information Systems Management* **32** (3), pp. 177-191.

Labadie, C. Legner, C., Eurich M. & Fadler, M.,FAIR Enough? Enhancing the Usage of Enterprise Data with Data Catalogs, *in* 'Proceedings of the 2020 22nd IEEE Conference on Business Informatics (CBI)', Antwerp, Belgium, 2020, pp. 201–210.

LaPlante A. & Sharma, B (2016), *Architecting Data Lakes*, 2nd ed., O'Reilly.

Lefebvre, H., Legner, C., & Fadler, M. (2021), Data democratization: toward a deeper understanding, *in* 'Proceedings of the 42nd International Conference on Information Systems', ICIS, Austin, USA.

Lim, E.P., Chen, H. & Chen, G., 'Business intelligence and analytics: Research directions', *ACM Transactions on Management Information Systems (TMIS)* **3**(4), pp. 1–10.

Marjanovic, O. & B. Dinter, B (2018), Learning from the History of Business Intelligence and Analytics Research at HICSS: A Semantic Text-mining Approach, *Communications of the Association for Information Systems* **43**(40), Atlanta, USA.

Mayring, P. (2014), Qualitative content analysis: theoretical foundation, basic procedures and software solution, Social Science Open Access Repository (SSOAR).

Myers, M.D., Newman, M. (2007), The qualitative interview in IS research: Examining the craft, in: Information and Organization, **17**(1), pp 2-26.

Michalczyk, S., Nadj, M., Azarfar, D., Maedche, A. & Gröger, C. (2020), A State-Of-The-Art Overview and Future Research Avenues of Self-Service Business Intelligence and Analytics, *in* 'Proceedings of the 28th European Conference on Information Systems', ECIS.

Miles, M. B., Huberman, A. M. & Saldaña, J. (2014), *Qualitative data analysis: A methods sourcebook*, Sage.

Mucha, T. M., Ma, S. & Kaveh, A. (2022), Beyond MLOps: The Lifecycle of Machine Learning-based Solutions, *in* 'Proceedings of the 2022 Americas Conference on Information Systems', AMCIS, Minneapolis, USA.

Munappy, A.R., Mattos, D.I., Bosch, J. Olsson, H.H. & Dakkak, A. (2020), From Ad-Hoc Data Analytics to DataOps, *in* 'Proceedings International Conference on Software and System Processes', ICSSP20, Seoul, Republic of Korea, pp. 165-174.

Namyslo, N. & Baars, H. (2022), Harnessing the Business Potential of Self-Service Machine Learning for Forecasting Warranty Costs – Insights from a Case Study in the Automotive Sector, *in* 'Proceedings Pacific Asia Conference on Information Systems', PACIS 2022, Taipei (Taiwan) and Sydney (Australia).

Ooms, R. & Spruit, M. (2020), Self-service data science in healthcare with automated machine learning, *Applied Sciences* **10** (9), 2992.

Oreščanin, D. & Hlupić, T. (2021), Data Lakehouse-a Novel Step in Analytics Architecture, *in* 'Proceedings 44th International Convention on Information, Communication and Electronic Technology', MIPRO, Opatija, Croatia, pp. 1242–1246.

Ravitch, S. M., & Riggan, M. (2012), *Reason & rigor: How conceptual frameworks guide research*, Sage.

Sánchez-Gordón, M., & Colomo-Palacios, R. (2018), Characterizing DevOps culture: a systematic literature review, *in* 'Proceedings International conference on software process improvement and capability determination', Thessaloniki, Greece, pp. 3–15.

Seddon, P.B., Constantinidis, D., Dod, H. (2012), How does business analytics contribute to business value? *in* 'Proceedings 33rd international conference on information systems', ICIS, Orlando, 2012.

Sharda, R., Delen, D. & Turban, E (2015), *Business Intelligence and Analytics – Systems for Decision Support*, Pearson.

Thomson, W.J.J. & van der Walt, J.S. (2010), Business intelligence in the cloud, *South African Journal of Information Management* **12** (1).

van der Goes, M. (2021), Scaling Enterprise Recommender Systems for Decentralization, *in* 'Proceedings 15th ACM Conference on Recommender Systems', RecSys21, Amsterdam, Netherlands, pp. 592–594.

vom Brocke, J., Simons, A., Niehaves, B., Riemer, K., Plattfaut, R. & Cleven, A. (2009), Reconstructing the Giant: On the Importance of Rigour in Documenting the Literature Search Process, *in* 'Proceedings of the 17th European Conference on Information Systems', Verona, Italy, pp. 1–12.

Walsham, G. (1995), Interpretive case studies in IS research: nature and method, in: European Journal of Information Systems (EJIS), **4**(2), pp. 74-81.

Webster, J., & Watson, R. T. (2002), 'Analyzing the Past to Prepare for the Future: Writing a literature Review', *MIS Quarterly,* **26**(2), pp. xiii-xxiii.

Xu, J. Naseer, H., Maynard, S., & Filippou, J. (2021), Leveraging Data and Analytics for Digital Business Transformation through DataOps: An Information Processing Perspective, *in* 'Proceedings Australasian Conference on Information Systems', Sydney, Australia.

Yin, R. K. (2018), *Case study research and applications – design and methods*, SAGE.

Boosting Benefits, Offsetting Obstacles—The Impact of Explanations on AI Users' Task Performance

Marie Christine Walter, Hanna Rebecca Broder, and Maximilian Förster

Abstract Artificial Intelligence (AI) bears the potential to inform human decision-making in a large variety of domains. However, its "black box" character poses an obstacle to human agency in interaction with AI-based decision support. A possible solution comes from the research field of Explainable AI (XAI), which generates explanations that reveal AI's functioning to users. Our research on XAI focuses on understanding the immediate and prolonged effect of XAI-based decision support on task performance. To this end, we conducted a randomized between-subjects online experiment with 289 participants performing the task of image classification. We find that explanations along AI decisions boost the positive effect of AI-based decision support on task performance during interaction. Furthermore, explanations can counterbalance the potential negative effect on prolonged task performance, which manifests after AI-based decision support is being withdrawn. Our findings contribute to understanding the impact of XAI on the outcome of human-AI interaction.

Keywords Explainable artificial intelligence · Task performance · Decision support systems · Online experiment

1 Introduction

In recent years, Artificial Intelligence (AI) technologies have made enormous advances and have been applied in a large variety of domains (Enholm et al. 2021; Minh et al. 2022). These include, among others, autonomous cars in mobility (Minh

---

M. C. Walter · H. R. Broder · M. Förster (✉)
Institute of Business Analytics, University of Ulm, Ulm, Germany
e-mail: maximilian.foerster@uni-ulm.de

M. C. Walter
e-mail: marie.walter@uni-ulm.de

H. R. Broder
e-mail: hanna.broder@uni-ulm.de

D. Beverungen et al. (eds.), *Solutions and Technologies for Responsible Digitalization*,
Lecture Notes in Information Systems and Organisation 75,
https://doi.org/10.1007/978-3-031-80122-8_7

et al. 2022), defect detection in manufacturing (Joung et al. 2019), and breast cancer diagnostics in healthcare (Kaymak et al. 2017). AI bears potential to augment human decision-making based on its ever-evolving predictive performance, thus empowering decision makers to form their decisions together with the available technology (Berente et al. 2021). To illustrate, AI models can for example be implemented to assist physicians in breast cancer diagnostics through early identification of cancerous spots based on histopathological image classification (e.g., Kaymak et al. 2017).

However, many AI systems are considered "black boxes"—the reasons for their decisions remain opaque to their users (Guidotti et al. 2019). This "black box" character poses obstacles to leverage AI's potential for augmented decision-making (e.g., Wachter et al. 2018). First, the "black box" character represents an impediment for human agency, which is reflected in users often blindly following the AI system's decisions or not using the system at all (Brasse et al. 2023). Second, the "black box" character poses an obstacle to learning from AI, as it prevents users from scrutinizing AI outcomes and understanding AI insights (Berente et al. 2021).

Against this backdrop, the research field of Explainable AI (XAI) aims to improve human-AI collaboration by automatically generating explanations along AI systems' outputs (Adadi and Berrada 2018). Explanations are meant to reveal the functioning and knowledge of AI systems for their users (Arrieta et al. 2020; Meske et al. 2022). Thereby, they shall improve user interaction with AI-based decision support systems (Berente et al. 2021): First, explanations aim to improve immediate user interaction with AI resulting in better decisions. Second, explanations aim to enable users to learn from the knowledge of the AI system which remains hidden otherwise (Brasse et al. 2023).

XAI research has achieved considerable progress in the development of novel XAI approaches in recent years (Arrieta et al. 2020). At the same time, the research field is criticized for an insufficient understanding of the impact of explanations on human-AI interaction (Brasse et al. 2023). First promising studies have generated interesting insights on the impact of explanations on perception and behavioral intention of users, including trust (e.g., Banovic et al. 2023), perception of AI (e.g., Dodge et al. 2019), and behavioral use intentions (e.g., Conati et al. 2021). Recent works have further investigated the influence of XAI on the outcome of human-AI interaction, i.e., task performance. Existing studies indicate a positive impact of XAI-based decision support compared to no decision support on task performance (Schemmer et al. 2022a), find a persuasive effect of XAI-based decision support on advice following (e.g., Bansal et al. 2011; van der Waa et al. 2021), and indicate the potential of XAI-based decision support to improve task performance compared to opaque AI-based decision support (Buçinca et al. 2020; Lai and Tan 2019). So far, extant understanding is limited to the effect of XAI on task performance during user interaction with AI-based decision support systems. Studies to date neglect the potential prolonged effect of explanations on task performance, i.e., their effect after users have interacted with AI-based decision support systems.

We contribute to this research gap by addressing the open question whether explanations have an immediate and a prolonged effect on task performance of users of

AI-based decision support systems. To this end, we pose the following research question: How do automatically generated explanations along AI decisions influence task performance during and after interaction with an AI-based decision support system?

To investigate this question, we conduct an online experiment with 289 participants performing the task of image classification. Participants are randomly assigned to three groups: a control group receiving no support and two treatment groups. One treatment group receives AI-based decision support, the second treatment group receives AI-based decision support paired with automatically generated visual explanations. We analyze explanations' immediate effects on users' task performance during interaction with AI-based decision support systems as well as their prolonged effect on task performance after interaction, i.e., when decision support is withdrawn. We find that while AI-based decision support improves users' immediate task performance, additional provision of explanations along AI decisions further boosts this effect. Moreover, additional provision of explanations along AI decisions can counterbalance the potential negative prolonged effect of AI-based decision support on task performance, which may manifest once support is withdrawn. Our findings contribute to a better understanding of the impact of XAI on immediate and prolonged task performance of users of AI-based decision support systems.

The remainder of this paper is structured as follows: Sect. 2 provides an overview of the theoretical background and related work. In Sect. 3, we describe our case setting, study procedure, participants, measurement, and analysis methods used. Then, in Sect. 4, we present our results based on an online experiment comparing the immediate and prolonged effect of AI-based decision support and XAI-based decision support on task performance. We critically discuss implications and limitations of our research and provide directions for future research in Sect. 5. Finally, we conclude with a summary.

2 Theoretical Background and Related Work

2.1 Explanations in AI

The research field of XAI addresses AI's opacity: XAI aims at making AI's reasoning more accessible, while at the same time maintaining AI's high performance (Adadi and Berrada 2018). To this end, XAI provides methods to automatically generate explanations along AI decisions. These approaches can be categorized according to scope of explainability and model dependency. Scope of explainability can be global or local. Global approaches aim at explaining the functioning of an entire AI model, while local approaches aspire to explain specific outcomes (Payrovnaziri et al. 2020; Vilone and Longo 2020). For example, in the context of breast cancer diagnostics, global explanations may outline the most relevant criteria that are leveraged for the AI's identification of cancerous histopathology images. In contrast, local explanations may expose which criteria influenced a specific cancerous spot identified. Model dependency distinguishes between model-specific approaches, i.e., generating explanations for individual (classes of) AI models, and model-agnostic approaches, i.e., generating explanations for various (classes of) AI models (Adadi and Berrada 2018; Arrieta et al. 2020). Recently, considerable progress in the development of novel XAI approaches has been made (Adadi and Berrada 2018; Arrieta et al. 2020).

Explanations resulting from approaches outlined above aim at improving user interaction with AI, which manifests itself in four key goals (Meske et al. 2022). First, one target of explanations is to enable humans to evaluate AI, e.g., to detect its flaws (Meske et al. 2022). A second goal of explanations is to improve AI models, i.e., to increase their accuracy based on a better understanding of their functioning (Arrieta et al. 2020). A third goal of explanations is to justify AI's decisions, thus making the AI's reasoning more transparent and accountable for users and those affected by its decisions (Arrieta et al. 2020; Adadi and Berrada 2018). Finally, a fourth objective of explanations is to allow users to "learn from the algorithm's working and results in order to gain deep knowledge" (Meske et al. 2022, p. 57).

2.2 *Impact of Explanations on User Behavior*

Literature emphasizes that clarifying the role of explanations can make significant contributions to the ongoing discussion of human-AI interaction (Sundar 2020). In fact, it is still poorly understood how XAI-based explanations affect user behavior (Brasse et al. 2023). Research on the impact of explanations on user behavior focuses on use of AI systems, users' cognitive evaluations of AI, and the outcome of user interaction with AI, such as task performance (Rzepka and Berger 2018). These effects are driven by user, task, and context, as well as system characteristics (Rzepka and Berger 2018). XAI addresses one key system characteristic, namely, the opacity of AI, which shapes user interaction with AI (Berente et al. 2021). Thus, research on the role of explanations along AI decisions is considered highly relevant for managing AI (Berente et al. 2021).

Recently, empirical research on the impact of XAI-based explanations on user behavior has emerged. Existing studies explore the impact of explanations on a range of behavioral and perceptional constructs, including trust (Banovic et al. 2023; Bayer et al. 2021; Jussupow et al. 2021; Shin 2021; Yan and Xu 2021), perception of AI (Dodge et al. 2019; Jussupow et al. 2021), behavioral use intentions (Conati et al. 2021; Hamm et al. 2021; Kim et al. 2023), disclosure of personal information (Yan and Xu 2021), understanding of AI (Elshawi et al. 2019), and advice acceptance (Bayer et al. 2021; Schemmer et al. 2022b). First insights on positive effects of XAI on actual use of AI systems (e.g., Conati et al. 2021), users' cognitive evaluations of AI interactions (e.g., Shin 2021), and the outcome of respective interactions (e.g., Bayer et al. 2021) have been uncovered.

2.3 Impact of Explanations on Task Performance

Often, the ultimate desired outcome of user interaction with AI is increased task performance (Rzepka and Berger 2018). Extant literature suggests a positive effect of AI decision support on task performance (Rzepka and Berger 2018) with improved decision quality (e.g., Batra and Antony 2001), reduced error incidents, and enhanced productivity growth (e.g., Furman and Seamans 2019).

The question whether additional provision of explanations along AI-based decision support can enhance the positive impact of AI support on users' task performance increasingly attracts the attention of researchers (Schemmer et al. 2022a). A synthesis of existing empirical studies (e.g., Bansal et al. 2021; Buçinca et al. 2020; Carton et al. 2020; Fügener et al. 2021; Lui et al. 2021; van der Waa et al. 2021) by Schemmer et al. (2022a) suggests a positive effect of XAI-based decision support compared to no decision support on task performance. Further studies find a persuasive effect of XAI-based decision support on advice following (e.g., Bansal et al. 2011; van der Waa et al. 2021) and indicate XAI-based explanations' potential to improve task performance compared to opaque AI-based decision support (Buçinca et al. 2020; Lai and Tan 2019). More concretely, Buçinca et al. (2020) propose a significant difference between XAI-based decision support and AI-based decision support regarding task performance in predicting fat content of meals. This insight is complemented by the findings of Lai and Tan (2019), which demonstrate a positive impact of XAI-based explanations along AI-based decision support on task performance in deception detection.

So far, studies on the impact of XAI on task performance are limited to investigating the impact of explanations along AI-based decision support during user interaction. These studies are closely connected to XAI's goal of justifying AI decisions. However, XAI also aims to facilitate learning from AI (Meske et al. 2022). Thus, the question arises whether provision of explanations along AI-based decision support can not only help to improve immediate task performance (i.e., during user interaction with AI), but also prolonged task performance (i.e., after user interaction with AI).

Against this background, we aim to investigate whether XAI-based explanations have an immediate and a prolonged effect on task performance of users of AI-based decision support systems. We formulate the following two hypotheses:

H1: XAI-based explanations alongside AI-based decision support have a positive impact on task performance during interaction with the AI.

H2: XAI-based explanations alongside AI-based decision support have a positive impact on task performance after interaction with the AI.

3 Methodology

We test our hypotheses by means of an online experiment in which participants perform an image classification task. We statistically compare task performance between (1) a control group receiving no decision support, (2) users of AI-based decision support, and (3) users of AI-based decision support paired with automatically generated explanations during and after interaction with the system. In the remainder of this section, we provide an overview of the case setting, study procedure and participants, as well as measurement and analysis.

3.1 Case Setting

We implemented and conducted an online experiment based on an application where users' task is to classify the city of origin in Google Street View images. All images originated from four cities in Germany and in Israel—Berlin, Hamburg, Jerusalem, and Tel Aviv. We selected the four cities based on popularity (size and touristic status) and distinctive differences with regards to architecture. Moreover, we considered appropriate task difficulty, i.e., the images were featuring more obvious differences between Middle Eastern and Western European cities and more subtle differences between cities in the same country. Thus, the task is relevant to various image classification tasks in practice, e.g., breast cancer diagnostics. In this case, an AI might detect cancerous spots on histopathology images, with more obvious and more subtle indicators, and include explanations to elaborate on its classifications.

As a data set, we extracted 15.000 images from Google Street View in January 2022. The images were divided into 80% training and 20% test data images (cf. Gholamy et al. 2018). To generate AI-based decisions for classifying the city of origin in Google Street View images, we trained a neural network with a MobileNetV2 architecture, which constitutes a State-of-the Art and typical black box AI model for image classification (cf. Sandler et al. 2018; Xiang et al. 2019). After optimizing the parameters of the model on the training data, it achieved an accuracy of 0.88 on the test data images.

To automatically generate explanations along the AI-based decisions, we implemented the XAI method LIME (cf. Ribeiro et al. 2016). LIME is a prominent model-agnostic XAI method which is suitable for the task of image classification (Wanner et al. 2020). It produces visual explanations, which highlight areas of a respective image that are especially relevant for the AI's decision. To ensure that explanations are representative for the chosen XAI method and meaningful for users in our study, we conducted a combination of functionally-grounded and human-grounded evaluation as proposed by Förster et al. (2020). First, we leveraged functionally-grounded evaluation to verify that explanations are stable and valid by systematically assessing a range of LIME parametrizations with respect to stability and validity measures (cf. e.g., Visani et al. 2022). Second, to ensure that explanations are meaningful for users in our study, we leveraged human-grounded evaluation and adjusted LIME parameters based on textual feedback on the helpfulness of explanations from a pre-study with 15 participants (cf. Förster et al. 2020).

3.2 Study Procedures and Participants

The experiment was conducted through an online application, which could be accessed via browsers on mobile devices or computers. Participants were randomly assigned to three groups: control group (no decision support), treatment group AI (AI-based decision support), and treatment group XAI (AI-based decision support paired with visual explanations). The experiment consisted of three parts.

In the first part, all participants received an introduction to their task and answered demographic questions (gender, year of birth, highest degree of education). Further, we assessed users' expertise in terms of prior visits to Israel and/or Germany. We also informed participants that they would receive a performance-based remuneration to incentivize them to carry out their task as well as possible. In addition, we informed them about the presence of attention checks in all parts of the experiment.

In the second part, participants received treatment according to their random assignment. All participants conducted eight rounds performing their task, i.e., classifying the city of origin in a Google Street View image. Per round, the control group only received an image to be matched to one of the four cities (Berlin, Hamburg, Jerusalem, Tel Aviv) without any further information. Treatment group AI was presented the image paired with a recommendation from the AI decision support system. Treatment group XAI was shown the image paired with the same recommendation as treatment group AI and an additional LIME explanation. Figure 1 depicts an exemplary round for treatment group XAI in the second part of the experiment, where the XAI-based explanation highlights the palm trees, i.e., pixels which were particularly relevant for the AI's decision "Tel Aviv". Apart from explanations (and recommendations), interfaces for treatment group AI (and the control group) looked similar.

After having completed eight rounds, participants moved to the third part of the experiment, where all treatment conditions from the second part were removed. All participants conducted five more rounds performing their task. Per round, all participants only received the image to be classified without any further information. One of the five images served as an attention check, with an image that obviously originated from Berlin, as it included a town sign with the city name on it.

For our experiment, we recruited 300 participants, which passed all attention checks, from the platform Clickworker. We chose the number of participants through a G * Power analysis (cf. Faul et al. 2009) based on the results of a pre-study. Despite the attention checks, our study attracted 11 so-called speeders and cheaters, as is typical for online platforms (Ford 2017). We identified those participants based on conspicuously short and long completion times and excluded them from the analysis. The final sample consists of a size of 289 participants with $n = 99$ participants in the

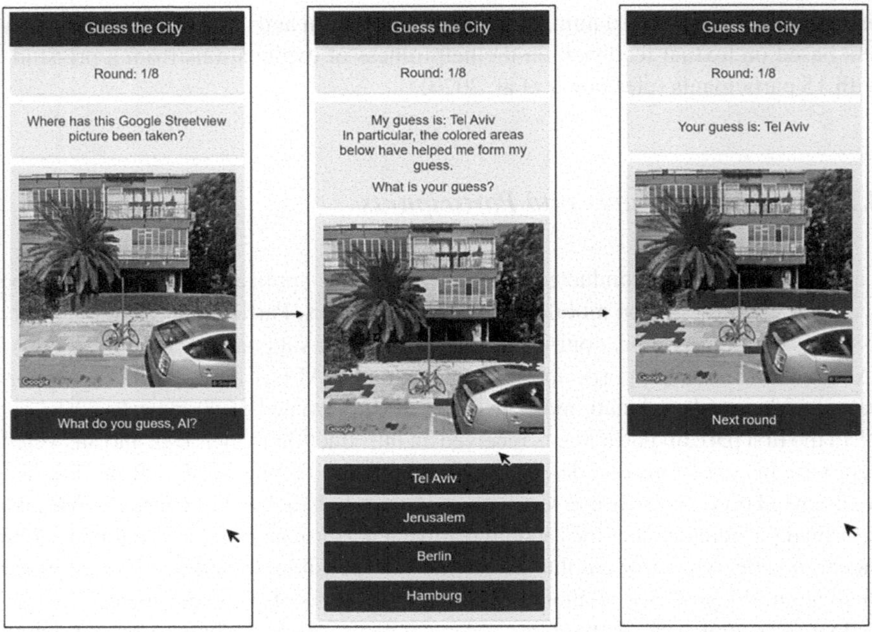

Fig. 1 Screenshots illustrating one round for treatment group XAI

control group, n = 97 participants in treatment group AI, and n = 93 participants in treatment group XAI. Every participant received 1.58 EUR financial compensation. The top 50% participants according to task performance additionally received a performance bonus of 1.00 EUR. Among the 289 participants, 164 participants identified as male and 125 as female. The average age of participants was 37 years. Participants came from 34 different nations, with the majority of participants from Germany (145 participants), followed by Brazil (26 participants). Expertise was measured as a binary variable across all groups and refers to users' prior visits to Israel or Germany, i.e., having visited one of the countries (1) versus not having visited one of the countries (0): 181 participants had visited one of the two countries, while 108 had visited neither Israel nor Germany. Overall, the three groups did neither differ significantly in demographic variables nor in expertise.

3.3 Measurement and Analysis

To test our hypotheses and to investigate the impact of automatically generated explanations along AI decision support systems, we assessed users' task performance during and after treatment by assessing the number of accurately classified images. First, we measured task performance during treatment, which refers to the eight rounds in the second part of the experiment when users were supported by the AI-based decisions support system (treatment group AI), the AI-based decision support system paired with visual explanations (treatment group XAI) or no decision support system (control group). Task performance scores ranged from 0 to 8 for all groups. Second, we measured task performance after treatment, which refers to the four rounds (plus attention check round) in the third part of the experiment after treatment conditions were withdrawn for all three groups. Here, task performance scores ranged from 0 to 4 for all groups.

The focus of this paper is to analyze the immediate and prolonged effect of XAI-based explanations along AI decision support on task performance. To this end, we not only analyze the difference between AI-based decision support and XAI-based decision support, but also the impact of AI-based decision support and XAI-based decision support compared to no support. To assess the impact of (X)AI-based decision support on users' task performance, we compare either treatment group with the control group. To determine the difference in impact of AI-based decision support and XAI-based decision support, we compare the constructs' distributions between the two treatment groups. For statistical comparison, we chose the Mann–Whitney U-test as a non-parametric alternative to the t-test since we cannot assume normality, as confirmed by the Shapiro–Wilk test.

4 Results

This section is dedicated to our findings. First, we analyze the impact of XAI-based explanations along AI decision support on task performance during interaction. Second, we describe the effect of XAI-based explanations along AI decision support on task performance after interaction.

4.1 Impact of Explanations on Task Performance During Interaction with the Decision Support System

We analyze the effect of automatically generated explanations on task performance during user interaction with an AI-based decision support system.

Results support our first hypothesis: Users being assisted by AI decisions paired with explanations, i.e., participants in treatment group XAI, perform significantly better than users being assisted by AI decisions only, i.e., participants in the treatment group AI ($U = 5567.00$, $p < 0.01$). Users in treatment group XAI perform best (mean = 6.13, median = 6.00, STDV = 1.71), while users in treatment group AI perform better (mean = 5.27, median = 5.00, STDV = 2.16) than users without decision support, i.e., participants in the control group (mean = 3.69, median = 4.00, STDV = 1.63).

Mann–Whitney U tests reveal that all group differences in task performance are significant at the 1% level or lower. The effect of providing AI decision support in combination with corresponding explanations is large as indicated by the rank biserial correlation r resulting from a Mann–Whitney U test comparing treatment group XAI and the control group (U = 7782.00, r = 0.69, $p < 0.001$) (cf. Cohen 2013). The impact of the provision of AI support on task performance is higher than the impact of the provision of explanations in addition to AI support: A Mann–Whitney U test comparing treatment group AI and the control group (U = 6940.50, r = 0.45, $p < 0.001$) indicates a medium effect, while a Mann–Whitney U test comparing treatment group XAI and treatment group AI (U = 5567.00, r = 0.23, $p < 0.01$) indicates a small effect (cf. Cohen 2013).

4.2 Impact of Explanations on Task Performance After Interaction with the Decision Support System

We analyze the effect of automatically generated explanations on task performance after users have interacted with an AI-based decision support system.

Results support our second hypothesis: After decision support is being withdrawn, users having been assisted by AI decisions paired with explanations, i.e., participants in treatment group XAI, perform significantly better than users having been assisted by AI decisions only, i.e., participants in the treatment group AI (U = 5190.00, r = 0.15, $p < 0.05$). Task performance after interaction with the system of treatment group AI (mean = 2.40, median = 2.00, STDV = 1.03) is lower than respective task performance of treatment group XAI (mean = 2.67, median = 3.00, STDV = 0.94) and the control group (mean = 2.69, median = 3.00, STDV = 1.10). Mann–Whitney U tests show that differences in task performance after decision support is being withdrawn between treatment group AI and the control group (U = 5515.50, r = 0.15, $p < 0.05$) as well as between treatment group XAI and treatment group AI (U = 5190.00, r = 0.15, $p < 0.05$) are significant at the 5% level. According to a Mann–Whitney U test, treatment group XAI and the control group do not significantly differ in task performance after decision support is being withdrawn (U = 4698.50, r = 0.02, $p = 0.40$).

5 Discussion

With our work, we aimed to expand existing literature on the impact of XAI-based explanations on task performance. We performed our analysis using an AI-based application, which allows users to classify the city of origin in Google Street View images and conducted an online experiment with three groups, receiving (1) no decision support, (2) AI-based decision support, and (3) XAI-based decision support (i.e.,

AI-based decision support paired with automatically generated explanations). We examined the immediate effect and the prolonged effect of XAI-based explanations on users' task performance.

5.1 Implications for Research and Practice

The results contribute to research in two ways:

First, our study demonstrates that XAI-based explanations can boost the benefit of AI for users' task performance during interaction with AI-based decision support. Our results demonstrate that while AI-based decision support alone already improves task performance ($p < 0.001$), additional provision of explanations leads to further improvements compared to mere AI support ($p < 0.01$). While the positive impact of AI on task performance has already been indicated by prior research (Rzepka and Berger 2018), in particular our insights on explanations' value-add for task performance beyond the effect of mere AI-based decision support contribute to the ongoing discussion on the effect of XAI- compared to AI-based decision support (Schemmer et al. 2022a). Our findings highlight the positive immediate impact of automatically generated explanations along AI-based decision support systems on users' task performance, which has so far only been investigated by a few papers (Buçinca et al. 2020; Lai and Tan 2019). We contribute to this discussion by putting XAI's compared to AI's effect sizes into perspective with the impact of AI support being higher (medium effect size) than the impact of further providing paired explanations (small effect size). This distinction leads us to emphasize the incremental impact of explanations in improving users' task performance. These findings underpin the potential of XAI to yield additional performance improvements for users interacting with AI-based decision support systems.

Second, our study is the first to indicate that explanations can counterbalance the potential negative prolonged effect on users' task performance that manifests when an AI-based decision support is being withdrawn. We find that users of an XAI-based decision support system show higher task performance after the interaction than users of an AI-based decision support system ($p < 0.05$). In our study, despite the positive effect of AI-based decision support on task performance during the interaction, users of the AI-based decision support system show even lower task performance after interaction compared to users that have not received any support before ($p < 0.05$). This finding is of particular relevance given the ongoing discussion on whether users' immediate performance improvements during interaction with (X)AI-based decision support occur because users actually incorporate the AI's advice into their own decision-making (cf. Lai et al. 2019) or simply because they blindly (over-) rely on the AI's advice (cf. Jacovi et al. 2021; Schemmer et al. 2022b). Blind advice utilization would equally lead to an improvement in task performance during user interaction with the AI if AI's performance outweighs human performance (Wang et al. 2008). However, it is expected to cause a performance decline as a prolonged effect after decision support is withdrawn. Our results on task performance suggest that—once the decision support is withdrawn—users who received AI-based decision support perform worse compared to those that received no decision support before. In contrast, those who received XAI-based decision support perform equally to those that received no decision support before. Thus, our findings provide a first indication of the actual risk of opaque AI-based decision support to cause blind (over-)reliance, while XAI-based explanations have the potential to counteract the prolonged negative effect of AI-based decision support.

Next to these theoretical implications, our findings indicate two practical implications for organizations and developers, who intend to leverage the potential of AI for employees:

First, XAI-based decision support systems are more effective to assist employees in their tasks than AI-based decision support systems. Our results suggest that users of XAI-based decision support systems significantly outperform users of AI-based decision support systems. By equipping, for instance, physicians with XAI-based decision support for breast cancer diagnostics, they are expected to make more accurate decisions. Thus, organizations considering introducing AI-based decision support should contemplate the introduction of XAI-based decision support while weighing expected performance improvements against a potential risk of overreliance resulting from the provision of explanations as indicated by prior studies (Schemmer et al. 2022b).

Second, XAI can counterbalance the potential negative effect of AI-based decision support on employees' prolonged task performance. The results of our study indicate that users being supported by AI decisions in their task might perform worse after the decision aid is withdrawn, compared to users not being supported by AI before. As discussed above, leveraging AI bears the risk of inappropriate usage such as blindly following or rejecting AI decisions (Jacovi et al. 2021). This might lead to deterioration of employees' skills. The provision of explanations along AI decisions enables users to comprehend the AI's inner workings and to question the AI's outcomes during interaction. Our results show that this can counterbalance the negative effect of AI-based decision support on users' prolonged task performance. Thus, organizations and developers can leverage XAI methods to prevent potential deterioration of employees' skills resulting from inappropriate usage of AI.

5.2 Limitations and Future Research

While our research presents first interesting insights on the impact of XAI on immediate and prolonged task performance, several limitations remain and might serve as a starting point for future research. Our focus on one specific use case results in two limitations, which are associated with limited external validity. First, the use case, despite being modelled to exhibit characteristics of real-life (X)AI applications, such as breast cancer diagnostics, is nevertheless artificial and thus limits external validity. Second, our use case encompassed lay users only despite the image classification task being equally relevant to domain experts in an organizational context. While lay users remain a critical group of (X)AI-based decision support, it is necessary to equally understand how explanations' immediate and prolonged effect on task performance differs for expert users. Apart from these limitations, third, limited cognitive abilities of participants, which are inherent in human-based experiments, might reduce the internal validity of our results. Future studies might address these points by designing field experiments with application-grounded evaluations (Doshi-Velez and Kim 2018), designed for actual users being directly affected and personally invested in their decisions. Fourth, in our study, we only investigated explanations resulting from LIME, representing a well-established but rather simple XAI approach. In the future, it could be interesting to examine how other XAI approaches impact task performance. Fifth, our study has exploratory character and aims to provide a first step towards a better understanding of the immediate and prolonged effect of explanations along AI decisions on task performance. While our work provides empirical insights that automatically generated explanations enhance the immediate and prolonged effect on task performance for users interacting with AI-based decision support systems, we did not investigate the underlying root causes for this effect. We hope that our work serves as a starting point for further in-depth studies. In particular, prolonged effects of XAI, e.g., on learning, should be further investigated and theoretically undermined. Sixth, in our experiment we only measured task performance during and after treatment as well as expertise as one important indicator for initial human task performance, however, we did not measure initial task performance. Future studies could also measure task performance prior to any treatment and compare with task performance during and after interaction with an AI. Thereby, future research might contribute to better understand whether explanations can indeed help to learn from AI.

6 Conclusion

In recent years, considerable progress has been made in the development of novel XAI approaches. However, XAI research is often criticized for an insufficient understanding of the impact of explanations on user behavior. In this paper, we addressed the open question of how XAI-based explanations along AI-based decision support influence users' immediate and prolonged task performance. We tested our hypotheses by means of an online experiment with 289 participants performing the task of image classification. In our experiment, users were randomly assigned to three groups, i.e., a control group receiving no decision support and two treatment groups receiving AI- or XAI-based decision support. Our results reveal that while AI-based decision support has an immediate positive effect on users' task performance, additional provision of explanations along AI decisions further boosts this effect. Further, the results demonstrate that additional provision of explanations along AI-based decision support can counterbalance the potential negative effect of AI-based decision support on prolonged task performance once decision support is withdrawn. In short, findings suggest that explanations can boost immediate benefits and offset prolonged obstacles of user interaction with AI. With our findings, we contribute to understanding the impact of XAI on immediate and prolonged task performance of users of AI-based decision support systems.

References

Adadi, A. & Berrada, M. (2018), Peeking Inside the Black-Box: A Survey on Explainable Artificial Intelligence (XAI), *IEEE Access* **6**, 52138–52160.

Arrieta, A. B., Díaz-Rodríguez, N., Del Ser, J., Bennetot, A., Tabik, S., Barbado, A., Garcia, S., Gil-Lopez, S., Molina, D., Benjamins, R., Chatila, R. & Herrera, F. (2020), Explainable Artificial Intelligence (XAI): Concepts, Taxonomies, Opportunities and Challenges toward Responsible AI, *Information Fusion* **58**, 82–115.

Banovic, N., Yang, Z., Ramesh, A. & Liu, A. (2023), Being Trustworthy is Not Enough: How Untrustworthy Artificial Intelligence (AI) Can Deceive the End-Users and Gain Their Trust, *in* 'Proceedings of the ACM on Human-Computer Interaction', ACM, pp. 1–17.

Bansal, G., Wu, T., Zhou, J., Fok, R., Nushi, B., Kamar, E., Ribeiro, M. T. & Weld, D. (2021), Does the Whole Exceed its Parts? The Effect of AI Explanations on Complementary Team Performance, *in* 'CHI Conference on Human Factors in Computing Systems (CHI '21)', ACM.

Batra, D. & Antony, S. (2001), Consulting Support during Conceptual Database Design in the Presence of Redundancy in Requirements Specifications: An Empirical Study, *International Journal of Human-Computer Studies* **54**, 25–51.

Bayer, S., Gimpel, H. & Markgraf, M. (2021), The Role of Domain Expertise in Trusting and Following Explainable AI Decision Support Systems, *Journal of Decision Systems*, 1–29.

Berente, N., Bin, G. & Recker, J. (2021), Managing Artificial Intelligence, *MIS Quarterly* **45**(3), 1433–1450.

Bertrand, A., Belloum, R., Eagan, J. R. & Maxwell, W. (2022), How Cognitive Biases Affect XAI-Assisted Decision-Making: A Systematic Review, *in* 'Proceedings of the 2022 AAAI/ACM Conference on AI, Ethics, and Society', pp. 78–91.

Brasse, J., Broder, H., Förster, M., Klier, M. & Sigler, I. (2023), Explainable Artificial Intelligence in Information Systems: A Review of the Status Quo and Future Research Directions, *Electronic Markets* **33**(26).

Buçinca, Z., Lin, P., Gajos, K. Z. & Glassman, E. L. (2020), Proxy Tasks and Subjective Measures Can Be Misleading in Evaluating Explainable AI Systems, *in* 'Proceedings of the 25th International Conference on Intelligent User Interfaces', pp. 454–464.

Carton, S., Mei, Q. & Resnick, P. (2020), Feature-Based Explanations Don't Help People Detect Misclassifications of Online Toxicity, *in* 'Proceedings of the International AAAI Conference on Web and Social Media', pp. 95–106.

Cohen, J. (2013), *Statistical Power Analysis for the Behavioral Sciences*. 2nd Edition. Erlbaum Associates.

Conati, C., Barral, O., Putnam, V. & Rieger, L. (2021), Toward Personalized XAI: A Case Study in Intelligent Tutoring Systems, *Artificial Intelligence* **298**, 103503.

Dodge, J., Liao, V., Zhang, Y., Bellamy, R. & Dugan, C. (2019), Explaining Models: An Empirical Study of How Explanations Impact Fairness Judgment, *in* 'Proceedings of the 24th International Conference on Intelligent User Interfaces', pp. 275–285.

Doshi-Velez, F., & Kim, B. (2018), Considerations for Evaluation and Generalization in Interpretable Machine Learning, *in* 'Explainable and Interpretable Models in Computer Vision and Machine Learning', Springer, pp. 3–17.

Elshawi, R., Al-Mallah, M. H. & Sakr, S. (2019), On the Interpretability of Machine Learning-based Model for Predicting Hypertension, *BMC Medical Informatics and Decision Making* **19**(146), 1–32.

Enholm, I. M., Papagiannidis, E., Mikalef, P. & Krogstie, J. (2021), Artificial Intelligence and Business Value: A Literature Review, *Information Systems Frontiers* **24**(5), 1709–1734.

Faul, F., Erdfelder, E., Buchner, A. & Lang, A.-G. (2009), Statistical Power Analyses Using G*Power 3.1: Tests for Correlation and Regression Analyses, *Behavior Research Methods* **41**, 1149–1160.

Förster, M., Klier, M., Kluge, K., & Sigler, I. (2020), Fostering Human Agency: A Process for the Design of User-Centric XAI Systems, *in* 'Proceedings of the 41st International Conference on Information Systems. A Virtual AIS Conference', AIS.

Ford, J. B. (2017), Amazon's Mechanical Turk: A Comment, *Journal of Advertising* **46**(1), 156–158.

Fügener, A., Grahl, J., Gupta, A. & Ketter, W. (2021), Will Humans-In-The-Loop Become Borgs? Merits and Pitfalls of Working with AI, MIS Quarterly **45**(3), 1527–1556.

Furman, J. & Seamans, R. (2019), AI and the Economy, *Innovation Policy and the Economy* **19**, 161–191.

Gholamy, A., Kreinovich, V. & Kosheleva, O. (2018), Why 70/30 or 80/20 Relation Between Training and Testing Sets: A Pedagogical Explanation, Technical report, Computer Science Commons.

Guidotti, R., Monreale, A., Ruggieri, S., Turini, F., Giannotti, F. & Pedreschi, D. (2019), A Survey of Methods for Explaining Black Box Models, *ACM Computing Surveys* **51**(5), 1–42.

Hamm, P., Wittmann, H. F. & Klesel, M. (2021), Explain it to Me and I will Use it: A Proposal on the Impact of Explainable AI on Use Behavior, *in* 'Proceedings of the 42nd International Conference on Information Systems', AIS.

Jacovi, A., Marasovic, A., Miller, T. & Goldberg, Y. (2021), Formalizing Trust in Artificial Intelligence: Prerequisites, Causes and Goals of Human Trust in AI, *in* 'Proceedings of the 2021 ACM Conference on Fairness, Accountability, and Transparency', ACM, pp. 624–635.

Joung, B. G., Leea, W. J., Huanga, A. & Sutherlanda, J. W. (2019), Development and Application of a Method for Real Time Motor Fault Detection, *in* 'Proceedings of the 8th International Conference on Through-Life Engineering Services', Elsevier B.V., pp. 94–98.

Jussupow, E., Meza Martínez, M. A., Mädche, A. & Heinzl, A. (2021), Is This System Biased? – How Users React to Gender Bias in an Explainable AI System, *in* 'Proceedings of the 42nd International Conference on Information Systems', AIS, pp. 1–17.

Kaymak, S., Helwan, A. & Uzun, D. (2017), Breast Cancer Image Classification Using Artificial Neural Networks, *Procedia Computer Science* **120**, 126–131.

Kim, S. S. Y., Watkins, E. A., Russakovsky, O., Fong, R. & Monroy-Hernández, A. (2023), Help Me Help the AI: Understanding How Explainability Can Support Human-AI Interaction, *in* 'Proceedings of the 2023 CHI Conference on Human Factors in Computing Systems', ACM, pp. 1–17.

Lai, V. & Tan, C. (2019), On Human Predictions with Explanations and Predictions of Machine Learning Models: A Case Study on Deception Detection, *in* '2019 Proceedings of the Conference on Fairness, Accountability, and Transparency', ACM, pp. 29–38.

Lui, H., Lai, V. & Tan, C. (2021), Understanding the Effect of Out-of-Distribution Examples and Interactive Explanations on Human-AI Decision Making, *in* 'Proceedings of the ACM on Human-Computer Interaction', pp. 1–45.

Meske, C., Bunde, E., Schneider, J. & Gersch, M. (2022), Explainable Artificial Intelligence: Objectives, Stakeholders, and Future Research Opportunities, *Information Systems Management* **39**(1), 53–63.

Minh, D., Wang, H. X., Li, Y. F. & Nguyen, T. N. (2022), Explainable Artificial Intelligence: A Comprehensive Review, *Artificial Intelligence Review* **55**(5), 3503–3568.

Payrovnaziri, S. N., Chen, Z., Rengifo-Moreno, P., Miller, T., Bian, J., Chen, J. H., Liu, X. & He, Z. (2020), Explainable Artificial Intelligence Models using Real-World Electronic Health Record Data: A Systematic Scoping Review, *Journal of the American Medical Informatics Association* **27**(7), 1173–1185.

Ribeiro, M. T., Singh, S. & Guestrin, C. (2016), "Why Should I Trust You?": Explaining the Predictions of Any Classifier, *in* 'Proceedings of the 22nd ACM SIGKDD International Conference on Knowledge Discovery and Data Mining', ACM, pp. 1135–1144.

Rzepka, C. & Berger, B. (2018), User Interaction with AI-Enabled Systems: A Systematic Review of IS Research, *in* 'Proceedings of the 39th International Conference on Information Systems', AIS.

Sandler, M., Howard, A., Zhu, M., Zhmoginov, A. & Chen, L.-C. (2018), MobileNetV2: Inverted Residuals and Linear Bottlenecks, *in* 'Proceedings of the 2018 IEEE Conference on Computer Vision and Pattern Recognition', IEEE, pp. 4510–4520.

Schemmer, M., Hemmer, P., Nitsche, M., Kühl, N. & Vössing, M. (2022a), A Meta-Analysis of the Utility of Explainable Artificial Intelligence in Human-AI Decision-Making, *in* 'Proceedings of the 2022 AAAI/ACM Conference on AI, Ethics, and Society', ACM, pp. 617–626.

Schemmer, M., Kühl, N., Benz, C. & Satzger, G. (2022b), On the Influence of Explainable AI on Automation Bias, in 'Proceedings of the 30th European Conference on Information Systems'.

Shin, D. (2021), The Effects of Explainability and Causability on Perception, Trust, and Acceptance: Implications of Explainable AI, *International Journal of Human-Computer Studies* **146**.

Sundar, S. S. (2020), Rise of Machine Agency: A Framework for Studying the Psychology of Human–AI Interaction (HAII), *Journal of Computer-Mediated Communication* **25**(1), 74–88.

van der Waa, J., Nieuwburg, E., Cremers, A. & Neerincx, M. (2021), Evaluating XAI: A Comparison of Rule-based and Example-based Explanations, *Artificial Intelligence* **291**.

Vilone, G. & Longo, L. (2020), 'Explainable Artificial Intelligence: A Systematic Review', *ArXiv*.

Visani, G., Bagli, E., Chesani, F., Poluzzi, A. & Capuzzo, D. (2022), Statistical Stability Indices for LIME: Obtaining Reliable Explanations for Machine Learning Models, *Journal of the Operational Research Society* **73**(1), 91–101.

Wachter, S., Mittelstadt, B. & Russell, C. (2018), Counterfactual Explanations Without Opening the Black Box: Automated Decisions and the GDPR, *Harvard Journal of Law & Technology* **31**(2), 841–887.

Wang, L., Jamieson, G. A., & Hollands, J. G. (2008), Selecting Methods for the Analysis of Reliance on Automation, *in* 'Proceedings of the Human Factors and Ergonomics Society Annual Meeting', **52**(4), pp. 287–291.

Wanner, J., Herm, L.-V., Heinrich, K., Janiesch, C., & Zschech, P. (2020), White, Grey, Black: Effects of XAI Augmentation on the Confidence in AI-based Decision Support Systems, *in* 'Proceedings of the 41st International Conference on Information Systems', AIS.

Xiang, Q., Wang, X., Li, R., Zhang, G., Lai, J. & Hu, Q. (2019), Fruit Image Classification Based on MobileNetV2 with Transfer Learning Technique, *in* 'Proceedings of the 3rd International Conference on Computer Science and Application Engineering', ACM, pp. 1–7.

Yan, A. & Xu, D. (2021), AI for Depression Treatment: Addressing the Paradox of Privacy and Trust with Empathy, Accountability, and Explainability, *in* 'Proceedings of the 42nd International Conference on Information Systems', AIS.

Artificial Intelligence Explainability Requirements of the AI Act and Metrics for Measuring Compliance

Fabian Walke, Lars Bennek, and Till J. Winkler

Abstract Explainability in artificial intelligence (AI) is crucial for ensuring transparency, accountability, and risk mitigation, thereby addressing digital responsibility, social, ethical and ecological aspects of information system usage. AI will be regulated in the European Union (EU) through the AI Act. This regulation introduces requirements for explainable AI (XAI). This paper examines which requirements for XAI are regulated and which metrics could be used for measuring compliance. For this purpose, legal texts from the European Parliament and Council were analyzed in order to ascertain XAI requirements. Additionally, XAI taxonomies and metrics were collected. The results reveal, that the AI Act provides abstract regulations for explainability, making it challenging to define specific metrics for achieving explainability. As a solution, we propose a socio-technical metric classification for measuring compliance. Further studies should analyze forthcoming explainability requirements to make AI verifiable and minimize risks arising from AI.

Keywords XAI · Measurement · Assessment · Taxonomy · European union

F. Walke (✉) · L. Bennek · T. J. Winkler
FernUniversität in Hagen, Chair of Information Management, Hagen, Germany
e-mail: fabian.walke@fernuni-hagen.de

L. Bennek
e-mail: lars.bennek@studium.fernuni-hagen.de

T. J. Winkler
e-mail: till.winkler@fernuni-hagen.de

T. J. Winkler
Copenhagen Business School, Department of Digitalization, Frederiksberg, Denmark

D. Beverungen et al. (eds.), *Solutions and Technologies for Responsible Digitalization*,
Lecture Notes in Information Systems and Organisation 75,
https://doi.org/10.1007/978-3-031-80122-8_8

1 Introduction

With artificial intelligence (AI) and the emergence of generative AI, such as ChatGPT and other advanced AI models, the topic of AI and machine learning (ML) has reached a new level and is now more than ever attracting the interest of experts and laypeople alike. AI is a generic term for a sub-field of computer science for which no uniform definition exists (Buxmann and Schmidt 2019). AI covers several research areas, such as ML, natural language processing (NLP), speech, vision and robotics (Mukhamediev et al. 2022). With the publication of the AI strategy of the European Commission (2018) and the German federal government (2020) as well as the European Commission's (EC) proposal of the 'Artificial Intelligence Act' (AIA) (European Commission 2021), this technology is also receiving special attention from politicians.

In the AIA, AI is assigned to different risk levels: unacceptable risk, high risk, low risk and minimal risk. While unacceptable-risk systems are to be banned, high-risk systems are subject to different requirements, including transparency and interpretability. The ethics guidelines of the EC (2019) specify this requirement: The entire decision-making process must be recorded and documented, and an "understandable explanation of the algorithmic decision-making processes" is required, as far as possible. Article 13 (1) AIA stipulates with regard to transparency that users must be able to interpret and use the results appropriately. Explainable artificial intelligence (XAI) is a field of research that has emerged in response to the increasing needs for transparency and interpretability of AI. XAI is crucial for digital responsibility, because it ensures that decision-making processes of AI systems can be traced and understood, thereby enabling accountability and transparency. XAI has also social implications related to information systems, as it can help mitigate the potential risks of biases, discrimination, and other negative impacts on individuals and society. With regard to ethical and ecological implications of information systems, XAI can help ensure that AI is developed and used in a way that is aligned with ethical principles and environmental sustainability goals.

Linardatos et al. (2021) provide a taxonomy that divides XAI methods into black-box and white-box models. Zhou et al. (2021) summarize XAI metrics and assign them to different explanation types. Sovrano et al. (2022) go one step further and compare metrics with explainability requirements of the AIA. They note that future research would need to consider these metrics in the light of future legislative changes. This paper builds on the findings of Sovrano et al. (2022). The first objective of this paper is to determine whether adjustments are to be expected with regard to the explainability requirements of the European Council (Council) based on the general approach on the AI Act (AIA-Council; European Council 2022b) and the opinion on the AI Act of the Legal Affairs Committee of the European Parliament (EP) (AIA-EP; European Parliament 2022). The second objective is to investigate, based on Sovrano et al. (2022), which metrics can be used to measure the compliance with AI explainability requirements. The consideration of XAI metrics in this paper, however, is only seen as an introductory approach to the topic of compliance and XAI metrics. This leads to the research questions of this paper: RQ1: *Which requirements for XAI arise from the AIA, AIA-Council, AIA-EP?* RQ2: *Which metrics could be used to measure compliance with XAI requirements?* This paper applies a literature review and document analysis to address the research questions, which are described in the next section (Sect. 2), followed by the results (Sect. 3) and the discussion and conclusion (Sect. 4) of this research paper.

2 Methodology

The study employs a literature review and a document analysis to achieve the research objectives. The literature review is based on the framework for literature reviewing from vom Brocke et al. (2009), consisting of five phases: definition of scope, conceptualization, literature search, analysis and synthesis, and research agenda. The scope of our literature review can be systematized referring to the taxonomy of Cooper (1988) as recommended by vom Brocke et al. (2009). Cooper (1988) subdivides literature reviews into six characteristics: focus, goal, perspective, coverage, organization, and audience of the paper which are further divided into categories (Table 1). Some categories of these six characteristics are mutually exclusive while other characteristics allow multiple categories. The focus of this paper lies on research outcomes and practices. Our primary goal is the integration of the AIA, AIA-Council and AIA-EP with regard to requirements for XAI and the integration with appropriate metrics from the literature to measure compliance of AI explainability requirements. Our secondary goal is to show central issues regarding XAI literature in the form of taxonomies. We choose a neutral perspective for the literature review, the presentation of the analysis and synthesis of the results. The coverage of the literature is central (reviewing the topic pivotal to the XAI topic) and the organization of the papers is conceptual. Our target groups are specialized scholars, general scholars and practitioners in the field of AI (Table 1).

The conceptualization (vom Brocke et al. 2009) is based on the AIA, AIA-Council and AIA-EP legal texts, academic literature and grey literature regarding general XAI topics and also regarding metrics to measure compliance with the AI explainability requirements. The literature search consisted of techniques of keyword search, backward and forward search in different sources (citation indexing services, bibliographic databases, publications) (vom Brocke et al. 2015). As we only focus on a central coverage of the literature regarding the XAI topic, we provide an abbreviated description of the search process. The penultimate phase is the analysis and synthesis of the found literature, which is consists of five sub-steps (overview [1], taxonomies [2], requirements [3], analysis [4], metrics and synthesis [5]; see Sect. 3). Sub-step 1 and 2 provide for RQ1 and RQ2 a basic understanding of the current discussion in literature on taxonomies, XAI requirements and compliance, while sub-step 3 and 4 focus on RQ1 and sub-step 5 on RQ2. We follow a concept matrix approach (Salipante et al. 1982; Webster and Watson 2002) for the presentation of the results (i.a. taxonomies [2] in Table 2). With regard to the explainability requirements from

Table 1 Positioning of this paper within the taxonomy of Cooper (1988)

Characteristic	Categories				
Focus	**Research outcomes**		Research methods	Theories	**Practices or applications**
Goal	**Integration**			Criticism	**Central issues**
Perspective	**Neutral representation**			Espousal of position	
Coverage	Exhaustive		Exhaustive (selective citation)	Representative	**Central or pivotal**
Organization	Historical			**Conceptual**	Methodological
Audience	**Specialized scholars**	**General scholars**		**Practitioners**	General public

The selected categories from the Cooper (1988) taxonomy

the AIA, we analyzed the passages listed in the literature in the context of XAI (requirements [3]; Table 3). Since the views of the EP (AIA-EP) and the Council (AIA-Council) are also decisive at the end of the ordinary legislative procedure and these have not yet been taken into account by the literature, the AIA-Council and AIA-EP published in December 2022 are therefore considered. The AIA-EP was selected because the Legal Affairs Committee of the EP has exclusive competences with regard to Article 13, 14 AIA, which are relevant for explainability. We analyzed the AIA, AIA-EP and AIA-Council (Table 4) and summarized the results in a concept-matrix (Table 5), whereby we apply a document analysis in the form of a content analysis (Mayring 2022) for these legal texts. The content analysis consists of defining the units of analysis, such as articles, paragraphs, or sections, based on the research question. We also determine categories related to the research question, such as the requirements for transparency and explainability of AI. We analyzed the documents with qualitative content analysis techniques and we identified passages related to the research question by searching for the words "transparen*", "interpret*", "explain*" and "understa*" in the documents. When new passages with an XAI context were identified, these have also been integrated in our results. Then we collected XAI metrics from the literature and structured them with regard to the findings of the previous steps (metrics and synthesis [5]; Table 6). In the last phase, the analysis and synthesis of the literature results into a research agenda (Sect. 4).

Table 2 Concept-matrix and analysis of XAI taxonomies

Expression	Adadi and Berrada (2018)	Arrieta et al. (2019)	Arya et al. (2019)	Islam et al. (2022)	Linardatos et al. (2021)	Vilone and Longo (2020)
Intrinsic versus Post-hoc	x	x	x	x	x	x
Model specific versus agnostic	x	x			x	x
Problem type						x
Local versus Global	x		x	x	x	x
Input type				x	x	x
Result type		x	x	x		x
Static versus interactive			x			
Data versus model			x			
Surrogate versus visualisation			x			

Table 3 Concept-matrix and analysis of XAI legal requirements literature

AIA passage	Ebers (2021a)	Hacker and Passoth (2020)	Sovrano et al. (2022)
Recital 38		x	x
Recital 47	x		x
Article 13(1)	x	x	x
Article 13(2)	x	x	
Article 13(3)		x	
Article 14(4)(c)		x	x
Article 14(4)(d)		x	x
Article 29(4)		x	x
App. IV(2)(b)			x

Table 4 Analysis of the AIA-EP and AIA-Council (new passages marked with asterisk*)

AIA	Analytical results
Recital 80 a*	**AIA-EP**: New recital clarifying that an explanation should consider the expertise and knowledge of the average user. For AI systems that are not capable of issuing an explanation, this should be stated
Article 4a*	**AIA-EP:** Inclusion of a definition of transparency. Transparency means both traceability and explainability, as well as informing the user that they are interacting with an AI
Article 13 (1)	**AIA:** Sufficient transparency to allow users to interpret and use the results **AIA-Council:** Sufficient transparency for users and providers to understand and use the system **AIA-EP:** Sufficient transparency to enable users and providers to understand how the system works (further requirements in the following line)
Article 13 (1)	**AIA-EP:** Addition to the transparency requirement: An AI result must be interpretable by providers and users. The user should understand the AI and generally know how the AI system works and what data it processes. Decisions made by AI should be explainable by those affected by them
Article 13 (3) (b)	**AIA-EP:** The instruction manual of an AI system contains information on the degree to which it can provide an explanation for decisions
Article 13 (3) (ea)*; Article 13 (3) (f)*	**AIA-EP and AIA-Council:** A description of the mechanisms included in the AI system that enable users to properly collect, store and evaluate the prescribed logs shall be added to the instructions manual

3 Results

The results are divided into five segments: *Overview (1), Taxonomies (2), Requirements (3), Analysis (4), Metrics and Synthesis (5).* Regarding *Overview (1)*, we provide a definition of XAI, present most important standards and ongoing standardization activities. In the course of the legislative process of the AIA, the definition of AI is a controversial point and one of the main points of criticism of the European Council (European Council 2022a). An AI system is thus defined by the Council (2022b) as follows: "[…] system that is designed to operate with elements of autonomy and that infers how to achieve a set of goals based on machine and/or human-generated data and inputs through machine learning and/or logic- and knowledge-based concepts, and produces system-generated outputs such as content (generative AI systems), predictions, recommendations, or decisions that influence the environment with which the AI systems interact" (Article 3 No. 1, AIA-Council). The definition is based on the more detailed definition of the EC's High Level Expert Group on AI (AI-HLEG). In its policy paper (AI HLEG 2018), AI-HLEG calls for AI systems to be developed in such a way that humans can understand the steps or their basis. In the context of XAI, interpretability and explainability are partly differentiated and partly used synonymously (Markus et al. 2021; Schaaf et al. 2021). The variety in the literature of different definitions is not only limited to interpretability (e.g. Doshi-Velez and Kim 2017; DIN & DKE 2022) and explainability (e.g. Adadi

Table 5 Concept-matrix of AIA explainability requirements

AIA passage	Requirement	AIA	AIA-EP	AIA-Cou
Article 13(1)	Users must be able to interpret and use the results of a high-risk AI system appropriately	x	x	
Article 13(1)	The results of an AI system must be interpretable by users and providers according to the state of the Article Users and providers should understand how the AI system works and know what data is being processed		x	
Article 13(1)	Users and providers must be able to understand and use the system appropriately		x	x
Article 13(3)(b) No. (ii)	The accuracy level of the AI system shall be specified in the instructions for use	x	x	x
Article 13(3)(b) No. iii a)	The instruction manual of an AI system contains information on the degree to which it can provide an explanation for decisions		x	
Article 13(3)(b) No. v)	The user manual of an AI system contains information about the training, validation and test data sets used	x	x	x
Article 14	A human oversight must be enabled to correctly interpret the results of a high-risk AI system. In particular, the characteristics of the system and the existing interpretation tools and methods must be taken into account	x	x	x
Appendix IV No. 2 (b)	Detailed documentation of: System design specifications, in particular general logic of the AI system and algorithms; Main design decisions including rationale and assumptions; Main classification decisions; What is to be optimised by the system and how important each parameter is; Decisions on possible trade-offs in terms of technical solutions to meet requirements in Title III, Chapter 2 (including, for example, Article 13 and 14)	x		x

Table 6 XAI metrics (adapted from Sovrano and Vitali 2023; Sovrano et al. 2022, 2021)

Focus	Metrics and source
Social	*Satisfaction, Trust, Mental Models, Curiosity* (Hoffman et al. 2018)
Socio-technical	*Performance* (Hoffman et al. 2018; Buçinca et al. 2020); *Usability* (Dieber and Kirrane 2022); *Effectiveness* (Sovrano and Vitali 2021; Wang and Yin 2021); *Human-Grounded Benchmark* (Mohseni et al. 2021); *System Causability Scale* (Holzinger et al. 2020)
Technical	*Performance Difference, Number of Rules, Number of Features, Stability* (Rosenfeld 2021); *Fidelity* (Vilone and Longo 2020; Lakkaraju et al. 2017); *Completeness* (Vilone and Longo 2020); *Monotonicity, Non-sensitivity, Effective complexity* (Nguyen and Martínez 2020); *Unambiguity, Interpretability, Interactivity* (Lakkaraju et al. 2017); *Relevance Mass Accuracy, Relevance Rank Accuracy* (Arras et al. 2022); *Proximity, Sparsity, Adequacy* (Keane et al. 2021); *Non-Representativeness, Diversity* (Nguyen and Martínez 2020); *Degree of Explainability* (Sovrano and Vitali 2023)

and Berrada 2018; Miller 2017), it also extends to other terms such as explanation (e.g. Montavon et al. 2018; Gilpin et al. 2018), interpretation (Montavon et al. 2018), transparency (e.g. Lipton 2016; Arrieta et al. 2019), post-high interpretability (Lipton 2016), comprehensibility (Arrieta et al. 2019), completeness (Gilpin et al. 2018) and fidelity (Markus et al. 2021). A much respected (Arrieta et al. 2019; Miller 2017; Waltl and Vogl 2018) taxonomy of conceptualizations is provided by Lipton (2016), who distinguish between *transparency* (how the model works; subdivided into simulatability, decomposability, algorithmic transparency) *and post-hoc interpretability* (descriptive, additional information; distinguished in textual descriptions, visualizations, location explanations and explanation by example).

The AIA does not provide a definition on XAI in its current version. On the part of the Legal Affairs Committee of the European Parliament (AIA-EP), the inclusion of a definition of transparency in the AIA has been proposed, which is based on *traceability* and *explainability*, without defining these terms. From the AIA, the outstanding importance of harmonized standards is evident (Article 40), so that in this paper, in addition to the transparency definition of the AIA-EP, the definitions of Deutsches Institut für Normung e. V. and the German Commission for Electrical, Electronic and Information Technologies in DIN & VDE (DIN & DKE 2022) for explainability, interpretability and transparency are mentioned hereafter, which in turn refer to definitions of the International Organization for Standardization (ISO 2020, 2022) and International Software Testing Qualifications Board (ISTQB 2021). According to DIN & DKE (2022) explainability describes the desired property of an AI system that factors that led to an automated AI decision can be understood by a person. Interpretability is the degree of comprehensibility of the functioning of an underlying AI technology and transparency is the availability of an open, understandable and accessible presentation of information on functional aspects of an AI system—this includes, among other things, the explainability of the AI system, but also the comprehensibility of the data protection concept or information on quality assurance processes during development. The definition by Lipton (2016) on the other hand, offers a more in-depth analysis of the terminology, enables a more differentiated view of XAI and can therefore be used as a supplementary source to gain a more comprehensive understanding of the topic. The concretization of legislation belongs to the European Committee for Standardization (CEN), European Committee for Electrotechnical Standardization (CENELEC) and European Telecommunications Standards Institute (ETSI). Standards of international standardization organizations such as ISO and the International Electrotechnical Commission (IEC) can in principle be adopted if they are in line with European fundamental values and human rights. In the field of AI, CEN and CENELEC work together to review existing international standards, to check their transferability or to develop them themselves (Ebers 2021b; European Commission 2023). The ongoing standardization activities with reference to XAI (DIN & DKE 2022; ETSI 2023; European Commission 2023) are 'Explicability and transparency of AI processing' (DGR/SAI-007), 'Artificial Intelligence—Life Cycle Processes and Quality Requirements—Part 3: Explainability' (DIN SPEC 92,001–3) and 'Information technology—Artificial intelligence—Objectives and approaches for explainability of ML models and AI systems' (ISO/IEC TS 6254).

Regarding *Taxonomies (2)*, we present a concept-matrix of literature based taxonomies. To shed light on XAI, taxonomies of XAI are first examined on the basis of the literature. Taxonomies for XAI already exist, some are subject to a similar logic, but they vary in their expression. Table 2 compares these taxonomies according to their respective expression (as the unit of analysis). In summary, the different XAI taxonomies show that none of the taxonomies cover all the expressions. For this paper it is not necessary to commit to one taxonomy, as they could complement each other.

Intrinsic expression (Table 2) means, AI is directly interpretable due to its transparent nature and *Post-hoc* uses as a tool a method that explains a model after it has been trained (Arya et al. 2019). Post-hoc methods may be applicable only to *specific* AI models or *agnostically* to all AI models (Arrieta et al. 2019). Vilone and Longo (2020) distinguish in their taxonomy between classification and regression based on the underlying *problem type*. *Local* describes an explanation of a single prediction and *global* that the explanation refers to the overall model (Arya et al. 2019). Vilone and Longo (2020) list numeric/categorical, pictorial, textual *input* data and time series and Linardatos et al. (2021) divide *input* data into tables, texts, images and graphs. Islam et al. (2022) distinguish between numbers, rules, text and visualization, while Arrieta et al. (2019) and Arya et al. (2019) distinguish between table, picture and text as *results*. *Static* means, that the explanation remains unchanging and does not respond to user feedback, while *interactive* allows the user to receive different types of explanations through an exchange of information and questions until the user is satisfied (Arya et al. 2019). *Data versus model* means, the explanation refers to the data or to the model (Arya et al. 2019). *Surrogate* describes a second, simpler model that approximates a more complex model and *visualization* enables interpretation by visualizing the explanation or parts of it (Arya et al. 2019). The analysis in Table 2 shows, that the expressions problem type, static versus interactive, data vs. model and surrogate vs. visualization are less frequently taken into account in the literature.

The *Requirements (3)* for XAI from a legal perspective are explained hereafter. In April 2021, the EC proposed the AIA, which is designed to regulate AI in the future. In order to speed up the legislative process, the Council presented its general approach to the EP in December 2022 and thus communicated its position on AIA to the EP (AIA-Council). The EP is currently still in its first reading (EUR-Lex 2023). The responsible committees have already submitted various opinions, but a common position has not yet been voted on (EUR-Lex 2023; Zenner 2022). The opinion of the Legal Affairs Committee of the EP has already been published (AIA-EP). In the ordinary legislative procedure, there is ultimately a law agreed between the Council and the EP. The EC can exert influence through opinions after its proposal (European Parliament 2021).

The AIA takes a risk-based approach, distinguishing between AI systems that pose an unacceptable, high, moderate or minimal risk. While the former AI systems are prohibited, so-called high-risk AI systems are subject to extensive requirements, e.g. with regard to technical documentation, data quality, recording and storage obligations or transparency and explainability requirements (Ebers 2021a). Ebers (2021a), Hacker and Passoth (2020) and Sovrano et al. (2022) each examine the AIA with regard to transparency and XAI requirements. Table 3 shows which legal passages they deal with in each case, whereby Article 13 AIA has been identified as the core of the AI explainability requirements, which is why the focus of our paper is on this article. Hacker and Passoth (2020) note that in the various articles explainability serves different goals, namely enabling action (Article 13 II, Article 52 AIA), technical performance (Article 13 III lit. b AIA), protection against risks (Article 13 III lit. b AIA) and conformity with law (Article 13 I AIA). The transparency requirement from Article 52 AIA aims in particular to ensure that persons are informed, even in the case of moderate-risk systems, that they are dealing with an AI system or that the content presented has been artificially generated. This type of transparency will not be considered in the further course, as it is not transparency in the sense of the definition set of this literature review. The recital 61 AIA underlines the key role of standards for compliance. Compliance with harmonized standards should at the same time enable proof of compliance with the requirements. In addition, technical specifications are conceivable in the areas for which no standards exist.

Article 13 (1) AIA is of central importance with regard to explainability: "High-risk AI systems shall be designed and developed in such a way to ensure that their operation is sufficiently transparent to enable users to interpret the system's output and use it appropriately. An appropriate type and degree of transparency shall be ensured, with a view to achieving compliance with the relevant obligations of the user and of the provider set out in Chapter 3 of this Title." (Article 13 (1) AIA). Hacker and Passoth (2020) state with regard to the required transparency that Article 13 AIA does not require a global explainability of an AI system and that the transparency requirement primarily serves to ensure compliance with the law of the AIA itself. In sum, the AIA would offer a range of specifications for technical transparency, but would not provide for any meaningful explanations for the persons affected by AI decisions (Hacker and Passoth 2020). Ebers (2021a) agrees with this criticism. The requirements of Article 13 AIA are a step in the right direction in terms of explainability, but do not provide individual rights. Moreover, these are not further specified in the AIA but remain formulated in general terms. How AI becomes explainable would be left to the provider of the AI (Ebers 2021a). Sovrano et al. (2022) see the AI explainability requirements from the AIA as pursuing two goals: Firstly, to enable users to use AI correctly and secondly, to comply with the legal requirements from the AIA itself. What Sovrano et al. (2022), Ebers (2021a) and Hacker and Passoth (2020) have in common is that they only refer to the AIA, but not to the AIA-Council and AIA-EP, which is carried out by the present paper in the segment of analysis (4).

In addition, there are already further legal requirements for explainability. A central role is played by the General Data Protection Regulation (GDPR), which introduces transparency obligations in the context of personal data. For example, the information required by Articles 13, 14 of the GDPR must be provided to the data subject in a precise, transparent, comprehensible and easily accessible form and in clear and simple language in accordance with Article 12 of the GDPR (Kaulartz and Braegelmann 2020). In the case of an automated decision permitted under Article 22 (1), (4) of the GDPR, the data subject must also be provided with meaningful information about the logic involved, among other things, in accordance with Article 15 (1) (h) of the GDPR (Hacker and Passoth 2020). However, even beyond the GDPR, there are legal requirements that do not specifically relate to AI, but from which the need for explainability may already arise, for example in subject areas such as product liability or contract law (Hacker and Passoth 2020). Especially in the area of criminal proceedings, constitutional principles may also be relevant, for example with regard to the rule of law's obligations to give reasons, the right to a fair trial, the principle of democracy or effective legal protection (Kaulartz and Braegelmann 2020).

The *Analysis (4)* is based on the methodology described in Sect. 2, on the previously mentioned literature (Hacker and Passoth 2020; Ebers 2021a; Sovrano et al. 2022) in Table 3 and on the AIA, AIA-EP, AIA-Council documents. As a result, we present our analytical results in Table 4 and a concept matrix of AIA explainability requirements in Table 5. Table 5 summarizes the AI explainability requirements based on the passages with XAI reference. Only those were taken into account that refer directly or indirectly to the explainability of the AI system or its results. Similar requirements mentioned in more than one document are merged while different descriptions of the requirements are presented individually. It can be seen that the EP in particular proposes further elaboration on explainability. The EP requires both: the AI system must be understandable, and the AI result must be interpretable for the user. The definition of transparency is also new. The Council proposes a loosening by replacing the interpretation of the AI result with an understanding of the AI system in Article 13 (1) AIA-Council. Overall, it could be identified that all three organizations (EC, EP, Council) stick to the explainability, in the sense that there is no significant tightening or loosening of the explainability, and partly only changes in the phrasing. The requirements in the AIA will remain abstract and details will be regulated in specific standards.

Regarding *Metrics and Synthesis (5),* Adadi and Berrada (2018) show in their XAI study that only 5% of the scientific papers examined evaluate interpretability. Regarding legal requirements for explainability, the question arises how it can be determined whether these requirements are met. In the following, an overview of the terminology and taxonomy of metrics will be provided. Based on this, various XAI metrics are presented and classified. In ML, metrics are used to evaluate and compare the performance of a model. Metrics such as recall, which is the ratio of correctly identified positive cases to all actual positive cases, are used for this purpose (Erickson and Kitamura 2021). In the context of XAI, according to Sovrano et al. (2022), metrics are used to quantitatively assess the quality of explainability in ML. The terms 'assess' and 'evaluate' are used synonymously. In the context of this paper the terms are used as follows: In order to be able to quantitatively assess or evaluate the quality of explainability, this is measured by means of metrics. In the research field of XAI metrics, initial taxonomies have already been established. Doshi-Velez and Kim (2017) distinguish between application-, people- and function-related evaluation. Zhou et al. (2021) take up this division and assign an explanatory type (model-based, attribution-based, example-based) and explanatory properties to a series of quantitative metrics. Sovrano and Vitali (2023) summarize the dimensions of these taxonomies and come to a total of seven dimensions: evaluation type (quantitative or qualitative), model specificity (model-agnostic), supported media (textual information, images), supported format (case-based explanation, rule-based), information format (natural language, rule-based, others), supporting theory (e.g. cognitive science), subject-based (human evaluation) and measured criteria (carnap's criteria of adequacy).

Sovrano and Vitali (2023) and Sovrano et al. (2021, 2022) also provide an overview of different XAI metrics. Based on these metrics from the literature (Sovrano and Vitali 2023; Sovrano et al. 2022, 2021), the information systems (IS) research focus of this paper, and the fact that the AIA will remain abstract, we have classified the metrics for measuring the explainability of AI into three focus systems: Social systems (human focus), social-technical systems (focus on human-technology interaction) and technical systems (focus on AI technology) (Table 6). The different systems are considered as a focus in which a predominant proportion of either social, socio-technical or technical system components of the metrics is given. In addition to the socio-technical perspective, a quality-related service perspective (Walke and Winkler 2022; Walke et al. 2023) on metrics could also be conceivable for future classifications. XAI metrics (Table 6) could be used for measuring AI explainability requirements compliance. The social focus system addresses the question, if an AI system explains how it works, how do we know whether the explanation works and the user has achieved a pragmatic understanding of the AI (Hoffman et al. 2018)? The users' satisfaction with the explanation provided, or trust, mental models and curiosity can be suitable social XAI metrics. The socio-technical focus system addresses the bridge between the user and the technical AI system or XAI tool itself. A prominent possible XAI metric is usability (Dieber and Kirrane 2022), which can be understood as the outcome of use of an AI system or XAI tool, meaning the interaction between humans and technology. The technical focus system describes pure technical XAI metrics. Technical XAI metrics are, among others, the performance difference between the agent's model (black box) and the performance of the logic presented as an explanation (best observed transparent model), the quantified number of rules in the agent's explanation (agent's output), the number of features used to construct the explanation (e.g. image processing focuses on pixels, but for example edges are inherently more interpretability), or the stability of the agent's explanation (ability to robustly handle small noise perturbations) (Rosenfeld 2021).

4 Discussion and Conclusion

In this paper, we investigated which requirements the AIA places on XAI and which metrics could be used to measure compliance. The requirements presented in the analysis of the literature in Table 5 in Sect. 3 are diverse and affect both users and providers. Depending on the final regulation text, global explainability or both global and local explainability will remain a requirement. The instructions for use must include detailed information on how the system works and the data sets used to ensure appropriate interpretation of the results. In addition, human supervision is required to interpret the results correctly. Documenting design specifications and decisions is an important step in ensuring the transparency and comprehensibility of AI systems. It can be seen that the requirements are partly specific, partly abstract. On the one hand, it is specified that the degree of accuracy of the AI system must be stated in the instructions manual, and on the other hand that the result must be interpretable, without defining interpretability separately, which can lead, in conjunction with the large number of definitions of interpretability, to legal uncertainty.

In summary, it can be said that the AIA regulates explainability requirements in a binding manner, as the EP, the Council and the EC agree. According to the analyzed legal texts of the EP and the Council, explainability will be regulated with no significant changes, so the requirement of explainability will remain. The EP, in particular, has expanded its explanations on explainability. The requirements from the AIA listed by Ebers (2021a), Hacker and Passoth (2020) and Sovrano et al. (2022) could be confirmed overall. In addition, further insights were gained through the analysis of the AIA-Council and AIA-EP, i.a. with further explanations of the EP, more clarity is provided on explainability. Regarding the first research question (RQ1), which requirements for XAI are envisaged by the AIA, could thus be answered by confirming the AI explainability requirements from the literature and extending the requirements after analyzing the legal texts.

In all likelihood, however, the requirements in the AIA will remain abstract, while the details will be regulated in specific standards. In this respect, the metrics listed in the literature (Table 6) cannot be narrowed down in such a way that metric A or B reliably fulfils the AI explainability requirement C. In this light, a selection of concrete metrics for specific legal requirements cannot be made, but the proposed socio-technical metric classification could be used as an orientation for future compliance measurements. The second research question (RQ2), which metrics could be used to measure AI explainability requirements compliance, could therefore only be answered to the extent that a metrics-based compliance measurement of legal requirements of XAI must await concrete standards and cannot be based solely on proposals of the EC, EP or the Council. Nevertheless, focus areas in relation to social, socio-technical and technical system components could already be collected to enable future measurements.

This paper shows that explainability will remain an important part of regulation even after the trilogue negotiations, so organizations can already prepare for appropriate action. A preparatory action could be to consider explainability in the development and select appropriate metrics from the paper's catalog. As a research agenda can be stated: After the final AIA publication and concretization through harmonized standards, further research should be carried out, comparable to the present paper in a timely manner, to analyze the practicability of the defined AI explainability requirements. With a timely analysis, digital responsibility with regard to social, ethical and environmental aspects of AI can be taken into account and possible risks and dangers arising from AI can be counteracted. An important result of this paper is, that the AIA basically prescribes XAI, but remains abstract. A future AIA, associated guidelines and harmonized standards are the basic prerequisite for putting XAI and any metrics into practice.

References

Adadi, A. and Berrada, M. (2018), "Peeking Inside the Black-Box: A Survey on Explainable Artificial Intelligence (XAI)", *IEEE Access*, Vol. 6, pp. 52138–52160.

AI HLEG (2018), *Eine Definition der KI: Wichtigste Fähigkeiten und Wissenschaftsgebiete.*, available at: https://www.bundesnetzagentur.de/DE/Fachthemen/Digitalisierung/Mittelstand/Downloads/Experten.pdf;jsessionid=A9275C1BF8EE50C73591799288D66689?__blob=publicationFile&v=2 (accessed 4 January 2023).

Arras, L., Osman, A. and Samek, W. (2022), "CLEVR-XAI: A benchmark dataset for the ground truth evaluation of neural network explanations", *Information Fusion*, Vol. 81, pp. 14–40.

Arrieta, A.B., Díaz-Rodríguez, N., Del Ser, J., Bennetot, A., Tabik, S., Barbado, A., García, S., Gil-López, S., Molina, D., Benjamins, R., Chatila, R. and Herrera, F. (2019), *Explainable Artificial Intelligence (XAI): Concepts, Taxonomies, Opportunities and Challenges toward Responsible AI*.

Arya, V., Bellamy, R.K.E., Chen, P.-Y., Dhurandhar, A., Hind, M., Hoffman, S.C., Houde, S., Liao, Q.V., Luss, R., Mojsilović, A., Mourad, S., Pedemonte, P., Raghavendra, R., Richards, J., Sattigeri, P., Shanmugam, K., Singh, M., Varshney, K.R., Wei, D. and Zhang, Y. (2019), *One Explanation Does Not Fit All: A Toolkit and Taxonomy of AI Explainability Techniques*.

Buçinca, Z., Lin, P., Gajos, K.Z. and Glassman, E.L. (2020), "Proxy tasks and subjective measures can be misleading in evaluating explainable AI systems", in Paternò, F., Oliver, N., Conati, C., Spano, L.D. and Tintarev, N. (Eds.), *Proceedings of the 25th International Conference on Intelligent User Interfaces, 17 03 2020 20 03 2020, Cagliari Italy*, ACM, New York, NY, USA, pp. 454–464.

Buxmann, P. and Schmidt, H. (2019), *Künstliche Intelligenz*, Springer Gabler, Berlin, Heidelberg.

Cooper, H.M. (1988), "Organizing knowledge syntheses: A taxonomy of literature reviews", *Knowledge in Society*, Vol. 1 No. 1, pp. 104–126.

Dieber, J. and Kirrane, S. (2022), "A novel model usability evaluation framework (MUsE) for explainable artificial intelligence", *Information Fusion*, Vol. 81, pp. 143–153.

DIN & DKE (2022), *Deutsche Normungsroadmap Künstliche Intelligenz. Ausgabe 2.*, available at: https://www.dke.de/resource/blob/2008010/776dd87a4b9ec18d4ab295025ccbb722/nr-ki-deutsch---download-data.pdf (accessed 6 March 2022).

Doshi-Velez, F. and Kim, B. (2017), *Towards A Rigorous Science of Interpretable Machine Learning.*

Ebers, M. (2021a), "Regulating Explainable AI in the European Union. An Overview of the Current Legal Framework(s)", *SSRN Electronic Journal.*

Ebers, M. (2021b), "Standardisierung Künstlicher Intelligenz und KI-Verordnungsvorschlag", *Recht Digital*, pp. 588–597.

Erickson, B.J. and Kitamura, F. (2021), "Magician's Corner: 9. Performance Metrics for Machine Learning Models", *Radiology. Artificial intelligence*, Vol. 3 No. 3, e200126.

ETSI (2023), *Explicability and transparency of AI processing. Details of 'DGR/SAI-007' Work Item.*, available at: https://portal.etsi.org/webapp/WorkProgram/Report_WorkItem.asp?WKI_ID=63078 (accessed 12 February 2023).

EUR-Lex (2023), *Verfahren 2021/0106/COD*, available at: https://eur-lex.europa.eu/legal-content/DE/HIS/?sortOrder=asc&uri=CELEX%3A52021PC0206 (accessed 4 February 2023).

European Commission (2018), *Künstliche Intelligenz für Europa*, available at: https://eur-lex.europa.eu/legal-content/DE/TXT/?uri=CELEX:52018DC0237 (accessed 28 October 2023).

European Commission (2019), *Mitteilung der Kommission an das Europäische Parlament, den Rat, den Europäischen Wirtschafts- und Sozialausschuss und den Ausschuss der Regionen Schaffung von Vertrauen in eine auf den Menschen ausgerichtete künstliche Intelligenz.*, available at: https://eur-lex.europa.eu/legal-content/DE/TXT/?uri=CELEX:52019DC0168 (accessed 29 October 2022).

European Commission (2021), *Proposal for a regulation of the European Parliament and of the Council laying down harmonised rules on artificial intelligence (Artificial Intelligence Act) and amending certain union legislative acts.*, available at: https://eur-lex.europa.eu/legal-content/DE/TXT/?uri=CELEX:52019DC0168 (accessed 29 October 2022).

European Commission (2023), *Rolling Plan for ICT standardization. Artificial Intelligence.*, available at: https://joinup.ec.europa.eu/collection/rolling-plan-ict-standardisation/artificial-intelligence-0 (accessed 12 February 2023).

European Council (2022a), *Gesetz über künstliche Intelligenz: Rat will sichere und die Grundrechte wahrende KI fördern.*, available at: https://www.consilium.europa.eu/de/press/press-releases/2022/12/06/artificial-intelligence-act-council-calls-for-promoting-safe-ai-that-respects-fundamental-rights/ (accessed 4 January 2023).

European Council (2022b), *Vorschlag für eine Verordnung des Europäischen Parlaments und des Rates zur Festlegung harmonisierter Vorschriften für künstliche Intelligenz (Gesetz über künstliche Intelligenz) und zur Änderung bestimmter Rechtsakte der Union—Allgemeine Ausrichtung.*, available at: https://data.consilium.europa.eu/doc/document/ST-14954-2022-INIT/de/pdf (accessed 4 January 2023).

European Parliament (2021), *Ordentliches Gesetzgebungsverfahren.*, available at: https://www.europarl.europa.eu/germany/de/europ%C3%A4isches-parlament/ordentliches-gesetzgebungsverfahren#shadowbox/1/ (accessed 5 February 2023).

European Parliament (2022), *Opinion of the Committee on Legal Affairs for the Committee on the Internal Market and Consumer Protection and theCommittee on Civil Liber-ties, Justice and Home Affairs on the proposal for a regulation of the Eu-ropean Parliament and of the Council laying down harmonised rules on ar-tificial intelligence (Artificial Intelligence Act) and amending certain Union Legislative Acts (COM(2021)0206—C9-0146/2021—2021/0106(COD))*, available at: https://www.europarl.europa.eu/doceo/document/JURI-AD-719827_EN.pdf (accessed 5 February 2023).

German Federal Government (2020), *Strategie Künstliche Intelligenz der Bundesregierung. Fortschreibung 2020.*, available at: https://www.ki-strategie-deutschland.de/files/downloads/201201_Fortschreibung_KI-Strategie.pdf (accessed 28 October 2022).

Gilpin, L.H., Bau, D., Yuan, B.Z., Bajwa, A., Specter, M. and Kagal, L. (2018), *Explaining Explanations: An Overview of Interpretability of Machine Learning.*

Hacker, P. and Passoth, J.-H. (2020), "Varieties of AI explanations under the law. From the GDPR to the AIA, and beyond.", in Holzinger, A., Goebel, R., Fong, R., Moon, T., Müller, K.-R. and Samek, W. (Eds.), *xxAI - Beyond Explainable AI*, Springer International Publishing.

Hoffman, R.R., Mueller, S.T., Klein, G. and Litman, J. (2018), *Metrics for Explainable AI: Challenges and Prospects.*

Holzinger, A., Carrington, A. and Müller, H. (2020), "Measuring the Quality of Explanations: The System Causability Scale (SCS): Comparing Human and Machine Explanations", *Kunstliche intelligenz*, Vol. 34 No. 2, pp. 193–198.

Islam, M.R., Ahmed, M.U., Barua, S. and Begum, S. (2022), "A Systematic Review of Explainable Artificial Intelligence in Terms of Different Application Domains and Tasks", *Applied Sciences*, Vol. 12 No. 3, p. 1353.

ISO (2020), *ISO/IEC TR 29119–11:2020 Software and systems engineering - Software testing - Part 11: Guidelines on the testing of AI-based systems.*

ISO (2022), *ISO/IEC 22989:2022 Information technology - Artificial intelligence - Artificial intelligence concepts and terminology.*

ISTQB (2021), *Certified Tester AI Testing (CT-AI) Syllabus. Version 1.0.*, available at: https://www.german-testing-board.info/wp-content/uploads/2021/10/ISTQB_CT-AI_Syllabus_v1.0.pdf (accessed 6 March 2023).

Kaulartz, M. and Braegelmann, T. (Eds.) (2020), *Rechtshandbuch Artificial Intelligence und Machine Learning*, C.H. Beck; Vahlen, München.

Keane, M.T., Kenny, E.M., Delaney, E. and Smyth, B. (2021), "If Only We Had Better Counterfactual Explanations: Five Key Deficits to Rectify in the Evaluation of Counterfactual XAI Techniques".

Lakkaraju, H., Kamar, E., Caruana, R. and Leskovec, J. (2017), *Interpretable & Explorable Approximations of Black Box Models.*

Linardatos, P., Papastefanopoulos, V. and Kotsiantis, S. (2021), "Explainable AI: A Review of Machine Learning Interpretability Methods", *Entropy*, Vol. 23 No. 1, p. 18.

Lipton, Z.C. (2016), *The Mythos of Model Interpretability.*

Markus, A.F., Kors, J.A. and Rijnbeek, P.R. (2021), "The role of explainability in creating trustworthy artificial intelligence for health care: A comprehensive survey of the terminology, design choices, and evaluation strategies", *Journal of Biomedical Informatics*, Vol. 113, p. 103655.

Mayring, P. (2022), *Qualitative Inhaltsanalyse: Grundlagen und Techniken,* 13., überarbeitete Auflage, Beltz, Weinheim, Basel.

Miller, T. (2017), *Explanation in Artificial Intelligence: Insights from the Social Sciences.*

Mohseni, S., Block, J.E. and Ragan, E. (2021), "Quantitative Evaluation of Machine Learning Explanations: A Human-Grounded Benchmark", in Hammond, T., Verbert, K., Parra, D., Knijnenburg, B., O'Donovan, J. and Teale, P. (Eds.), *26th International Conference on Intelligent User Interfaces, 14 04 2021 17 04 2021, College Station TX USA*, ACM, New York, NY, USA, pp. 22–31.

Montavon, G., Samek, W. and Müller, K.-R. (2018), "Methods for interpreting and understanding deep neural networks", *Digital Signal Processing*, Vol. 73, pp. 1–15.

Mukhamediev, R.I., Popova, Y., Kuchin, Y., Zaitseva, E., Kalimoldayev, A., Symagulov, A., Levashenko, V., Abdoldina, F., Gopejenko, V., Yakunin, K., Muhamedijeva, E. and Yelis, M. (2022), "Review of Artificial Intelligence and Machine Learning Technologies: Classification, Restrictions, Opportunities and Challenges", *Mathematics*, Vol. 10 No. 15, p. 2552.

Nguyen, A. and Martínez, M.R. (2020), *On quantitative aspects of model interpretability.*

Rosenfeld, A. (2021), "Better Metrics for Evaluating Explainable Artificial Intelligence: Blue Sky Ideas Track".

Salipante, P., Notz, W. and Bigelow, J. (1982), "A Matrix Approach to Literature Reviews.", *Research in Organizational Behavior*, Vol. 4, pp. 321–348.

Schaaf, N., Wiedenroth, S.J. and Wagner, P. (2021), *Erklärbare KI in der Praxis.*

Sovrano, F., Sapienza, S., Palmirani, M. and Vitali, F. (2021), "A Survey on Methods and Metrics for the Assessment of Explainability Under the Proposed AI Act", 8–10 December, Vilnius, Lithuania.

Sovrano, F., Sapienza, S., Palmirani, M. and Vitali, F. (2022), "Metrics, Explainability and the European AI Act Proposal", *J*, Vol. 5 No. 1, pp. 126–138.

Sovrano, F. and Vitali, F. (2021), "From Philosophy to Interfaces: an Explanatory Method and a Tool Inspired by Achinstein's Theory of Explanation", in Hammond, T., Verbert, K., Parra, D., Knijnenburg, B., O'Donovan, J. and Teale, P. (Eds.), *26th International Conference on Intelligent User Interfaces, 14 04 2021 17 04 2021, College Station TX USA*, ACM, New York, NY, USA, pp. 81–91.

Sovrano, F. and Vitali, F. (2023), *An Objective Metric for Explainable AI: How and Why to Estimate the Degree of Explainability.*

Vilone, G. and Longo, L. (2020), *Explainable Artificial Intelligence: a Systematic Review.*

vom Brocke, J., Simons, A., Niehaves, B., Niehaves, B., Reimer, K., Plattfaut, R. and Cleven, A. (2009), "Reconstructing the giant: On the importance of rigour in documenting the literature search process", available at: https://aisel.aisnet.org/ecis2009/161.

vom Brocke, J., Simons, A., Riemer, K., Niehaves, B., Plattfaut, R. and Cleven, A. (2015), "Standing on the Shoulders of Giants: Challenges and Recommendations of Literature Search in Information Systems Research", *Communications of the Association for Information Systems*, Vol. 37.

Walke, F. and Winkler, T.J. (2022), "The TIHP Framework—An Instrument for Measuring Quality of Hybrid Services".

Walke, F., Winkler, T.J. and Le, M. (2023), "Success of Digital Identity Infrastructure: A Grounded Model of eID Evolution Success.", *Proceedings of the 56th Hawaii International Conference on System Sciences*, Vol. 56.

Waltl, B. and Vogl, R. (2018), "Explainable Artificial Intelligence. The new frontier in legal informatics", 22.02.2018.

Wang, X. and Yin, M. (2021), "Are Explanations Helpful? A Comparative Study of the Effects of Explanations in AI-Assisted Decision-Making", in Hammond, T., Verbert, K., Parra, D., Knijnenburg, B., O'Donovan, J. and Teale, P. (Eds.), *26th International Conference on Intelligent User Interfaces, 14 04 2021 17 04 2021, College Station TX USA*, ACM, New York, NY, USA, pp. 318–328.

Webster, J. and Watson, R.T. (2002), "Analyzing the Past to Prepare For the Future: Writing a Literature Review", *MIS Quarterly*, Vol. 26 No. 2.

Zenner, K. (2022), "Digitizing Europe. Documents and Timelines: The Artificial Intelligence Act (part 3).".

Zhou, J., Gandomi, A.H., Chen, F. and Holzinger, A. (2021), "Evaluating the Quality of Machine Learning Explanations: A Survey on Methods and Metrics", *Electronics*, Vol. 10 No. 5, p. 593.

Improving the Efficiency of Human-in-the-Loop Systems: Adding Artificial to Human Experts

Johannes Jakubik, Daniel Weber, Patrick Hemmer, Michael Vössing, and Gerhard Satzger

Abstract Information systems increasingly leverage artificial intelligence (AI) and machine learning (ML) to generate value from vast amounts of data. However, ML models are imperfect and can generate incorrect classifications. Hence, human- in-the-loop (HITL) extensions to ML models add a human review for instances that are difficult to classify. This study argues that continuously relying on human experts to handle difficult model classifications leads to a strong increase in human effort, which strains limited resources. To address this issue, we propose a hybrid system that creates artificial experts that learn to classify data instances from unknown classes previously reviewed by human experts. Our hybrid system assesses which artificial expert is suitable for classifying an instance from an unknown class and automatically assigns it. Over time, this reduces human effort and increases the efficiency of the system. Our experiments demonstrate that our approach outperforms traditional HITL systems for several benchmarks on image classification.

Keywords Human-in-the-loop systems · Artificial experts · Human-AI collaboration · Unknown data

---

J. Jakubik (✉) · D. Weber · P. Hemmer · M. Vössing · G. Satzger
Karlsruhe Institute of Technology, Karlsruhe, Germany
e-mail: johannes.jakubik@kit.edu

D. Weber
e-mail: daniel.weber@kit.edu

P. Hemmer
e-mail: patrick.hemmer@kit.edu

M. Vössing
e-mail: michael.voessing@kit.edu

G. Satzger
e-mail: gerhard.satzger@kit.edu

D. Beverungen et al. (eds.), *Solutions and Technologies for Responsible Digitalization*, Lecture Notes in Information Systems and Organisation 75,
https://doi.org/10.1007/978-3-031-80122-8_9

1 Introduction

AI-based information systems have become increasingly prevalent and powerful over the last decade (e.g., Berente et al. 2021). Yet, predictions (i.e., classification) of the incorporated machine learning (ML) models are subject to uncertainty and may be incorrect. As a result, human experts are often tasked with reviewing the predictions of these models to identify and override errors (Dellermann et al. 2019a; Grønsund and Aanestad 2020, Jakubik et al. 2022). In these so-called human-in- the-loop (HITL) systems, a model might classify the majority of instances automatically. However, instances that are difficult for the model are assigned to a human expert for manual review. This concept makes HITL systems a viable means for human-AI collaboration and has promoted their applications in domains such as medicine (Bodén et al. 2021; Cai et al. 2019) and manufacturing (Cimini et al. 2020). However, these systems typically still require a significant amount of human effort (Agnisarman et al. 2019).

In HITL systems, detecting data from unknown classes to forward them to a human expert is essential to guarantee high levels of accuracy—especially in high-stake decision- making like the medical domain, finance, or autonomous driving (Sanchez et al. 2022).

For example, when a model encounters an image of an "unfamiliar" traffic sign, it should treat it as unknown rather than attempting to match it to an existing class. However, this approach requires human experts to "build" knowledge regarding the novel class the instance belongs to. To address this issue and to reduce the required human effort, an approach is required that can incrementally learn from unknown data (Keswani et al. 2022).

In this work, we aim to improve the efficiency of HITL systems. We train additional ML models—called *artificial experts*—that mimic the human expert's knowledge regarding classes that are unknown to the general ML model (i.e., the model trained to solve the task). Our so-called *AI-in-the-Loop* (AIITL) system creates (i.e., trains) multiple artificial experts based on the knowledge incrementally acquired from human expert in traditional HITL systems. The AIITL system then allocates instances that are recognized as unknown to suitable artificial experts. To achieve this, we reinterpret out-of-distribution (OOD) detectors as an allocation mechanism.

Each artificial expert is responsible for a separate set of classes unknown to the general model and uses an OOD detector to independently "claim" instances for classification that it considers to stem from one of the classes in their respective set. Data instances that the OOD detector deems to originate from an unknown class are rejected by the individual artificial expert. The human expert is only consulted when none or multiple artificial experts claim an instance for "their" set of classes. The human expert then provides his or her knowledge by assigning the instance to the correct artificial expert or instantiates a new one responsible for the novel class. The overall objective of the system is to reduce human effort while maintaining classification accuracy. Following Bansal et al. (2021), we optimize a utility metric represented by the combination of classification accuracy and human effort.

Overall, our contributions are as follows. First, we propose a novel technique for capturing human expert knowledge about unknown data instances and make it accessible by "creating" artificial experts. Second, we show that our approach outperforms traditional HITL systems by a large margin in terms of their utility—the combination of classification accuracy and human effort. Third, we reinterpret OOD detectors as allocation mechanisms for the collaboration of artificial and human experts—allowing for a coordination between artificial experts as ML models that can "claim" unknown instances. We provide our code at https://github.com/jhnnsjkbk/AIITL.

2 Background and Related Work

In the following, we review related work on HITL systems, the detection of data from unknown classes, and incremental learning.

2.1 Human-In-The-Loop Systems

AI-based systems including a "human-in-the-loop" enable a machine learning model to consult a human expert for instances that are difficult to classify (Dellermann et al. 2019a, b; Grønsund and Aanestad 2020; Jakubik et al. 2022). For example, in the medical domain, it is essential that machine learning models forward.

x-ray images that are difficult to classify (i.e., the model is uncertain about the prediction) to physicians for manual inspection. In the literature, several setups exist in which human experts augment and complement ML models: HITL systems are employed in supervised learning (e.g., Wang et al. 2016, Kamar 2016, Wu et al. 2021a, b), semi-supervised learning (e.g., Wrede and Hellander 2019, Weber et al. 2021), and reinforcement learning (e.g., Wu et al. 2022, Liu et al. 2019, Liang et al. 2017, Elmalaki 2021). However, these approaches generally require repetitive human effort that is growing with the number of unknown instances and the inaccuracy in detecting such instances. The resulting strain placed on human resources often renders HITL systems inefficient (see Agnisarman et al. 2019). Therefore, any approach that can reduce human effort required in these systems is highly desirable.

A literature search identified two recent works pursuing this objective, however with slightly different approaches: First, Keswani et al. (2022) consider a HITL system where the classifier is incrementally re-trained on novel, unseen data. For this re-training, the ML model acquires human expert knowledge for instances with low model confidence. Thus, the overall goal is to incrementally mimic several human experts with a *single ML model* in order to reduce subsequent effort. In contrast, we propose various separate artificial experts that individually learn to classify instances from specific domains and collaboratively classify novel instances in order to reduce human effort. Unlike the approach of Keswani et al. (2022), our technique does not require to train an additional deferral model for the collaboration of multiple agents in the system. Second, Wu et al. (2021a) have recently proposed the collaboration between two ML models in an HITL system. Their approach defers instances to human experts based on the alignment of these ML models as part of a multi-model collaboration. However, their work is specifically tailored to document layout analysis, while we propose a system to reduce the effort in HITL systems in general.

2.2 Detection of Data Instances from Unknown Classes

In our work, we make use of out-of-distribution detectors from the field of computer science and reinterpret them as allocation mechanisms. These OOD detectors allow to determine whether a data instance originates from an unknown class. The differentiation of known and unknown data is achieved based on whether unknown data originates from the same underlying distribution as known data or not. For example, everyday images of cars follow the same (or very similar distribution) but these images follow a different distribution than x-ray images from the medical domain. This approach can also be applied to distinguish more similar classes. In our case, we will consider classes from one dataset to be known, while classes from a range of other datasets are unknown and incrementally learned over time. In general, OOD detection aims at identifying data from unknown distributions (Liang et al. 2018, Lee et al. 2018, Hsu et al. 2020, Liu et al. 2020a, b, c)). Among the most widespread approaches for OOD detection are *ODIN* (Liang et al. 2018) and *Mahalanobis-based OOD* detection (Lee et al. 2018). These two approaches are popular benchmarks utilized in recent studies (Hsu et al. 2020, Liu et al. 2020a, b, c, Mohseni et al. 2020). In the context of HITL systems, OOD detection is typically considered during the training in active.

learning and few-shot learning (Han et al. 2021; Liu et al. 2020a, b, c; Wan et al. 2021) or for explainability (Bansal et al. 2018). Importantly, current literature finds a lack of handling detected unknown data in general (Geng et al. 2021). We later address this by using OOD detectors as allocation mechanisms and by processing detected data from unknown classes within our AIITL system.

2.3 Incremental Learning

Deep neural networks face severe difficulties when learning from evolving streams of training data. This phenomenon is often referred to as *catastrophic forgetting* (Mittal et al. 2021; Li & Hoiem 2017; Rebuffi et al. 2017) as—while adapting to the new classes— the performance of the ML model on the original classes deteriorates. That means the accuracy of ML models drops strongly, when the model is incrementally trained on new data. In the context of reducing human effort in

HITL systems, this implies that we cannot simply fine-tune our model incrementally based on acquired human expert knowledge without facing catastrophic forgetting. Retraining the model on the entire set of known and unknown data each time unknown instances emerge would result in high computational cost and, thus, does not represent a suitable alternative either.

To tackle catastrophic forgetting, class-incremental learning aims at making models more robust against new data that becomes available over time. Researchers have pro- posed approaches such as exemplar selection (e.g., Castro et al. 2018, Hou et al. 2019, Wu et al. 2019, Iscen et al. 2020, Liu et al. 2020c), forgetting-constraint (e.g., Li and Hoiem 2017, Rebuffi et al. 2017, Hou et al. 2019, Yu et al. 2020), and bias removal methods (e.g., Hou et al. 2019, Wu et al. 2019, Zhao et al. 2020). One of the most popular approaches in incremental learning is Deep Model Consolidation (Zhang et al. 2020). The approach consists of a general model for old (i. e., known) data and a separate model that is responsible for the new classes. We later follow a similar idea by generating separate models for novel data from unknown classes to reduce the human effort in HITL systems.

3 Methodology

The task of the AIITL system is to classify data from both known and unknown classes. We train a *general* model on data from the known classes. Unknown data originates from a set of unknown classes. The classification of an instance is then either conducted by the general model, one of *n* artificial experts, or a human expert. Our objective is to improve the utility of the system that is influenced by the level of human effort and the overall classification accuracy. The hybrid system is detailed in Fig. 1 and will be explained in the following.

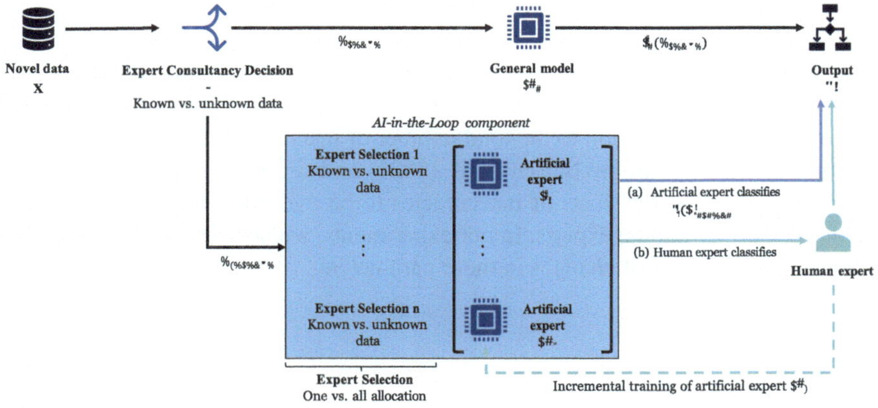

Fig. 1 Illustration of the AIITL system with artificial experts to support the human expert of a Human-in-the-Loop system

3.1 Notation

The objective of the AIITL system is to reduce repetitive manual reviewing effort of human experts. For this, artificial experts need to mimic human experts on data instances that are unknown for the general model. In line with our research questions, we developed a system of human and artificial experts that aid a general ML model in classifying images. For this, we design artificial experts as an optional support that actively try to classify instances—and only forward instances to a human expert that both the general model and none of the artificial experts could classify. We formalize our approach in the following. Let $\mathrm{X} \in \mathbb{R}^N$ and $\mathrm{Y} \in \mathbb{N}$ denote the input and target space of the AIITL system. The input space consists of the images that need to be classified by our system, while the target space refers to the classification outcomes for each of the input images. In our approach, we refer to known data by $\mathbf{X}_{known}$ and define data from unknown classes as $\mathbf{X}_{unknown}$. The overall task of the AIITL system is to provide a set of classifications $\mathbf{y}\hat{}$ for the input data instances carried out by either the general ML model, a maximum of n supplementary artificial experts, or a human expert. Each of the ML models (i. e., the general ML model and the artificial experts) are iteratively trained to classify data from a specific domain. This results in individual classification functions

$$f_p : \mathrm{X}^j \rightarrow \mathrm{Y}^j, \mathbf{X}^j \rightarrow \mathbf{y}^j \tag{1}$$

for each of the ML models in the AIITL system, where j refers to the index of the model. Note, that these functions are unknown a priori and are approximated by convolutional neural networks as $\hat{f}_p\ (\mathbf{X}^j) = \mathbf{y}^{\hat{}j}$ when training the AIITL system.

Following Bansal et al. (2021), we use a utility score that combines the system's accuracy $\phi(\mathbf{X}, \hat{f})$ and the human effort $\rho(\mathbf{X}, \hat{f})$ to approximate the efficiency of the AIITL system for our evaluation. It is defined as:

$$U(\mathbf{X},\hat{f}) = \alpha\, \phi(\mathbf{X},\hat{f}) - \beta\ \ \rho(\mathbf{X},\hat{f}) \tag{2}$$

with $\mathbf{X} = \cup_j \mathbf{X}^j$ and $\hat{f} = \cup_p \hat{f}_p$. Accuracy quantifies the classification quality of the AIITL system. Human effort refers to the number of instances that are classified by the human expert in relation to the total number of instances. For the calculation of the utility score, we follow Bansal et al. (2021) and set $\alpha = 1$ and $\beta = 0.5$. That means, that we consider costs of inaccuracies to be two times higher than cost of manual review by human experts. In our experiments, we later demonstrate that our results are robust against changes in these parameters.

3.2 Allocation Mechanisms

We implement two allocation stages that guide instances through the AIITL system. The *Expert Consultancy Decision* is part of the traditional HITL system, deciding whether an instance is known or unknown utilizing OOD detection. Instances from known classes are then classified by the general model, while unknown instances are passed to an expert for review. The *Expert Selection* allows us to defer detected unknown data to artificial experts that are incrementally trained using data and labels from the manual review of the human expert. For the Expert Selection, we reinterpret OOD detectors as allocation mechanisms. To this end, we fit an OOD detector for each of the artificial experts. The OOD detectors then claim an instance for the respective expert if the instance is considered to originate from a known class (i. e., the instance is drawn from the experts' training distribution). If an instance is claimed by none or multiple artificial experts, the instance is allocated to a human expert for manual review. In the following, we briefly introduce the employed allocation mechanisms:

- **ODIN** is an OOD detector based on temperature scaling and perturbations of the input data (Liang et al. 2018). Model- and domain-specific scores are compared to thresholds. Based on this score, an instance is either defined as originating from a known class or from an unknown class.
- **Mahalanobis-based OOD (MAHA)** computes scores based on input perturbation and the Mahalanobis-distance between the input and the closest class-conditional Gaussian distribution (Lee et al. 2018). These scores are leveraged to classify an instance to part of the set of known classes or stem from an unknown class.
- **Gating model** is a separate model from the field of so-called "Mixture of Experts" that is trained to allocate instances to the artificial experts (Jacobs & Nowlan 1991). In contrast to the OOD detectors, this model is explicitly trained on allocating data instances to artificial experts.

4 Experiments

In the following, we describe our experimental setup. For the evaluation, we use popular datasets for image classification (e.g., CIFAR-10, SVHN). We evaluate the AIITL system under incremental data availability over 30 discrete steps. After training the general model, known and unknown data incrementally appears over the 30 steps. We train the "candidate" artificial experts on the labels that are iteratively generated by human experts during manual reviewing. In our implementations, we simulate a single human expert and assume a perfect classification accuracy for all input instances following related.

literature (e.g., Bansal et al. 2021). We evaluate the performance of the AIITL system in a separate test batch (i.e., after the 30 steps of incremental learning).

We use a small proportion of the data from manual reviewing for validation and test of the artificial experts. We split the remaining data in 80% data for training and 20% for test. We then utilize the accuracy of artificial experts on the test set as indicator when a specific artificial experts should be included in the AIITL system. This is in line with Bansal et al. (2021), who utilize the model confidence, but more directly related to the utility metric. When the test accuracy of an artificial expert exceeds a threshold of 95%, the system includes the artificial expert and considers it during the allocation of detected unknown data.

4.1 Benchmarks

Our evaluation procedure uses three benchmarks. First, we employ the general model from the HITL system without the option of a manual review from the human experts. This benchmark can be considered as a full automation baseline and prevents human effort but is likely to have a low classification accuracy in the presence of unknown data. Second, we utilize a traditional HITL system, where the general model classifies known instances, and the human expert is consulted for manual reviewing of the unknown instances. This HITL system also constitutes the initial version of each AIITL system (i.e., step 1) and allows us to assess the merit of introducing artificial experts over the steps. Finally, we compare the AIITL system with the HITL system under *perfect* allocation of unknown data, which is an upper bound in terms of classification accuracy.

4.2 Datasets

For our experiments, we build a dataset out of four well-known image classification datasets. While CIFAR-10 (Krizhevsky 2009) is used to train the general model and, thus, represents the known classes, three others represent unknown data classes: SVHN (Netzer et al. 2011), MNIST (Lecun et al. 1998) and Fashion-MNIST (Xiao et al. 2017). CIFAR-10 consists of 60,000 images of ten different classes (e.g., airplane, car, truck). Fashion-MNIST contains 60,000 images of Zalando's articles from ten different classes. MNIST consists of 60,000 images of handwritten digits and SVHN includes 600,000 images of printed digits from pictures of house number plates from Google Street View. We utilize the predefined train-test splits for the datasets.

4.3 *Training*

We employ a Wide-ResNet-28–10 architecture (Zagoruyko & Komodakis 2016) for the general model and a total of three artificial experts, where each artificial expert will be responsible for a separate set of unknown data. For the gating model, we make use of a DenseNet-121 (Huang et al. 2016) pretrained on ImageNet (Russakovsky et al. 2014). We train the general model for 200 epochs with a batch size of 256 and SGD as the optimizer with a learning rate of 0.1. The artificial experts are iteratively trained for 300 epochs with a 128 batch size using the SGD optimizer with a learning rate of 0.1. All models were trained on a NVIDIA A100 GPU.

4.4 *Results*

We present the utility scores of the AIITL system and the proposed baselines in Fig. 2. After 30 steps of incremental learning, we observe that the proposed hybrid system outperforms the *perfect* HITL system with all allocation mechanisms. While the performance of the HITL system under perfect allocation results in an utility of 0.51, our system achieves scores of 0.92 based on the allocation using the gating model, 0.73 with allocation based on the Mahalanobis method, and 0.61 for allocation based on the ODIN method. This suggests that even when we assume a perfect allocation of known and unknown images (i.e., the general model only classifies known images and the human expert only reviews unknown images), the HITL system is less efficient than our hybrid system.

Table 1 reports the accuracy and human effort of the initial HITL system from step 1 (i.e., a traditional HITL system with imperfect allocation using allocation mechanisms) and the resulting AIITL system after 30 steps. The AIITL system outperforms the HITL system (i.e., in the absence of artificial experts) both in terms

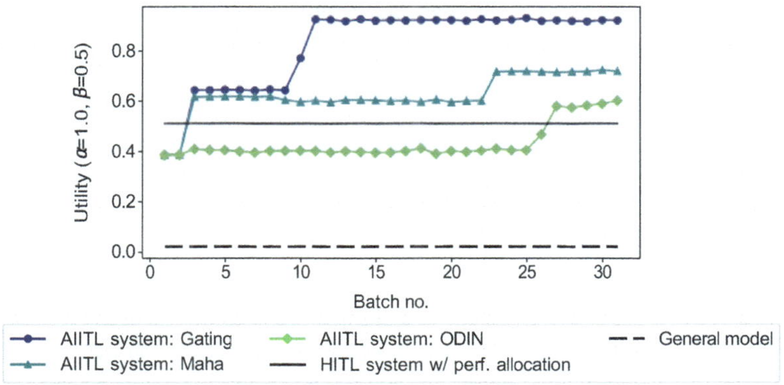

Fig. 2 Utility score of the AIITL system for different allocation mechanisms and baselines

Table 1 Overview of accuracy and human effort of the AIITL system after 30 steps compared to the performance of a traditional HITL system

	HITL	AIITL		
		Gating	MAHA	ODIN
Human effort $\rho(X, \hat{f})$	0.73	**0.00**	0.39	0.27
Accuracy $\phi(X, \hat{f})$	0.75	**0.92**	**0.92**	0.74
Utility $U(X, \hat{f})$	0.39	**0.92**	0.73	0.61

Best performances are highlighted in bold

of accuracy and human effort for allocation based on the gating model and MAHA. The accuracy increases by 17 pp from 75 to 92%. The human effort is reduced by 73 pp and 34 pp by the gating model and MAHA, respectively. For the allocation based on ODIN the accuracy slightly declines from 75 to 74%, while the human effort is reduced significantly from 0.73 to 0.27. Overall, this demonstrates that the suggested hybrid system improves the efficiency strongly compared to HITL systems.

5 Analyzing the Influence of Varying Weights for Human Effort on the System Efficiency

We conduct sensitivity analyses to better comprehend the influence of the weight of human effort in Eq. 2. For that, we vary the weight of human effort and depict examples in Fig. 3. Across experiments, we find consistent improvements of our hybrid system over traditional HITL systems. In addition, we evaluate when traditional HITL systems become preferable in our experiments and found that HITL systems improve over our hybrid system only when human effort is more than ten times less important than accuracy (i.e., $\beta < 0.1$). In our experiments, AIITL systems consistently outperform HITL systems when accuracy is less than ten times more important than human effort (i.e., $\beta > 0.1$). Overall, our results demonstrate strong increases in the efficiency of the proposed hybrid AIITL system compared to traditional HITL systems.

5.1 Applying the Hybrid System in the Context of Semantically Similar Classes

In the previous section, we focused on unknown classes that originate from other datasets than the training dataset for the general model (e.g., the general model was trained on CIFAR-10 images, while unknown data originates from SVHN). In this section, we show that our hybrid system improves the efficiency of HITL systems even when we sample a range of classes of the training set to be known, while

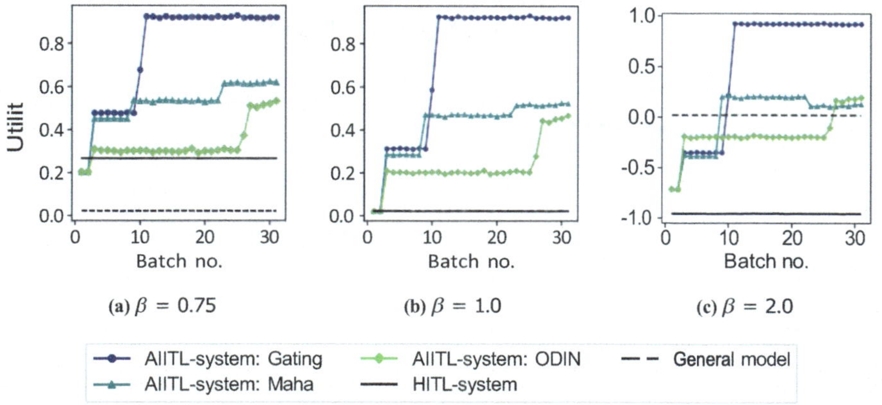

Fig. 3 Sensitivity analysis regarding the influence of the weight of human effort β on the overall utility of the AIITL system and the baselines ($\alpha = 1$)

other classes of this dataset are treated as unknown. For this, we select the first six classes of CIFAR-10 to be known, while we consider the remaining four as unknown classes. For example, the classes "car" and "deer" represent known classes, while the semantically similar classes "truck" and "horse" represents unknown classes (see Fig. 4).

We then train the general model on the known classes, while a single artificial expert and the human expert are later responsible for classifying the four unknown classes. Following common practice for detecting unknown classes that are part of the same set as known classes, we utilize softmax thresholding as a simple baseline to detect unknown instances (Geng et al. 2021). We present our results in Fig. 5. Overall, we observe that our hybrid system outperforms the traditional HITL system, the HITL system under perfect allocation, and the general model by a large margin. Our results are in line with the previous findings and demonstrate that the AIITL

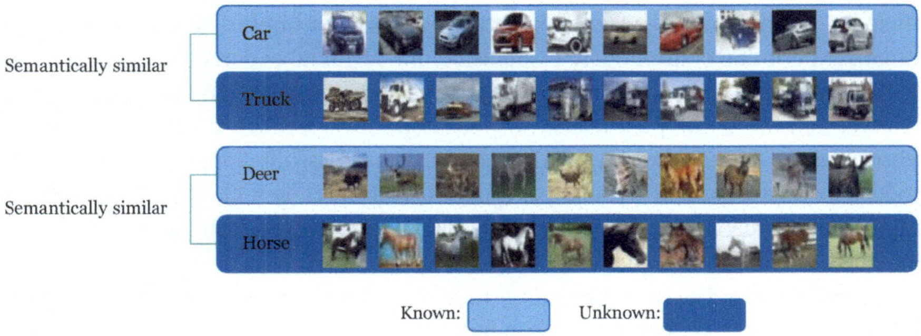

Fig. 4 Visual examples of semantically similar classes that are considered as known and unknown classes respectively. The general model is trained on known classes, while the artificial experts learn to classify unknown classes based on incremental feedback from the human expert

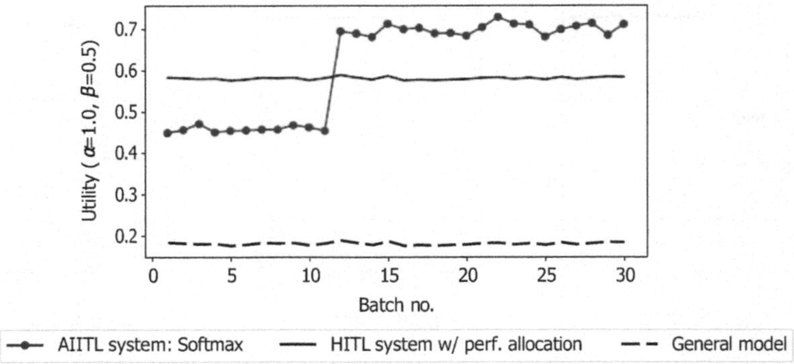

Fig. 5 Utility score of our hybrid system and baselines in a setting where unknown classes originate from the same dataset as known classes. Graphs depict performances on the CIFAR-10 dataset, where six classes are considered to be known, while the remaining four classes are treated as unknown

system can be leveraged in contexts where known and unknown classes are very similar.

6 Discussion

Our work results in a range of implications for research and practice in the field of HITL systems and hybrid systems that leverage both ML and human expert knowledge.

First, we observe inefficiencies in traditional HITL systems that are created by allocation of tasks to a human expert that are difficult to classify for the ML model. This results in substantial human effort that ultimately can inhibit the application of HITL systems in general. We demonstrate that a hybrid team of artificial and human experts can significantly reduce the human effort and thereby increase the efficiency of the overall system. For practitioners, this implies that knowledge of domain experts can continuously be ingested into artificial experts (i.e., ML models) that can support human experts on repetitive tasks. This frees human capacities for creative, and more complex tasks. For research, our approach demonstrates that a hybrid team of human and artificial experts can successfully support a general ML model in the presence of data that originates from unknown classes. Especially in real-world applications, well-defined processes to handle data from unknown classes is essential to ensure a required level of system accuracy.

Second, we observe two interesting trade-offs in the design of our hybrid system that need to be taken account for when utilizing our approach in real-world applications: (a) the choice of the allocation mechanism and (b) the required accuracy level of artificial experts to include them in the hybrid team. For the choice of the allocation mechanism, we observe a trade-off between the efficiency level (i.e., utility score) and the capability of adapting to data from unknown classes. For example, the gating model achieves a very strong utility, while it is limited in the ability to detect data from novel classes. The human expert first needs to feed the gating model with a sufficient number of instances from the encountered unknown class so that the gating model is able to allocate instances from that class correctly. On the other hand, ODIN and MAHA techniques achieve slightly lower performances (still outperforming traditional HITL systems by a large margin) but are adapting more quickly to a novel set of unknown classes. When designing hybrid systems in practice, it is critical to carefully select a suitable allocation mechanism. The second trade-off refers to the accuracy of artificial experts that is required to include the expert in the hybrid system. Generally, the higher the accuracy of an artificial expert, the better the overall performance of the system. However, achieving an increased performance of the artificial experts typically requires a higher amount of labeled data and, therefore, of manual reviews by the human expert. Defining the required level of accuracy of the artificial expert in applications in research and practice will require an in depth understanding of the costs of misclassifications (i.e., inaccuracies) and the costs of manual reviews by the human expert.

Third, we see exciting parallels between our hybrid system and the field of human-AI collaboration as well as complementary team performance. In the latter, human and AI achieve a joint accuracy that none of them would have achieved individually. These approaches focus on maximizing the accuracy, while we add an additional dimension by focusing on the human effort. Coupling these approaches may result in even more promising performances in terms of the overall efficiency of the system.

As any research, ours is not free of limitations. While we evaluated our approach on a wide range of image classification datasets, evidence from the field of, for example, natural language and from structured data is missing. Moreover, the approach needs to be validated in real-world situations with domain experts representing the "human-in- the-loop" to assess actual cost savings and efficiency improvements. Thus, as a next step, we want to explore variations of AIITL systems in different use cases and on real-world datasets. Finally, while our approach is general, we evaluated our approach in a linear setting due to computational limitations, meaning that the number of artificial experts linearly increased with the number of unknown domains. It will be interesting for future research to investigate how e.g., a constant number of artificial experts performs in settings with an increasing number of unknown domains. Thus, additional research on the optimal number of artificial experts is necessary. To increase the practical applicability, we are interested in exploring additional mechanisms to assess when an artificial expert should be included in the system.

7 Conclusion

In this work, we argue that consulting human experts for manual review of difficult model classifications leads to a strong increase in human effort. Retraining an ML model on incrementally appearing novel classes is not an alternative as it leads to a signifi- cantly declining performance on the base classes—a phenomenon called "catastrophic forgetting". To improve the efficiency of HITL systems, we introduce several artificial experts that learn to classify data from unknown classes based on the manual review from human experts. The resulting hybrid system of human and artificial experts improves the efficiency of HITL systems by reducing human effort and is robust against catastropic forgetting. We additionally introduce allocation mechanisms within our hybrid system that allow us to automatically assign detected unknown data to a suitable artificial expert. Overall, we find that our hybrid system outperforms traditional HITL systems by a large margin in terms of their utility—the combination of classification accuracy and human effort—across a range of benchmarks.

References

Agnisarman, S., Lopes, S., Madathil, K. C., Piratla, K. & Gramopadhye, A. (2019), 'A Survey of Automation-Enabled Human-In-The-Loop Systems For Infrastructure Visual Inspection', *Automation in Construction* **97**, 52–76.

Bansal, G., Nushi, B., Kamar, E., Horvitz, E. & Weld, D. S. (2021), Is the Most Accurate AI the Best Teammate? Optimizing AI for Teamwork, *in* 'Proceedings of the Thirty- Fifth AAAI Conference on Artificial Intelligence (AAAI-21)', Vol. 35, AAAI Press,
pp. 11405–11414.

Bansal, G., Weld, D. S. & Allen, P. G. (2018), A Coverage-Based Utility Model for Iden- tifying Unknown Unknowns, *in* 'Proceedings of the Thirty-Second AAAI Conference on Artificial Intelligence (AAAI-18)', Vol. 32, AAAI Press.

Berente, N., Gu, B., Recker, J. & Santhanam, R. (2021), 'Managing artificial intelligence', *MIS quarterly* **45**(3).

Bodén, A. C., Molin, J., Garvin, S., West, R. A., Lundström, C. & Treanor, D. (2021), 'The human-in-the-loop: An evaluation of pathologists' interaction with artificial intelligence in clinical practice', *Histopathology* **79**(2), 210–218.

Cai, C. J., Reif, E., Hegde, N., Hipp, J., Kim, B., Smilkov, D., Wattenberg, M., Viegas, F., Corrado, G. S., Stumpe, M. C. et al. (2019), Human-centered tools for coping with imperfect algorithms during medical decision-making, *in* 'Proceedings of the 2019 CHI Conference on Human Factors in Computing Systems', pp. 1–14.

Castro, F. M., Marín-Jiménez, M. J., Guil, N., Schmid, C. & Alahari, K. (2018), End-to- end incremental learning, *in* 'Proceedings of the European conference on computer vision (ECCV)', pp. 233–248.

Cimini, C., Pirola, F., Pinto, R. & Cavalieri, S. (2020), 'A human-in-the-loop manufac- turing control architecture for the next generation of production systems', *Journal of Manufacturing Systems* **54**, 258–271.

Dellermann, D., Calma, A., Lipusch, N., Weber, T., Weigel, S. & Ebel, P. (2019a), The Future of Human-AI Collaboration: A Taxonomy of Design Knowledge for Hybrid Intelligence Systems, *in* ‘Proceedings of the Fifty-Second Hawaii International Conference on System Sciences (HICSS)’, University of Hawaii at Manoa, AIS, IEEE Computer Society Press, pp. 2611–2620.

Dellermann, D., Ebel, P., Söllner, M. & Leimeister, J. M. (2019b), ‘Hybrid Intelligence’, *Business and Information Systems Engineering* **61**(5), 637–643.

Elmalaki, S. (2021), Fair-iot: Fairness-aware human-in-the-loop reinforcement learning for harnessing human variability in personalized iot, *in* ‘Proceedings of the Interna- tional Conference on Internet-of-Things Design and Implementation’, pp. 119–132.

Geng, C., Huang, S. J. & Chen, S. (2021), ‘Recent Advances in Open Set Recogni- tion: A Survey’, *IEEE Transactions on Pattern Analysis and Machine Intelligence* **43**(10), 3614–3631.

Grønsund, T. & Aanestad, M. (2020), ‘Augmenting the algorithm: Emerging human-in- the-loop work configurations’, *Journal of Strategic Information Systems* **29**(2). Article no.: 101614.

Han, L., Dong, X. & Demartini, G. (2021), Iterative Human-in-the-Loop Discovery of Unknown Unknowns in Image Datasets, *in* ‘Proceedings of the Ninth AAAI Conference on Human Computation and Crowdsourcing (HCOMP)’, Vol. 9, AAAI Press, pp. 72–83.

Hou, S., Pan, X., Loy, C. C., Wang, Z. & Lin, D. (2019), Learning a unified classifier incrementally via rebalancing, *in* ‘Proceedings of the IEEE/CVF Conference on Computer Vision and Pattern Recognition’, pp. 831–839.

Hsu, Y.-C., Shen, Y., Jin, H. & Kira, Z. (2020), Generalized ODIN: Detecting Out-of- distribution Image without Learning from Out-of-distribution Data, *in* ‘Proceedings of the IEEE/CVF Conference on Computer Vision and Pattern Recognition (CVPR)’, IEEE Computer Society, pp. 10951–10960.

Huang, G., Liu, Z., van der Maaten, L. & Weinberger, K. Q. (2016), Densely Connected Convolutional Networks, *in* ‘Proceedings of the IEEE Conference on Computer Vision and Pattern Recognition (CVPR)’, IEEE Computer Society, pp. 4700–4708.

Iscen, A., Zhang, J., Lazebnik, S. & Schmid, C. (2020), Memory-efficient incremental learning through feature adaptation, *in* ‘European conference on computer vision’, Springer, pp. 699–715.

Jacobs, R. A. & Nowlan, S. J. (1991), ‘Adaptive Mixture of Local Experts’, *Neural Computation* **3**(1), 79–87.

Jakubik, J., Blumenstiel, B., Vössing, M. & Hemmer, P. (2022), Instance Selection Mechanisms for Human-in-the-Loop Systems in Few-Shot Learning, *in* ‘Proceedings of the Seventeenth International Conference on Wirtschaftsinformatik (WI)’, Vol. 6, AIS.

Kamar, E. (2016), Directions in Hybrid Intelligence: Complementing AI Systems with Human Intelligence, *in* ‘Proceedings of the Twenty-Fifth International Joint Confer- ence on Artificial Intelligence (IJCAI)’, AAAI Press, pp. 4070–4073.

Keswani, V., Lease, M. & Kenthapadi, K. (2022), ‘Designing Closed Human-in-the-loop Deferral Pipelines’, *arXiv preprint* arXiv:2202.04718 .

Krizhevsky, A. (2009), Learning Multiple Layers of Features from Tiny Images, Techni- cal report, University of Toronto, Toronto.

Lecun, Y., Bottou, L., Bengio, Y. & Haffner, P. (1998), ‘Gradient-Based Learning Applied to Document Recognition’, *Proceedings of the IEEE* **86**(11), 2278–2324.

Lee, K., Lee, K., Lee, H. & Shin, J. (2018), A Simple Unified Framework for Detecting Out-of-Distribution Samples and Adversarial Attacks, *in* ‘Advances in Neural Infor- mation Processing Systems (NeurIPS)’, Vol. 31, Curran Associates, pp. 7167–7177.

Li, Z. & Hoiem, D. (2017), ‘Learning without forgetting’, *IEEE transactions on pattern analysis and machine intelligence* **40**(12), 2935–2947.

Liang, H., Yang, L., Cheng, H., Tu, W. & Xu, M. (2017), Human-in-the-loop reinforce- ment learning, *in* ‘2017 Chinese Automation Congress (CAC)’, IEEE, pp. 4511–4518. Liang, S., Li, Y. & Srikant, R. (2018), Enhancing The Reliability of Out-of-distribution Image Detection in Neural Networks, *in* ‘Proceedings of the Sixth International Conference on Learning Representations (ICLR)’, ICLR.

Liu, A., Guerra, S., Fung, I., Matute, G., Kamar, E. & Lasecki, W. (2020a), Towards Hybrid Human-AI Workflows for Unknown Unknown Detection, *in* ‘Proceedings of the World Wide Web Conference (WWW)’, ACM, pp. 2432–2442.

Liu, W., Wang, X., Owens, J. D. & Li, Y. (2020b), Energy-based Out-of-distribution De- tection, *in* 'Advances in Neural Information Processing Systems (NeurIPS)', Vol. 33, Curran Associates, pp. 21464–21475.

Liu, Y., Su, Y., Liu, A.-A., Schiele, B. & Sun, Q. (2020c), Mnemonics training: Multi-class incremental learning without forgetting, *in* 'Proceedings of the IEEE/CVF conference on Computer Vision and Pattern Recognition', pp. 12245–12254.

Liu, Z., Wang, J., Gong, S., Lu, H. & Tao, D. (2019), Deep reinforcement active learning for human-in-the-loop person re-identification, *in* 'Proceedings of the IEEE/CVF international conference on computer vision', pp. 6122–6131.

Mittal, S., Galesso, S. & Brox, T. (2021), Essentials for class incremental learning, *in* 'Proceedings of the IEEE/CVF Conference on Computer Vision and Pattern Recogni- tion', pp. 3513–3522.

Mohseni, S., Pitale, M., Yadawa, J. & Wang, Z. (2020), Self-Supervised Learning for Gen- eralizable Out-of-Distribution Detection, *in* 'Proceedings of the Thirty-Fourth AAAI Conference on Artificial Intelligence (AAAI-20)', Vol. 34, AAAI Press, pp. 5216– 5223.

Netzer, Y., Wang, T., Coates, A., Bissacco, A., Wu, B. & Ng, A. Y. (2011), Reading Digits in Natural Images with Unsupervised Feature Learning, *in* 'Workshop on Deep Learning and Unsupervised Feature Learning of the Twenty-Fifth Conference on Neural Information Processing Systems (NeurIPS)', Curran Associates.

Rebuffi, S.-A., Kolesnikov, A., Sperl, G. & Lampert, C. H. (2017), iCaRL: Incremental classifier and representation learning, *in* 'Proceedings of the IEEE conference on Computer Vision and Pattern Recognition', pp. 2001–2010.

Russakovsky, O., Deng, J., Su, H., Krause, J., Satheesh, S., Ma, S., Huang, Z., Karpathy, A., Khosla, A., Bernstein, M., Berg, A. C. & Fei-Fei, L. (2014), 'ImageNet Large Scale Visual Recognition Challenge', *International Journal of Computer Vision* **115**, 211– 252.

Sanchez, T., Caramiaux, B., Thiel, P. & Mackay, W. E. (2022), Deep learning uncertainty in machine teaching, *in* '27th International Conference on Intelligent User Interfaces', pp. 173–190.

Wan, S., Hou, Y., Bao, F., Ren, Z., Dong, Y., Dai, Q. & Deng, Y. (2021), 'Human-in- the-Loop Low-Shot Learning', *IEEE Transactions on Neural Networks and Learning Systems* **32**(7), 3287–3292.

Wang, H., Gong, S., Zhu, X. & Xiang, T. (2016), Human-in-the-loop person re- identification, *in* 'European conference on computer vision', Springer, pp. 405–422.

Weber, V., Piovano, E. & Bradford, M. (2021), It is better to verify: Semi-supervised learning with a human in the loop for large-scale nlu models, *in* 'Proceedings of the Second Workshop on Data Science with Human in the Loop: Language Advances', pp. 8–15.

Wrede, F. & Hellander, A. (2019), 'Smart computational exploration of stochastic gene regulatory network models using human-in-the-loop semi-supervised learning', *Bioinformatics* **35**(24), 5199–5206.

Wu, J., Huang, Z., Hu, Z. & Lv, C. (2022), 'Toward human-in-the-loop ai: Enhancing deep reinforcement learning via real-time human guidance for autonomous driving', *Engineering*.

Wu, X., Ma, T., Li, X., Chen, Q. & He, L. (2021a), 'Human-In-The-Loop Document Layout Analysis', *arXiv preprint* arXiv:2108.02095 .

Wu, X., Xiao, L., Sun, Y., Zhang, J., Ma, T. & He, L. (2021b), 'A Survey of Human-in- the-loop for Machine Learning', *arXiv preprint* arXiv:2108.00941 .

Wu, Y., Chen, Y., Wang, L., Ye, Y., Liu, Z., Guo, Y. & Fu, Y. (2019), Large scale incremental learning, *in* 'Proceedings of the IEEE/CVF Conference on Computer Vision and Pattern Recognition', pp. 374–382.

Xiao, H., Rasul, K. & Vollgraf, R. (2017), 'Fashion-MNIST: a Novel Image Dataset for Benchmarking Machine Learning Algorithms', *arXiv preprint* arXiv:1708.07747 .

Yu, L., Twardowski, B., Liu, X., Herranz, L., Wang, K., Cheng, Y., Jui, S. & Weijer, J. v. d. (2020), Semantic drift compensation for class-incremental learning, *in* 'Proceedings of the IEEE/CVF Conference on Computer Vision and Pattern Recognition', pp. 6982– 6991.

Zagoruyko, S. & Komodakis, N. (2016), Wide Residual Networks, *in* 'Proceedings of the Twenty-Seventh British Machine Vision Conference (BMVC)', BMVA Press. Article no.: 87.

Zhang, J., Zhang, J., Ghosh, S., Li, D., Tasci, S., Heck, L., Zhang, H. & Kuo, C.-C. J. (2020), Class-incremental learning via deep model consolidation, *in* 'Proceedings of the IEEE/CVF Winter Conference on Applications of Computer Vision', pp. 1131– 1140.
Zhao, B., Xiao, X., Gan, G., Zhang, B. & Xia, S.-T. (2020), Maintaining discrimina- tion and fairness in class incremental learning, *in* 'Proceedings of the IEEE/CVF Conference on Computer Vision and Pattern Recognition', pp. 13208–13217.

Automated Knowledge Extraction from IS Research Articles Combining Sentence Classification and Ontological Annotation

Sebastian Huettemann

Abstract Manually analyzing large collections of research articles is a time- and resource-intensive activity, making it difficult to stay on top of the latest research findings. Limitations of automated solutions lie in limited domain knowledge and not being able to attribute extracted key terms to a focal article, related work, or background information. We aim to address this challenge by (1) developing a framework for classifying sentences in scientific publications, (2) performing several experiments comparing state-of-the-art sentence transformer algorithms with a novel few-shot learning technique and (3) automatically analyzing a corpus of articles and evaluating automated knowledge extraction capabilities. We tested our approach for combining sentence classification with ontological annotations on a manually created dataset of 1000 sentences from Information Systems (IS) articles. The results indicate a high degree of accuracy underlining the potential for novel approaches in analyzing scientific publications.

Keywords Knowledge extraction · Sentence classification · Ontological analysis · Few-shot learning · Natural language processing

1 Introduction

Studying research contributions has a long tradition in IS. In 2000, Claver et al. (2000) set out to analyze research in the IS discipline by examining articles in MISQ and Information & Management within a 17-year time frame. In 2003, Lee et al. (2003) studied the technology acceptance model's past, present, and future by analyzing roughly a hundred articles from leading IS journals. More recently in 2018, Kupfer (2018) analyzed over 1000 conference articles to craft an overview of research methods employed in IS.

S. Huettemann (✉)
Berlin School of Economics and Law, Berlin, Germany
e-mail: sebastian.huettemann@hwr-berlin.de

D. Beverungen et al. (eds.), *Solutions and Technologies for Responsible Digitalization*, Lecture Notes in Information Systems and Organisation 75,
https://doi.org/10.1007/978-3-031-80122-8_10

These exemplary projects have something in common: They indicate that there is an ever-present need for extracting knowledge from the existing body of literature in IS to inform researchers about related work, potential knowledge gaps, and future research directions. These approaches unfortunately share another aspect: they highly depend on manual labor as analyzing hundreds of research articles tends to be an extremely time- and resource-intensive activity.

Research builds on cumulative knowledge and the identification of ongoing research conversations in a specific field. In the field of IS, however, the amount of existing research seems to have already surpassed human limits to comprehension. Larsen et al. (2019) recently demonstrated that conventional approaches to literature reviews tend to miss most of the relevant literature. A trend aggravated by the growing number of publications. As human capabilities to analyze the ever-growing body of research are limited, we must ask the question of how such endeavors can be supported by developing and advancing computational methods for knowledge extraction and synthesis.

Today, researchers are supported by various technologies enabling organizing and querying available knowledge. Scopus (Elsevier 2015), Web of Science (Thomson-Reuters 2015), Google Scholar (Google Scholar 2023), and Semantic Scholar (AI2 2021) are only a few examples of widely used academic search engines. However, albeit providing various search options, none of these solutions is able to sufficiently extract domain knowledge from articles, such as theories, research methods, topics, and technologies.

Tate et al. (2015) highlighted the potential of performing ontological meta-analyses for reviewing, mapping, and visualizing the current body of knowledge in a domain. They referred to Ramaprasad and Syn (2015) who developed an approach to identify under-researched areas by mapping literature to an ontological framework of the IS discipline. This relates to recent calls for novel approaches to improve the discoverability of knowledge in IS. Larsen et al. (2020) and Wagner et al. (2021) underline the importance of ontological indexing to enable automated knowledge mining from scientific articles.

However, extracting domain-specific terminology can lead to ambiguous results as extracted key terms from an article could either refer to a focal article, related work, or background information. To correctly attribute detected terms, we need to be able to analyze and classify contextual information, i.e., a sentence in which key terms are embedded. Consider the following sentences: “We attempt to build a new adaptive behavior theory.” versus “Smith et al. attempted to build a new adaptive behavior theory.” Extracting the term *adaptive behavior theory* out of both sentences would not be sufficient as it cannot be inferred whether the term belongs to a focal article or related work.

In contrast, being able to correctly attribute key terms from a domain ontology to articles could generate additional metadata that describes the contents of articles in greater detail. Such metadata could enable additional filters in search engines or quantitative analyses over large collections of documents to aggregate mentions of specific theories, methods, topics, or technologies.

Therefore, we ask the following research questions: *RQ1: How can we classify sentences in research articles to correctly attribute scientific key terms to a focal article? RQ2: Which state-of-the-art machine learning model performs best in classifying sentences from research articles?*

We contribute to the development of automated methods for knowledge extraction from large collections of research articles by (1) developing a framework for sentence classification that supports the correct attribution of extracted key terminology, (2) comparing state-of-the-art open-source transformer models with a novel few-shot learning technique for classifying sentences, and (3) evaluating the potential of our approach on a corpus of conference articles and providing a use case example. We share the annotated data for training and testing our models via a GitHub repository (Huettemann 2023).

2 Theoretical Background

Our approach for inferring the correct attribution of extracted key terms relates to research in three areas: (1) ontological analysis of research articles where our approach can contribute to automatically extracting necessary data, (2) domain ontologies in IS that are necessary to map the text of research articles to domain-specific concepts, and (3) sentence classification to infer the attribution of extracted key terms by classifying the surrounding context.

2.1 Ontological Analysis of Research Articles

Automatically extracting knowledge from research articles in the IS discipline can serve several purposes, e.g., populating theory repositories, identifying knowledge gaps, supporting the conduct of literature reviews, and increasing transparency regarding the evolution of the discipline. Some examples of knowledge extraction include Li et al. (2020) who proposed TheoryOn, a search engine that allows for directly searching constructs and their relationships in scientific texts, Anisienia et al. (2021) who proposed the application of transfer learning with a deep learning model for extracting research methods, and Eckle-Kohler et al. (2013) who used natural language processing and machine learning techniques to extract research methods based on a taxonomy.

In contrast to methods that focus on extracting individual aspects, incorporating domain ontologies could lead to a more comprehensive extraction of knowledge from research articles. Ramaprasad et al. (2015) proposed a method for semi-automated ontological meta-analysis and synthesis to automatically derive insights from large collections of documents (Tate et al. 2015). Cameron et al. (2017) applied this approach to the domain of mHealth and demonstrated that such analyses lead to detailed quantitative insights. One example of the application IS is the research from

La Paz et al. (2020) who created an ontological overview of twenty-five years of research in the Information Systems Journal.

2.2 Domain Ontologies in IS

Scholars in IS created different taxonomies to capture and hierarchically organize key terms that describe specific aspects within the IS discipline. Barki et al. (1988, 1993) proposed a classification schema containing 1300 key terms in IS, organized for instance into theories, information technologies, IS management, or IS usage. More recent approaches addressed rather specific areas, such as e-commerce (Gregg and Scott 2008), mobile applications (Nickerson et al. 2013), and digital platforms (Springer and Petrik 2021).

Mueller et al. (2022) presented a more comprehensive ontology that captures IS key terminology in a hierarchical and interconnected manner. This IS Ontology comprises 2700+ key terms including theories, topics, methods, technologies, and other relevant categories. These terms are hierarchically organized, implying "is a"—relationships, e.g., *machine learning* is a *data analysis method* is a *methodological entity*. This structure allows for aggregating findings along upper categories so that for instance all key terms classified as *data analysis method* can be collected. It further includes around 380,000 synonyms for its key terms, aiming to enhance detection capabilities. We, therefore, integrated the IS Ontology into our approach to detect key terms in sentences.

2.3 Sentence Classification

Sentence classification in scientific publications can be used to support information retrieval systems (Neves et al. 2019), knowledge graph population (Oelen et al. 2021), or to predict citation intents (Cohan et al. 2019). Brack et al. (2022) used transformer-based language models for sequential sentence classification in abstracts and full papers from biomedicine, computer graphics, chemistry, and computational linguistics. Gonçalves et al. (2020) classified sentences in abstracts by using a deep learning approach based on a convolutional layer and a bi-directional gated recurrent unit. Asadi et al. (2019) classified sentences in existing datasets from biochemistry and computer graphics by using logistic model trees, sequential minimal optimization, and a data fusion technique. Jin and Szolovits (2018) performed sequential sentence classification in medical science abstracts with a hierarchical sequential labeling network. We did not find any approaches to sentence classification using few-shot learning as a technique to reduce the effort in manually annotating sentences.

3 Methodology

In this section, we present our approach to infer the correct attribution of extracted key terms from scientific publications. We developed a sentence classification framework to guide the annotation of training data. We selected a set of state-of-the-art transformer models for classifying sentences and created training data as well as a gold standard for testing the models' performance.

3.1 Development of a Sentence Classification Framework

We developed a framework for sentence classification to infer the correct attribution of extracted key terms from scientific publications. We infer this attribution by classifying the context of the terms—the sentence.

We defined the following criteria for creating a corpus of articles that served as the basis for developing the framework and the data for training and testing the machine learning models: (1) the articles in the corpus should reflect current publication standards and practices in IS, (2) the articles should be randomly selected and the final corpus should contain more than 100 articles to assure a sufficient variety in sampled sentences, and (3) the articles should be open-access so that the annotated dataset can be shared with other researchers. We searched for open-access publications in journals of the Senior Scholars' Basket (AIS 2021), and randomly selected 117 open-access articles from these journals' web pages covering a timeframe from 2012 until 2020 (AIS corpus). The complete list of articles can be found in our GitHub repository (Huettemann 2023).

We used Grobid (2022) for text extraction from PDF documents and spaCy (Honnibal and Montani 2021) for sentence segmentation and key term detection to detect terms that are included in the IS Ontology (Mueller et al. 2022). Only sentences that contained such terms were extracted. Table 1 illustrates the final framework.

To develop the framework, we performed qualitative coding using elements from grounded theory as suggested by Saldaña (2013). In the first round of coding, we sampled 1525 sentences from the articles in our corpus containing IS-related key terminology and used the sentence categories from the Academic Phrasebank (John Morley 2018) as a starting point. We performed descriptive coding (Saldaña 2013) to categorize the sentences into four classes: background, method, related work, and results. Our initial assumption was that all classes, except for related work, would relate to a focal article. However, we found that some sentences described general background knowledge that could also not be attributed to a focal article.

Throughout a second round of coding, we added more detailed categories to better differentiate between sentence classes (see Table 1). In a third round of coding, we performed code mapping (Saldaña 2013) to refine and group the categories. We found that key terms from the IS Ontology contained in sentences belonging to the detailed categories a to d could directly be attributed to an article. Sentences in subclass

Table 1 Framework for sentence classification

Class	Detailed category	Description	Examples
1. Related to article	a. Purpose and section contents	Sentences that describe the focus of an article (e.g. aim, purpose, method); Sentences that describe the content of article sections	"In this study, we performed …" "In the next section, we describe …"
	b. Method details	Sentences that describe a method (case study, survey, experiment) or a procedure in detail	"We evaluated our system in a series of experiments" "The data comprised 20 discussion threads"
	c. Research questions and hypotheses	Sentences stating a research question or a hypothesis	"RQ1: How can X influence Y?" "H1: A causes B"
	d. Results	Sentences that describe results or contributions; Sentences that contain performance comparisons	"Our primary contributions are …" "We present empirical evidence for …"
2. Related Work	e. Statement of related work	Sentences must contain a citation and refer to related work	"Smith developed a method that …" "According to Smith, X is defined as …"
3. Background information	f. Definitions	Sentences that contain a definition and no cite	"X is defined as …"
	g. Future work	Sentences that imply directions for future work	"Future work could address X"
	h. General information	Sentences that contain more general statements without a citation	"Online communities provide organizations with new opportunities"

e referred to statements associated with a reference. Subclasses f to h indicated general information that did not describe the contents of a focal article. After the third round of coding, further analysis of the literature did not provide additional information.

3.2 Few-Shot Learning and Model Selection

Few-shot learning refers to training machine learning models with only a few training examples. As training state-of-the-art deep learning models typically requires large amounts of data, few-shot learning can be used to fine-tune a model that has already been trained on large datasets to adjust the model to a specific context (Beltagy et al. 2022). In 2022, researchers from Hugging Face, Intel Labs, and the UKP Lab introduced Setfit, a novel framework for few-shot fine-tuning of Sentence Transformers (Tunstall et al. 2022). Compared to other few-shot learning techniques, this framework can be used with less complex models and less training data while still producing highly accurate results.

We defined several criteria for selecting a set of models for our experiments. The models should (1) reflect state-of-art in natural language processing, (2) be publicly available to ensure replicability, (3) have demonstrated very good overall performance, and should preferably have been trained on specific scientific datasets.

We identified sentence-transformers as state-of-the-art in natural language processing (Wolf et al. 2020) and selected three general purpose sentence-transformer models that were extensively tested and evaluated as reported by HuggingFace (Hugging Face 2023i): *paraphrase-mpnet-base-v2* (Reimers and Gurevych 2019; Hugging Face 2023f), *all-MiniLM-L6-v2* (Hugging Face 2023g), and *distilbert-base-uncased-finetuned-sst-2-english* (Hugging Face 2023c). These models were the top downloaded models for text classification and sentence similarity with over 2.5 m downloads each. We have also included the model *bert-base-uncased* (Hugging Face 2023b) which was developed by Devlin et al. (2019) and marks a seminal work introducing Bidirectional Encoder Representations from Transformers.

Furthermore, we identified three models that were fine-tuned on scientific datasets: *multicite-multilabel-scibert* was trained on citation context analysis (Lauscher et al. 2022; Hugging Face 2023e), *longformer-scico* was fine-tuned to detect technical concepts in scientific publications (Cattan and Johnson 2021; Hugging Face 2023d), and *specter* implemented a novel method for embedding scientific documents (Cohan et al. 2020; Hugging Face 2023h).

We did not include GPT models in our approach as the latest version, GPT-4, was released after the submission deadline for the conference. As of to date, GPT-4 is only available via the application ChatGPT and an API. It is not possible to download the model, and the capabilities for fine-tuning are limited. Furthermore, recent research points to GPT models providing different outputs for identical inputs (OpenAI 2023; Reiss 2023; Susarla et al. 2023). We therefore conclude that fine-tuning GPT-4 would require in-depth testing of different prompting strategies which would exceed the scope of this research.

Table 2 Class distribution in final dataset

Class	# Sentences	% Sentences
1. Related to article	1096	33.5
2. Related work	656	46.4
3. Background information	1516	20.1

3.3 Development of Training Data

We performed two iterations of training and validating the selected models. In the first iteration, we used the 1525 sentences that we annotated throughout the development of the sentence classification framework for training (see Sect. 3.1). We applied a 70/20/10-split for training, validation, and testing. For testing the impact of changes in hyperparameter settings, we performed several experiments with *multicite-multilabel- scibert* and *paraphrase-mpnet-base-v2.* Adjusting the batch size and number of epochs as well as increasing the number of iterations higher than 20 did not lead to increases in F1 scores. We noticed improvements in F1 scores the more examples we used for each class in the training set.

In the second iteration, we therefore annotated an additional sample of 1743 sentences from the AIS corpus (see Sect. 3.1). The author annotated these sentences according to the classification framework and we combined this new dataset with the previously annotated set of 1525 sentences, resulting in a total of 3268 sentences.

To further improve the performance, we compared the predictions of *multicite-multilabel-scibert* and *paraphrase-mpnet-base-v2* against manual annotations. When both models predicted a class that deviated from manual annotation, we often found classification errors made by the annotator. After performing tenfold cross-validation, we reviewed predictions for the entire dataset and noticed 230 instances of potentially misclassified sentences, roughly seven percent of the dataset. For each of these sentences, we decided if re-labeling was justified and adjusted the annotation for 198 sentences. Table 2 shows the class distribution in the final dataset.

3.4 Development of a Gold Standard

We created a corpus of scientific articles from the International Conference in Wirtschaftsinformatik (WI corpus). We downloaded conference articles from the AIS eLibrary (2022) and removed articles in German as the current approach only works for articles in the English language. This resulted in 506 articles from the years 2015, 2017, 2019, 2021, and 2022. We extracted all sentences from the PDF documents and performed an automated search for IS-related key terms. Only sentences that contained key terms from the IS Ontology were included in the analysis.

We created a gold standard with a sample of this data. To become familiar with the coding process and to discuss deviating results, the author and a master student in IS each manually annotated a sample of 250 sentences by applying the sentence classification framework (see Sect. 3.1). After this, both annotators created a gold standard by manually annotating a new sample of 1000 sentences from the WI-corpus. For each sentence, the annotators assigned one of three possible classes: *belongs_to_article, related_work,* or *background_information.* In addition, the annotators assessed whether the identified key terms in a sentence could be attributed to the focal article by assigning *yes* or *no.*

The sentence "Our study provides a useful framework for interdisciplinary research." contains for instance the key term *framework.* For such sentences, we would use the labels *belongs_to_article* and *yes.* A sentence such as "DevOps is practiced by Facebook [29]" would be classified as *related_work* and *no.*

For the task of sentence classification, both annotators independently assigned the same labels in 866 out of 1000 cases. This resulted in a Cohen's Kappa of 0.79 and fell into the category of substantial agreement (Landis and Koch 1977; SciKit Learn 2022). For the task of assessing whether an identified key term could be attributed to a focal article, both annotators independently assigned the same labels in 889 out of 1000 cases. This resulted in a Cohen's Kappa of 0.77 and fell into the category of substantial agreement (Landis and Koch 1977; SciKit Learn 2022). Throughout discussing the results, the annotators assigned final labels for sentences with deviating classes.

4 Experiments and Results

4.1 Evaluation of Sentence Classification Framework

We assumed that only key terms in sentences classified as *belongs_to_article* describe a focal article. Key terms in other sentence classes either describe related work or provide background information. To test this assumption and thereby evaluate the sentence classification framework, we analyzed the annotations in the gold standard for the task of assessing whether an identified key term could be attributed to a focal article. Table 3 shows the sentence classes and the number of extracted key terms from the IS Ontology regarding whether those describe a focal article. The results confirmed our initial assumption and show that the classification can be used to infer key term attribution in articles.

4.2 Comparison of Model Performance

To identify the best model for the task of inferring the attribution of ontological key terms, we trained and tested the models in two scenarios: Regular fine-tuning (Hugging Face 2023a) and few-shot learning with Setfit (Tunstall et al. 2022). We

Table 3 Key term attribution in sentence classes

Sentence-class	Describes focal article	Describes focal article %	Does not describe focal article	Does not describe focal article %	Total
Belongs to article	401	99.3	3	0.7	410
Related work	1	0.4	232	99.6	233
Background information	0	0.0	357	100.0	357

used the training dataset of 3268 sentences (see Sect. 3.3): 70% of the data were used for training, 20% for validation, and 10% for final testing. We performed tenfold cross-validation so that each model was trained and validated 10 times on different portions of the dataset.

For the reporting of our results, we used standard measures in natural language processing. We calculated macro and weighted average F1 scores where F1 = 2 * (precision * recall)/(precision + recall). Macro average F1 scores provide an unweighted average of F1 scores for individual classes whereas weighted average F1 scores take class imbalance into account (SciKit Learn 2023b).

We applied the following hyperparameters for few-shot learning with Setfit: batch_size = 64, num_iterations = 20, num_epochs = 1, loss_class = CosineSimilarityLoss. For regular fine-tuning, we applied: per_device_train_batch_size = 32, num_train_epochs = 20, learning_rate = 2e-5, and weight_decay = 0.01. The training was performed on Nvidia v100 GPUs. Table 4 shows the results.

We have also trained a multinomial Naive Bayes classifier (SciKit Learn 2023a) to provide a naive benchmark. For this classifier, we removed stopwords from training data, performed word stemming, and transformed all words into lowercase. We applied a bag-of-words approach and performed tenfold cross-validation. This resulted in average macro and weighted F1 scores of 0.678 and 0.686, respectively.

Table 4 Average F1 scores of selected models

Model	Regular fine-tuning		Few-shot learning	
	Macro F1	Weighted F1	Macro F1	Weighted F1
multicite-multilabel-scibert	0.951	0.948	0.953	0.950
paraphrase-mpnet-base-v2	0.943	0.938	0.950	0.945
longformer-scico	0.950	0.945	0.941	0.936
bert-base-uncased	0.938	0.932	0.941	0.936
distilbert-base-uncased-finetuned-sst-2-english	0.935	0.932	0.939	0.935
all-MiniLM-L6-v2	0.928	0.932	0.930	0.925
allenai-specter	0.945	0.940	0.945	0.940

4.3 Evaluation of Gold Standard

To find out how well the models generalize to a different dataset, we compared the models by predicting sentence classes for the 1000 sentences in the gold standard (see Sect. 4.4). We show the detailed results for the best-performing model, *multicite-multilabel-scibert*, in Table 5. Figure 1 provides an additional perspective on the classification performance by illustrating the confusion matrix.

We identified two relevant types of errors: (1) the model classifies a sentence that belongs to an article into a different class, and (2) the model classifies a sentence that belongs to a different class as *belongs_to_article*. We regard the first type of error as less critical. As we want to detect key terms that describe an article, this error means that some key terminology is not detected at all. The second type of error is regarded as more severe because key terminology that describes related work or background information is falsely classified as *belongs_to_article*. The confusion matrix shows that the second type of error occurs less frequently than the first one. Only 19 sentences were wrongly classified as *belongs_to_article*.

Table 5 Results for sentence classification on a sample of WI-conference articles

Classes and averages	Precision	Recall	F1 score	Number of sentences
belongs_to_article	0.95	0.82	0.88	410
related_work	0.92	0.97	0.94	233
background_information	0.85	0.94	0.89	357
macro average	0.9	0.91	0.9	1000
weighted average	0.9	0.9	0.9	1000

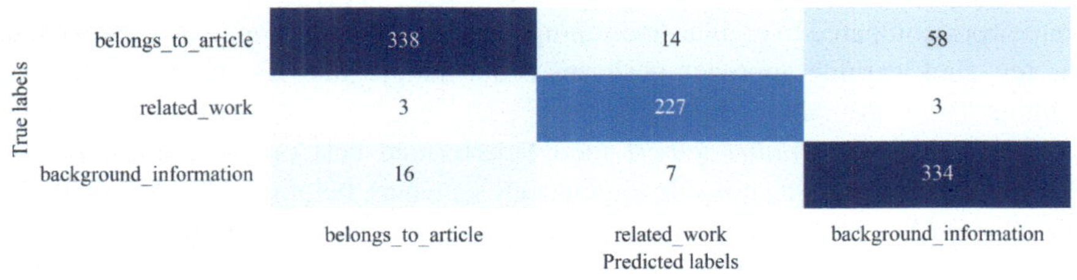

Fig. 1 Confusion matrix

5 Discussion

5.1 Discussion of Results

Referring to RQ1, classifying sentences according to the proposed classification framework proved to be a promising approach to attribute keywords to a focal article as shown in Sect. 4.1. In a sample of 1000 sentences from the WI corpus, we only found four cases where a key term could not be attributed correctly based on the sentence class (see Table 3). In the first case, a specific term was not included in the IS Ontology. Therefore, *Twitter spam* was incorrectly detected as *email spam.* The second case refers to a negated statement where the term *quantitative study* was detected although it was not contained in a focal article: "First, while we derived the conceptual model from theoretical accounts and complementary, exploratory interviews, a rigorous validation (i.e. in terms of a *quantitative study*) is still lacking." In the third case, the term *software support* was detected, although the term *support* was used as a verb: "We reached out to the three online shop vendors to inquire whether their *software supports* personalized price discrimination."

One sentence classified as *related_work* was ambiguous as the first half of the sentence referred to a focal article whereas the second half described related work: "To consider this, these organizational goals were taken into account when developing the *framework* in accordance to Hilty, who further differentiates between rebound effect perspectives of private households, enterprises and states."

For the task of sentence classification (RQ2), we found only small differences in the F1 scores of the models, ranging between 0.925 and 0.951 (see Table 4). This indicates that training with a limited amount of data—as performed in this research—results in good performance across models based on a transformer architecture. Interestingly, we noticed almost no improvement by applying a few-shot learning framework compared to regular fine-tuning (see Sect. 4.2). We can only assume that the few-shot learning approach performs better than regular fine-tuning when less training data is available.

The *multicite-multilabel-scibert* model performed best on the gold standard. Although the model was not able to detect all sentences belonging to a focal article (recall = 0.82), it performed very well in predicting the correct classes for the detected sentences (precision = 0.95). These results suggest that important keywords are overlooked in some cases, but are rarely incorrectly attributed to an article.

An analysis of misclassified sentences showed that classification errors mainly occurred in cases where sentences contained ambiguous signals, making it hard to infer if mentioned findings relate to a focal article or related work. In those cases, considering additional context information, such as adjacent sentences or the relative position in the article might improve classification results.

5.2 Limitations

One limitation of our approach is the dependence on a domain ontology. As research progresses, new terms are introduced regularly. If such terms are not included in an ontology, they would be missed. We, therefore, need ways to update a domain ontology with current terminology to make our approach sustainable. Semi-automated approaches could for instance identify author-generated keywords from recent articles where a language model could search for similar key terms in an ontology to recommend placing those into the existing hierarchy.

Another limitation relates to the definition of the class *belongs_to_article* in the classification framework. Currently, one of the main indicators for this class is the usage of personal pronouns, e.g., "We performed a case study". However, for articles written in the passive voice, additional indicators must be present to perform a correct classification, e.g., "In this article, a case study is performed." For sentences written in the passive voice without any indicators, adding additional context information from adjacent sentences might be a way to improve classification performance.

5.3 Implications

With the presented approach, we hope to inform the design of novel tools and technologies that support researchers in more quickly gaining insights from analyzing literature. The approach could for instance be implemented in systems aiming to perform semi-automated systematic literature reviews, especially assessing reviews that synthesize the literature to identify trends, research gaps, and under-researched areas as suggested by Leidner (2018). As a use case example, we searched for the top 5 research methods in the WI corpus (see Sect. 4.4). Based on ontological key terms in sentences that describe the contents of an article, Table 6 shows the number of articles that used a specific method. In contrast to manual approaches, this analysis was not conducted over days or weeks, but in minutes.

Implementing our approach in search engines or domain-specific databases such as the AIS Library (2023) could enable semantic filter options making it possible to identify articles that discuss specific theories, methods, or topics. Furthermore, the

Table 6 Top 5 research methods in WI corpus by article count

Research method	2015	2017	2019	2021	2022	Total
Literature study	48	47	53	60	71	279
Design science	35	38	35	39	48	195
Qualitative interview	39	35	34	41	38	187
Survey	37	27	43	36	30	173
Conceptual modeling	33	24	22	13	18	110

approach could support research in novel directions where a collection of articles could be dynamically filtered according to ontological key terms to enable automated summarization of findings through the use of large language models such as ChatGPT. Understanding whether fine-tuning large language models on ontologically indexed data could potentially help in reducing the phenomenon of hallucination (Susarla et al. 2023) might be a future research direction.

6 Conclusion

We see the main contribution of this article in the following points:

1. Developing a framework for classifying sentences in scientific publications
2. Creating an annotated dataset of 3268 sentences from open-access publications that we made publicly available, enabling researchers to build up on our findings
3. Comparing and evaluating state-of-the-art sentence transformer algorithms with a novel few-shot learning technique
4. Performing and evaluating sentence classification on the WI corpus and providing a use case example for automated knowledge extraction capabilities.

We showed that a combination of sentence classification and ontological annotation can support researchers in extracting domain knowledge from large corpora of research articles in a fraction of the time usually required.

Future work could further improve prediction accuracy by including additional context information when training language models, such as adjacent sentences, paragraphs, or positional information of sentences within an article. Semi-automated methods for updating domain ontologies will make our approach more sustainable. Furthermore, conducting user studies where researchers use our approach in a practical setting might lead to novel methods to conduct semi-automated analyses of scientific literature.

References

AI2 (2021), Semantic Scholar | AI-Powered Research Tool, https://www.semanticscholar.org/, Accessed: 15.11.2021.

AIS (2021), Senior Scholars' Basket of Journals, https://aisnet.org/page/SeniorScholarBasket, Accessed: 15.11.2021.

AIS eLibrary (2022), AIS Electronic Library - Proceedings of Wirtschaftsinformatik-Conference, https://aisel.aisnet.org/wi/, Accessed: 28.2.2023.

AIS Library (2023), Association for Information Systems (AIS) eLibrary, https://aisel.aisnet.org/, Accessed: 31.5.2023.

Anisienia, A., Mueller, R.M., Kupfer, A. & Staake, T. (2021), Research Method Classification with Deep Transfer Learning for Semi-Automatic Meta-Analysis of Information Systems Papers, *in* 'Hawaii International Conference on System Sciences (HICSS)'.

Asadi, N., Badie, K. & Mahmoudi, M.T. (2019), 'Automatic Zone Identification in Scientific Papers via Fusion Techniques', *Scientometrics* **119**(2), pp. 845–862.

Barki, H., Rivard, S. & Talbot, J. (1988), 'An Information Systems Keyword Classification Scheme', *MIS Quarterly* **12**(2), p. 299.

Barki, H., Rivard, S. & Talbot, J. (1993), 'A Keyword Classification Scheme for IS Research Literature: An Update', *MIS Quarterly* **17**(2), p. 209.

Beltagy, I., Cohan, A., Logan Iv, R., Min, S. & Singh, S. (2022), Zero- and Few-Shot NLP with Pretrained Language Models, *in* 'Proceedings of the 60th Annual Meeting of the Association for Computational Linguistics: Tutorial Abstracts' Association for Computational Linguistics, pp. 32–37.

Brack, A., Hoppe, A., Buschermöhle, P. & Ewerth, R. (2022), Cross-Domain Multi-Task Learning for Sequential Sentence Classification in Research Papers, *in* 'Proceedings of the 22nd ACM/IEEE Joint Conference on Digital Libraries (JCDL)' Association for Computing Machinery (ACM).

Cameron, J.D., Ramaprasad, A. & Syn, T. (2017), 'An ontology of and roadmap for mHealth research', *International Journal of Medical Informatics* **100**, pp. 16–25.

Cattan, A. & Johnson, S. (2021), SCICO: Hierarchical Cross-Document Coreference for Scientific Concepts, *in* 'Automated Knowledge Base Construction (AKBC)'.

Claver, E., González, R. & Llopis, J. (2000), 'An analysis of research in information systems (1981–1997)', *Information & Management* **37**(4), pp. 181–195.

Cohan, A., Ammar, W., van Zuylen, M. & Cady, F. (2019), Structural Scaffolds for Citation Intent Classification in Scientific Publications, *in* 'Proceedings of the 2019 Conference of the North American Chapter of the Association for Computational Linguistics: Human Language Technologies (NAACL)'.

Cohan, A., Feldman, S., Beltagy, I., Downey, D. & Weld, D. (2020), SPECTER: Document-level Representation Learning using Citation-informed Transformers, *in* 'Proceedings of the 58th Annual Meeting of the Association for Computational Linguistics'.

Devlin, J., Chang, M.-W., Lee, K. & Toutanova, K. (2019), BERT: Pre-training of Deep Bidirectional Transformers for Language Understanding, *in* 'Proceedings of NAACL-HLT'

Eckle-Kohler, J., Nghiem, T.-D. & Gurevych, I. (2013), Automatically assigning research methods to journal articles in the domain of social sciences: Automatically Assigning Research Methods to Journal Articles in the Domain of Social Sciences, *in* 'Proceedings of the American Society for Information Science and Technology', pp. 1–8.

Elsevier (2015), Scopus - the largest abstract and citation database of peer-reviewed literature: scientific journals, books and conference proceedings, http://www.elsevier.com/online-tools/scopus, Accessed: 29.4.2015.

Gonçalves, S., Cortez, P. & Moro, S. (2020), 'A Deep Learning Classifier for Sentence Classification in Biomedical and Computer Science Abstracts', *Neural Computing and Applications* **32**(11), pp. 6793–6807.

Google Scholar (2023), About Google Scholar, https://scholar.google.de/intl/de/scholar/about.html, Accessed: 6.3.2023.

Gregg, D.G. & Scott, J.E. (2008), 'A typology of complaints about eBay sellers', *Communications of the ACM* **51**(4), pp. 69–74.

GROBID (2022), GROBID - A machine learning software for extracting information from scholarly documents, https://github.com/kermitt2/grobid, Accessed: 30.6.2022.

Honnibal, M. & Montani, I. (2021), spaCy - Industrial-strength Natural Language Processing in Python, https://spacy.io/, Accessed: 17.11.2021.

Huettemann, S. (2023), GitHub Repository: Sentence Classification Data, https://github.com/sebastianhuettemann/sentence_classification, Accessed: 13.6.2023.

Hugging Face (2023a), Fine-tune a pretrained model, https://huggingface.co/docs/transformers/training, Accessed: 19.6.2023.

Hugging Face (2023b), Model Overview: bert-base-uncased, https://huggingface.co/bert-base-uncased, Accessed: 15.6.2023.

Hugging Face (2023c), Model Overview: distilbert-base-uncased-finetuned-sst-2-english, https://huggingface.co/distilbert-base-uncased-finetuned-sst-2-english, Accessed: 22.2.2023.
Hugging Face (2023d), Model Overview: longformer-scico, https://huggingface.co/allenai/longformer-scico, Accessed: 15.6.2023.
Hugging Face (2023e), Model Overview: multicite-multilabel-scibert, https://huggingface.co/allenai/multicite-multilabel-scibert, Accessed: 15.6.2023.
Hugging Face (2023f), Model Overview: paraphrase-multilingual-mpnet-base-v2, https://huggingface.co/sentence-transformers/paraphrase-multilingual-mpnet-base-v2, Accessed: 15.6.2023.
Hugging Face (2023g), Model Overview: sentence-transformers/all-MiniLM-L6-v2, https://huggingface.co/sentence-transformers/all-MiniLM-L6-v2, Accessed: 22.2.2023.
Hugging Face (2023h), Model Overview: specter, https://huggingface.co/allenai/specter, Accessed: 15.6.2023.
Hugging Face (2023i), Pretrained Models: Sentence-Transformers documentation, https://www.sbert.net/docs/pretrained_models.html, Accessed: 15.6.2023.
Jin, D. & Szolovits, P. (2018), Hierarchical Neural Networks for Sequential Sentence Classification in Medical Scientific Abstracts, *in* 'Proceedings of the 2018 Conference on Empirical Methods in Natural Language Processing' Association for Computational Linguistics, pp. 3100–3109.
John Morley (2018), *Academic Phrasebank 2018 Enhanced Edition*. The University of Manchester.
Kupfer, A. (2018), Research Methods in the Information Systems Discipline: A Literature Analysis of Conference Papers, *in* 'Americas Conference on Information Systems (AMCIS) 2018 Proceedings'.
La Paz, A., Merigó, J.M., Powell, P., Ramaprasad, A. & Syn, T. (2020), 'Twenty-five years of the Information Systems Journal: A bibliometric and ontological overview', *Information Systems Journal* **30**(3), pp. 431–457.
Landis, J.R. & Koch, G.G. (1977), 'The Measurement of Observer Agreement for Categorical Data', *Biometrics* **33**(1), p. 159.
Larsen, K.R., Hekler, E.B., Paul, M.J. & Gibson, B.S. (2020), 'Improving Usability of Social and Behavioral Sciences' Evidence: A Call to Action for a National Infrastructure Project for Mining Our Knowledge', *Communications of the Association for Information Systems*, pp. 1–17.
Larsen, K.R., Hovorka, D.S., Dennis, A.R. & West, J.D. (2019), 'Understanding the Elephant: The Discourse Approach to Boundary Identification and Corpus Construction for Theory Review Articles', *Journal of the Association for Information Systems*, pp. 887–927.
Lauscher, A., Ko, B., Kuehl, B., Johnson, S., Cohan, A., Jurgens, D. & Lo, K. (2022), MultiCite: Modeling realistic citations requires moving beyond the single-sentence single-label setting, *in* 'Proceedings of the 2022 Conference of the North American Chapter of the Association for Computational Linguistics: Human Language Technologies', pp. 1875–1889.
Lee, Y., Kozar, K.A. & Larsen, K.R.T. (2003), 'The Technology Acceptance Model: Past, Present, and Future', *Communications of the Association for Information Systems* **12**
Leidner, D. (2018), 'Review and Theory Symbiosis: An Introspective Retrospective', *Journal of the Association for Information Systems* **19**(06), pp. 552–567.
Li, J., Larsen, K. & Abbasi, A. (2020), 'TheoryOn: A Design Framework and System for Unlocking Behavioral Knowledge Through Ontology Learning', *MIS Quarterly* **44**(4), pp. 1733–1772.
Mueller, R.M., Huettemann, S., Larsen, K.R., Yan, S. & Handler, A. (2022), Toward an Information Systems Ontology, *in* 'Proceedings of the 17th International Conference on Design Science Research in Information Systems and Technology (DESRIST)'.
Neves, M., Butzke, D. & Grune, B. (2019), Evaluation of Scientific Elements for Text Similarity in Biomedical Publications, *in* 'Proceedings of the 6th Workshop on Argument Mining' Association for Computational Linguistics, pp. 124–135.
Nickerson, R.C., Varshney, U. & Muntermann, J. (2013), 'A method for taxonomy development and its application in information systems', *European Journal of Information Systems* **22**(3), pp. 336–359.
Oelen, A., Stocker, M. & Auer, S. (2021), Crowdsourcing Scholarly Discourse Annotations, *in* '26th International Conference on Intelligent User Interfaces' ACM, pp. 464–474.

OpenAI (2023), 'GPT-4 Technical Report', *arXiv*.

Ramaprasad, A. & Syn, T. (2015), 'Ontological Meta-Analysis and Synthesis', *Communications of the Association for Information Systems* **37**, https://aisel.aisnet.org/cais/vol37/iss1/7/, Accessed: 29.9.2021.

Reimers, N. & Gurevych, I. (2019), Sentence-BERT: Sentence Embeddings using Siamese BERT-Networks, *in* 'Proceedings of the 2019 Conference on Empirical Methods in Natural Language Processing and the 9th International Joint Conference on Natural Language Processing (EMNLP-IJCNLP)', pp. 3980–3990.

Reiss, M.V. (2023), 'Testing the Reliability of ChatGPT for Text Annotation and Classification: A Cautionary Remark', *arXiv* , http://arxiv.org/abs/2304.11085, Accessed: 15.6.2023.

Saldaña, J. (2013), *The coding manual for qualitative researchers.* SAGE Publications.

SciKit Learn (2022), Cohen's kappa: a statistic that measures inter-annotator agreement, https://www.scikit-learn/stable/modules/generated/sklearn.metrics.cohen_kappa_score.html, Accessed: 10.3.2023.

SciKit Learn (2023a), Naive Bayes classifier for multinomial models, https://www.scikit-learn/stable/modules/generated/sklearn.naive_bayes.MultinomialNB.html, Accessed: 19.6.2023.

SciKit Learn (2023b), SciKit Learn Metrics - sklearn.metrics.f1_score, https://www.scikit-learn/stable/modules/generated/sklearn.metrics.f1_score.html, Accessed: 5.3.2023.

Springer, V. & Petrik, D. (2021), Towards a Taxonomy of Impact Factors for Digital Platform Pricing, *in* Lecture Notes in Business Information Processing, Springer, pp. 115–124.

Susarla, A., Gopal, R., Thatcher, J.B. & Sarker, S. (2023), 'The Janus Effect of Generative AI: Charting the Path for Responsible Conduct of Scholarly Activities in Information Systems', *Information Systems Research.*

Tate, M., Furtmueller, E., Evermann, J. & Bandara, W. (2015), 'Introduction to the Special Issue: The Literature Review in Information Systems', *Communications of the Association for Information Systems* **37**.

Thomson-Reuters (2015), Web of Science - the world's leading source of scholarly research data, http://wokinfo.com, Accessed: 29.4.2015.

Tunstall, L., Reimers, N., Jo, U.E.S., Bates, L., Korat, D., Wasserblat, M. & Pereg, O. (2022), Efficient Few-Shot Learning Without Prompts, *in* '36th Conference on Neural Information Processing Systems (NeurIPS)'.

Wagner, G., Lukyanenko, R. & Paré, G. (2021), 'Artificial intelligence and the conduct of literature reviews', *Journal of Information Technology* **37**(2), pp. 209–226.

Wolf, T. et al. (2020), Transformers: State-of-the-Art Natural Language Processing, *in* 'Proceedings of the 2020 Conference on Empirical Methods in Natural Language Processing: System Demonstrations' Association for Computational Linguistics, pp. 38–45.

Beyond Binary Boundaries—Exploring the Potential of Categorical Variables in Counterfactual Explanations

Philipp Hühn and Simon Hofer

Abstract The rapid development of Artificial Intelligence (AI) has brought about significant changes in various industries. However, the opaqueness of AI systems leads to blind trust, distrust, or even avoidance of the systems altogether. Against this background, counterfactual explanation methods generate human-understandable explanations of how an AI system arrives at a given output. However, the thorough integration of categorical variables in the generation of counterfactual explanations remains a challenging research problem. In this paper, we investigate by means of a user study how a human-like handling of categorical variables affects users' perception of explanations for a state-of-the-art counterfactual explanation approach. The results show that using a human-like handling of categorical variables leads to the generation of explanations preferred by users. Moreover, we find that the handling of categorical variables affects users' perceptions of the concreteness, coherence, and relevance of the generated counterfactual explanations.

Keywords Explainable artificial intelligence · Counterfactual explanations · Categorical variables · User study

1 Introduction

Artificial Intelligence (AI) is rapidly evolving with significant impact on various industries (Boobier 2018), ranging from healthcare (Lee and Yoon 2021) and education (Chen et al. 2020) to finance (Kaur et al. 2020) and creative industries (Anantrasirichai and Bull 2022). However, besides its undeniable potential to revolutionize future ways of living, employing AI also bears significant challenges and risks. Insufficient data or biased data distribution can lead to incorrect training of

P. Hühn (✉) · S. Hofer
Ulm University, Institute of Business Analytics, Ulm, Germany
e-mail: philipp.huehn@uni-ulm.de

S. Hofer
e-mail: simon.hofer@uni-ulm.de

D. Beverungen et al. (eds.), *Solutions and Technologies for Responsible Digitalization*, Lecture Notes in Information Systems and Organisation 75,
https://doi.org/10.1007/978-3-031-80122-8_11

AI systems, resulting in discriminatory outcomes (Ferrer et al. 2021). Moreover, several AI systems are "black boxes," meaning that the reasons for their decisions remain opaque to their users, leading to blind trust or distrust, or even avoidance of the systems altogether (Herse et al. 2018). According to an expert group on AI appointed by the European Commission, the lack of trustworthiness in AI systems could lead to undesirable consequences and hinder their adoption (HLEG-AI 2019). To address these issues, the field of Explainable Artificial Intelligence (XAI) has emerged, providing methods to automatically generate human-understandable explanations of how an AI system arrives at a given output (Arrieta et al. 2020). However, current XAI methods for explanation generation are often criticized for their lack of user-centricity, which is detrimental to their goals (Förster et al. 2020). Incorporating insights from social science about how humans construct explanations, researchers consider counterfactual explanations to be particularly human-friendly (Miller 2019). Counterfactual explanation methods generate "what if" scenarios similar to the actual scenario but with an alternative model-output to enable users a better understanding of how the model arrived at a particular decision (Miller 2019; Verma et al. 2022). The inclusion of categorical variables is an important factor for user-centricity within counterfactual explanations (Förster et al. 2022; Warren et al. 2023). However, despite their ubiquity in real-world data, categorical variables have been largely neglected in counterfactual explanation research (Förster et al. 2022; van Looveren and Klaise 2021). Whereas in real-world datasets and human perception, categorical data can take various forms and exhibit linear or non-linear ordering, with features that possess varying degrees of similarity (Förster et al. 2022), prevailing approaches typically employ a 0/1 distance measure for all categorical variables (Dandl et al. 2020; Sharma et al. 2020). This simplistic approach does not adequately capture the intricate relationships both between and within categorical variables and counteracts user-centralization of the generated explanations (Förster et al. 2022; Mothilal et al. 2020; van Looveren and Klaise 2021). Aiming to improve the user-centricity of counterfactual explanations, Förster et al. (2022) developed a human-like approach to handle categorical variables.

Against this background, our research aims to examine the potential impact of employing a more human-like methodology to handle categorical variables on the users' perception of counterfactual explanations. To this end, we conduct a user study based on a state-of-the-art counterfactual explanation approach (Rasouli and Chieh Yu 2022) in which we investigate the influence of a human-like handling of categorical variables on user perception, e.g., their perceived relevance, coherence, and concreteness of the explanations. We find that explanations generated using a human-like handling of categorical variables are favored by users and perceived as significantly more relevant, coherent, and concrete. Additionally, we observe that the contrast between the hypothetical "what if" scenario and the actual scenario is perceived as significantly smaller and more feasible.

The remainder of this paper is structured as follows: Sect. 2 provides an overview of the theoretical background and related work and concludes with the research gap. In Sect. 3, we describe the methodology of our user study and subsequently, in Sect. 4, present its results. We critically discuss implications and limitations of our research and provide directions for future research in Sect. 5. Finally, we conclude with a summary.

2 Theoretical Background and Related Work

2.1 Counterfactual Explanations

The research field of XAI seeks to foster human understanding of AI systems by providing automatically generated explanations for their outputs (Arrieta et al. 2020). This requires that the explanations are designed in a “user-centric” manner to enable users to gain a deeper understanding of the reasoning behind the AI system’s decisions (Förster et al. 2020). User-centric XAI research is influenced by the way humans construct explanations, and therefore proposes counterfactual explanations (Miller 2019). These explanations consist of two key elements: the fact, which represents the event that resulted in the AI system’s output, and the foil, which represents an alternative event that would have led to a different output. The contrast between the fact and the foil forms the basis of the explanation (Lipton 1990; Wachter et al. 2018). One major objective of counterfactual explanation approaches is to keep the contrasts of these explanations small among other things to ensure their coherence (Förster et al. 2022; Miller 2019; Wachter et al. 2018).

In recent years, considerable progress has been made in the research area of counterfactual explanations, predominantly using optimization-based methods (Bhatt et al. 2020; Guidotti 2022; Verma et al. 2022). The search for a foil in optimization-based methods relies on the minimization of an objective function that encapsulates the method’s objectives (Wachter et al. 2018). This class of methods can be subcategorized into two distinct groups: those that employ gradient-based optimizers and those that employ gradient-free optimizers to find optimal foils (Guidotti 2022; Verma et al. 2022). Gradient-free optimization methods have certain advantages over gradient-based methods, including independence from model-specific information, applicability to categorical data, and improved computational efficiency (Guidotti 2022; Verma et al. 2022). Against this background, these algorithms are equally applicable to any kind of black box as well as white box models (Verma et al. 2022). Among the group of gradient-free optimization algorithms, genetic optimization algorithms exhibit promising potential (Dandl et al. 2020; Sharma et al. 2020). Genetic optimization algorithms draw inspiration from genetic principles, including gene coding, selection, mutation, and crossover, in order to identify the optimal solution. This involves creating a population of candidate solutions and repeatedly applying genetic operators to the population to generate new, potentially better solutions (Guo et al. 2010; Lambora et al. 2019). In contrast to traditional gradient-free optimization approaches performing a local stepwise search procedure by comparing nearby points and moving to the relative optimal points, genetic algorithms do not tend to get stuck in local optima (Guo et al. 2010; Jabbar et al. 2013; Lambora et al.

2019). Recently, a promising approach based on a genetic optimization algorithm was presented by Rasouli and Chieh Yu (2022). Their proposed algorithm CARE uses a multi-objective optimization technique leading to the generation of counterfactuals, that consider various trade-offs between the proposed objectives (Rasouli and Chieh Yu 2022). In addition, CARE contains various modules to satisfy properties for actionable recourse, such as validity or soundness which can be enabled or disabled according to a user's preferences.

2.2 *Categorical Variables in Counterfactual Explanations*

In the context of counterfactual explanations, categorical variables have been found to be more conducive to human understanding of an AI model's predictions than continuous variables (Warren et al. 2023). In light of this, literature emphasizes the inclusion of categorical variables as a critical factor in ensuring user-centricity in the context of counterfactual explanations (Förster et al. 2022; Warren et al. 2023). However, notwithstanding significant recent advances, counterfactual explanation methods have been found to fall short in the treatment of categorical variables (van Looveren and Klaise 2021). Categorical variables are frequently encountered in real-world applications and may exhibit linear (e.g., the interior condition of houses) or non-linear (e.g., real estate-type) ordering, with features that have varying degrees of similarity (e.g., a row-end house has more similarities to a semi-detached or single family home than to a villa or a commercial real estate property) (Förster et al. 2022; Russell 2019; van Looveren and Klaise 2021). Although the ability of genetic approaches to handle categorical data represents a significant advance over previous methods, they still lack the ability to account for the type or order of categorical variables (Dandl et al. 2020; Rasouli and Chieh Yu 2022; Sharma et al. 2020). They all use a simple matching system to calculate the distance for categorical variables: If the values within a categorical variable differ between two objects, the distance is set to 1, otherwise to 0 (Dandl et al. 2020; Rasouli and Chieh Yu 2022; Sharma et al. 2020). While this approach results in few categorical variables being changed, what matters to humans is not just whether a variable is changed but how it is changed (Förster et al. 2022). Exemplary, improving the interior condition of a house from 'simple' to 'normal' requires less effort than to 'luxurious'. Recent studies show that users perceive such differences in the similarity of values of categorical variables (Warren et al. 2023). Thus, a simple 0/1 distance measurement for categorical variables fails to capture the intricate relationships between and within categorical variables being perceived by humans (Mothilal et al. 2020; van Looveren and Klaise 2021).

2.3 Distance Measurement for Categorical Variables in Counterfactual Explanations

In the context of counterfactual explanations, a recently proposed approach with the primary objective to enhance the coherence and user-centricity includes also a novel technique for handling categorical variables (Förster et al. 2022). This technique presented by Förster et al. (2022) involves distinct treatment of linearly and non-linearly ordered categorical variables and an estimation of similarities between individual features of variables based on interrelations in the training data, specified in terms of Markov Chains. Because this approach, like human perception, assigns distinct similarities to different expressions of categorical variables, it handles categorical variables more human-like. In a nutshell, the estimation of the similarities is carried out by analyzing the impact of swapping categorical variable values of training data points on an estimated probability density function (PDF) (Förster et al. 2022). For this purpose, in the first step a Kernel Density Estimation (KDE) on the training data based on different kernels for linear and non-linear categorical variables is used to obtain an estimate for the PDF (Förster et al. 2021, 2022; Racine 2008). In the second step, Förster et al. (2022) estimate transition probabilities of features of categorical variables by swapping these features within training data points and analyzing the average effects on the KDE of these data points. These transition probabilities form the basis of the Markov Chains used to measure the distance of categorical variables (Förster et al. 2022). This distance measure aims to ensure the contrasts' closeness, sparseness, and feasibility by accounting for a potential ordering of categorical variables, as well as differences in the similarities of feature values of categorical variables (Förster et al. 2022). These characteristics are necessary for a counterfactual explanation to be perceived as coherent (Miller 2019). An evaluation of the approach, which includes further design decisions to increase coherence in addition to the distance measure, showed that its explanations are indeed perceived as more coherent compared to explanations generated using approaches presented by Wachter et al. (2018) and Sharma et al. (2020) that do not focus on coherence (Förster et al. 2022).

2.4 Research Gap

In summary, counterfactual explanations are a promising approach for generating user-centric explanations. However, prior research shows that proper handling of categorical variables is required to achieve this goal from the users' perspective. Nonetheless, despite the importance of categorical variables to users, a large proportion of current state-of-the-art approaches do not treat categorical variables as users perceive them. In their counterfactual explanation approach, Förster et al. (2022) take an important first step to a proper handling of categorical variables by using a more human-like measure to assess the distance between and within categorical variables. In an initial evaluation, Förster et al. (2022) showed that this handling of categorical variables in combination with other design decisions helps to increase the perceived coherence of explanations. However, beyond that, it has not yet been investigated how a human-like handling of categorical variables affects users' perception of counterfactual explanations. Against this background, our work aims to investigate the effects of human-like handling of categorical variables on the perception of counterfactual explanations in a user study. For this purpose, we implement a state-of-the-art counterfactual explanation approach once conventionally and once with the more human-like handling of categorical variables and compare the resulting explanations regarding user preference as well as their perceived relevance, concreteness, and coherence including the perception of the distance, sparsity, and feasibility of the explanations' contrasts.

3 Methodology

To investigate the impact of a more human-like handling of categorical variables on users' perceptions, we implemented and conducted an online user study using the oTree framework (Chen et al. 2016), in which participants were confronted with an AI-based price prediction for real estate objects. To explain the AI prediction, participants were presented with two explanations generated by a state-of-the-art counterfactual explanation approach using once it's conventional and once a more human-like handling of categorical variables. By means of assessing users' perception of several decisive characteristics of explanations in the context of XAI, we statistically analyze the effects of using a human-like handling of categorical variables.

3.1 Case Setting and Data Set

In order to assess the impact of incorporating a human-like handling of categorical variables in a state-of-the-art counterfactual explanation method on users' perceptions, it is necessary to instantiate this method in a use-case where categorical variables play a major role. Against this background, we choose house-price prediction as our use-case, as both numerical and categorical variables have a major impact on house-prices. As a basis for this use-case, we utilized a data set containing data from a large online marketplace for houses in Germany (Förster et al. 2022). The data set contains 52,557 rows where each row represents a house sold in Germany including its price as well as characteristic information of the houses contained in 20 structured variables.

3.2 AI Model and XAI Approach

Following Förster et al. (2022), we used 13 variables (6 numerical and 7 categorical variables) to train a gradient boosting model classifying the houses with an accuracy of about 80% into 8 price ranges. We decided to use a black box gradient boosting model because, although all approaches presented in this paper are equally applicable to white box models, the application on black box models is particularly relevant in the context of XAI. To generate explanations for the predictions, we used a promising state-of-the-art counterfactual explanation approach known as CARE, which uses a multi-objective genetic optimization to generate counterfactuals (Rasouli and Chieh Yu 2022). This approach allows for the consideration of various trade-offs among the proposed objectives. CARE emphasizes the coherence of explanations and therefore represents a good starting point for investigating the impact of a human-like handling of categorical variables developed in the context of coherence on user perception. In addition to coherence, CARE provides modules designed to satisfy properties for actionable recourse, such as validity or soundness, which can be customized based on user preferences. Overall, CARE constitutes an effective counterfactual explanation approach that has demonstrated its superiority over several other state-of-the-art algorithms (Rasouli and Chieh Yu 2022). However, in line with the customary practice in the research field of counterfactual explanations, CARE is based on a simple 0/1 distance measure for categorical variables. We instantiated CARE using all available modules in the objective function (Rasouli and Chieh Yu 2022) as well as the human-like distance measure for categorical variables presented by Förster et al. (2022). Based on this, we further instantiated an adoption of CARE where the conventional 0/1 distance measure used in CARE is replaced by the more human-like distance measure proposed by Förster et al. (2022). In the following, we refer to this instantiation as CARE_CAT. By making use of information on the similarities between values of categorical variables contained in the density of the training data (cf. Sect. 2.3), within CARE_CAT deviations of foil candidates from the fact in categorical variables result in a different evaluation of their distance, depending on the deviating variable and values. For example, a change from the interior condition 'simple' to 'normal' is penalized less than a change to 'luxurious'. We expect that this awareness of the relationships within the values of categorical variables in the generation process of counterfactual explanations will lead to the generation of explanations that are more in line with human expectation since the changes in categorical variables follow more human-like progression (with non-binary steps). To ensure comparability, we used the same parametrizations including the probability threshold, number of populations and generations, and constraints for CARE and CARE_CAT. We used both CARE and CARE_CAT to generate valid foils for facts randomly selected from the test data set. Table 1 shows two exemplary foils generated using CARE and CARE_CAT to explain the price classification of the gradient boosting model for the same fact.

Table 1 Exemplary foils from the user study generated using CARE and CARE_CAT

Variable	Fact	Foil CARE	Foil CARE_CAT
Building type	Single fam. home	Single fam. home	Single fam. home
Year constructed	1956	1956	1956
Living space	131 m^2	152 m^2	131 m^2
No. of rooms	5	5	5
No. of floors	1	1	1
Lot area	1347 m^2	947 m^2	964 m^2
Heating type	Central heating	Central heating	Central heating
Cellar	Yes	Yes	Yes
Building condition	Needs renovation	Needs renovation	Refurbished
Interior condition	Simple	Luxurious	Normal
Parking lots	2	2	2
County	Ostvorpommern	Ostvorpommern	Ostvorpommern
State	Mecklenburg-Vorpommern	Mecklenburg-Vorpommern	Mecklenburg-Vorpommern
Price class in € (k)	100–200	200–300	200–300

3.3 Study Procedure and Participants

We conducted the user study utilizing an online survey deployed using the oTree framework (Chen et al. 2016), accessible via web browsers on both mobile and desktop devices. The study consisted of three phases. During the initial phase, participants were provided with a concise introduction to the use-case, as well as a description of their task. The participants were informed that they will be presented with several examples of AI-generated house price estimates and that for each estimation two additional houses with either higher or lower price estimations will be provided to increase their understanding of how the AI model works. This introductory phase was designed to establish a clear understanding and context for the subsequent tasks assigned to the participants. Within the second phase of the study, participants were required to perform seven rounds of a task. In each round, they were presented with a house that was put up for sale, with its price classification estimated by the AI. In addition, the participants were presented with two alternative houses, generated using CARE and CARE_CAT, to elucidate the AI's prediction. The selection of houses put up for sale was performed using random sampling from the test data.

The two alternative houses were presented to the participants in a randomized order, with the first house displayed always referred to as "Alternative property 1" and the second house referred to as "Alternative property 2". Based on this information, the participants were asked to answer questions about their perception of the explanations (cf. Measurement and Analysis). During the third and final phase of the study, participants were requested to provide demographic information, including their gender, age, and highest level of education. In addition, participants were asked to indicate their level of proficiency in the task, which encompassed details regarding their previous experience in buying or selling a house within the last decade, their familiarity with handling real estate transactions on a regular basis, and their general knowledge of the real estate domain.

We recruited 65 participants to partake in our study. Upon analysis, we excluded two participants from the study due to their unusually short completion times and homogeneous responses to the questions posed. Thus, the remaining sample size amounted to 63 participants, ranging in age from 20 to 70 years, of whom 36 identified as male, 25 identified as female, 1 identified as non-binary, and 1 opted not to disclose their gender. All participants had at least a secondary education and exhibited predominantly average knowledge concerning housing-related matters.

3.4 Measurement and Analysis

To investigate the impact of using a human-like handling of categorical variables, in line with recommendations from literature, we assessed different proven constructs of the users' perception of the explanations (Haque et al. 2023). First, we asked the participants which of the two explanations they preferred for comprehending the prediction made by the AI (*Preference*). Second, we let the users compare the explanation pair with respect to the characteristics found to be the most decisive in the context of XAI, namely *Relevance*, *Coherence*, and *Concreteness* (Förster et al. 2020). Third, we asked the users to compare the explanations with respect to the properties of the explanations' contrasts, the human-like handling of categorical variables proposed by Förster et al. (2022) was designed to provide an improvement, i.e., the *Distance*, *Sparsity*, and *Feasibility* of the contrasts. Following the methodology employed by Förster et al. (2020) we utilized a single-choice question ("Alternative property 1" or "Alternative property 2") to assess the users' *Preference* concerning the explanations. The comparisons of the perception of the characteristics of the explanations (i.e., *Relevance*, *Coherence*, and *Concreteness*) as well as of their contrasts' properties (i.e., *Closeness*, *Sparsity*, and *Feasibility*) were conducted using 7-point Likert-Scales ranging from "(− 3) Definitely alternative property 1" to "(3) Definitely alternative property 2". We calculated the average ratings of all constructs for each of the explanation pairs shown to the participants. In total, 42 pairs of explanations have been rated by multiple users in the study. Based on the average ratings we employed one-sided t-tests to statistically evaluate if the human-like handling of categorical variables implemented in CARE_CAT has a positive effect on the aforementioned constructs.

4 Results

We conducted a user study to investigate whether the use of a human-like handling of categorical variables in the generation process of a state-of-the-art counterfactual explanation method affects users' perception of the explanations. In the following, we describe the results based on the user study.

First, we find that, on average, users select the explanations generated with CARE_CAT significantly more often as their preferred explanation (cf. Table 2, *Preference*). Further examination demonstrates that for the majority of the explanation pairs, more users preferred the explanations generated by CARE_CAT (cf. Fig. 1).

Second, we analyzed the impact of the human-like handling of categorical variables on the most decisive characteristics of explanations in the context of XAI. This analysis shows that the human-like handling of categorical variables has a significant positive impact on users' perception of all three characteristics, namely *Relevance*, *Coherence*, and *Concreteness*. The results further indicate that *Coherence* is the characteristic most greatly impacted with a mean effect of 0.412 (cf. Table 2).

Third, analyzing the users' perceptions of the explanations' contrasts' properties we find that integrating a human-like handling of categorical variables significantly increases the perceived *Closeness* and *Feasibility* (cf. Table 2). However, we do not detect a significant effect of the human-like handling of categorical variables on the perceived sparsity of the explanations' contrasts (cf. Table 2). A more detailed analysis shows that although the perception of *Closeness* exhibits to be most strongly influenced on average, with a mean effect of 0.454, the perception varies between the pairs of explanations (cf. Fig. 2). This indicates that although using the human-like handling of categorical variables on average leads to a significant increase in perceived *Closeness* of explanations, it does not consistently represent users' perceptions well.

Table 2 Results of the user study, ***: $p < 0.01$, **: $p < 0.05$

Construct	Mean effect	STDV	Test-statistic (*p*-value)
Preference	0.282***	0.734	2.485 (0.009)
Relevance	0.362**	1.101	2.127 (0.020)
Coherence	0.412***	0.966	2.782 (0.004)
Concreteness	0.386**	1.050	2.379 (0.011)
Closeness	0.454**	1.576	1.866 (0.035)
Sparseness	0.117	1.720	0.443 (0.330)
Feasibility	0.398***	1.048	2.464 (0.009)

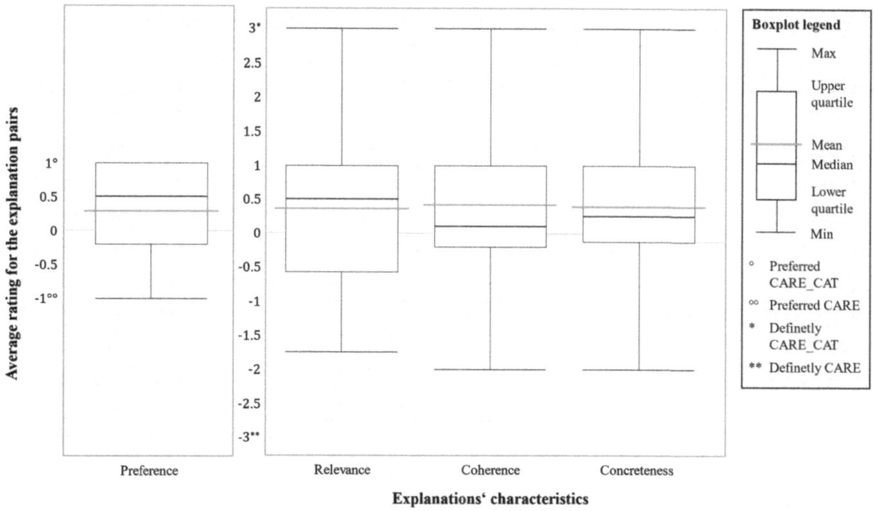

Fig. 1 Users' preferred explanation type and assessment of explanations' characteristics

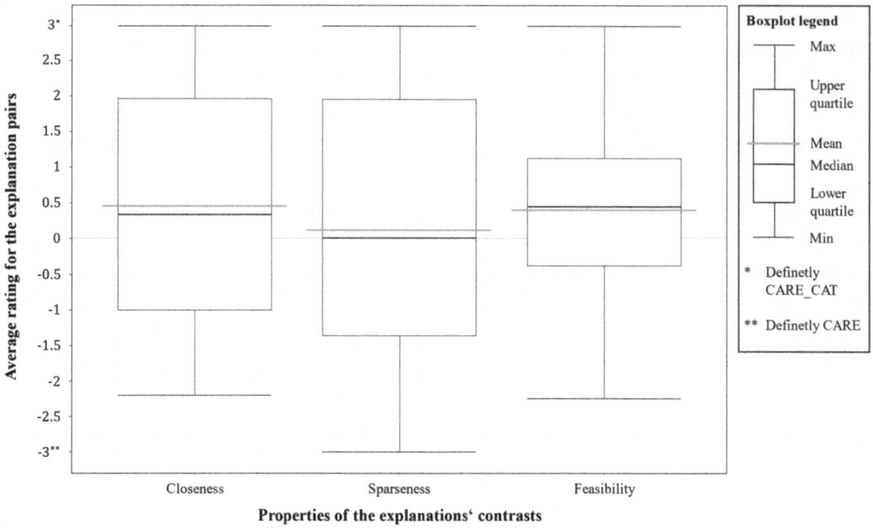

Fig. 2 Users' assessment of the properties of the explanations' contrasts

5 Discussion

With our work, we aim to expand existing research on counterfactual explanations by examining the potential of using a human-like handling of categorical variables in the generation process of counterfactual explanations. Therefore, we conducted an online user study on the impact of using the human-like handling of categorical variables proposed by Förster et al. (2022) within a state-of-the-art counterfactual explanation approach (Rasouli and Chieh Yu 2022). Our results contribute to research in two ways.

First, our results demonstrate that explanations generated using a human-like handling of categorical variables are preferred by its recipients. More concretely, we show that using the human-like distance handling proposed by Förster et al. (2022) in the counterfactual explanation approach CARE (Rasouli and Chieh Yu 2022) enables the generation of explanations that are significantly preferred over explanations generated using the conventional 0/1 distance of CARE ($p < 0.01$). While Förster et al. (2022) have previously evaluated the joint effect of their human-like handling of categorical variables in conjunction with other design decisions by evaluating their entire methodology against other algorithms, our study pioneers the investigation of whether the use of this human-like handling of categorical variables has a demonstrable impact on user preferences.

Second, our study specifically shows that using a human-like handling of categorical variables significantly increases users' perception of the relevance ($p < 0.05$), coherence ($p < 0.01$), and concreteness ($p < 0.05$) of the generated explanations as well as the perceived closeness ($p < 0.05$) and feasibility ($p < 0.01$) of their contrasts. This underscores the importance of the distance measurement for categorical variables in generating counterfactual explanations, as the relevance, coherence, and concreteness of explanations are the criteria deemed to be the foremost decisive attributes of explanations in the context of XAI (Förster et al. 2020). The effects on the coherence of the explanations as well as on the closeness and feasibility of their contrasts were to be expected since the human-like handling of categorical variables was developed for these purposes. However, the effect on the relevance and concreteness of the explanations was less clear. Given that the literature emphasizes the importance of categorical variables within counterfactual explanations because they make the explanations easier to understand, it is plausible that a human-like inclusion of categorical variables in counterfactual explanations also increases the users' perception of their relevance and concreteness. Our analysis did not reveal any statistically significant influence on the perceived sparsity of the explanations. This result was expected, as both the conventional 0/1 distance measure for categorical variables used in CARE and the human-like handling of categorical variables used in CARE_CAT favor sparsity.

In addition to these theoretical implications, our findings indicate two practical implications for organizations and developers. First, we have demonstrated the state-of-the-art counterfactual explanation method CARE (Rasouli and Chieh Yu 2022) in a novel use-case, thereby answering the call for future application of CARE within different settings and encouraging practitioners to apply CARE in practice. Second, in the context of our study, we have successfully enabled the transferability of the promising human-like handling of categorical variables proposed by Förster et al. (2022) to other counterfactual explanation approaches, using CARE as an example. Our findings serve to validate the viability of using this distance measure in other approaches and highlight its potential for seamless integration in other counterfactual explanation approaches.

6 Conclusion

Despite the fact that research on counterfactual explanations has made tremendous progress in recent years, state-of-the-art algorithms still lack a human-like handling of categorical variables. In this paper, we integrated such a human-like handling into a state-of-the-art counterfactual explanation approach. We assessed the impact of this integration via a user study involving 63 participants, comparing users' perceptions of explanations generated using the human-like handling of categorical variables with those generated using the conventional 0/1 distance measure. Our study is the first to explore the effects of using a human-like handling of categorical variables in a counterfactual explanation approach. Our contribution to research and practice is threefold. First, our research shows that counterfactual explanation approaches should incorporate information available about categorical variables embedded in the data or additionally available, including but not limited to the order and similarity of categorical features. Second, our user study indicates that the use of human-like handling of categorical variables in counterfactual explanation approaches has a significant effect on users' perceptions of the concreteness, coherence, and relevance of the generated explanations, as well as their perceived closeness to the fact and the feasibility of their contrast. Third, our research demonstrates that the promising human-like handling of categorical variables proposed by Förster et al. (2022) can be effectively integrated into other counterfactual explanation approaches, as exemplified by its successful implementation in CARE. By validating the transferability and potential for seamless integration of this distance measure in our study, we contribute to a broader scientific understanding of its utility and expand the scope of its applicability in state-of-the-art approaches. While our research provides interesting insights, several limitations remain and may serve as a starting point for future research. First, our research focused on a particular counterfactual explanation approach. Even though this approach is considered as state-of-the-art and exhibits promising potential, it is crucial for future research to analyze the effects of integrating a human-like handling of categorical variables into other approaches. It is reasonable to expect that such an integration would not pose significant challenges, given the successful transferability observed in our study. Second, we only investigated the impact of one approach for a more human-like handling of categorical variables. Given the absence of adequate distance measures for categorical variables in state-of-the-art counterfactual explanation approaches, future research must prioritize the investigation and development of alternative human-like distance measures. Third, our study was conducted with only 63 participants and focused on users' perceptions of the explanations. Even though assessing users' perceptions is a typical and recommended approach within the context of XAI, an analysis of users' behavior within a larger user study could provide additional insight into the effectiveness of incorporating a human-like handling of categorical variables into counterfactual generation approaches. For example, it would be of high interest to investigate on users' performance under different treatments in a setting measuring the task performance. Future research should aim to examine the impact of incorporating a human-like distance measurement in counterfactual explanation approaches on user behavior to further validate our findings.

References

Anantrasirichai, N. & Bull, D. (2022), 'Artificial intelligence in the creative industries: a review', *Artificial Intelligence Review* **55**, 589–656.

Arrieta, A. B., Díaz-Rodríguez, N., Del Ser, J., Bennetot, A., Tabik, S., Barbado, A., Garcia, S., Gil-Lopez, S., Molina, D., Benjamins, R., Chatila, R. & Herrera, F. (2020), 'Explainable Artificial Intelligence (XAI): Concepts, taxonomies, opportunities and challenges toward responsible AI', *Information Fusion* **58**, 82–115.

Bhatt, U., Xiang, A., Sharma, S., Weller, A., Taly, A., Jia, Y., Ghosh, J., Puri, R., Moura, J. M. F. & Eckersley, P. (2020), Explainable machine learning in deployment, *in* 'Proceedings of the 2020 Conference on Fairness, Accountability, and Transparency', pp. 648–657.

Boobier T. (2018), *Advanced analytics and AI: impact, implementation, and the future of work*. John Wiley & Sons.

Chen, D. L., Schonger, M. & Wickens, C. (2016), 'oTree—An open-source platform for laboratory, online, and field experiments', *Journal of Behavioral and Experimental Finance* **9**, 88–97.

Chen, L., Chen, P. & Lin, Z. (2020), 'Artificial Intelligence in Education: A Review', *IEEE Access* **8**, 75264–75278.

Dandl, S., Molnar, C., Binder, M. & Bischl, B. (2020), Multi-Objective Counterfactual Explanations, *in* 'Proceedings of International Conference on Parallel Problem Solving from Nature', pp. 448–469.

Ferrer, X., van Nuenen, T., Such, J. M., Cote, M. & Criado, N. (2021), 'Bias and Discrimination in AI: A Cross-Disciplinary Perspective', *IEEE Technology and Society Magazine* **40**(2), 72–80.

Förster, M., Hühn, P., Klier, M. & Kluge, K. (2021), Capturing Users' Reality: A Novel Approach to Generate Coherent Counterfactual Explanations, *in* 'Proceedings of the 54th Hawaii International Conference on System Sciences (HICSS)', pp. 1274–1283.

Förster, M., Hühn, P., Klier, M. & Kluge, K. (2022), 'User-centric explainable AI: design and evaluation of an approach to generate coherent counterfactual explanations for structured data', *Journal of Decision Systems*.

Förster, M., Klier, M., Kluge, K. & Sigler, I. (2020), 'Evaluating Explainable Artificial Intelligence – What Users Really Appreciate', *in* 'Proceedings of the 28th European Conference on Information Systems (ECIS), An Online AIS Conference'.

Guidotti, R. (2022), 'Counterfactual explanations and how to find them: literature review and benchmarking', *Data Mining and Knowledge Discovery*.

Guo, P., Wang, X. & Han, Y. (2010), The enhanced genetic algorithms for the optimization design, *in* '2010 3rd International Conference on Biomedical Engineering and Informatics', IEEE, pp. 2990–2994.

Haque, A. B., Islam, A. N. & Mikalef, P. (2023), 'Explainable Artificial Intelligence (XAI) from a user perspective: A synthesis of prior literature and problematizing avenues for future research', *Technological Forecasting and Social Change* **186**.

Herse, S., Vitale, J., Tonkin, M., Ebrahimian, D., Ojha, S., Johnston, B., Judge, W. & Williams, M. (2018), Do You Trust Me, Blindly? Factors Influencing Trust Towards a Robot Recommender System, *in* 'Proceedings of the 27th IEEE International Symposium on Robot and Human Interactive Communication (RO-MAN)', IEEE, pp. 7–14.

HLEG-AI (2019), Ethics Guidelines for Trustworthy AI, European Commission.

Jabbar, M. A., Deekshatulu, B. L. & Chandra, P. (2013), 'Classification of Heart Disease Using K-Nearest Neighbor and Genetic Algorithm', *Procedia Technology* **10**, 85–94.

Kaur, N., Sahdev, S. L., Sharma, M. & Siddiqui, L. (2020), 'Banking 4.0: 'The Influence of Artificial Intelligence on the Banking Industry & How AI Is Changing the Face of Modern Day Banks'', *International Journal of Management* **11**(6).

Lambora, A., Gupta, K. & Chopra, K. (2019), Genetic Algorithm- A Literature Review, *in* '2019 International Conference on Machine Learning, Big Data, Cloud and Parallel Computing (COMITCon)', IEEE, pp. 380–384.

Lee, D. & Yoon, S. N. (2021), 'Application of Artificial Intelligence-Based Technologies in the Healthcare Industry: Opportunities and Challenges', *International journal of environmental research and public health* **18**(1).

Lipton, P. (1990), 'Contrastive Explanation', *Royal Institute of Philosophy Supplement* **27**, 247–266.

Miller, T. (2019), 'Explanation in artificial intelligence: Insights from the social sciences', *Artificial Intelligence* **267**, 1–38.

Mothilal, R. K., Sharma, A. & Tan, C. (2020), Explaining machine learning classifiers through diverse counterfactual explanations, *in* 'Proceedings of the 2020 Conference on Fairness, Accountability, and Transparency (FAT)', pp. 607–617.

Racine, J. S. (2008), 'Nonparametric Econometrics: A Primer', *Foundations and Trends in Econometrics* **3**(1), 1–88.

Rasouli, P. & Chieh Yu, I. (2022), 'CARE: coherent actionable recourse based on sound counterfactual explanations', *International Journal of Data Science and Analytics*.

Russell, C. (2019), Efficient Search for Diverse Coherent Explanations, *in* 'Proceedings of the Conference on Fairness, Accountability, and Transparency (FAT)', ACM Press, pp. 20–28.

Sharma, S., Henderson, J. & Gosh, J. (2020), CERTIFAI: A Common Framework to Provide Explanations and Analyse the Fairness and Robustness of Black-box Models, *in* 'Proceedings of the AAAI/ACM Conference on AI, Ethics, and Society', pp. 166–172.

van Looveren, A. & Klaise, J. (2021), 'Interpretable Counterfactual Explanations Guided by Prototypes', *in 'Proceedings of the Conference in Machine Learning and Knowledge Discovery in Databases'*, Springer, pp. 650–665.

Verma S., Dickerson J. & Hines K. (2022), 'Counterfactual Explanations for Machine Learning: A Review', *ArXiv*. arXiv:2010.10596v3

Wachter, S., Mittelstadt, B. & Russell, C. (2018), 'Counterfactual Explanations Without Opening the Black Box: Automated Decisions and the GDPR', *Harvard Journal of Law & Technology* **31**(2), 841–887.

Warren G., Byrne R. MJ & Keane M. T (2023), 'Categorical and Continuous Features in Counterfactual Explanations of AI Systems ', *in* 'Proceedings of the 28th International Conference on Intelligent User Interfaces', ACM, pp. 171–183.

How Engineers Perform Data Science Work: Designing Hybrid Roles

Amelie L. Schmid and Manuel Wiesche

Abstract As of today, organizations are still struggling to derive consistent value from data science projects. The basic relevance of domain knowledge for data science work can be considered as common sense. Engineers, in particular, offer a unique view of emerging data science work based on their critical role within traditional industries. As a constraint, current studies on data science work consider domain experts as rather passive, and engineering-related studies are rare. To further explore these challenges, the present study analyses the data science work of 30 engineers at an international automotive supplier. By investigating three cases, the evolvement of hybrid data science work can be derived, by combining two perspectives: engineering and data science. Thus, engineers actively incorporate the data science perspective, particularly when development activities involve minimal participation of data scientists. This contribution significantly enhances existing knowledge by demonstrating how engineers embrace the data scientists' perspective and perform hybrid data work.

Keywords Data science work · Data scientists · Engineers · Hybrid practice · Transformation of work

A. L. Schmid (✉) · M. Wiesche
TU Dortmund University, Dortmund, Germany
e-mail: amelie.schmid@tu-dortmund.de; amelie.schmid@de.bosch.com

M. Wiesche
e-mail: manuel.wiesche@tu-dortmund.de

A. L. Schmid
Robert Bosch GmbH, Reutlingen, Germany

D. Beverungen et al. (eds.), *Solutions and Technologies for Responsible Digitalization*, Lecture Notes in Information Systems and Organisation 75,
https://doi.org/10.1007/978-3-031-80122-8_12

1 Introduction

During the last years, data science projects have gained significant importance as an essential approach for organizations to leverage the vast amounts of available data. However, organizations often face major challenges with data science projects like long project cycles, never-ending pilots, or even failed projects (Joshi et al. 2021). This results in the inability to extract meaningful insights and create consistent business value (Günther et al. 2017). One of the key issues lies in the existence of an expertise gap between data scientists and the domain experts, with their specialized knowledge in a specific domain (Kayabay et al. 2022). In this context, it is already acknowledged that a close collaboration between data scientists and domain experts is a success factor for data science implementation as well as the performing of data science work, respectively (van den Broek et al. 2021). It can be explained by the fact that—in contrast—a forced technology implementation might generate a feeling of fear, which leads to a rejecting attitude among the domain experts (Pachidi et al. 2021; Tams 2022). This holds particularly true for highly educated groups like engineers, who might react negatively to a new technology if they feel attacked by it (Anthony 2018).

However, current studies regarding the collaboration of domain experts and data scientists consider the role of domain experts as rather passive, with only limited specific contribution towards the emerging data science work. Instead, domain experts are asked to simply provide their domain knowledge and share their know-how in a way that the data scientists are able to make use of it in the further development process (Lebovitz et al. 2021; Park et al. 2021; Sambasivan and Veeraraghavan 2022). As a consequence, the resulting data science work is predominantly performed by the data scientist.

In-depth, the current insights regarding data science work of domain experts are predominantly grounded on studies within business-related areas like in HR (van den Broek et al. 2021), sales (Pachidi et al. 2021), or consulting (Strich et al. 2021). However, the professional group of engineers is of particularly high relevance, as they represent a key subject for the ongoing digital transformation within traditional industries while facing at the same time fundamental changes with respect to their existing tasks and roles (Azmi et al. 2018; Muhuri et al. 2019). Furthermore, the special characteristic of engineers within organizations, e.g., being conceptually driven as well as their critical contribution towards product development and innovation, request to take a differentiated look at this group of domain experts (Bechky 2003; Menzel et al. 2007).

Considering the relevance of domain knowledge for successful data science work (van Giffen and Ludwig 2023), the present work aims to expand the existing perspective of data scientists by focusing on the unique role of engineers. Thus, the following research question is answered: *How do engineers perform data science work?*

The data science work of engineers is analyzed based on 30 semi-structured interviews within an automotive supplier. The evolvement of a hybrid work practice, which is predominantly performed by the domain experts, is illustrated. Finally, the interconnection of the given work practices of engineers and the incorporation of new work practices of data scientists is discussed.

2 Theoretical Background

2.1 Data Science Work and Engineering Work

Recently, data science has gained increasing attention within organizations, as it can be used to gather new insights and create additional value from data (Günther et al. 2017). So far, no consistent designation for data science and its work practices exists. The used terms and definitions within information systems (IS) research range from naming a specific method like the usage of AI (Strich et al. 2021), big data, (Provost and Fawcett 2013), machine learning (Meyer et al. 2014) or robotics (Willcocks 2020). Moreover, these specific fields are summarized and only generic terms like data-driven work (Brynjolfsson et al. 2011) or data work (Parmiggiani et al. 2022) are applied. In order to frame the scope of our study, we refer to data science as the practice of analyzing large-scale data to get a glimpse on decision-making and taking actions (Abbasi et al. 2016; Crisan et al. 2021; Passi and Sengers 2020). Basically, the work of a data scientist is characterized by the detection of correlations and patterns within a defined data set. The overall goal of their work is to reveal insights based on data, even though these might not be generalizable, due to the missing direct link to the underlying reasons and causalities (Provost and Fawcett 2013). Thus, *data science work* is driven by rationality, objectivity and neutrality. The behavior of data scientists is evidenced-based, with the goal to diminish human bias (Agarwal and Dhar 2014; Davenport 2018; Jones 2019; Power et al. 2019).

In contrast, an exact understanding of the specific problem is of great importance for *engineering work*. That means that engineers apply their specific domain knowledge to generate solutions and use, e.g., physical approaches to generalize their results (Anderson et al. 2010; Sheppard et al. 2006). Moreover, the behavior of engineers is rather conceptual, having the goal of designing, e.g., new products (Bechky 2003). Engineers apply different strategies to guide others towards a particular meaning during the development process. Thus, engineers might want to utilize data to support an intended preference (Barley et al. 2012). It can be concluded that the basic approach and goal of data science work differs from engineering work to a large extent.

2.2 Transformation of Knowledge Work

It is already well known that work practices change based on increasing technological usage (Vaast and Walsham 2005). Also, data science offers tremendous new opportunities and creates different demands for the work of any domain expert (Leitner-Hanetseder et al. 2021). In the present study, work is defined as "the use of human, informational, physical, and other resources to produce products/services" (Alter 2013). Especially in the knowledge work context, data science has a major impact (Lebovitz et al. 2021).

In general, it is usually assumed that the transformation of knowledge work does not originate from the domain experts themselves. Instead, work transformation might be triggered by a forced IT system implementation (Soh et al. 2003; Vaast and Walsham 2005) or activated by an external market change (Nelson and Irwin 2014). In both cases, domain experts face numerous challenges. The negative effects of a forced work transformation are already well known: research on forced IT system implementations gave evidence on issues like decreasing job satisfaction due to less job control on the side of the employee (Bala and Venkatesh 2013) or challenges regarding workarounds and unintended use (Boudreau and Robey 2005). Prior studies have additionally focused on work transformation, where external market change caused an adaptation of the working mode without any alternative. For example, Nelson and Irwin (2014) illustrate how librarians had to change their work as an reaction towards the emerging internet. The so-called "paradox of expertise" lead to the fact that they refrained from integrating the new technology into their working mode by themselves, although the capabilities were available.

Moreover, current studies consider data science applications which are predominantly developed by data scientists and not by domain experts (Strich et al. 2021; van den Broek et al. 2021; Waardenburg et al. 2022; Zhang et al. 2020). One reason is the lack of capability of domain experts to apply data science, especially in business professions with limited data-related understanding (Oberländer et al. 2020). Instead, data scientists are requested to closely align their developing activities with the domain experts in order to integrate the specific knowledge into the technology, as domain-specific knowledge is a crucial success factor for data science work (Lebovitz et al. 2021; van den Broek et al. 2021). However, during the collaboration of domain experts and data scientists, additional challenging effects, such as limited or even lacking communication between the two groups, occur. Maintaining a common motivation and consistently following joint goals represent further issues that hinder successful collaboration and data science work (Mao et al. 2019). As a consequence, the domain experts might not be able to interpret and evaluate the outcome of the developed algorithms, as the internal logic is unknown (Zhang et al. 2020).

All the mentioned challenges might be tackled by granting domain experts an active role in the development of data science. Therefore, it is essential to overcome the knowledge boundary between data scientists and domain experts (Waardenburg et al. 2022). In the IS context, the active participation in workforce advice networks during an IT system implementation serves as a first example for that. Such a high employee interaction at the workplace during the implementation phase has a positive influence on job performance (Sykes et al. 2014). However, most studies consider the formation of data science work from data scientist's point of view and leave domain experts with the passive attitude of providing and sharing domain knowledge only (Park et al. 2021).

To conclude, it remains unclear how domain experts perform data science work independently form the strong influence of data scientists. This holds especially true if the development of data science applications take place by themselves, e.g., due to the given data and understanding of engineering. Thus, it is necessary to put a focus on data science work based on engineers' application of data science.

3 Methodology

In this research, we chose a qualitative research approach to examine data science work, performed by the domain expert instead of the data scientist. Specifically, we analyzed data science work by engineers within three cases. We find the qualitative approach particularly helpful, as it allows to adapt a research process towards the evolving research context in an iterative manner (Charmaz 2014; Corbin and Strauss 2015). Thus, it enables the answering of "how" questions (Langley 1999; van de Ven and Huber 1990).

3.1 Data Collection and Immersion into the Field

The analysis is based on a study within one of the biggest suppliers within the automotive industry, which is developing and manufacturing semiconductors and sensors as well as electronic control units (ECUs) at 40 plants and locations worldwide. We choose the automotive industry because it is a strategically relevant showcase for the complex digitalization process of traditional companies and related engineers. The analysis includes frequent visits to the field over the course of 12 months (Walsham 1995). Thereby, we have involved ourselves deeply into the context in order to truly understand the ecosystem (Johns 2006).

We chose three cases within the organization, as the analytical conclusions of multiple-case designs are generally more powerful and robust compared to single-case designs (Miles et al. 2020; Yin 2010). Case similarity and case variability served as guiding principles for the selection of cases (Kirsch 1997; Orlikowski 1993). To ensure case similarity, we chose the organizational area related to the production of ECUs as the overall context of the study. The utilization of data science plays a major role in this entire area, as it had been increasingly applied at different points along the entire ECU value stream. Thus, the environmental conditions and the data availability can be considered as a common ground. However, the cases varied in terms of involved engineers, departments, functions, specific tasks, stakeholders, and localization.

Table 1 represents an overview of the three selected cases: (1) Supplier, (2) Research & Development (R&D) and (3) Manufacturing. Each case has been selected based on a specific purpose within the overall research (Yin 2010). Case 1 was chosen as it involvd engineers who closely interact with external suppliers. The engineers selected from the R&D departments of case 2 bring in the perspective of highly educated employees having scientific backgrounds in physics, chemistry, and material science. Case 3 serves as a good field of investigation, as it is related to the core process of the company, and the involved engineers need to meet the highest quality standards.

In order to generate a profound picture, we sampled 30 engineers across all three cases from different hierarchical levels, a varied degree of data science knowledge and working experience, as well as a mixture of backgrounds and work roles (Patton 2009). Data was collected using semi-structured interviews (Miles et al. 2020). Within these interviews our primary goal was to elaborate on the emerging data science work practice. For that purpose, in a first step, we asked the participants to describe their current tasks in detail. Subsequently, this was followed by the elaboration of the new work practices with a focus on recent changes based on increasing data availability. The preliminary interview guideline was further optimized by follow-up questions as data collection progressed (Miles et al. 2020). The duration of the interviews was ~ 54 min.

Even though interviews were the primary data source, we collected further qualitative data to enhance the fundamental understanding and to receive a clearer picture of the phenomenon (Walsham 1995). The data included different documentations of the reported data science use cases which have been created for internal management

Table 1 Overview of the three cases

Characteristics	Case 1: Supplier	Case 2: R&D	Case 3: Manufacturing
Traditional work design	Manual claim management of each individual material; shipment of the broken part to the supplier; discussion with supplier ex-post, based on the physical product.	Product development by using domain knowledge; decision-making based on experience of the employees, as well as analytical models, basic statistics/simulation.	Manufacturing problems are solved by reacting to emerging issues; evaluation of the situation by an operator at the line; non-systematic quality management.
Work design with data science application	Claim management based on manufacturing data from production lines; no shipment of broken parts; exchange of data.	Data-driven product development; decision-making based on data models by using manufacturing data as well as field data.	Systemized problem analysis and solving using manufacturing data and visualization; data-driven quality assurance.

reviews. In addition, we participated two times at a 2-day workshop with representatives of the relevant functions, where the current data science projects have been elaborated and discussed.

3.2 Data Analysis

To obtain a profound overview of the key messages during the data collection process, we applied memoing and wrote a short summary with the most relevant statements after each interview (Glaser 1978). These memos helped to remember all relevant data during the data collection process. Consecutively, we were able to get back to the raw data during the data analysis. We transcribed all interviews, resulting in 482 pages of qualitative data, which serves as the primary data of this study.

The data analysis followed an iterative procedure. Qualitative data analysis software (MAXQDA) was used to gather, organize, and analyze the data in a clear and transparent manner. We coded all interview transcripts systematically, applying grounded theory practice (Corbin and Strauss 2015; Sarker et al. 2018). In a first step, open coding was used to assign appropriate labels to the interview passages which summarized the key message in a short phrase (Miles et al. 2020). Here, we identified the general work characteristics in applying data science. During the data analysis process, the persistence of the former engineering work practices became evident. That is why we used axial coding for the identification of connections between the subcodes (Strauss 1978). We were able to map the former engineering work practices as well as the new data science work practices to each work element. Finally, we applied selective coding to further develop and combine the dimensions, resulting in the final consolidation (Fig. 1) (Glaser 1978). The whole coding process followed an iterative procedure through several rounds of reviewing and rewriting (Miles et al. 2020).

4 Results

The present work targets on a deeper understanding of data science work performed by engineers. As a result, a hybrid data science practice is presented, illustrating that engineers combine (i) elements from their established work practices and (ii) the new work practices of data scientists. The characteristics of the hybrid role can be detailed by the following four relevant work elements: (i) approach, (ii) analytical diagnosis, (iii) problem categorization and (iv) decision-making (Fig. 2). Each of these categories and the respective characteristics of the two roles will be elaborated in the following.

Combining a reactive and a predictive approach. Both the reactive and predictive aspects are highly relevant for data science work of engineers within all three cases.

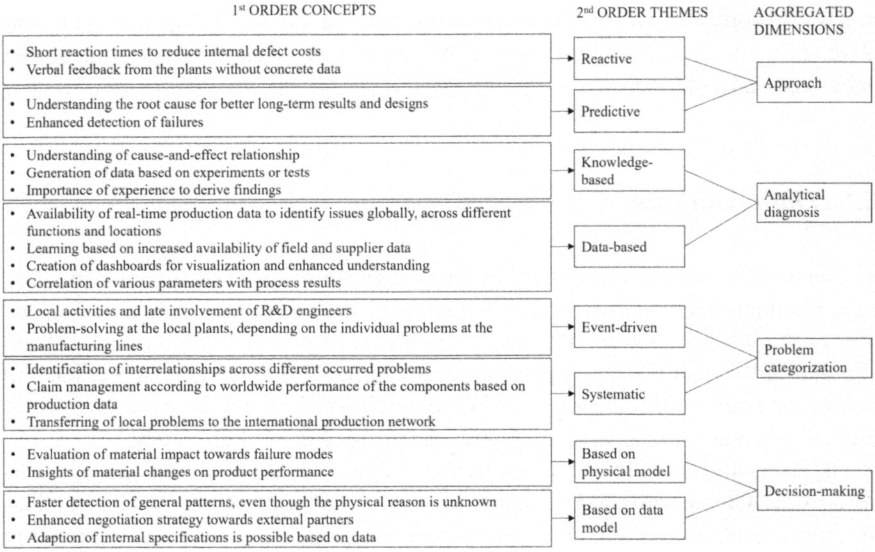

Fig. 1 Illustration of the coding process

Fig. 2 Hybrid practice of data science work

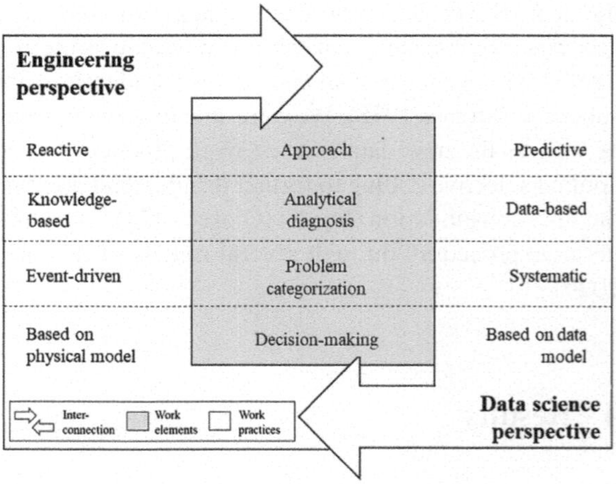

On the one hand side, the *reactive* work practices are well established since engineers need to support in problem solving during the manufacturing process. Short reaction times are needed, as internal errors cause a high internal cost. The collaboration between R&D and manufacturing requires staying reactive under specific circumstances:

> The major pain point is that we get a lot of verbal feedbacks from the plants regarding their problems. They are saying: [...] last night we had 10 failure pieces, please support us. (#28)

Nevertheless, identifying such incidents is an important baseline to learn for the future. Here, the application of data science is essential. Thus, the reactive working approach is strengthened by the *predictive* perspective. The proactive usage of data tremendously increases the speed of product development and the failure detection. Additionally, the adaptation of current operational processes can improve the quality of future work. As a result, plants can trigger improvements, such as machine settings with reference to identified errors. All in all, this targets to prevent reoccurring issues based on the same root cause.

In addition, by means of the explorative identification of similar error structures, future issues can be avoided. Such an early warning systems helps to keep the operations running within defined control limits, as potential issues are detected in advance. The roll-out and the proactive integration of the developed solution into future products by the workers from R&D ensures a reduction or even elimination of specific failures. Such a mindset of forward-thinking in R&D helps to introduce fundamentally new ideas:

> With much more detail, we can clearly identify the root cause in comparison to a hypothesis [...]. And now, we can understand: 'Ok, if I do this, it will make this happen, and at the end of the line, we will have a good result because I understand what is happening in between.' [...] And this also allows the team (...) to make better designs from scratch. (#27)

Analytical diagnosis based on knowledge and data. Engineers have acquired profound domain knowledge during their studies, and several years of working experience complement the knowledge level to a great extent. Hence, *knowledge-based* diagnosis is of great importance for certain operations. One respondent highlights the benefits of knowledge application, like an intense and autonomous analysis of any problem. For that purpose, a deeper involvement in the field is necessary to deal with the situation and to deduce a solution simply based on domain knowledge.

> The bottom line of my work is to build up knowledge. And I believe that this will remain the same and that you will continue to need the expertise, the experience. (#22)

However, in some situations, the exact identification of failures and error patterns is complex. This can even lead to an entire lack of understanding on relevant topics or occurring issues. To address this issue, data science is essential for conducting a complementary *data-based* analysis. Facts and figures enhance the problem diagnosis in various ways. In a first step, a detailed visualization of the manufacturing data can help to get a general feeling for the respective circumstances:

> Even the development who is very, very far away from production can check and see that: 'ok, we have a problem at this and this station and that pressfit force has been increased for the past two hours.' [...] And then [...] I see: 'ok, the force increase is caused by this supplier batch of the pins.' And this is making it much easier to detect the root cause of the problem. (#26)

This is valid if visualizations of relevant information are continuously available and always up to date. Using real-time data enables a constant tracking of the manufacturing process. In this way, the influence and effects of individual activities of workers from R&D or manufacturing can be identified immediately:

> But for such regular queries I created a Tableau dashboard. [...] There you see nicely: after we made the change here, that we got a nice improvement. From B/C to mainly A, but also a little bit of B still there. And to track that effectiveness, I just quickly made a dashboard. (#13)

Considering case 2, it can be concluded that the application of data science even leads to a systematic verification of already existing knowledge-based assumptions. In this context, the scope of the current work within R&D can be expanded since it is now possible to investigate relevant aspects by means of available data. In the past, models were built up and – in some cases – no clear explanation could be found. Today and in the future, data science application offers the possibility to check and calibrate these already existing models based on the data. Thus, so far open questions, e.g., regarding the maximum storage time of printed circuit boards (PCBs), can now finally be answered:

> What is the right storage time of PCBs [printed circuit boards]? That is very difficult to check on the development side. We try to anticipate the ageing process, like calculating how much oxide growth I have. But in the end, you can also say: 'Hey, the truth is in the field, right'? Let's see how old the PCBs are, whether we see a correlation, for example, that PCBs which are one year old have a higher defect rate than completely fresh PCBs. (#30)

Using event-driven and systematic problem categorization. Our data reveal that problem categorization is another important component, which is a relevant data science work practice. As already indicated, in the context of problem solving, the established work practices of engineers are rather *event-driven*. Case 3 shows that single, specific events must be analyzed in order define a solution for the specific problem. In particular, this holds if the occurring issue needs to be solved fast. Timing is another crucial factor that explains an apparently randomized way of working:

> The difficulty is: I always have the problems in the plants at different point in time. That's tricky because today plant A calls, tomorrow plant B calls. (#09)

This event-driven way of working results in work being categorized as single issues. Local on-site teams are set up and start to work jointly on the specific issue. Such an event-driven procedure has to be guided by a *systematic*, all-time solution of the problem. As one key aspect, data science shifts the perspective and generates the required holistic view. It needs to be taken care that single events at specific local plants are excluded from the data, as to prevent local effects distorting the overall picture. Such local events are, among others, incorrect machine settings or local environmental conditions which are not design-related or linked to the specific component.

As an essence, the systematic problem categorization focuses on the global perspective and distinguishes between real global pain points and specific location-dependent effects. The availability of manufacturing data offers the opportunity to detect the root cause of a problem at any line in a structured way. The priority of local effects is decreased, and the focus is set on global incidences which can be solved with much more effectiveness. In this way, it is possible to identify interrelationships of different order, which can cause further possible occurring issues. Thus, it fundamentally changes the problem categorization with respect to the claim management procedure. Even the work with external partners is changing, as the systematic usage of data provides a new basis for collaboration. This can be illustrated by the following example of case 1, which describes how the work practice with external suppliers is adapted:

> It is possible to make a claim of the performance of the components based on production data. This means that not only individual cases can be claimed, but also the global performance of different plants as well as differences in the performance of different suppliers. (#29)

The systematic problem categorization can also help to implement continuous improvement methods within the international production network. In this way, problems are not only solved at that single point in time but are also faster detected in case of similar occurrences at the different locations:

> We share all information in an international lesson learned network so that everyone in the organization can make use of a holistic approach and transfer it to their cases. (#03)

Decision-making grounding on physical model and data model. In the daily work, engineers have to make countless decisions, using physical and data models as a combination. Decisions *based on physical models* do not necessarily require a large amount of data for verification. Instead, engineers build a basis for the decision through the application of models which are referring to physical laws. These physical models are available for every engineering topic, such as mechanics, hardware, or manufacturing development. They serve as an important baseline for decision-making in the R&D area, like the selection of the appropriate material in the product design:

> If I change the material from copper to iron, I would like to know if this has an influence on my failure mode, e.g., the temperature cycling performance. My physical model tells me that stress and strain can cause cracks in the solder joint [...] and that iron promotes this more than copper, as the coefficient of thermal expansion is more critical. I have not recorded a single data point; I have derived analytically from physical models that this is going in the wrong direction. (#02)

The analytical derivation of the cause-and-effect relationship based on physics of failure enables this verification without the application of data science. In contrast, data and, thus, the application of data science is the fundamental prerequisite for deriving decisions based on data models. This holds for decisions within all three cases, such as the selection of a supplier (case 1), product development decisions (case 2), or decisions regarding the right way to solve occurring problems (case 3). By using the data model approach, it is possible to identify issues which cannot be explained solely by a physical model. Instead, it is possible to see further indications which might cause an issue. One example is the correlation between the results and a certain supplier, which enables insights into their respective performance and creates a better basis for negotiation:

> Based on the data, we can try to change the specification for the PCB [printed circuit board] shrinkage for the PCB (reflow) cycles. It is hard work, but based on our statistic regression, we see that the range of the currently defined specification is too big, and we can reduce it. (#28)

However, the accuracy of decision-making based on data models is strongly dependent on their granularity and level of detail. It is important to have a comprehensive description, leading, in the best case scenario, to a digital twin that contains any relevant element of the real world. At the final stage, the algorithm is even able to develop and recognize its own patterns with huge amount of data. It is important to mention that the examples of the decision-making aspects illustrate how the two poles of the physical model and data model approach interact with each other. At the first glance, decisions by data models based on probabilities can be taken, which do not require any domain knowledge. However, the physical reason behind these failures is still lacking and unclear. Digging deeper into the topic shows that results from the data model are not enough and, hence, have to be explained by a physical reason:

> Of course, based on the data, we would only see that the workpiece carrier is causing the issue and when we check it physically, we know this is being caused by the loose screw. (#26)

Combining engineering and data science work practices towards an interconnected hybrid practice. To sum up, engineer perform data science work by integrating data science practices into their existing role. Depending on the phenomenon, it can be required to apply the sophisticated engineering work practices. However, the merger with data science leads to the creation of the new hybrid practice. As a result, the feedback loop can be closed by the interconnection of both work practices:

> Particularly regarding our manufacturing, we can close this circle, because at the end of the day, we always view our work as CIP [continuous improvement process]. And if we include the feedback, we can look at how we can improve. (#20)

Finally, it can be recognized that both perspectives are strongly interwoven and in constant interaction. The traditional approach serves even as a baseline for fueling the data science perspective. For example, the generated data from event-driven issues within case 3 are an important prerequisite for further enhancing the R&D process:

> We have developed an IDC [internal defects cost] reduction cycle. Here we have both, the backward integration to existing products and forward integration for new products. (#02)

5 Discussion

The scope of the present study is to understand the design of data science work by engineers. The integration of data science into the existing work of the domain expert leads to the evolvement of hybrid data science work. Hence, the content of the current literature is expanded in two ways. First, it is introduced that the domain experts are the drivers of their data science work. Second, we show that engineering domain experts embed data science into their existing work, resulting in the hybrid practice.

5.1 Theoretical and Practical Contributions

For data scientists, it is already well known that they utilize data to construct new ways of working (Muller et al. 2019). In contrast, domain experts were so far considered as being passive in the sense of performing data science work (Jung et al. 2022; van den Broek et al. 2021). In the present work, we broaden this limited view and illustrate a new work setting that engineers themselves create. Consequently, data science work is performed by domain experts which leads to the fact that engineers question their existing boarder criteria. Moreover, the workers even calibrate and verify their established work results by means of data science.

Among others, this can be emphasized, e.g., in the sense of decision-making. Here, the solely application of data science results in uncertainty and missing underlying explanations (Lebovitz 2019; Lebovitz et al. 2022; Provost and Fawcett 2013). Nonetheless, work practices of engineering like the understanding of physical causalities, remain relevant. As a result, the combination of engineering and data science allows profound understanding, which provides further evidence on the relevance of the hybrid work practices. Prior studies already emphasized the importance of creating hybrid systems in the context of machine learning, as AI can only partially solve problems (Zhang et al. 2020). Within this work, we illustrate such a hybrid approach in the context of data science and provide, for the first time, a detailed explanation of the hybrid practice that is demanded. In addition, it serves as a detailed example for an emergent evolvement of digital transformation, as domain experts continuously realize value from the adjustment of their work (Koch et al. 2021).

The findings further extent recent studies investigating the impact of technology on work (van den Broek et al. 2021; Willcocks 2020). As an example, Strich et al. (2021) show that the old tasks of consultants were eliminated by an AI system. However, we demonstrate that domain experts do not discard the existing work practices. Instead, data science complements the established work, and it becomes part of the existing job. In this way, we contribute to research which recognizes that technology will rather modify than completely replace existing jobs (Bughin 2018; Huysman 2020) as well as research on the evolvement of an "IT identity" (Carter and Grover 2015). We extent this body of knowledge by illustrating two underlying success criteria concerning domain experts: First, the stronger contribution compared to the data scientists, and second, the capability to perform new data science work by themselves.

As an outcome, we derive contributions to practice from this study. First, it provides a more differentiated view on the establishment of new data roles within organizations. Major aspects of domain experts should be kept to a large extend, instead of pushing a hard transformation from classical engineers towards data scientists. This procedure helps to overcome obstacles and to convince additional domain experts to go into the same direction. Second, the results of this study reveal that the commitment towards data science application plays a crucial role for the successful implementation. It is, therefore, important to share the success story within the company to influence others.

5.2 Limitations and Future Research

The present study is subject to some limitations. The qualitative approach and the selective sample size result in restrictions on the overall generalizability of the results, as the data collection is limited to the domain-specific context with a focus on the automotive industry. An effort was spent to counteract this obstacle by selecting three different cases within the overall context. However, further research could seek to widen this perspective and compare the results to domain experts from different industries.

Finally, our work focusses on the specific characteristics of the created hybrid data science work while disregarding the respective transformation process towards that hybrid practice. It might be interesting to see how the transformation path works and whether the well-known "Model of Institutionalizing" (Reay et al. 2006) also holds in the data science context.

References

Abbasi A., Sarker S. and Chiang R. (2016) "Big Data Research in Information Systems: Toward an Inclusive Research Agenda," *Journal of the Association for Information Systems* 17(2), 1–32.

Agarwal R. and Dhar V. (2014) "Editorial — Big Data, Data Science, and Analytics: The Opportunity and Challenge for IS Research," *Information Systems Research* 25(3), 443–448.

Alter S. (2013) "Work System Theory: Overview of Core Concepts, Extensions, and Challenges for the Future," *Journal of the Association for Information Systems* 14(2), 72–121.

Anderson K. J. B., Courter S. S., McGlamery T., et al. (2010) "Understanding engineering work and identity: a cross-case analysis of engineers within six firms," *Engineering Studies* 2(3), 153–174.

Anthony C. (2018) "To Question or Accept? How Status Differences Influence Responses to New Epistemic Technologies in Knowledge Work," *Academy of Management Review* 43(4), 661–679.

Azmi A., Kamin Y., Noordin M., et al. (2018) "Towards Industrial Revolution 4.0: Employers' Expectations on Fresh Engineering Graduates," *International Journal of Engineering and Technology* 7(28), 267–272.

Bala H. and Venkatesh V. (2013) "Changes in Employees' Job Characteristics During an Enterprise System Implementation: A Latent Growth Modeling Perspective," *MIS Quarterly* 37(4), 1113–1140.

Barley W. C., Leonardi P. M. and Bailey D. E. (2012) "Engineering Objects for Collaboration: Strategies of Ambiguity and Clarity at Knowledge Boundaries," *Human Communication Research* 38(3), 280–308.

Bechky B. A. (2003) "Sharing Meaning Across Occupational Communities: The Transformation of Understanding on a Production Floor," *Organization Science* 14(3), 312–330.

Boudreau M.-C. and Robey D. (2005) "Enacting Integrated Information Technology: A Human Agency Perspective," *Organization Science* 16(1), 3–18.

Brynjolfsson E., Hitt L. M. and Kim H. H. (2011) "Strength in Numbers: How Does Data-Driven Decisionmaking Affect Firm Performance? In: *Proceedings of the 32nd International Conference on Information Systems: (*eds Dennis F. Galletta and Ting-Peng Liang), Shanghai, China, December 4–7.

Bughin J. (2018) "Why AI isn't the Death of Jobs," *MIT Sloan Management Review.*

Carter M. and Grover V. (2015) "Me, My Self, and I(T): Conceptualizing Information Technology Identity and its Implications," *MIS Quarterly* 39(4), 931–957.

Charmaz, K. (2014). Grounded Theory in Global Perspective. Qualitative Inquiry, 20(9), 1074–1084. https://doi.org/10.1177/1077800414545235

Corbin J. M. and Strauss A. L. (2015) *Basics of Qualitative Research: Techniques and Procedures for Developing Grounded Theory*. Los Angeles: SAGE.

Crisan A., Fiore-Gartland B. and Tory M. (2021) "Passing the Data Baton: A Retrospective Analysis on Data Science Work and Workers," *IEEE transactions on visualization and computer graphics* 27(2), 1860–1870.

Davenport T. H. (2018) *The AI Advantage*. The MIT Press.

Glaser B. G. (1978) *Theoretical sensitivity*. Mill Valley, Calif.: Soc. Pr.

Günther W. A., Rezazade Mehrizi M. H., Huysman M., et al. (2017) "Debating Big Data: A Literature Review on Realizing Value from Big Data," *The Journal of Strategic Information Systems* 26(3), 191–209.

Huysman M. (2020) "Information Systems Research on Artificial Intelligence and Work: A Commentary on "Robo-Apocalypse cancelled? Reframing the automation and future of work debate"," *Journal of Information Technology* 35(4), 307–309.

Johns G. (2006) "The Essential Impact of Context on Organizational Behavior," *Academy of Management Review* 31(2), 386–408.

Jones M. (2019) "What we talk about when we talk about (Big) Data," *The Journal of Strategic Information Systems* 28(1), 3–16.

Joshi M., Su N., Austin R., et al. (2021) "Why So Many Data Science Projects Fail to Deliver. Available at: https://sloanreview.mit.edu/article/why-so-many-data-science-projects-fail-to-deliver/.

Jung J. Y., Steinberger T., King J. L., et al. (2022) "How Domain Experts Work with Data: Situating Data Science in the Practices and Settings of Craftwork," *Proceedings of the ACM on Human-Computer Interaction* 6(CSCW1), 1–29.

Kayabay K., Gökalp M. O., Gökalp E., et al. (2022) "Data Science Roadmapping: An Architectural Framework for Facilitating Transformation towards a Data-driven Organization," *Technological Forecasting and Social Change* 174, 121264.

Kirsch L. S. (1997) "Portfolios of Control Modes and IS Project Management," *Information Systems Research* 8(3), 215–239.

Koch H., Chipidza W. and Kayworth T. R. (2021) "Realizing value from shadow analytics: A case study," *The Journal of Strategic Information Systems* 30(2), 101668.

Langley A. (1999) "Strategies for Theorizing from Process Data," *Academy of Management Review* 24(4), 691.

Lebovitz S. (2019) "Diagnostic Doubt and Artificial Intelligence: An Inductive Field Study of Radiology Work. In: *Proceedings of the 40th International Conference on Information Systems:* (eds H Krcmar and J Fedorowicz), Munich.

Lebovitz S., Levina N. and Lifshitz-Assa H. (2021) "Is AI Ground Truth Really True? The Dangers of Training and Evaluating AI Tools Based on Experts' Know-What," *MIS Quarterly* 45(3), 1501–1526.

Lebovitz S., Lifshitz-Assaf H. and Levina N. (2022) "To Engage or Not to Engage with AI for Critical Judgments: How Professionals Deal with Opacity When Using AI for Medical Diagnosis," *Organization Science* 33(1), 126–148.

Leitner-Hanetseder S., Lehner O. M., Eisl C., et al. (2021) "A Profession in Transition: Actors, Tasks and Roles in AI-based Accounting," *Journal of Applied Accounting Research* 22(3), 539–556.

Mao Y., Wang D., Muller M., et al. (2019) "How Data Scientists Work Together With Domain Experts in Scientific Collaborations," *Proceedings of the ACM on Human-Computer Interaction* 3(GROUP), 1–23.

Menzel H. C., Aaltio I. and Ulijn J. M. (2007) "On the way to creativity: Engineers as intrapreneurs in organizations," *Technovation* 27(12), 732–743.

Meyer G., Adomavicius G., Johnson P. E., et al. (2014) "A Machine Learning Approach to Improving Dynamic Decision Making," *Information Systems Research* 25(2), 239–263.
Miles M. B., Huberman A. M. and Saldaña J. (2020) *Qualitative data analysis: A methods sourcebook*. Los Angeles, London, New Delhi, Singapore, Washington DC, Melbourne: SAGE.
Muhuri P. K., Shukla A. K. and Abraham A. (2019) "Industry 4.0: A bibliometric analysis and detailed overview," *Engineering Applications of Artificial Intelligence* 78, 218–235.
Muller M., Lange I., Wang D., et al. (2019) "How Data Science Workers Work with Data. In: *Proceedings of the 2019 CHI Conference on Human Factors in Computing Systems: (*eds S Brewster, G Fitzpatrick, A Cox and V Kostakos), Glasgow Scotland Uk, 2019 May 09 05 2019, pp. 1–15. New York, NY, USA: ACM.
Nelson A. J. and Irwin J. (2014) ""Defining What We Do—All Over Again": Occupational Identity, Technological Change, and the Librarian/Internet-Search Relationship," *Academy of Management Journal* 57(3), 892–928.
Oberländer M., Beinicke A. and Bipp T. (2020) "Digital competencies: A review of the literature and applications in the workplace," *Computers & Education* 146, 103752.
Orlikowski W. J. (1993) "CASE Tools as Organizational Change: Investigating Incremental and Radical Changes in Systems Development," *MIS Quarterly* 17(3), 309.
Pachidi S., Berends H., Faraj S., et al. (2021) "Make Way for the Algorithms: Symbolic Actions and Change in a Regime of Knowing," *Organization Science* 32(1), 18–41.
Park S., Wang A. Y., Kawas B., et al. (2021) "Facilitating Knowledge Sharing from Domain Experts to Data Scientists for Building NLP Models. In: *26th International Conference on Intelligent User Interfaces: (*eds T Hammond, K Verbert, D Parra, B Knijnenburg, J O'Donovan and P Teale), College Station TX USA, 14 04 2021 17 04 2021, pp. 585–596. New York, NY, USA: ACM.
Parmiggiani E., Østerlie T. and Almklov P. G. (2022) "In the Backrooms of Data Science," *Journal of the Association for Information Systems* 23(1), 139–164.
Passi S. and Sengers P. (2020) "Making Data Science Systems Work," *Big Data & Society* 7(2), 205395172093960.
Patton M. Q. (2009) *Qualitative research & evaluation methods*. Thousand Oaks, Calif.: SAGE.
Power D. J., Cyphert D. and Roth R. M. (2019) "Analytics, bias, and evidence: the quest for rational decision making," *Journal of Decision Systems* 28(2), 120–137.
Provost F. and Fawcett T. (2013) "Data Science and its Relationship to Big Data and Data-Driven Decision Making," *Big data* 1(1), 51–59.
Reay, T., Golden-Biddle, K., & Germann, K. (2006). Legitimizing a New Role: Small Wins and Microprocesses of Change. The Academy of Management Journal, 49(5).
Sambasivan N. and Veeraraghavan R. (2022) "The Deskilling of Domain Expertise in AI Development. In: *CHI Conference on Human Factors in Computing Systems: (*eds S Barbosa, C Lampe, C Appert, DA Shamma, S Drucker, J Williamson, et al.), New Orleans LA USA, 29 04 2022 05 05 2022, pp. 1–14. New York, NY, USA: ACM.
Sarker S., Xiao X., Beaulieu T., et al. (2018) "Learning from First-Generation Qualitative Approaches in the IS Discipline: An Evolutionary View and Some Implications for Authors and Evaluators (PART 1/2)," *Journal of the Association for Information Systems* 19, 752–774.
Sheppard S., Colby A., Macatangay K., et al. (2006) "What is engineering practice?," *International Journal of Engineering Education* 22(3).
Soh C., Kien Sia S., Fong Boh W., et al. (2003) "Misalignments in ERP Implementation: A Dialectic Perspective," *International Journal of Human-Computer Interaction* 16(1), 81–100.
Strauss A. L. (1978) *Qualitative Analysis for Social Scientists*. Cambridge University Press.
Strich F., Mayer A.-S. and Fiedler M. (2021) "What Do I Do in a World of Artificial Intelligence? Investigating the Impact of Substitutive Decision-Making AI Systems on Employees' Professional Role Identity," *Journal of the Association for Information Systems* 22(2), 304–324.
Sykes T. A., Venkatesh V. and Johnson J. L. (2014) "Enterprise System Implementation and Employee Job Performance: Understanding the Role of Advice Networks," *MIS Quarterly* 38(1), 51–72.

Tams S. (2022) "Helping Older Workers Realize Their Full Organizational Potential: A Moderated Mediation Model of Age and IT-Enabled Task Performance," *MIS Quarterly* 46(1).
Vaast E. and Walsham G. (2005) "Representations and Actions: The Transformation of Work Practices with IT use," *Information and Organization* 15(1), 65–89.
van de Ven A. H. and Huber G. P. (1990) "Longitudinal Field Research Methods for Studying Processes of Organizational Change," *Organization Science* 1(3), 213–219.
van den Broek E., Sergeeva A. and Huysman Vrije M. (2021) "When the Machine Meets the Expert: An Ethnography of Developing AI for Hiring," *MIS Quarterly* 45(3), 1557–1580.
van Giffen B. and Ludwig H. (2023) "How Siemens Democratized Artificial Intelligence," *MIS Quarterly Executive* 22(1).
Waardenburg L., Huysman M. and Sergeeva A. V. (2022) "In the Land of the Blind, the One-Eyed Man Is King: Knowledge Brokerage in the Age of Learning Algorithms," *Organization Science* 33(1), 59–82.
Walsham G. (1995) "Interpretive case studies in IS research: nature and method," *European Journal of Information Systems* 4(2), 74–81.
Willcocks L. (2020) "Robo-Apocalypse Cancelled? Reframing the Automation and Future of Work Debate," *Journal of Information Technology* 35(4), 286–302.
Yin R. K. (2010) *Case Study Research: Design and Methods.* Los Angeles, California: SAGE.
Zhang Z., Nandhakumar J., Hummel J. T., et al. (2020) "Addressing the Key Challenges of Developing Machine Learning AI Systems for Knowledge-Intensive Work," *MIS Quarterly Executive*, 221–238.

Business Process Management

Through the Lens of Cognitive Functions and Contextual Factors—A Study of the Action Potentials of Artificial Intelligence in Business Process Management

Simon Meierhöfer and Claudius-Merlin Dorner

Abstract Artificial intelligence (AI) is currently one of the most prevalent technological breakthroughs. The nature of AI provides a multitude of action potentials in business process management (BPM). However, the diversity and complexity of underlying tools and methods of AI make it difficult for organizations to determine appropriate use cases in business processes, the central unit of BPM. At this point, organizations lack knowledge on how to conceptualize the use of AI in BPM. Against this background, we investigate the action potentials of individual cognitive functions of AI across different contextual factors of business processes by combining an online survey with an interview study by means of a mixed-methods approach. The results provide researchers and practitioners with a comprehensive overview of the action potentials of AI in BPM.

Keywords Artificial intelligence · Business process management · Cognitive functions · Contextual factors

S. Meierhöfer (✉)
Branch Business & Information Systems Engineering of the Fraunhofer FIT, Bayreuth, Germany
e-mail: simon.meierhoefer@fit.fraunhofer.de; simon.meierhoefer@fim-rc.de; simon.meierhoefer@uni-bayreuth.de

FIM Research Center, Bayreuth, Germany

University of Bayreuth, Bayreuth, Germany

C.-M. Dorner
Technical University of Munich, Munich, Germany
e-mail: claudius-merlin.dorner@tum.de

D. Beverungen et al. (eds.), *Solutions and Technologies for Responsible Digitalization*, Lecture Notes in Information Systems and Organisation 75,
https://doi.org/10.1007/978-3-031-80122-8_13

1 Introduction

Rapidly increasing data volumes, powerful computing capabilities, and advanced learning algorithms are leading to growing interest among researchers and practitioners in artificial intelligence (AI) (Haenlein and Kaplan 2019). Coupled with numerous application scenarios, AI provides organizations with tremendous action potentials, especially in business process management (BPM), as it promises to make business processes productive and efficient (Koehler 2018). However, the diversity and complexity of underlying tools and methods of AI make it difficult for organizations to determine appropriate use cases in business processes (Di Francescomarino and Maggi 2020).

To remain competitive in the digital age, organizations must continuously adapt their business processes to the dynamic environment (vom Brocke et al. 2014). In this dynamic environment, business processes are exposed to an ever-increasing amount of data (Reichert and Weber 2012). More concretely, business processes produce and consume more and more data that require aggregation to create value (Koehler 2018). For business processes as the heart of value creation, AI promises unprecedented opportunities to enhance productivity and efficiency. This in turn results in benefits such as improved products and services (Wamba-Taguimdje et al. 2020).

Despite these unprecedented opportunities, organizations lack knowledge on how to conceptualize the use of AI in BPM. To date, scientific work thematizes numerous application scenarios for the productive and efficient use of AI in BPM, but does not provide a comprehensive overview of the action potentials. For example, Koehler (2018) examines the role of contemporary tools and methods of AI in business processes, but only considers the action potentials to innovate business processes. From another point of view, Kulkov (2021) investigates the impact of AI on business processes, but only discusses the action potentials for core and support business processes. Finally, Knoch et al. (2020) study the action potentials of AI for the automatic gathering of process-related sensor information, whereas Aleksander (2017) explores the use of AI-based robots in business processes. Despite these valuable strands, respective contributions do not provide insights into what type of AI technology provides action potentials for what type of business process. These discrepancies mean that AI initiatives in the context of business processes often fail to achieve the aspired results as researchers and practitioners struggle to understand how to conceptualize the use of AI in BPM (Di Francescomarino and Maggi 2020). To address this issue, we state the following research question: What are the action potentials of individual cognitive functions of AI across different contextual factors of business processes?

To address this issue, we combined an online survey with an interview study by means of a mixed-methods approach. Building on Hofmann et al. (2020), who propose seven cognitive functions of AI, and vom Brocke et al. (2016), who provide six contextual factors of business processes, we investigate the action potentials of AI in BPM. In this way, we not only contribute to research by providing a comprehensive overview of the action potentials of individual cognitive functions across different contextual factors, but also to practice by highlighting application scenarios for the productive and efficient use of AI in BPM.

2 Theoretical Background

2.1 Artificial Intelligence

As one of the most prevalent technological breakthroughs, AI currently causes an inarguable wave of excitement among researchers and practitioners alike (Haenlein and Kaplan 2019). However, there is still no uniform definition of the term AI due to the lack of a precise understanding of intelligence itself (Koehler 2018). Moreover, AI refers to an umbrella term that covers a wide range of underlying tools and methods rather than a specific technology (Stone et al. 2016). In the context of this work, we follow Rai et al. (2019) and understand AI as the ability of machines to perform cognitive functions that we associate with the human mind.

Over time, the research community has evolved and refined the term AI in many ways to describe the nascent technology with common characteristics. For example, Russell and Norvig (2016) split the relevant aspects that define AI into four categories: thinking humanly, thinking rationally, acting humanly, and acting rationally. In line with this, a growing body of literature has recently started to study AI through the lens of cognitive functions (Wang and Wang 2006). Drawing on psychological science, cognitive functions are one way to examine the intelligence of the human brain (Rai et al. 2019). To do so, Rai et al. (2019) cluster cognitive functions into perceiving, reasoning, learning, interacting with the environment, problem-solving, decision-making, and demonstrating creativity. From another point of view, Vocke et al. (2019) distinguish between learning and reasoning as core cognitive functions. Besides, literature also separates cognitive functions from a capability perspective. For example, Rzepka and Berger (2018) divide cognitive functions into acting autonomously, learning user behaviors, perceiving and reacting to the environment, and understanding natural language. Similarly, Bawack et al. (2019) derive the cognitive functions of learning, sensing, acting, and comprehending.

Since the categorization of the functionalities of AI is blurred, Hofmann et al. (2020) combine views from existing work and introduce seven comprehensible and practically applicable solution classes of cognitive functions. The resulting conceptualization pays tribute to a finite set of cognitive functions that cover the domain entirely in terms of the modular functions of AI and facilitate an understanding of the technological features of AI. In Table 1, we summarize the individual cognitive functions with a description and exemplary sources.

Table 1 Overview of individual cognitive functions

Description	Exemplary references
Perceiving refers to the ability to capture environmental input and assimilate it for processing	Bawack et al. (2019), Rai et al. (2019), Russell and Norvig (2016), Rzepka and Berger (2018)
Recognizing describes the ability to identify an object by associating it with a concept or category	Bawack et al. (2019), Rzepka and Berger (2018)
Reasoning refers to the ability to identify cause-effect pairs and derive conclusions	Rai et al. (2019), Russell and Norvig (2016), Vocke et al. (2019)
Predicting describes the ability to estimate future events or conditions	Agrawal et al. (2018)
Decision-making refers to the ability to choose between discrete alternatives	Rai et al. (2019), Russell and Norvig (2016)
Generating describes the ability to produce or create something new	Hofmann et al. (2021), Rai et al. (2019)
Acting refers to the ability to do something to achieve a certain purpose	Bawack et al. (2019), Russell and Norvig (2016), Rzepka and Berger (2018)

2.2 Business Process Management

BPM is the art and science of overseeing how organizations perform work to achieve consistent results and benefit from improvement opportunities (Dumas et al. 2013). As the core of BPM, business processes refer to a series of measurable activities that generate value to achieve a specific business objective (Davenport 1993). Nowadays, organizations typically manage a variety of business processes in different contexts (vom Brocke et al. 2016). Depending on the context, business processes have individual requirements and pursue different goals that organizations must consider when managing them. To establish a common ground that promotes theoretical understanding and practical application of the role of context in business processes, vom Brocke et al. (2016) propose a framework to structure the context in which BPM can be applied along disjoint categories of contextual factors. In Table 2, we summarize the different types of contextual factors with a description and exemplary sources.

2.3 Relevant Work

To enable competitive work in the digital age, organizations must constantly search for ways to improve or innovate their business processes (Kerpedzhiev et al. 2021). In this context, information technology provides organizations with tremendous action potentials (Dumas et al. 2013). While scientific work has comprehensively investigated this interplay, recent advances in contemporary tools and methods of AI

Table 2 Overview of different contextual factors

Description	Exemplary references
Value contribution describes how high the share of a business process in the output of an organization is. (i.e., core, support, and management)	Gibb et al. (2006), Osterloh and Frost (2006), Ould (1995)
Repetitiveness indicates how often a business process with the same or a similar workflow is carried out. (i.e., repetitive, non-repetitive)	Lillrank and Liukko (2004), Schafermeyer et al. (2010), Tenhiälä (2011)
Knowledge-intensity describes how specialized the required knowledge of a business process is. (i.e., knowledge-intensive, non-knowledge-intensive)	Davenport (2005), Işik et al. (2013), Marjanovic and Freeze (2012)
Creativity indicates how much creative thinking ability is required for the execution of a business process. (i.e., creative, non-creative)	Hall and Johnson (2009), Seidel et al. (2010)
Interdependence describes how intertwined a business process is with another one. (i.e., interdependent, non-interdependent)	Schöpp and Frick (2012), Tenhiälä (2011)
Variability indicates how often a business process needs to be changed over time to achieve the defined goal. (i.e., variable, non-variable)	Arnold and Laue (2014), Gebauer and Lee (2008), Lillrank and Liukko (2004)

provide unprecedented opportunities to enhance productivity and efficiency in business processes (Koehler 2018). For example, AI can perform activities in business processes faster or simpler (Maggi and Marrella 2021). Further, AI can take over routines in business processes and even adapt to new situations without human inference (Koehler 2018).

Although scientific work indicates that AI provides a multitude of action potentials in BPM, it is still unclear what type of AI technology provides action potentials for what type of business process. Building on individual requirements and different goals of business processes, it is even more difficult for organizations to determine in which context AI creates value. However, to determine appropriate use cases for the productive and efficient use of information technology, a fit with business processes is imperative (vom Brocke and Rosemann 2015). To unfold this, research and practice alike require a structured overview by means of a collective framework that bridges the gap between AI and BPM. However, as both AI and BPM are broad and elusive terms that are difficult to study in an integrated manner, we abstract them into more specific concepts. For AI, we follow Hofmann et al. (2020), who describe individual cognitive functions that cover the entire spectrum of underlying tools and methods of AI. For BPM, we follow vom Brocke et al. (2016), who describe different contextual factors that are crucial for successfully managing business processes. As a result, in Fig. 1, we present a collective framework that conceptualizes the interplay between AI and BPM using cognitive functions and contextual factors.

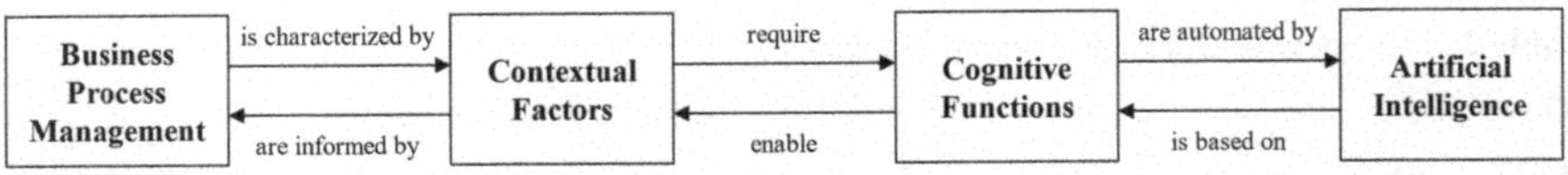

Fig. 1 Collective framework of contextual factors and cognitive functions

3 Research Methodology

To pursue the research objective, we adopted a mixed-methods approach, combining a quantitative and a qualitative study to gather multiple perspectives on the phenomenon under study (Venkatesh et al. 2013, 2016). In the first phase, we conducted an online survey with 32 experts in the fields of AI and/or BPM to collect initial quantitative insights. In the second phase, we conducted an interview study with seven experts from academia and industry to synthesize further qualitative data. This approach had two purposes: First, corroboration, as mixed methods allow an assessment of the credibility of the results by drawing inferences from the quantitative to the qualitative results and vice versa. Second, meaningfulness, as mixed methods provide a more conclusive and even richer explanation of the results.

3.1 Online Survey

To collect initial quantitative insights on the action potentials of individual cognitive functions across different contextual factors, we set up an online survey using the tool LimeSurvey. In iterative loops, we jointly worked out the structure and design of the online survey within the author team to ensure that the questionnaire covered all relevant aspects. Before distributing the questionnaire to potential participants, we conducted a pre-test with four fellow researchers to check the applicability and understandability of the online survey. After minor changes, we circulated the online survey among 150 potential participants with knowledge in the fields of AI and/or BPM via institutional email addresses and public LinkedIn accounts, with each expert receiving the same questionnaire. The data collection occurred from October to December 2022, while participation was voluntary and without incentives. In the end, we received 32 completed responses for further analysis. The core competency of the participants was AI ($n = 3$), BPM ($n = 25$), or both AI and BPM ($n = 4$). Further, the job position of the participants was distributed between chief executive officers ($n = 6$), decision-makers ($n = 16$), researchers ($n = 6$), and other professionals ($n = 4$). Finally, the average age of the participants was 42 years and the average work experience in the fields of AI and/or BPM was 11.8 years. Building on the different educational and functional backgrounds, we incorporated a cross-domain perspective on the research topic. In Fig. 2, we provide an overview of the participants in the online survey.

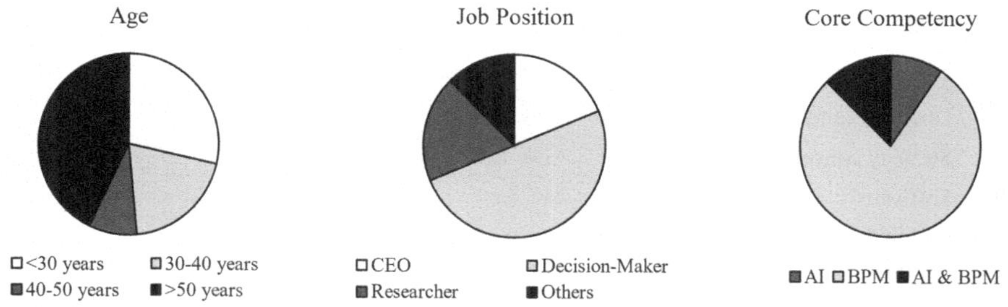

Fig. 2 Overview of the participants in the online survey

The questionnaire was structured as follows: We opened the online survey with an introduction to the research project and the theoretical underpinnings to ensure a proper understanding among the participants. The participants were then asked about their age, job position, core competency, as well as educational and functional background. As an ex-ante precaution against common method bias, we assured the respondents of the anonymity of their answers and stated that there were no right or wrong answers (Podsakoff et al. 2003). Before we started the questionnaire, we explained each cognitive function and each contextual factor in detail and illustrated them with an example. Afterward, the participants were asked to determine the action potentials of each individual cognitive function across each different contextual factor. To facilitate the assignment, we provided the participants with response categories according to the principles of Baur and Blasius (2014). For this purpose, we used a 5-point Likert scale with subdivisions from 0 = not important, 1 = less important, 2 = moderately important, 3 = very important, and 4 = extremely important (Schaeffer and Presser 2003).

3.2 *Interview Study*

To synthesize further qualitative data on the action potentials of individual cognitive functions across different contextual factors, we opted for a qualitative empirical research method on top of the online survey (Goldkuhl 2012). Following the guidelines of Myers and Newman (2007), we conducted seven semi-structured interviews with domain experts in the fields of AI and/or BPM. To limit bias, we recruited interview partners with different academic backgrounds and industry affiliations according to the principles of purposive sampling (Etikan 2016). Further, we only considered domain experts with more than five years of professional experience to ensure that the interview partners could assess the current state of research and development in the fields of AI and/or BPM. The expert interviews lasted between 35 and 65 min each and were moderated by one co-author via video conference. To ensure

Table 3 Overview of the participants in the interview study

ID	Position	Industry	Core competency	Experience (years)	Size (staff)
P1	Doctoral candidate	Research	AI & BPM	> 5	~ 120
P2	Strategy consultant	IT-consulting	AI & BPM	> 15	~ 5800
P3	Software development head	Finance	AI	> 10	~ 4100
P4	AI director	IT-services	AI	> 25	~ 300
P5	IT lead consultant	IT-consulting	BPM	> 5	~ 75,000
P6	Data scientist	Healthcare	AI	> 10	~ 400
P7	Data analyst	Production	AI	> 15	~ 70

data integrity, we recorded and transcribed the expert interviews for further analysis and reference. In Table 3, we summarize relevant information about the domain experts in the interview study.

The semi-structured interviews followed a guideline with four main sections: (1) an introduction to the research project and the theoretical underpinnings, (2) a brainstorming on examples that illustrate the action potentials of individual cognitive functions across different contextual factors, (3) a critical discussion of the results from the online survey combined with another brainstorming on examples, and (4) an interview conclusion including lessons learned for further elaboration. Throughout the expert interviews, we continuously sought to synthesize new insights to reflect and amplify the results from the online survey. We stopped the analysis after seven expert interviews as the interview partners raised no significant new issues and the aspects mentioned became increasingly repetitive. In this way, we could assume theoretical saturation within the author team (Eisenhardt 1989).

4 Results

To determine the action potentials of individual cognitive functions across different contextual factors, we calculate the mean score of the responses from the online survey. Using a 5-point Likert scale with subdivisions from 0 to 4, we split the action potentials into three categories. A score below 1.75 indicates a low action potential (light gray), a score between 1.75 and 2.75 represents a medium action potential (medium gray), and a score above 2.75 represents a high action potential (dark gray). In Table 4, we illustrate how the action potentials of individual cognitive functions vary across different contextual factors.

Overall, there are four salient clusters. First, cognitive functions have a high action potential for all levels of value contribution. Here, the action potential ranges from moderately important to extremely important. Second, cognitive functions have a high action potential for non-repetitive, knowledge-intensive, creative, interdependent, and variable contextual factors. Third, cognitive functions have a low action

Table 4 Action potentials of cognitive functions across contextual factors

		Contextual Factors													Ø
		Value contribution			Repetitive		Knowledge-int.		Creative		Interdependent		Variable		
		Core	Support	Mgmt	Yes	No	Yes	No	Yes	No	Yes	No	Yes	No	
Cognitive Functions	Perceiving	2,50	2,69	2,88	1,81	3,13	2,97	1,91	2,88	1,94	2,78	1,97	3,00	2,16	2,51
	Recognizing	2,84	2,97	3,03	2,13	3,28	3,31	1,91	2,81	2,13	3,00	2,13	3,22	2,28	2,69
	Reasoning	2,47	2,13	2,88	1,53	2,94	2,97	1,28	2,16	1,56	2,84	2,03	2,88	1,44	2,24
	Predicting	2,50	2,38	3,09	1,19	2,78	3,06	1,19	2,25	1,56	3,06	1,56	3,09	1,47	2,25
	Decision-making	3,19	2,53	3,56	1,47	2,78	2,91	1,41	2,44	1,66	3,13	2,13	3,00	1,66	2,45
	Generating	3,19	2,22	2,94	1,56	2,59	2,63	1,38	3,09	1,66	2,38	1,69	2,69	1,31	2,25
	Acting	3,50	2,97	2,88	2,69	2,66	3,09	2,16	2,59	2,34	2,91	2,47	2,94	2,09	2,71
Ø		2,88	2,55	3,04	1,77	2,88	2,99	1,60	2,60	1,83	2,87	2,00	2,97	1,77	

potential for repetitive, non-knowledge-intensive, non-creative, non-interdependent, and non-variable contextual factors. Fourth, the cognitive functions of perceiving, recognizing, and acting are prevalent with a high action potential across all contextual factors, whereas the cognitive functions of reasoning, predicting, decision-making, and generating are only dominant with a high action potential in certain contextual factors.

4.1 A Cognitive Function Perspective

Perceiving is very mature regarding its use in business processes (P1-P7). The ability to perceive information is a prerequisite for the existence of all other cognitive functions (P3). Specifically, perceiving entails the collection of relevant information that enables AI systems to perform cognitive functions (P1). Predominant examples of such AI systems in the context of business processes include Alexa or Google Assistant that utilize sensors to perceive information (P1, P4). However, the experts also pointed out that perceiving is not carried out by standalone AI systems, but combined with IoT systems. As such, AI systems process the data collected by IoT systems (P2).

Recognizing is very mature regarding its use in business processes (P1-P7). The experts rated the ability to recognize objects as the farthest advanced and most common cognitive function (P2). Predominant examples of such AI systems in the context of business processes include machine learning algorithms, such as supervised or unsupervised learning (P1, P3, P5, P6). Accordingly, recognizing enables the detection of discrepancies and inconsistencies in business processes (P1, P2, P4).

Reasoning is mature regarding its use in business processes (P1-P7). In general, reasoning constitutes a continuation of perceiving and recognizing that often builds on the combination of both (P2, P7). Predominant examples of such AI systems in the context of business processes involve regression analysis to find, analyze, and create clusters or patterns (P1, P2, P4, P7). Further, reasoning allows to reveal structures in business processes (P1).

Predicting is mature regarding its use in business processes (P1-P7). The experts emphasized numerous application scenarios based on a mix of statistical methods and deep learning algorithms to make predictions (P2, P3). Predominant examples of such AI systems in the context of business processes refer to predictive maintenance (P2, P5). However, AI systems for predicting are often inaccurate due to multiple influencing factors (e.g., data quality, data quantity) (P6).

Decision-making is mature regarding its use in business processes (P1-P7). Predominant examples of such AI systems in the context of business processes involve decision trees (P1, P4). However, there are restrictions to the standalone usability of decision-making, as AI systems can only provide recommendations, while decisions are subject to human actors (P1, P5). Further, due to the opaque nature of AI systems, the process of decision-making is limited regarding explainability and replicability (P4).

Generating is less mature regarding its use in business processes (P1-P7). The experts mentioned only a limited number of application scenarios, indicating a need for research and development to make generating feasible (P2, P6). Predominant examples of such AI systems in the context of business processes are, so far, restricted to chatbots that can generate answers to questions or generative adversarial networks that can generate artificial artifacts (P1, P5).

Acting is very mature regarding its use in business processes (P1-P7). Predominant examples of such AI systems in the context of business processes refer to established approaches such as robotic process automation (P1, P3, P7). However, the experts stated that acting builds on decision-making. Specifically, AI systems can only act when there is a decision with accurate and precise results present (P2, P3).

In Table 5, we list exemplary statements from the interview partners to ensure transparency and replicability of the results.

4.2 A Contextual Factor Perspective

Core processes have a high action potential. However, the use of AI is limited to individual application scenarios (P1, P2). On the one hand, trust is often not as high that organizations are reluctant to use AI in core processes (P1). On the other hand, regulatory restrictions regarding the processing of sensitive data along core processes play an impeding role (P3). **Support processes** have a medium action potential. Depending on the type of support process, AI allows the augmentation or automation of human actors (P4). **Management processes** have a high action potential. While there are application scenarios where AI performs monitoring or forecasting activities (P1, P2, P4), management decisions are subject to human actors (P1). Here, AI rather takes over supportive functions by providing relevant information to make decisions (P2).

Repetitive processes have a low action potential. The experts highlighted that standardized automation approaches are already sufficient, while the use of AI is more of an overkill (P1, P7). **Non-repetitive processes**, in contrast, have a high

Table 5 Exemplary statements from the interview partners

Cognitive functions	Exemplary statements	Source
Perceiving	Perceiving is more about sensor data. It is less of a standalone application of AI, but rather in the direction of IoT systems	P2
	I would mainly refer to visual and camera sensors as applications for perceiving	P4
Recognizing	Recognizing is already quite mature in practical applications, but […] it always depends on the amount of accessible and available amount of training data	P1
	Recognizing provides many use cases in the field of image or text recognition	P6
Reasoning	Clustering is probably the typical example here. If you have a large data set […], then a clustering algorithm can provide estimations	P1
	Finding patterns is a typical use case when it comes to reasoning	P7
Predicting	There are also approaches for predicting to inform optimal purchasing processes, especially in the case of more expensive commodities	P2
	Important is the data basis as good predictions depend on influencing factors	P3
Decision-making	In the end, the model […] never decides itself. It can only make a recommendation while someone else makes the decision	P5
	From a data set, you can run the decision model based on a decision tree	P4
Generating	Generating is relatively immature, so practical use cases are limited so far	P5
	No AI will generate a strategy. What it can generate are certain factors or characteristics	P6
Acting	The technological maturity is not yet such that acting functions could be easily implemented in business processes	P3
	RPA or AI, in most cases it is the combination of both that enables autonomy	P7

action potential. As unknown sequences or unstructured flows of business processes require continuous interpretation, there are valuable avenues for the use of AI (P2, P4).

Knowledge-intensive processes have a high action potential. The experts stated that AI allows the generation of insights and provision of recommendations by analyzing information from business processes, although extracting relevant knowledge is tricky (P3). Hence, the use of AI depends critically on the accessibility and availability of data (P7). **Non-knowledge-intensive processes**, in contrast, have a low action potential. Here, a lack of data leads to almost no avenues for the use of AI (P1, P5).

Creative processes have a high action potential. The experts pointed out that creativity in the context of business processes can increasingly be covered by AI (P2, P7). However, AI can only provide supportive functions and help human actors to create something new or ingenious (P2, P5). **Non-creative processes**, in contrast, have a low action potential. However, as long as the required creativity does not reach the capabilities of human actors, there are at least a few avenues for the use of AI (P5, P6).

Interdependent processes have a high action potential. The experts reiterated the dependency between business processes and data as interdependent processes mean interdependent data (P6). Building on the linkage between business processes, AI can uncover commonalities and differences among business processes, allowing the seamless transfer and enhancement of data (e.g., sequence, flow) (P2). **Non-interdependent processes**, in contrast, have a low action potential. Here, no linkage between business processes exists, so there are almost no avenues for the use of AI (P2, P6).

Variable processes have a high action potential. Unlike conventional approaches that require manual adaptation of business processes to work in a dynamic environment, AI enables an automatic adaptation of business processes to new situations (P2). **Non-variable processes**, in contrast, have a low action potential. Here, a balance must be struck between adaptations of business processes that a machine can take over and adaptations of business processes that require human inference (P2, P6).

5 Discussion

Overall, we find that in the context of business processes, some cognitive functions currently provide a low action potential, but may evolve in the future. In contrast, other cognitive functions may continue to provide a low action potential at all, even as more sophisticated tools and methods of AI emerge. More concretely, the results indicate that the cognitive functions of perceiving, recognizing, and acting have a high action potential in business processes associated with a wide range of potential application scenarios. Consistent with existing literature, these cognitive functions are most advanced for the productive and efficient use in business processes (Knoch et al. 2020). In contrast, the cognitive function of generating has a low action potential in business processes, which limits potential application scenarios. Here, Huang and Rust (2018) come to similar conclusions by pointing out that AI cannot comprehensively map complex activities that rely on human intelligence. Similarly, Aleksander (2017) mentions that AI cannot holistically mimic human intelligence, but rather provide supportive functions. Accordingly, in the context of business processes, AI assumes an augmenting rather than an automating role and still requires human inference. This finding coincides with perspectives from the cognitive function of decision-making. According to Daugherty and Wilson (2018), AI can provide suggestions for decision-making, but the decision itself is subject to human actors. Similarly, for the cognitive function of predicting, Agrawal et al. (2018) emphasize that a prediction is not a decision and still requires human inference. Finally, for the cognitive function of reasoning, Daugherty and Wilson (2018) point out that AI can identify clusters or patterns in business processes, but does not provide a logical understanding for a subsequent interpretation.

5.1 Theoretical and Practical Implications

From a theoretical perspective, the study provides researchers with a solid foundation to better grasp what type of AI technology provides action potentials for what type of business process. Building on the collective framework, the results thus foster a comprehensive understanding of enabling and limiting contextual factors regarding the use of cognitive functions and vice versa. From a practical perspective, the study provides managers with a guide on where to start or proceed when exploring the action potentials of individual cognitive functions across different contextual factors. By highlighting application scenarios for the productive and efficient use of AI in BPM, organizations can either search for a distinct cognitive function to solve a problem in a particular contextual factor or vice versa. At the same time, the collective framework serves as an opportunity space for organizations to uncover action potentials for improving or innovating business processes with the help of AI. Altogether, the study closes the knowledge gap on how to conceptualize the use of AI in BPM.

5.2 Limitations and Future Research

The study has several limitations that stimulate future research. First, we restricted the interview study to insights from professionals with a provider perspective (e.g., consultants, researchers). Future research should take a broader view and also consider a user perspective to gain additional insights into the action potentials of individual cognitive functions across different contextual factors. At this point, the general role of AI in BPM should also be investigated in more detail. Second, we provide only an overview of what type of AI technology provides action potentials for what type of business process by highlighting real-world examples. However, to ensure the successful use of AI in BPM, organizations require further guidance to find a distinct cognitive function to solve a problem in a particular contextual factor or vice versa. Future research should provide a method or model to guide managers in comparing and selecting appropriate use cases. Third, we focused on a status-quo reporting of the action potentials. However, as more sophisticated tools and methods of AI emerge, cognitive functions will progressively advance. Future research should take this as motivation to conduct a longitudinal study and investigate how existing action potentials evolve over time or whether new ones even emerge.

6 Conclusion

In the wake of recent developments, AI is currently one of the most prevalent technological breakthroughs that provides a multitude of action potentials in business processes, the central unit of BPM (Koehler 2018). However, the diversity and complexity of underlying tools and methods of AI make it difficult for organizations to determine appropriate use cases in business processes (Di Francescomarino and Maggi 2020). To close the knowledge gap on how to conceptualize the use of AI in BPM, we view AI through the lens of individual cognitive functions and analyze BPM through the lens of different contextual factors. Combining an online survey with an interview study with experts in the fields of AI and/or BPM by means of a mixed-methods approach, the results reveal that the action potentials of individual cognitive functions vary across different contextual factors. Most notably, we find that: First, cognitive functions do not provide a high action potential across the entire spectrum of contextual factors, but rather unfold only in distinct ones with a high action potential. Second, the action potentials of cognitive functions range from not important to extremely important, revealing different maturity levels of underlying tools and methods of AI. Building on these results, the present work provides a solid foundation to bridge the gap between AI and BPM and explore the emerging field even further in future research.

References

Agrawal, A., Gans, J. & Goldfarb, A. (2018), *Prediction Machines: The Simple Economics of Artificial Intelligence*, Harvard Business Review Press.

Aleksander, I. (2017), 'Partners of Humans: A Realistic Assessment of the Role of Robots in the Foreseeable Future', *Journal of Information Technology* 32(1), 1–9.

Arnold, O. & Laue, R. (2014), 'Überblick über Ansätze zur Modellierung von Variabilität in Geschäftsprozessmodellen', *HMD Praxis der Wirtschaftsinformatik* 51(5), 627–642.

Baur, N. & Blasius, J. (2014), *Methoden der empirischen Sozialforschung*, Springer.

Bawack, R., Wamba, S.F. & Carillo, K.D.A. (2019), 'Artificial Intelligence in Practice: Implications for Information Systems Research', *Proceedings of the 25th Americas Conference on Information Systems (ICIS), Cancun.*

Davenport, T.H. (1993), *Process Innovation: Reengineering Work Through Information Technology*, Harvard Business School Press.

Davenport, T.H. (2005), *Thinking for a Living: How to Get Better Performances and Results from Knowledge Workers*, Harvard Business Review Press.

Daugherty & Wilson. (2018), ISBN-13: 978–1633693869.

Di Francescomarino, C. & Maggi, F.M. (2020), 'Preface to the Special Issue on Artificial Intelligence for Business Process Management 2018', *Journal on Data Semantics* 9(1), 1.

Dumas, M., La Rosa, M., Mendling, J. & Reijers, H.A. (2013), *Fundamentals of Business Process Management*, Springer.

Eisenhardt, K.M. (1989), 'Building Theories from Case Study Research', *Academy of Management Review* 14(4), 532–550.

Etikan, I. (2016), 'Comparison of Convenience Sampling and Purposive Sampling', *American Journal of Theoretical and Applied Statistics* 5(1), 1–4.

Gebauer, J. & Lee, F. (2008), 'Enterprise System Flexibility and Implementation Strategies: Aligning Theory with Evidence from a Case Study', *Information Systems Management* 25(1), 71–82.

Gibb, F., Buchanan, S. & Shah, S. (2006), 'An Integrated Approach to Process and Service Management', *International Journal of Information Management* 26(1), 44–58.

Goldkuhl, G. (2012), 'Pragmatism vs Interpretivism in Qualitative Information Systems Research', *European Journal of Information Systems* 21(2), 135–146.

Haenlein, M. & Kaplan, A. (2019), 'A Brief History of Artificial Intelligence: On the Past, Present, and Future of Artificial Intelligence', *California Management Review* 61(4), 5–14.

Hall, J.M. & Johnson, M.E. (2009), 'When Should a Process Be Art, Not Science?', *Harvard Business Review Press* 87(3), 58–65.

Hofmann, P., Jöhnk, J., Protschky, D. & Urbach, N. (2020), 'Developing Purposeful AI Use Cases – A Structured Method and Its Application in Project Management', *Proceedings of the 15th International Conference on Wirtschaftsinformatik (WI), Potsdam.*

Hofmann, P., Rückel, T. & Urbach, N. (2021), 'Innovating with Artificial Intelligence: Capturing the Constructive Functional Capabilities of Deep Generative Learning', *Proceedings of the 54th Hawaii International Conference on System Sciences (HICSS), Honolulu.*

Huang & Rust. (2018). https://doi.org/10.1177/1094670517752459

Işik, Ö., Mertens, W. & van den Bergh, J. (2013), 'Practices of Knowledge Intensive Process Management: Quantitative Insights', *Business Process Management Journal* 19(3), 515–534.

Kerpedzhiev, G.D., König, U.M., Röglinger, M. & Rosemann, M. (2021), 'An Exploration into Future Business Process Management Capabilities in View of Digitalization', *Business & Information Systems Engineering* 63(2), 83–96.

Knoch, S., Herbig, N., Ponpathirkoottam, S., Kosmalla, F., Staudt, P. & Porta, D., *et al.* (2020), 'Sensor-based Human–Process Interaction in Discrete Manufacturing', *Journal on Data Semantics* 9(1), 21–37.

Koehler, J. (2018), 'Business Process Innovation with Artificial Intelligence: Levering Benefits and Controlling Operational Risks', *European Business & Management* 4(2), 55–66.

Kulkov, I. (2021), 'The Role of Artificial Intelligence in Business Transformation: A Case of Pharmaceutical Companies', *Technology in Society* 66(2), 1–11.

Lillrank, P. & Liukko, M. (2004), 'Standard, Routine and Non-Routine Processes in Health Care', *International Journal of Health Care Quality Assurance* 17(1), 39–46.

Maggi, F.M. & Marrella, A. (2021), 'Preface to the Special Issue on Artificial Intelligence for Business Process Management 2019', *Journal on Data Semantics* 10(1–2), 1–2.

Marjanovic, O. & Freeze, R. (2012), 'Knowledge-Intensive Business Process: Deriving a Sustainable Competitive Advantage through Business Process Management and Knowledge Management Integration', *Knowledge and Process Management* 19(4), 180–188.

Myers, M.D. & Newman, M. (2007), 'The Qualitative Interview in IS Research: Examining the Craft', *Information and Organization* 17(1), 2–26.

Osterloh, M. & Frost, J. (2006), *Prozessmanagement als Kernkompetenz: Wie Sie Business Reengineering strategisch nutzen können*, Gabler.

Ould, M.A. (1995), *Business Processes: Modelling and Analysis for Re-engineering and Improvement*, Wiley.

Podsakoff, P.M., MacKenzie, S.B., Lee, J.-Y. & Podsakoff, N.P. (2003), 'Common Method Biases in Behavioral Research: A Critical Review of the Literature and Recommended Remedies', *Journal of Applied Psychology* 88(5), 879–903.

Rai, A., Constantinides, P. & Sarker, S. (2019), 'Next Generation Digital Platforms: Toward Human-AI Hybrids', *MIS Quarterly* 43(1), 1–9.

Reichert, M. & Weber, B. (2012), *Enabling Flexibility in Process-aware Information Systems: Challenges, Methods, Technologies*, Springer.

Russell, S.J. & Norvig, P. (2016), *Artificial Intelligence: A Modern Approach*, Pearson Higher Education.

Rzepka, C. & Berger, B. (2018), 'User Interaction with AI-enabled Systems: A Systematic Review of IS Research', *Proceedings of the 39th International Conference on Information Systems (ICIS), San Francisco.*

Schaeffer, N.C. & Presser, S. (2003), 'The Science of Asking Questions', *Annual Review of Sociology* 29(1), 65–88.

Schafermeyer, M., Grgecic, D. & Rosenkranz, C. (2010), 'Factors Influencing Business Process Standardization: A Multiple Case Study', *Proceedings of the 43rd Hawaii International Conference on System Sciences (HICSS), Honolulu.*

Schöpp, C. & Frick, N. (2012), 'Massenprozessmanagement bei Dienstleistungen', *Multikonferenz Wirtschaftsinformatik (MKWI), Braunschweig.*

Seidel, S., Shortland, K., Court, D. & Elzinga, D. (2010), 'Managing Creativity-intensive Processes: Learning from Film and Visual Effects Production', *Handbook on Business Process Management 2*, 515–538.

Stone, P., Brooks, R., Brynjolfsson, E., Calo, R., Etzioni, O. & Hager, G., *et al.* (2016), 'Artificial Intelligence and Life in 2030: One Hundred Year Study on Artificial Intelligence', *Stanford University.*

Tenhiälä, A. (2011), 'Contingency Theory of Capacity Planning: The Link between Process Types and Planning Methods', *Journal of Operations Management* 29(1-2), 65–77.

Venkatesh, V., Brown, S. & Sullivan, Y. (2016), 'Guidelines for Conducting Mixed-methods Research: An Extension and Illustration', *Journal of the Association for Information Systems* 17(7), 435–494.

Venkatesh, V., Brown, S.A. & Bala, H. (2013), 'Bridging the Qualitative-Quantitative Divide: Guidelines for Conducting Mixed Methods Research in Information Systems', *MIS Quarterly* 37(1), 21–54.

Vocke, C., Constantinescu, C. & Popescu, D. (2019), 'Application Potentials of Artificial Intelligence for the Design of Innovation Processes', *Procedia CIRP* 84, 810–813.

vom Brocke, J., Mathiassen, L. & Rosemann, M. (2014), 'Business Process Management', *Business & Information Systems Engineering* 6(4), 189.

vom Brocke, J. & Rosemann, M. (2015), *Introduction, Methods, and Information Systems*, Springer.

vom Brocke, J., Zelt, S. & Schmiedel, T. (2016), 'On the Role of Context in Business Process Management', *International Journal of Information Management* 36(3), 486–495.

Wamba-Taguimdje, S.-L., Fosso Wamba, S., Kala Kamdjoug, J.R. & Tchatchouang Wanko, C.E. (2020), 'Influence of Artificial Intelligence (AI) on Firm Performance: The Business Value of AI-based Transformation Projects', *Business Process Management Journal* 26(7), 1893–1924.

Wang, Y. & Wang, Y. (2006), 'Cognitive Informatics Models of the Brain', *IEEE Transactions on Systems, Man, and Cybernetics, Part C (Applications and Reviews)* 36(2), 203–207.

Process and Strategy Mining in Real-Time Strategy Games

Nico Elbert, Nikolai Stein, and Christoph M. Flath

Abstract In this study, we introduce a data-driven approach for process mining in real-time strategy (RTS) games, which serve as a proxy for corporate decision processes. By analyzing decision sequences in gaming environments, we uncover strategic behaviors impacting performance and match outcomes. Our methodology leverages game data, enriching process mining research and providing implications for strategic planning in business process management.

Keywords Process mining · Data-driven · Game data · Real-time strategy games

1 Introduction

Demonstrating process mining on real corporate data can be challenging due to limited access caused by concerns about data privacy, regulatory restrictions, and considerations of competitive advantage. In many cases, companies are reluctant to share their data, as it may contain sensitive information that could harm their business if misused, and regulatory restrictions can limit data sharing with outside parties even further. Despite these challenges, there is growing recognition of the substantial benefits that process mining, contingent upon realistic data, can bring to organizations. To overcome these challenges, companies can use synthetic or simulated data as a means to showcase and understand the potential benefits of process mining. However, the use of synthetic or simulated data has limitations, as it may not accurately reflect the complexities and nuances of real-world processes. To explore the

N. Elbert (✉) · N. Stein · C. M. Flath
Julius-Maximilians-Universität Würzburg, 97070 Würzburg, Germany
e-mail: nico.elbert@uni-wuerzburg.de

N. Stein
e-mail: nikolai.stein@uni-wuerzburg.de

C. M. Flath
e-mail: christoph.flath@uni-wuerzburg.de

D. Beverungen et al. (eds.), *Solutions and Technologies for Responsible Digitalization*,
Lecture Notes in Information Systems and Organisation 75,
https://doi.org/10.1007/978-3-031-80122-8_14

potentials of these methods, competitive real-time strategy (RTS) games can serve as a great proxy for the analysis of decision-making in complex environments under time pressure. Within this context, game data serves as a controlled experimental environment (Wagner 2006), as previously demonstrated by other business-related academic studies, such as the works of Clement (2023), Künn et al. (2023), and Ching et al. (2021). Table 1 relates typical challenges in RTS games to corporate decision-making. Game histories of RTS matches are persisted in log files. These files contain event logs of every given action command in the game and hence contain rich data on player behavior, such as the sequences of actions taken by players, the resources they allocate, and the strategic decisions they make. By analyzing these logs, researchers can generate insights into player behavior and decision-making that can be used to inform and improve process mining and process discovery techniques in a competitive rational environment. Using data-driven approaches for this purpose ensures the general applicability of the techniques implemented. In this paper, we propose a data-driven, zero-domain knowledge approach for analyzing player behavior and strategies in RTS games. Our goal is to identify action sequences used by players and evaluate their impact on the outcome of competitive duels. The contribution of this paper is two-fold. First, we present a novel approach for using process mining techniques to analyze and model player strategies and behavior with zero-domain knowledge. Second, this approach not only sheds light on the behavior corresponding to the performance of players in these games, but also highlights the potential of game data as a proxy for other process mining examples. Players in this environment act highly rationally and develop skills over a long period of time. The high availability of data, combined with its similarities to other real-world processes, makes it an attractive option for process and strategy mining studies and should find appreciation in information systems research. The following sections will be organized as follows: First, we review related work in the field. Second, we describe our methodology and approach, highlighting the key steps of the process mining technique. Third, we present our results, and finally we discuss their implications.

2 Related Work

Numerous studies have investigated gameplay data in RTS games, utilizing both domain knowledge and data-driven techniques for identifying strategic patterns and predicting player behaviors. Dereszynski et al. (2011) and Synnaeve and Bessiere (2011) have employed statistical learning and Bayesian networks to analyze StarCraft II matches, focusing on build orders and additional features. These studies go beyond mere identification of strategic states, exploring the potential to incorporate partial observability into models to optimize player behavior and suggest future actions. Hayes and Beling (2018) took a different approach and used unsupervised hierarchical clustering to classify build orders in StarCraft II, analyzing a substantial dataset of 7647 matches. They developed an effective clustering algorithm with a unique distance matrix based on the military composition at specific

Table 1 Analogies between challenges in corporate decision-making and RTS games

Aspect	RTS games	Corporate decision-making
Resource management	Troops, buildings, resources	Financial resources, manpower, physical assets
Planning and strategy	Building base, expanding territory, defeating enemies	Achieving goals (e.g., increasing profits, expanding into new markets)
Risk assessment	Assessing risk of attacking enemy territories or building new structures	Assessing risk in business ventures
Adaptability	Adapting to changes in game environment (e.g., new enemy tactics, resource shortages)	Adapting to changes in market or business environment (e.g., new competitors, changes in consumer behavior)
Time management	Making decisions quickly and efficiently	Making decisions in a timely manner

times. Determining the optimal number of clusters involved using the average inter-cluster distance, intra-cluster distance, and setting a minimum size threshold for the smallest cluster. Further analysis through a principal component analysis provided insight into the differences between clusters. This analysis allowed for the prediction of an opponent's strategy based on the player's faction using a Bayesian inference model, demonstrating the predictive power of these analytical approaches. While these studies provide significant contributions, the current work adds the concept of process mining to the analysis of game data and introduces game data within the process mining domain. Process mining, as described by van Zelst et al. (2021), utilizes event data to provide a detailed understanding of processes, and shares similarities with the granular level of analysis used in this work. Within process mining, process discovery aims to construct a process model, such as a Petri net, as an abstract representation of an event log, with the objective is to create a model that offers valuable understanding of the captured behavior in the log (Van Dongen et al. 2009). We extend upon previous works by applying process mining techniques to examine the patterns and strategies in RTS games, a novel approach to studying gaming data. By abstracting the data into the right level of granularity, we are able to better understand player actions, bridging the gap between the hypothesized game strategies and the actual actions taken by players. With PM^2, Van Eck et al. (2015) presents a suitable methodology to tackle such a process mining project. We use the majors steps of this methodology as orientation framework for our project.

3 Methodology and Approach

Our data-driven approach is designed to elucidate game dynamics by delineating clusters of distinct strategies and common behavioral patterns, without the prerequisite of domain knowledge. As shown in Fig. 1, our approach consists of several key steps derived from the process mining methodologies by Van Eck et al. (2015) alongside data mining techniques (Van Der Aalst 2012, 2016). Before clustering game states, we perform several steps, including collection of game recordings, extraction of event logs, identification of important features and parameters, and aggregation and summarization of game state information. Our approach aims to produce two outcomes. First, we seek to adapt and extend the clustered state transition graphs presented in previous research by Dereszynski et al. (2011) and Synnaeve and Bessiere (2011), by leveraging the graphs behavior capturing capabilities, similar to Petri net models as described (Van Dongen et al. 2009). Second, we aim to compare these game state clusters at the point where they hold the clearest strategic information in order to identify distinct strategies. In the context of our approach, a game log corresponds to a graph $\mathcal{G}(S, A)$ transitioning between states s in discrete Steps, with one new state s after every action a. $\mathcal{S}$ is defined as the sum of all possible states. $a_t \in A$ describes an action that has been performed at point $t \in T$ in the game with T being the overall game time. With a suitable aggregation, as described below, this results in a comprehensive representation of the development of a game, guaranteeing an appropriate level of information, as proposed by El-Nasr et al. (2021). For our approach, the resulting state nodes within the graphs $\mathcal{G}(S, A)$ are then clustered to identify strategic behavioral patterns. We conduct our research using data from Age of Empires 2 (AOE2) matches, an RTS game in which players control a civilization, collect resources, build structures, train armies, and engage in combat with the ultimate goal of defeating their opponents. Players must make strategic choices about resource allocation, technology research, unit production, and combat tactics. Since the different military unit types have strengths and weaknesses in a rock-paper-scissors manner, their composition based on the opponent's choice is crucial for success; this leads to common decision sequences similar to chess openings. AOE2 has a well-established competitive scene, with numerous tournaments and leagues featuring all skill levels. For the present research, we focus on 1 vs. 1 matches.

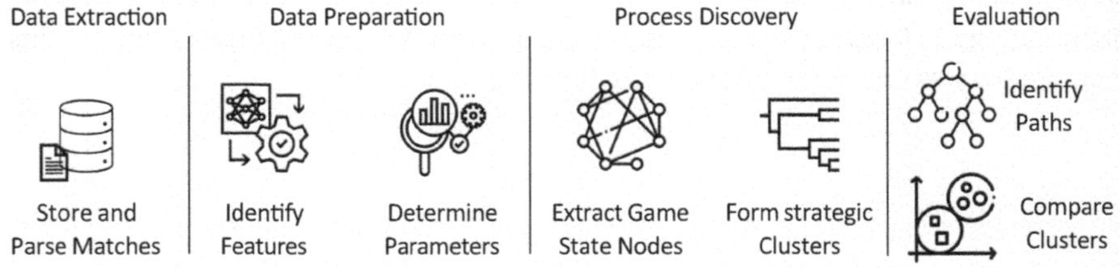

Fig. 1 Overview of strategy mining approach

3.1 Data Extraction

A total of 225,398 record files of 1 vs. 1 AOE2 matches were collected for this study. The matches were obtained by scraping the leaderboard of 166,625 players from AOE2Insights,[1] the leading platform for the AOE2 community, between January 1st and September 1st 2022. Scraped record files contain only general settings, player action commands, and initial positions. This would provide sufficient information for the game engine to simulate the course of the match, but doesn't contain actual information if an action could be completed successfully within itself. The resulting event log for every game contains the following information for each action:

- **Timestamp** at which an action command was given.
- **Type** of action, such as *Create Unit, Move, Build, Target,* etc.
- **Parameters** relevant for the action, e.g., unit/build type.
- **Payload** of the action command, containing additional information, e.g., performing or target object id, number of units, etc.
- **Player** performing the action.
- **Position** where the action takes place, specified by x,y coordinates.

To capture a player's skill level, every player is associated with an Elo rating. The Elo rating system (Elo 1978) is used to capture the relative skill levels of players in two-player zero-sum games and finds application in various fields. We analyze the Elo distribution among the matches and the underlying player structure, since they hold information about expected skill ability of the respective players for every game. To differ decision patterns for different skill levels, three Elo level brackets are introduced, as previously proposed by Anderson et al. (2017) in a chess context. Since the distribution is skewed towards higher Elo ratings, these brackets are set to be "Low Elo", representing the lowest 45% of matches up to a rating of 1062, "Medium Elo" representing the next 45% up to a rating of 1501 and finally the bracket "High Elo", representing the top 10%.

3.2 Data Preparation

Feature Identification To garner a data-driven comprehension of the game dynamics, the identification of pertinent features and corresponding actions is imperative. To achieve this, we train and evaluate an XGBoost model, as introduced by Chen and Guestrin (2016), to predict the results of the matches based on the collected data. The model provides insights into feature relevance by determining the importance of each feature in improving the accuracy of the validation results. For evaluation, we summarize over 400 single features in their respective masterdata categories provided by the game. For every 120 s time interval in the game, we train an independent model, predicting the match outcome based on the current aggregated game

[1] aoe2insights.com.

state. The training was conducted under two scenarios: one with incomplete information, only encompassing the actions from one player's perspective, as denoted by $\mathcal{G}_p(S_p, A_p)$, and the other with complete information, incorporating the perspectives of both players, as represented in the original graph $\mathcal{G}(S, A)$. The results show that complete and incomplete information scenarios develop similarly in the early stages, and hence the same elements are relevant. The results of the different time-dependent XGBoost models for the complete perspective are depicted in Fig. 2. In the dataset, which contains event logs of actions a, the finest granular representation of game state s is encapsulated by the number of specific action commands executed until a certain point in time, such as *create unit* x, as depicted in the initial graph $\mathcal{G}(S, A)$. To better generalize the game states and player behavior, we divide a match into disjoint observation intervals $\mathcal{I} = I_1, \ldots, I_n$ of a consistent length l, such that $\cup_{i=1}^{n} I_i = T$. The length l is dependent on the measure for game progress, e.g., 120 s of game time. The starting point of an interval I_i is given by $t_i^{start} = (i-1) \cdot l$ and the end point by $t_i^{end} = t_i^{start} + l = i \cdot l$. $\tilde{a}_i$ is the union of all actions a_t that have been performed within an observation interval I_i as $\tilde{a}_i = \cup_{t \in I_i} a_t$. Accordingly $\tilde{a}_i$ represents the transition between the states $\tilde{s}_i$ and $\tilde{s}_{i+1}$. This aggregated set of States $\tilde{S} \subset S$ results in the graph $\mathcal{G}(\tilde{S}, \tilde{A})$. Further we only consider the one player perspective for each player, as represented by $\mathcal{G}_p(S_p, A_p)$ with S_p being the states observed by player p, resulting of all actions A_p. In the next aggregation step, in order to simplify the action space, we summarize over action categories and define new action vectors $\hat{a}_i$ that contain the aggregation of all actions $\tilde{a}_i$ belonging to the same action category. For example, $\tilde{a}_i$ contains the information how many units of light and heavy cavalry have been produced. Both numbers get summed up under $\hat{a}_i$, resulting in a new set of States $\hat{S}$ and the graph $\mathcal{G}(\hat{S}, \hat{A})$ First, we define the set of actions of category c, denoted as $A_c \subseteq A$, where A is the set of all actions. Now, we define the mapping function $\mathcal{M} : A_c \rightarrow \hat{a}_{c,i}$, where $\hat{a}_{c,i}$ represents the aggregated actions of category c within the observation interval I_i. To aggregate the actions of category c within each observation interval I_i, modify the union expression as follows: $\hat{a}_i = \cup_{t \in I_i} \mathcal{M}(a_t \cap A_c)$. Here, $\hat{a}_i$ represents the aggregated actions of category c within the observation interval I_i. The results in Fig. 2 indicate a strong impact of military units on the accuracy of the prediction of the XGBoost model. Therefore, a game state representation that captures the composition of created units, as proposed by, can be appropriate to identify patterns. Given the high number of unit types, we aggregate them in a unit category. As Fig. 2 shows, economic units, buildings, and technologies also contribute significantly to accuracy. Therefore, the economic elements, similar to the military, are considered in the event logs and find representation in a game state encoding. This allows us to narrow the game state graph $\mathcal{G}$, to only capture the relevant actions $\hat{A}^* \subset \hat{A}$, resulting in the reduced sum of all states $\hat{S}^*$ and the reduced graph $\mathcal{G}(\hat{S}^*, \hat{A}^*)$. To competently compare between military and economic features, only the respective units find a representation based on their absolute numbers, as well as the resources spent on them. As depicted in Fig. 3 the resource spending rate differs significantly between the Elo rates and the winning and losing perspectives. Hence, the use of resource spending as an estimator for game progress allows us to compare strategies excited with different velocity due to a different resource spending rate, since the number of made decisions remains the same. To differentiate between levels of skill within decision sequences, we examine bracketing over the Elo groups, as well as over time frames or total resources spent. Analogously to the time frame slices as observation intervals, we also slice the resource spending in 500 resource intervals as an alternative representation. This results in the four different approaches for game state graphs G depicted in Fig. 4, narrowing the captured actions down to the set scope of nits $\hat{A}^* \subset \hat{A}$ and aggregating them under the defined observation intervals I_i in $\mathcal{G}(\tilde{S}, \tilde{A}^{r})$.

Parameterization To identify the point in the matches, at which game states contain the purest strategic information and create meaningful and comparable results, a number of parameters must be determined. The number of game state nodes significantly varies over the scenarios. To minimize the noise in the game state data Dereszynski et al. (2011) use a 25% threshold on their edges, with a limited number

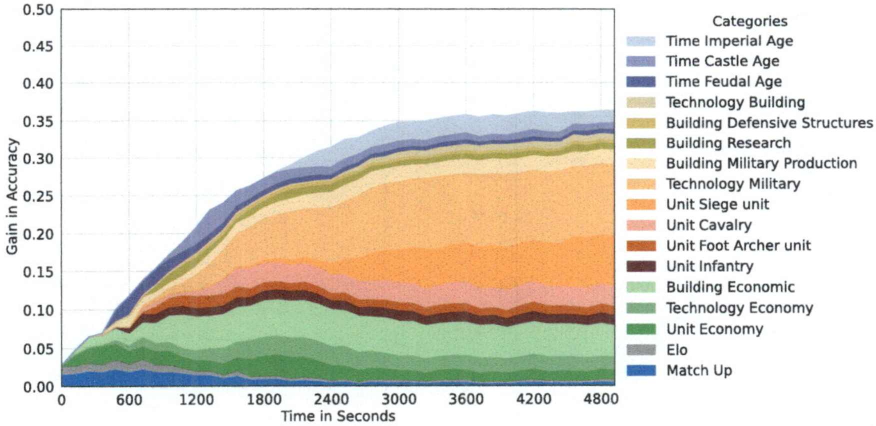

Fig. 2 Validation results of the XGBoost model under complete information

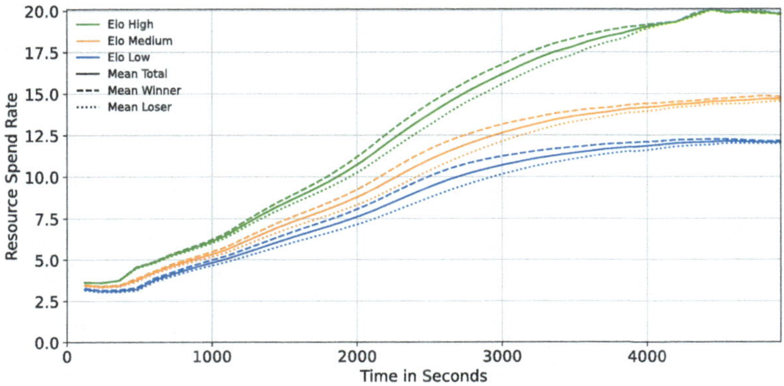

Fig. 3 Resource spending rates per second over time and Elo ratings

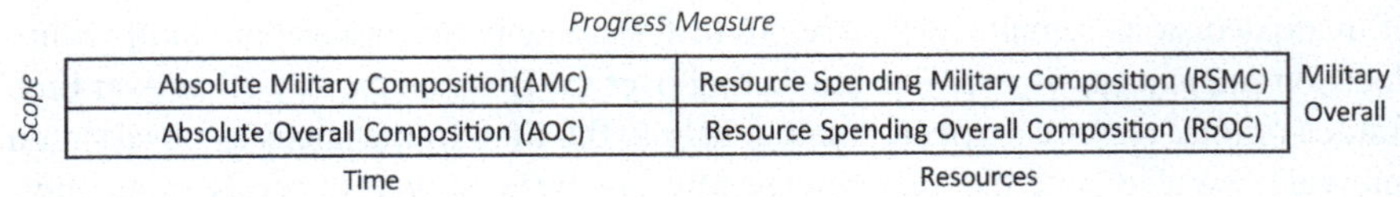

Fig. 4 Alternative game state representations

of discrete nodes. To ensure comparability in all scenarios, we determine a shared threshold of 50 by finding a suitable shared elbow point, based on the number of remaining nodes per threshold value. Since the number of states increases with the number of possible actions, the number of nodes increases significantly over time. Hence, the majority of nodes that do not meet the threshold are found in the later stages of the games, which are not the focus of this approach. Figure 5 supports this assumption, since the plot for the remaining nodes peaks significantly earlier than for the total nodes. Table 2 provides an overview of node counts for all scenarios and Elo groups.

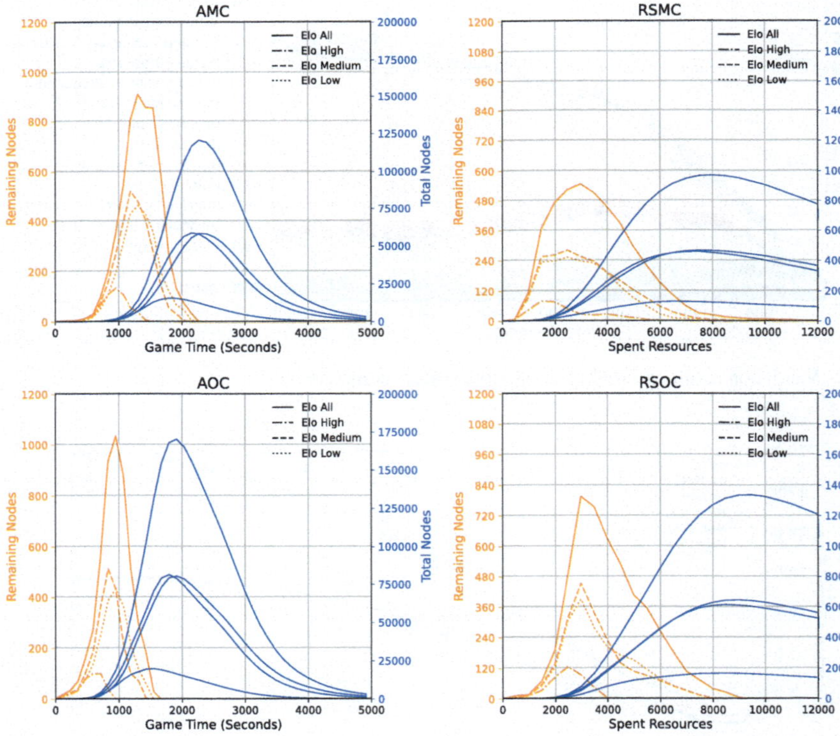

Fig. 5 Number of total and remaining nodes over the game progress measures g over scenarios and Elo ratings with the set threshold of 50

Table 2 Number of total nodes, remaining nodes and their share over the scenarios and Elo ratings for a threshold value of 50

	Elo	AMC	AOC	RSMC	RSOC
Total nodes	All	1,573,418	2,337,368	2,764,686	4,351,266
	High	190,657	266,524	393,962	607,369
	Medium	749,918	1,100,517	1,334,280	2,114,862
	Low	793,309	1,176,365	1,236,306	1,892,789
Remaining nodes	All	5,773	4,998	4,363	4,979
	High	566	388	384	410
	Medium	2,861	2,075	2,124	2,078
	Low	2,827	2,130	1,867	2,017
Share	All (%)	0.37	0.21	0.16	0.11
	High (%)	0.30	0.15	0.10	0.07
	Medium (%)	0.38	0.19	0.16	0.10
	Low (%)	0.36	0.18	0.15	0.11

3.3 Process Discovery

Node Creation We create the nodes for the different scenarios and Elo ratings using the described parameters in $\mathcal{G}(\hat{S}^*, \hat{A}^*)$. Each state node contains important information, such as the game progress measure (current time frame or step of spent resources) and a discrete game state is included in each node, consisting of the keys and values of the categories, as demonstrated in Fig. 6, e.g., *Infantry_8*, representing 8 produced infantry units until the end of observation interval. We also derived a label, from each game state and tracked the matches that visited that state, noting whether it was visited as a win or a loss, which allowed us to compare strategies later. Furthermore, incoming and outgoing edges were included to and from other nodes, and we calculated the mean win-rate over all visits. Finally, we also included information regarding the Elo distribution within the node.

Clustering After creating the nodes, our goal is to cluster them. To distinguish different strategies and merge similar strategies during the course of a game, we vectorize the game state nodes and compare them, using normalized cosine similarity as proposed by Steinbach et al. (2000). Based on the resulting distance matrix, we perform hierarchical clustering for every observation interval using the average-linkage method by Murtagh and Contreras (2012). A part of the resulting dendogram for the clustering of the AMC at 600 s is depicted in Fig. 6. To maintain comparability of game states across different stages of a game and various scenarios, we determine a maximum number of clusters by evaluating the mean intra-cluster distance for multiple observation intervals of the different scenarios, using the elbow method. The maximum number of clusters is set to 20. After clustering, we aggregate and store all available information regarding the clusters. In each cluster node, the information

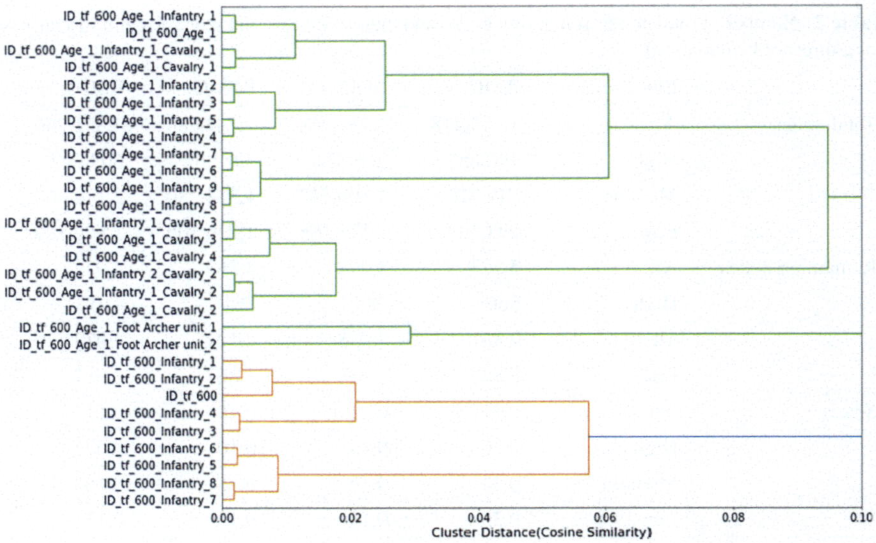

Fig. 6 Excerpt of the dendogram for the agglomerative clustering of AMC game state nodes for all Elo ratings after 600 s of game time

of the underlying nodes are aggregated and annotated with further information, such as game state distribution within the cluster weighted by the number of visits of the underlying nodes.

3.4 Evaluation

With this information, we generate and evaluate two different types of output. First we create a directed graph with weighted edges and further feature encoding from the provided cluster, node and edge information, visualizing the decision patterns over the course of the game progress, similar to a Petri net. Second, we compare the formed clusters against each other at the earlier set focus game progress value derived from Fig. 5.

4 Results

The procedure we have described yields in a directed decision sequence graphs, as illustrated for AMC in Fig. 7, and allows for an evaluation of clusters within the focus game states for the different scenarios, capturing player behavior similar to a Petri net (Van Dongen et al. 2009). The graph evolves from top to bottom along the game progress measure, with each step layer of nodes representing the game state after one observation interval. The symbols used symbolize the dominating category within the cluster, while the node size and edge weight denote the number of visits, and the color indicates the mean win rate within the nodes. Nodes are ordered from left to right by the dominant category within the cluster. In the AMC graph, the win rate over the nodes is correlated with the number of actions performed within the cluster. Because the graph is divided into time frames, a higher number of actions equates to a higher resource spending rate per node. The AMC graph exhibits multiple frequently used paths over the course of the game. Longer edges generally signify a switch in the dominating key, while shorter edges suggest that the two nodes share the same key. In contrast to the AMC graph, in the RSMC graph (not shown here), all nodes at one level possess the same amount of resource spending. Consequently, the graph encodes only strategic directions, and not skill measures. This results in nodes exhibiting less divergent win rates, as wins and losses tend to balance each other out. The results of the evaluation of the clusters in the focus game states are presented in Figs. 8 and 9. Figure 8 displays the weighted mean intra-cluster distances. To ensure a similar number of nodes for better comparability, we randomly subsampled each of the datasets to match the size of the high Elo dataset for every iteration. For AMC, the intra-cluster distance slightly decreases, while the inter-cluster distance marginally increases with higher Elo ratings. The intra-cluster distance for AOC and RSMC behaves similarly, although their all Elo subsample exhibits lower means than the low and medium Elo subsets. The inter-cluster distances either stagnate or reduce towards higher Elo ratings. For RSOC, the intra-cluster distance significantly escalates from low to medium Elo and then stagnates towards high Elo. Figure 9 compares the different clusters at the focus game states of the different scenarios based on their win rate in a heat map. Our results also include the cluster frequency. Clusters are ordered by their mean win rate and labelled with placeholders. Extreme values in the win rate heat map often correlate with a low frequency, despite the setting of multiple minimum thresholds. The AOC heat map in Fig. 9 contains a certain skill encoding based on the spending rate, leading to a divergent distribution of generally winning and losing clusters. The RSOC heat maps are less structured. They feature a grid of main cluster match-ups surrounded by low-frequency extreme values. The match-ups of the frequent main clusters showcase numerous match-ups with high and low win rates.

5 Discussion

Our results, focusing on a data-driven process and a strategy mining approach, yield several findings. We compared different game progress measures—time and resources—to ascertain suitable scenarios for different applications. We found that time-based scenario views prove more effective in pinpointing skilled players and facilitating highly accurate outcome predictions. In contrast, resource-based views permit strategic comparisons that are not influenced by skill level or a correlated spending rate. In the time-based approach, clusters manifest as a blend of skill

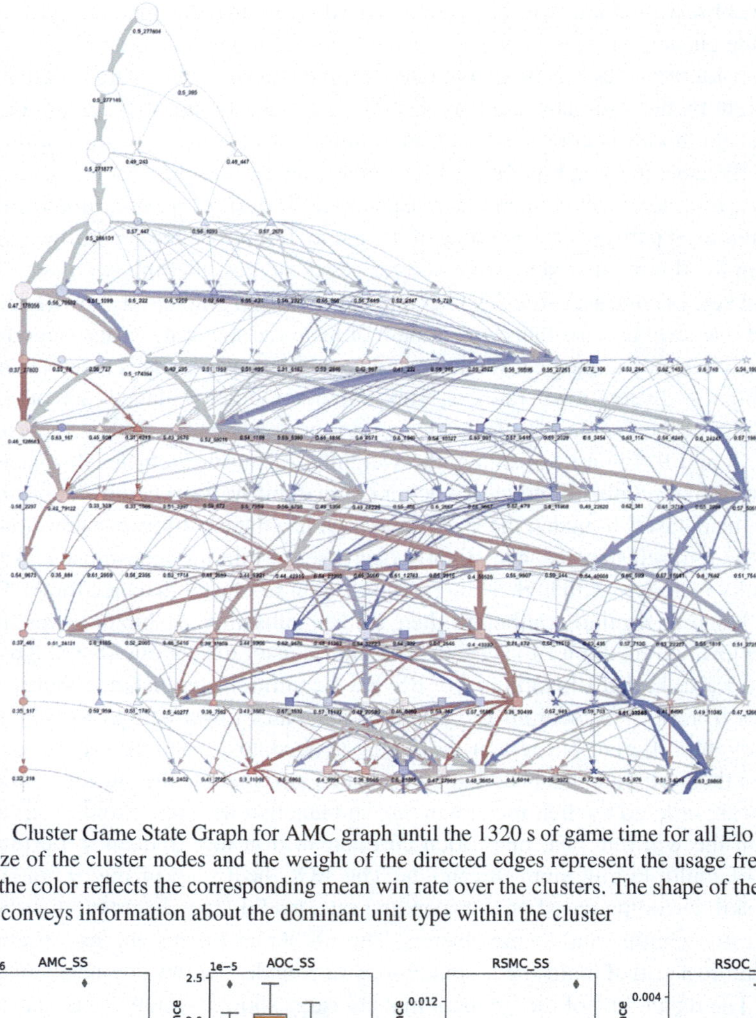

Fig. 7 Cluster Game State Graph for AMC graph until the 1320 s of game time for all Elo classes. The size of the cluster nodes and the weight of the directed edges represent the usage frequency, while the color reflects the corresponding mean win rate over the clusters. The shape of the cluster nodes conveys information about the dominant unit type within the cluster

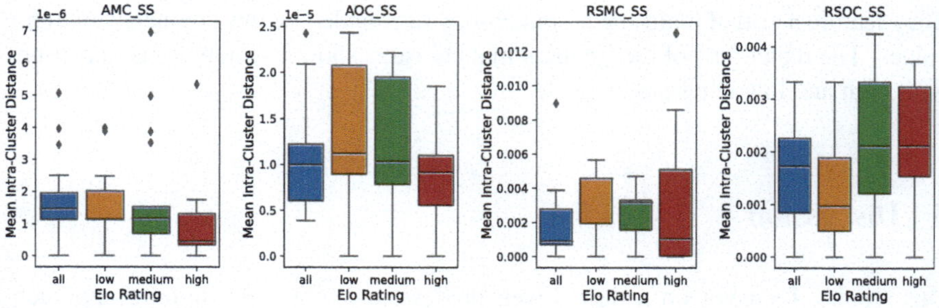

Fig. 8 Weighted mean intra-cluster distance in the focus game states

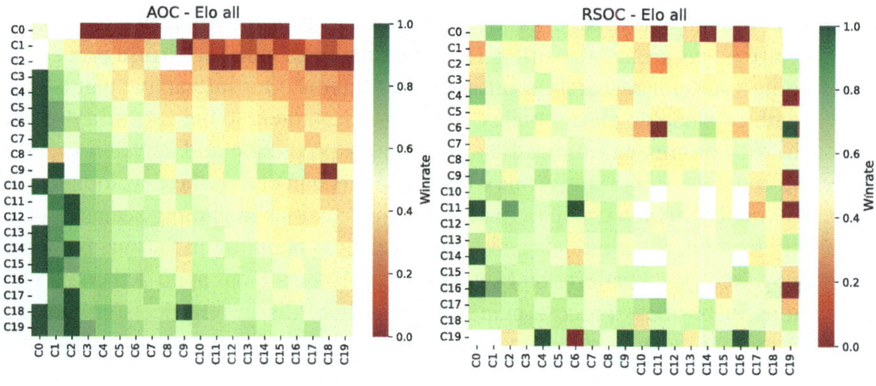

Fig. 9 Win rates for cluster match ups for AOC and RSOC

and strategic decisions. However, in the resource-based approach, clusters represent purely strategic decisions. The study uncovered various strategic patterns, demonstrating that approaches based on military composition are most effective in creating distinct clusters. We identified different kinds of common edges when examining the graphs. Particularly noteworthy are the edges in the game state graphs marking transitions from a win rate below 0.5 to a win rate above 0.5, and vice versa. These edges signal turning points in strategy or performance. It is interesting to note that the game state graphs for both clusters evolved over time, forming distinct branches with minimal horizontal interaction. As indicated in Sect. 4, these horizontal edges typically signify switches in the dominating key, so we can interpret these branches as strategic paths sharing common keys but differing in skill levels or purity. Achieving the cleanest possible results from the clusters and graphs necessitates selecting an appropriate level of aggregation for the game states. By fine-tuning parameters and refining our approach, we can utilize the results of this analysis to derive actions for improvement from any given state. While we provide insights into the specific game analyzed, these insights hold less relevance compared to our data-driven approach. The focus is on the methodology and the potential applications of this approach in a variety of other domains.

6 Conclusion and Future Research

In conclusion, this study presents an innovative, data-driven strategy for process mining in the realm of real-time strategy (RTS) games. Focusing on player decision sequences, we have uncovered critical patterns that illuminate strategic choices and their impacts on game outcomes. Our approach uniquely demonstrates the potential of game data as a comprehensive, complex, and accessible resource for the process mining community, offering an unprecedented environment for the development, testing, and improvement of process mining techniques. By doing so, we transcend the need for domain knowledge, making our approach broadly applicable and adaptable. The use of game data also offers intriguing parallels with real-world processes, affirming its value for research in information systems. Our interactive game state graphs, with expandable cluster nodes, stands as a testament to the versatility of our approach, with promising implications for strategy prediction and decision support in diverse contexts. Importantly, our work's insights can enrich the development of predictive models, which can anticipate strategic decisions in gaming scenarios and potentially beyond. Such models can inform strategic planning in various fields by recognizing behavioral patterns and key features. Moreover, our approach could find applications in business process management, where discerning decision-making patterns can significantly enhance operational efficiency and strategic planning. Looking ahead, we encourage the application of our methodology to multiple esports and real-world datasets, allowing for a rigorous evaluation of its efficacy and adaptability. This will facilitate a critical comparison of our methods against known benchmarks, providing an insight into their capacity to generate new domain knowledge. In summary, this study contributes significantly to the process mining community by showcasing the potential of game data as a fertile ground for research. Our work not only paves the way for enriching the field of process mining but also positions game data as an invaluable and cost-effective resource for domains where data access may be challenging or expensive. Our study underscores the power of data-driven approaches in extracting rich insights into complex processes across various domains, independent of prior domain knowledge.

References

Anderson, A., Kleinberg, J. & Mullainathan, S. (2017), 'Assessing human error against a benchmark of perfection', *ACM Transactions on Knowledge Discovery from Data (TKDD)* **11**(4), 1–25.

Chen, T. & Guestrin, C. (2016), Xgboost: A scalable tree boosting system, *in* 'Proceed- ings of the 22nd ACM SIGKDD International Conference on Knowledge Discovery and Data Mining', KDD '16, Association for Computing Machinery, New York, NY, USA, p. 785–794.

Ching, K., Forti, E. & Rawley, E. (2021), 'Extemporaneous coordination in specialist teams: The familiarity complementarity', *Organization Science* **32**(1), 1–17.

Clement, J. (2023), 'Missing the forest for the trees: Modular search and systemic inertia as a response to environmental change', *Administrative Science Quarterly* **68**(1), 186–227.

Dereszynski, E., Hostetler, J., Fern, A., Dietterich, T., Hoang, T.-T. & Udarbe, M. (2011), Learning probabilistic behavior models in real-time strategy games.

El-Nasr, M., Nguyen, T., Canossa, A. & Drachen, A. (2021), *Game Data Science*, OUP Oxford.

Elo, A. E. (1978), 'The rating of chessplayers, past and present. Arco Pub., New York'.

Hayes, R. & Beling, P. (2018), 'Unsupervised hierarchical clustering of build orders in a real-time strategy game', *The Computer Games Journal* **7**.

Künn, S., Palacios, J. & Pestel, N. (2023), 'Indoor air quality and strategic decision making', *Management Science* .

Murtagh, F. & Contreras, P. (2012), 'Algorithms for hierarchical clustering: an overview', *Wiley Interdisciplinary Reviews: Data Mining and Knowledge Discovery* **2**(1), 86–97.

Steinbach, M., Karypis, G. & Kumar, V. (2000), 'A comparison of document clustering techniques'.

Synnaeve, G. & Bessiere, P. (2011), A bayesian model for opening prediction in rts games with application to starcraft, pp. 281–288.

Van Der Aalst, W. (2012), 'Process mining: Overview and opportunities', *ACM Transac- tions on Management Information Systems (TMIS)* **3**(2), 1–17.

Van Der Aalst, W. (2016), *Process mining: data science in action*, Vol. 2, Springer.

Van Dongen, B. F., Alves de Medeiros, A. & Wen, L. (2009), 'Process mining: Overview and outlook of petri net discovery algorithms', *Transactions on Petri Nets and Other Models of Concurrency II: Special Issue on Concurrency in Process-Aware Informa- tion Systems* pp. 225–242.

Van Eck, M. L., Lu, X., Leemans, S. J. & Van Der Aalst, W. M. (2015), Pm^2: a process mining project methodology, *in* 'Advanced Information Systems Engineering: 27th International Conference, CAiSE 2015, Stockholm, Sweden, June 8–12, 2015, Proceedings', Springer, pp. 297–313.

van Zelst, S. J., Mannhardt, F., de Leoni, M. & Koschmider, A. (2021), 'Event abstraction in process mining: literature review and taxonomy', *Granular Computing* **6**, 719–736.

Wagner, M. G. (2006), On the scientific relevance of esports., *in* 'International conference on internet computing', Las Vegas, NV, pp. 437–442.

Enterprise Modeling and Business Ecosystems

Treating the End of the Data Life Cycle as a First-Class Citizen in Data Engineering

Daniel Tebernum and Falk Howar

Abstract Evolving regulatory frameworks, digital decarbonization, or new management challenges due to exponential data growth are bringing end-of-life data management to the forefront and making it an important building block in data engineering. However, the end of the data life cycle and in particular its management has received little attention in literature and practice. We argue this is partly due to the lack of an overarching model that creates a common understanding that data engineering experts and practitioners can build upon. We present Destroy Claims, which provides a standardized and comprehensive description of the end of the data life cycle and a corresponding architectural proposal for its integration. We demonstrate the feasibility of the solution through a use case inspired by practice, an evaluation gathered from expert discussions, and a survey. The results indicate that the proposed solution is a promising approach to support end-of-life data management in practice.

Keywords End of data life cycle · Data deletion management · Data model · Data deletion architecture · Data catalog

1 Introduction

Both research and practice have established a widely accepted view that efficient management of data can have a positive impact on business agility (Otto 2015; Tallon et al. 2013). However, current considerations in data engineering rarely address the end of the data life cycle, and even more so, they fail to encompass its management (Tebernum et al. 2021, 2023). With only 121 relevant publications in 23 years, data deletion has not received much attention, even across communities (Tebernum

D. Tebernum (✉)
Data Business, Fraunhofer ISST, Dortmund, Germany
e-mail: daniel.tebernum@isst.fraunhofer.de

F. Howar
Software Engineering, TU Dortmund University, Dortmund, Germany
e-mail: falk.howar@tu-dortmund.de

D. Beverungen et al. (eds.), *Solutions and Technologies for Responsible Digitalization*, Lecture Notes in Information Systems and Organisation 75,
https://doi.org/10.1007/978-3-031-80122-8_15

and Howar 2023). This is surprising as there are many benefits to addressing and professionalizing end-of-life data management.

First, evolving regulatory frameworks, i.e., laws and standards, highlight the need for data deletion management (see e.g., (European Commission 2016) and NIST 800-88). Second, the reduction of cost is of high relevance with regard to rising storage costs (see e.g., Google Cloud (2023a)). Next, the topic of digital decarbonization has gained importance (Jackson and Hodgkinson 2022) with events like the European energy crisis (Council of the EU 2022), and the fact that large parts of the data that are collected and stored only get used once (Trajanov et al. 2018) creates awareness for a more efficient use of limited resources. In addition, deleting data of poor quality is crucial to prevent unwanted propagation inside a company and possibly resulting negative influence on processes and products (Chae et al. 2014). Furthermore, privacy and security should be considered. For instance, data may be irretrievably and verifiably deleted before old storage media are sold (Klonowski et al. 2019), or must be deleted to prevent social engineering attacks. Consequently, also in the domain of data ecosystems and data spaces, data sovereignty considerations may require data deletion (Jung et al. 2022, p. 133). Finally, it is essential to consider technical factors such as the requirement to delete corrupted, invalid, or noisy data (Othon et al. 2019) and the need for efficient computations through the removal of unnecessary data Gao et al. (2019), Reardon et al. (2012), Lin et al. (2009), and Pachpor and Prakash (2018).

Consequently, the question arises why, despite the variety of relevant reasons for end-of-life data management, the subject is underrepresented in literature and practice. With the help of expert interviews, we identified two relevant factors: (1) in general, there is a missing unified understanding of the end of the data life cycle; (2) particularly in practice, there is a lack of comprehensive solutions on which to build for managing the end of the data life cycle. Therefore, the following research questions arise:

- RQ1: *How can the end of the data life cycle be modelled comprehensively?*
- RQ2: *How can such a model and its interpretation be integrated into a software architecture to support end-of-life data management?*

To address these research questions, two artifacts are developed. Our first artifact is a model that can describe the end of the data life cycle in a uniform way. Using this model, a common understanding, planning capabilities, and an automated execution of the end of the data life cycle can be achieved. To the best of our knowledge, there is no purpose-built solution that comprehensively and holistically models the end of the data life cycle. Our second artifact is an architectural proposal for the integration of the model into software. With our artifacts we want to support the establishment of the end of the data life cycle as first-class citizen in data engineering.

The remainder of this paper is organized as follows. First, in Sect. 2 we discuss the research methodology and describe our research process. In Sect. 3 we describe our two artifacts in detail. Section 4 demonstrates the applicability in the context of a real-world use case. A comprehensive analysis of the evaluation of our artifacts, including discussions on limitations and future work are part of Sect. 5.

Section 6 addresses related work. Finally, we summarize our results and describe methodological limitations.

2 Methodology

The results presented in this paper were developed utilizing the Design Science Research (DSR) Methodology. DSR is widely used and shaped by the Information Systems (IS) community (Österle et al. 2010). It focuses on the derivation and iterative development of artifacts. This work is based on the DSRM Process Model by Peffers et al. (2007) (see Fig. 1).

Motivation: See Sect. 1.

Objectives: To identify what can be leveraged to support end-of-life data management, we sought a real-world perspective. We conducted interviews with experts having between 5 and 15 years of experience. Among the interviewees were four software developers from the industry focussing on data engineering in mobile communication, automotive, machine learning, banking, and pharmacy. We also interviewed two business engineers from the research community with a focus on cloud platforms and data management to reflect a perspective that is not purely technical. Semi-structured interviews, which lasted one hour on average, were carried out through video calls and were subsequently recorded and transcribed. The main guiding questions were "*What comes to your mind about data deletion?*", "*When do you delete data?*", *and* "*What would push you to delete data?*". In addition, we prepared a miroboard where we presented previous research results and also our own ideas for discussion. We evaluated the interviews by applying an open coding on the transcripts according to the Grounded Theory Methodology (Glaser et al. 1968; Corbin and Strauss 1990). We then isolated the essence of the open codes in axial codes. The evaluation of the interviews identified two objectives to be addressed. First, it must be possible to describe the end of the data life cycle in a way that supports an unified understanding. This objective is supported by increased occurrence of the axial codes *standard*, *model* and *transparency*. Second, to support end-of-life data management, a system architecture must be designed that addresses data deletion as a first-class citizen. We derived this objective because of an increased occurrence of

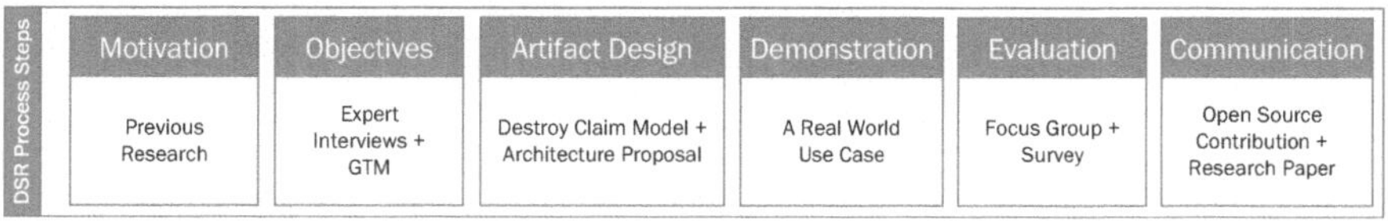

Fig. 1 Research process based on Peffers et al. (2007, p. 54)

the codes *architecture*, *component*, and *automatic*. These two objectives are reflected in RQ1 and RQ2. The list of codes are available at Zenodo.[1]

Artifacts Design: We developed two types of artifacts. In addition to our own ideas, insights from the expert interviews and our previous publication (Tebernum and Howar 2023) were also used for the design of the artifacts. The first artifact (A1) is the Destroy Claim Model, which we specifically designed to model and standardize the end of the data life cycle. This artifact of type model pays directly into RQ1. The second artifact (A2) is an architectural proposal on how to manage, distribute, and automate the end of the data life cycle in a real environment. This artifact of type architecture pays directly into RQ2.

Demonstration: The artifacts are utilized in a real-world use case. Through this, we show that the artifacts can be used for certain classes of problems. The demonstration was carried out using prototypical implementations. The use case demonstrated with screenshots is available online.[2] Further details are described in Sect. 4.

Evaluation: As the basis for our evaluation, we chose (1) focus groups (Hollander 2004) to foster a rich discussion and (2) the Strategic DSR Evaluation Framework (Venable et al. 2012) as a structured feedback mechanism. First, we presented our artifacts to nine data and software engineering experts. Among these were the four software engineers interviewed in the objectives DSR phase. We were able to recruit five additional software engineers ranging from 3 to 20 years of experience. Three from the industry with a focus on software architectures and data pipelines and two from research. A whiteboard was prepared for the virtual discussion rounds, which were performed in groups of three. On the whiteboard, previous publications and the existing research results of this work were shown. The experts were given detailed explanations of both the technical details and the demonstrated use case. Then a discussion was initiated in which the experts were invited to address ideas and problems. These were collected and refined on the whiteboard. Second, for structured feedback, the experts were given a questionnaire with 37 5-point Likert scale questions derived from the taxonomy of DSR evaluation methods by Prat et al. (2015). The results of the discussion and questionnaire are discussed in Sect. 5.

Communication: Communication is done through this paper, which informs the scientific community about our research project. Also, results were published as an open-source contribution on GitHub (Tebernum 2023; Tebernum and Atamantschuk 2023).

[1] https://doi.org/10.5281/zenodo.8046369.

[2] https://doi.org/10.5281/zenodo.8046369.

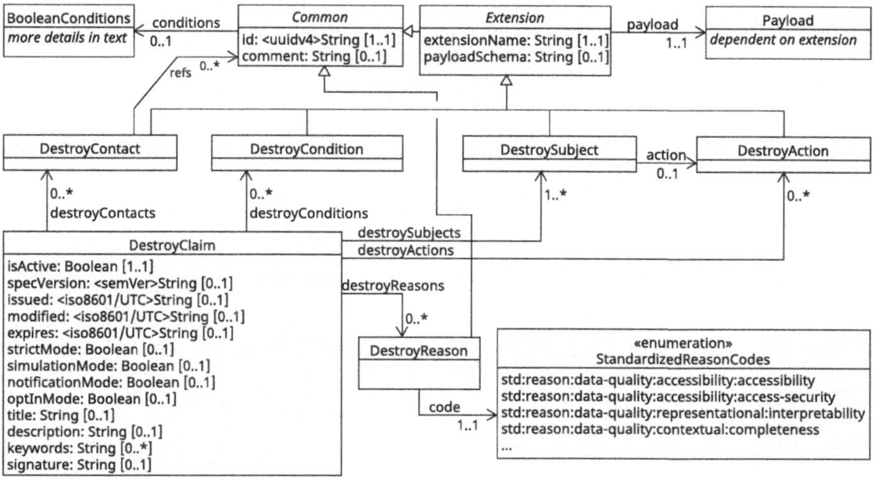

Fig. 2 Destroy claim model

3 Contribution

3.1 The Destroy Claim Model (A1)

This artifact contributes directly to RQ1. The aim is to comprehensively describe the end of the data life cycle for arbitrary data. In one of our previous research papers, we developed a data deletion taxonomy, which is derived from an extensive systematic literature review (Tebernum and Howar 2023). We used this as a basis to iteratively develop the model. In short, the questions of *what*, *when*, *where*, *how*, *why*, and who must be answered. Based on this, we developed an abstract model. It can be derived into concrete persistence formats according to one's own needs. E.g., a specific derivation in JSON has been generated and published on GitHub Tebernum (2023). Figure 2 shows the final iteration of the artifact.

Due to space constraints, the model is only described in general terms. More details can also be found on GitHub. The *DestroyClaim* class can be seen as the entry point of the model. It contains higher-level properties that pursue several purposes. On the one hand, there are descriptive properties that should enable human actors to better understand the Destroy Claim (see Table 1). On the other hand, it contains instructions on how to interpret the Destroy Claim (see Table 2).

Another important aspect is the specification of a deletion reason. We were able to identify a set of 52 reasons *why* one would want to delete data (see Tebernum and Howar 2023) and standardized them.[3] It is possible to have none or several *destroyReasons* and to also define custom ones.

[3] https://github.com/DaTebe/dstroyclaims/blob/9a8a6e5e432312175cc439f333c45620924400fc/docs/destroy-reasons.md.

Table 1 Destroy claim properties (descriptive)

Property	Description
id	The unique id to identify a destroy claim
title	An easy to understand title that describe what the destroy claim is about
description	A detailed description of the destroy claim
keywords	Keywords which tag the destroy claim
issued	Date of formal issuance of the destroy claim
modified	Date on which the destroy claim was last modified
comment	A human readable comment
signature	A cryptographic signature to establish trust in the destroy claim

Table 2 Destroy claim properties (interpretive)

Property	Description
isActive	Indicates if a destroy claim is active. If isActive is false, the destroy claim MUST NOT be executed
specVersion	Indicates which version of the destroy claim model specification was used to generate this destroy claim (currently only 1.0.0 available)
expires	As of the specified date, the destroy claim MUST NOT be executed and can be deleted
strictMode	If DCA (see Sect. 3.2) should act in strict mode or normal mode (for this and all other modes see GitHub (Tebernum 2023))
simulationMode	If DCA should act in simulation mode or real mode
notificationMode	If DCA should act in notification mode or silent mode
optInMode	If DCA should ask for permission or can execute the Destroy Claim on its own

Extension is a concept that greatly increases the flexibility of the model. It quickly became apparent that the use cases for deleting data are extremely heterogeneous and that it is not possible to develop a single rigid model to describe the end of the data life cycle. For this reason, the aspects of *what*, *when*, *where*, *who*, and *how* can be replaced by individual solutions. An extension should have a unique *extensionName* to distinguish between them. Each type of extension can define its individual *payload*, in which the modeling power required for the use case is given. For an extension, it must be clearly defined when it evaluates positively and when it evaluates negatively. There are four concrete variants of an extension. *DestroyContact* is used to model *who* has responsibilities. The extension can indicate responsibilities using *refs* that link to other parts of the Destroy Claim. *DestroySubject* is used to address the data to be deleted. The addressing should be as precise as possible so that incorrect data is not selected and deleted. Here, for example, content hashes or UUIDs can be used to address data.

Under *DestroyCondition*, the conditions can be modeled when the end of the data life cycle is reached. Here, aspects of *when*, *where* and *who* are to be modeled. For example, one could formulate three conditions stating that a certain file must be deleted when the year 2024 is reached, one is outside of Germany and one belongs to a certain department. *DestroyAction* is used to describe *how* data should be deleted. Here one can model, for example, whether memory areas are to be overwritten several times or whether the hardware must be destroyed.

A great promise of a unified model is that different parties can interpret the model in the same way. The use of *Extension* makes this goal no longer achievable without further ado. Therefore, we have designed a standard library of extensions to promote a common understanding and increase the chances that Destroy Claims can be understood outside one's own technical or organizational boundaries.[4]

Finally, we increased the flexibility of the Destroy Claims by using Boolean conditions.

By default, all extension evaluations are combined using a Boolean AND. Each extension, the *DestroyClaim* class, and the *DestroyReason* class can use Boolean algebra to influence a positive or negative evaluation outcome. For this purpose, the evaluation results of other extensions can be used and linked with the help of Boolean operators.

E.g., one can model that a Destroy Subject S_1 may only be deleted if another Destroy Subject S_2 is also deleted and only one of two additional conditions is met $((S_1 \Rightarrow S_2) \wedge (C_1 \oplus C_2))$.

3.2 An Architectural Integration Proposal (A2)

This artifact deals with the question of how to integrate A1 into software and thus support end-of-life data management. This artifact contributes to RQ2.

First, we need a trusted source for managing Destroy Claims. A data catalog is software that inventories all kinds of data by storing corresponding metadata. We suggest modelling the end of the data life cycle in a data catalog or similar.

Second, we designed the concept of the so-called Destroy Claim Agents (DCAs).

The DCA is a software component that receives and interprets Destroy Claims from one or more trusted sources and executes the end of the data life cycle in the environment. A DCA has two required interfaces. The *IDestroyClaim* interface allows the DCA to connect to one or more trusted sources for receiving Destroy Claims. The interface should be implemented according to the use case and can, for example, implement filters to query only relevant Destroy Claims or decide between a pull or push strategy.

[4] https://github.com/DaTebe/destroyclaims/blob/9a8a6e5e432312175cc439f333c45620924400fc/docs/std-extensions.md.

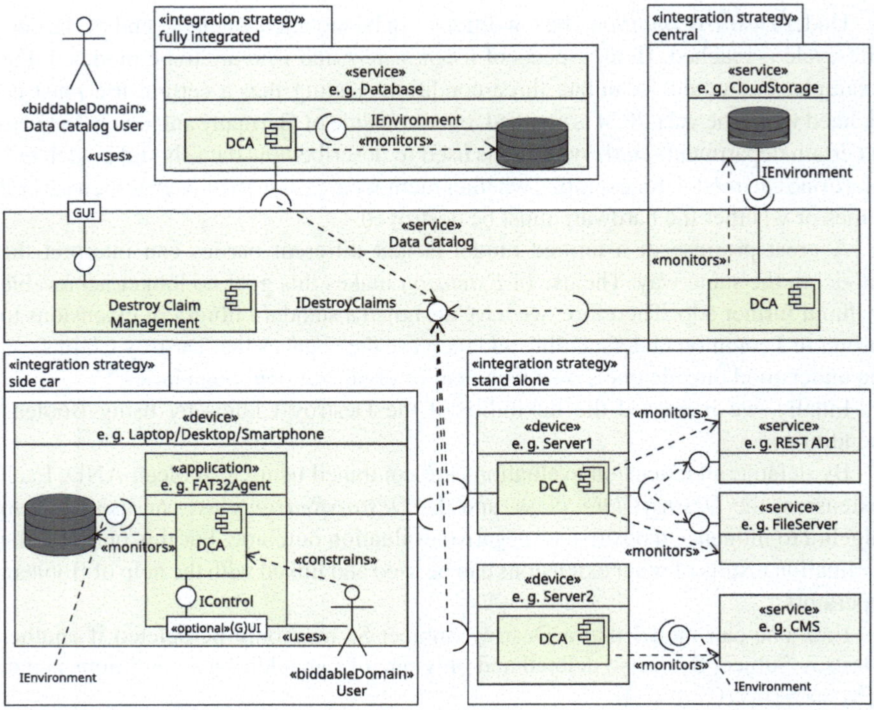

Fig. 3 Architectural proposals for destroy claim and DCA integration

The *IEnvironment* interface connects the DCA to its environment. The DCA has two duties that it must implement. First, the DCA must monitor the environment to determine whether Destroy Claims are applicable. Second, the DCA must be able to interact with the persistence layer of the environment to be able to delete data. The DCA also has one optional provided interface *IControl* that e.g., a human actor can use to consent to the execution of Destroy Claims or to configure the environment to be monitored. A detailed description of how a DCA has to evaluate and execute Destroy Claims is available on GitHub.[5]

Third, we want to provide an overview of how Destroy Claims and DCAs can be integrated into software architectures. Our four integration proposals can be seen in Fig. 3. In the following we will briefly characterize them.

Central: Using this integration strategy, there is only one central DCA. This strategy is best used when one does not have the capacity to manage multiple DCAs and when one DCA is sufficient to manage a potentially heterogeneous data landscape. In the best case, you do not have to take care of the deployment of the DCA, but it may already be part of a data catalog or other trusted sources for Destroy Claims. A

[5] https://github.com/DaTebe/destroyclaims/blob/9a8a6e5e432312175cc439f333c45620924400fc/docs/destroy-claim.md/dca-evaluating-and-executing-A-destroy-claim.

central DCA component may not gain an overview of the entire data landscape, because either the technologies in use are not supported or they are not accessible from a central point. In addition, the DCA must be configured to explicitly monitor and control certain systems.

Stand alone: For most parts, this integration strategy is the same as *central*. The difference is that several individual DCAs divide up the data landscape. To avoid unwanted interference between DCAs, they should (if possible) strictly separate the data landscape between them. This integration strategy should be applied when the various environments are in different contexts, e.g. have distinct responsibilities due to corporate structures. The operation of several DCAs will lead to an increased amount of administrative work.

Fully integrated: In this integration strategy, the DCA becomes an integral part of the service. This has the advantage that one no longer has to explicitly take care of the DCA. It only needs to be configured from which trusted source the Destroy Claims are to be obtained, when *IDestroyClaims* is implemented using a pull strategy. In addition, the DCA will be very much aligned with the existing data and technologies, which will likely make it more robust. This type of integration is suitable when a service is implemented from scratch. The costs would otherwise probably exceed the benefits. One disadvantage may be that it may not be able to be customised to interpret further extensions, but that you are dependent on the vendor of the specific service.

Side car: This integration strategy is similar to the *fully integrated* one. The DCA is not part of the service here, but lives alongside it. However, it is completely dependent on the life cycle of the service. If the service is stopped, the DCA is also terminated. The example in Fig. 3 shows a DCA inside an application that monitors the file system of an operating system. When the operating system and its file system is shut down, the DCA is also stopped. This strategy has the advantage that it is easy to deploy and scale alongside the service. It should be noted that the management of many DCAs can be difficult and resources are bound more quickly than, for example, with the central strategy.

4 Demonstration

The demonstration is performed using implemented prototypes of the artifacts. We extended the open source data catalog DIVA to support Destroy Claims (Tebernum and Atamantschuk 2023). Here, our concrete derivation of the model using JSON is implemented. Users can utilize the *DestroyClaimManagement* component to create and configure Destroy Claims via a web interface. Furthermore, the *IDestroyClaims* interface was implemented that enables external applications to retrieve Destroy Claims using a pull strategy. We also implemented a DCA with the *destroyclaim-js* library, which can also be found in our Destroy Claim GitHub repository (Tebernum 2023).

The use case itself deals with modeling the end of the data life cycle of file-based data. It was derived from real cases in the business world, where employees work with e.g. *Word*, *PowerPoint*, or *Photoshop*. Files are copied from different systems, such as the company's network or the internet, to one's local device. If the data is no longer to be used for various reasons, e.g. because it is out of date or has errors, employees may not be aware of this. They are currently encouraged to detect and remove obsolete data by themselves. We have set up a system that implements the sidecar integration strategy (see Fig. 3). We used DIVA as our trusted source and to inventory the file-based data. Users can model a Destroy Claim when they inventory data in DIVA. A DCA with a graphical interface was implemented that creates an index of the locally available data on the devices of the employees. When the end of the data life cycle is reached, the employees are informed via a pop-up. If the Destroy Claim is running in *optInMode*, the user can still decide whether to agree to the claim.

5 Evaluation

During the focus groups, several topics emerged that should be considered in future artifact iterations. An important point was that Destroy Claims are only useful if they are mostly automatically generated. It was suggested that there must be standardized blueprints that can be applied to classes or types of data. Data catalogs were identified as a useful component to perform this automation. The experts suggested that the Destroy Claims themselves must also be deleted at some point and whether there are Destroy Claims for Destroy Claims. We address this by setting an expiration date after which a Destroy Claim is no longer valid. Destroy Claims that are valid forever, for example because they address illegal data, would in fact theoretically exist forever. The general consensus was that this could probably only be a problem on a global scale where one has no control over the environment. Another point that was addressed was that a deletion, that is dependent on another deletion, is only possible if a single DCA monitors the environments in which the two data sets occur. There is no provision for multiple DCAs to collaborate. The experts argue that some data deletion could never be executed because of this. Another limitation concerns the intervals at which a Destroy Claim should be tested, as their applicability can change quickly depending on the conditions set. Strategies for regular evaluation of Destroy Claims need to be developed, and experts have suggested that evaluation strategies or claim priority could be included in the model's next iteration. While explaining the Detroy Claim model, two participants highlighted the similarity of the concrete JSON implementation to ODRL (Iannella and Villata 2018), and it should be considered whether a concrete instantiation of the model and the transfer of standard extensions to the ODRL world are feasible and beneficial. In addition to the gaps addressed, the experts also identified use cases that the authors had not considered.

One idea was to have a global system, maybe based on the blockchain technology, in which Destroy Claims could be collected. Creators of intellectual property can e.g., file claims for pirated copies. Another expert imagined placing signatures of viruses, spam and the like there. One question that came up here was about trustworthiness. The experts agreed that with digital signatures and trusted publishers, it could work. The experts also pointed out that even if the model is not used one-to-one in practice, it is a good basis for deriving more specialized profiles.

In order to get systematic feedback, the experts were given a survey after the focus group sessions (see Fig. 4). To provide an initial overview of the success of the project, some general questions were asked (Q01-Q03). It can be noted that the responses from the participants were consistently positive. Therefore, we can be confident that we are on the right track in making the end of the data life cycle a first-class citizen in data engineering. Following, a series of questions is asked to check whether artifact A1 achieves its objectives (Q04-Q11). Here, too, the assessment is predominantly positive.

However, it is striking that Q07 is predominantly answered neutrally. The participants don't seem to have any experience or assessment as to whether it is financially worthwhile to implement the solution. It is generally difficult to obtain reliable statistics in this regard. Nevertheless, it would be interesting to look at this aspect more closely in the future. The next block deals with the structure of A1 (Q12-Q15). This, too, is predominantly perceived positively. In detail, future iterations should look at whether A1 can be made simpler (Q13), as it can become objectivly quite complex to create and interprete Destroy Claims. Next, there is a series of questions dealing with the effect of A1 on the environment (Q16-Q25). There are a few points to discuss here. First of all, it is noticeable that most of the participants would not use the artefact A1 themselves (Q16). We suspect that the solution creates far too much overhead for individuals and is not a good fit in this context. This is supported by the fact that the artifact is considered useful for data engineers, who create enterprise-wide solutions and work in bigger environments (Q17). When we look at Q18, we have many neutral reports when it comes to ease of use and deployment. This is a good sign that the respondents answered mindfully, as they do not have any empirical data in this regard. The question whether the solutions have side effects on the environment (Q20), are negatively evaluated. We believe, this reflects the fear that deleting data will lead to unwanted states in which e.g., dead references are created or parts of the whole system no longer work. In the future, a clear focus in research should be on how to minimize side effects, by e.g., looking into formal guarantees or at least well-tested implementation patterns. The next set of questions pertains to the adaptability of A1 to future challenges (Q26-Q29). Again, the responses were consistently positive. This can further support the practical implementation of A1, as the necessary flexibility is present in case of required adjustments. Finally, questions were asked whether artifact A2 is achieving its objectives (Q30-Q37). Overall, the responses here are also very positive. Noteworthy is Q30, where all participants have consistently responded with *strongly agree*. We see this as an indicator that A2 makes a valuable contribution in supporting end-of-life data management. Also, the question about the performance of A2 (Q37) was predominantly answered neutrally.

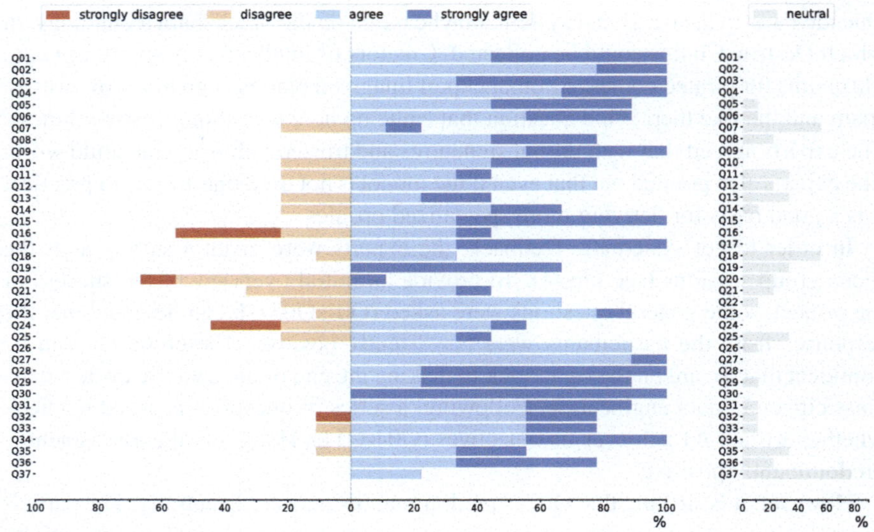

General:
Q01 Modelling the end of the data life cycle is important. **Q02** Destroy Claims have the potential to professionalize the end of the data life cycle. **Q03** A data catalog is the right place to model the end of the data life cycle.

Goal-based: (A1) The Destroy Claim Model...
Q04 ... is generally/in theory suitable/relevant to model the end of the data life cycle. **Q05** ... is suitable/relevant for modelling the end of the data life cycle in practice. **Q06** ... correctly achieves its goal. **Q07** ... has a return on investment that justifies the implementation costs. **Q08** ... is generally valid/applicable in the topic of modeling the end of the data life cycle. **Q09** ... can be technically implemented. **Q10** ... can be used in the context of existing technologies. **Q11** ... is economically reasonable.

Structure-based: (A1) The Destroy Claim Model...
Q12 ... is complete. **Q13** ... follows the KISS (Keep it small, stupid!) principle. **Q14** ... is simple to understand. **Q15** ... is consistent.

Environment-based: (A1) The Destroy Claim Model...
Q16 ... is something I would personally use/ would be useful to me. **Q17** ... is useful for data engineers. **Q18** ... can be easily deployed/used. **Q19** ... is ethically justifiable. **Q20** ... has no side effects. **Q21** ... converges with the business goals of my company. **Q22** ... has no negative impact on (my) business. **Q23** ... can be integrated into existing technologies. **Q24** ... uses innovative technologies. **Q25** ... has no negative impact on the technology in use.

Evolution-based: (A1) The Destroy Claim Model...
Q26 ... is robust enough to withstand increasing stress. **Q27** ... can be scaled (e.g. to work globally). **Q28** ... can be adapted into other contexts. **Q29** ... can be modified for future challenges.

Activity-based: (A2) The implementation and integration strategies for Destroy Claims...
Q30 ... increase the awareness to model the end of the data life cycle. **Q31** ... increase the acceptance to model the end of the data life cycle. **Q32** ... increase trust in the data. **Q33** ... increase confidence in deleting data. **Q34** ... can (theoretically) cover my personal data deletion use cases. **Q35** ... correspond to the KISS (Keep it small, stupid!) principle. **Q36** ... are consistent. **Q37** ... are performant

Fig. 4 Survey results and questions

Again, this shows that the participants filled out the questionnaire mindfully, as they could not have any information in this regard.

6 Related Work

The end of the data life cycle is a phase that is not considered in many data life cycle models ranging from research (Lenhardt et al. 2014; Kowalczyk 2017; Wissik and Ďurčo 2016; Ma et al. 2014; Faundeen et al. 2013; Allard 2012; Patel 2016), metadata (Catteau et al. 2006; Kosch et al. 2005), agriculture (Demestichas and Daskalakis 2020) to big data (Khan et al. 2014; Demchenko et al. 2014) and machine learning (Miao et al. 2017). If it is mentioned (Yu and Wen 2010; Michota and Katsikas 2015; Lin et al. 2014; Chaki and Chaki 2015; Ofner et al. 2013), it is only in passing and without reference to further literature. Likewise, data management frameworks that investigate the end of the data life cycle provide, at best, general guidelines for deleting data (Shah et al. 2021). In practice, technical solutions are found that feature end-of-life data management. For example, in the context of data life cycle policies in proprietary software such as Microsoft Azure (2023), Google Cloud (2023b) or in the form of usage policies in ODRL (2018). These solutions have in common that they do not consider the end of the data life cycle in more detail, but describe it as a by-product in the form of yet another action on data to be performed under certain conditions. To the best of our knowledge, there is no work in research that deals with modelling the end of the data life cycle or its management in a central and comprehensive way or addresses it in the context of data engineering.

7 Conclusion

Despite the fact that the end of the data life cycle and its management are becoming increasingly important, there is little to no attention in literature and practice. Our expert interviews indicate, that this is due to a missing common ground that creates a shared understanding among data engineering experts and practitioners. We address this by providing two DSR artifacts. First, Destroy Claims which comprehensively model the end of the data life cycle. Second, an architectural proposal that describes how end-of-life data management can be integrated into software utilizing Destroy Claims. The technical feasibility was demonstrated using prototypes that were implemented and made publicly available. Our evaluation found that the artifacts were mostly positively received and adequately addressed the objectives.

While Chap. 5 has already addressed limitations and future work related to the artifacts, this section will focus on methodological constraints. Firstly, it is important to acknowledge the potential for selection bias given the small sample size of six interviews and nine participants in the evaluation. Additionally, the coding process was conducted solely by the authors, raising the possibility that the derived objectives may not accurately represent the broader population of data engineers. Lastly, in terms of methodological considerations and future research, it is essential to deploy the artifacts in real-world scenarios to better assess their usefulness.

However, this undertaking requires substantial effort and costs, as the artifacts intervene very fundamentally in existing software systems. Therefore, we will initially conduct smaller-scale studies before undertaking larger-scale implementations.

Acknowledgements The authors acknowledge the financial support by the Federal Ministry for Economic Affairs and Climate Action of Germany in the project Smart Design and Construction (project number 01MK200016F).

References

Allard, S. (2012), "Dataone: Facilitating eScience Through Collaboration." *Journal of eScience Librarianship* 1 (1).

Catteau, O., Philippe V., and Julien B. (2006), "A Generic Representation Allowing for Expression of Learning Object and Metadata Lifecycle." In *Proceedings of the 6th IEEE International Conference on Advanced Learning Technologies, ICALT 2006, Kerkrade, the Netherlands, July 5–7, 2006*, 30–32. IEEE Computer Society. URL: https://doi.org/10.1109/ICALT.2006.1652357

Chae, B. Kevin, Yang C., Olson, D., & Sheu, C. (2014), "The Impact of Advanced Analytics and Data Accuracy on Operational Performance: A Contingent Resource Based Theory (RBT) Perspective." *Decision Support Systems* 59: 119–26.

Chaki, S., & Chaki, S. (2015), "The Lifecycle of Enterprise Information Management." *Enterprise Information Management in Practice: Managing Data and Leveraging Profits in Today's Complex Business Environment*, 7–14.

Corbin, J. M, & Strauss, A. (1990), "Grounded Theory Research: Procedures, Canons, and Evaluative Criteria." *Qualitative Sociology* 13 (1): 3–21.

Council of the EU, G. S. o. t. C. (2022), "Energy Crisis: Three EU-Coordinated Measures to Cut down Bills." 2022. URL: https://www.consilium.europa.eu/en/infographics/eu-measures-to-cut-down-energy-bills/.

Demchenko, Y., De Laat, C., & Membrey, P. (2014), "Defining Architecture Components of the Big Data Ecosystem." In 2014 International Conference on Collaboration Technologies and Systems (CTS), 104–12. IEEE, pp. 104–112.

Demestichas, K., & Daskalakis, E. (2020), "Data Lifecycle Management in Precision Agriculture Supported by Information and Communication Technology." Agronomy 10 (11): 1648.

European Commission. (2016), "Regulation (EU) 2016/679 of the European Parliament and of the Council of 27 April 2016 on the Protection of Natural Persons with Regard to the Processing of Personal Data and on the Free Movement of Such Data, and Repealing Directive 95/46/EC (General Data Protection Regulation) (Text with EEA Relevance)." European Commission. URL: https://eur-lex.europa.eu/eli/reg/2016/679/oj

Faundeen, J. L, Burley T. E., Carlino, J., Govoni, D. L., Henkel,H. S., Holl, S., Hutchison,V. B.,Martin, E., Montgomery, E.T., Ladino, C. C. et al. (2013), *The United States Geological Survey Science Data Lifecycle Model*. US Department of the Interior, US Geological Survey Reston, VA, USA.

Gao, B., Chen, B., Jia, S. & Xia, L. (2019), "eHIFS: An Efficient History Independent File System." In *Proceedings of the 2019 ACM Asia Conference on Computer and Communications Security*, 573–85.

Glaser, B. G., Strauss A. L. & Strutzel E. (1968), "The Discovery of Grounded Theory; Strategies for Qualitative Research." *Nursing Research* 17 (4): 364.

Google Cloud. (2023a), "Announcement of Pricing Changes for Cloud Storage." URL: https://cloud.google.com/storage/pricing-announce. [Online; accessed 6-June-2023].

Google Cloud. (2023b), "Object Lifecycle Management." URL:https://cloud.google.com/storage/docs/lifecycle. [Online; accessed 7-June-2023].

Hollander, J. A. (2004), "The Social Contexts of Focus Groups." *Journal of Contemporary Ethnography* 33 (5): 602–37.

Hubert Ofner, M., Straub K., Otto,B. & Oesterle, H. (2013), "Management of the Master Data Lifecycle: A Framework for Analysis." *Journal of Enterprise Information Management* 26 (4): 472–91.

Iannella, R. & Villata, S. (2018), "ODRL Information Model 2.2." *W3C*. URL: https://www.w3.org/TR/odrl-model/.

Jackson, T. W. & Hodgkinson, I. A. T. (2022), "Keeping a Lower Profile: How Firms Can Reduce Their Digital Carbon Footprints." *Journal of Business Strategy*, no. ahead-of-print.

Jung, C., Dörr, D., Otto, B., Ten Hompel, M. & Wrobel, S. (2022), "Data Usage Control." *Designing Data Spaces: The Ecosystem Approach to Competitive Advantage*, 129–46.

Khan, N., Yaqoob, I., Hashem, I. A. T., Inayat, Z., Mahmoud Ali, W. K., Alam, M., Shiraz, M. & Gani, A. (2014), "Big Data: Survey, Technologies, Opportunities, and Challenges." *The Scientific World Journal* 2014.

Klonowski, M., Struminski, T. & Sulkowska, M. (2019), "Universal Encoding for Provably Irreversible Data Erasing." In *ICETE (2)*, 137–48.

Kosch, H., Böszörményi, L., Döller, M., Libsie, M., Schojer, P. & Kofler, A. (2005), "The Life Cycle of Multimedia Metadata." *IEEE Multim.* 12 (1): 80–86.

Kowalczyk, S. T. (2017), "Modelling the Research Data Lifecycle." *Int. J. Digit. Curation* 12 (2): 331–61. URL: https://doi.org/10.2218/ijdc.v12i2.429

Lenhardt, W, Ahalt, S., Blanton, B., Christopherson, L. & Idaszak, R. (2014), "Data Management Lifecycle and Software Lifecycle Management in the Context of Conducting Science." *Journal of Open Research Software* 2 (1).

Lin, C.-W., Hong, T.-P. & Lu, W.-H. (2009), "An Efficient FUSP-Tree Update Algorithm for Deleted Data in Customer Sequences." In *2009 Fourth International Conference on Innovative Computing, Information and Control (ICICIC)*, 1491–94. IEEE.

Lin, L., Liu, T., Hu, J. & Zhang, J. (2014), "A Privacy-Aware Cloud Service Selection Method Toward Data Life-Cycle." In *2014 20th IEEE International Conference on Parallel and Distributed Systems (ICPADS)*, 752–59. IEEE.

Ma, X., Fox, P., Rozell, E., West, P. & Zednik, S. (2014), "Ontology Dynamics in a Data Life Cycle: Challenges and Recommendations from a Geoscience Perspective." *Journal of Earth Science* 25: 407–12.

Miao, H., Li, A., Davis, L. S. & Deshpande, A. (2017), "Towards Unified Data and Lifecycle Management for Deep Learning." In *33rd IEEE International Conference on Data Engineering, ICDE 2017, San Diego, CA, USA, April 19–22, 2017*, 571–82. IEEE Computer Society. URL: https://doi.org/10.1109/ICDE.2017.112.

Michota, A. & Katsikas, S. (2015), "Designing a Seamless Privacy Policy for Social Networks." In *Proceedings of the 19th Panhellenic Conference on Informatics*, 139–43.

Microsoft Azure. (2023), "Optimize Costs by Automatically Managing the Data Lifecycle." URL: https://learn.microsoft.com/en-us/azure/storage/blobs/lifecycle-management-overview. [Online; accessed 7-June-2023].

ODRL. (2018), "ODRL Information Model 2.2." URL: https://www.w3.org/TR/odrl-model/. [Online; accessed 7-June-2023].

Österle, H., Winter, R. & Brenner, W. (2010), *Gestaltungsorientierte Wirtschaftsinformatik: Ein Plädoyer für Rigor Und Relevanz*. Infowerk.

Othon, M, Mile, S., de Melo, A., Junior, A. & Arruda, A.(2019), "EVALUATION OF THE REMOVAL OF ANOMALIES IN DATA COLLECTED BY SENSORS."

Otto, B. (2015), "Quality and Value of the Data Resource in Large Enterprises." *Information Systems Management* 32 (3): 234–51.

Pachpor, N. N. & Prakash P. S. (2018), "Improving the Performance of System in Cloud by Using Selective Deduplication." In *2018 Second International Conference on Electronics, Communication and Aerospace Technology (ICECA)*, 314–18. IEEE.
Patel, D. (2016), "Research Data Management: A Conceptual Framework." *Library Review* 65 (4/5): 226–41.
Peffers, K., Tuunanen, T., Rothenberger, M. A. & Chatterjee, S. (2007), "A Design Science Research Methodology for Information Systems Research." *Journal of Management Information Systems* 24 (3): 45–77.
Prat, N., Comyn-Wattiau, I. & Akoka, J. (2015), "A Taxonomy of Evaluation Methods for Information Systems Artifacts." *Journal of Management Information Systems* 32 (3): 229–67.
Reardon, J., Capkun, S. & Basin, D. (2012), "Data Node Encrypted File System: Efficient Secure Deletion for Flash Memory." In *21st USENIX Security Symposium (USENIX Security 12)*, 333–48.
Shah, S. I. H., Peristeras, V. & Magnisalis, I. (2021), "DaLiF: A Data Lifecycle Framework for Data-Driven Governments." *J. Big Data* 8 (1): 89.
Tallon, P. P., Ramirez, R. V. & Short, J. E. (2013), "The Information Artifact in IT Governance: Toward a Theory of Information Governance." *Journal of Management Information Systems* 30 (3): 141–78.
Tebernum, D. (2023), *Destroy Claims* (version 1.2.1). URL: https://github.com/DaTebe/destroyclaims.
Tebernum, D., Altendeitering, M. & Howar, F. (2021), "DERM: A Reference Model for Data Engineering." In *Proceedings of the 10th International Conference on Data Science, Technology and Applications, DATA 2021, Online Streaming, July 6–8, 2021*, edited by Christoph Quix, Slimane Hammoudi, and Wil M. P. van der Aalst, 165–75. SCITEPRESS. URL: https://doi.org/10.5220/0010517301650175.
Tebernum, D., Altendeiterind, M. & Howar, F. (2023), "A Survey-Based Evaluation of the Data Engineering Maturity in Practice."
Tebernum, D. & Atamantschuk, S. (2023), *DIVA - Data Inventory and Valuation Approach* (version 4.1.0). URL: https://github.com/FraunhoferISST/diva.
Tebernum, D. & Howar, F. (2023), "Structuring the End of the Data Life Cycle."
Trajanov, D., Zdraveski, V., Stojanov, R. & Kocarev, L. (2018), "Dark Data in Internet of Things (IOT): Challenges and Opportunities." In *7th Small Systems Simulation Symposium*, 1–8.
Venable, J., Pries-Heje, J. & Baskerville, R. (2012), "A Comprehensive Framework for Evaluation in Design Science Research." In *LNCS*, 7286:423–38. URL: https://doi.org/10.1007/978-3-642-29863-9_31.
Wissik, T. & Ďurčo, M. (2016), "Research Data Workflows: From Research Data Lifecycle Models to Institutional Solutions." In *Selected Papers from the CLARIN Annual Conference 2015, October 14–16, 2015, Wroclaw, Poland*, 94–107. 123. Linköping University Electronic Press.
Yu, X. & Wen, Q. (2010), "A View about Cloud Data Security from Data Life Cycle." In *2010 International Conference on Computational Intelligence and Software Engineering*, 1–4.

Managing Cybersecurity and Other Fraud Risks in Small and Medium Enterprises—A Framework to Build a Fraud Management Program in Times of Digitalization

Michaela K. Trierweiler and Barbara Krumay

Abstract Fraud, particularly cybercrime, is an emerging worldwide risk that targets not only large but also small and medium enterprises (SME). SMEs are especially vulnerable because they often have limited resources in terms of money, staff, and IT knowledge. Because of the role SMEs play in the European economy, reducing their vulnerability has gained more importance. Therefore, this study considers the question of how to minimize fraud in SME-related digital and socio-technical work environments. Based on a design science research approach, we developed a fraud management framework to allow SMEs to identify individual fraud risks and establish an individual fraud management program based on the framework at hand. To be adaptable to different industries and sizes of SMEs, we propose a modular concept of documents and workshop material that includes occupational and cyber-fraud cases because previous fraud management concepts often handled only one of them.

Keywords Fraud management · Framework · SME · IT security · GRC

1 Introduction

Digitalization and digital transformation offer new opportunities for SMEs but also pose many challenges. Because 9 out of 10 enterprises in the European Union are SMEs-providing two-thirds of all jobs (European Commission 2020) they play an important role in the European economy (Lee et al. 2012; Li et al. 2016). Not only their importance and number but also their vulnerability make them lucrative targets

M. K. Trierweiler (✉) · B. Krumay
Institute for Business Informatics—Information Engineering, Johannes Kepler University Linz—JKU Business School, Linz, Austria
e-mail: mkt.jku@gmail.com

B. Krumay
e-mail: barbara.krumay@jku.at

D. Beverungen et al. (eds.), *Solutions and Technologies for Responsible Digitalization*, Lecture Notes in Information Systems and Organisation 75,
https://doi.org/10.1007/978-3-031-80122-8_16

for criminals (ACFE 2020a; Barth et al. 2020; E&Y 2018; Kempf 2015; Ponemon 2017). They were the most common victims of fraud (approx. 30%), suffering the highest financial losses and experiencing significant negative impacts compared to bigger companies (ACFE 2020a, 2018, 2016). SMEs face specific occupational fraud risks (ACFE 2018) but are also vulnerable to cyber-fraud (Ritchie 2021). These risks evolve from the limited resources in terms of money, staff, and IT knowledge of SMEs. Further, they are more likely to lack internal controls (ACFE 2020a) and proper risk management, since they focus on operations but fail to invest into IT security staff or even staff trained in regulatory compliance (Asti 2021). Fraud and cybersecurity breaches thus tend to go undetected in SMEs since identifying such events and formal documentation methods to report or learn are missing. Especially micro-SMEs (European Commission 2016), having fewer than 10 employees, show a flat organizational structure and combine different functions in one role. This makes active fraud prevention, often requiring segregation of duties, difficult to establish. A compliant corporate culture is rarely established in a structured way. Fraudsters often target accounting, although it is a well-protected and legally regulated area. Besides this target, identity theft, bribery, asset misappropriation, and corruption are other common frauds (ACFE 2022). Due to rapidly implemented information and communication technology (ICT) during the COVID-19 crisis, the number of threats even increased, as weaknesses in the implantation made attacks easier (Schöber and Schmitz 2020). This situation led to a significant increase in cyber-fraud, payment fraud, or identity theft (ACFE 2020b; Buil-Gil et al. 2020; Deloitte Poland 2020; Pasculli 2020). Risks also evolve from the use of shadow IT (Schuster 2021), i.e., unregulated, and unsupervised ICT (Ritchie 2021).

However, besides shadow IT, the increasing digitalization challenges companies. The omnipresence of widely used IT tools makes them vectors for fraud attacks (e.g., email phishing attempts). To detect and prevent from attacks and fraud, specific software and hardware tools enable real-time or big data analytics (Derksen 2013; Holzenthal 2014), and even AI (Spindler and Kögel 2020) can be used. However, in SMEs, highly technological measures are rarely used, and IT-related fraud management measures are rarely discussed in SME contexts (Trierweiler 2022). Current research focuses mainly on organizational measures without providing comprehensive guidelines. Research in this context is—to the best of our knowledge—neither related to information systems (IS) research nor considers cyber-fraud risk. However, the main source of risk and fraud is not the technology per se but the people handling it (Jeong et al. 2019). For example, phishing attacks happen often beyond technology and are connected to people's risk taking and decision making (Abroshan et al. 2021). Because companies operate in an ICT landscape embedded within a socio-technical business environment where people and technology work jointly, both must be considered.

Existing fraud management concepts, such as the BSI Grundschutz (BSI 2022) or the NIST Cybersecurity Framework (NIST 2013) are mainly addressing bigger companies. Even large auditing firms offer services targeted to bigger corporations. However, these approaches do not fit SMEs' situation because they rely on trained staff and established structures in a company. Since SMEs have lately become targets of attacks and fraud, concepts suited to the personnel resources, organizational situation, and technical possibilities of SMEs (Bada and Nurse 2019) are necessary. This research aims to fill this gap by developing a fraud management framework (FMF) for SMEs that overcomes potential limitations (e.g., very complex to understand and handle; no holistic view). Therefore, we ask how a fraud management framework should look to fit into different SME contexts and cover company-specific fraud risks of occupational and cyber-fraud while considering given resources. To answer this question, a multivocal literature review was conducted (Trierweiler 2022) to gain insights and build a knowledge base for a better artifact (Peffers et al. 2007). We apply a design science research (DSR) approach to create an FMF as an ensemble artifact (Sein et al. 2011) that fits different SME contexts. The ensemble artifact is modular and combines documents (templates, such as FCM-03_FraudPolicyTemplate) and workshops (development and evaluation, such as FCM-02_CounterMeasureSelection&KPI) to support the creation of a fraud management program within a relatively short time frame of just a few months.

This research contributes to the existing field in two ways: first, it bridges epistemic research and applied sciences by creating a new artifact; second, this artifact supports practitioners in SMEs to minimize fraud risks in their individual contexts. This new approach uses the man-technology-organization (MTO) concept (Ulich 2013), since current work situations are mainly socio-technical (Bostrom et al. 2009). Therefore, an effective fraud management system requires collaboration among technology (e.g., IT security aspects), organizational procedures (e.g., four-eyes principle), and workers (e.g., awareness training and ethical culture). Accordingly, the new framework shows characteristics like comprehensiveness, but also needs to be research-based, compatible with SMEs' fraud risk needs, and easy to understand. The last condition clearly influences the design and notation used to build the artifact. Our approach was piloted with an SME for evaluation as a proof of concept and to refine the design and details of the presented FMF in the sense of an action design research approach (Sein et al. 2011).

The remainder of this paper is structured as follows: Sect. 2 describes the state of the field regarding fraud management. Section 3 depicts the methodological approach, including the considerations for the real-world application of the artifact and the evaluation procedure. Section 4 explains the design considerations and components of the framework artifact, followed by an in-depth discussion related to the current literature. Finally, a conclusion, limitations, and future work are described.

2 State of Field

Compared to other criminal activities, fraud is often seen as a white-collar crime, i.e., a crime targeting financial or property loss (Braithwaite 1985). White collar crime covers not only delicts directly harming an organization (e.g., asset misappropriation), but also crimes (e.g., corruption, money laundering) committed for the benefit of the company (Heißner 2014). The main elements that constitute fraud are the harm done to a party resulting from action by another party (Bologna and Lindquist 1995). So far, fraud has been mainly discussed from a legal point of view as well as in accounting and auditing literature. Legal entities define fraud based on characteristics such as intention, deception, and damage to a third party. For example, the European Parliament names Articles 310(6) and 325 of the Treaty on the Functioning of the European Union (Pouwels 2022), the German criminal law in §263 and §263a (Bundesamt für Justiz n.d.), Austrian criminal law §146 (jusline.at 1975), to name just some legal foundations. Occupational fraud, i.e., fraud committed by an employee within the organization, covers three main categories: asset misappropriation (e.g., theft of cash, misuse of inventory), corruption (e.g., bribery, economic extortion), and financial statement fraud (e.g., net income understatements) (ACFE 2022). This scheme for occupational fraud, often referred to as the fraud tree (ACFE 2022; Wells 2001), addresses misconduct on different levels of an organization, from higher-level management to employees on the operational level (Henselmann and Hofmann 2010). Overall, misconducts addressed in the fraud tree cover undesired and non-compliant behavior (Heißner 2014).

Reasons for committing fraud are various, yet they follow a general scheme (Dorminey et al. 2012). The recently developed fraud models (Marks 2020) are mainly based on the so-called fraud triangle (Cressey 1952), a work done by Donald Cressy in the 1950s. In its very basic form, the fraud triangle addresses three conditions: pressure, opportunity, and attitude or rationalization (Kassem and Higson 2012; Wells 2014). Furthermore, it has been stated that fraud is related to the level of trust a person enjoys (Kassem and Higson 2012). The fraud triangle, however, was the starting point for other fraud models, such as the fraud diamond, adding capability as the fourth dimension (Wolfe and Hermanson 2004). Capability in this context includes the intelligence, creativity, and experience of the fraudster (Henselmann and Hofmann 2010), which may also include technical and computational skills as preconditions to committing IT-based fraud. Lately, academic research has identified another dimension: arrogance (e.g., Christian et al. 2019; Fuad et al. 2020; Maulidiana and Triandi 2020; Muhsin et al. 2018; Nindito 2018), making the fraud pentagon.

Thus, the relevance of fraud management has gained some attention, especially in the financial management and auditing literature (e.g., Amasiatu and Shah 2018; Cortesão et al. 2005; Soomro et al. 2019). Although research on fraud management focuses on schemes and frameworks, it also addresses the involved parties: fraud managers and offenders (Gill 2011). It has been shown that fraud managers recognize changes in the way frauds are committed relative to technology (Gill 2011), resulting in a "fraudogenic" environment (Button and Cross 2017). Fraud management is widely based on the above-mentioned fraud models (i.e., fraud triangle, fraud diamond, fraud pentagon) to detect fraudulent activities (Indarto and Ghozali 2016; Kassem and Higson 2012; Roden et al. 2016; Umar et al. 2020).

However, fraud management extends beyond pure detection and encompasses prevention and response to fraud, including mitigation and remediation (Cappelli et al. 2012; Girgenti and Hedley 2011). Fraud management frameworks exist at the governmental (e.g., U.S. Government Accountability Office 2015) and organizational levels, e.g., the COSO framework (COSO 2013). Existing fraud framework approaches related to SMEs mainly address occupational fraud but lack a clear position toward IT-related issues and do not adopt a holistic view (Trierweiler 2022). Six lately analyzed approaches (Trierweiler 2022) focus on employee fraud (Dawson 2015; Yearwood 2011), a specific industry (steel logistics in Thailand; Phuttima et al. 2014), or a business situation (internal controls for purchasing in the automotive sector in Malaysia; Aris et al. 2013). Or they focused on fraud reporting (Çalıyurt 2012) and the development of a fraud policy (Lincke and Green 2012). Common to all identified approaches is their conceptual nature, lacking evidence for applicability in the real world.

In addition, other disciplines offer frameworks that are transferable to fraud management, such as COBIT-2019 (ISACA 2019) or the NIST Cybersecurity Framework (NIST 2013). Both have been addressed in the context of SMEs (Andenmatten 2018; Asprion and Burda 2019; Johnson 2016; The MEP National Network 2020) but with a different focus on security. An effective fraud management approach comprises measures for prevention, detection, and response (Girgenti and Hedley 2011), which also apply to cybersecurity risks. Nowadays, IT security breaches and occupational fraud are intertwined: occupational fraud is often conducted within (e.g., changing a financial record) or via an information system (e.g., a phishing attack).

3 Methodology

The goal of this study is to develop a fraud management framework (FMF) for SMEs that overcomes potential limitations found in existing concepts. We adopt a DSR approach (Gregor and Hevner 2013; Hevner et al. 2004; Iivari 2015; Peffers et al. 2007) to develop an alternative FMF based on a recently published multivocal literature review identifying six SME-related fraud management approaches (Trierweiler 2022). Because of the scarce IT-related measures in the academic literature, we used grey literature to fill the gap. Therefore, the research entry point related to an objective-centered solution (Peffers et al. 2007) relies on the idea of an existing knowledge base (Hevner 2007). To safeguard consistency and integrate empirical sources, we further relied on domain-specific notation principles (e.g., Frank 2013) for explanation and description as well as action design research (ADR) for evaluation (Maccani et al. 2015; Sein et al. 2011) and refinement of the framework. From a methodical perspective, incremental artifact evaluation with incremental delivery of features is also a characteristic of ADR (Haj-Bolouri et al. 2018; Sein et al. 2011). Therefore, this FMF artifact was developed using an agile sprint approach.

To achieve a proof-of-concept state, a naturalistic evaluation (Iivari and Venable 2009) in a real-world SME was conducted, involving a second researcher creating and leading the feedback interviews to minimize bias. The piloting SME company has 10 employees with different levels of experience, from software developers to administrative staff. Security and fraud management are the responsibility of the CEO. The evaluation occurred from September until November 2022, involving the CEO of the company as well as people from the administrative staff to ensure validity, applicability (i.e., ease of use, understandability), and utility (e.g., Peffers et al. 2012; Prat et al. 2014). The pilot study was following the intended routine that a SME needs to apply to build its own fraud management program from this framework: The process starts with a briefing of the management and building a small ADR team of practitioners from the SME and the two researchers. To gain firsthand insights into the fraud management of the SME, a self-assessment questionnaire is filled out by SME management aiming at the identification of the fraud risk areas. Information from this self-assessment form is incorporated into a workshop with all SME project members to ensure the same knowledge base about fraud and the project in general. After this kickoff, a second workshop is conducted to perform the fraud risk analysis that is based on a comprehensive fraud glossary, consisting of over 120 fraud risks from different categories. At least the main areas of occupational and cyber-fraud need to be assessed by the SME. The results are then summarized and prepared for further use to define MTO-based fraud countermeasures. Their definition is typically finalized in another workshop to be SME bespoke as possible. After this definition phase, the implementation in the SME's context is necessary, which can be completed as a workshop (our case) or as a pure planning activity. The stages and workshops are supported by different documents constituting the ensemble artifacts of the FMF at hand.

After each workshop sessions, expert interviews (Atteslander et al. 2010; Döring and Bortz 2016) comprising 14 questions for aspects of utility (length, language, applicability, prerequisite of knowledge, needed time to work with), validity (scope and completeness perception), and efficacy (perceived impact and usefulness to the SME and to other SME contexts) were conducted to further evaluated the artefact. Answers were recorded and noted in form of a 5-point Likert scale (Brown 2010). The analysis of the answers was used to refine the components of the FMF for SMEs. In total, 21 documents were evaluated, and 16 documents were applied by the piloting SME. This extended evaluation was applied to gain feedback as comprehensive as possible.

Because of the complex nature of the matter to be addressed by the DSR project (e.g., Venable et al. 2012), the development of the artifact was done in different design cycles (Sein et al. 2011; vom Brocke and Buddendick 2006). An architectural construct (Trierweiler 2021), which is a meta-artifact (Iivari 2015) and developed in a first design cycle, was used to further design and build the content, sub-components, and their connections as well as the appropriate granularity of the information we show in this paper. This second design cycle was split into alpha and beta phases (see Sein et al. 2011) and connected to the evaluation as described above.

4 Results

Based on the DSR approach, we created an artifact that exists in two expressions: First, a meta-artifact, which comprises an architecture (Trierweiler 2021). It holds five connected dimensions (called "tiers"), with processes and sub-processes on a generic level. Second, a generalized artifact was produced to address a class of problems (Wieringa 2014). This artifact, further referred to as FMF for SMEs, contains self-explanatory information, template documents and workshop supporting material. However, it might require some external accompaniment and consultancy as well as project management and change management skills depending on the individual SME's knowledge.

4.1 Prerequisites and Design Considerations

Fraud prevention in an organization can best be achieved by having an effective and visible antifraud program (Vona 2008) embedded in a corporate culture of ethical standards and the organization's governance and risk considerations. From the existing literature and based on the evaluation, we identified certain requirements and design considerations related to the SME context, i.e., scope and completeness; usability and handling; modularity; limitations of staff; cost efficiency; comprehensiveness; data protection and topic sensitivity. Table 1 represents some findings from the evaluation.

We identified scope and completeness, referring to the extension of the scope beyond existing framework as well as achieving completeness of aspects as requirements. Many authors (e.g., Aris et al. 2013; Bungartz 2010; Cika 2017; Dawson 2015; Dimitrijević et al. 2020; Lachney 2020; Tazilah and Hussain 2015), refer to existing models to address prerequisites and design, such as the COSO model. It describes the components of an antifraud program as a process consisting of the following steps (Vona 2008): performing fraud risk assessments, building a control environment adverse to fraud, designing, and implementing fraud controls and countermeasures, sharing and training the fraud program, establishing monitoring activities, and responding to fraudulent activities. However, we identified the need to further extend the scope: from internal, staff-, and organizational-related controls responding mainly to classical occupational fraud risks (ACFE 2022) to IT-related fraud situations, addressing current threats resulting from today's digital world and socio-technical work environments. In addition, the framework was further extended, integrating information about fraud incident response activities and possibilities to find additional support in case an SME lacks the knowledge in-house. Therefore, the FMF for SMEs considers more and different aspects of content than previous approaches. In the evaluation, two additional aspects were identified and added to the FMF for SMEs, resulting in the documents FCM-08_ConflictOfInterestForm, and FMF-02_DocumentsExplanation.

Table 1 Evaluation findings

Topic	Findings	Implications
FMF overall	Works well; positive evaluation results in general	Keep approach
Dual language	Applying German and English in the same document reduced the understandability	Split documents to single language
Modular concept	Worked well; SME could use only the relevant documents	Keep approach
Usage for different SME contexts	Documents are perceived to work universally; split into a golden-rule version and a more comprehensive one suggested	Rework and split document
Transfer/reusage FRA results into the next stages	Transfer of documents that are not directly connected made usage and transfer of results a bit cumbersome	Idea to support it by an IS in future
Sequencing of documents	During application, we found that they should be applied in another area (tier)	Move documents to correct tier
Redundancies, text length, style	Redundancies were spotted; repetition allows a document to stand independently; some explanations could be more to the point	Check and rework documents

Furthermore, SMEs need a framework that is easy to use (usability) and does not require additional training (handling), allowing them to concentrate on the content. Therefore, the FMF for SMEs uses standard office products that are widespread and well-known. To address an international context, the framework allows a multi-language approach. However, based on the evaluation, the documents need to be separated for not confusing the employees. To fit different sizes and industries of SMEs, a modular design (modularity) was identified as a design consideration. The FMF for SMEs compiles of best practices, domain knowledge, and additional information. It is organized in form of well-structured multiple documents. Drawing from the example of other frameworks (BSI 2022; NIST 2013), documents were indexed in relation to the main components. The documents can be used stand-alone or in combination according to the needs for building the SME specific fraud management program. The documents are either templates and forms, that are instantiated on use (e.g., in workshops) or information documents. The piloting SME, for example, did not instantiate a new IT security policy based on the proposed template (FCM-03), but used their existing one.

SMEs are clearly challenged by the number of people they employ. Role-based access to systems or segregation of duties, particularly in finance and accounting, therefore is hard to achieve. Consequently, not all fraud countermeasures, such as establishing a four-eyes principle when releasing money in an investment situation, are feasible. Since there is no clear-cut recommendation on measures, the FMF for SMEs considers workshops to discuss measures and build individual solutions. In the same manor, the limited financial resources of SMEs need to be considered. Accordingly, cost-efficiency of solutions is vital, making the use of existing tools (e.g., standard office products) more feasible rather than developing or buying a specific information system that also requires costly training.

SMEs have specific characteristics independent from the industry they operate in, but do not have the resources to implement different, industry-specific frameworks. Therefore, comprehensiveness as well as to encompass all risk areas is vital. Thus, a fraud glossary was compiled to build the baseline for the fraud risk analysis. It is used for the risk assessment and to contribute to the awareness for specific risks. It also influences subsequent documents of the framework.

Due to the need to protect internal data and the topic sensitivity, an SME might hesitate to integrate external players. To overcome these issues, documents in the FMF for SMEs foresee non-disclosure agreements. Internally, documents related to the fraud management program holding sensitive data need to be maintained and controlled in an archive within the SME with a confidentiality clause to safeguard data protection.

4.2 The FMF for SMEs

The FMF for SMEs (Fig. 1) consists of five major interconnected components ("tiers"): Risk assessment (FRA), incident responses/forensics (FIR), fraud countermeasures (FCM), external support (FES), and implementation (FMFI). The FMF for SMEs addresses *risk assessment* to identify the individual fraud risk. It touches on *incident responses and forensics* because the need for risk management is often realized after an incident has occurred. The core part of the framework uses *fraud countermeasures* related to fraud types along the MTO concept (Ulich 2013) to enable the selection of suitable measures. In addition, the proposed framework suggests where to find *external support* and suggests a roadmap for *implementation*. A *continuous improvement cycle* follows the implementation to keep the measures current. The framework provides a series of documents related to each tier, marked with an abbreviation for the tier (e.g., FRA) and a consecutive number. The documents are either templates, that need to be instantiated or hold necessary information. Workshops are directly related to some documents, as in the workshops these documents are used as the basis for instantiated documents (fitting the SME) or discussed to gain a common understanding. To reflect the process related to the FMF for SMEs, a sequence for use and run through is proposed in four stages (see Sect. 4.3).

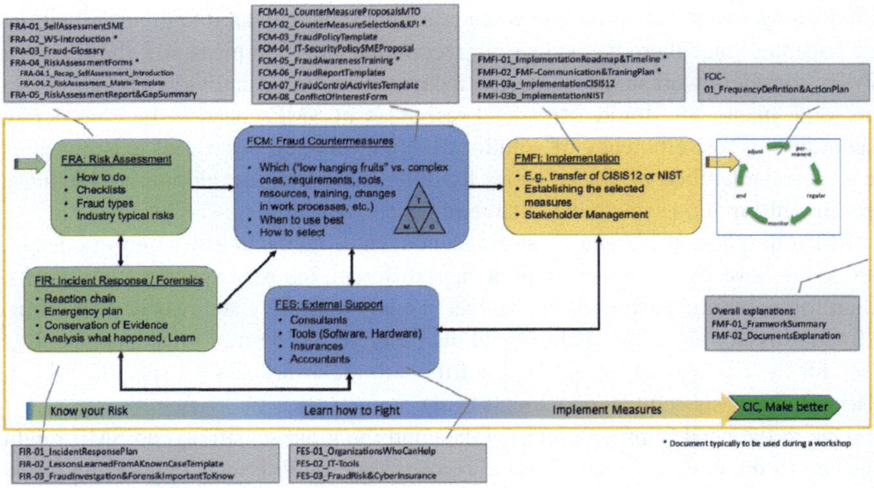

Fig. 1 FMF for SMEs

4.3 Sequence of Use and Run Through

Although the FMF for SMEs is modular and offers the possibility to use the documents independently, they follow a process, based on a logical and chronological sequence. The sequence is divided in four stages: (1) know your risk, (2) learn how to fight, (3) implement measures, and (4) CIC, make better.

Stage 1: Know Your Risk. This stage allows to identify, learn about, and prioritize individual fraud risks. It includes a fraud risk self-assessment as well as workshops with relevant stakeholders to identify the risk, its impact, and prioritization, based on documents indexed with FRA (fraud risk assessment). If the need to create a fraud management program is caused by a recent incident, the assessment could also start by analyzing the incident based on documents indexed with FIR (incident responses/ forensics).

Stage 2: Learn How to Fight. This second stage focuses on learning, i.e., how the fraud schemes are conducted, what are most common warning signals and what collusion strategies are. The SME shall understand what countermeasures could be suitable in the specific context, considering the SME's resources, balancing people (employee-related), technology, and organizational (processes) means. A workshop with relevant stakeholders of the SME is proposed to cover the learning process. Documents indexed with FCM (fraud countermeasures) support this stage. They provide support to capture the decisions for certain measures, but also templates to create a fraud and an IT-security policy, forms to design internal controls and to establish a fraud reporting process. Depending on the SME's situation of resources and know-how, external tools or support might be required at this stage. Documents dealing with outside-resources and information like IT tools or cyber-security insurance to carry-over the burden, are indexed with FES (fraud external support).

Stage 3: Implement Measures. In the third stage the implementation of measures applies. Within the identified countermeasures, there might be quick wins, i.e., measures that could be installed easily without consuming significant time or money. Other measures might require more investigation or planning as well as some investments because other external resources, such as IT security experts or technical equipment or software must be paid. Considering this, a plan for implementation and a kind of rollout strategy that includes some budgeting must be developed. The FMF for SMEs proposes a training and communication plan. When an SME has no procedures for such change management or rollouts, this FMF offers implementation strategies derived from established IT security frameworks and adapted to fraud management needs; see documents indexed with FMFI (fraud management framework implementation).

Stage 4: CIC, Make better. Stage 4 calls for the establishment of continuous improvement cycle (indexed FCIC) of the implemented fraud management program. It is necessary to keep it current and to adapt it to organizational changes, new fraud schemes, and technological developments. Determining an appropriate frequency to re-assess fraud risks and to adapt the countermeasures to the changed needs is proposed.

5 Discussion

The goal of this study was to develop a FMF for SMEs that overcomes potential limitations found in existing frameworks, such as non-comprehensiveness and lack of implementation in a real SME situation to proof applicability. Specific conditions found in SMEs (e.g., scarce financial and human resources; segregation of duties) hinder SMEs from using existing frameworks—such as COSO, COBIT, or NIST—that focus mainly on larger companies and often not directly on fraud management. In addition, fraud management seems to be successful only when it considers people, technology, and the organization. Therefore, in the FMF for SMEs, we combine measures targeting the specific SME aspects while integrating prevention, detection, and response tailored to an SME's needs. Following the man-technology-organization (MTO) concept (Ulich 2013) in the FCM tier the sociotechnical nature is considered (Bostrom et al. 2009).

To mitigate fraud and cybersecurity risks, it is relevant to understand "why" to mitigate the risk by ensuring a good security and awareness program by building or verifying organic policies and procedures (Asti 2021). To understand the "why" is part of the risk assessment and helps the SME to understand the individual fraud risks and how to prioritize them in accordance with given resources. The FMF for SMEs considers this point of "vulnerability management" (Ritchie 2021) by starting with the tier of the fraud risk assessment. What is different compared to other approaches is the comprehensive fraud glossary, fostering as the basis of the fraud risk assessment. The glossary incorporates different areas of fraud from which the SME can select during the assessment (occupational fraud, cyber-fraud, bid manipulation, and insurance fraud as well as other industry-specific areas). By evaluating these fraud areas, an SME can narrow the types of fraud; assess the impact in terms of reputation, financial loss, and business continuity; and prioritize. In addition, some summary documentation is needed to enable the SME to properly communicate the results of the fraud risk assessment within the organization. Although it seems obvious to start with a risk assessment, fraud management literature or conceptions often neglect this aspect; they assume that the fraud risk is known. However, research showed (Asti 2021) that SMEs tend to be less aware of their risks. With respect to SMEs' limited resources, a fraud training program is a measure of low cost and effort and a "must-have" and should comprise all different kinds of identified fraud. Building a "human firewall" is a key element addressing cybersecurity (Jeong et al. 2019) even when an SME has no dedicated IT knowledge. The FMF at hand provides preset training material that can be tailored with guidance to an SME situation. To complete the understanding of one's fraud vulnerability and to build a response plan to a suspected fraud case or a cybersecurity breach, the risk assessment is supported by the fraud incident response section to extend our fraud management approach compared to other approaches.

Although anti-fraud training is a key element, education is not sufficient as a stand-alone measure The awareness and willingness of an organization must be documented and enforced by dedicated policies—such as a fraud and IT security policy—which should also consider teleworking from home. A lack of these basic concepts (Ritchie 2021) is still common. The FMF at hand provides policy templates compiled from literature as best practices. In any case, an SME should have a legal consultation and review before handing out the policies to the organization.

A fraud management program is not valid if it is not launched. Therefore, the tier of fraud management implementation uses classical project management tools and makes proposals for an implementation roadmap and a communication plan. If an SME wants to use the given FMF as a blueprint and develop the fraud management program without external consultancy, we propose two adaptations from cybersecurity frameworks to allow an application of the framework in a self-management approach (FMFI-3a,b). One is based on the CISIS12® approach, a compliance information security management system in 12 steps (IT-Sicherheitscluster e.V. 2022; ISIS12-Netzwerk 2020). The second proposal focuses on the five stages of the NIST cybersecurity framework (identify, protect, detect, respond, recover; The MEP National Network 2020) applying them to fraud management, including a classification of measures as man-, technology-, or organization-related.

Shortcomings that emerged from the small set of academic literature used were considered. First, the approaches found in academic literature lack comprehensiveness in terms of the industries and types of fraud they cover. Therefore, the FMF at hand uses a modular document concept and a comprehensive fraud glossary as baselines. Second, the current literature has not shown evaluation or proof-of-concept.

This issue was addressed by implementing the FMF in a real-world SME context, considering that this fraud management framework will be easily understood by SME stakeholders. Therefore, the documents must be provided in the local language.

6 Conclusion, Limitations, and Future Research

Because of their importance and number, SMEs play a significant role in the European economy. At the same time, they are impacted by the effects of digital transformation in a positive as well as negative way. To address occupational fraud and IT security (cyber-fraud) risks, we provide a comprehensive fraud management framework for SMEs that overcomes potential limitations found in existing concepts of addressing only specific industries or fraud types or by being too big and complex for SMEs. In addition to a clear structure and process for implementation, we also provide information in the form of documents specifically designed for SMEs. We developed the artifact in two design cycles. The first cycle was an architectural design to determine the structure and content of a framework that would be applicable in real-world contexts. The second designed artifact was built with all the details and applied in a real-world SME context to demonstrate its proof of concept and to evaluate the artifact. Based on insights captured during this pilot study through interviews conducted by another researcher to minimize bias, the framework was refined to its current state. The framework consists of different documents that could be used in a modular concept, which allows a holistic approach but also flexible use and adaptations to the individual SME situation—such as size, industry, and resources. Further, it gives a structure to manage fraud rather than react on occasion and allows creation of awareness of the risk of fraud—because people are key to fraud management.

This research has some limitations. First, it has been applied to only one piloting company because fraud management is a sensitive topic that requires the establishment of trust between the researchers and the company beforehand. However, during evaluation, we assessed more components (documents) than used by the piloting SME and asked questions about perception of usability in other SME contexts. Therefore, we believe that the FMF for SMEs is generic enough to be applied in different contexts. Second, the scarce academic literature used as the basis may be an issue. By adding grey literature, we aimed to control this issue and build a broad base for designing each component of our framework. However, further research can be derived from these two limitations. Not only should the framework be tested and evaluated in additional SMEs from various industries, but also the study should be replicated after some time when the state of the field and the literature might be broader. Third, the transfer of results from the risk assessment to the next stages to select countermeasures was a bit cumbersome because this was a manual procedure prompted by the given document's approach. Here, one can think of an IS-supported version of the framework to be developed. However, such an application must consider the data protection statements and topic sensitivity of fraud by limiting accesses.

References

Abroshan, H., Devos, J., Poels, G., Laermans, E., 2021. Phishing Happens Beyond Technology: The Effects of Human Behaviors and Demographics on Each Step of a Phishing Process. IEEE Access 9, 44928–44949. https://doi.org/10.1109/ACCESS.2021.3066383

ACFE, 2016. Report to the Nations on Occupational Fraud and Abuse—2016 Global Fraud Study. Association of Certified Fraud Examiners, Austin, Texas, USA.

ACFE, 2018. Report to the Nations—2018 Global Fraud Study on Occupational Fraud and Abuse. Association of Certified Fraud Examiners, Austin, Texas, USA.

ACFE, 2020a. Report to the Nations—2020 Global Fraud Study on Occupational Fraud and Abuse. Association of Certified Fraud Examiners Inc., Austin, Texas, USA.

ACFE, 2020b. Fraud in the Wake of COVID-19: Benchmarking Report [WWW Document]. URL https://www.acfe.com/covidreport.aspx (accessed 6.18.20).

ACFE, 2022. The Fraud Tree—occupational fraud and abuse classification systems.

Amasiatu, C.V., Shah, M.H., 2018. First party fraud management: framework for the retail industry. IJRDM 46, 350–363. https://doi.org/10.1108/IJRDM-10-2016-0185

Andenmatten, M., 2018. COBIT 2019—Das neue Enterprise Governance Modell für Informationen und Technologien. Disruptive agile Service Management. URL https://blog.itil.org/2018/11/cobit-2019-das-neue-enterprise-governance-modell-fuer-informationen-und-technologien/ (accessed 6.19.20).

Aris, N.A., Arif, S.M.M., Othman, R., Chantrathevi, T., Tapsir, R., 2013. Internal Control Mechanism Framework for Fraud Prevention in Small Medium Automotive Industry, in: 2013 IEEE Symposium on Humanities, Science and Engineering Research (SHUSER). Malaysia, pp. 594–598.

Asprion, P.M., Burda, D., 2019. COBIT—Enzyklopädie der Wirtschaftsinformatik [WWW Document]. Enzyklopädie der Wirtschaftsinformatik—Online Lexikon. URL https://www.enzyklopaedie-der-wirtschaftsinformatik.de/wi-enzyklopaedie/lexikon/daten-wissen/Grundlagen-der-Informationsversorgung/COBIT (accessed 6.19.20).

Asti, A., 2021. Cyber Defense Challenges from the Small and Medium-Sized Business Perspective.

Atteslander, P., Cromm, J., Grabow, B., Klein, H., Maurer, A., Siegert, G., 2010. Methoden der empirischen Sozialforschung, 13., neu bearbeitete und erweiterte Auflage. ed, ESV basics. Erich Schmidt Verlag, Berlin.

Bada, M., Nurse, J.R.C., 2019. Developing cybersecurity education and awareness programmes for Small and medium-sized enterprises (SMEs). ICS 27, 393–410. https://doi.org/10.1108/ICS-07-2018-0080

Barth, M., Hellemann, N., Kob, T., Krösmann, C., Morgenstern, U., Tschersich, T., Ritter, T., Shulman, H., Trapp, D., Wintergerst, R., 2020. Spionage, Sabotage und Datendiebstahl—Wirtschaftsschutz in der vernetzten Welt (No. Studienbericht 2020). Bitkom e.V., Berlin.

Bologna, J., Lindquist, R.J., 1995. Fraud auditing and forensic accounting: new tools and techniques, 2nd ed. ed. Wiley, New York.

Bostrom, R.P., Gupta, S., Thomas, D., 2009. A Meta-Theory for Understanding Information Systems Within Sociotechnical Systems. Journal of Management Information Systems 26, 17–48. https://doi.org/10.2753/MIS0742-1222260102

Braithwaite, J., 1985. White Collar Crime. Annu. Rev. Sociol. 11, 1–25. https://doi.org/10.1146/annurev.so.11.080185.000245

Brown, S., 2010. Likert Scale Examples for Surveys [WWW Document]. URL https://www.extension.iastate.edu/Documents/ANR/LikertScaleExamplesforSurveys.pdf

BSI, Bundesamt für Sicherheit in der Informationstechnik (Ed.), 2022. IT-Grundschutz-Kompendium, Edition 2022. ed, Unternehmen und Wirtschaft. Reguvis Fachmedien GmbH, Köln / Bonn.

Buil-Gil, D., Miró-Llinares, F., Moneva, A., Kemp, S., Díaz-Castaño, N., 2020. Cybercrime and shifts in opportunities during COVID-19: a preliminary analysis in the UK. European Societies 1–13. https://doi.org/10.1080/14616696.2020.1804973

Bundesamt für Justiz, n.d. § 263a StGB—Einzelnorm.

Bungartz, O., 2010. Effiziente und effektive Interne Kontrollsysteme, in: Bassen, A., Wagenhofer, A. (Eds.), Controlling und Corporate-Governance-Anforderungen Verbindungen, Maßnahmen, Umsetzung. Erich Schmidt Verlag, Berlin, pp. 131–157.

Button, M., Cross, C., 2017. Technology and Fraud: The 'Fraudogenic' Consequences of the Internet Revolution, in: McGuire, M.R., Holt, T.J. (Eds.), The Routledge Handbook of Technology, Crime and Justice. (Author version of this article).

Çalıyurt, K.T., 2012. Reporting Fraud Using the Fraud-Free Company Model: A Case for the SMEs in Emerging Economies?, in: Çaliyurt, K., Idowu, S.O. (Eds.), Emerging Fraud. Springer Berlin Heidelberg, Berlin, Heidelberg, pp. 3–18.

Cappelli, D., Moore, A., Trzeciak, R., 2012. The CERT guide to insider threats: how to prevent, detect, and respond to information technology crimes (theft, sabotage, fraud), The Sei series in software engineering. Addison-Wesley, Upper Saddle River, NJ.

Christian, N., Basri, Y.Z., Arafah, W., 2019. Analysis of Fraud Triangle, Fraud Diamond and Fraud Pentagon Theory to Detecting Corporate Fraud in Indonesia. The International Journal of Business Management and Technology 3, 73–78.

Cika, N., 2017. An Analysis of Practices of Internal Controls in Small and Medium Enterprises in Albania. Journal of Accounting & Management (2284-9459) 7, 87–97.

Cortesão, L., Martins, F., Rosa, A., Carvalho, P., 2005. Fraud Management Systems in Telecommunications: a practical approach.

COSO, Committee of Sponsoring Organizations of the Treadway Commission, 2013. Guidance on Internal Control [WWW Document]. www.coso.org. URL https://www.coso.org/pages/ic.aspx (accessed 6.9.21).

Cressey, D.R., 1952. Application and Verification of the Differential Association Theory. The Journal of Criminal Law, Criminology, and Police Science 43, 43–52. https://doi.org/10.2307/1138991

Dawson, S., 2015. Internal control/anti-fraud program design for the small business: a guide for companies not subject to the Sarbanes-Oxley Act, Wiley corporate F&A series. Wiley, Hoboken.

Deloitte Poland, 2020. The impact of COVID-19 on the fraud risks faced by organisations

Derksen, O., 2013. Fraud Analyse von Massendaten in Echtzeit, in: Deggendorfer Forum zur digitalen Datenanalyse (Ed.), Big Data—Systeme und Prüfung. Schmidt, Berlin, pp. 45–59.

Dimitrijević, D., Karapavlović, N., Milutinović, S., 2020. Fraud prevention measures in Serbian small and medium-sized enterprises: Existence and effectiveness. Ekonomika preduzeća 68, 369–382. https://doi.org/10.5937/EKOPRE2006369D

Döring, N., Bortz, J., 2016. Forschungsmethoden und Evaluation in den Sozial- und Humanwissenschaften, 5. vollständig überarbeitete, aktualisierte und erweiterte Auflage. ed, Springer-Lehrbuch. Springer, Berlin Heidelberg.

Dorminey, J., Fleming, A.S., Kranacher, M.-J., Riley, R.A., 2012. The Evolution of Fraud Theory. Issues in Accounting Education 27, 555–579. https://doi.org/10.2308/iace-50131

European Commission, 2016. SME definition.

European Commission, 2020. User guide to the SME Definition. Publications Office of the European Union, Luxembourg.

E&Y, 2018. Global Forensic Data Analytics Survey 2018: How can you disrupt risk in an era of digital transformation? Ernst & Young Fraud Investigation & Dispute Services.

Frank, U., 2013. Domain-Specific Modeling Languages: Requirements Analysis and Design Guidelines, in: Reinhartz-Berger, I., Sturm, A., Clark, T., Cohen, S., Bettin, J. (Eds.), Domain Engineering. Springer Berlin Heidelberg, Berlin, Heidelberg, pp. 133–157. https://doi.org/10.1007/978-3-642-36654-3_6

Fuad, K., Lestari, A.B., Handayani, R.T., 2020. Fraud Pentagon as a Measurement Tool for Detecting Financial Statements Fraud, in: Proceedings of the 17th International Symposium on Management (INSYMA 2020). Atlantis Press, Vung Tau City, Vietnam. https://doi.org/10.2991/aebmr.k.200127.017

Gill, M., 2011. Fraud and recessions: Views from fraudsters and fraud managers. International Journal of Law, Crime and Justice 39, 204–214. https://doi.org/10.1016/j.ijlcj.2011.05.008

Girgenti, R.H., Hedley, T.P. (Eds.), 2011. Managing the risk of fraud and misconduct: meeting the challenges of a global regulated, and digital environment. McGraw-Hill, New York.

Gregor, S., Hevner, A.R., 2013. Positioning and Presenting Design Science Research for Maximum Impact. MISQ 37, 337–355. https://doi.org/10.25300/MISQ/2013/37.2.01

Haj-Bolouri, A., Purao, S., Rossi, M., Bernhardsson, L., 2018. Action Design Research in Practice: Lessons and Concerns. Presented at the Twenty-Sixth European Conference on Information Systems (ECIS2018), Portsmouth, UK.

Heißner, S., 2014. Täter und Delikte, in: Erfolgsfaktor Integrität. Springer Fachmedien Wiesbaden, Wiesbaden, pp. 37–70. https://doi.org/10.1007/978-3-658-05608-7_2

Henselmann, K., Hofmann, S., 2010. Accounting fraud: case studies and practical implications. Erich Schmidt, Berlin.

Hevner, A.R., 2007. A Three Cycle View of Design Science Research. Scandinavian Journal of Information Systems 19, 87–92.

Hevner, A.R., March, S.T., Park, J., Ram, S., 2004. Design Science in Information Systems Research. MIS Quarterly 28, 75–105.

Holzenthal, F., 2014. IT-gestützte Geldwäsche- und Betrugsbekämpfung in Banken und Versicherungen Mehrwert durch einen holistischen GRC-Ansatz. ZRFC, GRC-Report 3/14, 140–143.

Iivari, J., 2015. Distinguishing and contrasting two strategies for design science research. European Journal of Information Systems 24, 107–115. https://doi.org/10.1057/ejis.2013.35

Iivari, J., Venable, J.R., 2009. Action research and design science research—Seemingly similar but decisively dissimilar, in: ECIS 2009 Proceedings Presented at the 17th European Conference on Information Systems, Verona, Italy.

Indarto, S.L., Ghozali, I., 2016. Fraud diamond: Detection analysis on the fraudulent financial reporting. RGC 6, 116–123. https://doi.org/10.22495/rcgv6i4c1art1

ISACA, Information Systems Audit and Control Association, 2019. COBIT 2019 framework introduction and methodology.

ISIS12-Netzwerk, 2020. Handbuch zur effizienten Gestaltung von Informationssicherheit für Kleine und Mittlere Organisationen (KMO). IT-Sicherheitscluster e. V., 93053 Regensburg, Regensburg.

IT-Sicherheitscluster e.V., 2022. Was ist CISIS12®? CISIS12®. URL https://cisis12.de/was-ist-cisis12/ (accessed 3.5.23).

Jeong, J., Mihelcic, J., Oliver, G., Rudolph, C., 2019. Towards an Improved Understanding of Human Factors in Cybersecurity, in: 2019 IEEE 5th International Conference on Collaboration and Internet Computing (CIC). Presented at the 2019 IEEE 5th International Conference on Collaboration and Internet Computing (CIC), pp. 338–345. https://doi.org/10.1109/CIC48465.2019.00047

Johnson, C., 2016. Sizing Up the NIST Cybersecurity Framework. NIST Taking Measure. URL https://www.nist.gov/blogs/taking-measure/sizing-nist-cybersecurity-framework (accessed 6.19.20).

jusline.at, 1975. § 146 StGB (Strafgesetzbuch), Betrug—JUSLINE Österreich.

Kassem, R., Higson, A., 2012. The New Fraud Triangle Model. JETEMS 3, 191–195.

Kempf, D., 2015. Ohne Schutzschild. IT-Security Channel Compendium.

Lachney, K., 2020. An Exploration of Internal Controls and Their Impact on Employee Fraud in Small Businesses. Journal of Forensic and Investigative Accounting 12, 21–44.

Lee, Y., Shin, J., Park, Y., 2012. The changing pattern of SME's innovativeness through business model globalization. Technological Forecasting and Social Change 79, 832–842. https://doi.org/10.1016/j.techfore.2011.10.008

Li, W., Liu, K., Belitski, M., Ghobadian, A., O'Regan, N., 2016. E-Leadership through Strategic Alignment: An Empirical Study of Small- and Medium-sized Enterprises in the Digital Age. Journal of Information Technology 31, 185–206. https://doi.org/10.1057/jit.2016.10

Lincke, S., Green, D., 2012. Combating IS fraud: A teaching case study, in: AMCIS 2012 Proceedings. Presented at the Americas Conference on Information Systems (AMCIS), Seattle, Washington, pp. 578–584.

Maccani, G., Donnellan, B., Helfert, M., 2015. Action Design Research: A Comparison with Canonical Action Research and Design Science, in: At the Vanguard of Design Science: First Impressions and Early Findings from Ongoing Research Research-in-Progress Papers and Poster Presentations from the 10th International Conference. Presented at the DESRIST 2015, Dublin, Ireland.

Marks, J., 2020. Fraud Pentagon—Enhancements to the Three Conditions Under Which Fraud May Occur. BoardAndFraud. URL https://boardandfraud.com/2020/05/21/fraud-pentagon-enhancements-to-the-fraud-triangle-and-under-which-fraud-may-occur/ (accessed 1.5.21).

Maulidiana, S., Triandi, T., 2020. Analysis of Fraudulent Financial Reporting Through the Fraud Pentagon Theory, in: Proceedings of the 2nd International Seminar on Business, Economics, Social Science and Technology (ISBEST 2019). Atlantis Press, South Tangerang, Indonesia. https://doi.org/10.2991/aebmr.k.200522.042

Muhsin, Kardoyo, Nurkhin, A., 2018. What Determinants of Academic Fraud Behavior? From Fraud Triangle to Fraud Pentagon Perspective. KSS 3, 154. https://doi.org/10.18502/kss.v3i10.3126

Nindito, M., 2018. Financial Statement Fraud: Perspective of the Pentagon Fraud Model in Indonesia. Academy of Accounting and Financial Studies Journal.

NIST, National Institute of Standards and Technology, 2013. NIST Cybersecurity Framework [WWW Document]. www.nist.gov. URL https://www.nist.gov/cyberframework (accessed 3.11.23).

Pasculli, L., 2020. COVID19-related fraud risks and possible anti-fraud measures (Written evidence submitted to the Treasury Committee on the Economic Impact of Coronavirus) (No. EIC0792). Coventry University.

Peffers, K., Tuunanen, T., Rothenberger, M.A., Chatterjee, S., 2007. A Design Science Research Methodology for Information Systems Research. Journal of Management Information Systems 24, 45–77. https://doi.org/10.2753/MIS0742-1222240302

Peffers, K., Rothenberger, M., Tuunanen, T., Vaezi, R., 2012. Design Science Research Evaluation, in: Design Science Research in Information Systems. Advances in Theory and Practice. Springer Berlin Heidelberg, Berlin, Heidelberg, pp. 398–410. https://doi.org/10.1007/978-3-642-29863-9_29

Prat, N., Comyn-Wattiau, I., Akoka, J., 2014. Artifact Evaluation in Information Systems Design Science Research - A Holistic View. Presented at the Proceedings - Pacific Asia Conference on Information Systems, PACIS 2014, p. 16.

Phuttima, S., Rueangsirasak, W., Chaisricharoen, R., 2014. Fraud Detection System for Steel Logistic SME Business on Cloud Services Model. Presented at the 2014 4th Joint International Conference on Information and Communication Technology, Electronic and Electrical Engineering (JICTEE), IEEE, Chiang Rai, Thailand. https://doi.org/10.1109/JICTEE.2014.6804088

Ponemon, 2017. 2017 State of Cybersecurity in Small & Medium-Sized Businesses (SMB). Ponemon Institute LLC.

Pouwels, A.C.J., 2022. Combating fraud and protecting the EU's financial interests | Fact Sheets on the European Union | European Parliament [WWW Document]. URL https://www.europarl.europa.eu/factsheets/en/sheet/32/combating-fraud-and-protecting-the-eu-s-financial-interests (accessed 3.10.23).

Ritchie, D., 2021. Cyber insecurity—Resliience for the new normal. CIR—Continuity Insurance & Risk 16–19.

Roden, D.M., Cox, S.R., Kim, Joung Yeon, 2016. THE FRAUD TRIANGLE AS APREDICTOR OF CORPORATE FRAUD. Academyof Accounting and Financial Studies Journal 20, 80–92.

Schöber, P., Schmitz, P., 2020. Hochkonjunktur für die Schatten-IT [WWW Document]. IT-Business. URL https://www.it-business.de/hochkonjunktur-fuer-die-schatten-it-a-973554 (accessed 10.23.20).

Schuster, H., 2021. Schatten-IT im Homeoffice gefährdet Unternehmens-IT [WWW Document]. IT-Business. URL https://www.it-business.de/schatten-it-im-homeoffice-gefaehrdet-unternehmens-it-a-1010689 (accessed 3.29.21).

Sein, Henfridsson, Purao, Rossi, Lindgren, 2011. Action Design Research. MIS Quarterly 35, 37–56. https://doi.org/10.2307/23043488

Soomro, Z.A., Ahmed, J., Shah, M.H., Khoumbati, K., 2019. Investigating identity fraud management practices in e-tail sector: a systematic review. JEIM 32, 301–324. https://doi.org/10.1108/JEIM-06-2018-0110

Spindler, M., Kögel, H., 2020. Erkennung von Versicherungsbetrug mit künstlicher Intelligenz (Faktenpapier No.9), AI: Science over Fiction. Bitkom Bundesverband Informationswirtschaft, Telekommunikation und neue Medien e.V., Berlin.

Tazilah, M.D.A.B.K., Hussain, N.B.C., 2015. The Importance of Internal Control in SMEs: Fraud Prevention & Detection. Presented at the International Conference on Business, Accounting, Finance, and Economics (BAFE 2015), Malaysia.

The MEP National Network, 2020. MANUFACTURERS GUIDE TO CYBERSECURITY—For Small and Medium-Sized Manufacturers.

Trierweiler, M.K., 2022. IT-based Fraud Management Approaches in Small and Medium Enterprises—A Multivocal Literature Review, in: Wirtschaftsinformatik 2022 Proceedings. Presented at the 17th International Conference on Wirtschaftsinformatik (WI22), Nürnberg, Germany.

Trierweiler, M.K., 2021. Development of an IT-supported Anti-Fraud-Framework for SMEs: An Architectural Concept for Risk Management Using the 'Man-Technology-Organization' Approach, in: CEUR Workshop Proceedings of 7th International Workshop on Socio-Technical Perspective in IS Development (STPIS'21), Trento, Italy, pp. 204–215.

U. S. Government Accountability Office, 2015. A Framework for Managing Fraud Risks in Federal Programs | U.S. GAO [WWW Document]. URL https://www.gao.gov/products/gao-15-593sp (accessed 3.11.23).

Ulich, E., 2013. Arbeitssysteme als Soziotechnische Systeme—eine Erinnerung. Journal Psychologie des Alltagshandelns 6.

Umar, H., Partahi, D., Purba, R.B., 2020. Fraud Diamond Analysis In Detecting Fraudulent Financial Report. IJSTR 9, 6638–6646.

Venable, J., Pries-Heje, J., Baskerville, R., 2012. A Comprehensive Framework for Evaluation in Design Science Research, in: Peffers, K., Rothenberger, M., Kuechler, B. (Eds.), Design Science Research in Information Systems. Advances in Theory and Practice: 7th International Conference, DESRIST 2012. Springer Berlin Heidelberg, Berlin, Heidelberg, pp. 423–438. https://doi.org/10.1007/978-3-642-29863-9_31

vom Brocke, J., Buddendick, C., 2006. Reusable Conceptual Models-Requirements Based on the Design Science Research Paradigm. Presented at the DERIST 2006, Claremont, CA, USA.

Vona, L.W., 2008. Fraud risk assessment: building a fraud audit program. J. Wiley & Sons, Hoboken, NJ.

Wells, J.T., 2001. Enemies Within. Journal of Accountancy 192, 31–35.

Wells, J.T., 2014. Principles of fraud examination, Fourth edition. ed. Wiley, Hoboken, NJ.

Wieringa, R.J., 2014. Design science methodology for information systems and software engineering. Springer Berlin Heidelberg, New York, NY.

Wolfe, D.T., Hermanson, D.R., 2004. The Fraud Diamond: Considering the Four Elements of Fraud. CPA Journal 74.12, 38–42.

Yearwood, L.D.A., 2011. A Conceptual Framework for the Prevention and Detection of Occupational Fraud in Small Businesses (Master Thesis). Concordia University College of Alberta, Alberta Canada.

Digital Infrastructure, Internet of Things and CPS

Designing Digital Infrastructures for Industrial Data Ecosystems—A Literature Review

Anna Maria Schleimer and Estelle Duparc

Abstract Data ecosystems are driven by political and market demands but face strong barriers that require their own socio-technical infrastructure for their realization. In particular, the Industrial Internet of Things (IIoT) has distinct characteristics and requirements for software-based IIoT data ecosystem infrastructures to facilitate inter-organizational, trusted data sharing and value creation. However, the design and purposeful management of infrastructures are challenging, as they emerge organically. To identify opportunities and foundations for design knowledge contributions, this study assesses in a structured literature review a total of 415 papers about digital infrastructures for their applicability to data ecosystem settings considering data as main asset, data sovereignty, trust, and common value propositions. The findings suggest that industrial data ecosystems and digital infrastructure research are so far not connected, despite some implicit overlaps exist. Therefore, a research agenda is presented as well as a concept matrix with the main findings from existing infrastructural research.

Keywords Data ecosystem · Digital infrastructures · Data infrastructure · IIoT · Industrial data

1 Introduction

How to "work collaboratively and deal with industrial exposure, competitive advantages and confidentiality issues?" stated the World Economic Forum (2020, 8) when outlining the main challenges to accelerate the impact of the Industrial Internet

A. M. Schleimer (✉)
Data Business, Fraunhofer Institute for Software and Systems Engineering ISST, Dortmund, Germany
e-mail: anna.schleimer@isst.fraunhofer.de; anna.schleimer@tu-dortmund.de

A. M. Schleimer · E. Duparc
Chair of Industrial Information Management, TU Dortmund, Dortmund, Germany
e-mail: estelle.duparc@tu-dortmund.de

D. Beverungen et al. (eds.), *Solutions and Technologies for Responsible Digitalization*, Lecture Notes in Information Systems and Organisation 75,
https://doi.org/10.1007/978-3-031-80122-8_18

of Things (IIoT), especially for small and medium enterprises. The IIoT concept has traditionally a strong focus on modern sensor technology and hardware data collecting devices since IIoT builds upon the Internet of Things (IoT), "where common objects are regarded as things connected to an information internet" (Zhang et al. 2020, 1). Despite the traditionally strong emphasis on hardware, software and data processing aspects are key factors for IIoT success nowadays. The importance of software is reflected by the observation that "key revenue activities associated with IoT deal with platforms, applications and services", whereas the hardware segment decreased to only 30% (CBI June 2022; Jovanovic 2023). The following example outlines the benefits: Highly-connected IIoT devices enable companies in the logistic sector to "easily track their drivers' activities, vehicles' locations, and all goods' delivery status through a real-time logistics management system supported by heterogeneous networks and wide-deployed IIoT devices" (Huang et al. 2021, 1416–1417). This example illustrates that most scenarios cross enterprise boundaries and connect large system landscapes. Even complete data assets are not isolated, but may belong to multiple organizations and systems embedded in larger scenarios (Baars et al. 2021, 1). Hence, the implementation of the "new era [of] industrial system[s] requests a continuous chain of data sharing [...]" with data flowing among multiple parties (Zheng and Cai 2020, 968). But particularly the issues of data protection and security are impeding the realization of many promising application scenarios (Huang et al. 2021; Zheng and Cai 2020). Further, most existing ecosystems are predominantly created around a focal company (Baars et al. 2021, 2), raising strategic and business political concerns. To avoid dependencies and centralistic power structures, fair and balanced ecosystem approaches without an implicit "winner-takes-all" mentality gain increasingly attention (Wang 2021, 421).

Data ecosystems tackle these challenges by providing "infrastructures for the secure and reliable data exchange among organizations" (Capiello et al. 2020, 66). Within data ecosystems, data sovereignty is a key aspect, especially when it comes to sensitive industrial data (Jarke 2020; e.g., Gelhaar and Otto 2020). Recently, multiple consortia and initiatives emerged to build industrial data ecosystems (e.g., Catena-X 2023; Manufacturing-X 2022). The ecosystem viewpoint allows a peculiarly perspective on IIoT "in the light of joint value creation" (Adner and Kapoor 2010, 329). Thus, especially in the industrial sector, where IIoT technologies are being leveraged, the proliferation of data ecosystems across an organization requires a dedicated software infrastructure. Infrastructures are a new type of Information Systems (IS) artifact, and their scope extends far beyond individual systems. A traditional single-system view is "no longer sufficient to describe the challenges managers and chief information officers (CIOs) face today" (Fürstenau et al. 2019, 1319; Tilson et al. 2011). Thus, the 21st Century declares the "age of the digital infrastructure" (Elaluf-Calderwood et al. 2011, 1; Tilson et al. 2011). Infrastructures remain mostly invisible and become evident when they fail (Star and Ruhleder 1996)—or are lacking as in the case of data ecosystems for IIoT. Therefore, a strong need exists for knowledge about digital infrastructures for IIoT data ecosystems. In order to gather the existing knowledge from generic research on digital infrastructures and pave a way for future contributions, we pose the following research question:

What are white spots in existing research about industrial digital infrastructure for data ecosystems?

This paper is structured as follows: After introducing the topic (1), the background Sect. (2) provides fundamentals of industrial data ecosystems (2.1) and digital infrastructure (2.2). The following Sect. (3) describes the method and process steps of the structured literature review. The resulting findings are presented in form of a concept matrix (4) and discussed afterwards (5). An agenda for future research presents the conclusions of the white spot assessment (6.1) followed by the summary including the contributions and limitations (6.2).

2 Background

2.1 Industrial Data Ecosystems

Generally speaking, ecosystems describe "a group of interacting firms that depend on each other's activities" (Jacobides et al. 2018, 2256). More concrete and from a strategic perspective, ecosystems are a structure of a "multilateral set of partners that need to interact in order for a focal value proposition to materialize" (Adner 2017, 42). While ecosystems are often understood as loose affiliations to a focal organization, the structural view focuses on "activities and actors over which [a] focal organization may have no control, and with whom they have no direct contact" (Adner 2017, 44). Data ecosystems are a special form of ecosystems, where the particular challenges and concerns about data in inter-organizational settings are addressed. While software and hardware infrastructure remain important aspects as well, data ecosystems emphasize data as standalone-asset and "data-based resource[s], such as datasets and data sources" (Oliveira and Lóscio 2018, 7). Data ecosystems are defined as "a set of networks composed by autonomous actors that directly or indirectly consume, produce or provide data and other related resources" where each "actor performs one or more roles and is connected to other actors through relationships, in such a way that actors collaboration and competition promotes Data Ecosystem self-regulation" (Oliveira and Lóscio 2018, 4). The connection between autonomous actors is fundamentally based on their own interests or business models (Oliveira and Lóscio 2018, 7). These actors are usually understood as individual organizations who are competing yet cooperating and have a so-called co-opetition relationship with each other (Tiwana 2014). Within an IIoT context, actors can also describe autonomous devices that interact to exchange information. For example, a group of sensors that share data depending on their location and applicable legislation, or different policies defined by their different owners. Industrial data have characteristics, that challenge the technical and organizational design of data ecosystems. They are of high value and, thus, highly protected private data, as well as often heterogeneous types, may include time-sensitive streaming data, as well as occur in large volumes (Dai et al. 2020). This is in contrast to, for example, static geographical map data, or publicly available open data.

2.2 Digital Infrastructures

While the term infrastructure is often used to just describe one particular hardware technology, such as broadband services, digital infrastructures are a dedicated concept to emphasize socio-technical perspectives on"a new stage in the evolution of IT" and emphasize how "IT has become deeply socially embedded, and is coordinated across diverse socio-technical worlds" (Tilson et al. 2011, 26). The six characteristics of [information] infrastructures are being enabling, shared, open, socio-technical, heterogeneous, and building upon an installed base (Hanseth and Monteiro 1998, 10). Infrastructures are not sharply defined "through a distinct set of functions" nor have "strict boundaries" like applications (Tilson et al. 2011, 26). Instead, they are system collectives enabling generativity. This way, infrastructures support or enable a wide range of functionalities in contrast to being tied to single, strictly defined application scenarios (Hanseth and Monteiro 1998, 10).

Different research streams emerged to deal with the genesis of digital infrastructures and have different assumptions about their emergence: In the network view, a designer or policy maker "would seek to facilitate translation of interests and technology inscriptions" (Koutsikouri et al. 2017, 4714) following actor-network thinking (Callon 1984; Latour 1987). Second, the complexity perspective emphasizes the "adaptation processes of heterogeneous actors" (e.g., Braa et al. 2007). Third, the relational view focuses on a "community of practice" and sense-making (Koutsikouri et al. 2017, 4714; Vaast and Walsham 2009). In summary, active design as a form of intervention in an evolution is treated with skepticism because infrastructures are understood as emergent, evolutionary, and therefore not fully controllable or manageable phenomena. In 2010, Hanseth and Lyytinen (2010) formulated a design theory in the form of design principles for information infrastructures to address especially early growth and bootstrap problems[1] (Koutsikouri et al. 2017, 4714).

With regard to a dedicated infrastructure for data as main asset, a commonly used definition for data infrastructure does not exist. Swanson (2021, 3) states "that data becomes infrastructure when its provision is consolidated in a network open to a community of use". Others define the derm data infrastructure according to Bharadwaj (2000) in a resource-based-view perspective as a "technological resource consisting of hardware and software components that are necessary for collecting, storing, processing, analyzing, and sharing data and information across the organization" (Madhala et al. 2022, 4). Following this preliminary work, as a

[1] According to (Koutsikouri et al. 2017, 4714), the design principles can be summarized as "design initially for usefulness; build upon existing installed bases; expand installed base by persuasive tactics to gain momentum; make the design of IT capability as simple as possible; and modularize the digital infrastructure" (Hanseth and Lyytinen 2010).

working definition, we define the term data infrastructures in this article from a data ecosystem perspective as a socio-technical structure necessary for collecting, storing, processing, analyzing, and in particular sharing data and information across organizations. Despite some research streams follow the perspective that an infrastructure, including those for data, can not be actively designed and shaped, an infrastructure for data is "an effortful accomplishment" (Swanson 2021, 5). It requires purposeful action and investment. Thus, an active design is necessary to progress and satisfy user and market demands.

3 Structured Literature Review

To analyze existing knowledge on digital infrastructure design, this study performs a structured literature review (Webster and Watson 2002). This research method creates replicable findings in a systematic approach and requires a process documentation of each step during the data collection and analysis. A five-step approach following the one of vom Brocke et al. (2009) structures the process: The definition of the review scope (I), the conceptualization of the topic (II), literature search (III), literature analysis and synthesis (IV), and future research agenda (V).

To clearly define the review scope (I), we employ the taxonomy after Cooper (1988). The study focusses on research outcomes, (design) theories, and applications (such as managerial knowledge) regarding the design of data ecosystems. The goal is to apply existing knowledge of digital infrastructures to data ecosystems design. To this end, we conduct an exhaustive, selective, and structured literature review from a neutral perspective. The study addresses specialized scholars of IS and engineering, but also practitioners in the field of data sharing, data management, and data ecosystems who are concerned with socio-technial aspects fo their implementation.

Second, the outline of the most fundamental concepts, as well as challenges and terms provides an overview of the topic (II). Recent journal papers and conference proceedings that deal with the topic of digital infrastructures and data ecosystems provide such insights. Additionally, a backward-search of most relevant articles led to an overview of key issues and concepts.

In the third step (III), we searched for the keywords "data infrastructure" and "software infrastructure" in the title, abstract, and keywords of A- and B-ranked journals as well as relevant IS conferences listed in the scopus or AISEL databases. Since these results are not comprehensive, the search was extended to the more general search string "digital infrastructure". The terms mentioned were searched for individually, because there were none to very limited search results returned when combined directly with the term "data ecosystem".

Afterwards (IV), the literature analysis and synthesis started with a screening of abstracts. The selected articles provide insights into the design of digital infrastructures or their particular characteristics in mechanisms like evolution, creation, emergence, or implementation. Papers that did not focus on the standalone concepts

Table 1 Search result metrics

Database	Search String in abstract and title	Results	Refined	Selected
AISEL + Scopus	Data infrastructure	20	7	3
	Software infrastructure	4	2	2
	Digital infrastructure	391	108	36
Total		415	117	41

of "digital infrastructure", "data infrastructure", or "software infrastructure" were dismissed.

Additionally, also papers without inter-organizational settings or large enterprises were discarded. For example, those papers that solely focused on single technologies such as broadband, or isolated applications. Also, articles that do not contain research results but were still identified through the search mechanisms, such as tables of contents or planned research projects, are not helpful in answering the research question and are therefore discarded. The colloquial and interdisciplinary use of the term "digital infrastructure" leads to many non-target articles. Therefore, step four is repeated to exclude further irrelevant articles based on a detailed analysis of the content. The result is the detailed analysis presented as concept matrix (Webster and Watson 2002), described in the following Sect. 4. The structured literature review concludes with a research agenda (V), presented in Sect. 6.1. The research agenda provides the basis for enhancing or developing the identified whitespots.

See Table 1.

4 Concept Matrix

A coding process was used to assess the identified literature in a concept matrix. In the matrix, contributions containing direct characteristics or application scenarios of data ecosystems are marked with an "x". As well, implicit references to data ecosystems frequently occurred, which are marked with a bracketed "(x)". Next to the direct occurrence of the data ecosystem concept, further related concepts were identified: Value proposition as a pre-requisite, active infrastructure design activities, passive evolution or emergence activities, data assets, data sovereignty, and trust: The term "value proposition" refers to a joint value proposition that is addressed by the infrastructure according to the structural understanding by Adner (2017). Then, the keywords about active and passive design outlines whether the assumption of an organic, rather passive evolving infrastructural emergence and evolution is assumed, or if more active design and influence activities exist (as summarized, e.g., by Koutsikouri et al. 2017). Further, the focus on data as standalone-asset and accompanying concepts relevant for data ecosystems, namely data sovereignty and trust, are assessed (Capiello et al. 2020; Oliveira and Lóscio 2018). To further understand the context of the findings, also the domain of focus is noted. The complete result table can be requested online.[2] Table 2 presents an shortened version due to space restrictions. It includes all entries with at least three relevant data ecosystem related findings.

5 Discussion

The results show that none of the studies on digital infrastructure deal in depth and explicitly with data ecosystems, and few address IIoT scenarios. However, indirectly the characteristics or challenges of data ecosystems become. For example, some papers refer to a "digital jungle" (Zimmer et al. 2019; Niemimaa and Zimmer 2020), which which accounts for the heterogeneity, openness and loose coupling of ecosystem members. The following section provides a comprehensive, non-exhaustive outline of the main findings that are relevant in IIoT data ecosystem context. Next to adressing management and design issues, which make the most of all findings, also some findings relate to software and technological emergence issues.

5.1 Design and Management Findings

With regard to the ability to control and manage infrastructures in an innovation setting, Bygstad et al. (2017, 11) find that solutions were not simply implemented in a top-down manner, rather they resulted from continuous innovation and negotiation. Similarly, Osmundsen and Bygstad (2022, 158) identify how infrastructures are continuously developed and how interactions between different organizational roles are designed to make or give sense. To further analyze the negotiations, Elaluf-Calderwood et al. (2011) address large-scale networks of different organizations through a lense of tussles and control points to study collaboration, conflict, and control in digital infrastructures (Elaluf-Calderwood et al. 2011, 3–4). They note that "Cyberlaw scholars [are] concerned with the legal regulation of the Internet against abuse [and are going to] provide a complementary view of infrastructure development" through modalities such as laws, social norms, markets, and architecture or code (Elaluf-Calderwood et al. 2011, 6; Lessig 2000). These observations are also reflected in the data ecosystem field, as many development activities are pursued in associations' working groups and consortia dealing with legal and architectural topics (e.g., IDSA 2023).

Specific growth tactics are suggested by Koutsikouri et al. (2018, 1014) in the form of adding services, inventing processes, opening identifiers, and providing interfaces. Augustsson et al. (2019) focus on managerial challenges in the form of the effects of control efforts and drifts. Their findings highlight that "infrastructure evolution cannot be separated from changes related to customers and resources" (Augustsson

[2] https://bit.ly/WI23-conceptmatrix-DI.

Table 2 Shortened concept matrix

Author	Value proposition	[Active] Infrastructure Design & innovation	[Passive]Infrastructure evolution or emergence	Data asset focus	Data ecosystem	Data sovereignty	Trust	Domain
Andersen and Bogusz (2017)		(x)	(x)		(x)			Finance, blockchain
Andersen and Bogusz (2019)		(x)	(x)		(x)			Finance, blockchain
Augustsson et al. (2019)	(x)	x	x					IT service industry
Blaschke et al. (2016)	x	(x)			x			–
Bygstad and Hanseth (2018)	(x)	x			(x)			Healthcare
Bygstad and Øvrelid (2020)	(x)		x		(x)			Healthcare
Bygstad et al. (2017)	(x)		x		(x)			Healthcare
Drechsler et al. (2022b)	(x)	x	x		(x)			IIoT, manufacturing
Drechsler et al. (2022a)		x	x		(x)			IIoT, manufacturing
Elaluf-Calderwood et al. (2011)	x	x		(x)	(x)		(x)	Mobile telecommunication
Hanseth and Modol (2021)		(x)	x		(x)		(x)	Healthcare
Knol et al. (2014)		x		x	(x)		x	Logistics, sea cargo

(continued)

Table 2 (continued)

Author	Value proposition	[Active] Infrastructure Design & innovation	[Passive]Infrastructure evolution or emergence	Data asset focus	Data ecosystem	Data sovereignty	Trust	Domain
Koutsikouri et al. (2017)	(x)	(x)	x		(x)			Public transportation
Madhala et al. (2022)	x	(x)		x	(x)			Cross-industry
Miller et al. (2011)	(x)					x	x	–
Osmundsen and Bygstad (2022)	(x)	x	x					Energy
Slavova and Constantinides (2017)	x	x		(x)	(x)			Energy
Spagnoletti et al. (2022)			(x)	(x)	(x)			Online black markets
Swanson (2021)	x	x	x	x	(x)			–
Tilson et al. (2011)			x		(x)		(x)	Mobile operating systems
Ure et al. (2009)		x	(x)		x	(x)		Healthcare
Zorina and Dutton (2021)	(x)	(x)			(x)			Residential Internet

et al. 2019, 71). For a deeper understanding of the role of contextual factors, Koutsikouri et al. (2017, 4718) consider contextual triggers as important. They identify three contextual triggers for infrastructure evolution, namely “adding service value”, “creating design attractors”, and “lowering infrastructure barriers” (Koutsikouri et al. 2017, 4722). These findings are relevant for the data ecosystems field, as many activities are started with specific economic motivations that depend on a concrete market situation, for example, the Gaia-X association that responds to a market “dominated by a few players offering a hyper-verticalised model” (Gaia-X AISBL 2023). From a more technical perspective, Henfridsson and Bygstad (2013) identify configurations of the contextual conditions “loosely coupled architecture” and “decentralized control” that lead to mechanisms of scaling, adoption, and innovation. Fürstenau et al. (2019, 1335) tackle the issue of embeddedness and find three processes that embed systems in digital infrastructures. They identify a parallel process, a competitive process, and a spanning process of different systems in relation to their digital infrastructure. Other studies emphasize how architectural and governance choices evolve during a project’s trajectory. They imply a need to “simultaneously align policy goals, partners’ expectations, market availability, and resources” (Kempton et al. 2020). The focus on architectural configuration and implication of architectural design are apparent in data ecosystem studies as well, as the concept brings along concrete distributed architecture concepts with organizational implications (e.g., Curry 2020).

5.2 *Software-Related Findings*

In addition to the management-oriented findings, some articles also observe software and technology-oriented aspects. Fink et al. (2020, 252) address software libraries, that emerge as digital infrastructure. The standardized code packages become boundary resources when they are offered outside of an organization. Andersen and Bogusz (2019, 16) emphasize how development practices, especially code forking in open-source projects, lead to new organizing practices. This is in particular interesting for data infrastructures, as they mainly base on software and code with a strong emphasis on open-source software. To focus on the particular characteristics of data, Swanson (2021, 8) suggests a conceptual framework for data infrastructures divided between two main pillars of usage and provision. In direct relation to the ecosystem lens, Blaschke et al. (2016, 2) mention the changing situation towards service ecosystems and argue that digital infrastructures have to be more closely examined in this context. The study provides six theoretical foundations of digital infrastructure on the theoretical basis of service-dominant logic and complexity theory. The identified theoretical bases are integrity, elasticity, and ambidexterity (Blaschke et al. 2016, 8,9). Also, Zorina and Dutton (2021, 159) suggest four types of symbiotic and parasitic interactions to elaborate on the distinctive development paths in ecologies of multiple actions that can be transferred to IIoT data ecosystems. Other studies draw conclusions from studying the infrastructure of online black markets, which “operate in absence of formal rules, legal protection, social legitimacy and despite conflicting goals among actors" (Spagnoletti et al. 2022, 1811). With their unique setting of aversive forces "and a negative global impact of its social outcomes" (Spagnoletti et al. 2022, 1812), they are very specific cases. Yet, in their technology and governance structures, they show some features of data ecosystems, which are automated networks for data exchange in a zero-trust setting as well. One identified mechanism is the commoditization of widely diffused services that attract new buyers and vendors, as well as ensuring the security of transactions through decentralized systems due to the absence of a central actor, who is trusted by all parties (Spagnoletti et al. 2022, 1820).

However, few articles refer explicitly to the value derived by an infrastructure. Madhala et al. (2022, 5) suggest data, data-related human resources, and data infrastructure as precedent to data analytics capabilities and, thus, business performance. Bygstad et al. (2017, 11) found that digital infrastructure can support process innovation, while at the same time process innovation also aids the digital infrastructure yet seeing them as conflicting forces.

6 Conclusions

6.1 Research Agenda

The findings show that none of the articles mention data ecosystems as a dedicated goal for their designed infrastructure. While some indirect descriptions of data ecosystems concepts are evident, such as, for example, data sharing and interorganizational settings, the knowledge mostly targets a focal company instead of a complete network. Also, IIoT settings are rare. Especially, aspects of data sovereignty and trust, that are related to policy management and interoperability, as well as privacy and security, are missing so far. Even if studies refer to settings around organizations, the involved parties are implicitly different departments or affiliated users. In an IIoT context, the different actors can also be agents in the form of devices or services owned by competing parties, that have to be organized with an appropriate data infrastructure. The analysis of existing literature leads to five categories of topics that research about IIoT data ecosystems should address. The identified concepts can be a starting point for further studies of infrastructures from a data ecosystem perspective.

Active data ecosystem design towards data infrastructures

- Purposeful design knowledge is required to build and shape data infrastructures, despite they are not in full managerial control.
- The unit of analysis and design needs to be the shared value proposition and ecosystem without having a single focal company as (implicit) main actor.

- The particular characteristics of data assets and required tools for managing, sharing, and ensuring trust in zero-trust settings need to be elaborated.
- The high needs for automatization, scalability, and reliability should be examined in design knowledge.
- The foundational concept "data infrastructure" needs to be carefully defined and delineated from generic infrastructure perspectives.
- Discussion on suitable organizational forms and process models to pursue data infrastructure design activities have to be assessed.

Trust and data sovereignty

- The aspects of trust and informed decisions in data ecosystems need to be addressed not only from social policy or political perspectives but also from a technology and IS design perspective.
- The socio-technical processes of providing information that enables trustful, autonomous, and decentral decisions have to be elaborated.
- A connection between legal and technology-oriented fields is required to elaborate on how regulations or incentives can fuel infrastructural dynamics.

Software infrastructure

- The software development and standardization process for data infrastructure purposes needs to be better understood as infrastructures are different from closed applications or single functionalities. For example, to satisfy longevity or standardization demands.
- The characteristics of inter-organizational, infrastructural software development have to be better understood, such as the role of open-source projects or different, heterogeneous implementations of the same infrastructural components.
- The difference between software infrastructure in contrast to hardware-dominated infrastructure needs to be understood to enable purposeful research on their design challenges. For example, they might have different financing demands as their re-use demands low marginal costs.

Value orientation

- For a purposeful design of infrastructures for data ecosystems, the common value proposition should be clearly formulated and measurable.
- Dangerous and costly deadlock situations in design processes need to be understood and avoided. Mechanisms to align shared interests are required, in the face of conflicting or contrary demands.

Domain-specific knowledge

- The particular characteristics of the industrial domain, especially IIoT devices as participants in ecosystems, need to be understood.
- The domain-relevant legislation (e.g., data privacy) and its implications have to be incorporated in socio-technical infrastructure designs.

- For different domains, different infrastructure needs might exist.

7 Summary and Limitations

In sum, the findings show that the design issues of infrastructures are a relevant topic in IS research, especially since the last two decades. However, in light of the design needs for data ecosystems in the industrial domain using IIoT technologies, the findings often remain too general or are not addressing key targets. This presents a wide path for future research, to further elaborate on the particularities of industrial data in data ecosystems and the design of software-dominated infrastructures. In terms of scientific contributions, our research addresses the conceptual blurriness around "digital infrastructure", "software infrastructure", and "data infrastructure" by explaining and connecting them. Thus, the structured literature review provides a synthesis of the findings of multiple studies from the infrastructure research stream. The outlined findings can aid practitioners and researchers, especially from the industrial data ecosystem community, in design processes by pointing to a selection of relevant studies. Furthermore, the research agenda forms a basis for future research addressing the design of industrial data ecosystems and sheds light on the existing whitespots. Future researchers are pointed towards the remaining knowledge gaps. In terms of managerial contributions, the comprehensive summary provides purposeful insights into findings from the field of digital infrastructure that can be applied to industrial data ecosystem projects. The results illustrate the challenges and approaches towards inter-company, data-driven value creation. Thus, the results support companies in creating new possibilities of value co-creation based on a distinct infrastructure for IIoT data assets based on shared interests and values.

The limitations of this study are on the one hand due to the often imprecise use of the word infrastructure, which challenges to find dedicated articles according to our definition. Especially, when no further definition or description of the infrastructure understanding was given. Additionally, the search process depends on the exact wording, so that deviations in terms or other phrases, such as cyberinfrastructure, infrastructuring, or similar terms might not be included. Additionally, despite pursuing a neutral and systematic literature review, due to human errors the analysis might face some bias and limitations. Future studies could apply automated approaches to solve this.

Acknowledgements This work has been supported by the German Federal Ministry for Economic Affairs and Climate Action in context of the Gaia-X 4 KI project (no. 19A21011E).

References

Adner, Ron (2017). Ecosystem as Structure. Journal of Management 43 (1), 39–58. https://doi.org/10.1177/0149206316678451.

Adner, Ron/Kapoor, Rahul (2010). Value creation in innovation ecosystems: how the structure of technological interdependence affects firm performance in new technology generations. Strategic Management Journal 31 (3), 306–333. https://doi.org/10.1002/smj.821.

Andersen, J. V./Bogusz, Claire Ingram (2017). Patterns of Self-Organising in the Bitcoin Online Community: Code Forking as Organising in Digital Infrastructure. In: Proceedings of the 17th International Conference on Information Systems, ICIS 2017.

Andersen, J. V./Bogusz, Claire Ingram (2019). Self-organizing in blockchain infrastructures: Generativity through shifting objectives and forking. Journal of the Association for Information Systems 20 (9), 11.

Augustsson, N.-P./Nilsson, A./Holmström, J./Mathiassen, L. (2019). Managing digital infrastructures: negotiating control and drift in service provisioning. International Journal of Business Information Systems 30 (1), 51–78. https://doi.org/10.1504/IJBIS.2019.097045.

Baars, Henning/Tank, Ann/Weber, Patrick/Kemper, Hans-Georg/Lasi, Heiner/Pedell, Burkhard (2021). Cooperative Approaches to Data Sharing and Analysis for Industrial Internet of Things Ecosystems. Applied Sciences 11 (16), 7547. https://doi.org/10.3390/app11167547.

Bharadwaj, Anandhi S. (2000). A resource-based perspective on information technology capability and firm performance: an empirical investigation. Mis Quarterly, 169–196.

Blaschke, Michael/Haki, M. Kazem/Riss, Uwe/Winter, Robert/Aier, Stephan (2016). Digital infrastructure: A service-dominant logic perspective. In: Proceedings of the 16th International Conference on Information Systems, ICIS 2016, Dublin, Irland.

Braa, J./Hanseth, Ole/Heywood, A./Mohammed, W./Shaw, V. (2007). Developing Health Information Systems in Developing Countries: The Flexible Standards Strategy. Mis Quarterly 31 (2), 381. https://doi.org/10.2307/25148796.

Bygstad, Bendik/Hanseth, Ole (2018). Transforming digital infrastructures through platformization. Proceedings of the 26th European Conference on Information Systems, ECIS 2018.

Bygstad, Bendik/Hanseth, Ole/Siebenherz, A./Øvrelid, E. (2017). Process innovation meets digital infrastructure in a high-tech hospital. Proceedings of the 25th European Conference on Information Systems, ECIS 2017.

Bygstad, Bendik/Øvrelid, E. (2020). Architectural alignment of process innovation and digital infrastructure in a high-tech hospital. European Journal of Information Systems 29 (3), 220–237. https://doi.org/10.1080/0960085X.2020.1728201.

Callon, Michel (1984). Some Elements of a Sociology of Translation: Domestication of the Scallops and the Fishermen of St Brieuc Bay. The Sociological Review 32 (1_suppl), 196–233. https://doi.org/10.1111/j.1467-954X.1984.tb00113.x.

Capiello, Cinzia/Gal, Avigdor/Jarke, Matthias/Rehof, Jakob (2020). Data Ecosystems: Sovereign Data Exchange among Organizations (Dagstuhl Seminar 19391). https://doi.org/10.4230/DagRep.9.9.66.

Catena-X (2023). Catena-X Automotive Network. Available online at https://catena-x.net/ (accessed 3/7/2023).

CBI (2022). The European market potential for (Industrial) Internet of Things. Available online at https://www.cbi.eu/market-information/outsourcing-itobpo/industrial-internet-things/market-potential (accessed 2/16/2022).

Cooper, Harris M. (1988). Organizing Knowledge Syntheses: A Taxonomy of Literature Reviews. Knowledge in Society 1 (1), 104. https://doi.org/10.1007/BF03177550.

Curry, Edward (2020). Real-time Linked Dataspaces : Enabling Data Ecosystems for Intelligent Systems. Springer Nature.

Dai, Hong-Ning/Wang, Hao/Xu, Guangquan/Wan, Jiafu/Imran, Muhammad (2020). Big data analytics for manufacturing internet of things: opportunities, challenges and enabling technologies. Enterprise Information Systems 14 (9-10), 1279–1303. https://doi.org/10.1080/17517575.2019.1633689.

Drechsler, Katharina/Grisold, Thomas/Gau, Michael/Seidel, Stefan (2022a). Digital Infrastructure Evolution: A Digital Trace Data Study. In: Proceedings of the International Conference on Information Systems, ICIS 2022, Kopenhagen, Denmark.

Drechsler, Katharina/Grisold, Thomas/Seidel, Stefan (2022b). Cascading Digital Options and the Evolution of Digital Infrastructures: The Case of IIoT. In: Proceedings of the International Conference on Information Systems, ICIS 2022, Kopenhagen, Denmark.

Elaluf-Calderwood, Silvia/Herzhoff, Jan/Sørensen, Carsten/Eaton, Ben (2011). Mobile digital infrastructure innovation towards a tussle and control framework. 19th European Conference on Information Systems, ECIS 2011.

Fink, Lior/Shao, Jianhua/Lichtenstein, Yossi/Haefliger, Stefan (2020). The ownership of digital infrastructure: Exploring the deployment of software libraries in a digital innovation cluster. Journal of Information Technology 35 (3), 251–269. https://doi.org/10.1177/0268396220936705.

Fürstenau, Daniel/Baiyere, Abayomi/Kliewer, Natalia (2019). A dynamic model of embeddedness in digital infrastructures. Information Systems Research 30 (4), 1319–1342.

Gaia-X AISBL (2023). Vision and Mission. The demand in practice. Available online at https://gaia-x.eu/what-is-gaia-x/vision-and-mission/ (accessed 4/3/2023).

Gelhaar, Joshua/Otto, Boris (2020). Challenges in the Emergence of Data Ecosystems. In: Proceedings of the Pacific Asia Conference on Information Systems, PACIS 2020, 175.

Hanseth, Ole/Lyytinen, Kalle (2010). Design Theory for Dynamic Complexity in Information Infrastructures: The Case of Building Internet. Journal of Information Technology 25 (1), 1–19. https://doi.org/10.1057/jit.2009.19.

Hanseth, Ole/Modol, Juan Rodon (2021). The dynamics of architecture-governance configurations: an assemblage theory approach. Journal of the Association for Information Systems 22 (1), 5.

Hanseth, Ole/Monteiro, Eric (1998). Understanding information infrastructure. Unpublished Manuscript, Retrieved on 6th September from http://heim.ifi.uio.no/~oleha/Publications/bok.pdf.

Henfridsson, Ola/Bygstad, Bendik (2013). The generative mechanisms of digital infrastructure evolution. MIS Quarterly: Management Information Systems 37 (3), 907–931. https://doi.org/10.25300/MISQ/2013/37.3.11.

Huang, Cheng/Liu, Dongxiao/Ni, Jianbing/Lu, Rongxing/Shen, Xuemin (2021). Achieving Accountable and Efficient Data Sharing in Industrial Internet of Things. IEEE Transactions on Industrial Informatics 17 (2), 1416–1427. https://doi.org/10.1109/TII.2020.2982942.

IDSA (2023). International Data Spaces Association e.V. Available online at https://internationaldataspaces.org/we/the-association/.

Jacobides, Michael G./Cennamo, Carmelo/Gawer, Annabelle (2018). Towards a theory of ecosystems. Strategic Management Journal 39 (8), 2255–2276. https://doi.org/10.1002/smj.2904.

Jarke, Matthias (2020). Data Sovereignty and the Internet of Production. In: Schahram Dustdar/Eric Yu/Camille Salinesi et al. (Eds.). Advanced Information Systems Engineering. Cham, Springer International Publishing, 549–558.

Jovanovic, Bojan (2023). Internet of Things statistics for 2022 - Taking Things Apart. Available online at https://dataprot.net/statistics/iot-statistics/.

Kempton, Alexander Moltubakk/Grisot, Miria/Brænden, Kristin/Aanestad, Margunn (2020). Infrastructural tuning in public-private partnerships.

Knol, Arjan J./Klievink, Bram/Tan, Yao-hua (2014). Data Sharing Issues and Potential Solutions for Adoption of Information Infrastructures: Evidence from a Data Pipeline Project in the Global Supply Chain over Sea. In: Bled eConference, 40.

Koutsikouri, Dina/Henfridsson, Ola/Lindgren, Rikard (2017). Building digital infrastructures: Towards an evolutionary theory of contextual triggers. Proceedings of the Annual Hawaii International Conference on System Sciences 2017-January.

Koutsikouri, Dina/Lindgren, Rikard/Henfridsson, Ola/Rudmark, D. (2018). Extending digital infrastructures: A typology of growth tactics. Journal of the Association for Information Systems 19 (10), 1001–1019. https://doi.org/10.17705/1jais.00517.

Latour, B. (1987). Science in Action: How to Follow Scientists and Engineers Through Society. Harvard University Press.

Lessig, Lawrence (2000). Code and Other Laws of Cyberspace", Basic Books, 1999 Paul M. Schwartz,"BEYOND LESSIG'S CODE FOR INTERNET PRIVACY: CYBERSPACE FILTERS, PRIVACY-CONTROL, AND FAIR INFORMATION PRACTICES". Wisconsin Law Review 2000, 743.

Madhala, Prashanth/Li, Hongxiu/Helander, Nina (2022). Building Data Analytics Capabilities for Value Creation: A Resource-Based View. In: Proceedings of the Pacific Asia Conference on Information Systems, PACIS 2022.

Manufacturing-X (2022). Available online at https://www.plattform-i40.de/IP/Redaktion/DE/Downloads/Publikation/Manufacturing-X.pdf?__blob=publicationFile&v=14.

Miller, John/Hoffmann/David (2011). Sponsoring trust in tomorrow's technology: Towards a global digital infrastructure policy. International Data Privacy Law. https://doi.org/10.1093/idpl/ipr006.

Niemimaa, Marko/Zimmer, Markus Philipp (2020). Cultivating a 'Digital Jungle': Toward a Hybrid Governance Perspective on Infrastructure Evolution. In: Proceedings of the 24th Pacific Asia Conference on Information Systems; PACIS 2020.

Oliveira, Marcelo Iury S./Lóscio, Bernadette Farias (2018). What is a Data Ecosystem? In: Marijn Janssen/Soon Ae Chun/Vishanth Weerakkody (Eds.). Proceedings of the 19th Annual International Conference on Digital Government Research Governance in the Data Age - dgo '18, the 19th Annual International Conference, 30.05.2018 - 01.06.2018. Delft: Netherlands, ACM Press, 1–9.

Osmundsen, Karen/Bygstad, Bendik (2022). Making sense of continuous development of digital infrastructures. Journal of Information Technology 37 (2), 144–164. https://doi.org/10.1177/02683962211046621.

Slavova, Mira/Constantinides, Panayiotis (2017). Digital infrastructures as platforms: The case of smart electricity grids. Proceedings of the 25th European Conference on Information Systems, ECIS 2017.

Spagnoletti, Paolo/Ceci, Federica/Bygstad, Bendik (2022). Online Black-Markets: An Investigation of a Digital Infrastructure in the Dark. Information Systems Frontiers 24 (6), 1811–1826. https://doi.org/10.1007/s10796-021-10187-9.

Star, Susan Leigh/Ruhleder, Karen (1996). Steps Toward an Ecology of Infrastructure: Design and Access for Large Information Spaces. Information Systems Research 7 (1), 111–134. https://doi.org/10.1287/isre.7.1.111.

Swanson, E. Burton (2021). When Data Becomes Infrastructure and Our Lives Depend On It. In: ECIS 2021 Research Papers.

Tilson, David/Sørensen, Carsten/Lyytinen, Kalle (2011). The paradoxes of change and control in digital infrastructures: The mobile operating systems case. Proceedings of the 10th International Conference on Mobile Business, ICMB 2011. https://doi.org/10.1109/ICMB.2011.45.

Tiwana, Amrit (2014). Platform ecosystems. Aligning architecture, governance, and strategy. Amsterdam, Elsevier/MK Morgan Kaufmann.

Ure, Jenny/Procter, Rob/Lin, Yu-Wei/Hartswood, Mark/Anderson, Stuart/Lloyd, Sharon/Wardlaw, Joanna/Gonzalez-Velez, Horacio/Ho, Kate (2009). The development of data infrastructures for eHealth: A socio-technical perspective. Journal of the Association for Information Systems 10 (5), 415–429. https://doi.org/10.17705/1jais.00197.

Vaast, Emmanuelle/Walsham, Geoff (2009). Trans-Situated Learning: Supporting a Network of Practice with an Information Infrastructure. Information Systems Research 20 (4), 547–564. https://doi.org/10.1287/isre.1080.0228.

vom Brocke, Jan/Simons, Alexander/Niehaves, Bjorn/Reimer, Kai/Plattfaut, Ralf/Cleven, Anne (2009). Reconstructing the Giant: On the Importance of Rigour in Documenting the Literature Search Process. In: Proceedings of the 17th European Conference on Information Systems. Verona: Italy.

Wang, Ping (2021). Connecting the Parts with the Whole: Toward an Information Ecology Theory of Digital Innovation Ecosystems. MIS quarterly 45 (1), 397–422. https://doi.org/10.25300/MISQ/2021/15864.

Webster, Jane/Watson, Richard T. (2002). Analyzing the past to prepare for the future: Writing a literature review. Mis Quarterly (26(29), xiii–xxiii.

World Economic Forum (2020). Accelerating the Impact of Industrial IoT in Small and Medium-Sized Enterprises: A Protocol for Action. White Paper. Available online at https://www3.weforum.org/docs/WEF_Accelerating_the_Impact_of_IIoT.pdf.

Zhang, Pinjia/Wu, Yang/Zhu, Hongdong (2020). Open ecosystem for future industrial Internet of things (IIoT): Architecture and application. CSEE Journal of Power and Energy Systems. https://doi.org/10.17775/CSEEJPES.2019.01810.

Zheng, Xu/Cai, Zhipeng (2020). Privacy-Preserved Data Sharing Towards Multiple Parties in Industrial IoTs. IEEE Journal on Selected Areas in Communications 38 (5), 968–979. https://doi.org/10.1109/JSAC.2020.2980802.

Zimmer, Markus Philipp/Niemimaa, Marko/Xu D./Jiang J./Kim H.-W. (2019). Navigating in the digital jungle: Articulating combinatory Affordances of digital infrastructures for Collaboration. Proceedings of the 23rd Pacific Asia Conference on Information Systems, PACIS 2019.

Zorina, Aljona/Dutton, William H. (2021). Theorizing actor interactions shaping innovation in digital infrastructures: The case of residential internet development in Belarus. Organization Science 32 (1), 156–180. https://doi.org/10.1287/ORSC.2020.1389.

Software in the Manufacturing Industry: A Review of Security Challenges and Implications

Yannick Landeck, Dian Balta, Martin Wimmer, and Christian Knierim

Abstract Software defines digital infrastructures in the manufacturing industry, connecting services and computation resources to machines and devices. These infrastructures aim at increased flexibility, scalability, and a wider application portfolio for automated manufacturing processes. At the same time, the complexity of securing software increases dramatically. Threats to confidentiality, integrity, and availability of software can result in critical losses for automated industrial production and impact manufacturing companies. In order to map existing and emerging security challenges, we present the results of a hermeneutic literature review structured along abstraction levels and vertical integration of software. Based on this structure, we derive implications for academia and practice focused on system integrators, developers, and security auditors of digital infrastructures. Thereby, we discuss courses of action mapped to software security black boxes, infrastructure heterogeneity, and the adaptation of security for operational usage.

Keywords Software security · Manufacturing · Literature review

1 Introduction

As software is transforming the manufacturing industry, production is increasingly defined by digital infrastructures. Out of this transformation emerges an ecosystem that is comprised of software suppliers for manufacturing processes (cf. e.g. Alcácer

Y. Landeck (✉) · D. Balta
fortiss GmbH, Munich, Germany
e-mail: landeck@fortiss.org

D. Balta
e-mail: balta@fortiss.org

M. Wimmer · C. Knierim
Siemens AG, Munich, Germany
e-mail: martin.r.wimmer@siemens.com

C. Knierim
e-mail: christian.knierim@siemens.com

D. Beverungen et al. (eds.), *Solutions and Technologies for Responsible Digitalization*, Lecture Notes in Information Systems and Organisation 75,
https://doi.org/10.1007/978-3-031-80122-8_19

and Cruz-Machado (2019)) and technological innovations such as infrastructure-as-code (cf. e.g. (Rahman et al., 2019)). Due to the heterogeneity of software suppliers, this ecosystem is similar to established Cloud service platforms like Amazon Web Services[1] or Microsoft Azure.[2]

The transformation increases the dependency of the manufacturing industry on software along two key dimensions. On one hand, the **abstraction of software increases** (cf. e.g. (Baldini et al., 2017)). For instance, software functionality is not defined in a piece of code or imported as a library any more, but rather consumed as an abstract service. On the other hand, the boundaries of **vertical integration of software** are blurring (cf. e.g. (Boyes et al., 2018)). For instance, software controlling a machine can be managed in the Cloud rather than being installed from a disk or a USB stick.

Although both academia and practice have recognised the increasing dependency of manufacturing on software and its consequences in terms of security, no mapping between the aforementioned key dimensions exists. For instance, extant work investigates Cloud computing security (Tabrizchi and Rafsanjani 2020) or analyses the applicability of the IEC 62443 standard (Leander et al. 2019). Furthermore, topics of interest are software supply chain risk management issues (cf. (NIST, 2023)) and the need for a high common level of security in the European Union as constituted in the NIS2 Directive (cf. (Negreiro, 2023)).

To address this shortcoming, we focus on the research question: **What are security challenges and implications for the manufacturing industry in the light of increased abstraction and vertical integration of software?** The paper presents the results of a hermeneutic literature review on security challenges associated to the two dimensions. We derive implications that these challenges will have on the work of salient stakeholders related to software in manufacturing: system integrators, developers, and security auditors. The analysis dimensions and relevant stakeholders were identified by critically assessing the security challenges during our review process (cf. Sect. 3). To argue the implications for stakeholders, we propose courses of action towards current and emerging security challenges.

The paper is structured as follows. In Sect. 2, we describe the background of architectural software patterns, vertical software integration in manufacturing, and software security. In Sect. 3, we describe the methodology we follow. Section 4 frames software security in manufacturing and gives an overview on related literature studies. In Sect. 5, we summarise the security challenges found in our literature review. Section 6 discusses the implications that we derive from our findings and presents courses of actions for stakeholders. Finally, Sect. 7 concludes the paper.

---

[1] https://aws.amazon.com/.

[2] https://azure.microsoft.com/.

2 Background

2.1 Development of Architectural Software Patterns

Architectural software patterns express a fundamental structural organization schema for software systems (Buschmann et al. 1996). There is a recognisable evolution of software architectures from monolithic applications towards microservices and lately minimal coupling of functional components (Dragoni et al. 2017; Leitner et al. 2019).

Software Monoliths: (Dragoni et al., 2017) define a monolith as "a software application whose modules cannot be executed independently". Monoliths are characterised by tight coupling, vertical scaling and strong dependence (Ibrahim et al. 2019). (Lewis and Fowler, 2014) highlight two problems of evolving monoliths: the difficulty to keep a modular structure and that scaling of a module requires scaling of the entire application.

Service-oriented Architecture: Service-oriented architecture (SOA) is structuring software as services which are centered around representing certain business capabilities (Papazoglou 2003). SOA services achieve flexibility by decoupling their interfaces from their implementation (Dragoni et al. 2017).

Microservices emerged as an evolution of SOA. They reduce the complexity of applications and focus on the programming of simple services that effectively implement a single functionality (Dragoni et al. 2017). (Lewis and Fowler, 2014) give a definition of microservices and highlight their characteristics of being organised around business capabilities, characterised by decentralised governance, and designed to evolve.

Minimal Coupling of Functional Components: Function as a Service (FaaS) emerged as an implementation of software architectures that trend towards minimal coupling of functional components (Perez et al. 2019). It separates the writing of application code from the management of its deployment and underlying infrastructures (Bocci et al. 2021). The short-running functions in a FaaS environment are triggered by events, and then executed on-demand in an isolated environment (Leitner et al. 2019).

Development Towards Higher Levels of Software Abstraction: Even prior to the development of FaaS, the shift from monoliths to SOA has introduced new concepts of software abstraction. Thus, systems became more modular and interchangeable (Dragoni et al. 2017). Therefore, monoliths usually represent a **low level**, SOA a **medium level**, and FaaS a **high level** of software abstraction. With increased abstraction, more of the service and function implementation is hidden from other components.

2.2 Vertical Software Integration in Manufacturing

A frequently used model for the hierarchical framing of manufacturing is the **Reference Architectural Model Industrie 4.0 (RAMI 4.0)**. RAMI 4.0 is an abstract three-dimensional reference model capturing the dimensions of system hierarchy levels, information layers, and the lifecycle and value stream (Hankel and Rexroth 2015). "Vertical integration" of information systems refers to the technological support of organisational units across multiple system hierarchy levels of RAMI 4.0, from products and field devices up to enterprise level and the connected world (Jasperneite et al. 2020). Since software plays an essential role in these systems (Hasselbring 2000), we present different technological approaches to **vertical software integration** and analyse their impact on security.

Cloud: The National Institute of Standards and Technology (NIST) defines Cloud computing as "a model for enabling ubiquitous, convenient, on-demand network access to a shared pool of configurable computing resources" (Mell and Grance 2011). These resources (e.g. servers, applications, services) can be rapidly provisioned and released with minimal efforts for management and little service provider interaction (Mell and Grance 2011).

Edge: Edge computing is a paradigm used to move computation to the edge of the network (Donno et al. 2019). It was introduced to leverage Cloud computing infrastructures and process data closer to its source (Shi et al. 2016). Edge computing also presents benefits regarding data security and privacy, since sensitive information stays inside the network boundaries of a company (Roman et al. 2018).

Fog: Fog computing can arguably be considered as an implementation of Edge computing (Donno et al. 2019). It was introduced as an extension to Cloud computing, e.g. through content delivery networks (Shojafar et al. 2017). It provides computation, storage and networking services between end devices, Edge computing and Cloud servers (Roman et al. 2018; Satyanarayanan 2017).

IIoT: The Internet of Things (IoT) comprises the extension of network connectivity and computing capability to devices and sensors (Rose et al. 2015). The Industrial Internet of Things (IIoT) is the use of IoT technologies for the promotion of goals distinctive to industry (Boyes et al. 2018). Academia and practice established several reference architectures (cf. e.g. (Lin et al., 2017)) to describe the integration of IIoT devices, with software playing a major role in these systems.

IACS: Industrial Automation and Control Systems (IACS) or Industrial Control Systems (ICS) is a collective term typically used to describe different control systems (Boyes et al. 2018). In a guide to ICS security, the NIST states that, initially, ICS were isolated systems running proprietary protocols and specialised hardware and software (Stouffer et al. 2014). Since ICS have many characteristics that differ from traditional IT systems, vertically integrating software across hierarchy levels in manufacturing (cf. RAMI 4.0) poses challenges to security (Stouffer et al. 2014).

PERA: The Purdue Enterprise Reference Architecture (PERA) (Williams 1994) is another well-recognised model to frame software in manufacturing environments into hierarchical levels (Chen et al. 2008) and analyse security (cf. e.g. (Zografopoulos et al., 2021)). Levels 0 to 2 of PERA comprise IACS. Level 3 describes manufacturing operation systems for site management. Level 4 consists of systems for business operations, e.g. planning and logistics. Finally, level 5 comprises enterprise service management targeting functionalities such as analytics and reporting (Williams 1994).

2.3 Software Security

(Furnell et al., 2021) indicate a growing trend for senior business management to be held answerable for the reliable and secure operation of their information systems. The manufacturing domain is affected by this trend and is required to guarantee security in the context of technological advances that cause changes to IT infrastructures (Chhetri et al. 2018). Security approaches need to identify risks to critical infrastructures before they are victim to attacks (Chhetri et al. 2018). Information system security is commonly measured by the **CIA triad**: confidentiality, integrity, and availability (Basu et al. 2018; Samonas and Coss 2014). These aspects represent the building blocks for designing secure systems (Zissis and Lekkas 2012).

Confidentiality, often discussed in the context of privacy, refers to security activities that only grant authorised parties or systems access to protected data (Zissis and Lekkas 2012). **Integrity** targets the protection of system assets against modifications that harm information structures, sabotage processes, or reduce the value of data (Samonas and Coss 2014). **Availability** refers to the property of a system being accessible upon demand by an authorised entity and to carry on operations even in atypical situations (Zissis and Lekkas 2012).

With software serving as the foundation of digital infrastructures, the confidentiality, integrity and availability (CIA) triad frames the view on software security. Moreover, the latter needs to be driven by analysing protective mechanisms, assurance, and emerging challenges (Furnell et al. 2021).

3 Methodology

In this paper, we follow a qualitative and hermeneutic research approach (Klein and Myers 1999). Based on the methodology of (Boell and Cecez-Kecmanovic, 2014), we conducted a literature review following the process of two major hermeneutic circles: "*search and acquisition*" and "*analysis and interpretation*". We selected this approach in accordance with (Klein and Myers, 1999), since it suits the nature and context of our research in terms of depth, breadth and heterogeneity of research disciplines involved. We decided against a systematic review (Kitchenham and Charters 2007), since the definition of a comprehensive research question was not feasible at the beginning of our research and the analysis dimensions had to be identified first.

We followed the initial idea of analysing the security challenges of software in manufacturing. Consequently, we entered the "**search and acquisition**" circle to select, acquire, and read literature from the multi-dimensional field of software security (Boell and Cecez-Kecmanovic 2014). We gathered initial input by combining the keywords "security" and "security challenges" with terminology identified in our problem analysis (e.g. Cloud, IIoT, SOA) in Google Scholar. As recommended by (Webster and Watson, 2002), we started with highly cited papers of leading journals (e.g. (Combe et al., 2016; Marin et al., 2022)) and pursued backward and forward search. By this, we identified central terms and main authors of the research field and refined our approach to searching (Boell and Cecez-Kecmanovic 2014).

Next, we entered the "**analysis and interpretation**" circle of the hermeneutic approach. By this, we accumulated knowledge and experience that was used as a starting point for additional "search and acquisition" iterations. As suggested by (Boell and Cecez-Kecmanovic, 2014), there was not a clear timely separation between the two circles. We rather followed an iterative approach towards reaching a point of saturation. After seven iterations, we reached a point of saturation indicated by diminishing novelty (Boell and Cecez-Kecmanovic 2014) regarding the challenges for software security in manufacturing.

The second circle involved a deeper interaction with extant work. It involves the following iterative steps: **(1) reading; (2) mapping and classifying; (3) critical assessment; (4) argument development; (5) research problem/questions; and (6) searching** (Boell and Cecez-Kecmanovic 2014). In total, we read (1) and reviewed 134 publications published between 2005 and 2023. We mapped and classified (2) each publication by identifying major concepts, conceptual frameworks, and historical developments (cf. (Boell and Cecez-Kecmanovic, 2014)) of software security in manufacturing. For instance, the analysis of (Shafiei et al., 2021) motivated us to include the concept of Function as a Service (FaaS) in our next search iteration, since it is crucial for current developments of software architectures.

Next, by critically assessing (3) the security challenges addressed by each publication, we identified the two dimensions of our analysis: abstraction levels and vertical integration of software. Furthermore, we identified a research gap in the lack of intersection coverage in literature when analysing both dimensions and the concept of security (cf. Section 4). Thus, we gained additional knowledge on the research field and applied it to subsequent search iterations. Based on the assessment of literature, we developed arguments (4) on how to address the discovered gap. We gathered security challenges for software in manufacturing and pursued an argumentative-deductive analysis (Wilde and Hess 2007) to derive implications for system integrators, developers, and security auditors. Similar to the analysis dimensions, the relevance of these stakeholders was also identified during the critical assessment of literature.

These implications shaped the research problem/question (5) of our review. In particular, we analysed courses of action for each of the stakeholders addressing software security black boxes, infrastructure heterogeneity, and the adaptation of security for operational usage (as described in Sect. 6). Similar to the preceding steps of the hermeneutic circle, newly generated knowledge and experience influenced the subsequent "*search and acquisition*" (6) circle.

4 Framing Software Security in Manufacturing

4.1 Literature Coverage Along the Two Analysis Dimensions

Figure 1 sketches the coverage in literature for software security in manufacturing. First, it aligns technological approaches to vertical software integration with levels of the PERA model. Our analysis showed that the distinction between operational technology (OT) and information technology (IT) is blurring. For instance, the Industrial Internet of Things (IIoT) is a characteristic concept that is merging the two technologies (Boyes et al. 2018). Nevertheless, the IIoT reflects software systems which are no longer dedicated to one level of the PERA model, but can be vertically integrated from the field level (level 0) up to the enterprise services level (level 5). Second, Fig. 1 presents the intersection coverage in literature regarding security of software abstraction and vertical integration. In this representation, we aggregate software security literature of the PERA levels 3, 4, and 5 since the concepts of Edge and Fog computing complemented by Cloud computing cause software to be vertically integrated already (Donno et al. 2019). A distinct view on security of the individual levels and their coverage in literature is subject of future work, but not in the scope of our research.

Our analysis shows that the security of software monoliths is well discussed since we found an extensive coverage in literature (84 publications) addressing either the challenges of monoliths in particular or software security in general, which we

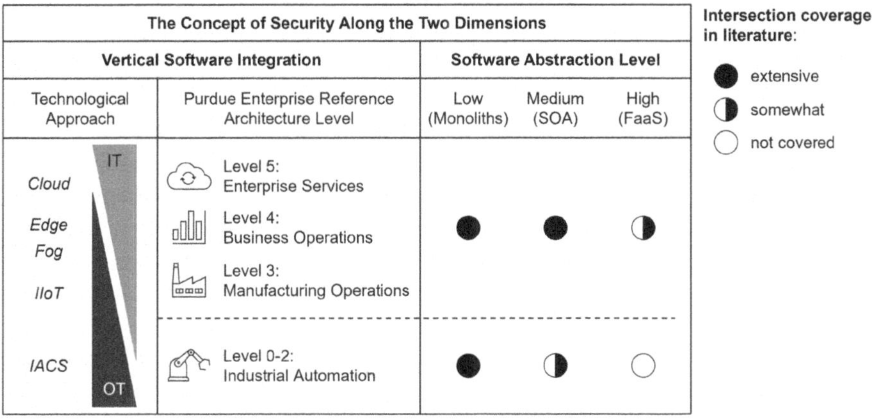

Fig. 1 A sketch of literature coverage on the concept of security for software in manufacturing

assigned to a low abstraction level. For instance, software integration in manufacturing usually requires security to focus more on integrity and availability than on confidentiality. The latter being important on higher integration levels (Tuptuk and Hailes 2018).

SOA (20 publications) is well-established for levels 4 and 5 (Dragoni et al. 2017) and is increasingly integrated on level 3 as well (cf. e.g. (Homay et al., 2019)). We found an extensive coverage in literature regarding security of SOA on these levels. On the contrary, SOA is usually not found on the levels 0–2 (Komoda 2006) which is reflected by the identified literature only somewhat covering the topic of security.

FaaS (30 publications) causes software to be even more vertically integrated along all levels (Leitner et al. 2019). Consequently, FaaS shifts into the focus of research on the levels 3–5 (Eismann et al. 2021). However, the literature we identified only somewhat covered FaaS security. Thus, our analysis shows that the investigation of security for FaaS implementations is extendable. As for FaaS security on levels 0–2, the identified literature did not cover the intersection of the two dimensions, possibly caused by FaaS considered to not fit the uses cases on lower levels. Additionally, work on FaaS security is often focusing on confidentiality (cf. e.g. (Bocci et al., 2022)), which is often secondary for manufacturing compared to integrity and availability (Tupa et al. 2017).

In summary, there is a lack of coverage in literature on security when considering the intersection of higher abstraction levels and increased vertical integration of software. We address this gap by reviewing security challenges for software in manufacturing and derive implications for stakeholders in the industry.

4.2 Related Work

There are several literature reviews on the security of IoT. For instance, (Kouicem et al., 2018) conduct a top-down survey and propose a taxonomy of security solutions in IoT. (Aly et al., 2019) present guidelines to IoT security issues and describe threats, challenges, solutions, and countermeasures proposed in literature. (Tange et al., 2020) conduct a systematic survey of IoT security and present a range of security requirements and discuss Fog computing opportunities. Although these reviews highlight several security challenges addressed in this paper, they are missing a manufacturing perspective and stakeholder-dependent implications. Furthermore, they are not reviewing developments towards higher levels of software abstraction.

Literature reviews on (smart) manufacturing security discuss cyber-physical security efforts (Elhabashy et al. 2019) or strategies, methodologies, and techniques to mitigate attacks (Junior et al. 2021). (Bahrami and Rouzbahani, 2021) conduct a bibliometric analysis on cybersecurity of smart manufacturing execution systems and present an empiric analysis. These reviews put emphasis on manufacturing systems, but lack in the analysis of software integration approaches and developments towards FaaS. In this paper, we are aiming to fill this gap by analysing literature from the perspective of both analysis dimensions.

5 Findings: Security Challenges for Software in Manufacturing

5.1 Security Challenges Related to the Software Abstraction Level

Below, we will present the results of our literature review on security challenges in terms of confidentiality, integrity, and availability regarding the software abstraction level, summarised in Table 1.

Security Challenges of Monoliths: Monoliths struggle with limited scalability due to their architectural constraints (Fritzsch et al. 2019). Delayed release cycles (Ahmadvand and Ibrahim 2016) can prolong the integration of security patches and thus hamper the CIA triad. Furthermore, monolithic systems suffer from dependencies (Merkel 2014), hampering the adaptation of security practices and the CIA triad (Sun et al. 2011). The rigid structure of monoliths causes their deployment and maintenance to be complex (Ahmadvand and Ibrahim 2016). Every change made requires a rebuild of the entire system, hampering availability (Villamizar et al. 2015).

Table 1 Summary of derived security challenges related to software abstraction levels

Software abstraction level	Summarised security challenges	Exemplary sources
Low (monoliths)	Delayed integration of security patches hampering CIA triad	Ahmadvand and Ibrahim (2016), Sun et al. (2011), Fritzsch et al. (2019)
	Preserving CIA triad for highly dependent systems	Merkel (2014), Dragoni et al. (2017), Sun et al. (2011)
	Hampered availability due to difficult maintenance	Villamizar et al. (2015), Fritzsch et al. (2019), Sun et al. (2011)
Medium (SOA)	Network vulnerabilities can compromise CIA triad	Yu et al. (2019), Combe et al. (2016), Makris et al. (2022)
	Application segregation and isolation to preserve CIA triad	Caprolu et al. (2019), Varghese et al. (2016), Yu et al. (2019)
	Evaluating integrity of third-party components	Takabi et al. (2010), Enck and Williams (2022), Ibrahim et al. (2019)
High (FaaS)	Large attack surfaces hampering integrity of functions	Marin et al. (2022), Schleier-Smith et al. (2021), Candel et al. (2023)
	Confidentiality and availability of platform orchestration	Li et al. (2021), Wen et al. (2022), Mondal et al. (2022)
	Unknown sources for event triggers hampering integrity	Marin et al. (2022), Shafiei et al. (2021), O'Meara and Lennon (2020)

Security Challenges of SOA: SOA is decoupling systems and thus introducing security concerns to the CIA triad caused by vulnerabilities of networks and communications (O'Brien et al. 2005; Subashini and Kavitha 2011). To secure microservices and preserve all aspects of the CIA triad, researchers have highlighted the importance of achieving application segregation and isolation (Caprolu et al. 2019; Ibrahim et al. 2019; Yu et al. 2019). Managing the security of containers, which are commonly used for microservice deployment, is a prominent challenge in research and practice (Bui 2015; Combe et al. 2016; Sultan et al. 2019). Furthermore, (Enck and Williams, 2022) and others highlight the challenge of evaluating the integrity of third-party components and the software supply chain (Hashizume et al. 2013; Takabi et al. 2010).

Security Challenges of FaaS: FaaS exposes larger attack surfaces than regular SOA, hampering the integrity of functions (Schleier-Smith et al. 2021). Research points out the challenge of guaranteeing confidentiality and availability regarding FaaS deployment platforms and their orchestration (Mondal et al. 2022; Wen et al. 2022). Securing those platforms poses a challenge (Candel et al. 2023) since the statelessness of functions hinders policy enforcement (Li et al. 2021). (O'Meara and Lennon, 2020) highlight the danger of execution flow manipulation that harms integrity, also reflecting the challenge of handling unknown sources for event triggers (Marin et al. 2022; Shafiei et al. 2021).

5.2 Security Challenges Related to Vertical Software Integration

In the following, we will present the results of our review on security in terms of confidentiality, integrity, and availability of vertical software integration, summarised in Table 2.

Preserving confidentiality for multi-tenant applications is a frequently mentioned security challenge in Cloud computing (Almorsy et al. 2016; Hashizume et al. 2013; Takabi et al. 2010). Furthermore, it is challenging to evaluate the obscurity of Cloud platform orchestration and management regarding confidentiality and availability (Jegan et al. 2020; Jonas et al. 2019; Marin et al. 2022).

Edge, Fog, and IIoT systems are characterised by a high heterogeneity of devices and networks (Bhat et al. 2020; Roman et al. 2018; Xiao et al. 2019). These devices often have limited computational resources which makes security mechanisms like policy enforcement, authentication, and authorisation a challenge (Shafiei et al. 2021; Sicari et al. 2015; Zeyu et al. 2020). This hampers all aspects of the CIA triad. Vulnerabilities of devices and endpoints pose cyber and physical threats to systems that hamper integrity (Ashibani and Mahmoud 2017; Kim et al. 2018; Yaacoub et al. 2020). Additionally, (Jegan et al., 2020) address the urgency of preventing attacks from new attack vectors that get exposed by vertical software integration.

Table 2 Summary of derived security challenges related to vertical software integration

Vertical software integration	Summarised security challenges	Exemplary sources
	Data confidentiality of multi-tenant applications	Zissis and Lekkas (2012), Hashizume et al. (2013), Behl and Behl (2012)
	Confidentiality and availability of obscure platform orchestration	Jegan et al. (2020), Wen et al. (2021), Jonas et al. (2019)
	Preserving CIA triad with limited resources of devices	Zeyu et al. (2020), Xiao et al. (2019), Roman et al. (2018)
	Mitigating cyber and physical threats to preserve integrity	Yaacoub et al. (2020), Makris et al. (2022), Ibrahim et al. (2019)
	Ensuring availability, reliability and resilience of critical systems	Wells et al. (2014), Ashibani and Mahmoud (2017), Yaacoub et al. (2020)
	Protecting hardware and networks in order to preserve CIA triad	Wen et al. (2021), Jegan et al. (2020), Ly and Jin (2016)
	Achieving availability of connections to legacy systems	Krotofil and Gollmann (2013), Ly and Jin (2016), Humayed et al. (2017)

Due to their criticality, IACS require high availability, reliability and resilience (Wells et al. 2014; Yaacoub et al. 2020). IACS pose the challenge of efficiently protecting hardware, function endpoints, and interfaces (Ly and Jin 2016; Wen et al. 2021) to preserve all aspects of the CIA triad in an increasingly connected environment (Ashibani and Mahmoud 2017; Chhetri et al. 2017). Availability of legacy systems, which are generally difficult to maintain and evolve, has to be preserved (Humayed et al. 2017; Krotofil and Gollmann 2013).

6 Discussion: Implications for Stakeholders in Manufacturing

The results of our literature review highlight the challenges to software security in manufacturing from two perspectives: software abstraction levels and vertical software integration. Moreover, our results highlight the temporal perspective of software security. Short term challenges are faced in practice and handled in research (e.g. software monoliths for OT are existing for decades) (Stouffer et al. 2014; Tuptuk and Hailes 2018). On the contrary, studies of emerging, long-term challenges are still in their infancy (e.g. FaaS has yet to impact OT) (Bocci et al. 2021; Li et al. 2021).

Table 3 Courses of action for stakeholders regarding each dimension of security challenges

	Software security black boxes	Heterogeneity of devices and networks	Adaptation of security approaches for OT
System integrator	Make security measurable at the deepest possible system level in order to evaluate black boxes	Define system boundaries and describe the required/allowed device interactions	Analyse and formulate security requirements of OT environments
Developer	Be able to provide as much evidence on software security as possible	Make software adaptable to dynamic security environments	Design software that adapts to OT security requirements
Security auditor	Define a language to communicate and assess security of software	Target the automation of assurance assessments regarding software security	Make security requirements of integration environments comparable

We argue that the basis for tackling security challenges has to be set in order to address long-term goals of securing software for manufacturing (cf. Table 3). Due to the characteristics of the gathered security challenges in Sect. 5, we group the derived security challenges along three dimensions: software security black boxes, heterogeneity of devices and networks, adaptation of security approaches for OT.

Additionally, we map the implications to three salient stakeholders. **System integrators** have domain-specific knowledge of manufacturing facilities and are also responsible for the task of software integration. **Developers** refer to software developers that define vertical software integration by designing applications for multiple PERA levels. **Security auditors** are third-party stakeholders that are associated with the task of assessing and evaluating software security in systems. Their role is increasingly established to provide assurance of system security (Rushby and Bloomfield 2022), e.g. to assure compliance to industrial security standards (Leander et al. 2019).

6.1 Software Security Black Boxes

The obscure security of software, e.g. in the context of FaaS, can be seen as "software security black boxes", since system integrators are not able to evaluate software security (Li et al. 2021). Therefore, they are inclined to make software security measurable at the deepest possible level. They are inclined to define thresholds for security compliance which the black boxes can be tested against (Wen et al. 2022). (Halabi and Bellaiche, 2017) propose an approach to making Cloud service provider security quantifiable. Its applicability in manufacturing is subject to future research.

Developers face the challenge to prove secure development and suitable software security to make themselves trustworthy. They must be able to provide as much evidence on security of their product as possible without reducing its value (Enck and Williams 2022). The software bill of materials (SBOM) is a promising approach to providing application metadata but covers only very specific aspects of security and lacks in terms of performance and adaptability (Xia et al. 2023).

Finally, the obscurity of software security makes it difficult for auditors to assess a systems' compliance to security requirements. A security auditor needs to pursue activities in order to define a policy language for communication and assessment of software security (Li et al. 2021). The three-dimensional model for software security evaluation proposed by (Han et al., 2014) can serve as a first step in this direction.

6.2 Heterogeneity of Devices and Networks

The heterogeneity of devices and networks, e.g. in the Industrial Internet of Things (IIoT), is introducing several security challenges. System integrators are required to define physical and logical boundaries of systems and describe the required/allowed software interactions (Ashibani and Mahmoud 2017). Following this thought, (Giaretta et al., 2019) propose Security-by-Contract and Fog computing to secure IoT systems.

For developers, we believe that engineering activities have to put emphasis on making software adaptable to dynamic security environments (Kim et al. 2018). (Neureiter et al., 2016) discuss the topic of domain-specific security-by-design using a model based approach, which could serve as one way to guide developers.

Finally, security auditors need to target the continuous assurance of software security, e.g. by following the concept suggested by (Rushby and Bloomfield, 2022). We believe that the challenge of heterogeneity cannot be dealt with by one stakeholder, but has to be approached jointly across the manufacturing industry.

6.3 Adaptation of Security Approaches for OT

Security demands in manufacturing require the adaptation of security approaches when targeting vertical software integration. System integrators are required to specifically analyse and formulate the security requirements of their domain (Krotofil and Gollmann 2013). (Giorgini et al., 2005) propose a combination of ownership, permission, and delegation to model security requirements. This could be a starting point for investigations in the manufacturing domain.

Correspondingly, developers need to adapt software to security requirements of lower vertical integration levels, e.g. a higher focus on integrity and availability (Pennekamp et al. 2019). We highlight the evaluation of software supply chain security since integrated vulnerabilities can harm aspects of the CIA triad (Enck and Williams 2022).

Finally, activities of security auditors have to put their focus on making software security requirements of different integration environments comparable (Wang et al. 2010). A formal modelling approach regarding domain-specific security requirements can set the direction of further research (Giorgini et al. 2005).

7 Conclusion

This paper presents the results of a hermeneutic literature review of security challenges for software in manufacturing.

We pursue an interpretative approach to the review of literature. As a basis for our analysis, we studied publications from different disciplines with focus on security of software in manufacturing. We interpreted the results along two derived dimensions: increased software abstraction and vertical integration of software. Our interpretation shows that there is a clear lack of research on FaaS for OT. Moreover, it shows that research on security regarding SOA for OT as well as FaaS for IT is still developing.

In a consequent hermeneutic cycle of analysis and interpretation, we derived three dimensions of security challenges (software security black boxes, heterogeneity of devices and networks, adaptation of security approaches for OT) and mapped them to three salient stakeholders (system integrators, developers, and security auditors). Moreover, we interpreted potential courses of action for these stakeholders and mapped them to the challenges' dimensions.

Although we followed the principles of interpretation (Klein and Myers 1999) and hermeneutic review of literature (Boell and Cecez-Kecmanovic 2014), we acknowledge that our research has a number of limitations and presents perspectives for future research endeavors. First, the scope of our literature review is broad which implies that we might not have achieved the level of detail necessary for tackling particular and detailed security issues and threats in practice. This leaves room for future work to narrow down the latter and analyse as well as prescribe concrete actions. For instance, concrete protection and assurance mechanisms (Furnell et al. 2021) for the emerging challenges could be studied. Second, our research provides projections of security challenges that are yet to be supported by empirical evidence in practice. This is the case, since the nature of security implies multiple managerial and technological perspectives (cf. (Furnell et al., 2021)). Our research covers both intensively studied intersections (e.g. security of monoliths for IT) as well as emerging intersections (e.g. security of FaaS in OT). This should be of value for researchers towards building concrete hypothesis for empirical studies as well designing artefacts for constructivistic studies.

We believe that our results are beneficial for both academia and practice. We encourage future research to build on our findings and the described limitations of our study. Practitioners can apply our results to guide stakeholders towards the definition of a mid- to long-term security strategy and particular courses of action.

References

Ahmadvand, M. and Ibrahim, A. (2016) , Requirements Reconciliation for Scalable and Secure Microservice (De)composition, *in* '2016 IEEE 24th International Requirements Engineering Conference Workshops (REW)', IEEE, Beijing, China, pp. 68–73.

Alcácer, V. & Cruz-Machado, V. (2019) , 'Scanning the Industry 4.0: A Literature Review on Technologies for Manufacturing Systems', *Engineering Science and Technology, an International Journal* **22**(3), 899–919.

Almorsy, M., Grundy, J. & Müller, I. (2016) , 'An analysis of the cloud computing security problem', 1609.01107 .

Aly, M., Khomh, F., Haoues, M., Quintero, A. & Yacout, S. (2019) , 'Enforcing security in Internet of Things frameworks: A Systematic Literature Review', *Internet of Things* **6**, 100050.

Ashibani, Y. & Mahmoud, Q. H. (2017) , 'Cyber physical systems security: Analysis, challenges and solutions', *Computers & Security* **68**, 81–97.

Bahrami, A. H. & Rouzbahani, H. M. (2021) , 'Cyber security of smart manufacturing execution systems: A bibliometric analysis', *AI-Enabled Threat Detection and Security Analysis for Industrial IoT* pp. 105–119.

Baldini, I., Castro, P., Chang, K., Cheng, P., Fink, S., Ishakian, V., Mitchell, N., Muthusamy, V., Rabbah, R. & Slominski, A. (2017) , 'Serverless computing: Current trends and open problems', *Research advances in cloud computing* pp. 1–20.

Basu, S., Bardhan, A., Gupta, K., Saha, P., Pal, M., Bose, M., Basu, K., Chaudhury, S. & Sarkar, P. (2018) , Cloud computing security challenges & solutions-A survey, *in* '2018 IEEE 8th Annual Computing and Communication Workshop and Conference (CCWC)', IEEE, Las Vegas, NV, pp. 347–356.

Behl, A. & Behl, K. (2012) , An analysis of cloud computing security issues, *in* '2012 World Congress on Information and Communication Technologies', IEEE, Trivandrum, India, pp. 109–114.

Bhat, S. A., Sofi, I. B. & Chi, C.-Y. (2020) , 'Edge Computing and Its Convergence With Blockchain in 5G and Beyond: Security, Challenges, and Opportunities', *IEEE Access* **8**, 205340–205373.

Bocci, A., Forti, S., Ferrari, G.-L. & Brogi, A. (2021) , 'Secure FaaS orchestration in the fog: How far are we?', *Computing* **103**(5), 1025–1056.

Bocci, A., Forti, S., Ferrari, G.-L. & Brogi, A. (2022) , Type, pad, and place: Avoiding data leaks in Cloud-IoT FaaS orchestrations, *in* '2022 22nd IEEE International Symposium on Cluster, Cloud and Internet Computing (CCGrid)', IEEE, Taormina, Italy, pp. 798–805.

Boell, S. K. & Cecez-Kecmanovic, D. (2014) , 'A Hermeneutic Approach for Conducting Literature Reviews and Literature Searches', *Communications of the Association for Information Systems* **34**.

Boyes, H., Hallaq, B., Cunningham, J. & Watson, T. (2018) , 'The industrial internet of things (IIoT): An analysis framework', *Computers in Industry* **101**, 1–12.

Bui, T.(2015) , 'Analysis of Docker Security'.

Buschmann, F., Meunier, R., Rohnert, H., Sommerlad, P. & Stal, M. (1996) , *Software Patterns*, Wiley: Eaglewood Cliffs, NJ, USA.

Candel, J. M. O., Elouali, A., Gimeno, F. J. M. & Mora, H.(2023) , Cloud vs Serverless Computing: A Security Point of View, *in* 'International Conference on Ubiquitous Computing and Ambient Intelligence', Springer, pp. 1098–1109.

Caprolu, M., Di Pietro, R., Lombardi, F. & Raponi, S. (2019) , Edge Computing Perspectives: Architectures, Technologies, and Open Security Issues, *in* '2019 IEEE International Conference on Edge Computing (EDGE)', IEEE, Milan, Italy, pp. 116–123.

Chen, D., Doumeingts, G. & Vernadat, F. (2008) , 'Architectures for enterprise integration and interoperability: Past, present and future', *Computers in Industry* **59**(7), 647–659.

Chhetri, S. R., Faezi, S., Rashid, N. & Al Faruque, M. A. (2018) , 'Manufacturing Supply Chain and Product Lifecycle Security in the Era of Industry 4.0', *Journal of Hardware and Systems Security* **2**(1), 51–68.

Chhetri, S. R., Rashid, N., Faezi, S. & Al Faruque, M. A. (2017) , Security trends and advances in manufacturing systems in the era of industry 4.0, *in* '2017 IEEE/ACM International Conference on Computer-Aided Design (ICCAD)', IEEE, pp. 1039–1046.

Combe, T., Martin, A. & Di Pietro, R. (2016) , 'To Docker or Not to Docker: A Security Perspective', *IEEE Cloud Computing* **3**(5), 54–62.

Donno, M. D., Tange, K. & Dragoni, N. (2019) , 'Foundations and Evolution of Modern Computing Paradigms: Cloud, IoT, Edge, and Fog', **7**, 13.

Dragoni, N., Giallorenzo, S., Lafuente, A. L., Mazzara, M., Montesi, F., Mustafin, R. & Safina, L. (2017) , 'Microservices: Yesterday, today, and tomorrow', *Present and ulterior software engineering* pp. 195–216.

Eismann, S., Scheuner, J., van Eyk, E., Schwinger, M., Grohmann, J., Abad, C. L. & Iosup, A. (2021) , 'Serverless Applications: Why, When, and How?', *IEEE Software* **38**(1), 32–39.

Elhabashy, A. E., Wells, L. J. & Camelio, J. A. (2019) , 'Cyber-Physical Security Research Efforts in Manufacturing – A Literature Review', *Procedia Manufacturing* **34**, 921–931.

Enck, W. & Williams, L. (2022) , 'Top Five Challenges in Software Supply Chain Security: Observations From 30 Industry and Government Organizations', *IEEE Security & Privacy* **20**(2), 96–100.

Fritzsch, J., Bogner, J., Zimmermann, A. & Wagner, S. (2019) , From Monolith to Microservices: A Classification of Refactoring Approaches, *in* J.-M. Bruel, M. Mazzara & B. Meyer, eds, 'Software Engineering Aspects of Continuous Development and New Paradigms of Software Production and Deployment', Vol. 11350, Springer International Publishing, Cham, pp. 128–141.

Furnell, S., Haskell-Dowland, P., Agrawal, M., Baskerville, R., Basu, A., Bishop, M., Cuellar, J., Foresti, S., Futcher, L. & Gal-Oz, N. (2021) , Information security and privacy–challenges and outlook, *in* 'Advancing Research in Information and Communication Technology', Springer, pp. 383–401.

Giaretta, A., Dragoni, N. & Massacci, F. (2019) , Protecting the Internet of Things with Security-by-Contract and Fog Computing, *in* '2019 IEEE 5th World Forum on Internet of Things (WF-IoT)', IEEE, Limerick, Ireland, pp. 1–6.

Giorgini, P., Massacci, F., Mylopoulos, J. & Zannone, N. (2005), Modeling security requirements through ownership, permission and delegation, *in* '13th IEEE International Conference on Requirements Engineering (RE'05)', IEEE, Paris, France, pp. 167–176.

Halabi, T. & Bellaiche, M. (2017), 'Towards quantification and evaluation of security of Cloud Service Providers', *Journal of Information Security and Applications* **33**, 55–65.

Han, Z., Li, X., Feng, R., Hu, J., Xu, G. & Feng, Z. (2014) , A Three-Dimensional Model for Software Security Evaluation, *in* '2014 Theoretical Aspects of Software Engineering Conference', IEEE, Changsha, pp. 34–41.

Hankel, M. & Rexroth, B. (2015) , 'The reference architectural model industrie 4.0 (rami 4.0)', *Zvei* **2**(2), 4–9.

Hashizume, K., Rosado, D. G., Fernández-Medina, E. & Fernandez, E. B. (2013) , 'An analysis of security issues for cloud computing', *Journal of Internet Services and Applications* **4**(1), 5.

Hasselbring, W. (2000) , 'Information system integration', *Communications of the ACM* **43**(6), 32–38.

Homay, A., Zoitl, A., de Sousa, M. & Wollschlaeger, M. (2019) , A Survey: Microservices Architecture in Advanced Manufacturing Systems, *in* '2019 IEEE 17th International Conference on Industrial Informatics (INDIN)', IEEE, Helsinki, Finland, pp. 1165–1168.

Humayed, A., Lin, J., Li, F. & Luo, B. (2017) , 'Cyber-Physical Systems Security—A Survey', *IEEE Internet of Things Journal* **4**(6), 1802–1831.

Ibrahim, A., Bozhinoski, S. & Pretschner, A. (2019) , Attack graph generation for microservice architecture, *in* 'Proceedings of the 34th ACM/SIGAPP Symposium on Applied Computing', ACM, Limassol Cyprus, pp. 1235–1242.

Jasperneite, J., Sauter, T. & Wollschlaeger, M. (2020) , 'Why We Need Automation Models: Handling Complexity in Industry 4.0 and the Internet of Things', *IEEE Industrial Electronics Magazine* **14**(1), 29–40.

Jegan, D. S., Wang, L., Bhagat, S., Ristenpart, T. & Swift, M. (2020) , 'Guarding Serverless Applications with SecLambda'.

Jonas, E., Schleier-Smith, J., Sreekanti, V., Tsai, C.-C., Khandelwal, A., Pu, Q., Shankar, V., Carreira, J., Krauth, K., Yadwadkar, N., Gonzalez, J. E., Popa, R. A., Stoica, I. & Patterson, D. A. (2019) , 'Cloud Programming Simplified: A Berkeley View on Serverless Computing'.

Junior, A. A. D. S., Pio, J. L. D. S., Fonseca, J. C., De Oliveira, M. A., Valadares, O. C. D. P. & Da Silva, P. H. S. (2021) , 'The State of Cybersecurity in Smart Manufacturing Systems: A Systematic Review', *European Journal of Business and Management Research* **6**(6), 188–194.

Kim, N. Y., Rathore, S., Ryu, J. H., Park, J. H. & Park, J. H. (2018) , 'A Survey on Cyber Physical System Security for IoT: Issues, Challenges, Threats, Solutions', *Journal of Information Processing Systems* **14**(6), 1361–1384.

Kitchenham, B. & Charters, S. (2007) , 'Guidelines for performing systematic literature reviews in software engineering EBSE Technical Report EBSE-2007-01', *Keele, Staffs, and Durham, UK* .

Klein, H. K. & Myers, M. D. (1999) , 'A Set of Principles for Conducting and Evaluating Interpretive Field Studies in Information Systems', *MIS Quarterly* **23**(1), 67.

Komoda, N. (2006) , Service Oriented Architecture (SOA) in Industrial Systems, *in* '2006 IEEE International Conference on Industrial Informatics', IEEE, Singapore, pp. 1–5.

Kouicem, D. E., Bouabdallah, A. & Lakhlef, H. (2018) , 'Internet of things security: A top-down survey', *Computer Networks* **141**, 199–221.

Krotofil, M. & Gollmann, D. (2013) , Industrial control systems security: What is happening?, *in* '2013 11th IEEE International Conference on Industrial Informatics (INDIN)', IEEE, Bochum, Germany, pp. 664–669.

Leander, B., Čaušević, A. & Hansson, H. (2019) , Applicability of the IEC 62443 standard in Industry 4.0 / IIoT, *in* 'Proceedings of the 14th International Conference on Availability, Reliability and Security', ACM, Canterbury CA United Kingdom, pp. 1–8.

Leitner, P., Wittern, E., Spillner, J. & Hummer, W. (2019) , 'A mixed-method empirical study of Function-as-a-Service software development in industrial practice', *Journal of Systems and Software* **149**, 340–359.

Lewis, J. & Fowler, M. (2014), 'Microservices: A definition of this new architectural term', *MartinFowler. com* **25**, 14–26.

Li, X., Leng, X. & Chen, Y. (2021), 'Securing Serverless Computing: Challenges, Solutions, and Opportunities'.

Lin, S.-W., Miller, B., Durand, J., Bleakley, G., Chigani, A., Martin, R., Murphy, B. & Crawford, M. (2017), 'The industrial internet of things volume G1: Reference architecture', *Industrial Internet Consortium* **10**.

Ly, K. & Jin, Y. (2016), Security Challenges in CPS and IoT: From End-Node to the System, *in* '2016 IEEE Computer Society Annual Symposium on VLSI (ISVLSI)', IEEE, Pittsburgh, PA, USA, pp. 63–68.

Makris, A., Tserpes, K. & Varvarigou, T. (2022), 'Transition from monolithic to microservice-based applications. Challenges from the developer perspective', *Open Research Europe* **2**, 24.

Marin, E., Perino, D. & Di Pietro, R. (2022), 'Serverless computing: A security perspective', *Journal of Cloud Computing* **11**(1), 69.

Mell, P. & Grance, T. (2011), 'The NIST definition of cloud computing'.

Merkel, D. (2014), 'Docker: Lightweight linux containers for consistent development and deployment', *Linux j* **239**(2), 2.

Mondal, S. K., Pan, R., Kabir, H. M. D., Tian, T. & Dai, H.-N. (2022), 'Kubernetes in IT administration and serverless computing: An empirical study and research challenges', *The Journal of Supercomputing* **78**(2), 2937–2987.

Negreiro, M. (2023), 'The NIS2 Directive - A high common level of cybersecurity in the EU', *EPRS | European Parliamentary Research Service* .

Neureiter, C., Engel, D. & Uslar, M. (2016), 'Domain Specific and Model Based Systems Engineering in the Smart Grid as Prerequesite for Security by Design', *Electronics* **5**(4), 24.

NIST (2023), 'NIST Cybersecurity Framework 2.0 Concept Paper: Potential Significant Updates to the Cybersecurity Framework'.
O'Brien, L., Bass, L. & Merson, P. (2005), Quality Attributes and Service-Oriented Architectures:, Technical report, Defense Technical Information Center, Fort Belvoir, VA.
O'Meara, W. & Lennon, R. G. (2020) , Serverless Computing Security: Protecting Application Logic, *in* '2020 31st Irish Signals and Systems Conference (ISSC)', IEEE, Letterkenny, Ireland, pp. 1–5.
Papazoglou, M. (2003) , Service-oriented computing: Concepts, characteristics and directions, *in* 'Proceedings of the 7th International Conference on Properties and Applications of Dielectric Materials (Cat. No.03CH37417)', IEEE Comput. Soc, Rome, Italy, pp. 3–12.
Pennekamp, J., Henze, M., Schmidt, S., Niemietz, P., Fey, M., Trauth, D., Bergs, T., Brecher, C. & Wehrle, K. (2019) , Dataflow Challenges in an Internet of Production: A Security & Privacy Perspective, *in* 'Proceedings of the ACM Workshop on Cyber-Physical Systems Security & Privacy - CPS-SPC'19', ACM Press, London, United Kingdom, pp. 27–38.
Perez, A., Risco, S., Naranjo, D. M., Caballer, M. & Molto, G. (2019) , On-Premises Serverless Computing for Event-Driven Data Processing Applications, *in* '2019 IEEE 12th International Conference on Cloud Computing (CLOUD)', IEEE, Milan, Italy, pp. 414–421.
Rahman, A., Mahdavi-Hezaveh, R. & Williams, L. (2019) , 'A systematic mapping study of infrastructure as code research', *Information and Software Technology* **108**, 65–77.
Roman, R., Lopez, J. & Mambo, M. (2018) , 'Mobile Edge Computing, Fog et al.: A Survey and Analysis of Security Threats and Challenges', *Future Generation Computer Systems* **78**, 680–698.
Rose, K., Eldridge, S. & Chapin, L. (2015) , 'The internet of things: An overview', *The internet society (ISOC)* **80**, 1–50.
Rushby, J. & Bloomfield, R. (2022), 'Assessing Confidence with Assurance 2.0'.
Samonas, S. & Coss, D. (2014) , 'The CIA strikes back: Redefining confidentiality, integrity and availability in security.', *Journal of Information System Security* **10**(3).
Satyanarayanan, M. (2017) , 'The Emergence of Edge Computing', *Computer* **50**(1), 30–39.
Schleier-Smith, J., Sreekanti, V., Khandelwal, A., Carreira, J., Yadwadkar, N. J., Popa, R. A., Gonzalez, J. E., Stoica, I. & Patterson, D. A. (2021) , 'What serverless computing is and should become: The next phase of cloud computing', *Communications of the ACM* **64**(5), 76–84.
Shafiei, H., Khonsari, A. & Mousavi, P. (2021) , 'Serverless Computing: A Survey of Opportunities, Challenges and Applications'.
Shi, W., Cao, J., Zhang, Q., Li, Y. & Xu, L. (2016) , 'Edge Computing: Vision and Challenges', *IEEE Internet of Things Journal* **3**(5), 637–646.
Shojafar, M., Pooranian, Z., Naranjo, P. G. V. & Baccarelli, E. (2017) , 'FLAPS: Bandwidth and delay-efficient distributed data searching in Fog-supported P2P content delivery networks', *The Journal of Supercomputing* **73**(12), 5239–5260.
Sicari, S., Rizzardi, A., Grieco, L. & Coen-Porisini, A. (2015) , 'Security, privacy and trust in Internet of Things: The road ahead', *Computer Networks* **76**, 146–164.
Stouffer, K., Lightman, S., Pillitteri, V., Abrams, M. & Hahn, A. (2014) , 'Guide to Industrial Control Systems (ICS) Security', *NIST Special Publication* .
Subashini, S. & Kavitha, V. (2011) , 'A survey on security issues in service delivery models of cloud computing', *Journal of Network and Computer Applications* **34**(1), 1–11.
Sultan, S., Ahmad, I. & Dimitriou, T. (2019) , 'Container Security: Issues, Challenges, and the Road Ahead', *IEEE Access* **7**, 52976–52996.
Sun, Y., Nanda, S. & Jaeger, T. (2015) , Security-as-a-Service for Microservices-Based Cloud Applications, *in* '2015 IEEE 7th International Conference on Cloud Computing Technology and Science (CloudCom)', IEEE, Vancouver, BC, Canada, pp. 50–57.
Tabrizchi, H. & Kuchaki Rafsanjani, M. (2020) , 'A survey on security challenges in cloud computing: Issues, threats, and solutions', *The Journal of Supercomputing* **76**(12), 9493–9532.
Takabi, H., Joshi, J. B. & Ahn, G.-J. (2010) , 'Security and Privacy Challenges in Cloud Computing Environments', *IEEE Security & Privacy Magazine* **8**(6), 24–31.

Tange, K., De Donno, M., Fafoutis, X. & Dragoni, N. (2020) , 'A systematic survey of industrial Internet of Things security: Requirements and fog computing opportunities', *IEEE Communications Surveys & Tutorials* **22**(4), 2489–2520.

Tupa, J., Simota, J. & Steiner, F. (2017) , 'Aspects of Risk Management Implementation for Industry 4.0', *Procedia Manufacturing* **11**, 1223–1230.

Tuptuk, N. & Hailes, S. (2018) , 'Security of smart manufacturing systems', *Journal of Manufacturing Systems* **47**, 93–106.

Varghese, B., Wang, N., Barbhuiya, S., Kilpatrick, P. & Nikolopoulos, D. S. (2016) , 'Challenges and Opportunities in Edge Computing'.

Villamizar, M., Garces, O., Castro, H., Verano, M., Salamanca, L., Casallas, R. & Gil, S. (2015) , Evaluating the monolithic and the microservice architecture pattern to deploy web applications in the cloud, *in* '2015 10th Computing Colombian Conference (10CCC)', IEEE, Bogota, Colombia, pp. 583–590.

Wang, C., Wang, Q., Ren, K. & Lou, W. (2010) , Privacy-Preserving Public Auditing for Data Storage Security in Cloud Computing, *in* '2010 Proceedings IEEE INFOCOM', IEEE, San Diego, CA, USA, pp. 1–9.

Webster, J. & Watson, R. T. (2002) , 'Analyzing the Past to Prepare for the Future: Writing a Literature Review', *MIS Quarterly* **26**(2), xiii–xxiii.

Wells, L. J., Camelio, J. A., Williams, C. B. & White, J. (2014) , 'Cyber-physical security challenges in manufacturing systems', *Manufacturing Letters* **2**(2), 74–77.

Wen, J., Chen, Z. & Liu, X. (2022) , 'Software Engineering for Serverless Computing'.

Wen, J., Chen, Z., Liu, Y., Lou, Y., Ma, Y., Huang, G., Jin, X. & Liu, X. (2021) , An empirical study on challenges of application development in serverless computing, *in* 'Proceedings of the 29th ACM Joint Meeting on European Software Engineering Conference and Symposium on the Foundations of Software Engineering', ACM, Athens Greece, pp. 416–428.

Wilde, T. & Hess, T. (2007) , 'Forschungsmethoden der Wirtschaftsinformatik'.

Williams, T. J. (1994) , 'The Purdue enterprise reference architecture', *Computers in industry* **24**(2-3), 141–158.

Xia, B., Bi, T., Xing, Z., Lu, Q. & Zhu, L. (2023) , 'An Empirical Study on Software Bill of Materials: Where We Stand and the Road Ahead'.

Xiao, Y., Jia, Y., Liu, C., Cheng, X., Yu, J. & Lv, W. (2019) , 'Edge Computing Security: State of the Art and Challenges', *Proceedings of the IEEE* **107**(8), 1608–1631.

Yaacoub, J.-P. A., Salman, O., Noura, H. N., Kaaniche, N., Chehab, A. & Malli, M. (2020) , 'Cyber-physical systems security: Limitations, issues and future trends', *Microprocessors and Microsystems* **77**, 103201.

Yu, D., Jin, Y., Zhang, Y. & Zheng, X. (2019) , 'A survey on security issues in services communication of Microservices-enabled fog applications', *Concurrency and Computation: Practice and Experience* **31**(22).

Zeyu, H., Geming, X., Zhaohang, W. & Sen, Y. (2020) , Survey on Edge Computing Security, *in* '2020 International Conference on Big Data, Artificial Intelligence and Internet of Things Engineering (ICBAIE)', IEEE, Fuzhou, China, pp. 96–105.

Zissis, D. & Lekkas, D. (2012) , 'Addressing cloud computing security issues', *Future Generation Computer Systems* **28**(3), 583–592.

Zografopoulos, I., Ospina, J., Liu, X. & Konstantinou, C. (2021) , 'Cyber-Physical Energy Systems Security: Threat Modeling, Risk Assessment, Resources, Metrics, and Case Studies', *IEEE Access* **9**, 29775–29818.

Exploring Multi-agent Systems for Intermodal Freight Fleets: Literature-Based Justification of a New Concept

Dennis Maecker, Henning Gösling, Christoph Heinbach, and Friedemann Kammler

Abstract Freight transportation is increasingly connected with the automation of fleet assets by intelligent systems. This study emerges from the consortium research project Gaia-X 4 ROMS, which aims to develop a comprehensive approach for smart freight fleets in the field of parcel deliveries. Within this project, a novel type of multi-agent system (MAS) for the management of freight fleets is being developed. To determine the state of prior research and recent developments in this field, a systematic literature review was conducted and presented herein. The findings of the review demonstrate a lack of applied solutions in this topic, highlighting the need for a novel approach. Accordingly, a first framework for the envisioned multi-agent system, as conceptualized within the consortium research project, is presented in this work, serving as a basis for subsequent design phases.

Keywords Systematic literature review · Multi-agent system · Intelligent logistics · Smart freight fleet · Consortium research

D. Maecker (✉) · H. Gösling · C. Heinbach · F. Kammler
German Research Center for Artificial Intelligence (DFKI), Osnabrück, Germany
e-mail: dennis.maecker@dfki.de

H. Gösling
e-mail: henning.goesling@dfki.de

C. Heinbach
e-mail: christoph.heinbach@dfki.de

F. Kammler
e-mail: friedemann.kammler@dfki.de

D. Beverungen et al. (eds.), *Solutions and Technologies for Responsible Digitalization*, Lecture Notes in Information Systems and Organisation 75,
https://doi.org/10.1007/978-3-031-80122-8_20

1 Introduction

The e-commerce business reached a record sales revenue with more than $ 5 trillion in 2021 globally (Chevalier 2022), driving a continuous parcel delivery growth across nations. In Germany, for instance, the number of business-to-consumer (B2C) parcels delivered has increased by 16.6 per cent in the same year compared to 2020, leading to 15 million parcels delivered per day (BIEK 2022). Parcel delivery chains are composed of different freight transport legs (i.e., first-mile, long-haul, and last mile transport) and involve various operators (e.g., dispatcher, customs, delivery man) and resources (e.g., vans, trucks, trailers, delivery robots). A higher degree of automation in the parcel delivery chain is seen as an opportunity for logistics companies to cope with the enormous quantities of parcel deliveries within logistics networks (Dekhne et al. 2019). A central software for an automated management of the involved actors in intermodal parcel deliveries is often not applicable due to a fragmented business industry and the complex interdependencies inherent in such transportation systems. Instead, a multi-agent-based approach could be used in which each of the distributed actors involved in the different legs of the transport chain is represented by an autonomous software agent. The software agent then decides for an actor whether and when a task is executed. In this context, a MAS enables the decomposition of complex problems and efficient distribution of both data and control across physical boundaries (Jennings 2000; Wooldridgey and Ciancarini 2001). However, the multi-agent-based management of parcel deliveries while using state-of-the-art freight fleet resources like delivery robots and telematic-equipped trailers is a sparsely investigated topic. In this light, the consortium research project Gaia-X 4 ROMS (Remote Operation for Automated and Connected Mobility Services) (Gaia-X 4 Future Mobility n.d.) has been established. The consortium research project seeks further to contribute to the development of federated data ecosystems promoting data sovereignty and fair competition for distributed participants involved in the provision and consumption of data (Braud et al. 2021).

To obtain an overview of existing solutions for MAS in freight fleet management, several reviews and surveys were identified. This includes literature reviews conducted by Davidsson et al. (2005) and Falco and Robiolo (2019), indicating a lack of research in the field of MAS that were applied to automate processes in the transportation sector. Further, while academia has addressed MAS for city logistics (Taniguchi et al. 2020) or urban mobility (de Gauna et al. 2020), solutions for managing an intermodal freight fleet in its entirety, as it is planned in the consortium research project, remain yet scarce. To gain precise and holistic knowledge of the topic addressed, a systematic literature review was deemed necessary. The literature review revealed a research gap in this field and justifies a novel MAS concept for freight fleet management which is presented in this paper. Overall, the following research questions (RQ) guide the initial phases for a dedicated MAS solution:

RQ1: *What is the current state of research on the use of multi-agent systems for managing intermodal freight fleets?*

RQ2: *To what extent have these systems been implemented and applied in practice, hence what maturity level did they reach?*

RQ3: *Can a concept for a multi-agent system for managing intermodal freight fleets be justified by the findings of the literature review?*

To answer the research questions, the remainder of the paper is organized as follows. In Sect. 2, we establish a background of the topic addressed and present relevant definitions. Afterwards, in Sect. 3, we introduce the approach for our systematic literature review as one iteration in the design science research approach that is applied in our consortium research project. Subsequently, in Sect. 4, we present the findings of the literature review and propose a novel concept of a MAS for intermodal freight fleet management. Section 5 encompasses a discussion of the results and states implications for the research consortium process. Lastly, in Sect. 6, we emphasize the limitations of our paper, conclude our work, and provide an outlook for future research.

2 Background

MASs and transport logistics management have been the focus of significant attention in recent years, and their broad applicability has resulted in a range of definitions that varies among different disciplines. To provide a comprehensive understanding, it is important to outline the definitions of both MASs and transport logistics.

2.1 Multi-agent Systems

MASs are composed of several autonomous agents (Pitt 2021). According to Pitt (2021), each autonomous agent in a MAS represents a human being or an organization and is responsible for undertaking certain actions on its behalf in an intelligent way while continuously taking input from the environment or other agents into account. However, on a lower level of abstraction, an autonomous agent is "an embedded software process which encapsulates some notion of state and communicates with others by message passing" (Pitt 2021, p.18). Different architectures exist that can be used to develop autonomous agents. For example, when following the BDI architecture, an agent consists of a control loop with three states: belief revision (belief), option generation (desire), and action selection (intention) (Pitt 2021). Wahlster (2017) differentiates between autonomous systems that are robots with physical sensors and actors, and those that are software agents (or softbots) acting solely in digital environments. Apart from control loops which are necessary for self-regulation, autonomous systems may consist of actors, sensors, a knowledge base and mechanisms for learning, optimization, collaboration, and communication (Wahlster 2017).

2.2 *Intermodal Freight Fleets, Digitalization, and Software Agents*

Road freight transportation bridges the physical distances between shippers (e.g., retailer) and consignees (e.g., consumers) for delivering freight (e.g., finished products packaged in parcels) in the B2C business. A closer look into the transport chain for parcel deliveries reveals three transport stages: a first-mile transport from the shipper to a depot, a long-haul transport between two depots, and a last-mile transport from the depot to another consignee (Brabänder and Braun 2020). This situation is accompanied by an intense technological transformation of the road freight sector focusing on data-driven business opportunities leading to intermodal fleet operations combining freight fleets, customer orders, and the operational activities of both transport and fleet operators (Akac et al. 2020; Farquharson et al. 2021). The wave of digital innovations consequently aims at the automation of road freight transportation addressing: (1) mobile delivery robots that can navigate autonomously through urban areas for the first- and last-mile transport of parcels and that can track their own status and those of the parcels (Asdecker 2020), (2) autonomous trucks for the long-haul transports between depots mostly on highways (Sternberg et al. 2020), (3) telematic units that can continuously track the status of trucks, swap bodies, trailers, and their load during long-haul transports (Heinbach et al. 2022c), (4) intelligent data services that can be used to improve forecasts and planning (Birkel et al. 2020), and (5) digital platforms to exchange road freight orders and transport orders between platform participants and to optimize order assignments (Heinbach et al. 2022a). MASs are especially applicable for the automation of the order management in intermodal freight fleets, because a multi-agent-based approach does not include a central control instance and can thus better cope with the fragmented business industry in the transport logistics sector.

3 Research Methods

This section presents a comprehensive outline of the methodologies employed in this study, detailing the systematic approach taken in the consortium research project for the literature review and the development of the new MAS concept.

3.1 *Design Science Research Process (DSRP) of a Consortium Research Project*

The research of the MAS for freight fleet management, as part of the consortium research project, employs a consortium research methodology that is structurally aligned to the Design Science Research Process (DSRP) framework, following

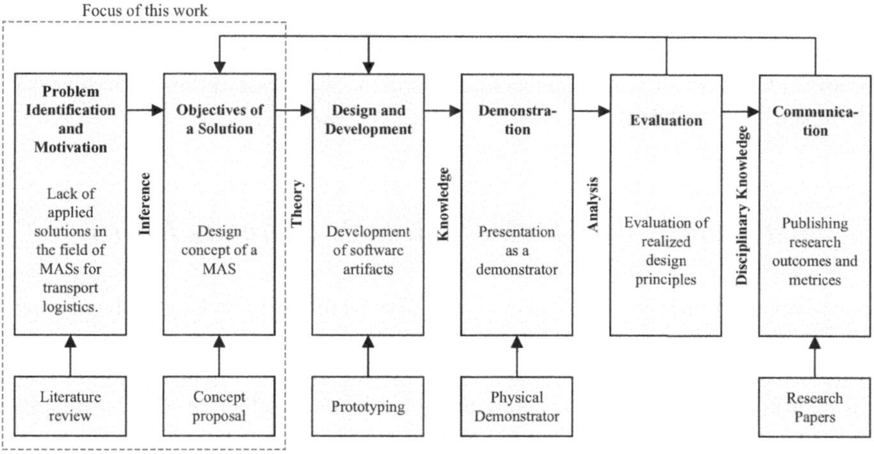

Fig. 1 Design science research process (DSRP) model as described by Peffers et al. (2007)

Österle and Otto (2010). One of the key advantages of this approach is that it facilitates knowledge exchange with the practitioner community. To navigate the development, the DSRP as proposed by Peffers et al. (2007) provides a basic framework for designing and evaluating solutions to complex problems. The methodology consists of several iterative steps as depicted in Fig. 1. The outcomes of the research within the consortium research project, encompassing the first two steps, are presented in this work.

In the methodology of evidence-based software engineering, a systematic literature review aims to accumulate all evidence on a research question (Kitchenham et al. 2009), but also identifies research gaps (Kitchenham 2004), and most notably aids the decision-making process in the development of software artifacts (Dyba et al. 2005). In the context of our consortium research project, the systematic literature review in this work corroborates our research approach and demonstrates the absence of prior investigations in this field, thus highlighting the necessity for a novel MAS concept for freight fleet management. Due to the scope of our project on the logistics sector, which focuses generally on the transport of goods and not on the transport of humans (Muchna et al. 2017), we did not include papers that describe a human-centered MAS for the management of passenger traffic. In the second step, the research requirements and basic design features of the system were gathered in close collaboration with practitioners, following the recommended procedure of Sonnenberg and vom Brockeb (2012) and the closely related Action Design Research (ADR) methodology proposed by Sein et al. (2011). In this process, the relevant technologies and actors were identified. As a result, concepts were derived for the software agents to represent the various actors and resources with their respective responsibilities in a given transport chain. These concepts for the different types of software agents were iteratively refined and evaluated with the practitioners. For this end, the online collaboration tool Miro was used (Miro n.d.). In addition, the importance of integrating state-of-the-art technology such as delivery robots and telematic-enabled trailers as well as having a sovereign data exchange within a dataspace in the broader context of Gaia-X were identified as further critical objectives of the research project (Heinbach et al. 2022b).

3.2 Methodology Used for the Systematic Literature Review

To answer RQ1 using empirical evidence and facilitate knowledge advancement and further developments, our literature review must prioritize transparency and replicability throughout the rigor review process, thereby mitigating potential bias and ensuring comprehensive research outcomes. Thus, to adhere to these principles, a research protocol was established (Snyder 2019; Tranfield et al. 2003).

To precisely address the subject of MASs, and to ensure that only relevant studies are included while avoiding those for e.g., agent-based simulations, the string multi-agent was selected. To further narrow down the application area of the MAS, the string fleet management was incorporated. Additionally, to focus on freight and differentiate from other types of transportation (e.g., public transport), a third string freight was introduced. Hence, to ensure a comprehensive search that aligns to our research question, the search term multi-agent AND (fleet management) AND freight was selected.

For the purpose of a comprehensive literature review, several electronic databases were identified and included in the search process, namely SpringerLink, ScienceDirect, AISel, Wiley, IEEE, ACM, JSTOR and Scopus (Gusenbauer and Haddaway 2020; Charband and Navimipour 2016; de Gauna et al. 2020). In accordance with Kitchenham (2004), primary studies of all types of outlets are included in the search to counter a possible publication bias. EndNote serves as the primary reference management tool utilized for this systematic literature review, complemented by Excel for quantitative analysis and reporting of the search process at each step. To include all research evidence with regard to the initially formulated research question, the primary studies are not filtered by year of publication. As suggested by Kitchenham (2004), no additional language filtering was conducted in order to avoid a language bias (Rothstein et al. 2005). After retrieving all search results, studies are filtered by accessibility of full text in the first step, followed by a successive relevance assessment of titles and abstracts with respect to RQ1, i.e., the relevance with respect to the development of MASs for freight fleet management. To prevent inadvertent exclusion of relevant research, broader inclusion criteria were applied when screening the titles and abstract. Hence, all studies covering concepts of intelligent systems or recent innovations for transportation problems were included. Eligible studies undergo a rigorous full-text evaluation to ensure stricter inclusion criteria are met, allowing only those studies to be included that explicitly address MASs for transportation problems. Additionally, related approaches like agent-based modeling are excluded, and only studies concerning transport logistics and road-based transport

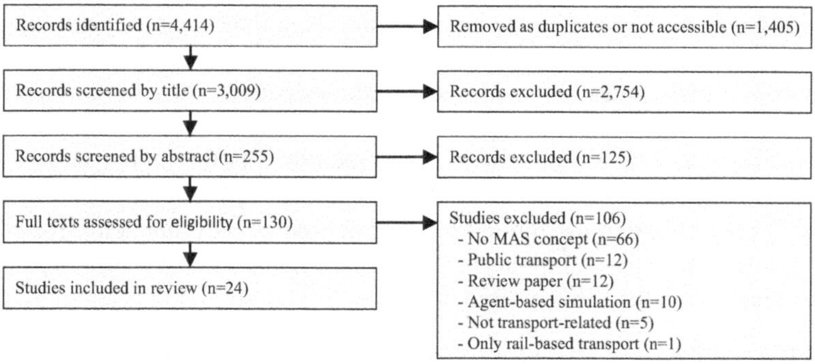

Fig. 2 Flow diagram of the literature screening process, based on Page et al. (2021)

in the transport chain are included in order to comply with RQ1 and the scopes of the research consortium project.

4 Literature Review Results and Arising Concept Proposal

Building upon the preceding sections that laid out the context and methodology, this section endeavors to deliver the outcomes of the literature review and proposes a novel concept of using a MAS for freight fleet management, which was developed in the consortium research project. This section follows the Preferred Reporting Items for Systematic Reviews and Meta-Analyses (PRISMA) statement (Moher et al. 2009; Liberati et al. 2009) that provides a standardized reporting guideline ensuring the completeness and transparency of systematic reviews.

4.1 Results of the Systematic Literature Review

Study Selection Process Fig. 2 illustrates the process of data selection in this study based on the research protocol as defined in Sect. 3. In the first step, 4414 studies were identified by searching the online databases with the defined search string. The 130 studies that emerged from the sequential process of screening the titles and abstracts were then subjected to a full-text assessment to determine their eligibility in addressing research question RQ1, leading to 24 included studies for the review.[1] The excluded reports of this last step were subsequently categorized based on their respective reasons for exclusion, as listed in Fig. 2.

[1] Comprehensive bibliographic information relating to each subsequent phase of the screening process, following the initial title screening, can be accessed here: bit.ly/WI2023_397.

Data Synthesis To investigate the temporal trends in the research topic, the publication dates of each study included in the literature review were extracted. The distribution of these dates was analyzed to identify patterns of scholarly interest in the subject over time. Even though no filtering based on the year of publication was applied to the studies, the earliest study identified in the review dates back to 1994, suggesting that the subject of MASs for fleet management is a relatively recent research topic. Although the limited number of studies prevents definitive conclusions regarding the temporal trends in the field, the analysis underscores a persistent scholarly interest in the subject since 2005.

Data Abstraction This part aims to assess the current state of research and maturity of MAS solutions in freight fleet management (RQ1, RQ2). Further, the concepts to be extracted from the individual studies were delineated based on the requirements of the consortium research project. Firstly, the assessment focused on determining whether the specific study pertains to the domain of logistics, specifically parcel delivery, as this is the main focus of the consortium research project. Additionally, it was assessed whether the agents act as representatives of the supply chain entities (e.g., trailers, depots) to allow for a direct agent-based representation and responsibility of a physical entity. The prospect of physical distribution of the system is also contemplated, as the consortium research project necessitates not only the deployment of agents on a single server, but their migration capability of agents to fleet assets, such as delivery robots. As stated before, the transport chain for parcel delivery comprises the stages of first- and last-mile delivery, as well as the long-haul transport between depots. To comprehend and efficiently respond to the complex interdependencies of logistics processes at a system-level, it is essential to adopt a holistic perspective that considers all segments of the transport chain as a unified system. Accordingly, these three transport chain segments were defined as the concepts to be extracted from the literature. Closely tied to this is the concept of intermodality, as presented in Sect. 2.2. Lastly, the concept of maturity was introduced as similarly done by Davidsson et al. (2005). In this work, the maturity of a MAS is assessed based on three stages: (1) proposed concept or ontology, (2) implemented or tested MAS, (3) the deployment of a MAS in an applied fleet management system. The abstracted data was then aggregated into a concept matrix as proposed by Webster and Watson (2002), shown in Table 1. From the high-level perspective provided in Table 1 it is notable that there is a low density in concepts abstracted from the studies. Of the 24 studies surveyed, only ten explicitly combine agents with transport entities. Other approaches consider the agents as representatives of regions (Dorer and Calisti 2005a, b), or specific tasks, such as optimization (Miliauskas 2022), or as representatives of companies and parties (van der Putten et al. 2006; Robu et al. 2008; Teo et al. 2012, 2014). The solution of Maestro et al. (2021) is representing carriers by virtual organizations of agents, that are each individually responsible for certain tasks, e.g., optimization or urban traffic information. The majority of the papers that did not explicitly address parcel delivery consider rather focused topics, e.g., the pickup-and-delivery problem (Kozlak 2007) or delivery in the presence of flooding events (de Oliveira et al. 2017) without detailing the nature of goods. Other works state different types of goods, such as art, furniture and computers (Falk et al. 1994), or containers (Wojtusiak et al. 2012).

Further fields of interest in the analyzed literature were bidding and auction mechanisms (Los et al. 2020, 2022; Mes et al. 2008, 2013; van der Putten et al. 2006; Robu et al. 2008), ontologies (Giret et al. 2018; Miliauskas 2022) or assessing the impact of transport measures on MAS-based delivery systems (Holmgren et al. 2012; Teo et al. 2012, 2014). Moreover, several works take into account the influence of traffic on the distribution of urban goods (Boussier et al. 2009; Gómez-Marín et al. 2018, Koźlak 2007). Only two studies reached the highest stage of a deployed system (Maturity 3), namely the two contributions by Dorer and Calisti (2005a, b), in which the Living Systems Adaptive Transportation Networks (LS/ATN) framework is proposed that is deployed with one of the logistics partners (Dorer and Calisti 2005b). However, the system is deployed in a centralized manner, integrating into an existing traffic management system (Dorer and Calisti 2005b). It has to be noted however, that Dorer and Calisti (2005a) additionally present tests for a physically distributed agent-based approach. Although not assigned to the highest maturity stage, the closely connected works of van der Putten et al. (2006) and Robu et al. (2008) were developed in close collaboration with the European logistics service provider Vos logistics, with plans for deployment of the proposed MAS (van der Putten et al. 2006). Another approach of potential significance was formulated by Funk et al. (1999), which covers a holonic MAS for rail-based inter-depot logistics and road-based pickups and deliveries. Yet, this solution was proposed only at the stage of a prototypic simulation. In view of RQ1, it can thus be concluded that there is a high research interest in MAS for fleet management. Nevertheless, the current literature predominantly focuses on specific problems, the last-mile delivery for instance, or particular mechanisms such as auctioning or bidding, rather than considering the complete transport chain on a system level as done within our consortium research project. Further, concerning RQ2 it can be summarized that the majority of the proposed MAS were at a stage in which tests or simulations were presented (Maturity 2). However, only two studies reached the highest stage of a deployed system (Maturity 3).

4.2 Proposition of a Novel Concept

The previous section revealed the lack of applied MAS solutions for the integrated and automated management of an intermodal freight fleet consisting of vehicles for the first-mile, long-haul and last-mile transport of parcels. Therefore, this section is justified by the finding in Sect. 4.1 and aims to answer RQ3 by introducing a novel MAS. As proposed by Heinbach et al. (2022b), one objective of the MAS is to increase the automation in the order management of parcel deliveries. As a second objective, the MAS should include state-of-the-art technologies like delivery robots for the first- and last-mile deliveries and telematic-equipped trailers and swap bodies for the long-haul transport of parcels. The third objective is to realize horizontal and secure data flows between the software agents of the MAS and the distributed vehicles and

Table 1 Concept matrix of the analyzed literature according to Webster and Watson (2002)

Articles	Concepts							
	Agents representing physical resources	Distributed system	Parcel delivery	Intermodality	Part of transport chain			Maturity level
					First mile	Long-haul	Last mile	
Boussier et al. (2009)	•		•				•	1
Dorer and Calisti (2005a)		•			•		•	3
Dorer and Calisti (2005b)					•		•	3
Elfazziki et al. (2009)		•					•	2
Falk et al. (1994)	•				•		•	2
Funk et al. (1999)	•	•		•	•	•	•	2
Giret et al. (2018)	•	•	•	•	•		•	2
Gómez-Marín et al. (2018)	•		•		•		•	1
Holmgren et al. (2012)				•	•		•	2
Koźlak (2007)	•				•		•	2
Los el al. (2020)	•		•		•		•	2
Los et al. (2022)	•		•		•		•	2
Maestro et al. (2021)		•					•	1
Mes et al. (2008)	•				•		•	2
Mes et al. (2013)	•				•		•	2
Miliauskas (2022)		•						1
de Oliveira et al. (2017)							•	2

(continued)

Table 1 (continued)

Articles	Concepts							
	Agents representing physical resources	Distributed system	Parcel delivery	Intermodality	Part of transport chain			Maturity level
					First mile	Long-haul	Last mile	
van der Putten et al. (2006)					•		•	2
Robu et al. (2008)					•		•	2
Sitek et al. (2014)				•			•	2
Stinson and Mohammadian (2022)				•	•	•	•	2
Teo et al. (2012)			•		•		•	2
Teo et al. (2014)			•		•		•	2
Wojtusiak et al. (2012)		•				•		2
Total	10	7	7	5	17	3	22	

other resources. Based on these three main objectives, the functions of different actors and entities along the transport chain for parcel deliveries were defined and assigned to different types of software agents (see Fig. 3). More exactly, the desired MAS should cover the following software agents and functions to realize the objectives of a more automated management of systems for parcel deliveries that include delivery robots and telematic-equipped trailers and swap bodies: Firstly, a delivery agent (1) is needed representing a parcel delivery robot responsible for bidding for first- and last-mile transport orders, for optimizing the robot's tour, for sending driving commands to the robot, and for the management of customer interactions. Such a delivery agent could belong to a parcel delivery service company. A trailer agent (2), representing a physical swap-body or a trailer, should manage the long-haul transport, including the bidding for freight lists, tour optimization, and the insertion of workshop visits. The trailer agent could be hosted by a transport service company. As the handling of freight between the different types of vehicles takes place at depot facilities, a depot agent (3) is necessary. This agent should receive the estimated time of arrival (ETA) of delivery agents (1) and trailer agents (2) at depot facilities to coordinate appropriate docking procedures. Depot agents might run in the realm of freight forwarding companies. Further, an entity has to manage the connection between an external booking platform, which can be used by customers to create bookings for parcel deliveries, and the delivery agents and trailer agents. Thus, the booking agent (4) is defined that interfaces with the booking platform and divides shipping orders into freight orders (i.e., long-haul transport between depots) as well as transport orders for first- and last-mile (i.e., parcel pickups and deliveries). For instance, a booking agent could represent a shipper. Another function of the booking agent is to update the customers of a shipper about the current status of their parcel deliveries. Since each long-haul transport between two depots includes a multitude of parcels, a bordero agent (5) is necessary to combine freight orders into consolidated loading lists (so-called "borderos" (Oelfke 2005)). Bordero agents could belong to freight forwarding companies. Lastly, workshop facilities were identified as a relevant actor in the transport network, resulting in the workshop agent (6), responsible for handling maintenance orders initiated by trailer agents (2). Workshop agents might represent individual workshop companies and can bid for maintenance orders and optimize their schedules after winning an auction. Figure 3 illustrates a top-level conceptual framework of the MAS proposed in the consortium research project Gaia-X 4 ROMS.

The software agents are planned to be operational on a physically distributed system, thereby realizing the concept of decentralized fleet management. The third objective of the MAS—but also of the Gaia-X 4 ROMS consortium research project in general—is to have secure and horizontal data flows within the distributed system. To this end, we will follow the Gaia-X standards to create a federated and self-sovereign data ecosystem (Otto and Burmann 2021; Konietzko et al. 2022).

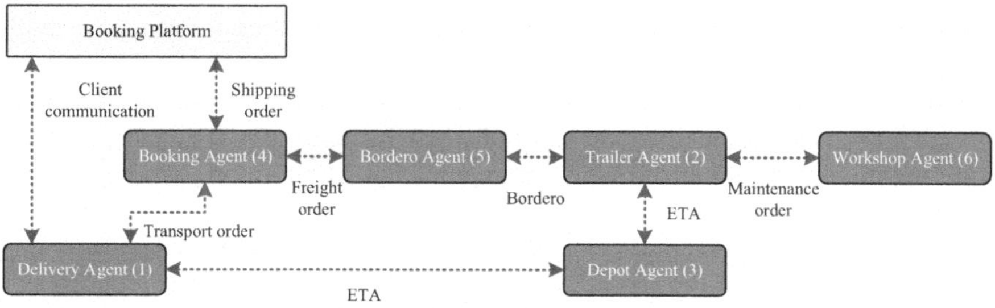

Fig. 3 Concept of the MAS comprising six different types of agents as well as an auxiliary booking platform

5 Discussion

Through a systematic review of existing literature, this study aims at providing a comprehensive understanding of the research concerning the application of MAS for intermodal freight fleet management (RQ1). This supports a deeper understanding and contextualization of the project within the research landscape. The results presented in Sect. 4.1 indicate a sustained level of interest in the topic in academia, while a notable research deficit in the current literature pertaining to the utilization of MASs in the logistics industry, especially parcel delivery, was identified. Subsequently, RQ2 was addressed by the observation that only in a limited number of studies (Dorer and Calisti 2005a, b; van der Putten et al. 2006; Robu et al. 2008), the presented MASs for managing freight fleets reached or approached the stage of deployment. Moreover, none of the solutions regard the entire intermodal transport chain. Further, all of the studies deviated in the core concepts from the one of the consortium research project, either by focusing on centralized deployment or incorporating agents not representing transport entities. This finding is corroborated by the related literature reviews, that were identified and presented in the introduction of this work (Sect. 1).

During the systematic literature analysis, various factors influencing the validity of this study were identified. First, during the screening process it became apparent that many studies do not strictly distinguish between the concepts of MASs and agent-based simulation or use these terms interchangeably. However, this issue predominantly occurred during the full-text assessments, suggesting that the exclusion process in previous steps was lenient enough to tolerate concepts of agent-based simulation (type-I error). This also implies a low rate of inadvertent exclusion of MASs (type-II error), satisfying the requirement of a comprehensive review. Further, as outlined in Sect. 4.1, not all studies identified in the initial retrieval could be accessed, potentially introducing an unknown degree of publication bias that could not be addressed. Finally, the data retrieval and screening was conducted by a single researcher, increasing the likelihood of selection bias (Dyba et al. 2005). However, a rigorous research protocol was established beforehand (Sect. 3.2) to ensure objectivity and reproducibility of the selection process. Regarding the data abstraction outlined in Sect. 4.1, concepts were derived from examining the consortium research project and identified in the primary studies.

Nonetheless, it was not always evident whether a study addressed a specific concept. For instance, the distributability of a MAS concept was frequently implied by the mention of decentralized agent communication. Furthermore, as some studies covered abstract concepts of various logistics problems, it was not always clear how they were allocated to specific segments of the transport chain. One example in this context is the work of Elfazziki et al. (2009) in which an agent-based concept for general road transport is proposed with the focus on the negotiation and task-planning aspects.

Justified by the findings of the literature review, that revealed the lack of applied solutions for relevant MASs, Sect. 4.2 introduced a novel concept for a MAS, which was developed and evaluated within the consortium research project. The concept serves as an answer to RQ3 and represents a comprehensive approach to managing an intermodal freight fleet with a MAS. The derived concept features six agent types representing the intermodal fleet (trailer equipment and parcel delivery robots), logistics facilities (depots and workshops), and order processing aspects (bookings and borderos). The approach enables the holistic agent-based management of a freight fleet dedicated to parcel delivery.

6 Conclusions and Future Work

This work represents the fundamental research of the Gaia-X 4 ROMS project, a consortium research endeavor focusing on developing a MAS for an integrated management of intermodal freight fleets in order to increase the automation of parcel logistics and thereby cope with the increasing number of parcels deliveries. After conducting a thorough analysis of existing literature reviews, it can be inferred that the utilization of MASs in the field of logistics remains limited and the identified literature reviews do not cover the precise concepts of the MAS as envisaged by the consortium research project. This necessitated a systematic literature review confirming a lack of applied multi-agent-based approaches for the integrated management of intermodal transport chains. Hence, this work justifies the innovative MAS concept for intermodal freight fleet management, consisting of software agents for parcel delivery robots, trailers, depots, booking activities, consolidation activities, and workshops.

Additionally, the consortium research approach encourages continuous collaboration with practitioners, guaranteeing a high degree of applicability of our proposed solution in real-world logistics scenarios. The integration of the consortium research project into the Gaia-X project ensures adherence to state-of-the-art concepts of data security and sovereignty, making it designed for long-term and sustainable use. Given the ongoing expansion of the parcel delivery market and the rise of new technologies like IoT devices, it is reasonable to anticipate that innovative strategies, such as the proposed MAS concept presented in this study, will attain increased relevance in forthcoming years.

As outlined at the outset, this study serves as a foundation for the first steps in the consortium research project and highlights the necessity of a novel agent-based approach. Accordingly, detailed design principles for each type of software agent based on the work of Gregor et al. (2020) and Wahlster (2017) are being developed and will be presented in future work. Moreover, the agents' routines for self-regulation as well as the agents' optimization models, data models, learning models, and their interactions with stakeholders will be defined. Further on, the evaluations of the agents' design principles and of the agents' detailed technical concepts are being conducted to achieve a solid technical ground for prototyping along the phases of the DSRP.

Acknowledgements This paper was written as part of the project Gaia-X 4 ROMS—Support and Remote Operation of Automated and Networked Mobility Services (FKZ: 19S21005C). The joint project is funded by the German Federal Ministry of Economics and Climate Protection (BMWK). The authors are responsible for the content of this article.

References

Akac, A., Anagnostopoulou, A. & Nalmpantis, D. (2020), Digitalization in Freight Transport Services: Balkan Area, *in* 'Advances in Mobility-as-a-Service Systems', Springer International Publishing, pp. 1056–1065.

Asdecker, B. (2020), How Dare You Replace My Deliveryman?! Acceptance of Last-Mile Transportation Innovations–A Qualitative Perspective, *in* 'Proceedings of Americas Conference on Information Systems (AMCIS) 2020', AISeL, pp. 1–10.

Birkel, H., Kopyto, M. & Lutz, C. (2020), Challenges of Applying Predictive Analytics in Transport Logistics, *in* 'Proceedings of the 2020 on Computers and People Research Conference', ACM.

Boussier, J. M., Cucu, T., Ion, L., Estraillier, P. & Breuil, D. (2009), 'Goods distribution with electric vans in cities: Towards an agent-based simulation', *World Electric Vehicle Journal* **3**(3), 597–605.

Brabänder, C. & Braun, M. (2020), 'Bringing economies of integration into the costing of groupage freight', *Journal of Revenue and Pricing Management* **19**(6), 366–385.

Braud, A., Fromentoux, G., Radier, B. & Grand, O. L. (2021), 'The Road to European Digital Sovereignty with Gaia-X and IDSA', *IEEE Network* **35**(2), 4–5.

Bundesverband Paket und Expresslogistik e. V. (BIEK), KE CONSULT Kurte&Esser GbR (2022), 'Impulsgeber mit Innovationskraft, KEP-Studie 2022– Analyse des Marktes in Deutschland'. https://www.biek.de/files/biek/downloads/papiere/BIEK_KEP-Studie_2022.pdf. Accessed: 09.03.2023.

Charband, Y. & Navimipour, N. J. (2016), 'Online knowledge sharing mechanisms: a systematic review of the state of the art literature and recommendations for future research', *Information Systems Frontiers* **18**(6), 1131–1151.

Chevalier, S. (2022), 'Retail e-commerce sales worldwide from 2014 to 2026', Statista. https://www.statista.com/statistics/379046/worldwide-retail-e-commerce-sales/. Accessed: 02.03.2023.

Davidsson, P., Henesey, L., Ramstedt, L., Törnquist, J. & Wernstedt, F. (2005), 'An analysis of agent-based approaches to transport logistics', *Transportation Research* **13**(4), 255–271.

de Oliveira, Kelli, L., Lessa, D. A., Oliveira, E. & Gregório Calazans, B. F. (2017), 'Multi-agent modelling approach for evaluating the city logistics dynamic in a vulnerability situation: An exploratory study in Belo Horizonte (Brazil)', *Transportation Research Procedia* **25**, 1046–1060.

de Gauna, D. E. R., Villalonga, C. & Sanchez, L. E. (2020), 'Multi-agent systems in the field of urbane-mobility: A Systematic Review', *IEEE Latin America Transactions* **18**(12), 2186–2195.

Dekhne, A., Hastings, G., Murnane, J. & Neuhaus, F. (2019), 'Automation in logistics: Big opportunity, bigger uncertainty'. https://www.mckinsey.com/industries/travel-logistics-and-infrastructure/our-insights/automation-in-logistics-big-opportunity-bigger-uncertainty. Accessed: 12.06.2023.

Dorer, K. & Calisti, M. (2005a), An Adaptive Approach to Dynamic Transport Optimization, *in* F. Klügl, A. Bazzan & S. Ossowski, eds, 'Applications of Agent Technology in Traffic and Transportation', Birkhäuser Basel, Basel, pp. 33–49.

Dorer, K. & Calisti, M. (2005b), An Adaptive Solution to Dynamic Transport Optimization, *in* 'Conference on Autonomous Agents and Multiagent Systems', AAMAS '05, International Conference on Autonomous Agents and Multiagent Systems, Association for Computing Machinery, New York, NY, USA, p. 45–51.

Dyba, T., Kitchenham, B. & Jorgensen, M. (2005), 'Evidence-based software engineering for practitioners', *IEEE Software* **22**(1), 58–65.

Elfazziki, A., Nejeoui, A. & Sadgal, M. (2009), Modeling Multi-agent System of Management Road Transport: Tasks Planning and Negotiation, *in* E. Damiani, K. Yetongnon, R. Chbeir & A. Dipanda, eds, 'Advanced Internet Based Systems and Applications', International Conference on Signal-Image Technology and Internet-Based Systems, Springer Berlin Heidelberg, Berlin, Heidelberg, pp. 169–179.

Falco, M. & Robiolo, G. (2019), A Systematic Literature Review in Multi-Agent-Sytems: Patterns and Trends, *in* '2019 XLV Latin American Computing Conference (CLEI)', IEEE.

Falk, J., Spieck, S. & Mertens, P. (1994), Solving Logistical Problems with Partly Intelligent Agents, *in* B. Wolfinger, ed., 'Innovationen bei Rechen- und Kommunikationssystemen', World Computer Congress, Springer Berlin Heidelberg, Berlin, Heidelberg, pp. 459–465.

Farquharson, N., Mageto, J. & Makan, H. (2021), 'Effect of internet of things on road freight industry', *Journal of Transport and Supply Chain Management* **15**.

Funk, P., Vierke, G. & Bürckert, H.-J. (1999), *A Multi-Agent Systems Perspective on Intermodal Transport Chains*, Springer Berlin Heidelberg, Berlin, Heidelberg, pp. 159–170.

Gaia-X 4 Future Mobility (n.d.), 'Die Projektfamilie. GAIA-X 4 Future Mobility'. https://www.gaia-x4futuremobility.dlr.de/. Accessed: 08.03.2023.

Giret, A., Julian, V., Carrascosa, C. & Rebollo, M. (2018), An Ontology for Sustainable Intelligent Transportation Systems, *in* 'Highlights of Practical Applications of Agents, Multi-Agent Systems, and Complexity: The PAAMS Collection', Conference on Practical Applications of Agents and Multi-Agent Systems, Springer International Publishing, Cham, pp. 381–391.

Gómez-Marín, C. G., Arango-Serna, M. D. & Serna-Urán, C. A. (2018), 'Agent-based microsimulation conceptual model for urban freight distribution', *Transportation Research Procedia* **33**, 155–162.

Gregor, S., , Kruse, L., Seidel, S. & and (2020), 'Research perspectives: The anatomy of a design principle', *Journal of the Association for Information Systems* **21**, 1622–1652.

Gusenbauer, M. & Haddaway, N. R. (2020), 'Which academic search systems are suitable for systematic reviews or meta-analyses? Evaluating retrieval qualities of Google Scholar, PubMed, and 26 other resources', *Research Synthesis Methods* **11**(2), 181–217.

Heinbach, C., Beinke, J., Kammler, F. & Thomas, O. (2022a), 'Data-driven forwarding: a typology of digital platforms for road freight transport management', *Electronic Markets* **32**(2), 807–828.

Heinbach, C., Gösling, H., Meier, P. & Thomas, O. (2022b), 'Smart Managed Freight Fleet: Ein automatisiertes und vernetztes Flottenmanagement in einem föderierten Datenökosystem', *HMD Praxis der Wirtschaftsinformatik* **60**(1), 193–213.

Heinbach, C., Kammler, F. & Thomas, O. (2022c), Exploring Design Requirements of Fleet Telematics Systems Supporting Road Freight Transportation: A Digital Service Side Perspective. *Wirtschaftsinformatik 2022 Proceedings* **1**.

Holmgren, J., Ramstedt, L., Davidsson, P. & Persson, J. A. (2012), Multi-Agent-Based Simulation for Analysis of Transport Policy and Infrastructure Measures, *in* S. Cranefield & I. Song, eds, 'Agent Based Simulation for a Sustainable Society and Multi-agent Smart Computing', International Conference on Principles and Practice of Multi-Agent Systems, Springer Berlin Heidelberg, Berlin, Heidelberg, pp. 1–15. in Transport Logistics, *in* 'Proceedings of the 2020 on Computers and People Research Conference', ACM.

Jennings, N. R. (2000), 'On agent-based software engineering', *Artificial Intelligence* **117**(2), 277–296.

Kitchenham, B., Brereton, O. P., Budgen, D., Turner, M., Bailey, J. & Linkman, S. (2009), 'Systematic literature reviews in software engineering – A systematic literature review', *Information and Software Technology* **51**(1), 7–15.

Kitchenham, B. (2004), 'Procedures for performing systematic reviews', *Keele, UK, Keele University* **33**(2004), 1–26

Konietzko, E., , Tanrikulu, C., Schwarz, F., Lindow, K., & and (2022), 'How to Gaia-X? – Ein Vorgehensmodell zur erfolgreichen Teilnahme an interoperablen und dezentralen Datenökosystemen am Beispiel von Gaia-X', *Industrie 4.0 Management* **2022**(6), 54–58.

Koźlak, J. (2007), Learning in Cooperating Agents Environment as a Method of Solving Transport Problems and Limiting the Effects of Crisis Situations, *in* Y. Shi, G. D. van Albada, J. Dongarra & P. M. A. Sloot, eds, 'Computational Science – ICCS 2007', International Conference on Computational Science, Springer Berlin Heidelberg, Berlin, Heidelberg, pp. 872–879.

Liberati, A., Altman, D. G., Tetzlaff, J., Mulrow, C., Gotzsche, P. C., Ioannidis, J. P. A., Clarke, M., Devereaux, P. J., Kleijnen, J. & Moher, D. (2009), 'The PRISMA statement for reporting systematic reviews and meta-analyses of studies that evaluate healthcare interventions: explanation and elaboration', *BMJ* **339**(jul21 1), b2700–b2700.

Los, J., Schulte, F., Spaan, M. T. J. & Negenborn, R. R. (2020), 'Collaborative Vehicle Routing when Agents have Mixed Information Sharing Attitudes', *Transportation Research Procedia* **44**, 94–101.

Los, J., Schulte, F., Spaan, M. T. J. & Negenborn, R. R. (2022), An Auction-Based Multi-Agent System for the Pickup and Delivery Problem with Autonomous Vehicles and Alternative Locations, *in* M. Freitag, A. Kinra, H. Kotzab & N. Megow, eds, 'Dynamics in Logistics', International Conference on Dynamics in Logistics, Springer International Publishing, Cham, pp. 244–260.

Maestro, J. A., Rodriguez, S., Casado, R., Prieto, J. & Corchado, J. M. (2021), Comparison of Efficient Planning and Optimization Methods of Last Mile Delivery Resources, *in* H. Gao, R. J. Durán Barroso, P. Shanchen & R. Li, eds, 'Broadband Communications, Networks, and Systems', International Conference on Broadband Communications, Networks, and Systems, Broadnets, Springer International Publishing, Cham, pp. 163–173.

Mes, M., van der Heijden, M. & Schuur, P. (2008), 'Look-ahead strategies for dynamic pickup and delivery problems', *OR Spectrum* **32**(2), 395–421.

Mes, M., van der Heijden, M. & Schuur, P. (2013), 'Interaction between intelligent agent strategies for real-time transportation planning', *Central European Journal of Operations Research* **21**.

Miliauskas, A. (2022), *Automated Freight Brokerage Based on Multi-Agent Semantic Web Service Composition*, Springer International Publishing, Cham, pp. 141–155.

Miro (n.d.), 'Miro Online Collaboration Tool'. https://miro.com/. Accessed: 09.03.2023.

Moher, D., Liberati, A., Tetzlaff, J. & Altman, D. G. (2009), 'Preferred Reporting Items for Systematic Reviews and Meta-Analyses: The PRISMA Statement', *Journal of Clinical Epidemiology* **62**(10), 1006–1012.

Muchna, C., Brandenburg, H., Fottner, J. & Gutermuth, J. (2017), *Grundlagen der Logistik - Begriffe, Strukturen und Prozesse*, Springer-Verlag, Berlin Heidelberg New York.

Oelfke, D. (2005), Spediteursammelgutverkehr, *in* 'Speditionsbetriebslehre und Logistik', Gabler Verlag, pp. 111–116.

Österle, H. & Otto, B. (2010), 'Consortium Research', *Business & Information Systems Engineering* **2**(5), 283–293.

Otto, B. & Burmann, A. (2021), 'Europäische Dateninfrastrukturen', *Informatik Spektrum* **44**(4), 283–291.

Page, M. J., McKenzie, J. E., Bossuyt, P. M., Boutron, I., Hoffmann, T. C., Mulrow, C. D., Shamseer, L., Tetzlaff, J. M., Akl, E. A., Brennan, S. E., Chou, R., Glanville, J., Grimshaw, J. M., Hróbjartsson, A., Lalu, M. M., Li, T., Loder, E. W., Mayo-Wilson, E., McDonald, S., McGuinness, L. A., Stewart, L. A., Thomas, J., Tricco, A. C., Welch, V. A., Whiting, P. & Moher, D. (2021), 'The prisma 2020 statement: an updated guideline for reporting systematic reviews', *BMJ* **372**.

Peffers, K., Tuunanen, T., Rothenberger, M. A. & Chatterjee, S. (2007), 'A Design Science Research Methodology for Information Systems Research', *Journal of Management Information Systems* **24**(3), 45–77.

Pitt, J. (2021), *Self-Organising Multi-Agent Systems: Algorithmic Foundations of Cyber-Anarcho-Socialism*, World Scientific.

van der Putten, S., Robu, V., La Poutré, H., Jorritsma, A. & Gal, M. (2006), Automating Supply Chain Negotiations Using Autonomous Agents: A Case Study in Transportation Logistics, *in* 'Conference on Autonomous Agents and Multiagent Systems', AAMAS '06, International Conference on Autonomous Agents and Multiagent Systems, Association for Computing Machinery, New York, NY, USA, p. 1506–1513. research', *Information Systems Frontiers* **18**(6), 1131–1151.

Robu, V., Noot, H., La Poutré, H. & van Schijndel, W.-J. (2008), An Interactive Platform for Auction-Based Allocation of Loads in Transportation Logistics, *in* 'Conference on Autonomous Agents and Multiagent Systems', AAMAS '08, International Conference on Autonomous Agents and Multiagent Systems, International Foundation for Autonomous Agents and Multiagent Systems, Richland, SC, p. 3–10.

Rothstein, H. R., Sutton, A. J. & Borenstein, M. (2005), 'Publication bias in meta-analysis', *Publication bias in meta-analysis: Prevention, assessment and adjustments* pp. 1–7.

Sein, Henfridsson, Purao, Rossi & Lindgren (2011), 'Action Design Research', *MIS Quarterly* **35**(1), 37.

Sitek, P., Wikarek, J. & Grzybowska, K. (2014), A Multi-Agent Approach to the Multi-Echelon Capacitated Vehicle Routing Problem, *in* 'Highlights of Practical Applications of Heterogeneous Multi-Agent Systems. The PAAMS Collection', Springer International Publishing, Cham, pp. 121–132.

Snyder, H. (2019), 'Literature review as a research methodology: An overview and guidelines', *Journal of Business Research* **104**, 333–339.

Sonnenberg, C. & vom Brocke, J. (2012), Evaluation Patterns for Design Science Research Artefacts, *in* 'Communications in Computer and Information Science', Springer Berlin Heidelberg, pp. 71–83.

Sternberg, H., Chen, H., Hofmann, E. & Prockl, G. (2020), Autonomous Trucks: A Supply Chain Adoption Perspective, *in* 'Proceedings of the 53rd Hawaii International Conference on System Sciences', Hawaii International Conference on System Sciences (HICSS), United States, pp. 4534–4539.

Stinson, M. & Mohammadian, A. K. (2022), 'Introducing CRISTAL: A model of collaborative, informed, strategic trade agents with logistics', *Transportation Research Interdisciplinary Perspectives* Systematic review of the state of the art literature and recommendations for future **13**, 100539

Taniguchi, E., Thompson, R. G. & Qureshi, A. G. (2020), 'Modelling city logistics using recent innovative technologies', *Transportation Research Procedia* **46**, 3–12.

Teo, J. S., Taniguchi, E. & Qureshi, A. G. (2012), 'Evaluating City Logistics Measure in E-Commerce with Multiagent Systems', *Procedia - Social and Behavioral Sciences* **39**, 349–359. Seventh International Conference on City Logistics which was held on June 7- 9,2011, Mallorca, Spain.

Teo, J. S., Taniguchi, E. & Qureshi, A. G. (2014), 'Evaluation of Load Factor Control and Urban Freight Road Pricing Joint Schemes with Multi-agent Systems Learning Models', *Procedia - Social and Behavioral Sciences* **125**, 62–74. Eighth International Conference on City Logistics 17–19 June 2013, Bali, Indonesia.

Tranfield, D., Denyer, D. & Smart, P. (2003), 'Towards a Methodology for Developing Evidence-Informed Management Knowledge by Means of Systematic Review', *British Journal of Management* **14**(3), 207–222.

Wahlster, W. (2017), 'Künstliche Intelligenz als Grundlage autonomer Systeme', *Informatik-Spektrum* **40**(5), 409–418.

Webster, J. & Watson, R. T. (2002), 'Analyzing the Past to Prepare for the Future: Writing a Literature Review', *MIS Quarterly* **26**(2), xiii–xxiii. with electric vans in cities: Towards an agent-based simulation', *World Electric Vehicle Journal* **3**(3), 597–605

Wojtusiak, J., Warden, T. & Herzog, O. (2012), 'The learnable evolution model in agent-based delivery optimization', *Memetic Computing* **4**.

Wooldridgey, M. & Ciancarini, P. (2001), Agent-Oriented Software Engineering: The State of the Art, *in* 'Agent-Oriented Software Engineering', Springer Berlin Heidelberg, pp. 1–28.

Towards Hybrid Architectures: Integrating Large Language Models in Informative Chatbots

Arnold F. Arz von Straussenburg and Anna Wolters

Abstract Informative chatbots embedded in an organization-specific context can provide a reliable, interactive, and engaging source of information for users. However, traditional chatbot techniques have limitations in processing and understanding user input and generating human-like responses. On the other hand, the latest implementations of large language models show promising results in these domains but have limitations in providing accurate and up-to-date facts from domain-specific knowledge bases. With the advent of popular chatbots like ChatGPT, they are increasingly becoming part of organizations' digital infrastructure. In this research-in-progress paper, we argue that the strengths and weaknesses of traditional techniques and large language models are complementary. Therefore, we propose a hybrid chatbot architecture that utilizes inter-agent communication to compensate for disadvantages while enhancing the chatbot's abilities, as perceived by the user. This approach will form the basis for development and evaluation using Design Science Research (DSR) as part of our research.

Keywords Chatbots · Hybrid chatbot architecture · Large language models

1 Introduction and Motivation

Chatbots provide an interactive way to access information, perform tasks, and act as friendly interlocutors (Adamopoulou and Moussiades 2020a) They can be used in various sectors for different purposes to help organizations by providing a source of information with control over accuracy and topicality. However, challenges include understanding user intent, generating human-like responses, and maintaining data sources.

A. F. Arz von Straussenburg (✉) · A. Wolters
University of Koblenz, Koblenz, Germany
e-mail: arz@uni-koblenz.de

A. Wolters
e-mail: awolters@uni-koblenz.de

D. Beverungen et al. (eds.), *Solutions and Technologies for Responsible Digitalization*, Lecture Notes in Information Systems and Organisation 75,
https://doi.org/10.1007/978-3-031-80122-8_21

More powerful Large Language Models (LLMs) offer advanced chatbot capabilities beyond existing Natural Language Processing (NLP) and Machine Learning (ML) techniques, excelling in generating human-like text and understanding unstructured data sources (Brown et al. 2020). ChatGPT, an LLM-based chatbot trained with reinforcement learning from human feedback, has had a significant impact on the public since its release (OpenAI 2022). Despite their advantages, these new technologies still have drawbacks, including the potential to provide responses that are not supported by the underlying knowledge base. This may become a significant issue as chatbots become more integrated into organizations' digital infrastructure and operations. Furthermore, while commercial chatbots already use LLM (Shuster et al. 2022), there is limited research on using LLM for informative chatbots.

This paper not only contrasts established chatbot methods with LLM-based chatbots to understand their respective strengths and weaknesses but also pioneers the integration of LLMs and traditional chatbot technologies, proposing a novel hybrid approach aimed at improving efficacy and user experience in information retrieval tasks. Furthermore, we argue that a combination of both techniques can enable the creation of powerful chatbot architectures that mitigate weaknesses and emphasize strengths. To achieve this, the research paper addresses the following research questions: *What are the advantages and shortcomings of both traditional and LLM chatbots?* (RQ1) and *How can these approaches be integrated/combined to enable accurate informative chatbots that provide natural-sounding answers?* (RQ2).

2 Background

2.1 Classification of Chatbots

Chatbots, also referred to as conversational agents, digital assistants, interactive agents, or natural dialogue systems (Adamopoulou and Moussiades 2020b, 2020a; Diederich et al. 2019) are computer systems that enable humans to interact with computers using natural language (Lokman and Ameedeen 2019). While not all chatbots can be fit neatly into categories, several dimensions can classify the types of chatbots considered in scientific discourse, each with different characteristics that form the basis for our research. The combined chatbot classifications or taxonomies presented by (Adamopoulou and Moussiades 2020b), (Diederich et al. 2019), (Lokman and Ameedeen 2019), and (Hussain et al. 2019) are depicted in Table 1.

Chatbots can have different objectives, namely providing information, supporting users in fulfilling tasks, or focusing on conversing with their users (Adamopoulou and Moussiades 2020b; Diederich et al. 2019). There are also different approaches for processing input texts and generating responses. Rule-based techniques apply pattern-matching to understand the context and the user's intent (Adamopoulou and

Table 1 Chatbot classification

Dimension	Characteristics			
Knowledge domain	Open-domain/general-purpose	Closed-domain/domain-specific		
Service provided	Interpersonal	Intra-personal	Inter-agent	
Goal	Informative	Task-based	Conversational/non-task based	
Input processing/response generation	Rule-based	Retrieval-based	Generative	
Human-aid	Human mediation	Autonomous		
Permission	Open-source	Commercial		
Text processing	Word embeddings	Text-level (Latin alphabet)		
Interaction/communication mode	Text-based	Voice-based	Both	
Implementation	Programming	Modeling	Supervised learning	Hybrid
Language	Single language	Multi language		

Moussiades 2020b), while the most human-like response can be achieved by generating the answer using ML techniques, depending on the quality of the training data, the complexity of the users' input and other factors. Additionally, text processing might be performed using word embeddings or based on the text itself as represented by the Latin alphabet (Lokman and Ameedeen 2019). Chatbots can be implemented by programming, modeling, supervised learning, or applying a hybrid approach, combining the previous implementation techniques (Diederich et al. 2019). Moreover, users might interact with the chatbot via text, voice, or both, while the chatbot could support a single or multiple languages (Hussain et al. 2019; Diederich et al. 2019).

2.2 *Large Language Models*

An LLM is an advanced AI-based text model that sets itself apart from other text models by utilizing *massive* amounts of data, surpassing what is commonly referred to as big data (O'Leary 2022). The resulting pre-trained, often autoregressive deep learning models, aim at producing natural language text (Floridi and Chiriatti 2020) and often feature a massive number of parameters, far exceeding those of previous models. As a result, these models offer a versatile and task-agnostic foundation for a wide range of text-based tasks, such as text summarization or generation (Brown et al. 2020, p. 202).

Large organizations such as Google, OpenAI and Meta offer multiple commercial LLMs like Google's LaMDA (Thoppilan et al. 2022), T5 (Raffel et al. 2020), and BERT (Devlin et al., 2019) models, as well as OpenAI's GPT-4 and GPT-3.5, and Meta's BlenderBot 3 (Shuster et al. 2022) and LLaMA (Touvron et al. 2023). Out of these models, GPT-4 is currently the largest, consisting of 175 billion parameters, while the first and second generations used 110 M (GPT-1) and 1.5B (GPT-2) parameters, respectively (Floridi and Chiriatti 2020; Thoppilan et al. 2022). Besides commercial LLMs, there are also freely and publicly available models that are larger than GPT-2. Examples of these GPT-Neo (2.7B parameters) (Black et al. 2021), GPT-J-6B (Wang and Komatsuzaki 2021), and GPT-NeoX-20B (Black et al. 2022), which were developed by EleutherAI based on the GPT-NeoX platform (Andonian et al. 2021). Other examples are PanGu-α (13B) (Zeng et al. 2021) and FairSeq (2.7B, 6.7B, 13B) (Ott et al. 2019).

To apply pre-trained models to context-specific tasks, fine-tuning is typically required. This involves a supervised learning process that updates the weights of the training parameters and generally requires large datasets with thousands of labeled data instances (Brown et al. 2020). An example of a context-specific model is ChatGPT (OpenAI 2022). However, to avoid extensive fine-tuning, pre-trained LLMs can be used with one-shot or few-shot learning. These techniques involve in-context learning using 10–100 examples as prompts. Unlike fine-tuning, one-shot or few-shot learning doesn't update model parameters, but few-shot learning has shown promising results. Another variant is zero-shot learning, which does not use any demonstrations but relies on a natural language description of the task (Brown et al. 2020).

3 Research Method

Our research-in-progress aims to build a hybrid chatbot that integrates LLMs with informative approaches, for which we present the conceptualization in the given paper. Therefore, we are working in the field of design-oriented information systems research (Hevner et al. 2004; Österle et al. 2010), with the goal of designing an artifact, which is the hybrid chatbot. To achieve this, our research follows the DSR methodology proposed by Peffers et al. (2007). In this paper, Sect. 1 and Sect. 2 contribute to problem identification and motivation. Section 4 compares LLMs with informative chatbots, which helps define the objectives for hybrid chatbots. Then, we develop a concept and present a prototypical implementation in Sect. 5, which contributes to the design and development phase, as well as the demonstration. Since this manuscript is still in progress, we have yet to conduct a comprehensive demonstration and evaluation. In the future, the resulting artifact will be validated on the basis of a set of experts. However, by communicating our intermediate results, we contribute to the sixth phase of Peffers et al. (2007). This allows us to integrate feedback from our peers with upcoming process iterations.

4 Comparison of Different Chatbot Approaches

Existing research in chatbot development has established a general architecture that can be used to design chatbots for different categories, as shown in Fig. 1. This architecture, adapted from Adamopoulou and Moussiades (2020a), comprises three main components: NLP; dialogue management; and information retrieval, which involves gathering data from sources such as databases or the web. Different types of chatbots focus on different parts of the general architecture. Informative chatbots rely on comprehensive information retrieval to answer user queries, while conversational chatbots focus on dialogue management and user message analysis to sustain a conversation. The approach used for language understanding is also affected by the choice of input processing and response generation method.

As mentioned in Sect. 2, there are two approaches for developing chatbots: rule-based and ML-based. Rule-based chatbots are specific to a task and follow a decision tree-like path with hand-coded or structured knowledge (Adamopoulou and Moussiades 2020b; Ramesh et al. 2017). ML-based chatbots consider the dialogue context and do not require predefined responses but need (at least incremental) training on labeled datasets for new tasks, making them less applicable when a chatbot gains new knowledge (Adamopoulou and Moussiades 2020a). These chatbots are typically more focused on producing human-like responses.

Task-agnostic LLMs, like GPT-4, have created new possibilities for building chatbots. They differ from traditional ML approaches in implementation and capabilities, with LLMs being able to generalize and adapt to specific tasks using a relatively small amount of task-specific data and transfer downstream tasks easily (Brown et al. 2020). Given suitable training data and computational resources, they can cover an extensive range of topics, generate more organic responses, and update more efficiently than their traditional counterparts. However, there are also drawbacks to using LLMs. They can generate inappropriate text when inappropriate language is fed into them, and their generative nature may result in plausible but unsupported answers (O'Leary 2022). Moreover, LLMs require more computational resources and can be more expensive to operate than traditional chatbots. Thus, both chatbot approaches have their own advantages and drawbacks, which answers the first research question.

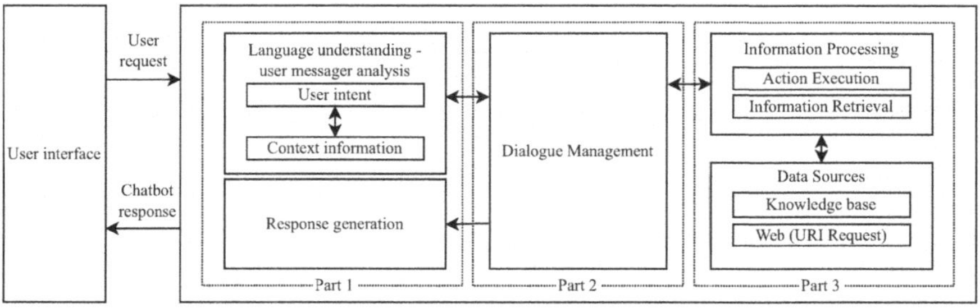

Fig. 1 General chatbot architecture

5 Towards Hybrid Chatbots

5.1 Design of a Hybrid Architecture

The difference between rule-based and ML-based traditional chatbots results in divergent integration with LLM approaches. Rule-based chatbots offer developers tight control over included information and answers, making them well-suited for informative chatbots. Thus, we focus on the integration with generative LLMs to enhance their ability to generate natural text in the following.

To balance the opposing strengths and weaknesses of both rule-based and LLM approaches, we propose a generic concept of a hybrid chatbot. Specifically, we plan to integrate LLMs into traditional informative chatbots, building on the notion of hybrid chatbot implementations presented by Diederich et al. (2019). The proposed hybrid chatbot will leverage a combination of chatbots with different approaches to provide the best possible architecture with their specific advantages. This can be achieved by chaining two interdependent chatbot components that are not functional on their own and combining them through inter-agent communication, as shown in Fig. 2.

The figure illustrates a traditional, rule-based chatbot on the right-hand side, which consists of all three parts of the architecture shown in Fig. 1: user message analysis and response generation (Part 1), dialogue management (Part 2), and information retrieval (Part 3) and a LLM-based chatbot, without Part 3 of the architecture, on the left-hand side. To overcome the limitations of Part 1 in the traditional chatbot, an LLM is utilized to analyze the incoming *user request* and transforms it via inter-agent communication, resulting in a *formatted user request*. This formatted user request provides the user intent and necessary context, like intents derived from previous questions, to the traditional chatbot. Subsequently, the traditional chatbot can accurately provide relevant information in a condensed manner (*traditional response*) by accessing the knowledge base. Finally, the chatbot response includes the output of the combined prompt, which includes the original user request, the traditional chatbot's response, and instructions on the answer format.

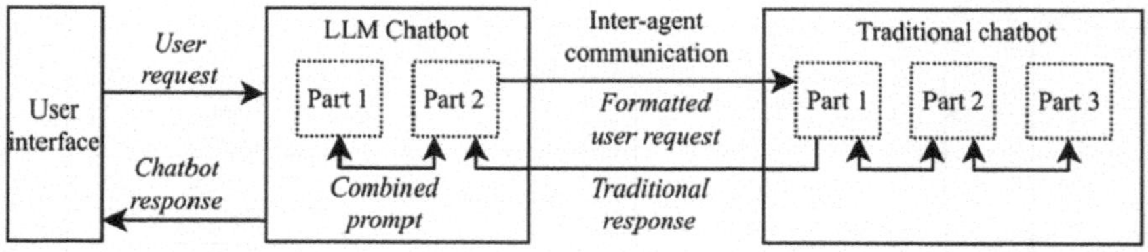

Fig. 2 LLM chatbot that enhances the answering capabilities of a traditional chatbot

5.2 *Implications*

The proposed architecture combines the accuracy guarantees of rule-based chatbots with the conversational capabilities of LLMs, which are often superior to those of rule-based chatbots. This hybrid architecture can be used to enhance existing traditional chatbots, allowing adoption in many application cases. These enhancements have the potential to significantly improve a variety of use cases in many organizations, like B2B customer service by providing prompt and precise responses to FAQs, reducing representatives' workload, and personalizing interactions to improve customer satisfaction and retention. Simultaneously, they enable a more personalized customer experience which can improve customer satisfaction and loyalty, acting as a key driver for retention.

6 Conclusion and Outlook

In this research-in-progress paper, we aim to enhance our understanding of how the combination of LLMs with established chatbot technologies can improve the reliability of informative chatbots. Drawing on existing chatbot classifications and architectures, we have concluded that addressing the possibility of including LLMs, such as GPT-4, in chatbot research is essential. By analyzing the strengths and weaknesses of different chatbot approaches, we propose a conceptualization of a hybrid chatbot implementation. We use inter-agent communication to combine a LLM and a traditional chatbot, creating an architecture that leverages the advantages of both. We argue that LLMs outperform traditional NLP methods in generating human-like responses while relying on the benefits of accessing structured information through the information retrieval part of a traditional chatbot. In this way, we ensure that the generated response is based on valid information. With this concept, we contribute to the research on developing hybrid chatbot architectures without restricting it to specific technologies. In the next step of our research, we will prototype the conceptualization and evaluate its ability to generate human-like responses and answer questions based on valid and reliable information. Future research needs to follow an iterative design process by taking multiple technologies into consideration, and by continuously adjusting the concept based on the latest evaluation results.

Acknowledgements This research has been funded by The Federal Ministry of Education and Research (BMBF) under Research Grant No. 16DHBKI039.

References

Adamopoulou, E., Moussiades, L., 2020a. Chatbots: History, technology, and applications. Machine Learning with Applications 2, 100006. https://doi.org/10.1016/j.mlwa.2020.100006

Adamopoulou, E., Moussiades, L., 2020b. An Overview of Chatbot Technology, in: Maglogiannis, I., Iliadis, L., Pimenidis, E. (Eds.), Artificial Intelligence Applications and Innovations. AIAI 2020. IFIP Advances in Information and Communication Technology. Springer, pp. 373–383. https://doi.org/10.1007/978-3-030-49186-4_31

Andonian, A., Anthony, Q., Biderman, S., Black, S., Gali, P., Gao, L., Hallahan, E., Levy-Kramer, J., Leahy, C., Nestler, L., Parker, K., Pieler, M., Purohit, S., Songz, T., Phil, W., Weinbach, S., 2021. GPT-NeoX: Large scale autoregressive language modeling in PyTorch. https://doi.org/10.5281/zenodo.5879544

Black, S., Biderman, S., Hallahan, E., Anthony, Q., Gao, L., Golding, L., He, H., Leahy, C., McDonell, K., Phang, J., Pieler, M., Prashanth, U.S., Purohit, S., Reynolds, L., Tow, J., Wang, B., Weinbach, S., 2022. GPT-NeoX-20B: An Open-Source Autoregressive Language Model, in: Proceedings of BigScience Episode #5 -- Workshop on Challenges & Perspectives in Creating Large Language Models. Presented at the Proceedings of BigScience Episode #5 -- Workshop on Challenges & Perspectives in Creating Large Language Models, Association for Computational Linguistics, Dublin & virtual, pp. 95–136. https://doi.org/10.18653/v1/2022.bigscience-1.9

Black, S., Gao, L., Wang, P., Leahy, C., Biderman, S., 2021. GPT-Neo: Large scale autoregressive language modeling with mesh-tensorflow. https://doi.org/10.5281/zenodo.5297715

Brown, T.B., Mann, B., Ryder, N., Subbiah, M., Kaplan, J., Dhariwal, P., Neelakantan, A., Shyam, P., Sastry, G., Askell, A., Agarwal, S., Herbert-Voss, A., Krueger, G., Henighan, T., Child, R., Ramesh, A., Ziegler, D.M., Wu, J., Winter, C., Hesse, C., Chen, M., Sigler, E., Litwin, M., Gray, S., Chess, B., Clark, J., Berner, C., McCandlish, S., Radford, A., Sutskever, I., Amodei, D., 2020. Language models are few-shot learners. Presented at the Advances in Neural Information Processing Systems.

Devlin, J., Chang, M.-W., Lee, K., Toutanova, K., 2019. BERT: Pre-training of Deep Bidirectional Transformers for Language Understanding. https://doi.org/10.48550/arXiv.1810.04805

Diederich, S., Brendel, A.B., Kolbe, L.M., 2019. Towards a Taxonomy of Platforms for Conversational Agent Design, in: Proceedings of 14th International Conference on Wirtschaftsinformatik. pp. 1100–1114.

Floridi, L., Chiriatti, M., 2020. GPT-3: Its Nature, Scope, Limits, and Consequences. Minds and Machines 30, 681–694. https://doi.org/10.1007/s11023-020-09548-1

Hevner, A.R., March, S.T., Park, J., Ram, S., 2004. Design Science in Information Systems Research. MIS Quarterly 28, 75–105. https://doi.org/10.2307/25148625

Hussain, S., Ameri Sianaki, O., Ababneh, N., 2019. A Survey on Conversational Agents/Chatbots Classification and Design Techniques, in: Barolli, L., Takizawa, M., Xhafa, F., Enokido, T. (Eds.), Proceedings of the Workshops of the 33rd International Conference on Advanced Information Networking and Applications (WAINA-2019). pp. 946–956. https://doi.org/10.1007/978-3-030-15035-8_93

Lokman, A.S., Ameedeen, M.A., 2019. Modern chatbot systems: A technical review, in: Advances in Intelligent Systems and Computing. Springer Verlag, pp. 1012–1023. https://doi.org/10.1007/978-3-030-02683-7_75

O'Leary, D.E., 2022. Massive data language models and conversational artificial intelligence: Emerging issues. Intelligent Systems in Accounting, Finance and Management 29, 182–198. https://doi.org/10.1002/isaf.1522

OpenAI, 2022. Introducing ChatGPT [WWW Document]. URL https://openai.com/blog/chatgpt (accessed 3.6.23).

Österle, H., Becker, J., Frank, U., Hess, T., Karagiannis, D., Krcmar, H., Loos, P., Mertens, P., Oberweis, A., Sinz, E.J., 2010. Memorandum zur gestaltungsorientierten Wirtschaftsinformatik. Schmalenbachs Z betriebswirtsch Forsch 62, 664–672. https://doi.org/10.1007/BF03372838

Ott, M., Edunov, S., Baevski, A., Fan, A., Gross, S., Ng, N., Grangier, D., Auli, M., 2019. fairseq: A fast, extensible toolkit for sequence modeling, in: Proceedings of NAACL-HLT 2019: Demonstrations.

Peffers, K., Tuunanen, T., Rothenberger, M.A., Chatterjee, S., 2007. A Design Science Research Methodology for Information Systems Research. Journal of Management Information Systems 24, 45–77.

Raffel, C., Shazeer, N., Roberts, A., Lee, K., Narang, S., Matena, M., Zhou, Y., Li, W., Liu, P.J., 2020. Exploring the Limits of Transfer Learning with a Unified Text-to-Text Transformer. https://doi.org/10.48550/arXiv.1910.10683

Ramesh, K., Ravishankaran, S., Joshi, A., Chandrasekaran, K., 2017. A Survey of Design Techniques for Conversational Agents, in: Kaushik, S., Gupta, D., Kharb, L., Chahal, D. (Eds.), Information, Communication and Computing Technology. Springer Verlag, pp. 336–350. https://doi.org/10.1007/978-981-10-6544-6_31

Shuster, K., Xu, J., Komeili, M., Ju, D., Smith, E.M., Roller, S., Ung, M., Chen, M., Arora, K., Lane, J., Behrooz, M., Ngan, W., Poff, S., Goyal, N., Szlam, A., Boureau, Y.-L., Kambadur, M., Weston, J., 2022. BlenderBot 3: a deployed conversational agent that continually learns to responsibly engage.

Thoppilan, R., De Freitas, D., Hall, J., Shazeer, N., Kulshreshtha, A., Cheng, H.-T., Jin, A., Bos, T., Baker, L., Du, Y., Li, Y., Lee, H., Zheng, H.S., Ghafouri, A., Menegali, M., Huang, Y., Krikun, M., Lepikhin, D., Qin, J., Chen, D., Xu, Y., Chen, Z., Roberts, A., Bosma, M., Zhao, V., Zhou, Y., Chang, C.-C., Krivokon, I., Rusch, W., Pickett, M., Srinivasan, P., Man, L., Meier-Hellstern, K., Morris, M.R., Doshi, T., Santos, R.D., Duke, T., Soraker, J., Zevenbergen, B., Prabhakaran, V., Diaz, M., Hutchinson, B., Olson, K., Molina, A., Hoffman-John, E., Lee, J., Aroyo, L., Rajakumar, R., Butryna, A., Lamm, M., Kuzmina, V., Fenton, J., Cohen, A., Bernstein, R., Kurzweil, R., Aguera-Arcas, B., Cui, C., Croak, M., Chi, E., Le, Q., 2022. LaMDA: Language Models for Dialog Applications.

Touvron, H., Lavril, T., Izacard, G., Martinet, X., Lachaux, M.-A., Lacroix, T., Rozière, B., Goyal, N., Hambro, E., Azhar, F., Rodriguez, A., Joulin, A., Grave, E., Lample, G., 2023. LLaMA: Open and Efficient Foundation Language Models. https://doi.org/10.48550/arXiv.2302.13971

Wang, B., Komatsuzaki, A., 2021. GPT-J-6B: A 6 Billion Parameter Autoregressive Language Model.

Zeng, W., Ren, X., Su, T., Wang, H., Liao, Y., Wang, Z., Jiang, X., Yang, Z., Wang, K., Zhang, X., Li, C., Gong, Z., Yao, Y., Huang, X., Wang, Jun, Yu, J., Guo, Q., Yu, Y., Zhang, Yan, Wang, Jin, Tao, H., Yan, D., Yi, Z., Peng, F., Jiang, F., Zhang, H., Deng, L., Zhang, Yehong, Lin, Z., Zhang, C., Zhang, S., Guo, M., Gu, S., Fan, G., Wang, Y., Jin, X., Liu, Q., Tian, Y., 2021. PanGu-α: Large-scale Autoregressive Pretrained Chinese Language Models with Auto-parallel Computation. https://doi.org/10.48550/arXiv.2104.12369

Innovative Prototypes and Impact of IS

Context-Aware Marketing Attribution Based on Survival Analysis

Kilian Züllig, Stefan Napirata, and Steffen Zimmermann

Abstract Companies increasingly invest in digital marketing channels to promote their products and services. While the expenditures for each marketing channel are known, the contribution of marketing channels to a successful conversion, and therefore the value they generate, is unknown, but highly relevant for strategic decision-making. In this paper, we develop a novel, context-aware additive hazard marketing attribution (CAHMA) model based on survival analysis to address this problem. In addition to channel-specific, time-decaying effects of marketing on the users' conversion rate, we control for the effects of contextual features, such as the device or country from which users interact with marketing channels. Based on a prototypical implementation, we demonstrate the model's applicability and evaluate it on real-world data from the industry. We find that CAHMA outperforms other models in terms of accuracy while offering unique interpretability of the results and hence, providing deep insights for practitioners into the effects of marketing.

Keywords Marketing attribution · Online advertising · Survival analysis · Conversion prediction

1 Introduction

Over the past decade, digital marketing has become the most important way for companies to reach potential new and existing customers to promote their products or services. Spending on digital marketing has more than doubled in the last 5 years

K. Züllig (✉) · S. Napirata · S. Zimmermann
Institute of Business Analytics, Ulm University, Ulm, Germany
e-mail: kilian.zullig@uni-ulm.de

S. Napirata
e-mail: stefan.napirata@uni-ulm.de

S. Zimmermann
e-mail: steffen.zimmermann@uni-ulm.de

D. Beverungen et al. (eds.), *Solutions and Technologies for Responsible Digitalization*, Lecture Notes in Information Systems and Organisation 75,
https://doi.org/10.1007/978-3-031-80122-8_22

and is expected to keep increasing in future (Statista, 2022b). Thereby, Big Data analytics enables businesses to provide customers with more targeted and personalized advertisements to motivate them to move along the purchase funnel toward the action desired by the advertising company, i.e., conversion (Kannan et al., 2016). Along their customer journey towards conversion, users typically have multiple interactions, i.e., touchpoints, with different marketing channels such as search engine advertising (SEA), display or social media advertising. While companies can easily quantify the exact amount spent for each marketing channel, their contribution to a successful conversion, and therefore the value generated from specific channels, is unknown. Marketing attribution is a strategy for determining the individual contribution of marketing channels to conversions and allocating the generated value accordingly. In order to measure and manage the efficiency of marketing and to improve its return on investment, marketing attribution has been recognized as a central task in digital marketing (Kannan et al., 2016), underlining the importance of accurate marketing attribution models. Yet, determining the accuracy of marketing attribution is not trivial, because there is no ground truth for the value generated by channels. Most likely, not even customers are aware of the exact influence that different marketing channels had on their own purchase decisions. In this vein, marketing attribution is a two-folded problem. First, an attribution strategy is necessary to allocate the value of conversions to marketing channels and second, a measurement of how well this allocation reflects reality is required. For the latter, it has become standard to assume that good marketing attribution models should also be good at predicting whether a customer journey leads to a conversion or not (Shao & Li, 2011). Aiming for the highest predictive accuracy, data-driven marketing attribution models tend to increase in complexity (e.g., Kumar et al., 2020). While predictive accuracy is indeed an important criterion for convincing managers of a model's credibility (Lodish, 2001), managers must understand how the results are generated in order to rely on them for strategic decisions (Little, 2004).

Existing literature proposes a variety of data-driven approaches (see e.g., Zaremba (2020) for an overview), with a recent trend towards neural-network-based models (e.g., Yang et al., 2020; Kumar et al., 2020; Yao et al., 2022). While these models may be best at predicting conversions, they strongly sacrifice on interpretability, especially regarding their black-box model structure. Consequently, practitioners are unlikely to rely on them for strategic decision-making, which is the ultimate purpose of attribution models (Romero Leguina et al., 2020).

On the other hand, there are advanced, data-driven models that also find application in the industry. Among these, Markov chains provide a comprehensible model structure and solid predictive accuracy (Anderl et al., 2013). While this seems promising, there are relevant aspects that cannot be modeled with Markov chains (Anderl et al., 2016). For example, the effect of a user's touchpoint with a marketing channel on the conversion probability obviously decreases over time, which cannot be accounted for by Markov chains. Models based on additive survival analysis (e.g. Zhang et al., 2014; Ji & Wang, 2017) also have a very intuitive and comprehensible model structure and, in addition, allow to incorporate such time-decaying effects. Even more, beyond time-dependencies, the environment and circumstances under which users interact with marketing channels (e.g., season or country) or, if available, user characteristics (e.g., users' demographics or preferences), might also have an impact on their conversion probabilities. This additional information can also be included in additive survival analysis models, using contextual features. Zhang et al. (2014), however, do not account for such contextual features. Ji & Wang (2017) significantly increase the complexity of their model when including contextual features, such that it loses interpretability, besides having some unresolved mathematical issues.[1]

In this paper, we propose a novel context-aware additive hazard marketing attribution model (CAHMA) based on survival analysis. The model assumes an intuitive, additive relationship between the effects of marketing channels and accounts for the influence of contextual features. Unlike Ji & Wang's (2017) model, we directly control for channel-independent but context-dependent effects, similar to how control variables are used in regression models. This allows to better separate context-specific effects and identify the "true" channel-specific effect of marketing. Based on a prototypical implementation, we demonstrate the applicability of CAHMA and evaluate it on a real-world dataset from GetYourGuide, a leading international booking platform for travel products. The data was provided by the platform in search of a new marketing attribution model with high predictive accuracy under the condition of strong interpretability of both the model structure and results. We find that CAHMA outperforms other interpretable data-driven marketing attribution models. Considering highly skewed data for marketing attribution, CAHMA is particularly accurate in detecting the relevant minority class, i.e., converting customer journeys. At the same time, CAHMA provides unique insights into the channel-independent effects of contextual features in addition to the channel-specific influence strength and time-decaying effect of marketing.

2 Context-Aware Additive Hazard Marketing Attribution Model

Before we present our model and its evaluation, we introduce the concepts of survival analysis which is commonly used to build models for censored time-to-event data (Lawless, 2011). Let T be a non-negative random variable describing the waiting time until the occurrence of an event (here, conversion of a user). The main goal of our model is to estimate the probability distribution of T, which is the basis for our marketing attribution and conversion prediction. Using standard notations from probability theory, $F(t)$ denotes the cumulative distribution function and $f(t)$ the probability density function of T. The survival function $S(t)$ is the counter probability that the conversion does not occur until time t. The hazard rate $\lambda(t)$ is defined as the probability of conversion within the next, infinitesimally small moment after time

[1] For a more detailed discussion of the related literature see: https://github.com/CAHMAchameleon/CAHMA.

t, given that the user has not converted until t. Applying basic calculus (see e.g., Lawless, 2011), one can derive the following two identities

$$(i) \quad S(t) = e^{-\int_0^t \lambda(s),ds}, \quad (ii) \quad f(t) = S(t)\lambda(t).$$

As $S(t)$ and consequently $f(t)$ depend only on the hazard rate, the random variable T, and therefore the entire model, is completely defined by the hazard rate $\lambda(t)$. We detail later, how modeling the hazard rate is sufficient to determine the marketing attribution and conversion prediction.

2.1 CAHMA Model

Based on survival analysis, we introduce our novel CAHMA model for context-aware marketing attribution. We denote users (i.e., potential customers) by $u \in \{1, \ldots, U\}$ and marketing channels by $k \in \{1, \ldots, K\}$. A touchpoint corresponds to an interaction of a user u with a marketing channel k and is denoted by a tuple $\left(a_l^u, t_l^u\right)$, where a_l^u denotes the marketing channel of the l-th interaction of user u and t_l^u denotes the timestamp of this interaction. The customer journey of a user u, consisting of l_u touchpoints, is defined as $J^u = \left\{\left(a_l^u, t_l^u\right)_{i=1}^{l_u}, Y^u, T^u, X^u\right\}$. At the end of a customer journey either a conversion or no conversion is observed, which is denoted by $Y^u \in \{0, 1\}$. Furthermore, every customer journey has a latest timestamp T^u, marking the end of the journey. If the customer journey leads to a conversion, i.e., $Y^u = 1$, then T^u is the time of conversion. If the customer journey does not lead to a conversion, i.e., $Y^u = 0$, then T^u corresponds to the end of the observation window. Additionally, we include available contextual features, e.g., the season or country in which the touchpoint was recorded. The vector X^u contains the contextual features observed during the customer journey of user u.

Similar to Zhang et al. (2014), we assume an additive effect between the channel-specific and time-dependent effect $\kappa_{a_l^u}(t)$ of each touchpoint. Extending the model of Zhang et al. (2014), we further account for the influence of contextual features in a time-independent baseline hazard $b(X)$. Therefore, the hazard rate for customer journey J^u at time t is given by

$$\lambda_u\left(t|J^u\right) = \begin{cases} b(\mathrm{X^u}) + \sum\limits_{\mathrm{t_l^u < t}} \kappa_{a_l^u}(t), & \text{for } \mathrm{t} \geq \mathrm{t_1^u} \\ 0, & \text{for } \mathrm{t} < \mathrm{t_1^u}. \end{cases}$$

In line with Zhang et al. (2014) and Ji & Wang (2017), we assume a positive influence of each touchpoint on the hazard rate, which fades over time. Hence, we model the channel-specific effect of each touchpoint on the instantaneous conversion probability of user u at time t by the kernel function $\kappa_{a_l^u}(t) = \beta_{a_l^u}\omega_{a_l^u}e^{-\omega_{a_l^u}\left(t-t_l^u\right)}$. For each interaction with channel k, i.e., if $a_l^u = k$, β_k represents the channel-specific influence strength of the touchpoint on the hazard rate and ω_k is the corresponding speed of decay over time. $(t - t_l^u)$ denotes the elapsed time since the l-th interaction. All β_k's must be non-negative, as otherwise, the hazard rate could be negative, which is impossible by the definition of a probability and the assumptions of survival analysis. We further constrain all ω_k's to be non-negative as well, to maintain the assumption of time-decaying effects of marketing.

The time-independent baseline hazard, introduced in the proposed method, allows controlling for channel-independent effects on the conversion probability that are instead driven by contextual features of user u. The baseline hazard is given by $b(X^u) = e^{\alpha_0 + \sum_{i=1}^{I} \alpha_i X_i^u}$, where each X_i^u represents one out of I different contextual feature from the feature vector X^u. The parameters $\alpha_i \in \{1, \ldots, I\}$ estimate the effects of contextual features and are not restricted in their domain. The coefficient α_0 is a constant. While different functional forms of the baseline are possible, we use an exponential function, ensuring that the baseline is always greater than zero. Moreover, the differences in the effects of two features can be easily analyzed and interpreted. By modeling a positive, time-independent baseline hazard we establish a mathematically correct survival analysis model and estimate a true probability distribution of the time to conversion.

Figure 1 illustrates an exemplary hazard rate for one customer journey over time, as assumed in our model. The horizontal line represents the context-dependent baseline hazard which is constant for one customer journey. Each kernel function $\kappa_k(t)$ corresponds to one peak that fades over time. When the user interacts with one of the marketing channels, the hazard rate increases (c.f. vertical increase). The influence strength β_k of a channel corresponds to the area between the curve and the dotted line below and the time-decaying effect ω_k defines the slope of the curve. The concept of the baseline, the influence strength, and the time-decaying effect allow for a very descriptive and understandable model structure with interpretable model parameters and results. For the sake of interpretability, we calculate the half-life of a channel, which is the time until the effect of a channel on the conversion rate is half its quantity. Using an exponential function, the half-life is constant over time, which facilitates interpretation.

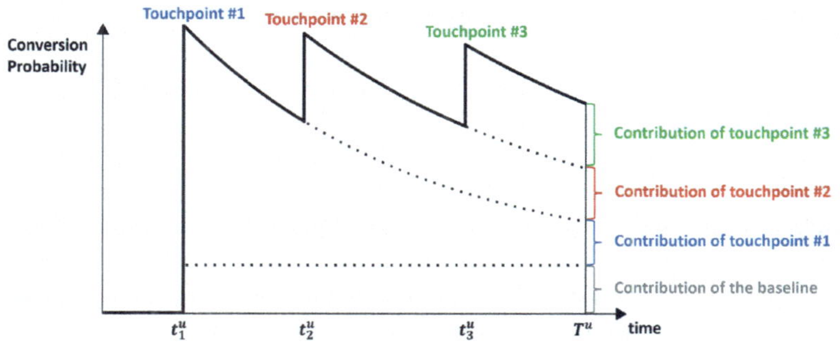

Fig. 1 Hazard rate

The central objective of marketing attribution is to take a retrospective view on customer journeys to assign value to individual touchpoints or channels. However, there is no ground truth for the assigned values making it impossible to directly evaluate the quality or accuracy of the attribution. Thus, an alternative measure for the quality of marketing attribution models is required. It is widely assumed that a marketing attribution model, that accurately captures the effects of marketing, should also perform well in the task of conversion prediction. Consequently, predictive accuracy is commonly used to evaluate the performance of the models instead of directly evaluating the marketing attribution. In the following, we first derive the marketing attribution strategy based on CAHMA before explaining how the method can predict conversions.

Marketing Attribution Strategy. Through its additive structure, the proposed model allows calculating the contribution of each touchpoint $\left(a_l^u, t_l^u\right)$ to the instantaneous conversion probability, i.e., the hazard rate, at any given time t from the value of the channel-specific kernel function $\kappa_k(t)$. In the case of a conversion, the contribution of a marketing channel is given by the relative contribution at conversion time T^u of all touchpoints in the customer journey that belong to that channel. Similar to previous models based on additive survival analysis (Zhang et al. (2014); Ji & Wang (2017), that is

$$attr_k^u = \frac{\sum_{t_l^u < T^u, a_l^u = k} \kappa_k(T^u)}{\sum_{t_l^u < T^u} \kappa_k(T^u)}.$$

The baseline hazard $b(X^u)$ models the context-dependent but channel-independent effect of marketing, which is collectively triggered by all touchpoints in the customer journey. Thus, we ignore the contribution of the baseline in the attribution. This is equivalent to distributing the effect of the baseline over all channels in the customer journey according to their relative contribution to the channel-specific effects.

Conversion Prediction. The proposed model allows to directly derive the conversion probability of users from the hazard rate by integrating over the time after their last interaction $t_{l_u}^u$. Hence, the conversion probability within a time window $\tilde{t}$ is given by

$$P\left(T \leq t_{l_u}^u + \tilde{t} | J^u\right) = 1 - e^{\tilde{t} b(X^u | J^u) - \sum_{l=1}^{l_u} \beta_{a_l^u} \left(e^{\omega_{a_l^u} \tilde{t}} - 1\right) e^{-\omega_{a_l^u} \left(t_{l_u}^u + \tilde{t} - t_l^u\right)}}.$$

It follows from this equation that for an infinitely large time window, i.e., $\tilde{t} \to \infty$, the baseline hazard will drive the survival function to zero and the probability of eventual conversion to 1. This property of survival analysis models ensures that the time to conversion T is a true random variable. In our practical context of marketing attribution, it can be argued that not every user will convert. However, our model only assumes that every user would theoretically convert within an infinite time window. The predicted conversion time may be too large to be observed if it exceeds the time during which a customer journey is trackable, or even the remaining lifetime of the user.

Parameter Estimation. We use maximum likelihood estimation to fit all parameters $\Theta = \{\alpha_0, \ldots, \alpha_I, \beta_1, \ldots, \beta_K, \omega_1, \ldots, \omega_K\}$ to the data. The objective log-likelihood function is given by

$$\log \mathcal{L}(\Theta) = \sum_{u \in U, Y^u=0} \log(S(T^u|J^u)) + \sum_{u \in U, Y^u=1} \log(S(T^u|J^u)\lambda(T^u|J^u)).$$

As there is an analytic solution for the gradients of our log-likelihood function, the optimization problem can be solved using any gradient optimization algorithm that allows for box constraints.[2]

2.2 *Demonstration and Evaluation*

Prototypical Implementation. The prototype of CAHMA is implemented in the programming language R. Calculating the log-likelihood function and its gradients requires operations on a very large number of grouped subsets of the data (i.e., single customer journeys). Using the open source package "data.table" from R, our prototype can handle substantial marketing attribution datasets even on a local computer. However, for a productive analytics environment, nowadays many companies rely on modern cloud computing platforms (Statista, 2022a) such as Microsoft Azure or Amazon AWS that allow for efficient distributed computing over large clusters with analytics engines like Apache Spark or Hadoop. To be able to leverage the advantages of such platforms, we apply the MapReduce programming model, which is the foundation for Spark or Hadoop. MapReduce allows distributing big datasets over large clusters to perform computations efficiently in parallel (Dean & Ghemawat, 2008). Due to the additive structure of the log-likelihood function and its gradients, their calculation can be decomposed into many smaller subproblems. Following MapReduce, these subproblems are then distributed over a cluster of worker processes for parallel computation (map) before aggregating the results in one global solution (reduce). While MapReduce together with data.table already enables efficient computations in R, the developed prototype can be transferred to Apache Spark to run even more efficiently on modern cloud computing platforms, further improving the practical applicability of CAHMA.

Dataset. To evaluate the prototype of CAHMA, we were provided with a real-world dataset by GetYourGuide. The dataset was provided in anonymized form. GetYourGuide invests heavily in its digital marketing campaigns to generate new and reattract previous customers. The dataset contains information on the interactions of potential

[2] For more details on the log-likelihood, its gradients and the optimization problem see https://github.com/CAHMAchameleon/CAHMA.

customers with various marketing channels used by GetYourGuide over a nine-month time window from June through February.[3] In total, the dataset contains almost 33 Mio. touchpoints of 14.8 Mio. unique users[4] and 11 distinct channels. Each record of the dataset represents one touchpoint. Additionally, the dataset contains the exact transaction time and contextual features such as the device which was used for an interaction or the country in which it was recorded.

Assuming that reconversions of users can be influenced by their marketing touchpoints, which occurred before their previous transactions, we do not restart customer journeys after conversions. Instead, all previous touchpoints of users are added to their subsequent customer journeys which extend beyond the users' previous transactions. By this approach, we aim to avoid underestimating the contribution of early touchpoints for repeated conversions. Overall, we obtain 14,950,959 distinct customer journeys, of which significantly less than 5% ended in conversions. This highlights the strong imbalance of the data. We randomly split the dataset into disjoint training and evaluation sets, each containing 50% of the customer journeys. This allows us to assess out-of-sample performance on unseen data, which is unbiased by overfitting. To enrich customer journeys with contextual features, we use dummy-coded variables of the devices on which, the countries in which, and the seasons during which the customer journeys were tracked. The dataset contains more than 200 different countries, with some of them having even less than 10 occurrences. Hence, we code the ten most relevant countries in terms of their frequency and conversion rate individually and segment the remaining countries into nine geographic regions to limit the number of required dummy variables. This coding is solely based on information from the training data to avoid any data leakage to the evaluation dataset. The seasons are defined as the three-month time windows of summer (June–August), fall (September–November), and winter (December–February). Spring is omitted because our data contains no records for this time frame. For the devices, we distinguish between Android, iOS, other mobile devices, and desktop computers. Beyond the described data preparation steps and basic data cleaning, including the removal of duplicates and incomplete records, we do not further manipulate the dataset, e.g., to reduce the imbalance. This way we ensure to evaluate CAHMA on a realistic dataset available in practice.

Competing Models. Because of their practical relevance, we compare our proposed model to existing additive survival analysis models, which are based on the same assumptions and the standard Markov chain model by Anderl et al. (2013). All models are trained and evaluated on the same datasets. The competing models are

- **AdditiveHazard** (Zhang et al., 2014): This model based on survival analysis provides the basis for our proposed model, using an additive hazard rate but without considering contextual features.

[3] For confidentiality reasons, we cannot provide details on commercially highly sensitive information such as the exact conversion rate or channel specifics.

[4] The dataset is limited to information associated with website visitors that have consented to the specific data collection according to data protection legislation.

- **AMTA** (Ji & Wang, 2017):This model is also based on survival analysis and provides an alternative approach that allows the inclusion of contextual features. The model considers contextual features by the users' intrinsic, time-independent conversion rate as an additional influence on conversion. The authors attempt to model the overall conversion probability as a joint distribution of the time-independent conversion probability and the marketing-induced conversion probability.
- **MarkovChain** (Anderl et al., 2013): This model is the current standard at GetYourGuide and, as already discussed, represents a popular choice for data-driven marketing attribution models among practitioners. As suggested by Anderl et al. (2013), we apply third-order Markov chains as it optimizes the general trade-off between predictive accuracy and model complexity which hinders interpretability.

Marketing Attribution. Figure 2 shows the contribution of the different channels based on the attribution generated by the four models. For comparison, the figure further includes the relative frequency with which the channels occur in the dataset. All models provide similar attributions, which appear to be correlated with the frequency of the channels. This supports the general plausibility of the results. The most remarkable differences between the overall frequency of channels and the attributed values can be observed for Channel 5, Channel 7, and Channel 9. All four models estimate Channel 5 to be significantly more relevant than suggested by its frequency. In all survival analysis models, the attribution of Channel 9 strongly deviates from the one in MarkovChain and the frequency of the channel, which suggests that Channel 9 is estimated to be much less influential. While the other survival analysis models assign significantly more value to Channel 7, CAHMA attributes only slightly more value to it than MarkovChain.

Predictive Accuracy. To access predictive accuracy, the Receiver-Operator-Characteristic (ROC) curve and the area under the ROC curve (AUC) is a standard metric for the performance of probabilistic classifiers. However, the dataset at hand is highly skewed with a conversion rate of significantly less than 5 %. For such highly skewed data, AUC tends to be overly optimistic in the measurement of an

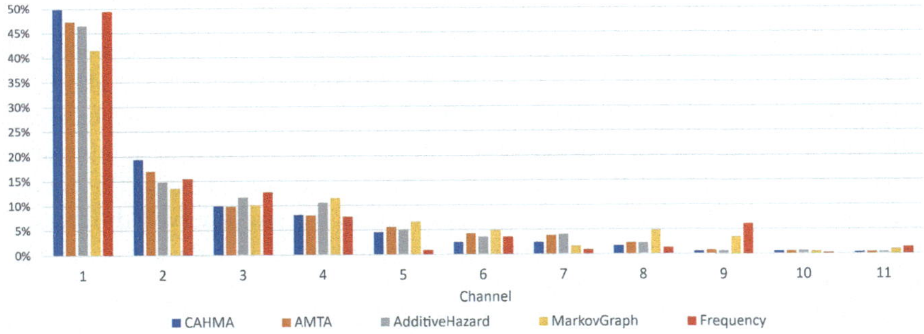

Fig. 2 Results of the attribution for the different models

algorithm's performance (Branco et al., 2016). In these cases, Precision-Recall (PR) curves are more informative (Davis & Goadrich, 2006; Saito & Rehmsmeier, 2015). Furthermore, marketing attribution models can only attribute value for customer journeys which actually lead to a conversion. Consequently, it is primarily important for these models to accurately detect and map converting customer journeys. Moreover, marketing data is right censored as it is unknown whether non-converting customer journeys terminated because the user actually did not convert or simply for technical reasons, such as the deletion of the tracked cookie. This induces noise in the negative majority class. As PR curves are more sensitive to improvements in the positive minority class (Davis & Goadrich, 2006; Loezer et al., 2020; Saito & Rehmsmeier, 2015),they are particularly suitable to evaluate marketing attribution models. Thus, we include the area under the PR curve (PR-AUC) as the primary, central metric to measure the predictive accuracy. Additionally, we report the ROC curve and AUC as a supplementary metric.

Panel A in Fig. 3 depicts the achieved ROC curves and corresponding AUC values for CAHMA and the competing models based on the out-of-sample performance on the evaluation set. CAHMA achieves a higher AUC value than AdditiveHazard and AMTA, as related models based on survival analysis. MarkovChain achieves a slightly higher AUC than CAHMA, however, the ROC curve of MarkovChain does not strictly dominate the curve of CAHMA. For low false positive rates, CAHMA's ROC curve increases much steeper and thus lies above MarkovChain's ROC curve in this region, indicating a faster initial increase in the true positive rate at a lower cost of false positives. Thus, CAHMA outperforms MarkovChain in predicting the important minority class. This outperformance becomes more evident when comparing the more informative PR curves of all models (c.f. Panel B in Fig. 3). Considering the PR-AUC, CAHMA significantly outperforms all competing models. Although significantly worse than CAHMA, both alternative survival analysis models also achieve a higher PR-AUC than MarkovChain. Overall, the results indicate that CAHMA is considerably better than the competing models at detecting converting customer journeys. The low PR-AUC of MarkovChain is driven by the sharp decline in its PR curve for low recall values. Hence, MarkovChain is more likely to miss converting customers, which is undesirable considering the highly skewed, right censored data and the objective to generate insights into why customers ultimately convert.

Interpretability. The general structure of MarkovChain is easy to understand and provides a transparent strategy for deriving the attribution. However, the ability to interpret the results is limited as MarkovChain cannot account for contextual features.

In contrast, additive survival analysis models in general have a significantly stronger interpretability of the results due to their model parameters. The model parameters of CAHMA give additional explanations for the observed differences between the frequency and the attribution of the channels and provide deeper insights into how the attribution was derived. Beyond the previous work by Zhang et al. (2014) and Ji & Wang (2017), we normalize the influence strength β_k to the interval from 0 % to 100 % and calculate the half-life of a channel's effect from its time-decaying property ω_k. This allows us to easily compare the parameters and analyze

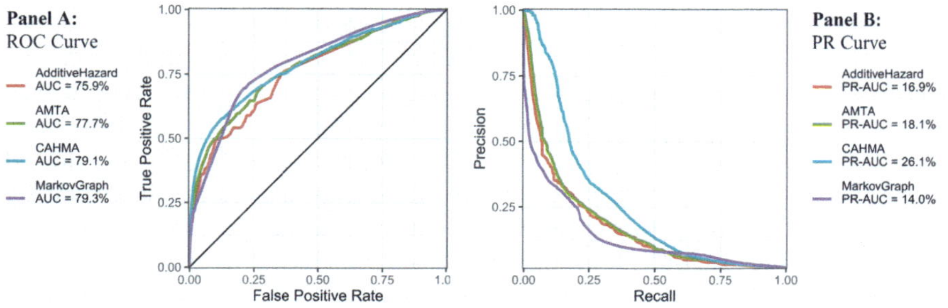

Fig. 3 Results of the conversion prediction using AUC and PR-AUC

how different channels exert their influence. Figure 4 shows the transformed values of the parameters β_k and ω_k. Channel 1 has a relatively small influence strength and a very low half-life, indicating that each time a user interacts with this channel, it only exerts a small influence that decays very quickly with time. However, due to its high frequency (c.f. Figure 2) in the dataset, Channel 1 adds a small effect very often and is thus still attributed the highest value. On the other hand, touchpoints with, e.g., Channel 5 or Channel 7 are very scarce but exert a much higher and/or longer-lasting influence and are thus still attributed a considerable value above their relative frequency.

In general, differences among the influence strengths and half-lives of marketing channels are very plausible. For example, each individual click on a search result when looking for tickets to attractions is likely to have less impact and to be forgotten more quickly than when a user is individually targeted by a personalized email or receives a link shared by a friend or idol. This interpretability of influence and persistency of channels over time is a key strength of additive survival analysis models.

In addition to the channel-specific influence strength of marketing and its half-life, CAHMA allows for determining the channel-independent effect of marketing. The

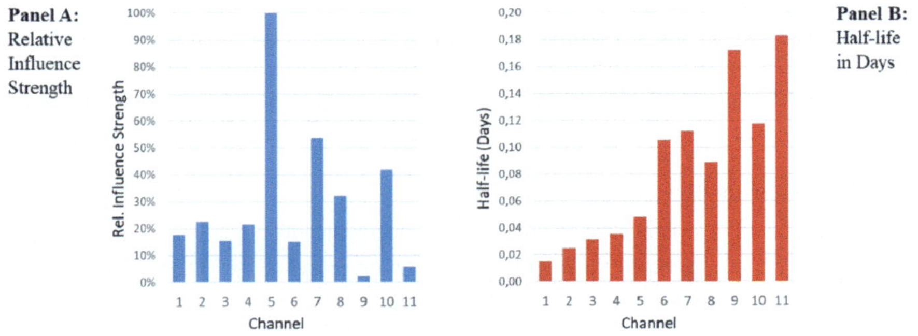

Fig. 4 Overview of model parameters

average contribution of the baseline hazard at conversion time is 4.72 %. As elaborated in Sect. 2.1, we distribute this contribution over all channels in the customer journeys to derive the marketing attribution. However, controlling for the influence of contextual features provides additional insights. Contextual features that are correlated with a high conversion probability will increase the baseline hazard rate and vice versa. As the baseline hazard is modeled by an exponential form, we can directly compare the influence on the baseline hazard of two contextual features with parameters α_1 and α_2. For example, the estimated parameters for the devices iOS and Android are 3.10 and 2.43, respectively. The resulting ratio $e^{3.10-2.43} = 1.95$ suggests, that, ceteris paribus, the channel-independent baseline hazard for iOS users is about 95 % higher than for Android users. Consequently, with an identical customer journey, iOS users would be more likely to convert. Overall, our model suggests that iOS users have the highest and users of other mobile devices have the lowest baseline hazard. Fall and winter have a substantially lower impact on a user's hazard rate compared to summer. In general, interactions from European countries have greater influence compared to other regions.

3 Discussion and Conclusion

Overall, as presented in Table 1, our proposed model meets the evaluation criteria very well. CAHMA showed high predictive accuracy compared to the competing models. This supports the validity of CAHMA's attribution. The high predictive accuracy of CAHMA does not come at the expense of interpretability. The structure of the proposed model is very comprehensible and inherits the strong interpretability of the results of additive survival analysis models. In addition, the baseline can be used to examine the extent to which different contextual features influence the user's probability to convert. This allows to directly compare these influences as well as determining the value generated by channel-independent marketing effects. The latter is not included in Ji & Wang's (2017) model. Therefore, our model enables a unique interpretation of the contextual features.

We contribute to the literature on data-driven marketing attribution models in general and to models based on survival analysis in particular. Adding a context-dependent baseline hazard allows to control for channel-independent effects of

Table 1 Summary of the evaluation results

Model	Predictive accuracy	Interpretability	
	PR-AUC (%)	Of the model	Of the results
Markov chain	14.0	+	
Additive hazard	16.9	+	+
AMTA	18.1	+	+
CAHMA	26.1	+	++

marketing and, thus, to better capture the "true" effect of marketing channels. Also, the baseline resolves the mathematical issue of previous additive survival models, as it aligns CAHMA with the assumptions of survival analysis and properties of probability theory.

With interpretability as an important criterion for marketing attribution models, our research has additional practical contributions. Estimating an influence strength and a half-life of the effect of each marketing channel generates further insights into "how" marketing channels exert their influence and affect users. This interpretation has not been the focus of researchers and is impossible to achieve for Markov chain models, which are commonly used in the industry. Integrating contextual features in our model in form of a baseline hazard enables flexible extension and adaption of the model to specific use cases and provides further interesting insights, as the effects of different contextual features on the user's conversion probability can be compared (c.f. Sect. 2.2). While we model contextual features such as the season or country in which the user interacted with the marketing channels, our model is not restricted to these kinds of features. For example, campaign-level data could be used in the baseline hazard as contextual features to further model the influence of campaign characteristics over various channels on the conversion probabilities of users. This would then allow for comparing the general, channel-independent effect of marketing campaigns in addition to channel-level marketing attribution. Altogether, by implementing a prototype of CAHMA as part of an applied research project with GetYourGuide, we demonstrate the practical value of the model. Considering its interpretability and flexible extensibility, we outline the valuable support that CAHMA can provide for strategic marketing decisions.

Our work has limitations that can serve as starting points for future research. First, we evaluate our model on one dataset which only covers 9 months of data missing the spring season. As spring is likely a busy season for the travel products, it would be interesting to analyze additional data to estimate the impact of the spring season. In general, it would be interesting to see, whether our results hold for other datasets from various industries. Furthermore, our dataset only contains online channels such as SEA, display or social media advertising and is solely click-based. However, impressions, i.e., touchpoints where a user sees an advertisement without clicking on it, and exposure to offline marketing can have a relevant influence on users' purchase decisions. Although we expect the proposed model to successfully process impressions and offline channels as well, this could be verified in future work. Third, the model could be evaluated using additional criteria such as robustness and algorithmic efficiency (Anderl et al., 2013). While our in- and out-of-sample predictive accuracy are stable and, as discussed, applying MapReduce promises good scalability, a more formal assessment of these criteria could be performed in future. Finally, future research could further analyze how CAHMA performs compared to neural networks despite their lack of interpretability. This would allow to quantify the trade-off between predictive accuracy and interpretability. Although interpretability is crucial, some practitioners may consider black-box models if the gain in predictive accuracy is sufficiently large.

Based on the proposed model, further extensions are possible and indicate promising research opportunities. While we model an exponential form for the baseline hazard to guarantee mathematical validity, other functional forms are possible. In the same vein, the approach of additive survival analysis is not limited to the implemented exponential kernel function for the channel-specific marketing effects. Alternative kernel functions to allow for different time-dependent effects could be investigated in future work. Finally, in line with the assumptions of survival models, our model assumes that every user converts within an infinite timeframe. To account for the fact that not every user does indeed convert, the proposed model could be extended by additionally considering the probability that the waiting time until conversion exceeds the time a user can be observed due to technical and lifetime restrictions. However, it must be ensured that the additional complexity does not impair the interpretability and thus practical relevance of the model.

References

Anderl, E., Becker, I., vonWangenheim, F. & Schumann, J. H. (2013), 'Putting attribution to work: A graph-based framework for attribution modeling in managerial practice', *SSRN Electronic Journal* .

Anderl, E., Becker, I., von Wangenheim, F. & Schumann, J. H. (2016), 'Mapping the customer journey: Lessons learned from graph-based online attribution modeling', *International Journal of Research in Marketing* **33**(3), 457–474.

Branco, P., Torgo, L. & Ribeiro, R. P. (2016), 'A survey of predictive modeling on imbalanced domains', *ACM Computing Surveys* **49**(2), 1–50.

Davis, J. & Goadrich, M. (2006), The relationship between precision-recall and roc curves, *in* 'Proceedings of the 23rd international conference on Machine learning - ICML '06', ACM, pp. 233–240.

Dean, J. & Ghemawat, S. (2008), 'Mapreduce', *Communications of the ACM* **51**(1), 107– 113.

Ji, W. & Wang, X. (2017), Additional multi-touch attribution for online advertising, *in* 'Proceedings of the AAAI Conference on Artificial Intelligence', AAAI, pp. 1360– 1366.

Kannan, P. K., Reinartz,W. & Verhoef, P. C. (2016), 'The path to purchase and attribution modeling: Introduction to special section', *International Journal of Research in Marketing* **33**(3), 449–456.

Kumar, S., Gupta, G., Prasad, R., Chatterjee, A., Vig, L. & Shroff, G. (2020), Camta: Causal attention model for multi-touch attribution, *in* '2020 International Conference on Data Mining Workshops (ICDMW)', IEEE, pp. 79–86.

Lawless, J. (2011), *Statistical Models and Methods for Lifetime Data*, 2nd edn, Wiley.

Little, J. D. C. (2004), 'Models and managers: The concept of a decision calculus', *Management Science* **50**(12_supplement), 1841–1853.

Lodish, L. M. (2001), 'Building marketing models that make money', *Interfaces* **31**(3_supplement), 45–55.

Loezer, L., Enembreck, F., Barddal, J. P. & de Souza Britto, A. (2020), Cost-sensitive learning for imbalanced data streams, *in* 'Proceedings of the 35th Annual ACM Symposium on Applied Computing', ACM, pp. 498–504.

Romero Leguina, J., Cuevas Rumin, A. & Cuevas Rumin, R. (2020), 'Digital marketing attribution: Understanding the user path', *Electronics* **9**(11), 1822.

Saito, T. & Rehmsmeier, M. (2015), 'The precision-recall plot is more informative than the roc plot when evaluating binary classifiers on imbalanced datasets', *PloS one* **10**(3), e0118432.

Shao, X. & Li, L. (2011), Data-driven multi-touch attribution models, *in* 'Proceedings of the 17th ACM SIGKDD international conference on Knowledge discovery and data mining - KDD '11', ACM, pp. 258–264.

Statista (2022*a*), 'Cloud computing: usage in companies in germany 2022', https://www.statista.com/statistics/459998/usage-of-cloud-computing-by-companies-in-germany/?locale=en. Accessed: 09.03.2023.

Statista (2022*b*), 'Digital advertising - worldwide', https://www.statista .com/outlook/dmo/digital-advertising/worldwide. Accessed: 09.03.2023.

Yang, D., Dyer, K. & Wang, S. (2020), 'Interpretable deep learning model for online multi-touch attribution', *arXiv preprint* arXiv:2004.00384 .

Yao, D., Gong, C., Zhang, L., Chen, S. & Bi, J. (2022), Causalmta: Eliminating the user confounding bias for causal multi-touch attribution, *in* 'Proceedings of the 28th ACM SIGKDD Conference on Knowledge Discovery and Data Mining', ACM, pp. 4342– 4352.

Zaremba, A. (2020), 'Conversion attribution:what is missed by the advertising industry? the opec model and its consequencesfor media mix modeling', *Journal of Marketing and Consumer Behaviour in Emerging Markets* **10**(1), 4–23.

Zhang, Y., Wei, Y. & Ren, J. (2014), Multi-touch attribution in online advertising with survival theory, *in* '2014 IEEE International Conference on Data Mining', IEEE, pp. 687–696.

A Prototype to Support Business Model Innovation Through Crowdsourcing and Artificial Intelligence

Arthur Klippenstein, Christoph Weskamp, Florian Laux, Florian Neuhaus, Karlson Pfannschmidt, Melissa Bülling, and Stephan Kassanke

Abstract The development of new and innovative business models is a central challenge for many companies, particularly for small and medium-sized companies. Information systems could support these companies by actively guiding them through a business model development process. However, the existing business model development tools only provide passive support for their users (e.g., digital whiteboards). Therefore, we set out to develop a prototype that actively supports its users by generating business model ideas. Informed by an existing design theory, we built a prototype relying on hybrid intelligence (i.e., the combination of human and artificial knowledge). The prototype iteratively generates new business model ideas by recombining existing knowledge, posts the ideas to a crowdsourcing platform for evaluation, and learns from the crowds' evaluation. This demonstration paper presents the prototype, the challenges we faced during its implementation, and directions for future research on machine-supported business model development.

A. Klippenstein · F. Neuhaus · S. Kassanke
Myconsult GmbH, Salzkotten, Germany
e-mail: klippenstein@myconsult.de

F. Neuhaus
e-mail: neuhaus@myconsult.de

S. Kassanke
e-mail: kassanke@myconsult.de

C. Weskamp · F. Laux · K. Pfannschmidt (✉)
Paderborn University, Paderborn, Germany
e-mail: karlson.pfannschmidt@uni-paderborn.de

C. Weskamp
e-mail: christoph.weskamp@uni-paderborn.de

F. Laux
e-mail: florian.laux@uni-paderborn.de

M. Bülling
UNITY AG, Büren, Germany
e-mail: melissa.buelling@unity.de

D. Beverungen et al. (eds.), *Solutions and Technologies for Responsible Digitalization*, Lecture Notes in Information Systems and Organisation 75,
https://doi.org/10.1007/978-3-031-80122-8_23

Keywords Business model development · Hybrid intelligence · Machine-generated ideas · Prototype

1 Motivation

The increasing speed of technological advancement and changing requirements forces companies to constantly reinvent their business models (Osterwalder et al. 2020). Business models describe a layer between a company's long-term strategy and everyday processes, and how companies create, deliver and capture value (Osterwalder and Pigneur 2010). A given product or service can be commercialized by a virtually unlimited number of business models and the right choice of model can determine the success of the product or service (Al-Debei and Avison 2010). Consequently, for many companies the innovation of existing and the development of new business models present key challenges. In particular, small and medium-sized companies struggle to systematically develop innovative business models (EFI 2023). Failing to do so, however, is likely to seriously hurt their competitiveness.

Software-supported business model development has the potential to guide companies through the business model development process. However, the existing software support focuses on the digitization of the analogous processes involved in business model development, instead of actively providing guidance to its users (Szopinski et al. 2020). A particularly promising approach to actively support users is the application of hybrid intelligence, which combines artificial intelligence with human knowledge (Dellermann et al. 2019a, b), thus providing a new level of support to its users. Moreover, the collaboration between humans and machines has the potential to generate more innovative ideas than either party could produce alone. So far hybrid intelligence has been used in the context of business model validation (e.g., Bao et al. 2011; Dellermann et al. 2019a, b), but not in the context of business model idea generation. In validation, artificial intelligence uses its computation capacities to analytically evaluate business models. By contrast, in idea generation different capabilities are required, as the artificial intelligence has to use combinatorial capabilities to generate new ideas in a creative process. Therefore, we propose and investigate the following research question:

How should a hybrid intelligence system be designed to support business model idea generation?

To answer this question and to realize the unused potential of information systems in business model development, we built a prototype that combines crowdsourcing with machine learning in a socio-technical system. A previously published design theory by John (2016) served as a starting point for a multi-year research project with the purpose of developing the aforementioned prototype. In this article, we present the current version of the prototype accompanied by insights as well as challenges, design choices and pitfalls occurring in the implementation of each component.

2 Related Literature

The field of business model research experienced rapid growth resulting in three different research strands including research focused on (1) business models as attributes of real firms, (2) business models as cognitive or linguistic schemas, and (3) business models as a formal conceptual representation of how a business functions (Massa et al. 2017). Business models are commonly defined as describing the mechanisms of how a company creates, delivers, and captures value (Teece 2010). Formal conceptual representations, especially modeling languages, provide a promising starting point for software-supported business model development. Within these languages, business models can be represented in a formal and structured way to simplify the processing of business model information by machines. A wide range of modeling languages exist in the literature. These modeling languages provide business developers with the necessary vocabulary and notations to present business models in a unified way. While all of these modeling languages offer different advantages and drawbacks (see John et al. 2017 for a detailed review), the Business Model Canvas emerged as the quasi-standard in research and practice (Osterwalder and Pigneur 2010). In support of this statement, the book introducing the Business Model Canvas has been sold over a million times and has been quoted more than 19,000 times (according to Google Scholar). The Business Model Canvas consists of nine building blocks describing different parts of the business model (e.g., value proposition, revenue streams, or customer relationships). For each building block one or multiple elements can be added to instantiate a business model (e.g., a subscription service is an element in the building block revenue streams). Due to its prominent position, a wide range of support tools have been developed specifically for the Business Model Canvas.

Szopinski et al. (2020) propose a taxonomy that aggregates and systematizes business model development from theory and practice. In total, they identify 24 software tools that use the Business Model Canvas as their foundation. In their taxonomy, they classify the features of the identified software into eleven feature dimensions across three overarching categories. First, the modeling category entails features of development tools that can be used to create business models. Second, the collaboration category is a collection of features enabling interactions between multiple business developers. Third and finally, the technical category consists of dimensions regarding software architecture and data exchange. Similarly, Ebel et al. (2016) developed a framework for developing business model development tools and identified 20 functions across four business model development phases (environmental analysis, business model design, implementation, and management) and two additional aspects (shared materials, community). Finally, Fritscher and Pigneur (2010) developed a tool that aims to replicate the sticky-note experience of using the business model canvas in a digital context. It can be noted that in all three cases all of the identified features and functions only passively support their users and do not provide active guidance to their users.

Early conceptualizations of machine-supported creative processes envisioned that machines and humans work together as colleagues to achieve more creative results (Lubart 2005). This vision has been supported by the recent development towards hybrid intelligence systems (i.e., systems where humans and machines interact at eye level). As these systems are particularly suitable for settings where machines alone struggle to deliver good results, they seem particularly applicable to facilitate complex and creative processes like business model development (Dellermann et al. 2019a, b). Therefore, this concept provides a promising foundation for a tool that actively supports its users during business model development. Hybrid intelligence combines the complementary strengths of humans and machines (Dellermann et al. 2019a, b) and leads to superior results, that neither actor could have achieved alone (Lofi and Maarry 2014). Machines can take over tasks that are time-consuming and resource intensive, while humans take over tasks that require intuition, creativity, or gut feeling (Dellermann et al. 2019a, b). Because humans and machines possess different strengths, a task that is easy to solve for humans may pose a significant challenge for machines and vice versa (Moravec 1988). Humans and machines can collaborate in different ways, or patterns (Lofi and Maarry 2014). For instance, the "crowd trainer" pattern suggests using large groups of humans (i.e., the crowd) as teachers for the machines.

Previous research has already identified the potential of hybrid intelligence for supporting creative processes in the business model context. Most related to our proposed prototype is an artifact developed for business model validation (Dellermann et al. 2018), which uses hybrid intelligence to improve business model evaluation by augmenting machine learning techniques with human expertise. The artifact also leverages crowdsourcing and artificial intelligence in a business model context, but targets a different phase of the business model development process by focusing on the validation of existing business models. The prototype presented in this study, by contrast, aims to support the creation of business model ideas, and therefore requires different functionalities. While the process of validation is an analytical process based on formal analysis and pattern recognition, the process of idea generation is a creative process based on the recombination of existing knowledge (Mumford and Gustafson 1988).

3 Design Theory

The proposed prototype is based on a previously published design theory by John (2016). Within this section, we briefly present the principles of form and function proposed by this theory. The design theory is based on the observation that human idea-generation processes rely on two cognitive abilities of humans: (1) building up knowledge and (2) flexible recombination of the accumulated knowledge. Following the blind variation/selective retention theory the idea-generation process can be broken down into two steps (Campbell 1960). First, humans use the ability to recombine their existing knowledge to develop a wide range of ideas to create novelty.

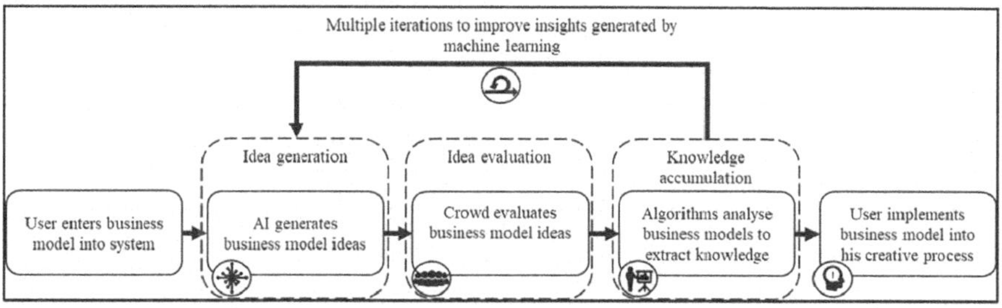

Fig. 1 Overview of the functionality of the artifact proposed by John (2016)

Second, to ensure that these novel ideas are also useful, humans evaluate them and select the most promising ideas as candidate solutions. In this step, humans also build knowledge on the attributes that constitute a promising idea and advance their knowledge for future idea generation. However, these abilities and processes are limited by the cognitive capacity of human idea generators (i.e., a human brain can only hold a limited amount of knowledge and can also only generate a limited number of ideas). The combination of machine learning and crowdsourcing can be used to alleviate these limitations of human cognition in idea generation. Following the ideas of the blind variation/selective retention theory, a tool integrating humans and machines should implement the following three subprocesses: idea creation, idea evaluation, and knowledge accumulation. To ensure continuous learning and process improvement these subprocesses should be carried out iteratively (see Fig. 1).

In the subprocess of idea creation machine learning can be leveraged to generate large and diverse sets of ideas. Humans generate ideas by creating novel yet useful recombinations of existing schemas from their domain knowledge (Mumford and Gustafson 1988). The idea creation step in the design theory follows the same principle, in that machines can use a database containing knowledge about business models and their possible characteristics to generate novel business model ideas by recombining these characteristics (Martins et al. 2015).

The previous step results in a new set of business model ideas that have yet to be evaluated. However, idea evaluation—and especially creativity assessment—are areas where machines struggle to perform as well as humans. For this reason, John (2016) proposes to rely on human judges for idea evaluation. Because the number of generated ideas can be very high, it would not be feasible to rely on a single human judge, whereas crowdsourcing can be used as a substitute by involving large and anonymous groups of people (Howe 2006). Crowdsourcing in particular offers two key benefits compared to evaluation by a few selected experts: (1) it generates a sufficient number of ratings for machine learning and (2) enables quick data collection. Large crowds can effectively reduce the time required to evaluate all the ideas, and, according to initial empirical observations, crowds can assess creativity at a level comparable to experts (e.g., Magnusson et al. 2014; Mollick and Nanda 2016) as long as they are familiar with the context of the ideas. To automate the process of idea evaluation, John (2016) suggests the utilization of a crowdsourcing platform with a web interface, to automatically post the ideas to a crowdsourcing platform where human judges can evaluate them.

Upon receiving the results from the crowdsourcing platform, the final subprocess of the design process, i.e., idea quality accumulation, can be triggered. The goal of this subprocess is to identify those combinations of idea attributes that increase idea quality. John (2016) proposes to apply supervised machine learning to the pairs of business model ideas and ratings to identify promising patterns and attributes. The generated insights can then be used to inform the future iterations of the idea generation subprocess, for instance by increasing the frequency with which promising attributes and combinations occur within the generated ideas. Each iteration of the process will produce more rating data on new ideas which can be used to train machine learning algorithms, resulting in more robust insights. Once the user is satisfied with the quality of the resulting ideas, the process can be terminated.

4 Development of the Prototype

In a three-year research project we implemented a prototype following the aforementioned design theory and in particular the principles of implementation. Within this section we present how each of the principles proposed by John (2016) was implemented during the project.

4.1 Business Model Representation

The first principle *domain construct* encompasses the need for a data structure to capture business model knowledge and specific business model information to ensure proper communication between the different subprocesses. This principle comes along with two design choices: the choice of a business modeling language and the technological implementation of this modeling language. To address the first design choice we reviewed the business modeling languages identified by John et al. 2017 with regard to nine criteria (e.g., semantic complete representation of business models or the capability to represent business models from different domains). In line with the observation that the Business Model Canvas emerged as a de-facto standard, we also find that it is best suited for the application in an idea generator. While it offers a systematic approach to structure business model attributes, the attributes themselves are usually presented in unstructured text data. This approach enables creative thinking by humans, but also has major drawbacks when it comes to machine processability. Without an appropriate level of standardization, algorithms will struggle to process the business models. A recommender system following John (2016) requires a fixed set of business model attributes for recombination. Thus, to address the second design choice regarding the domain construct principle, we used the building blocks of the Business Model Canvas as a starting point to develop a standardized business model representation in XML for our prototype. We created a hierarchical representation embedded in the existing logical structure of the Business Model Canvas by providing predefined attributes for each of its building blocks. The predefined attributes were collected during multiple iterations of focus groups involving business consultants and innovation researchers. The resulting data representation comprises 1928 nodes in total, out of which 33 are attributes that can be assigned 1882 unique values. Further, we developed a frontend, which simplifies the interaction with the business model representation. Figure 2 illustrates the entire business model representation and Fig. 3 the corresponding frontend.

To ensure a good balance between a suitable model for processing by machines and a rich description that is easy for humans to understand, we carried out multiple

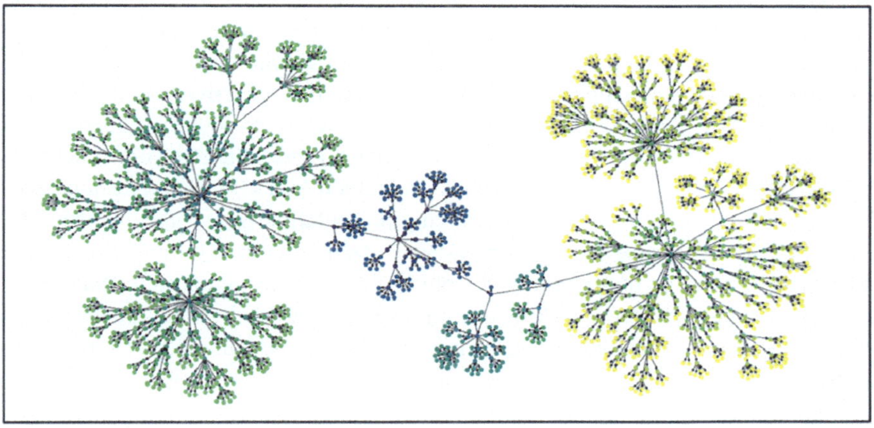

Fig. 2 Visualization of the hierarchical business model representation as a graph

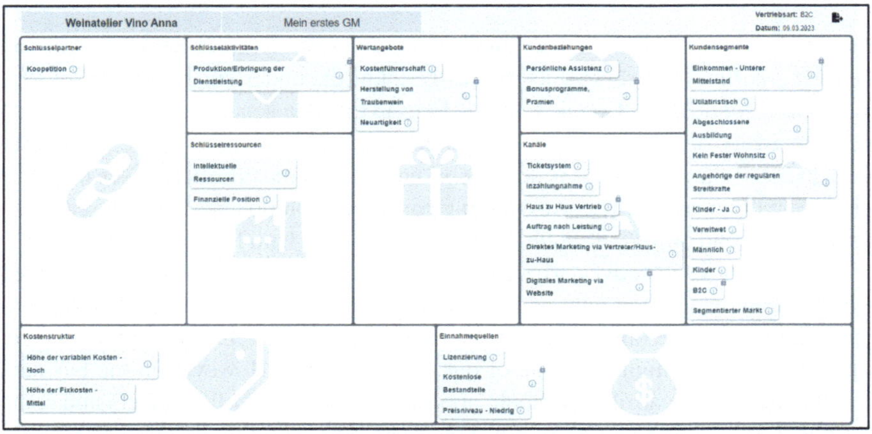

Fig. 3 Screenshot of the prototype's user interface displaying a business model

evaluations of the proposed business model representation. A first evaluation revealed that different value propositions of business models represented within our representation format were often indistinguishable from one another. This observation was mostly driven by a narrow set of available attributes for the value proposition within the data structure. For example, brick&mortar stores selling cars or clothing were almost indistinguishable from one another. To address this issue, we integrated additional comments and a statistically representative economic classification (i.e., the NACE classification[1]) to provide further industry-related information in the value proposition.

In order to generate further feedback for the frontend, we created a quantitative survey based on a case study. The goal was to conduct a preliminary evaluation of the system. The main characteristics investigated in the survey were the usefulness of the prototype, the user-friendliness of the interface, the intention to use the prototype, the overall impression, and especially the presentation of the results. The objective was to maximize the human interpretability of the resulting business model, while maintaining optimal machine readability. To achieve this objective, a tradeoff has to be made between the flexibility and the level of structure provided by the business model representation. A very flexible business model representation would enable its users to freely define the required business model attributes. Further, new attributes that have not been considered in the existing presentation format can be added by users (e.g., new technologies). By comparison, a well-structured presentation format induces restrictions on human creativity, but facilitates a machine's understanding of the presented business model. However, if humans do not understand the machine's proposition, because the underlying business model representation is not sufficiently descriptive, humans are unlikely to accept it.

4.2 Constrained Random Idea Generation

The next principles of implementation are the *cognitive procedures construct* and the *idea creation construct* which basically entail the underlying processes of idea generation (John 2016). Cognitive procedures in the idea generation process have to generate a very diverse set of ideas to properly cover the solution space (Szopinski et al. 2020). If the set of ideas is not diverse enough, promising alternatives might be missed simply because the corresponding part of the solution space is not searched. Further, a second objective should be to generate ideas with high initial quality.

In light of these objectives, we made the following design choice: Ideas are created using random generation with additional quality-ensuring constraints in our prototype. The random recombination of the attributes from our business model representation ensures a high coverage of our solution space. However, in the business model context some attributes should appear more frequently than others and some combinations of attributes should not at all occur. To account for these combinations,

[1] https://nacev2.com/en.

we introduce constraints to our idea generation, which ensure higher initial quality by avoiding the generation of unreasonable ideas. There are two types of constraints in our prototype: soft constraints and hard constraints. The soft constraints ensure the proper frequency of the attributes by predefining frequencies of single- and multiple-choice attribute occurrences. For single-choice attributes (e.g., gender), the system chooses one of the options uniformly at random. For multiple choice attributes (e.g., the type of customer relations), the prototype independently makes a random decision for each available option, where the frequency of chosen options is calibrated to be similar to the frequency observed in human business model generation. The hard constraints define clear combinations that should not occur in any generated ideas, because they are illogical. For instance, a business model targeted at kids should not specify information regarding customers' employment status. Under the consideration of the hard and soft constraints, our prototype automatically generates random recombinations of business model attributes. This approach ensures that the generated ideas cover a wide range of attributes and combinations, training the algorithm to make good recommendations.

With the implementation of the constrained random idea generation, we faced two challenges. First, in the early iterations of the process the average quality of the generated ideas was quite low because the prototype had not yet accumulated any knowledge. Only presenting ideas of low quality can potentially bias the crowd, because they have no high-quality ideas for anchoring their judgments. When a set of only low-quality ideas is distributed for idea evaluation, the ideas with slightly higher quality might receive inflated ratings. In response, we decided to enrich the sets of generated ideas with selected human-generated and curated ideas. Providing ideas with a wider range of quality should increase the quality gamut of the rated business models, and decrease the difficulty of idea evaluation for the crowd. It further allows the machine learning algorithm to be trained on good and bad ideas. In the long term, once sufficient knowledge has been accumulated by the prototype, the inclusion of human-generated ideas is no longer required. Second, most users of the prototype were set on keeping certain business model attributes fixed. For instance, some users who previously employed a business model based on a premium product or service were unwilling to switch to a less quality-oriented value proposition. Therefore, we integrated a feature to lock attributes, which signals that it should be included in every generated idea.

4.3 Crowdsourced Idea Evaluation

In the fourth principle of implementation, *idea evaluation and conversion constructs*, all design choices regarding the rating of ideas are included. This results in a number of design choices such as the choice of crowdworking platform, the representation of ideas on these platforms, and the information that should be provided alongside the ideas. Because machines struggle to evaluate creativity, John (2016) proposes to rely on a crowdsourcing platform. With regard to the first design choice (i.e.,

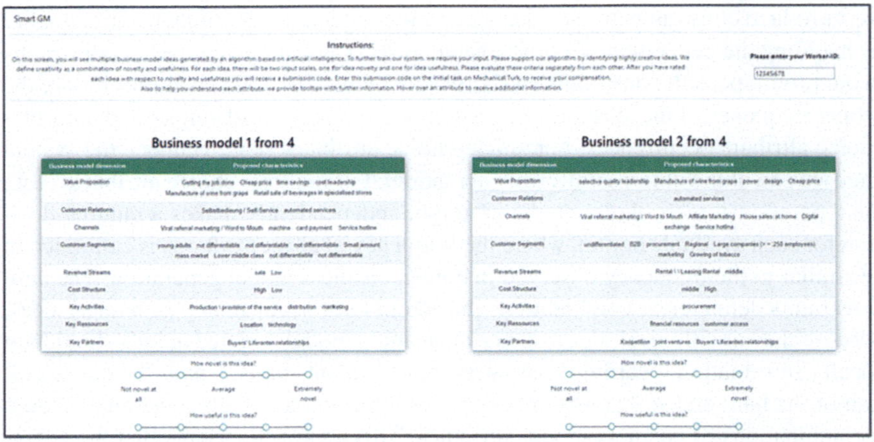

Fig. 4 Overview of the evaluation task posted to the crowdsourcing platform

the choice of crowdworking platform) our options were limited because when the research project started, only Amazon Mechanical Turk offered an interface with all the required features for an idea generator. Therefore, the prototype implements idea evaluation by automatically posting newly generated business model ideas to humans on Amazon Mechanical Turk. The second design choice regarding this principle of implementation focuses on the number of ideas to be evaluated by a single crowdworker. Upon completion of the idea generation subprocess, a large number of unevaluated business models is generated. Because it would be unreasonable to ask a single human worker to evaluate the entire set of ideas, it is broken down into smaller subsets of business model ideas. User studies regarding the cognitive load of our evaluation task revealed that subsets of four ideas led to an adequate cognitive load For each subset of ideas, an evaluation screen is automatically generated and posted to the crowd (see Fig. 4).

A third design choice had to be made regarding the choice of idea representation in the evaluation process. We evaluated two display modes: the Business Model Canvas and a table. We decided against using the canvas in the crowdsourced evaluation setting, mainly because crowdworkers would require prior knowledge to properly read the canvas as it is intended (i.e., starting with the center). By contrast, while a table loses some of the spatial information conveyed by a canvas, it enabled us to establish a predefined reading order for the crowdworkers. Thus, each idea is represented in an individual table, and each evaluation task also provides further instructions regarding the evaluation process. The final design choice refers to the choice of an appropriate evaluation mechanism. We conducted an online experiment to investigate the existing evaluation approaches and their applicability in a crowdworking context. The results indicate that intuitive evaluation approaches, like multidimensional rating scales or up- and down-voting systems, led to more accurate judgments in our setting.

Finally, when implementing the idea evaluation subprocess challenges arose when establishing the communication between humans and machines. The business model representation represents ideas in a rather abstract format which is easy to understand for machines but harder to understand for humans. A lack of common understanding between judges could introduce unwanted biases and noise to the evaluation data. To mitigate this challenge, we provided evaluators with additional information in the form of tooltips, which were implemented in the evaluation frontend. For each attribute, these tooltips provide an elaborate explanation and definition, thus reducing the risk of misunderstandings among the judges.

4.4 Knowledge Accumulation and Improved Idea Generation

In the final subprocess of an iteration, we have to extract and accumulate business model knowledge from the crowdsourced evaluations. This process is captured in the principle *idea quality aggregation*. Following John (2016), we choose a supervised machine learning model to process the business model ideas and the ratings provided by the crowd. The resulting model can be used to predict the rating for new business model ideas, to identify valuable attributes, and to generate improved business model ideas. In particular, the random idea generation can be improved by generating very large numbers of ideas and selecting only ideas with a high predicted quality for the next iteration. This approach scales with the size of the knowledge base. If the knowledge base grows larger, the machine learning model will become more reliable and will be able to identify higher quality ideas for future iterations. Further, the model can be used to provide additional outputs to the user, such as an analysis of important attributes.

Regarding knowledge accumulation, the data format poses multiple challenges for typical, off-the-shelf machine learning models, which usually require a numeric representation of a fixed size. Our business model representation overwhelmingly consists of single- and multiple-choice attributes, a rather untypical data format for machine learning. We addressed this challenge by employing binary encoding of the business models attributes—a commonly used technique in the field of machine learning. However, a possible downside of binary encoding is the large number of features it generates, which may result in insufficient generalization. Further, crowdsourcing platforms are often renowned for varying data quality characterized by a large amount of noise in the data. Additionally, each iteration requires a large number of generated ideas to cover the solution space. Because the overall number of evaluations will be subject to budget constraints, each iteration will only result in a moderate amount of data.

Therefore, we chose a robust model class, namely random forests, to be able to handle the challenging data format. Further, it provides the required functionality for downstream tasks (Breiman 2001). Finally, to ensure the optimal performance of the model, we developed a machine learning pipeline that uses cross-validation and

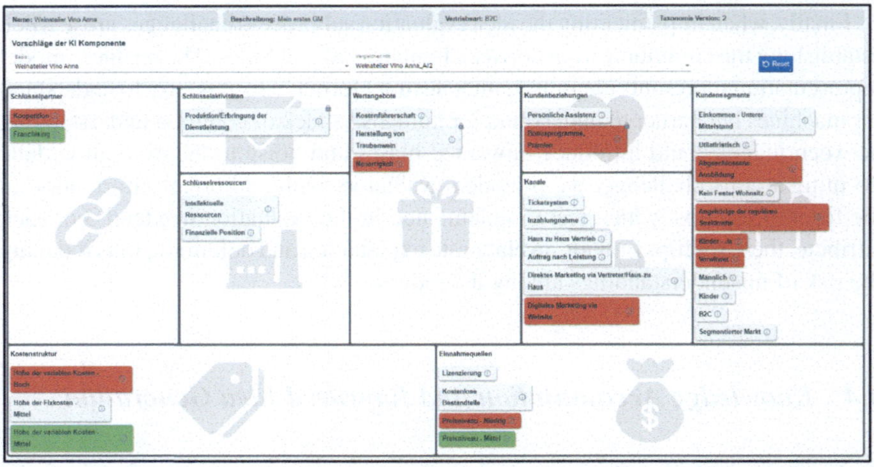

Fig. 5 Frontend displaying an automatically generated business model. The colors highlight attributes that have been changed from the initial business model

hyperparameter optimization, which avoids overfitting the model to the noisy data from the crowd.

Finally, the *overall* principle mainly encompasses the design choice, at which point the idea generation process should be terminated. Our prototype terminates once the user decides that a sufficient level of quality is reached. In case the user decides against another iteration and terminates the process, the business models deemed most promising by the model will be displayed as a result (see Fig. 5).

5 Discussion and Outlook

In this demonstration paper we have shown a software tool for machine-supported business model generation and some of the design choices we faced during its implementation. Following an established design theory, we built a prototype to investigate the potential of human–machine collaboration. So far, we used the prototype in a stylized example to investigate its functionality and conducted initial focus groups to investigate how users interact with the resulting business model ideas. The most consistent observation is that the resulting suggestions do indeed promote creativity. However, users also reported that the representation of business models in a static hierarchical representation can at times be rather abstract. Therefore, when confronted with the final ideas, users still had to transform the abstract output from the prototype into concrete ideas. In our evaluation, most users reported that this step actually resulted in more ideas they would not have come up with otherwise. The observation that even propositions that are perceived as rather abstract can be used to foster human creativity is intriguing but also highlights some remaining challenges for our prototype.

Compared to the expository instantiation provided in the initial design theory, our prototype provides a fully developed IT artifact. While there are some similarities between these artifacts (i.e., both use the business model canvas as the underlying representation), there are also differences. The expository instantiation implements idea evaluation with a one-dimensional rating scale and asks the local user to evaluate ideas, by contrast, our prototype uses a multidimensional rating scale on a crowdworking platform to gather feedback. Further, while the initial instantiation simply increases the frequency of popular attributes, our prototype uses an up-to-date machine learning model to determine the importance of certain attributes.

The observations made in our research project provide theoretical and practical contributions to the Information Systems community. On a theoretical level, we are the first to implement an information system following the design theory for business model generators (John 2016). By doing so, we were able to extend the knowledge of how the proposed principles of implementation should be instantiated and what challenges may arise. In particular, we describe the design choices we made to instantiate the design theory. On a practical level, a tool specifically designed to actively support the business model development process can provide its users with guidance, particularly if the users lack prior business model knowledge. But the recent technological advances in generative artificial intelligence challenge the design theory proposed by John (2016) in many aspects. Nowadays, generative artificial intelligence could also be used to develop business model ideas. Prompting ChatGPT to generate business model ideas results in a set of ideas structured in a Business Model Canvas. A key benefit is that these models have been trained on very large datasets with widespread information, and consequently provide higher flexibility compared to our predefined business model representation. However, information systems following John's design theory still provide a valuable contribution to practice as they can incorporate more recent information, trends and developments by actively engaging with humans. By contrast, systems based on generative artificial intelligence can only consider the information they are trained on. However, these approaches are not mutually exclusive to one another. For instance, future research could investigate information systems that replace the idea generation process proposed by John (2016) with generative artificial intelligence. Further, future research could also compare the effects of different degrees of formalization and standardization on creativity in innovation contexts such as business model development. It could also be investigated how a lesser degree of standardization could affect the evaluation quality of the crowd in hybrid intelligence approaches.

Overall, our prototype offers a first step toward business model development tools that actively support their users. Initial observations suggest that these tools can indeed foster creativity, but further research and evaluations will be needed to uncover the full potential of machine-supported business model generation.

Acknowledgements The authors gratefully acknowledge the financial support provided by the European Regional Development Fund (ERDF).

References

Al-Debei, M. M., & Avison, D (2010). 'Developing a unified framework of the business model concept' *European Journal of Information Systems* **19**(3),. 359–376.

Bao, J., Sakamoto, Y., & Nickerson, J. V. (2011). 'Evaluating Design Solutions Using Crowds'. in *Proceedings of the 17th Americas Conference on Information Systems*, Detroit, USA.

Breiman, L. (2001), 'Random Forests', *Machine Learning* **45**(1), 5–32.

Campbell, D. T. (1960), 'Blind variation and selective retention in creative thought as in other knowledge processes', *Psychological review* **67**(6), 380–400.

Commission of Experts for Research and Innovation (EFI), (2023). 'Research, innovation and technological performance in Germany - EFI Report 2023', EFI, Berlin.

Dellermann, D., Ebel, P., Söllner, M., & Leimeister, J. M. (2019), 'Hybrid Intelligence', *Business & Information Systems Engineering* 61(5), 637–643.

Dellermann, D., Lipusch, N., Ebel, P., and Leimeister, J. M. (2019). 'Design principles for a hybrid intelligence decision support system for business model validation', *Electronic Markets* **29**(3), 423–441.

Dellermann, D., Lipusch, N., & Li, M. (2018), 'Combining Humans and Machine Learning: A Novel Approach for Evaluating Crowdsourcing Contributions in Idea Contests', *in* 'Proceedings Multikonferenz Wirtschaftsinformatik'.

Ebel, P., Bretschneider, U., & Leimeister, J. M. (2016), 'Leveraging virtual business model innovation: a framework for designing business model development tools', *Information Systems Journal* **26**(5), 519–550.

Fritscher, B., & Pigneur, Y. (2010), 'Supporting Business Model Modelling: A Compromise between Creativity and Constraints', *in* 'Task Models and Diagrams for User Interface Design: 8th International Workshop, Revised Selected Papers', Springer, pp. 28–43.

Howe, J. (2006), 'The rise of crowdsourcing', *Wired magazine* 14(6), 1–4.

John, T. (2016), 'Supporting Business Model Idea Generation Through Machine-generated Ideas: A Design Theory', *in* 'ICIS 2016 Proceedings'.

John, T., Kundisch, D., & Szopinski, D. (2017), 'Visual Languages for Modeling Business Models: A Critical Review and Future Research Directions', *in* 'ICIS 2017 Proceedings'.

Lofi, C., & Maarry, K. E. (2014), 'Design Patterns for Hybrid Algorithmic-Crowdsourcing Workflows', *in* 'Proceedings IEEE 16th Conference on Business Informatics', IEEE, pp. 1–8.

Lubart, T. (2005), 'How can computers be partners in the creative process: Classification and commentary on the Special Issue', *International Journal of Human-Computer Studies* **63**(4–5), 365–369.

Magnusson, P. R., Netz, J., & Wästlund, E. (2014), 'Exploring holistic intuitive idea screening in the light of formal criteria', *Technovation* **34**(5-6), 315–326.

Martins, L. L., Rindova, V. P., & Greenbaum, B. E. (2015), 'Unlocking the Hidden Value of Concepts: A Cognitive Approach to Business Model Innovation', *Strategic Entrepreneurship Journal* **9**(1), 99–117.

Massa, L., Tucci, C. L., & Afuah, A. (2017), 'A critical assessment of business model research', *Academy of Management Annals* **11**(1), 73–104.

Mollick, E., & Nanda, R. (2016), 'Wisdom or Madness? Comparing Crowds with Expert Evaluation in Funding the Arts', *Management Science* **62**(6), 1533–1553.

Moravec, H. (1988), *The Future of robot and human intelligence: The Future of Robot and Human Intelligence.* Harvard University Press.

Mumford, M. D., & Gustafson, S. B. (1988), 'Creativity syndrome: Integration, application, and innovation', *Psychological bulletin* **103**(1), 27–43.

Osterwalder, A., & Pigneur, Y. (2010), *Business model generation: A handbook for visionaries, game changers, and challengers.* Wiley&Sons.

Osterwalder, A., Pigneur, Y., Etiemble, F., & Smith, A. (2020), *The invincible company.* Wiley&Sons.

Szopinski, D., Schoormann, T., John, T., Knackstedt, R., & Kundisch, D. (2020), 'Software tools for business model innovation: current state and future challenges', *Electronic Markets* **30**(3), pp. 469–494.

Teece, D. J. (2010), 'Business Models, Business Strategy and Innovation', *Long Range Planning* **43**(2–3), pp. 172–194.

Overcoming the Data Transparency Trade-Off: Designing a Blockchain-Based Delivery Invoice System for the Construction Industry

Jonathan Lautenschlager, Jan Stramm, Tobias Guggenberger, André Schweizer, and Artur Rösch

Abstract Blockchain's inherent characteristics render it a promising solution in collaborative supply chain networks. However, the technology still faces challenges in coopetition, as sharing business data on blockchains requires balancing the benefits of data transparency for process automation with concerns about exposing business information to competitors. This paper draws on design science research to iteratively design and develop a decentralized infrastructure that can address the coopetition aspects of digital delivery invoices in construction supply chains. As a result, design objectives and design principles are derived while experts thoroughly evaluate the prototype. Practical guidance for implementing digital delivery invoices is provided to enable coopetitive while secure data exchange. Our findings suggest that if construction companies want to prioritize network effects despite the growing complexity, they should establish channels and private data collections along with additional privacy-enhancing technologies to ensure secure data exchange across the entire supply chain.

Keywords Blockchain technology · Data transparency · Delivery invoices · Construction industry · Supply chain management

---

J. Lautenschlager (✉) · J. Stramm · T. Guggenberger
Branch Business and Information Systems Engineering of the Fraunhofer FIT, University of Bayreuth, Bayreuth, Germany
e-mail: jonathan.lautenschlager@fit.fraunhofer.com; jonathan.lautenschlager@fb3.fra-uas.de

J. Stramm
e-mail: jan.stramm@fit.fraunhofer.com; jan.stramm@fb3.fra-uas.de

T. Guggenberger
e-mail: tobias.guggenberger@fit.fraunhofer.com

J. Lautenschlager · J. Stramm
ditlab, Frankfurt University of Applied Sciences, Frankfurt, Germany

A. Schweizer · A. Rösch
TRUSTEQ GmbH, Cologne, Germany
e-mail: andre.schweizer@trusteq.de

D. Beverungen et al. (eds.), *Solutions and Technologies for Responsible Digitalization*, Lecture Notes in Information Systems and Organisation 75,
https://doi.org/10.1007/978-3-031-80122-8_24

1 Introduction

More and more industries have become aware of the potential benefits of digital and automated processes. Many companies have recognized that transitioning from analog, often paper-based, to digital processes significantly improves business performance (Bajpai and Misra 2022). They aim to increase process efficiency through automation and simplification potentially leading to cost savings. In particular, digitization can foster cost savings within the construction industry by increasing the automation of partly intricate and supportive construction planning processes and resulting supply chain transactions (Prebanic´ and Vukomanovic´ 2021). Thus, digitizing simple yet crucial processes such as the delivery invoice process of construction materials can bring significant business value to companies and their supply chains.

Nevertheless, the digital transformation of supportive construction processes is lagging due to several adoption challenges in practice (Demirkesen and Tezel 2021). Despite the presence of digital electronic data interchange (EDI) standardization and accompanying digital solutions over the past few decades, they have failed to adequately fulfil the market's requirements due to their centralized nature with specifically tailored functionalities. Furthermore, depending on the service provider, these solutions prioritize individual goals, resulting in dependencies and further hindering their widespread market adoption. Current construction industry concepts reflect this circumstance by facing the challenge of digital coopetition between stakeholders involved in their supply chains (Wilhelm 2011). Digital coopetition refers to the concurrent trade-off between the willingness to exploit collaboration benefits while maintaining market positions within competition among companies in a value network (Hoffmann et al. 2018). To do so, construction companies facilitate data-sharing platforms to collaboratively share sensitive business data to execute supportive construction planning processes (Li et al. 2019). The partial aspect of collaboration that requires the sharing of information and resources is leading to increased efficiency, cost reduction, improved supply chain visibility, and fostering innovation and new business models.

In that regard, Sternberg et al. (2020) highlight blockchain technology as a promising solution that brings many benefits to supply chains but faces challenges in the context of practical adoption. Blockchain's inherent potentials, such as enhanced product traceability, enhanced trust among stakeholders, and increased data availability, make it appealing for organizations to adopt decentralized solutions within collaborative supply chain network purposes (Azzi et al. 2019; Butijn et al. 2020; Guggenberger et al. 2020). However, sharing confidential business data on blockchains requires balancing the benefits of data transparency for process automation with concerns about disclosing sensitive business information to competing companies (Alt 2020; Guggenberger et al. 2022). Ultimately, this hinders the adoption of a blockchain solution in practice. For instance, various parties are involved in the delivery network of construction materials, including multiple suppliers and transporters delivering to the construction site as the recipient. In this scenario, the construction company at the building site desires to keep the bilateral details of individual partial deliveries within the supply chain confidential because sharing the information with unauthorized third parties could result in losing competitive advantages and neglecting antitrust regulations. Consequently, the competitive context in the construction industry requires a solution that unlocks collaboration benefits while balancing the protection of business interests and data protection.

In this context, privacy-enhancing features provided by modern blockchain frameworks, such as channels and private data collections, seem promising (Toufaily et al. 2021). Thus, within this paper, we design, develop and evaluate a decentralized infrastructure that can account for the aspects of the coopetition trade-off within the supply chain management in the construction industry (Kannengießer et al. 2020). Therefore, we ask:

> *RQ: How can blockchain technology help to digitize the process of handling delivery invoices in the construction industry supply chain while addressing the challenges associated with the coopetition trade-off?*

We address our research questions by following a design science research (DSR) approach. Thus, we iteratively developed, refined, and evaluated the prototype implementation of our decentralized system (Hevner 2004).

2 Theoretical Background

2.1 From Paper-Based to Electronic Delivery Invoice Processes

In the construction industry, different stakeholders exchange delivery invoices with each other to document the delivery of goods or services from one party to another and record payment for those goods or services. The current exchange of delivery invoices, typically paper-based, contains a record of orders and delivery details passed on to supply chain stakeholders to ensure they agree on the transaction details. This process involves multiple stakeholders in the construction industry supply chain, such as a construction company ordering building materials from a supplier, who then hires a transport and logistics company to deliver the materials to the construction site. Additionally, the process includes the participation of various employees from different supply chain stakeholders, which leads to a long and complex process with many steps. Figure 1 shows this exemplary and simplified process, including solely one additional stakeholder (Deutscher and Bautechnik-Verein 2022).

The many processing scenarios lead to several inherent challenges of the current complex paper-based delivery invoice process. For instance, the current delivery invoice process in the construction industry faces the inefficiency of a time-consuming and prone-to-error process, the lack of data transparency for improved construction process planning, security, and standardization of procedures as well

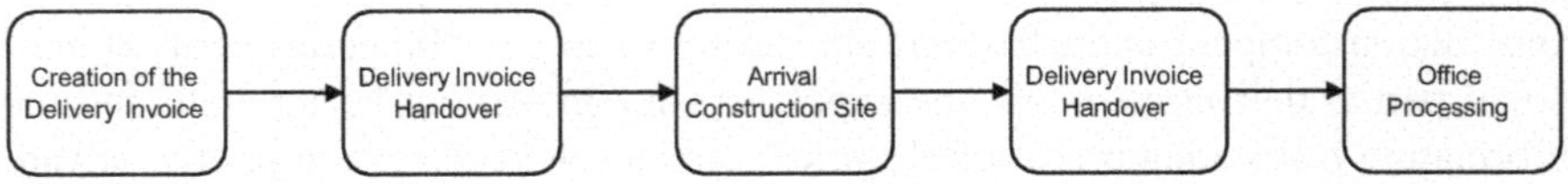

Fig. 1 Current delivery invoice process in the construction industry

as the lack of automation, interoperability, and traceability of delivery invoice processing. For instance, delivery invoices can contain specific and sensitive information such as a unique supplier identifier assigned by tax authorities, the quantity and description of the goods or services delivered and the agreed price. The delivery invoice is utilized as the basis for processing payments and reconciling records among the parties involved in the transaction. Nonetheless, because these invoices are predominantly paper-based, the back offices of construction companies have to wait for the site manager to deliver the paper-based documents physically or scan and email them to the back office, resulting in an inefficient process (Prebanić and Vukomanović 2021).

Besides paper-based processes, existing digital solutions in the construction industry use standardized data formats for EDI of digitized bills (Gibson and Bell 1990)—e.g., by using *XRechnung* or *EDIFACT*—to handle the processing of delivery invoices (Samuelson and Björk 2014; Wiehager 2021). Despite their promising potential, the effectiveness of digital solutions is limited due to market fragmentation and the absence of a universally accepted digital infrastructure solution that caters to the diverse needs of companies, regardless of their size. This suggests that current digital solutions, irrespective of their standardization and data formats, face significant challenges when it comes to practical implementation and widespread adoption in the business market (Demirkesen and Tezel 2021). The construction industry's unique requirements cannot be fully addressed by a single digital solution tailored to specific industry interests. Challenges such as partial services, change orders, retention payments, and industry-specific standards pose interoperability issues for current digital solutions. Achieving widespread acceptance requires collaboration among all stakeholders, including contractors, subcontractors, suppliers, authorities, and customers. However, in the construction industry, processing delivery invoices is complex due to rudimentary and differing information systems and supporting processes. Finally, the presence of centralized systems controlled by individual companies or domain-specific solutions hampers information flow and impedes widespread adoption and collaboration among stakeholders (Pagel 2019).

These concerns hinder the broad acceptance of digital invoicing solutions provided by single stakeholders, as companies prioritize antitrust compliance to may avoid legal consequences (Agdas and Ellis 2010; Anumba and Ruikar 2002). In this context, blockchain technology offers a promising solution that can meet these demands and leverage the advantages of an interoperable platform, particularly in terms of secure data exchange (Sternberg et al. 2020).

2.2 Blockchain Technology as Potential Solution

Blockchain technology has the potential to offer several benefits to the construction industry. Most importantly, it provides end-to-end traceability of the delivery invoices covering even complex supply chains. These traceability features can help to ensure that materials are delivered on time and in the correct quantity, faster decision-making resulting in increased efficiency striving for an enhancement on construction scheduling, and help to improve accountability.

A blockchain is a decentralized digital ledger built on a peer-to-peer network and replicated across multiple nodes to ensure fault tolerance (Butijn et al. 2020). It comprises stacks of transactions, referred to as blocks that are linked together through hash pointers, creating a chain (Beck et al. 2017). The nodes on the network use a *consensus mechanism* to decide which blocks to append and how to order transactions within a block (Wüst and Gervais 2018; Sedlmeir et al. 2022). As long as a majority of the network is reliable in some metric such as hash rate (*Proof of Work*), cryptocurrency share (*Proof of Stake*), or number or reputation of nodes (*Voting-based* or *Proof of Authority* Consensus), this reliability guarantees the correct execution of transactions and the practical immutability of the ledger. Transactions on a blockchain can represent a variety of activities (Butijn et al. 2020), such as exchanging goods or the execution of smart contracts (e.g., the exchange of construction material or the conclusion of a supply chain agreement). The ability to trust that a transaction will have the intended outcome and cannot be altered after the fact is referred to as digital trust (Sedlmeir et al. 2022).

Blockchains can be classified into two main categories: permissioned and permissionless blockchains. Permissionless blockchains allow any entity to participate in the consensus process, while permissioned blockchains require authorization for entities to take on this role. Public blockchains are accessible to anyone, while private blockchains are restricted to authorized entities (Wüst and Gervais 2018; Beck et al. 2018). Permissionless blockchains are *public*, i.e., any entity can download and read the corresponding state of the ledger. In contrast, permissioned blockchains are often—but not always—*private*, i.e., only authorized entities have read access (Rossi et al. 2019).

There are several blockchain technology implementations, each with unique characteristics and corresponding strengths and weaknesses, resulting in many blockchain frameworks. We investigated the use of *Hyperledger Fabric* as it is well-suited for enterprise and supply chain use cases (Sternberg et al. 2020). It is designed to be highly modular and configurable, allowing organizations to set up networks that meet their specific needs. Especially the support for channels allowing organizations to create sub-networks within a larger network, enabling them to keep certain transactions private and visible only to specific parties in defined private data collections. Explicit endorsement policies determine which specific nodes, known as endorsing peers, must endorse a transaction before it can be considered valid. These policies are specified in the chain code (smart contracts) and can be based on various factors, such as the identity of the submitting user or the specific assets involved in the transaction.

Both approaches allow for the sharing of sensitive information among a restricted set of participants while maintaining the integrity and immutability of the data on the blockchain (Androulaki et al. 2018).

3 Research Method

To conceptualize a prototype processing digital delivery invoices in the construction industry, we followed the DSR approach by Peffers et al. (2007). DSR entails the design and development of innovative and meaningful artifacts such as constructs, methods, models, or instantiations for a given problem in information systems (IS) (Hevner 2004; Gregor and Hevner 2013). We have developed a model in the form of a comprehensive decentralized prototype that proposes an IT solution for digital delivery invoices in the construction industry (Hevner 2004). We addressed the need for rigor and relevance (Peffers et al. 2007) by basing our work on previous research, practical insights from the research project, and corresponding elevated expert interviews. To significantly contribute to IS research, an IT artifact must address a relevant business need that may arise from the people, organizations, or technologies in an environment (Hevner 2004). As derived previously, the development of decentralized IT infrastructure for the digital delivery invoices that addresses current challenges of practical adoption in the construction industry that can unify a wide range of organizations and enterprises in the construction industry represents such a business need.

To derive design goals during our data collection, we rely on literature research and several project workshops on the prototype for digital delivery invoices in the construction industry. The ultimate goal of the research project is to advance the industry by exploring decentralized concepts and technologies that can facilitate the digital transformation of construction planning processes. In specific, our research project is embedded in a consortium project, which has allowed us to work with multiple consortium partners from the construction industry and IT experts to iteratively develop a decentralized system that addresses real-world application challenges. We are evaluating our decentralized system and corresponding prototype by gathering expert feedback from distributed technology and construction industry experts in nine ex-post interviews. Their experience is illustrated in Table 1 (Sonnenberg and Brocke 2012; Venable et al. 2016).

Table 1 Experts' professional background and experience in the ex post interviews

#	Organizational responsibility	Experience (years)	Interview duration (min)
1	Blockchain technology expert	≥ 3	61
2	Expert for decentralized technologies	≥ 5	59
3	Project manager for lean construction	≥ 3	56
4	Manager industrial solutions	≥ 8	49
5	CEO (IT consultancy)	≥ 10	31
6	IT consultant	≥ 3	53
7	Construction process management expert	≥ 10	54
8	Software engineer	≥ 3	54
9	Software developer (construction company)	≥ 5	52

4 Architecture and Prototype

4.1 Design Objectives

We focus on securely exchanging data within coopetitive supply chain scenarios to address our research question. Hence, we define design objectives which, on the one hand, ensure the fundamentally secure data exchange within a decentralized infrastructure (DO1) and, on the other hand, take into account the two partial aspects of coopetition—collaboration (DO2) and competition (DO3) (Bader et al. 2021; Bons et al. 2020; Lacity and Hoek 2021).

Design objective 1—Secure data exchange: Concerning the secure data exchange between supply chain stakeholders, the solution focuses on the data protection goals of confidentiality, integrity, availability, and authenticity. This focus ensures that delivery invoice data cannot be altered unnoticed or without authorization (integrity), the data is genuine (authenticity), and data can be accessed whenever needed (availability).

Design objective 2—Collaboration: Leveraging a secure and decentralized infrastructure, as well as digital delivery invoices processes, effective collaboration among the stakeholders in a supply chain is essential. This requires the ability to easily integrate various existing systems of construction companies into the decentralized network through modular connectivity options. The delivery invoice system should possess suitable interfaces allowing easy integration with third-party software, including enterprise resource planning (ERP), customer relationship management (CRM), and accounting systems. Furthermore, the solution must establish a decentralized system encompassing all construction goods and materials. This integrated approach is vital in providing construction companies with a comprehensive system that caters to the cooperation between various suppliers and ensures process reliability for all types of goods.

Design objective 3—Competition: When dealing with competitive supply chain scenarios, the solution must take into account the aspect of data confidentiality. The data exchange should only occur with authorized parties, and sensitive business data must be kept private from unauthorized third parties. However, the solution must automatically share sufficient data to expedite the processing of delivery invoices, particularly in downstream invoicing and invoice verification areas.

4.2 Blockchain Prototype Architecture: Functionalities and Definitions

Processing delivery invoices constitutes an inter-organizational process that can significantly benefit using blockchain technology (Butijn et al. 2020; Bons et al. 2020). We decided on Hyperledger Fabric as a suitable blockchain solution to exploit those benefits and to create a comprehensive and functional decentralized infrastructure, we systematize our decentralized system and prototype into three levels: *backend-, frontend-, and blockchain-layer*. It also incorporates an identity provider, which is utilized to establish and implement company-level rights and role concepts. This approach allows the company to integrate existing identity providers, avoiding redundant systems. The backend uses two databases to manage blockchain access and different construction companies. In regard, the prototype is designed to be adaptable and extensible based on the need for collaboration and the challenge of balancing competition. The prototype's backend and frontend components serve as a model for best practices that can be tailored to individual requirements. While authorization for different companies is controlled at the blockchain level, the backend allows user-specific administration. These administration features enable each company to customize its authorization process within the decentralized system of the blockchain delivery invoice system, thus promoting the competition requirement of data privacy. The decentralized systems technical implementation and schematic representation can be found in Fig. 2. The following chapters provide an in-depth explanation of the technologies and how they are implemented across the three levels.

Frontend-Layer: The system features various views tailored to different user needs. The views can be broadly divided into two categories: those required by companies for an overarching overview of their processes (both ongoing and completed) and those used by process participants for a more focused process view (e.g., weigher, driver, foreman). At the same time, the back office of a construction company may require an overall process view. The foreman at the construction site only needs a process view to, for instance, plan for the arrival of goods. The solution must create

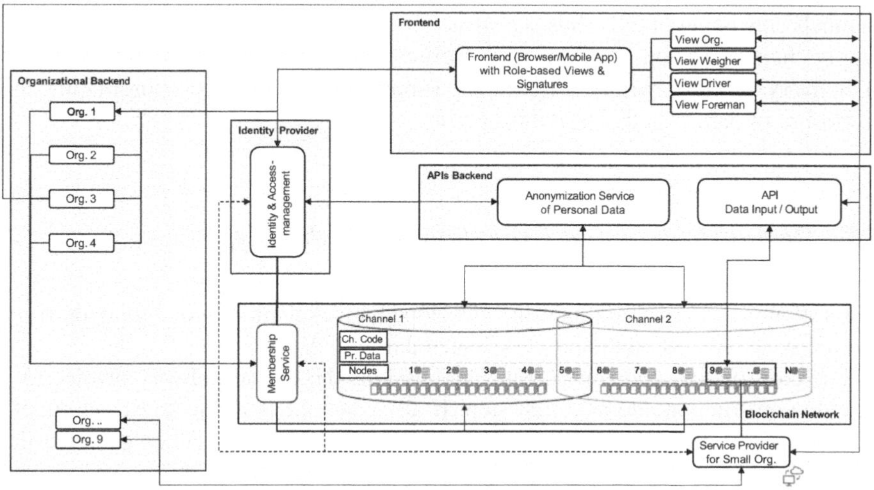

Fig. 2 Decentralized System for the Processing of Digital Delivery Invoices in the Construction Industry

and edit a delivery invoice process in this context. Therefore, the frontend layer solution allows transferring data from the inventory systems to the blockchain. In this course, the standardization of interfaces and the provision of signing data are necessary to implement the holistic and seamless process.

Backend-Layer: The backend is an intermediary layer between the blockchain and frontend that can be scaled and customized to meet the specific requirements of individual users. The respective organization determines the organizational backend functionalities and the corresponding software (e.g., choice of an ERP system) for connecting to the decentralized network system. Identity management for each organization can be handled by an identity provider, which, for instance, assigns individual identities to different employees within a company. The APIs backend extends the identity provider and makes the interaction possible via APIs. Moreover, small and medium-sized companies may not have the capacity to host a blockchain network node, so an external service provider such as a construction association or a regular service provider can take over this function. The membership service of the blockchain network is used for onboarding new companies, enabling connections through standardized protocols. However, specific interfaces for the connection must be defined in the case of individual implementation.

Blockchain-Layer: The blockchain layer consists of the membership service for onboarding new companies and dedicated channels for handling explicit building materials. In doing so, the privacy of delivery invoice data within each process is of utmost importance. In our prototype, we ensure this by creating dedicated channels for different types of construction goods (such as a channel for solely processing bulk material), and by establishing private data collections within those channels consisting of only those construction companies involved in that particular supply chain operation. Defining the specific participants involved in the exchange of delivery invoices within a particular supply chain assists in coordinating the disclosure of data to authorized third parties.

4.3 Demonstration and Execution of the Prototype

The following section outlines the developed blockchain-based digital delivery invoice system based on the process depicted in Fig. 2.

The construction company creates and assigns the digital delivery invoice to a specific construction site as a first step. If all stakeholders at the construction site are part of the decentralized infrastructure solution, they can either generate the corresponding construction site within the system or select an existing one. However, if stakeholders are not part of the decentralized infrastructure, they must manually input the delivery invoice information or use traditional paper-based methods to create and prepare the delivery invoice for transfer to the supplier. This process is carried out through the individual company's backend. Figure 3 provides a detailed overview of the completed delivery invoice process, which begins once the delivery invoice and construction site have been created. This marks the starting point of the digital process. Before the delivery invoice is accepted, the transporter inspects both the goods and the invoice itself. Acceptance or rejection of the delivery invoice can be done by scanning the QR code on the construction company's smartphone using their specific frontend solution. Alternatively, the manual entry and commenting of delivery invoice data is also possible. Parties involved may include comments on the delivery invoice, particularly crucial in goods damage or insufficient availability. The delivered goods and the corresponding invoice are transported to the designated location, and the involved parties may track their current location through GPS live tracking if agreed upon. In the detailed view, users can access a drop-down interface that displays information such as the QR code that needs to be scanned or the current location through GPS live tracking if necessary. This enables all parties to be informed about the expected delivery time and make necessary adjustments to subsequent processes. The foreman at the construction site checks the delivery invoice and goods before accepting them. They can accept or reject the delivery invoice by scanning the QR code from the carrier's smartphone. If a digital delivery invoice does not exist, one can be created from the QR code on the paper delivery invoice. Manual entry of delivery invoice data is also possible. Parties can add comments to the delivery invoice in the same manner as during the transportation of goods. Stakeholders can access the delivery invoice status from their back office anytime, as it is synchronized through the decentralized blockchain network. This allows for quicker and automatic adjustments, subsequent deliveries, or invoice audits if needed.

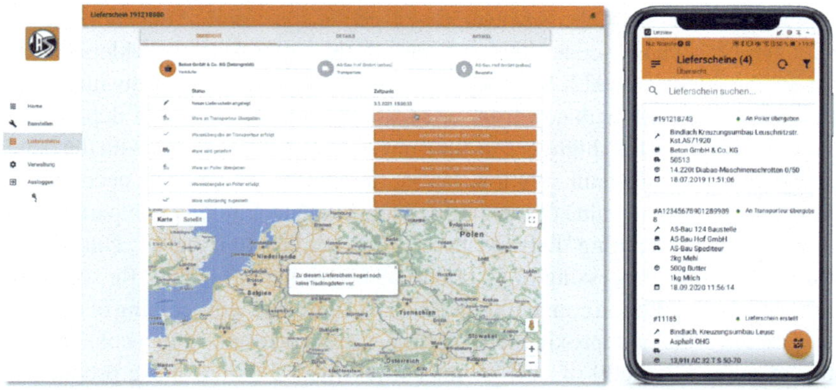

Fig. 3 Prototype overview

5 Evaluation and Discussion

During the development phase, we employed an iterative evaluation process to assess the feasibility of our artifact and the corresponding prototype with respect to the identified design goals. Our approach included a qualitative evaluation based on nine expert interviews (Sonnenberg and Brocke 2012; Venable et al. 2016). During these interviews, we presented our prototype architecture. The findings from the development of our system and the evaluation by the experts were finally incorporated into the definition of three design principles. These provide initial recommendations for action for building a decentralized solution for secure data exchange between companies in cooperative supply chain environments.

Design Principle 1: Implement a decentralized solution when the advantages of network effects in a coopetitive market outweigh the challenges of implementing such a complex solution. Pertinent research and our experts emphasize the beneficial effect for supply chains when implementing a blockchain solution. It offers inherent characteristics such as increased product traceability, enhanced trust among stakeholders, and increased data availability, especially in comparison to centralized stand-alone EDI solutions for invoice handling (Alt 2020; Toufaily et al. 2021; Bons et al. 2020). In this context, *expert 3 outlines that "the blockchain offers the advantage of rapid data exchange within its network, which in turn fosters trust among its users*". This may result in an enhancement of interoperability and, lastly, in a significant advantage within the construction scheduling and collaboration opportunities between network participants (DO2). However, implementing blockchain solutions poses a significant challenge, particularly for small and medium-sized enterprises (Sternberg et al. 2020). While the initial operating costs of running a blockchain node are minimal, the establishment of a company's system presents significant challenges. Bootstrapping the system involves various tasks, such as whitelisting IP addresses and integrating data pipelines with existing legacy systems. For instance, small and medium-sized construction companies can participate in the system and collaborate effectively (DO2). However, they face the constraint of managing server capacity and blockchain nodes either in-house or through service providers (expert 8) (Guggenberger et al. 2022; Sedlmeir et al. 2022). Additionally, firms must train their employees to work with new front-end features and maintain an IT department, which collectively leads to higher costs that may not be commensurate with the benefits of a potential blockchain solution. Hence, a careful evaluation is necessary to determine the long-term value of integrating blockchain technology compared to the existing process of handling delivery invoices. According to expert 7, considering the estimated annual processing of 50,000 to 60,000 delivery invoices for small and medium-sized construction companies in Germany, the current processing of delivery invoices incurs costs of approximately €4.50 per invoice resulting in a considerable amount of circa €250.000 of cost savings when may avoiding those proportionally by implementing a blockchain solution (Business Guides-Transport and Logistics: Blockchain Praxis 2021). Therefore, deciding to adopt blockchain technology requires outweighing the exact costs and corresponding cost savings of processing delivery invoices in the form of blockchain transactions in comparison to current and established operational process costs over time. Therefore, companies must carefully consider their primary implementation objectives. This entails determining whether their initial focus is on digitizing the delivery invoice to enhance process efficiency, which can potentially be achieved with less complexity through bilateral data exchange and the implementation of existing standardized solutions like EDI or digital invoice formats. Alternatively, companies may aim to fully leverage network effects to enhance the overall construction planning process (DO2). However, experts highlight the significance of secure data exchange (DO1), particularly regarding specific information such as, e.g., the quantity indicators of construction materials exchanged between stakeholders involved in the supply chain. This remains essential even with simpler data exchange solutions and is not fully addressed by such solutions compared to blockchain-based solutions (expert 1,2).

Design Principle 2: Implement private data collections and private channels to safeguard the inter-organizational data exchange processes from being disclosed to unauthorized third parties. The secure data exchange of the system was defined as a primary goal during development. While blockchain typically shows strengths in the area of availability and integrity, data confidentiality, however, has often been a challenge. When it comes to secure data exchange (DO1), our experts commend the selection of Hyperledger Fabric. In comparison to public blockchain solutions like Ethereum, Hyperledger Fabric provides a wider range of options for implementing access controls and ensuring data confidentiality for each organization involved. For instance, private data collections are one of the features that enable organizations to preserve the privacy of their data within private channels (experts 4, 6). Thus, only parties directly involved in the process can perform actions, such as changing the status of a delivery invoice. In this context, expert 2 agrees that the "*access to data should be managed as granular as possible, particularly when organizations potentially can view data which would be processed on other construction sides and within other supply chains*". Particularly, the opportunity to use private data collections allows the blockchain to be used without all information being shared in plain text with all parties (Guggenberger et al. 2022). In the developed system, delivery invoices are only stored on the process participants' servers. The information remains exclusively with the respective organizations, which is particularly crucial for coopetition between construction companies as they rely on a concealed data exchange due to market rivalries. Thus, high data integrity can be achieved through the distributed storage of the hashes while improving system automation and increasing process performance by avoiding unnecessary data storage (DO3). Expert 4 particularly emphasizes that *decentralized networks make a lot of sense, because at the end of the day, they strengthen the issue of security, but also trust and transparency*" while existing digital invoicing solutions are flawed in providing the necessary features for data integrity, thereby inhibiting widespread adoption. This is also due to the construction industry being subject to strict antitrust regulations, which prohibit the sharing of certain information like procurement prices with competitors, maintaining data privacy is not just desirable but also essential for ensuring legal compliance (experts 3, 4).

Design Principle 3: To ensure complete confidentiality of data, it is necessary to augment private data collections and channels with additional privacy-preserving technologies. During our evaluation, experts caution that although the provision of channels and private data collections for dedicated building materials enhances data security, it is still not a perfect solution to prevent unauthorized disclosure of sensitive information to third parties (experts 1, 3). While private data collections control access to data, they do not entirely prevent participants who are members of the private collection from viewing confidential data related to intermediate steps in the supply chain. This issue is particularly critical in complex supply chains involving multiple competing companies in the construction industry. For example, a participating company should not have visibility into the bilateral supply chain beyond its direct involvement. Therefore, experts suggest the prospective implementation of additional privacy-enhancing technologies (experts 1–3). For example, *Expert 1 emphasizes that "the utilization of blockchain technology using zero-knowledge proofs (ZKPs) becomes particularly intriguing when there is a requirement to document precise quantitative records of construction materials*". Integrating ZKPs enables cryptographic proof of data without revealing the actual data, while multiparty computations can address this issue and enhance data automation without compromising data confidentiality (DO1, DO3) (Sedlmeir et al. 2022). This approach provides a viable solution to avoid the trade-off between data disclosure and data automation within the context of complex supply chains in the construction industry.

6 Conclusion

Our research offers valuable practical insights into the challenges associated with implementing blockchain technology for digital delivery invoice processes in the construction industry. We specifically address the issue of managing data transparency associated with decentralized networks and the corresponding coopetition trade-off between collaboration and competition among participants in construction industry supply chains. Our findings indicate that construction companies should factor in the increased complexity of setting up and operating a corresponding network, such as hosting and maintaining a blockchain node, which may result in higher operational overhead costs. Construction companies must carefully evaluate whether setting up such a network pays off or may opt for potentially less complex solutions, such as the bilateral exchange of signed certificates which are gaining momentum and acceptance in research and practice (Guggenberger et al. 2023). However, if construction companies adopt blockchain-based solutions, the use of channels and private collections offers a promising option for processing fine-grained data, exchanging it securely and considering the trade-offs of coopetition in the supply chain. However, our research is not without limitations, which offers avenues for future research. We set the focus particularly on the coopetition trade-off as a challenge of adapting blockchain technology to process delivery invoices in the construction industry. However, other challenges, such as scalability, can also significantly impact the diffusion of our solution into practice. As such, our design objectives for the prototype are exclusively focused on secure data exchange, while there may be additional other design objectives for the overall implementation of such a solution that future research must consider. Also providing a comprehensive cost analysis is necessary to be able to fully evaluate the extent of the practical benefit. Concluding, this study takes a first step toward digital delivery invoices in the construction industry while exploring the coopetition trade-off as a significant challenge to be overcome in order to progress the adoption of blockchain solutions in practice.

Acknowledgements We gratefully acknowledge the Bavarian Ministry of Economic Affairs, Regional Development and Energy for their support and funding of the DLSB Project *DIK-2110-0006// DIK0395/03/* that made this paper possible. We also thank the editor and the anonymous reviewers for their highly valuable and constructive feedback.

References

Agdas, D., Ellis, R.D.: The potential of XML technology as an answer to the data interchange problems of the construction industry. Construction Management and Economics 28(7), 737–746 (Jul 2010), https://doi.org/10.1080/01446191003767503

Alt, R.: Electronic markets on blockchain markets. Electronic Markets 30(2), 181–188 (Jun 2020), https://doi.org/10.1007/s12525-020-00428-1

Androulaki, E., Barger, A., Bortnikov, V., Cachin, C., Christidis, K., Caro, A.D., Enyeart, D., Ferris, C., Laventman, G., Manevich, Y., Muralidharan, S., Murthy, C., Nguyen, B., Sethi, M., Singh, G., Smith, K., Sorniotti, A., Stathakopoulou, C., Vukolic´, M., Cocco, S.W., Yellick, J.: Hyperledger fabric. In: Proceedings of the Thirteenth EuroSys Conference. ACM (Apr 2018), https://doi.org/10.1145/3190508.3190538

Anumba, C., Ruikar, K.: Electronic commerce in construction—trends and prospects. Automation in Construction 11(3), 265–275 (Apr 2002), https://doi.org/10.1016/s0926-5805(01)00087-5

Azzi, R., Chamoun, R.K., Sokhn, M.: The power of a blockchain-based supply chain. Computers & Industrial Engineering 135, 582–592 (Sep 2019), https://doi.org/10.1016/j.cie.2019.06.042

Bader, L., Pennekamp, J., Matzutt, R., Hedderich, D., Kowalski, M., Lücken, V., Wehrle, K.: Blockchain-based privacy preservation for supply chains supporting lightweight multi-hop information accountability. Information Processing & Management 58(3), 102529 (May 2021), https://doi.org/10.1016/j.ipm.2021.102529

Bajpai, A., Misra, S.C.: Evaluation of success factors to implement digitalization in the construction industry. Construction Innovation (Dec 2022), https://doi.org/10.1108/ci-02-2022-0042

Beck, R., Avital, M., Rossi, M., Thatcher, J.B.: Blockchain technology in business and information systems research. Business & Information Systems Engineering 59(6), 381–384 (Nov 2017), https://doi.org/10.1007/s12599-017-0505-1

Beck, R., Müller-Bloch, C., King, J.L.: Governance in the blockchain economy: A framework and research agenda. Journal of the Association for Information Systems pp. 1020–1034 (2018), https://doi.org/10.17705/1jais.00518

Bons, R.W., Versendaal, J., Zavolokina, L., Shi, W.L.: Potential and limits of blockchain technology for networked businesses. Electronic Markets 30(2), 189–194 (Apr 2020), https://doi.org/10.1007/s12525-020-00421-8

Butijn, B.J., Tamburri, D.A., van den Heuvel, W.J.: Blockchains. ACM Computing Surveys 53(3) (Jul 2020), https://doi.org/10.1145/3369052

Demirkesen, S., Tezel, A.: Investigating major challenges for industry 4.0 adoption among construction companies. Engineering, Construction and Architectural Management (Apr 2021), https://doi.org/10.1108/ecam-12-2020-1059

https://dbv-s3-bucket.s3.eu-central-1.amazonaws.com/digitalisierung_der_lieferkette_im_betonbau_leitfaden_zur_entwicklung_ei ner_digitalen_anwendung_4191a8bf49.pdf

EW Business Guides-Transport & Logistics: Blockchain & Praxis (2021), https://newbusiness.at/magazin/new-business-guides/transport-und-logistik-guide-2021/blockchain-und-praxis

Gibson, G.E., Bell, L.C.: Electronic data interchange in construction. Journal of Construction Engineering and Management 116(4), 727–737 (Dec 1990), https://doi.org/10.1061/(asce)0733-9364(1990)116:4(727)

Gregor, S., Hevner, A.R.: Positioning and presenting design science research for maximum impact. MIS Quarterly 37(2), 337–355 (Feb 2013), https://doi.org/10.25300/misq/2013/37.2.01

Guggenberger, T., Schweizer, A., Urbach, N.: Improving interorganizational information sharing for vendor managed inventory: Toward a decentralized information hub using blockchain technology. IEEE Transactions on Engineering Management 67(4), 1074–1085 (2020)

Guggenberger, T., Sedlmeir, J., Fridgen, G., Luckow, A.: An in-depth investigation of the performance characteristics of hyperledger fabric. Computers & Industrial Engineering 173, 108716 (2022)

Guggenberger, T., Neubauer, L., Stramm, J., Völter, F., Zwede, T.: Accept me as I am or see me go: A qualitative analysis of user acceptance of self-sovereign identity applications. In: Proceedings of the Hawaii International Conference on System Sciences (2023)

Hevner, March, Park, Ram: Design science in information systems research. MIS Quarterly 28(1), 75 (2004), https://doi.org/10.2307/25148625

Hoffmann, W., Lavie, D., Reuer, J.J., Shipilov, A.: The interplay of competition and cooperation. Strategic Management Journal 39(12), 3033–3052 (Nov 2018), https://doi.org/ https://doi.org/10.1002/smj.2965

Kannengießer, N., Lins, S., Dehling, T., Sunyaev, A.: Trade-offs between distributed ledger technology characteristics. ACM Computing Surveys 53(2), 1–37 (May 2020), https://doi.org/10.1145/3379463

Lacity, M.C., Van Hoek, R.: What we've learned so far about blockchain for business (2021), https://sloanreview.mit.edu/article/what-weve-learned-so-far-about-blockchain-for-business/

Li, J., Greenwood, D., Kassem, M.: Blockchain in the built environment and construction industry: A systematic review, conceptual models and practical use cases. Automation in Construction 102, 288–307 (Jun 2019), https://doi.org/10.1016/j.autcon.2019.02.005

Pagel, P.: Bei der Übermittlung und Verarbeitung elektronischer Rechnungen müssen die geltenden Anforderungen an Datenschutz und Datensicherheit erfüllt sein". Wirtschaftsinformatik & Management 11(5), 342–346 (Aug 2019), https://doi.org/10.1365/s35764-019-00201-w

Peffers, K., Tuunanen, T., Rothenberger, M.A., Chatterjee, S.: A design science research methodology for information systems research. Journal of Management Information Systems 24(3), 45–77 (Dec 2007), https://doi.org/10.2753/mis0742-1222240302

Prebanic´, K.R., Vukomanovic´, M.: Realizing the need for digital transformation of stakeholder management: A systematic review in the construction industry. Sustainability 13(22), 12690 (Nov 2021), https://doi.org/10.3390/su132212690

Rossi, M., Mueller-Bloch, C., Thatcher, J.B., Beck, R.: "blockchain research in information systems: Current trends and an inclusive future research agenda". Journal of the Association for Information Systems pp. 1388–1403 (2019), https://doi.org/10.17705/1jais.00571

Samuelson, O., Björk, B.C.: Adoption processes for edm, edi and bim technologies in the construction industry. Journal of Civil Engineering and Management 19(Supplement_1), S172–S187 (Jan 2014), https://doi.org/10.3846/13923730.2013.801888

Sedlmeir, J., Lautenschlager, J., Fridgen, G., Urbach, N.: The transparency challenge of blockchain in organizations. Electronic Markets 32(3), 1779–1794 (Mar 2022), https://doi.org/10.1007/s12525-022-00536-0

Sedlmeir, J., Wagner, T., Djerekarov, E., Green, R., Klepsch, J., Rao, S.: A serverless distributed ledger for enterprises. In: Proceedings of the Annual Hawaii International Conference on System Sciences. Hawaii International Conference on System Sciences (2022). https://doi.org/10.24251/hicss.2022.886

Sonnenberg, C., Brocke, J.V.: Evaluation patterns for design science research artefacts. In: Communications in Computer and Information Science, pp. 71–83. Springer Berlin Heidelberg (2012). https://doi.org/10.1007/978-3-642-33681-2_7

Sternberg, H.S., Hofmann, E., Roeck, D.: The struggle is real: Insights from a supply chain blockchain case. Journal of Business Logistics 42(1), 71–87 (Mar 2020), https://doi.org/10.1111/jbl.12240

Toufaily, E., Zalan, T., Dhaou, S.B.: A framework of blockchain technology adoption: An investigation of challenges and expected value. Information & Management 58(3), 103444 (Apr 2021), https://doi.org/10.1016/j.im.2021.103444

Venable, J., Pries-Heje, J., Baskerville, R.: FEDS: a framework for evaluation in design science research. European Journal of Information Systems 25(1), 77–89 (Jan 2016), https://doi.org/10.1057/ejis.2014.36

Wiehager, S.: Datenqualität und Datenmanagement in der Bauwirtschaft. In: Agile Digitalisierung im Baubetrieb, pp. 79–106. Springer Fachmedien Wiesbaden (2021), https://doi.org/10.1007/978-3-658-34107-7

Wilhelm, M.M.: Managing coopetition through horizontal supply chain relations: Linking dyadic and network levels of analysis. Journal of Operations Management 29(7–8), 663–676 (Apr 2011), https://doi.org/10.1016/j.jom.2011.03.003

Wüst, K., Gervais, A.: Do you need a blockchain? In: IEEE Crypto Valley Conference on Blockchain Technology. IEEE (Jun 2018), https://doi.org/10.1109/cvcbt.2018.00011

Prescriptive Analytics, Mobility and Logistics

Punctuality Predictions in Public Transportation: Quantifying the Effect of External Factors

Tim Meyer-Hollatz, Nina Schwarz, and Tim Werner

Abstract Increasing availability of large-scale datasets for automatic vehicle location (AVL) in public transportation (PT) encouraged researchers to investigate data-driven punctuality prediction models (PPMs). PPMs promise to accelerate the mobility transition through more accurate prediction delays, increased customer service levels, and more efficient and forward-looking planning by mobility providers. While several PPMs show promising results for buses and long-distance trains, a comprehensive study on external factors' effect on tram services is missing. Therefore, we implement four machine learning (ML) models to predict departure delays and elaborate on the performance increase by adding real-world weather and holiday data for three consecutive years. For our best model (XGBoost) the average MAE performance increased by 17.33% compared to the average model performance when only trained on AVL data enriched by timetable characteristics. The results provide strong evidence that adding information-bearing features improve the forecast quality of PPMs.

Keywords Punctuality prediction · Public transportation · Machine learning · Automatic vehicle location

T. Meyer-Hollatz · N. Schwarz · T. Werner (✉)
Fraunhofer Institute for Applied Information Technology FIT, Branch Business and Information Systems Engineering, Augsburg, Germany
e-mail: tim.werner@fit.fraunhofer.de; tim.werner@hs-augsburg.de

T. Meyer-Hollatz
e-mail: tim.meyer-hollatz@fit.fraunhofer.de

N. Schwarz
e-mail: nina.schwarz@fit.fraunhofer.de; nina.schwarz@hs-augsburg.de

N. Schwarz · T. Werner
University of Applied Science Augsburg, Augsburg, Germany

D. Beverungen et al. (eds.), *Solutions and Technologies for Responsible Digitalization*, Lecture Notes in Information Systems and Organisation 75,
https://doi.org/10.1007/978-3-031-80122-8_25

1 Introduction

While research on human movement in time and space has already been around for several decades (Weiner 1997), disruptive technologies and new mobility concepts in smart cities usher the need to leverage large amounts of data for providing cleaner, safer, and more efficient urban transportation (Mehmood et al. 2017). Especially local public transportation can be a factor in reducing emissions, preventing accidents, and democratizing mobility (Torre-Bastida et al. 2018; Yang et al. 2015). Previous research highlights the impact of punctuality and arrival predictions as a significant factor for potential passengers to switch to public transportation (Olsson and Haugland 2004; Ibrahim and Borhan 2020), thereby leveraging artificial intelligence (AI) to solve societal challenges and provide more sustainable mobility. To this end, data-driven punctuality prediction models (PPMs) can significantly improve prediction performance (Shi et al. 2021) and amplify the reliability of public transportation when forecasting potential delays. Furthermore, data-driven PPMs allow local transportation companies to refine driving schedules, predict high volumes of passengers, and plan supporting trips.

Data-driven PPMs use historic train movements (HTM) consisting of AVL and timetable data as well as external factors to predict future transportation punctuality by abstracting rules and dependencies from previous disturbances such as labor strikes or severe snowfall and their effect on the mobility services (Ge et al. 2022; Zakeri and Olsson 2018). Although previous research has exemplarily shown that extreme weather conditions adversely affect punctuality in PT (Oneto et al. 2016; Tao et al. 2018) it has not yet investigated the potential increase in prediction performance by combining features from versatile data sources (Wang and Work 2015; Pongnumkul et al. 2014) and quantify the resulting impact. Therefore, it remains to be seen to what extent additional factors improve the PPMs overall performance over a long time period when compared to models solemnly built on HTM. Against this backdrop, we formulate the following research question (RQ):

> *How does enriching historical datasets with external factors influence the performance quality of punctuality predictions in public tram transportation?*

We address the RQ by implementing and training four state-of-the-art ML models on different combinations of features aggregated from HTM, weather, and holiday data to predict the expected departure delay with a time horizon of a few days in advance ahead as the limit for small-scale weather projections is between hours and days (Bauer et al. 2015; Jung et al. 2010). We compare their performance in an empirical case study to evaluate the effect of enriching HTM data with additional features. The historical punctuality dataset contains real-world AVL data of a medium-sized German city over three consecutive years resulting in 1.4 million Trips at 222 stations.

We contribute to existing research by quantifying the increase in prediction accuracy when adding exogenous features to a large HTM dataset. Compared to existing research, we increase the amount of exogenous data sources and refine their granularity with respect to time (hourly) and events (public holidays, vacations) for weather and holiday data, respectively. Then we utilize four different state-of-the-art ML models proposed by the literature as PPMs to test our RQ. We could not only confirm extant research on the impact of weather and holidays but could further extend the findings to a higher granularity and for a complete tram network over multiple years. Understanding the interplay between different data streams for additional prediction performance potential is essential for policymakers, mobility companies, and passengers alike to increase the service level in PT (Olsson and Haugland 2004; Ibrahim and Borhan 2020).

2 Problem Context and Theoretical Background

Research on punctuality prediction in PT has grown significantly over the last few years (Ghofrani et al. 2018; Spanninger et al. 2020) and has been addressed in various studies (Bešinović 2020; Ge et al. 2021). This development is strengthened by extended computing power and increased availability of larger datasets (Ghofrani et al. 2018). Following Ge et al. (2021), they can be comprised of endogenous data such as AVL, automatic fare collection (AFC), automatic passenger counting (APC), or rail network parameters (RNP) and exogenous data sources like weather, traffic, surveys, or social media. As a result, ML models have been developed to complement statistical approaches quantifying influencing factors on rail-based mobility (Hagenauer and Helbich 2017; Zúñiga et al. 2021).

The different approaches to predicting punctuality in public transportation can be classified by multiple aspects. One recent approach by Spanninger et al. (2020) distinguished research papers by categorizing them based on four characteristics. (I) First, which mathematical models are used for the analysis, e.g., time series analysis, artificial neural network. (II) Second, which input datasets are used to predict the delay. (III) Third, which type of output is considered, e.g., deterministic, single value prediction vs. stochastic, probability predictions. (IV) Fourth, based on the distinction between dynamic, based on real values at previous stations, and static forecasts, several hours or days in advance. As discussed in the introduction, this paper focuses on approaches that predict tram departure delays with a time horizon of a few days before the travel itinerary. Building on preliminary works by Ghofrani et al. (2018) and Spanninger et al. (2020), we focus on the theoretical background in characteristics (I) and (II) as they represent the focus of this research.

Spanninger et al. (2021) differentiate punctuality prediction models (PPM) as data-driven (based on historical punctuality records) or event-driven approaches (modeling the dependencies of sequential events). Due to the higher availability of data in the public transportation sector, data-driven approaches are increasingly the focus of ongoing research (Mesbah et al. 2015; Barabino et al. 2017; Shoman et al. 2020). Spanninger et al. (2021) further partition previous studies by their use of data sources, namely Historic Train Movements (HTM), Actual Delays (AD), Infrastructure Indicators (II), Timetable Properties (TP), and External Factors (EF) thereby differentiating between endogenous and exogenous factors as proposed by (Ge et al. 2021). Therefore, the key differences between data-driven PPMs in current research stem from different model selections or different datasets (Spanninger et al. 2020). Table 1 summarizes the most relevant publications with respect to this study, focusing on application area, data scope, selected features, implemented PPMs, and their evaluation metrics.

HTM datasets consisting of AVL and time table data are the basis for a wide range of data-driven approaches in the research field of punctuality predictions in public transportation (Wang and Work 2015; Shi et al. 2021; Spanninger et al. 2021; Ge et al. 2021). We can further differentiate these papers by comparing the different modes. Multiple research projects base their mobility predictions on HTM datasets for busses within urban regions (Pałys et al. 2022a, b; Mandelzys and Hellinga 2010) or trains covering larger distances (Yaghini et al. 2013; Pongnumkul et al. 2014; Shi et al. 2021; Marković et al. 2015). However, less attention is paid to PPMs for highly intertwined rail-based transportation (i.e. trams) within urban environments that show higher station frequencies and shorter distances (Rößler et al. 2021; Mesbah et al. 2015). Zychowski et al. (2018) predicted the travel time between two stations using a neural network.

The network was trained to conduct dynamic predictions using HTM features and information about the previous stop (Zychowski et al. 2018). In comparison, Mesbah et al. (2015) use weather and HTM features to predict travel time reliability.

Table 1 Overview of data-driven punctuality prediction models in current literature

Literature	Vehicle	Scope	Features	Models	Metric
Wang and Work (2015)	Train	2 years, 100k trips	HTM, AD	Regression	RMSE
Mesbah et al. (2015)	Tram	5 years –	HTM, AD, EF	Regression	R^2
Laifa et al. (2021)	Train	1 year 12k trips	HTM, AD, EF	LigthGBM	RME, RMSE, R^2
Shi et al. (2021)	Train	6 months 30k trips	HTM, AD	XGB, Bayesian	RMSE
Arshad and Ahmed (2021)	Train	2 months 1k trips	HTM, AD, EF	RF	MAE, RMSE, R^2, Accuracy
Zychowski et al. (2018)	Tram	– 20k trips	HTM	ANN	Accuracy
Zhong et al. (2022)	Bus	7 days 10k trips	HTM, AD	RF, KNN, ANN	MAE, MAPE
Nimpanomprasert et al. (2022)	Bus	1 year –	HTM, AD	ANN, LSTM	RMSE
Pałys et al. (2022a, b)	Bus	30 days –	HTM, AD	KNN, Regression	MAE, STD
This study	Tram	3 years 1,4m trips	HTM, AD, EF	LightGBM XGBoost, RF, KNN	MAE, RMSE

They leveraged an ordinary least square regression and limited the used HTM data to the morning peak timeframe (7 am - 9 am). The weather features were designed by calculating the average for the morning period as a stationary value (Mesbah et al. 2015). Many other studies extended their HTM data with weather events to test its effect on punctuality within PT on a time scale from several days to weeks (Ge et al. 2021). While the focus on weather impacts remains identical across all papers, the types of results vary. Among others, Zakeri and Olsson (2018) focus on the effects of serve weather conditions on the punctuality of trains in Norway. Oneto et al. (2016) followed a similar approach by dynamically predicting the delay of trains in Italy. Compared to Zakeri and Olsson (2018), Oneto et al. (2016) focused on the influence of regular weather conditions and compare multiple models. Besides weather, (Laifa et al. 2021; Mesbah et al. 2015) use holidays as an additional factor. However, evaluating the impact of holiday variables on the overall prediction quality is rare.

While the effects of external factors such as weather and holidays on public transportation have already been the focus of several studies (Oneto et al. 2016; Zakeri and Olsson 2018; Wei et al. 2018; Liu et al. 2017) it remains unclear to what extent these findings are applicable for tram-based mobility. Mesbah et al. (2015) and Zychowski et al. (2018) provide the first evidence but focus on either small sample data sets or limited time frames. Thus, an analysis of a complete tram network for multiple timeframes and years has—to the best of our knowledge—not been investigated before. Furthermore, we increase the granularity as compared to daily or weekly weather aggregations for weather features (Zakeri and Olsson 2018; Chen et al. 2004). In addition, this study contributes to the literature by answering the call for further research regarding the effect of holidays (Laifa et al. 2021). Lastly, the aforementioned results are verified by implementing four different PPMs, whichave seen promising results in previous works (Shi et al. 2021; Nimpanomprasert et al. 2022).

3 Methodology

This work builds on the Cross-Industry Standard Process for Data Mining (CRISP-DM), commonly applied in empirical studies, to quantify the effect of external factors on punctuality prediction in public transportation. The proposed method increases understanding and cross-project comparability by avoiding mistakes through a standardized and structured research approach (Wirth and Hipp 2000). We slightly modified the proposed method by omitting the deployment step, as it is not within the scope of this study, and extending the evaluation step with a comprehensive comparison. The modified CRISP-DM process consists of five different steps, namely "Business Understanding", "Data Understanding", "Data Preparation", "Modelling" and "Evaluation & Comparison" (Wirth and Hipp 2000) (Fig. 1).

"Business Understanding": First, CRISP-DM starts by covering business understanding to identify specific challenges and strategic barriers. For our study, business

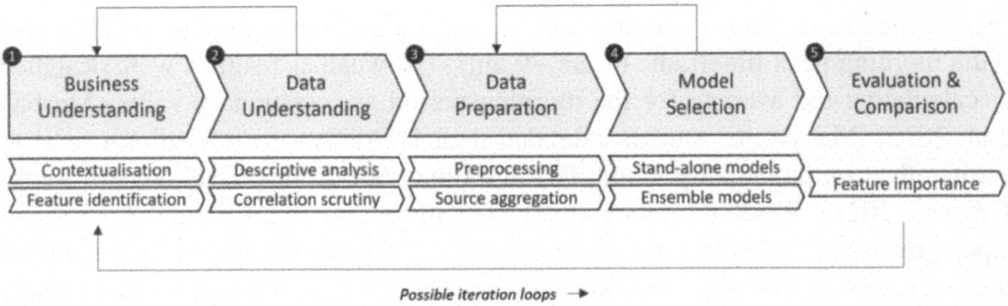

Fig. 1 Derived five-step process for the quantification of external punctuality factors

understanding was primarily used to identify that weather and holiday events as features to be considered in improving the prediction of punctuality in public transportation (Laifa et al. 2021; Zakeri and Olsson 2018; Oneto et al. 2016) and to better understand the impact of delays in public transportation services for mobility providers and their passengers (Ge et al. 2021). Furthermore, this step includes general knowledge of the punctuality predictions in public transportation which has been displayed in Sect. 2.

"Data Understanding": Second, CRISP-DM ensures a profound understanding of the collected data, tightly linking it to the subsequent data preparation. We collected our combined dataset from three different sources. Subsequently, we implemented correlation scrutiny and descriptive analysis. Section 4 introduces both the dataset and the preprocessing steps.

"Data Preparation": Third, CRISP-DM provides a framework to fulfill the quality requirements of the underlying data. We cleansed the data from outliers and invalid, false data points during this process.

"Model Selection": Fourth, CRISP-DM provides a standardized guideline for the modeling and selection process detailed in Sect. 5. This study utilizes four PPMs to quantify the effect of external features on punctuality performance in public transportation.

"Evaluation & Comparison": Fifth, CRISP-DM assists in evaluating and comparing derived results. In this study, we assess two different error measures to substantiate our findings and underline the robustness of our results since single error measurements may not provide a holistic picture (Botchkarev 2019). For better comparison to the literature, we use the mean absolute error (MAE) as the primary evaluation metric when presenting the results and derived our own metric to ensure comparability with the existing research in Sect. 6. Afterward, Sect. 7 critically reviews specific results and derives implications, limitations, and prospects for further research.

4 Data Understanding and Preparation

As formulated in our research question, we aim to quantify the impact of additional features on the punctuality prediction of intra-urban public transportation. Therefore, we integrated data from different sources to cover the various aspects that influence the punctuality of tramways. In a second consecutive step, we processed the aggregated datasets. Finally, we derived the features for the machine learning algorithms.

Data Aggregation

In Sect. 2, we discussed which features were used in the existing literature to predict the delay of public transportation. Based on this research, we identified three available datasets for our region of interest. The primary dataset provided by Stadtwerke Augsburg GmbH includes parts of AVL data of the tramline network of Augsburg from May 2019 until August 2022. It comprises over 25 million records for five tram lines, each detailing a tram stop, including the arrival and departure times. The weather dataset provided by Meteostat contains weather information for each station and hour within the historic train movements. Finally, the holiday dataset, provided by the German Ministerial Culture Conference, includes information about holidays, public holidays and long weekends during the same timeframe. The latter two are publicly accessible.

Preprocessing of Data

During the preprocessing steps, we excluded tram runs that had either transmission errors (e.g., wrong line number, no actual departure time) or corrupt data points (e.g., significant outliers). This procedure had several implications for our results. Foremost, our prediction focuses on tram delays and excludes tram breakdowns since they are indistinguishable from corrupted data points. Furthermore, our preprocessing methods reduced the number of records from 25 to 14 million.

Figure 2 shows an excerpt from the final dataset. The plot on the left-hand side illustrates the distribution of the departure delay across the considered data points. Most data records exhibit low and positive departure delays, indicating that trams tend to leave stations belated rather than too early, which aligns with the policy of tram providers. The remaining plots highlight increased departure delays during usual working times compared to evening hours and the effect of different geolocations of tram stations concerning departure delay.

Data Transformation and Feature Selection

After the preprocessing steps, our final dataset contains 14 million punctuality records. Based on the literature review conducted in Sect. 2 and multiple explorative data analysis, we focused on 16 features divided into three feature sets. The first set contains features describing the historic tram movements and time data. The remaining two sets of features describe external influences on the tram movements,

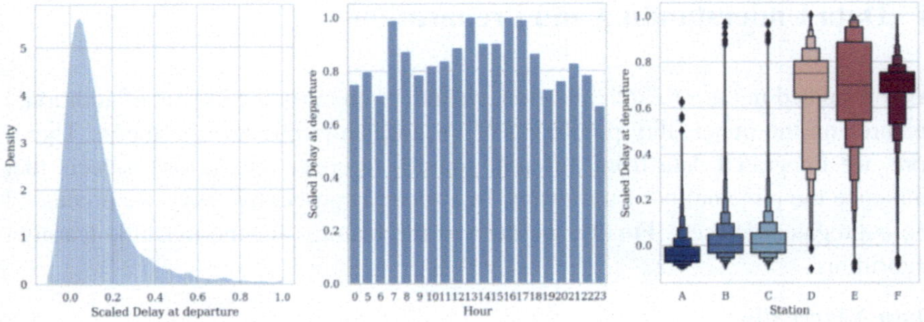

Fig. 2 Summary plots for the historic train movements

namely weather and holidays. Table 2 displays the variables and their respective specifications. As introduced in Sect. 1, this study forecasts the delay from multiple hours to days afront. The delay can be expressed in various formats reaching from different categories such as arrival delay (AD), dwell delay (DWD), driving time delay (DTD), and departure delay (DED) to different calculation methods, i.e., cumulative versus relative.

This study focuses on the DED, which is calculated as follows:

$$DED_i = AD_i + DWD_i, i \in \{1, \ldots, N\}, \tag{1}$$

where the arrival delay at station i is determined by

$$AD_i = AD_{i-1} + DWD_{i-1} + DTD_{i-1,i} \tag{2}$$

and $N \in \mathbb{N}$ is the number of stations within the transportation network. Altogether the DED combines potential arrival delays at station *i-1* (previous station), driving time delays between station i and *i-1*, and unscheduled waiting times at stations *i-1* and i and takes positive values in case of a departure delay and negative values in case of an early departure.

5 Model Selection, Fitting and Evaluation

After the data preprocessing, we conducted an intensive literature review to identify various ML models suited for DED prediction with reasonable optimization runtime and scalability for our datasets. We evaluated the selected models based on performance, accuracy, interpretability, and runtime.

Model selection

The ensemble models XGBoost, LightGBM, and the stand-alone KNN model improved the punctuality predictions or outperformed other comparable models'

Table 2 Description of all features used in this study

Variables	Values
Historic Tram Movements (HTM)	
Daily number of departures at a station	Numeric
Line number	Categorical
Direction	Binary
Weekday	Categorical
Hour	Categorical
One week rolling mean departure delay by stop	Numeric (s)
One year rolling mean departure delay by stop	Numeric (s)
One week rolling mean departure delay by line number	Numeric (s)
One year rolling mean departure delay by line number	Numeric (s)
Weather (W)	
Temperature	Categorical
Snow height	Numeric (mm)
Windspeed	Categorical
Precipitation	Categorical
Holiday (H)	
School holidays	Binary
Public holidays	Binary
Long weekend (bank holiday + extra day)	Binary

* The categories for the weather features are based onBaumgarte et al. (2022)

accuracy or runtime (Shi et al. 2021; Laifa et al. 2021; Pongnumkul et al. 2014). These studies were all based on HTM data. In addition, we chose a Random Forest Regressor (RF) as a fourth model since its implementation by Arshad and Ahmed (2021) has already achieved good prediction results for the combination of HTM and weather data considering different error measures.

Model fitting

Recent studies underline that tuned hyperparameters outperform the default settings of machine learning libraries. Therefore, searching for the best hyperparameter configuration has become increasingly important (Truong et al. 2019). However, tuning a model to find the best combination is costly. Besides higher costs, manual hyperparameter tuning leads to reduced reproducibility. Since this problem is widely acknowledged, several publications and libraries provide possible solutions (Hutter et al. 2019). Automated Machine Learning (AutoML) summarizes these solutions aiming to improve the availability of ML functionalities, reduce training costs, and improve reproducibility while maintaining high accuracy (Truong et al. 2019). Therefore, we leverage a recent AutoML library called FLAML. Researchers at Microsoft developed FLAML to balance the tradeoff between trial costs (i.e., CPU costs for training) and trial error (i.e., accuracy of the model) (Wang et al. 2021b). The framework uses Blendsearch for hyperparameter tuning, combining global and local search (Wang et al. 2021a). Overall, the first benchmarking results of FLAML suggest that it outperforms existing AutoML frameworks for shorter (1 h) and longer runs (4 h) (Wang et al. 2021b; Gijsbers et al. 2019).

We fitted every model separately using the provided learners and their corresponding hyperparameter spaces of the FLAML library to answer our RQ, leading to the best possible configurations within the selected time budget. We trained each model to minimize the mean absolute error using a holdout validation set containing 25% of the data, a fivefold cross-validation on the test set containing the remaining 75% of the entire dataset and no additional preprocessing. Considering the call for more comprehensible AI research, we provide an in-depth description of the hyperparameter tuning according to the specifications of Kühl et al., along with corresponding results upon request (Kühl et al. 2021).

Model evaluation

A common problem in punctuality prediction is that historic punctuality data underlies strict regulations in terms of publishing. The dependencies of the ML evaluation functions (e.g., MAE and RMSE) on the volatility of the test data set make them directly connected. This results in the fact that the MAEs per research project are not directly comparable, limiting the comparability between different studies. Based on prior works by Wang and Work (2015), we introduce an error metric that compares the mean of the differences between the planned departure times according to the timetable and the historic departure times ($DED_{timetable}$) and the mean of the predicted departure delay of the model ($DED_{predicted}$). The ratio between these two mean absolute errors, as defined in Eq. 3, acts as a quality metric for the result that is independent of the granularity of the baseline values. By reporting the quality metric and the model characteristics, such as mean absolute error (MAE), and root mean squared error (RMSE), we guarantee the comparability of our results.

$$QM = 1 - \frac{MAE(DED_{predicted})}{MAE(DED_{timetable})} = 1 - \frac{MAE_{model}}{MAE_{baseline}} \tag{3}$$

6 Results

This section presents the prediction performance results of our large-scale data-driven PPMs, focusing on the differences between historical and enriched feature sets. We evaluate our models using a fivefold cross-validation on the training dataset and summarize the resulting error metrics. To this end, our PPMs are presented on the x-axis. In contrast, the y-axis shows the previously introduced quality metric (3) (left-hand side) and the improvements compared to the baseline RMSE, which is calculated by using the RMSE instead of the MAE in Eq. 3 (right-hand side).

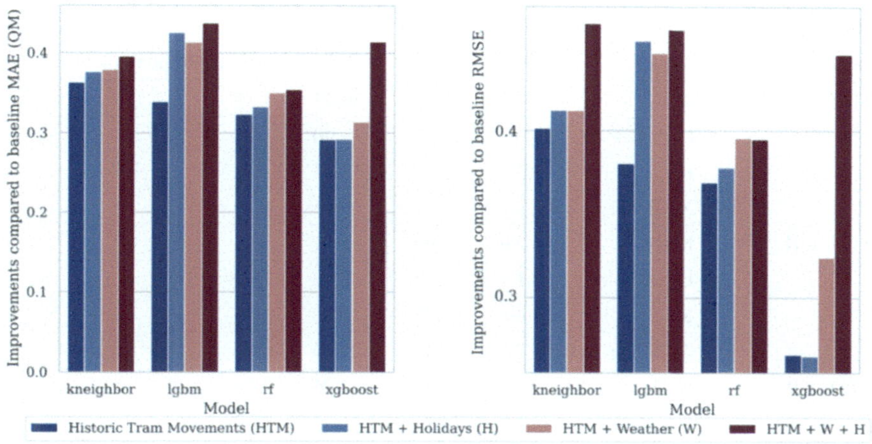

Fig. 3 Performance evaluation for PPMs benchmarked against the deviations in the train schedule

Figure 3 illustrates our results. The y-axis of the RMSE figure is scaled to ensure better readability of the results.

Considering both evaluation metrics, all models tend to improve performance when trained on enriched datasets. XGBoost exhibits the most significant relative improvements of 17.33% comparing historical data and the complete feature set. While the relative percentage might vary between the models, the overall tendency prevails—the larger the set of uncorrelated features, the better the quality metric. Overall, the RF model and the KNN improved gradually over each feature extension. Table 3 additionally provides an overview of the two-error metrics and our quality metric for each of the four data-driven PPMs grouped by the underlying dataset, HTM, HTM + W, HTM + H, and HTM + W + H, to increase understandability and comparability. We notice that all PPMs trained on the enriched dataset outperform the models trained exclusively on HTM data.

Moreover, they exhibit greater robustness and generalization abilities than their counterparts trained on singular aggregated data.

We benchmarked each feature against the results of the HTM data to link the improved model performance to the selected features. We achieved this by implementing four ML models for each feature set and comparing the tuple (model and feature set) to the HTM result of the same model while ruling out secondary effects since they are inherent in both training sets. Table 4 shows the average improvement for selected categorical features.

Table 3 Error metrics and standard deviation for all PPMs

Data-set	Model	MAE	RMSE	QM	Relative improvement (%)
HTM	KNN	57.75	81.70	36.33	–
	LightGBM	59.95	84.91	33.90	–
	RF	61.38	86.55	32.33	–
	XGBoost	64.26	99.37	29.15	–
HTM + H	KNN	56.54	79.94	37.66	2.11
	LightGBM	52.13	72.78	42.52	13.04
	RF	60.49	85.25	33.30	1.45
	XGBoost	64.22	99.47	29.19	0.06
HTM + W	KNN	56.27	79.94	37.96	2.56
	LightGBM	53.19	74.11	41.36	11.28
	RF	58.89	82.57	35.07	4.06
	XGBoost	62.21	92.61	31.41	3.20
HTM + W + H	KNN	54.79	70.91	39.59	5.13
	LightGBM	51.08	71.54	43.68	14.81
	RF	58.55	82.70	35.44	4.61
	XGBoost	53.12	74.18	41.43	17.33

Table 4 XGBoost MAE comparison for selected exogenous features

Exogenous event	XGBoost (HTM)	XGBoost (HTM + W/HTM + H)
Temperature below – 10 °C	58.61	55.68 (– 5.0%)
Precipitation over 50 $\frac{mm}{cm^2}$	59.18	56.39 (– 4.7%)
Fresh snow (30–60 cm)	56.50	53.89 (– 4.6%)
Evening hours of public holidays	58.53	58.37 (– 0.3%)

7 Discussion and Implications

This study quantifies the effect of exogenous factors on tram punctuality predictions building on the work of Mesbah et al. (2015). We implement four different ML models derived from relevant literature and analyze prediction performance by adding seven exogenous features to the HTM baseline dataset. We train all models on permutations of the large-scale exogenous datasets to study performance for each category as well as individual features to rule out secondary effects. The best overall model, LightGBM, yields an MAE of 51.08 s or 43.76% QM when trained on HTM enriched with four weather and three holiday features.

Our results have various managerial and academic implications. First, we provided academia with a method to quantify punctuality prediction results based on a quality metric that allows researchers to compare their findings across different datasets. Second, we show that AutoML methods can be used in the field of punctuality prediction to train profound PPMs with reasonable computational time. Third, we verify previous findings for urban tram networks and quantify the effect of enriching HTM data with exogenous factors while ruling out secondary effects. Fourth, we confirm our results on an entire transportation network containing multiple stations and lines compared to previous research, mainly focusing on single lines or single stations. Fifth, we study the effects of more exogenous data (holidays and weather) for a longer time period with finer granularity compared to relevant literature.

Although, to our knowledge, this is the first study to investigate an entire tram network, our findings are limited to one transportation network within one city. Furthermore, the number of weather stations could be increased to more precisely depict hyperlocal weather development. While we see a performance increase when adding more exogenous factors, further research should investigate its impact on computational power as well as financial and ecological costs. Finally, we encourage the research community to study both the influence of endogenous and exogenous factors based on explainable ML models and broaden the scope by adding more transportation networks to foster well-informed managerial decision-making within the PT sector.

8 Conclusion

In this study, we address the RQ of whether and to what extent exogenous factors influence the performance of PPMs in PT after adequate training and tuning efforts. We derive four state-of-the-art ML models from relevant literature presented in Sect. 2 and implement them on a large-scale mobility dataset with over 14 million real-world punctuality records of a medium-sized German city. Our results suggest a fundamental link between PPM performance improvement and enriched HTM data for tram mobility. By answering our research question, we contribute to investigating the correlation between external features and data-driven punctuality prediction models in public rail-based transport. We confirm extant research that weather and holiday features positively influence the overall model performance. We further extended the existing discourse by proving fine granular weather and holiday features influence the prediction quality and, therefore, the delay of trams within a whole tram network.

References

Arshad, Mohd/Ahmed, Muqeem (2021). Train Delay Estimation in Indian Railways by Including Weather Factors Through Machine Learning Techniques. Recent Advances in Computer Science and Communications 14 (4), 1300–1307. https://doi.org/10.2174/2666255813666190912095739.

Barabino, Benedetto/Di Francesco, Massimo/Mozzoni, Sara (2017). An Offline Framework for the Diagnosis of Time Reliability by Automatic Vehicle Location Data. IEEE Transactions

on Intelligent Transportation Systems 18 (3), 583–594. https://doi.org/10.1109/TITS.2016.258 1024.
Bauer, Peter/Thorpe, Alan/Brunet, Gilbert (2015). The quiet revolution of numerical weather prediction. Nature 525 (7567), 47–55. https://doi.org/10.1038/nature14956.
Baumgarte, Felix/Keller, Robert/Röhrich, Felix/Valett, Lynne/Zinsbacher, Daniela (2022). Revealing influences on carsharing users' trip distance in small urban areas. Transportation Research Part D: Transport and Environment 105, 103252. https://doi.org/10.1016/j.trd.2022.103252.
Bešinović, Nikola (2020). Resilience in railway transport systems: a literature review and research agenda. Transport Reviews 40 (4), 457–478. https://doi.org/10.1080/01441647.2020.1728419.
Botchkarev, Alexei (2019). A New Typology Design of Performance Metrics to Measure Errors in Machine Learning Regression Algorithms. Interdisciplinary Journal of Information, Knowledge, and Management 14, 45–76. https://doi.org/10.28945/4184.
Chen, Mei/Liu, Xiaobo/Xia, Jingxin/Chien, Steven I. (2004). A Dynamic Bus-Arrival Time Prediction Model Based on APC Data. Computer-Aided Civil and Infrastructure Engineering 19 (5), 364–376. https://doi.org/10.1111/j.1467-8667.2004.00363.x.
Ge, Liping/Sarhani, Malek/Voß, Stefan/Xie, Lin (2021). Review of Transit Data Sources: Potentials, Challenges and Complementarity. Sustainability 13 (20), 11450. https://doi.org/10.3390/su132011450.
Ge, Liping/Voß, Stefan/Xie, Lin (2022). Robustness and disturbances in public transport. Public Transport 14 (1), 191–261. https://doi.org/10.1007/s12469-022-00301-8.
Ghofrani, Faeze/He, Qing/Goverde, Rob M.P./Liu, Xiang (2018). Recent applications of big data analytics in railway transportation systems: A survey. Transportation Research Part C: Emerging Technologies 90, 226–246. https://doi.org/10.1016/j.trc.2018.03.010.
Gijsbers, Pieter/LeDell, Erin/Thomas, Janek/Poirier, Sébastien/Bischl, Bernd/Vanschoren, Joaquin (2019). An Open Source AutoML Benchmark. AutoML Workshop at ICML 2019.
Hagenauer, Julian/Helbich, Marco (2017). A comparative study of machine learning classifiers for modeling travel mode choice. Expert Systems with Applications 78, 273–282. https://doi.org/10.1016/j.eswa.2017.01.057.
Hutter, Frank/Kotthoff, Lars/Vanschoren, Joaquin (2019). Automated Machine Learning. Cham, Springer International Publishing.
Ibrahim, Ahmad Nazrul Hakimi/Borhan, Muhamad Nazri (2020). The Interrelationship Between Perceived Quality, Perceived Value and User Satisfaction Towards Behavioral Intention in Public Transportation: A Review of the Evidence. International Journal on Advanced Science, Engineering and Information Technology 10 (5), 2048. https://doi.org/10.18517/ijaseit.10.5.12818.
Jung, T./Miller, M. J./Palmer, T. N. (2010). Diagnosing the Origin of Extended-Range Forecast Errors. Monthly Weather Review 138 (6), 2434–2446. https://doi.org/10.1175/2010MWR3255.1.
Kühl, Niklas/Hirt, Robin/Baier, Lucas/Schmitz, Björn/Satzger, Gerhard (2021). How to Conduct Rigorous Supervised Machine Learning in Information Systems Research: The Supervised Machine Learning Report Card. Communications of the Association for Information Systems 48 (1), 589–615. https://doi.org/10.17705/1CAIS.04845.
Laifa, Hassiba/khcherif, Raoudha/Ben Ghezalaa, Henda Hajjami (2021). Train delay prediction in Tunisian railway through LightGBM model. Procedia Computer Science 192, 981–990. https://doi.org/10.1016/j.procs.2021.08.101.
Liu, Chengxi/Susilo, Yusak O./Karlström, Anders (2017). Weather variability and travel behaviour – what we know and what we do not know. Transport Reviews 37 (6), 715–741. https://doi.org/10.1080/01441647.2017.1293188.
Mandelzys, Michael/Hellinga, Bruce (2010). Identifying Causes of Performance Issues in Bus Schedule Adherence with Automatic Vehicle Location and Passenger Count Data. Transportation Research Record Journal of the Transportation Research Board 2143 (1), 9–15. https://doi.org/10.3141/2143-02.

Marković, Nikola/Milinković, Sanjin/Tikhonov, Konstantin S./Schonfeld, Paul (2015). Analyzing passenger train arrival delays with support vector regression. Transportation Research Part C: Emerging Technologies 56, 251–262. https://doi.org/10.1016/j.trc.2015.04.004.

Mehmood, Rashid/Meriton, Royston/Graham, Gary/Hennelly, Patrick/Kumar, Mukesh (2017). Exploring the influence of big data on city transport operations: a Markovian approach. International Journal of Operations & Production Management 37 (1), 75–104. https://doi.org/10.1108/IJOPM-03-2015-0179.

Mesbah, Mahmoud/Lin, Johnny/Currie, Graham (2015). “Weather” transit is reliable? Using AVL data to explore tram performance in Melbourne, Australia. Journal of Traffic and Transportation Engineering (English Edition) 2 (3), 125–135. https://doi.org/10.1016/j.jtte.2015.03.001.

Nimpanomprasert, Thummaporn/Xie, Lin/Kliewer, Natalia (2022). Comparing two hybrid neural network models to predict real-world bus travel time. Transportation Research Procedia 62, 393–400. https://doi.org/10.1016/j.trpro.2022.02.049.

Olsson, Nils O.E./Haugland, Hans (2004). Influencing factors on train punctuality—results from some Norwegian studies. Transport Policy 11 (4), 387–397. https://doi.org/10.1016/j.tranpol.2004.07.001.

Oneto, Luca/Fumeo, Emanuele/Clerico, Giorgio/Canepa, Renzo/Papa, Federico/Dambra, Carlo/Mazzino, Nadia/Anguita, Davide (2016). Advanced Analytics for Train Delay Prediction Systems by Including Exogenous Weather Data. In: 2016 IEEE International Conference on Data Science and Advanced Analytics (DSAA), 2016 IEEE International Conference on Data Science and Advanced Analytics (DSAA), Montreal, QC, Canada, 17.10.2016 - 19.10.2016. IEEE, 458–467.

Pałys, Łukasz/Ganzha, Maria/Paprzycki, Marcin (2022). Applying machine learning to predict behavior of bus transport in Warsaw, Poland.

Pałys, Łukasz/Ganzha, Maria/Paprzycki, Marcin (2022). Machine Learning for Bus Travel Prediction. In: International Conference on Computational Science. Springer, Cham, 703–710.

Pongnumkul, Suporn/Pechprasarn, Thanakij/Kunaseth, Narin/Chaipah, Kornchawal (2014). Improving arrival time prediction of Thailand's passenger trains using historical travel times. 11th Int. Joint Conf. on Computer Science and Software Engineering (JCSSE), 307–312. https://doi.org/10.1109/JCSSE.2014.6841886.

Rößler, David/Reisch, Julian/Hauck, Florian/Kliewer, Natalia (2021). Discerning Primary and Secondary Delays in Railway Networks using Explainable AI. Transportation Research Procedia 52, 171–178. https://doi.org/10.1016/j.trpro.2021.01.018.

Shi, Rui/Xu, Xinyue/Li, Jianmin/Li, Yanqiu (2021). Prediction and analysis of train arrival delay based on XGBoost and Bayesian optimization. Applied Soft Computing 109, 107538. https://doi.org/10.1016/j.asoc.2021.107538.

Shoman, Maged/Aboah, Armstrong/Adu-Gyamfi, Yaw (2020). Deep Learning Framework for Predicting Bus Delays on Multiple Routes Using Heterogenous Datasets. Journal of Big Data Analytics in Transportation 2 (3), 275–290. https://doi.org/10.1007/s42421-020-00031-y.

Spanninger, Thomas/Trivella, Alessio/Büchel, Beda/Corman, Francesco (2021). A Review of Train Delay Prediction Approaches. SSRN Electronic Journal. https://doi.org/10.2139/ssrn.3964737.

Spanninger, Thomas/Trivella, Alessio/Corman, Francesco (2020). Approaches for real-time train delay prediction. https://doi.org/10.3929/ethz-b-000420036.

Tao, Sui/Corcoran, Jonathan/Rowe, Francisco/Hickman, Mark (2018). To travel or not to travel: 'Weather' is the question. Modelling the effect of local weather conditions on bus ridership. Transportation Research Part C: Emerging Technologies 86, 147–167. https://doi.org/10.1016/j.trc.2017.11.005.

Torre-Bastida, Ana Isabel/Del Ser, Javier/Laña, Ibai/Ilardia, Maitena/Bilbao, Miren Nekane/Campos-Cordobés, Sergio (2018). Big Data for transportation and mobility: recent advances, trends and challenges. IET Intelligent Transport Systems 12 (8), 742–755. https://doi.org/10.1049/iet-its.2018.5188.

Truong, Anh/Walters, Austin/Goodsitt, Jeremy/Hines, Keegan/Bruss, C. Bayan/Farivar, Reza (2019). Towards Automated Machine Learning: Evaluation and Comparison of AutoML

Approaches and Tools. In: 2019 IEEE 31st International Conference on Tools with Artificial Intelligence (ICTAI), 2019 IEEE 31st International Conference on Tools with Artificial Intelligence (ICTAI), Portland, OR, USA, 04.11.2019 - 06.11.2019. IEEE, 1471–1479.

Wang, Chi/Wu, Qingyun/Huang, Silu/Saied, Amin (2021a). Economical Hyperparameter Optimization with Blended Search Strategy. In: The Ninth International Conference on Learning Representations (ICLR 2021).

Wang, Chi/Wu, Qingyun/Weimer, Markus/Zhu, Erkang (2021b). FLAML: A Fast and Lightweight AutoML Library. In: Fourth Conference on Machine Learning and Systems (MLSys 2021).

Wang, Ren/Work, Daniel B. (2015). Data Driven Approaches for Passenger Train Delay Estimation. In: 2015 IEEE 18th International Conference on Intelligent Transportation Systems, 2015 IEEE 18th International Conference on Intelligent Transportation Systems - (ITSC 2015), Gran Canaria, Spain, 15.09.2015 - 18.09.2015. IEEE, 535–540.

Wei, Ming/Corcoran, Jonathan/Sigler, Thomas/Liu, Yan (2018). Modeling the Influence of Weather on Transit Ridership: A Case Study from Brisbane, Australia. Transportation Research Record Journal of the Transportation Research Board 2672 (8), 505–510. https://doi.org/10.1177/0361198118777078.

Weiner, Edward (1997). Urban Transportation Planning in the United States. An Historical Overview. U.S. Department of Transportation.

Wirth, Rüdiger/Hipp, Jochen (2000). CRISP-DM: Towards a Standard Process Model for Data Mining. Proceedings of the 4th International Conference on the Practical Applications of Knowledge Discovery and Data Mining.

Yaghini, Masoud/Khoshraftar, Mohammad M./Seyedabadi, Masoud (2013). Railway passenger train delay prediction via neural network model. Journal of Advanced Transportation 47 (3), 355–368. https://doi.org/10.1002/atr.193.

Yang, Wenyue/Li, Tao/Cao, Xiaoshu (2015). Examining the impacts of socio-economic factors, urban form and transportation development on CO2 emissions from transportation in China: A panel data analysis of China's provinces. Habitat International 49, 212–220. https://doi.org/10.1016/j.habitatint.2015.05.030.

Zakeri, Ghazal/Olsson, Nils O. E. (2018). Investigating the effect of weather on punctuality of Norwegian railways: a case study of the Nordland Line. Journal of Modern Transportation 26 (4), 255–267. https://doi.org/10.1007/s40534-018-0169-7.

Zhong, Gang/Yin, Tingting/Li, Linchao/Zhang, Jian/Zhang, Honghai/Ran, Bin (2022). Bus Travel Time Prediction Based on Ensemble Learning Methods. IEEE Intelligent Transportation Systems Magazine 14 (2), 174–189. https://doi.org/10.1109/MITS.2020.2990175.

Zúñiga, Felipe/Muñoz, Juan Carlos/Giesen, Ricardo (2021). Estimation and prediction of dynamic matrix travel on a public transport corridor using historical data and real-time information. Public Transport 13 (1), 59–80. https://doi.org/10.1007/s12469-020-00255-9.

Zychowski, Adam/Junosza-Szaniawski, Konstanty/Kosicki, Aleksander (2018). Travel Time Prediction for Trams in Warsaw. In: International Conference on Computer Recognition Systems. Springer, Cham, 53–62.

The manufacturer's authorised representative in the EU is Springer Nature Customer Service Centre GmbH, Europaplatz 3, 69115 Heidelberg, Germany. If you have any concerns regarding our products, please contact ProductSafety@springernature.com

Printed and bound by CPI Group (UK) Ltd, Croydon, CR0 4YY
01/10/2026
02225957-0013